D0046228

An economic history of Britain since 1700, in three volumes by thirty-nine eminent historians and economists, this book will succeed the first edition of 'Floud and McCloskey' (published in 1981) as the leading textbook on its subject. The text has a firm economic basis, but emphasises the historical context and chronology and is written in straightforward and jargon-free English. It will appeal particularly to first and second year university students, but is also suitable for anyone interested in the history of the British economy. Volume 1 covers the period 1700–1860, that of Britain's rise to relative economic supremacy. Volume 2 discusses the period 1860–1939, that of the height of British economic power and of painful readjustment after 1914. Volume 3 considers the period since 1939, that of relative economic decline and of increasing involvement with the European Community.

THE ECONOMIC HISTORY OF BRITAIN SINCE 1700

SECOND EDITION

Volume 2: 1860–1939

THE ECONOMIC HISTORY OF BRITAIN SINCE 1700

SECOND EDITION

Volume 2: 1860–1939

Edited by RODERICK FLOUD *and*
DONALD McCLOSKEY

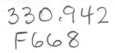

Published by the Press Syndicate of the University of Cambridge
The Pitt Building, Trumpington Street, Cambridge CB2 1RP
40 West 20th Street, New York, NY 10011–4211, USA
10 Stamford Road, Oakleigh, Melbourne 3166, Australia

First published 1981
Second edition 1994

Printed in Great Britain at the University Press, Cambridge

A catalogue record for this book is available from the British Library

Library of Congress cataloguing in publication data

The economic history of Britain since 1700/edited by Roderick Floud and Donald McCloskey. – 2nd ed.
p. cm.
Includes bibliographical references and index.
Contents: v. 1. 1700–1860 v. 2. 1860–1939 v. 3. 1939–1992.
1. Great Britain – Economic conditions. I. Floud, Roderick. II. McCloskey, Donald N.
HC254.5. E27 1993 330.941′07 93–20093

ISBN 0 521 41498 9 (v. 1) 0 521 41499 7 (v. 2)
ISBN 0 521 42520 4 (v. 1 pb) 0 521 42521 2 (v. 2 pb)
ISBN 0 521 41500 4 (v. 3) 0 521 42522 0 (v. 3 pb)

ISBN 0 521 41499 7 hardback
ISBN 0 521 42521 2 paperback

UP

To Lydia, Sarah, Daniel and Margaret

Contents

List of figures — *page* xi
List of tables — xiv
List of contributors — xvii
Introduction to first edition
RODERICK FLOUD *and* DONALD McCLOSKEY — xix
Introduction to second edition
RODERICK FLOUD *and* DONALD McCLOSKEY — xxv
Maps — xxvii

1 Britain, 1860–1914: a survey
RODERICK FLOUD — 1

2 Population, migration and regional development, 1870–1939
DUDLEY BAINES — 29

3 Entrepreneurship, 1870–1914
SIDNEY POLLARD — 62

4 Employment relations in manufacturing and international competition
WILLIAM LAZONICK — 90

5 The service industries
CLIVE LEE — 117

6 British agriculture, 1860–1914
CORMAC Ó GRÁDA — 145

7 Foreign investment and accumulation, 1860–1914
MICHAEL EDELSTEIN — 173

8 Imperialism: cost and benefit
MICHAEL EDELSTEIN — 197

9 Money in the economy, 1870–1939
FORREST CAPIE *and* GEOFFREY WOOD — 217

10 Economic fluctuations, 1870–1913
SOLOMOS SOLOMOU 247

11 Living standards, 1870–1914
MARY MACKINNON 265

12 The inter-war economy in a European mirror
BARRY EICHENGREEN 291

13 The macro-economics of the inter-war years
MARK THOMAS 320

14 Unemployment and the labour market in inter-war Britain
TIM HATTON 359

15 Industry and industrial organisation in the inter-war years
JAMES FOREMAN-PECK 386

Chronology 415
Bibliography 422
List of British Isles cities, towns, villages, parishes, counties, regions and other geographic landmarks cited 457
Index and glossary 469

Figures

1.1 Real GDP per worker, 1880–1914 *page* 3
1.2 Expectation of life at birth, 1801–1991 7
2.1 Death rates at various ages per million living, England and Wales, 1846–50, 1921–5, 1947 31
2.2 The decline in fertility in Britain, 1841–1931 39
2.3 The age structure of the British population, 1851–1951 43
2.4 Emigration (outward passenger movement) from Britain, 1825–1930 48
2.5 The estimated industrial distribution of the British labour force, 1851–1931 54
4.1 Rates of participation in the labour force, 1911 (England and Wales) 94
6.1 British sheep imports, 1865/9–1910/3 167
6.2 British mutton and lamb imports, 1880/5–1910/13 168
6.3 British beef imports, 1880/5–1910/13 169
6.4 British cattle imports, 1865/9–1910/13 170
6.5 The effects of free trade in corn 171
7.1 British savings and investment rates, 1850–1914 176
9.1 UK Consol yield and bank bill rate, 1870–1915 224
9.2 UK bank failures, 1870–1921 228
9.3 UK money base, 1919–39 235
9.4 Real and nominal exchange rate, 1920–31 235
9.5 UK and US interest rates, 1924–34 235
9.6 UK monetary aggregate (M0), 1924–34 236
9.7 US high-powered money, 1924–34 236
9.8 Annual changes in the retail price index, M3 and real GNP, 1920–39 238
10.1 The residual error of GDP, 1870–1914 249
10.2 Compromise and balanced GDP, 1870–1914 249
10.3 UK industrial production, 1870–1914 251
10.4 Home investment, 1870–1913 252
10.5 British agricultural production, 1855–1914 261

10.6 British agricultural output: cyclical component, 1870–1914 262
12.1 Per capita GDP for eight European countries and the UK, 1913–44 297
12.2 Post-war growth and the wartime set-back, 1913, 1920 and 1927 298
12.3 The nominal effective exchange rate for Britain and nine European countries, 1922–36 299
12.4 Post-war export growth and the wartime set-back, 1913, 1920 and 1927 300
12.5 Volume of British and European exports, 1921–36 301
12.6 Volume of British and European imports, 1921–36 301
12.7 Industrial production in Britain and Europe, 1922–37 302
12.8 Central bank discount rates, 1921–37 303
12.9 Money supply (M1) in Britain and Europe, 1925–37 303
12.10 Annual average rate of inflation in Britain and Europe, 1924–36 304
12.11 Unemployment rate in industry in Britain and Europe, 1921–37 305
12.12 Hourly earnings in industry, mines and transport in Britain and Europe, 1929–37 307
12.13 Industrial production of gold and non-gold countries, 1925–36 310
12.14 Investment as a share of GNP in Britain and Europe, 1925–37 314
13.1 Economic growth, 1900–50 321
13.2 Unemployment and the output gap, 1900–50 322
13.3 Unemployment and the output gap, 1918–38 324
13.4 A simple model of aggregate supply and aggregate demand 325
13.5a Prices and unemployment, 1918–38 328
13.5b The price level and the output gap, 1918–38 328
13.5c Inflation and unemployment, 1918–38 329
13.5d Inflation and the output gap, 1918–38 329
13.6a Consumption expenditures, 1920–38 330
13.6b Investment expenditures, 1919–38 330
13.6c International transactions, 1919–38 331
13.6d Government expenditures, 1919–38 331
13.7a Prices and the money supply, 1919–38 332
13.7b Exchange rates, 1920–38 332
13.7c Interest rates, 1919–38 333
13.8a Nominal wages, 1920–38 334
13.8b Real wage rates, 1913–38 334

13.8c Labour productivity, 1913–38 335
13.8d Unit labour costs, 1919–38 335
13.9 A model of aggregate supply and aggregate demand, 1918–21 336
13.10a A model of aggregate supply and aggregate demand, 1929–32 346
13.10b A model of the labour market, 1929–32 346
13.11 A model of aggregate supply and aggregate demand, 1932–7 349
14.1 Unemployment rate, 1921–38 360
14.2 The probability of leaving unemployment, 1929 370
14.3 Labour demand and supply 377
14.4a The real wage and employment: in aggregate, 1921–38 379
14.4b The real wage and employment: in manufacturing, 1921–38 379
14.5 Wage rates and the cost of living, 1921–38 382

Tables

1.1	Real GDP per worker, 1856–1913	*page* 3
1.2	Growth of output, inputs and total factor productivity, 1856–1973	5
1.3	Changes in the distribution of the national income, 1880–1913	8
1.4	The long-term growth of the British economy, 1700–1973	15
1.5	Growth of gross domestic product per man-year in the United Kingdom compared with six other industrial countries, 1873–1973	16
1.6	Occupational distribution of the working population, 1856–1911	18
1.7	Population growth and migration, England and Wales, 1841–1911	18
1.8	Growth in the quality of the labour input, 1856–1973	24
1.9	Capital formation proportions, 1851–1916	25
1.10	Capital formation proportions for the UK, 1873–1913	25
1.11	The components of domestic capital formation, 1851–1914	26
2.1	Population growth in Great Britain, 1861–1939	30
2.2	Death rates per 1,000 population, standardised by the age structure of the population in 1901	33
2.3	Employment and the labour force, UK, 1920–38	44
2.4	Age distribution of the male labour force, 1901, 1931 and 1951	44
2.5	Destinations of British emigrants (outward bound passengers) other than Europe, 1853–1930	48
2.6	Population growth and migration, England and Wales, 1841–1911	52
2.7	Wages of agricultural labourers, 1867–1907	57
2.8	Employment growth in Greater London, Lancashire and Clydeside, 1841–1911	60
4.1	Occupational distribution of the British labour force, 1911	93
4.2	Relative wages of selected workers by pay level, 1886–1926	94

4.3 Relative pay of selected workers by industry, 1886–1926 96
4.4 Union membership, density and work stoppages, 1893–1939 97
5.1 Output growth rates, 1861–1951 121
5.2 Labour input growth rates, 1861–1951 123
5.3 Employment in domestic service, 1851–1951 124
5.4 Employment in services, 1851–1951 124
5.5 Regional employment in services, 1871–1931 125
5.6 Labour productivity growth rates, 1861–1951 140
6.1 The trend in agricultural output and incomes, 1862–1914 146
6.2 Total factor productivity change in British agriculture, 1871–1911 149
6.3 Gross agricultural output of Great Britain, 1870–6 and 1904–10 151
6.4 Elasticities of supply of British agricultural products, 1874–1914 151
6.5 The size distribution of British farms, 1885–1915 159
6.6 Regional wage variation, 1790s–1890s 160
6.7 Reapers' wages and implied reaping rates, 1850 and 1860 161
6.8 The age structure of agricultural workers, 1871–1911 161
7.1 UK rates of savings and investment, 1830–1914 175
7.2 Realised rates of return to home and overseas railway securities, 1870–1913 184
7.3 Realised rates of return, aggregate indices, selected sub-periods, 1871–1913 184
8.1 Some conjectures on the gains from imperialism, 1870 and 1913 205
8.2 Average annual defence expenditures, 1860–1912 211
9.1 The proximate determinants of changes in the UK money supply, 1870–1913 227
9.2 Banks and bank branches, 1870–1920 228
9.3 Revenue and debt in the First World War, 1913–20 233
9.4 Money and prices from 1920 to 1932 244
10.1 Balanced GDP peak to peak growth rates, 1874–1913 253
10.2 Peak to peak growth rates for the volume of exports, 1866–1913 255
10.3 A sectoral analysis of the peak to peak phases in the British gross capital stock, 1862–1913 257
10.4 Peak to peak growth rates in broad money, 1873–1913 258
10.5 Market interest rates and ex-post-real interest rates, averaged over five cycles, 1873–1913 260

10.6 Weather variation over the peak to peak phases of agricultural production, 1866–1909 263
11.1 European per capita incomes, 1870–1910 271
11.2 Estimates of nominal and real wage changes, 1873–1913 272
11.3 Working-class cost of living indices, 1870–1913 272
11.4 Wage earners in the United Kingdom, selected sectors, 1881 and 1911, and average annual full-employment earnings, 1911 274
11.5 Indices of average full-time money earnings, selected sectors, 1880–1913 275
11.6 Estimated weekly per capita consumption, selected foods, 1860–1913 279
11.7 Death rates 1870–1914 281
11.8 Indoor pauperism, 1870–1909 285
14.1 Benefit to wage ratios for claimants to insurance benefits, 1937 364
14.2 Poverty lines and unemployment benefit rates, 1929/30 and 1936 366
14.3 Composition of the unemployed, 1928–38 368
14.4 The duration of unemployment, 1929–38 371
14.5 Regional unemployment rates, 1929, 1932, 1936 374
15.1 Professional salaries, 1913–37 396
15.2 Shares of value added in national income, 1930 401
15.3 Ratios of total productivity, US as a ratio to GB in three natural monopolies, 1927 and 1937 407
15.4 Regional labour productivity in industry, 1924 and 1935 411

Contributors

DUDLEY BAINES is Reader in Economic History at the London School of Economics

FORREST CAPIE is Professor of Economic History at City University Business School

MICHAEL EDELSTEIN is Professor of Economics at Queens College and the Graduate School of the City University of New York

BARRY EICHENGREEN is Professor of Economics at the University of California at Berkeley and a Research Associate of the National Bureau of Economic Research

RODERICK FLOUD is Provost of London Guildhall University and a Research Associate of the National Bureau of Economic Research

JAMES FOREMAN-PECK is Lecturer in Economics at the University of Oxford and a Fellow of St Antony's College

TIM HATTON is Reader in Economics at the University of Essex

WILLIAM LAZONICK is Professor of Economics at Columbia University

CLIVE LEE is Professor of Historical Economics at the University of Aberdeen

DONALD McCLOSKEY is Professor of Economics and of History at the University of Iowa

MARY MACKINNON is Professor of Economics at McGill University

CORMAC Ó GRÁDA is Associate Professor of Economics at University College, Dublin

SIDNEY POLLARD is Emeritus Professor of Economic History at the University of Bielefeld and Honorary Senior Fellow of the University of Sheffield

SOLOMOS SOLOMOU is Lecturer in Economics at the University of Cambridge

MARK THOMAS is Professor of History at the University of Virginia

GEOFFREY WOOD is Professor of Economics at City University Business School

Introduction to first edition

Roderick Floud & Donald McCloskey

Economic history is an exciting subject, a subject full of problems and controversy. It is exciting because in economic history one is constantly forced to ask the question – why? Why were steam engines brought into use at a particular point during the industrial revolution? Why did so many millions brave great dangers to emigrate to the New World? Why were so many unemployed in the depression of the 1930s? Why do parents today have fewer children than parents 200 years ago? Economic history is not, therefore, a story – still less a chronological story, for most events in economic history cannot be neatly dated. Instead it is a list of questions: some can be answered, some cannot, but it is the search for answers, and for the best way to seek answers, which gives the subject both its justification and its interest. 'Economic history concerns the dullest part of human life. Sex, art, aberrant behaviour, politics, bloodshed – it is largely devoid of these' (Parker 1971). Yet it is concerned instead with how people live most of their lives, how many people are born and how they die, how they earn and how they spend, how they work and how they play.

At the same time, economic history can be hard, boring and frustrating, both to write and to learn. Simply because it is concerned with how people have commonly lived, and why they have commonly behaved in a particular way, it is often difficult to discover relevant evidence; people, certainly most people, do not record in great detail for posterity what they buy or what they do at work, nor even how many children they have. The historian has to reconstruct the details of such behaviour from scattered and ambiguous evidence, and his reconstruction can often only be imprecise; few of the statements made in this book are, for that reason, entirely free from the possibility of error, and many represent only guesses. They are the best guesses made, when the book was written, by economic historians expert in their subject, but guesses nonetheless. Indeed, part of the fascination of economic history, although also one of the main causes of the controversies which rumble on for years in the scholarly journals of the subject, lies in making new guesses, and in working out what the effect on our knowledge of the past might be if we made different, but still sensible, guesses about the interpretation of evidence.

Even when we know, at least approximately, whether people ate white or brown bread, or at what age they married, they are very unlikely to have recorded for posterity why they ate white bread when their parents ate brown, or why they married at twenty-seven when their parents married at twenty-four. Even if they did so, their records would be inconclusive, for two reasons: first, people are poor at self-analysis; second, the factor which they choose as 'the' reason why is usually one among many joint reasons. In any case, the economic historian's interest is not normally in the behaviour of individuals, except as exemplars of the behaviour of society, or large groups within society, as a whole. While a political historian can reasonably hope to understand something of the political history of the nineteenth century by studying the life and thoughts of Queen Victoria or of Abraham Lincoln, the economic historian knows that the behaviour of any one individual has very little or no effect upon, and may even be totally different from, the observed behaviour of society as a whole. The fact that the marriage age in a parish is observed to have fallen from an average of twenty-seven in one generation to an average of twenty-four in the next does not show that all those who married did so at the age of twenty-four; nor, conversely, does the fact that two people married at twenty-nine invalidate the fact of the fall in the average.

The answer that we give to a question such as 'why did people marry at an earlier age than their parents' cannot therefore stem directly from the memories or writings of those who were doing the marrying. It can stem partly from such evidence, but only because such evidence helps to build up a set of the many possible reasons why people might have decided to marry earlier. This set of reasons, based partly on evidence from those who married and partly on the knowledge and common sense of the historian, is a necessary beginning to the task of explanation. Armed with it, the historian can begin to explore the evidence, and to see to what degree the behaviour which he observes fits best with one reason rather than another. He might begin, for example, with the belief that people are likely to marry if they are richer and can afford to set up house at an earlier age than their parents; if he finds after seeking for evidence of changes in income levels that on the contrary income levels fell at the same time as marriage became earlier, then that belief seems unlikely to be helpful, and another possible reason must be explored.

In other words, the historian uses evidence of the behaviour of individuals to help him to build up an expectation of how people might have behaved, against which he can contrast his observations of how they actually seem to have behaved. The expectation, or model as it is often called, is founded on assumptions about human behaviour, and therefore about the likely response of groups of individuals to changes in their circumstances. At its most simple, for example, the expectation might be that in general people buy less of a commodity as it becomes more expensive. The expectation may not always be correct for each individual, but it serves in general.

We need to have such expectations, or models, if we are to organise our thoughts and assumptions and apply them to the elucidation or solution of problems about what happened in history. If we do not, then we can only flounder in a mass of individual observations, unaware whether the individual behaviour which we observe is normal or aberrant. Models, therefore, cut through the diversity of experience and behaviour which we all know to characterise any human activity, and embody our judgement as to why people are likely to have behaved as they did.

If the models of historians are to be useful in analysing the past, then they must be carefully chosen. The economic and social historian deals in his work on past societies with subjects which are the concern of many analysts of contemporary society: economists, geographers, sociologists, political scientists. It is sensible for the historian to consider whether he may use their models to aid him in his work. In making the choice he must always be conscious that contemporary society is different from past society, and that a model may either have to be adapted to the requirements of historical analysis or, at the extreme, rejected as entirely inappropriate. But if the adaptation can be made then the historian is likely to gain greatly in his work from the insights of contemporary social scientists; these insights help him to expand and refine his model of the past.

These assertions are controversial. Not all historians accept that it is useful to apply models drawn from the social sciences to historical analysis. Not all, even today, would accept that the primary task of the historian is to explain; they would hold, instead, that description, the discovery of the record of what happened in the past, should be given pride of place. Most frequently, critics of the use of models and of the statistical methods which often accompany them claim that models cannot cope with the rich diversity of human behaviour in the past, that they simplify and therefore distort. Even mere statistical description – counting heads and calculating averages – has been attacked for dehumanising history and for replacing people by numbers.

Such attacks are based largely on misunderstanding. It is certainly true that models of human behaviour must simplify; indeed, that is their purpose, to enable the historian to concentrate on a restricted set of possible explanations for that behaviour, rather than being distracted by the diversity of individual deeds. It is also true that models concentrate on expectations of normal or average behaviour; again, this is deliberate and necessary if the normal is to be distinguished from the aberrant. The historian who uses models does not forget that diversity exists; indeed he makes use of that diversity, those different reactions to different circumstances, to help him to frame and then to improve his model. In some circumstances, no doubt, the diversity of the past may defeat the simplifying powers of the historian and the most complex of models, but such circumstances are no grounds for rejection of the use of models as a whole.

A more reasonable criticism of models and their application to history is that they are often themselves too simple, and that they embody unjustifiable assumptions about human behaviour. In later chapters of this book, for example, we make use of models which assume the existence of full employment, or of perfect mobility of labour; such models may lead to misleading results if such conditions do not obtain. Yet to criticise the use of one model in one set of circumstances does not show that all use of models is wrong. It shows simply that the historian, and the reader of this or any book, should be alert and critical and should not make silly errors; the same could be said of any scholarly work.

A third ground of criticism of the use of models and of statistical methods in history is better founded. Many social scientists use mathematical language to express their ideas and to formulate their models, while most historians, and even many social scientists, are not sufficiently familiar with mathematics to understand what is written. They do not appreciate that mathematics is often used merely as a shorthand, and are even less likely to appreciate that it is sometimes used merely to impress the unwary. Very reasonably, someone who does not understand may reject the ideas along with the language by which they are veiled, even though, in truth, the models can almost always be expressed in a language which is comprehensible to non-mathematicians.

This book has been written by economic and social historians who are expert in the use of models and of statistical methods in history, but are conscious of the fears, doubts and misunderstandings which such usage evokes. They wish to show that economic and social history is not diminished thereby but augmented, and that the results can be understood by anyone interested in historical problems. The economic and social history which they write, and which is discussed in this book, is sometimes called the 'new' economic and social history. The novelty of applying the methods of social science to history is by now about a quarter of a century old; it is often 'new' not so much in its aim nor even in its methods, but merely in the language which it uses. The results, however, are of great interest, and for this reason the authors have expressed their ideas in a language which any student of the subject can understand; where they have used a model or a statistical method which may be unfamiliar, it has been explained.

Together, the chapters in this book make up an economic history of England and Wales since 1700. The basic chronology and the evidence on which it is based are discussed, and the book as a whole provides a treatment of the most important themes in English social and economic history during the period of industrialisation and economic growth. Much has been left out, for the authors and editors have chosen to concentrate on the topics which are most problematical and yet where solutions to problems may be attainable. The book is divided into five overlapping chronological divisions, corresponding to the periods from 1700 to 1800, from 1780 to 1860, from 1860 to 1914, from 1900 to 1945, and from 1945 to the present day. Each division except the last begins with a general survey of the period, which is followed by a number of chapters which consider the main problems which have arisen in the historical interpretation of that period; each division except the first and last concludes with a chapter dealing with the social history of the period in relation to the economic changes which have been considered. The period since 1945 is treated as a whole in one, final, chapter. The book is divided into two volumes, with the break at 1860, although a number of chapters in both volumes bridge the break. Each volume has its own index and glossary, and its own bibliography; frequent references to sources and to further reading are given in the text, making use of the 'author–date' system of reference. In this system, books or articles are referred to in the text simply by the name of the author and the date of publication, for example (Keynes 1936); the bibliography is an alphabetical list of authors, with the date of publication immediately following the author's name. Thus (Keynes 1936) in the text has its counterpart as Keynes, J. M. 1936. *The General Theory of Employment, Interest and Money* in the bibliography.

The book has been planned and written by many hands. The Social Science Research Council of Great Britain generously made funds available both for an initial planning meeting and for a conference at which the first drafts of the chapters were discussed. The authors and editors are grateful to the SSRC for its generosity, and to Donald Coleman, Philip Cottrell, Jack Dowie, Malcolm Falkus, Jordan Goodman, Leslie Hannah, Max Hartwell, Brian Mitchell, Leslie Pressnell, John Wright and Tony Wrigley for attending the conference and making many helpful comments. Annabel Gregory, Alan Hergert, Nigel Lewis, and Ali Saad gave invaluable help in preparing the manuscript for publication.

Introduction to second edition

Roderick Floud & Donald McCloskey

The first edition, in 1981, had two volumes. This, the second, a dozen years later, has three. The change marks not only the expansion of the study of the last fifty years but also the acceleration of historical research on the British economy. From its beginnings in the late 1960s, with a thin, bright stream of predecessors back to the 1940s and before, the historical economics of Britain has flourished.

This edition, like the first, embodies a collaboration between British and North American authors which has been characteristic of the subject. Much of the underlying research, of which it is a synthesis, was first published in American journals such as *Explorations in Economic History* and the *Journal of Economic History*, as well as in the British *Economic History Review*. British and American economic historians have published their findings in those journals and, increasingly, in general interest journals of economics, reflecting a continuing interest among economists in the past of the first industrial nation. The British economy was the first to commercialise, industrialise, move to services and mature. Small wonder that economists have come to see Britain's history as a laboratory for economic science.

The materials used in that laboratory have become more varied during the 1980s. Two books in particular, each the product of years of research, have extended our knowledge of the fundamentals of the economy; Wrigley and Schofield (1981) have put *The Population History of England* on a firmer footing, while Matthews, Feinstein and Odling-Smee (1982) have given a magisterial account of *British Economic Growth*. But their work has been accompanied, on a lesser scale, by a host of economists and historians who have continued to explore both the central issues of economic history – growth, distribution, consumption – and the interconnections between those issues and topics of social, demographic and other forms of historical enquiry.

These enquiries have often been controversial. A political emphasis on the role of markets which was common to Reagan's America and Thatcher's Britain in the 1980s led to studies of such diverse topics as child labour, education and inter-war unemployment. Monetarists tested the power of money to explain British experience. From the left, a generation of economically trained Marxists challenged the optimistic view of Victorian economic performance which had characterised the first generation of cliometricians. Research into the distribution of income, into the speed of Britain's growth and the alleged decline of the British economy and into demographic history and the history of nutrition, mortality and morbidity has given rise to fierce challenge.

These controversies are reflected in the pages which follow. There is no agreement on many topics in British economic history and it is right that differences should be exposed rather than glossed over. The 1980s have, however, seen much less controversy than in previous decades about the methods of enquiry; the role of economic theory, of statistics and computing, whose use in economic history had been challenged but which now underpins all the chapters in these volumes. Underpin is the right word, for there is much less explicit quantification and theorising than in the first edition; it is still there, but the authors feel less need to expose it and less need to parade technical expertise and technical language.

As with the first edition, the style of the book owes much to discussion between the authors at a conference at which first drafts were presented to a critical and constructive audience of the authors themselves and invited commentators. The commentators were Bernard Alford, Sue Bowden, Andrew Dilnot, Peter Mathias, Roger Middleton, Geoffrey Owen, George Peden, Peter Wardley, Katherine Watson, and Tony Wrigley; the authors and editors are grateful to all of them for their help. The conference was made possible by grants from the Economic and Social Research Council, from the British Academy and from Cambridge University Press and it benefited from the hospitality and the pleasant surroundings of St Catharine's College, Cambridge. The production of the book has been greatly aided by the enthusiasm of Richard Fisher and the copy-editing of Linda Randall, together with other staff of Cambridge University Press.

It is salutary to remember, in considering a book which is to a large extent about technical change, that the first edition was produced without the aid of word processors, fax machines or electronic mail. Twelve years later all have been used but the travails of editorship remain, together with our wish to acknowledge, in overcoming them, the support of our wives, Cynthia and Joanne, and of our children to whom this edition, like the first, is dedicated.

ATLANTIC
OCEAN
SHETLAND ISLANDS
ORKNEY ISLANDS
North
Sea
SUTHERLAND
ROSS AND CROMARTY
HIGHLANDS
Culloden
Inverness
Aberdeen
HEBRIDES
SCOTLAND
Edinburgh
LOTHIANS
Glasgow
LOWLANDS
Firth of Clyde
BORDERS
NORTH-EAST
Newcastle
NORTHERN IRELAND
ULSTER
Belfast
NORTH-WEST
Irish Sea
Leeds
Hull
CONNAUGHT
R. Boyne
REPUBLIC OF IRELAND
Dublin
Liverpool
Manchester
Sheffield
LEINSTER
EAST MIDLANDS
NORTH WALES
Limerick
St George's Channel
WEST MIDLANDS
Birmingham
EAST ANGLIA
MUNSTER
WALES
ENGLAND
SOUTH WALES
HOME COUNTIES
Thames Estuary
London
SOUTH-EAST
Cardiff
Bristol Channel
Bristol
SOUTH-WEST
Southampton
Portsmouth
0 50 100 150 km
0 50 100 miles
Plymouth
English Channel
ISLES of SCILLY
FRANCE

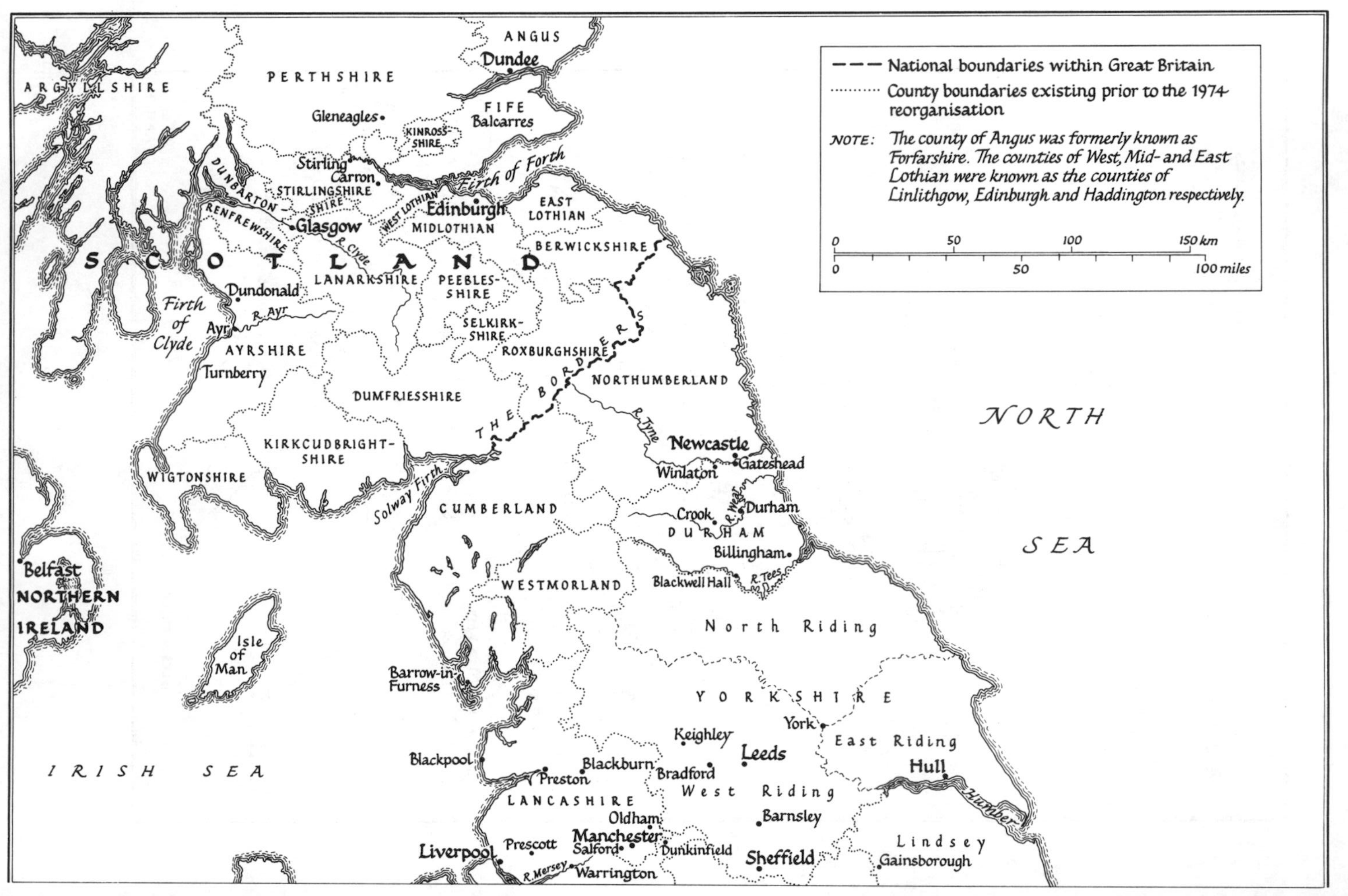

National boundaries within Great Britain
County boundaries existing prior to the 1974 reorganisation
NOTE: The county of Angus was formerly known as Forfarshire. The counties of West, Mid- and East Lothian were known as the counties of Linlithgow, Edinburgh and Haddington respectively.
0 50 100 150 km
0 50 100 miles
ARGYLLSHIRE
PERTHSHIRE
ANGUS
Dundee
FIFE
Balcarres
Gleneagles
KINROSS-SHIRE
Stirling
Carron
STIRLINGSHIRE
DUNBARTON-SHIRE
Firth of Forth
WEST LOTHIAN
Edinburgh
EAST LOTHIAN
MIDLOTHIAN
RENFREWSHIRE
Glasgow
R. Clyde
BERWICKSHIRE
SCOTLAND
Dundonald
LANARKSHIRE
PEEBLES-SHIRE
Firth of Clyde
Ayr
R. Ayr
SELKIRK-SHIRE
AYRSHIRE
ROXBURGHSHIRE
Turnberry
THE BORDERS
NORTHUMBERLAND
DUMFRIESSHIRE
R. Tyne
NORTH
KIRKCUDBRIGHT-SHIRE
Newcastle
Gateshead
Winlaton
WIGTONSHIRE
Solway Firth
CUMBERLAND
Crook
R. Wear
Durham
DURHAM
Billingham
SEA
Belfast
NORTHERN IRELAND
WESTMORLAND
Blackwell Hall
R. Tees
North Riding
Isle of Man
Barrow-in-Furness
YORKSHIRE
York
Keighley
East Riding
Leeds
Blackpool
Blackburn
Bradford
Hull
IRISH SEA
Preston
West Riding
Humber
LANCASHIRE
Barnsley
Oldham
Lindsey
Liverpool
Prescott
Manchester
Salford
Dunkinfield
Sheffield
Gainsborough
R. Mersey
Warrington

E N G L A N D
W A L E S
Anglesey
Carnarvon
CARNARVONSHIRE
FLINTSHIRE
FLINT
DENBIGHSHIRE
MERIONETHSHIRE
MONTGOMERYSHIRE
RADNORSHIRE
CARDIGANSHIRE
PEMBROKESHIRE
CARMARTHENSHIRE
BRECKNOCKSHIRE
Merthyr Tydfil
GLAMORGANSHIRE
Cardiff
Monmouth
MONMOUTHSHIRE
Forest of Dean
R. Severn
Macclesfield
Marston
CHESHIRE
Crewe
Burslem
Etruria
Stoke-on-Trent
STAFFORDSHIRE
DERBYSHIRE
Derby
Ash
Nottingham
NOTTINGHAMSHIRE
Gedling
Bottesford
Lincoln
LINCOLNSHIRE
Kesteven
Holland
The Wash
SHROPSHIRE
Ironbridge
Black Country
Dudley
Birmingham
Meriden
Edgbaston
Coventry
Warwick
WARWICKSHIRE
Shepshed
Leicester
LEICESTERSHIRE
RUTLAND
The Fens
CAMBRIDGESHIRE (ISLE OF ELY)
NORFOLK
Norwich
HEREFORDSHIRE
Hereford
WORCESTERSHIRE
GLOUCESTERSHIRE
NORTHAMPTONSHIRE
Northampton
HUNTINGDONSHIRE
Huntingdon
Bedford
BEDFORDSHIRE
Cambridge
WEST SUFFOLK
EAST SUFFOLK
Ipswich
Harwich
Banbury
OXFORDSHIRE
Oxford
BUCKINGHAMSHIRE
HERTFORDSHIRE
ESSEX
R. Thames
MIDDLESEX
London
Southend-on-Sea
Thames Estuary
Bristol
Newbury
BERKSHIRE
Bristol Channel
N
WILTSHIRE
Odiham
SURREY
KENT
Dover
The Weald
SOMERSET
HAMPSHIRE
WEST SUSSEX
EAST SUSSEX
Strait of Dover
Morchard Bishop
DEVON
Exeter
Dawlish
DORSET
Southampton
Portsmouth
Isle of Wight
CORNWALL
Plymouth
English Channel
FRANCE

1 Britain, 1860–1914: a survey

Roderick Floud

Introduction

At the end of the nineteenth century Britain possessed the wealthiest and most powerful economy that the world had ever known. The average income of its citizens was greater than that of any other country, the majority of the world's trade was carried out in its ships and financed by its institutions while its external investments surpassed those of all the other major economies combined. It had been the first nation to undergo industrialisation, the first to install modern transport networks, the first to develop the financial infrastructure required to support industry at home and commerce and investment abroad.

In the light of this success, it is odd indeed that historical accounts of the British economy between 1860 and 1914 have been dominated by discussions of failure. Even odder, such discussions have not normally been concerned with such themes as the extent of poverty, the high rates of infant mortality or the overcrowded slums, all of them aspects of the late Victorian and Edwardian economies which sat ill, in the eyes of many contemporary observers, with the high average income of British inhabitants and even more with the ostentation of its ruling classes. Instead, economic failure has been asserted because Britain was not rich enough, because its economy did not grow as rapidly as those of other rich nations, or because its managers and entrepreneurs did not grasp the opportunities presented by new markets and new technologies.

Judgement on the years from 1860 to 1914 depends crucially, therefore, on the choice of 'performance indicators'; it is necessary to decide which measure or measures of the success or failure of an economy to prefer. That decision, in its turn, will determine which evidence is sought and presented in the course of argument. For evidence, particularly evidence about the individual or aggregate behaviour of around 30 million people, is neither value-free nor immediately available or obvious; it needs to be carefully gathered, carefully weighed and tested for consistency and fitness for purpose.

The purpose of this chapter is therefore to set the scene for those chapters which follow by describing, with the use of some of that new evidence, the overall growth and development of the British economy between 1860 and 1914 and by analysing the main arguments used to understand that growth.

The record of aggregate growth

National income

The first performance indicator to be used is, appropriately, the most fundamental. People work to live, to produce income which they can then use to consume goods and services and to save to provide for their future needs. The average value of the work which its citizens undertake, in other words their average income, is thus the basic indicator of the success or otherwise of the economy of a nation. Figure 1.1 shows that average, in the form of a calculation of real gross domestic product per capita from 1880 to 1914.

Three preliminary points must be made about this calculation. First, the calculation is of 'real' product in the sense that allowance has been made for price changes, specifically for the falling prices of the late Victorian years and the rising prices of the Edwardian period. Second, it is of 'domestic' product, thus excluding the income which returned to Britain from investments overseas (see ch. 7); this income accrued largely to the upper classes but is excluded not for that reason but because the intention here is to measure the size of the domestic economy. Third, Figure 1.1, like all the evidence presented in this chapter, is an estimate, based on a myriad of underlying estimates of incomes and prices. Other estimates and other ways of making such estimates exist, and some of them give different results (Feinstein 1990c and ch. 10 below).

Figure 1.1 shows immediately that the economy did not grow smoothly from one year to the next. On the contrary, there were periods of rapid growth and others of decline, succeeding each other in what has often been seen as a regular pattern of fluctuations or cycles (ch. 10 below). To measure the growth of the economy, either over the whole time from 1880 to 1914 or for shorter periods within it, it is essential to measure that growth in such a way as to compare like with like; for this reason, it is now conventional to measure over the time periods shown in Table 1.1, where the end-dates represent peaks in average income. Peaks are preferred to troughs because, at the peaks, the output of the economy must have been close to that which was possible with the resources available at the time while, at the troughs, a variable amount of those resources was un-

Table 1.1. *Real GDP per worker, 1856–1913 (annual percentage growth rates)*

	Income data (1)	Expenditure data (2)	Output data (3)
Whole period			
1856–1913	1·01	1·03	0·95
Two long swings			
1856–82	1·18	1·26	1·15
1882–1913	0·86	0·84	0·79
Four phases			
1856–73	1·32	1·38	1·12
1873–82	0·90	1·03	1·20
1882–99	1·49	1·27	0·85
1899–1913	0·09	0·33	0·72

Note: Feinstein has revised these estimates. See Feinstein 1990c: 340–53 for details.
Source: Feinstein 1990c: 337.

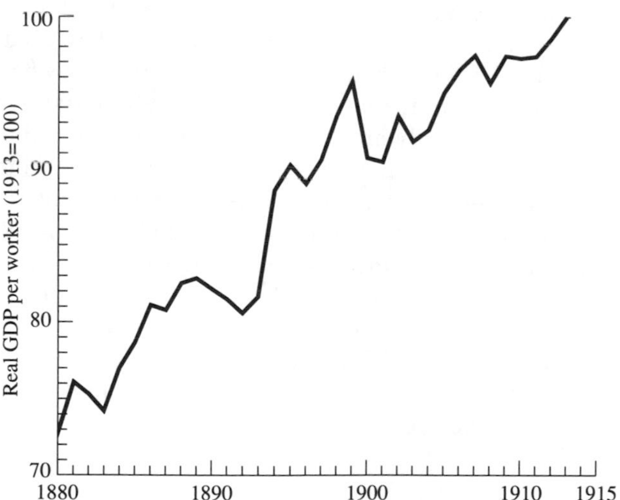

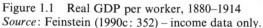

Figure 1.1 Real GDP per worker, 1880–1914
Source: Feinstein (1990c: 352) – income data only.

employed. Measurement between peaks thus gives an indication of the potential or capacity of the economy as it changes over time.

On the basis of this evidence, the British economy grew by about 1 per cent per annum throughout the period from 1860 to 1914. Growth was faster than this, though not by very much, in 1856–73 and 1882–99, and slower, though again not by very much, in 1873–82 and 1899–1913. While 1 per cent per annum may seem a small amount, particularly to those accustomed to post-Second World War economies which at least aspire to grow at 3–4 per cent per annum, as a compounded rate continued over fifty-four years it was sufficient to raise the average income of the British population by about 80 per cent. In addition, in using as the indicator of growth a 'per capita' indicator it is important not to forget that between the census years 1861 and 1911 the British population rose from 20.066 million to 36.070 million, a rise of 79.8 per cent. The absolute as well as the per capita growth of the economy was therefore substantial – nearly 80 per cent more people were each on average about 80 per cent better off.

Two questions immediately arise. The first is: was this a good or a bad performance? To answer this requires consideration of the whole debate about the success or failure of the British economy (see also ch. 15 below and vol. 3, ch. 11). The second question can be discussed now: how and why did this growth occur?

Economies grow for one of three reasons; because they obtain more resources or because they make better use of the resources they have got or because of a combination of these two causes. The substantial population growth of this period naturally brought with it growth in the labour force – a more elusive concept than population itself – which rose from 10.523 million in 1861 to 18.286 million in 1911, a rise of 73.8 per cent. But much of the productive potential of this increased number of workers was naturally used in feeding and otherwise providing for their own needs, so that this growth by itself does not provide an explanation for the overall increase in average incomes. To seek such an explanation it is necessary to look more broadly at all the resources available to the economy – labour, land, machinery, buildings – and at their separate and joint use in increasing output and incomes.

Productivity

A method which is often used to do this – and which will therefore be employed as the second 'performance indicator' – is the calculation of a measure known as total factor productivity. To understand this measure, begin by considering the more familiar term: labour productivity. This is normally used by economists and politicians to describe the average output

Table 1.2. *Growth of output, inputs and total factor productivity, 1856–1973*

	Annual percentage growth rates						
			Weights				
Period	Labour	Gross capital	Labour	Capital	Total inputs	Outputs	TFP
1856–73	0·0	1·9	0·59	0·41	0·8	2·2	1·4
1873–1913	0·9	1·9	0·57	0·43	1·3	1·8	0·5
1856–1973	0·2	2·0	—	—	0·8	1·9	1·1

Notes: 1. The estimates for the growth of labour do not include any allowance for improved quality, which is therefore included within the 'residual' estimate of TFP. If labour quality were included in inputs, TFP growth would be 1·4 per cent for 1856–73, 0·5 per cent for 1873–1913 and 1·1 per cent for 1856–1973.
2. No explicit estimates of weights were made for 1856–73, the weights being derived from the estimates for shorter periods.
3. Matthews *et al.* (1982: chs. 3–7, but especially ch. 7) discuss these estimates and their rationale in great detail. Those chapters should be carefully consulted.
Source: Matthews *et al.* (1982: 208, Tables 7.1 and 7.2). The calculation is as follows (with all figures being annual percentage growth rates):

(labour × weight of labour) + (capital × weight of capital) = total inputs

and output − total inputs = total factor productivity.

of a group of workers, usually in one factory or industry but sometimes in the economy as a whole. It is calculated by dividing the value of output by the number of workers. GDP per capita is such a measure; although it has been used so far as a measure of average income, it is exactly equivalent (though it may be calculated in a different way) to the average productivity of labour in the nation as a whole.

Calculations of labour productivity on their own do not take account of the fact that in a modern and mechanised economy production is not achieved simply by workers with their hands, but is carried out by workers in conjunction with capital equipment such as machines and factories. Output per worker can therefore be significantly altered by giving a worker a new machine, without any change in the amount of effort which he puts in; a man digging his garden with a spade might, for example, use a mechanical cultivator to speed up the job. Thus any calculation of the efficiency with which the economy uses its resources must include the effects of change in the amount of capital employed; it is for this reason that economists frequently calculate the capital–output ratio, which is analogous to the calculation of labour productivity or output per man.

Instead of output per unit of capital, however, the inverse is calculated, capital employed per unit of output, so that a fall in the capital–output ratio indicates a rise in the productivity of capital. During the late nineteenth century the capital–output ratio in Britain was about 4.0; this can be interpreted as meaning that on average the equipment used in production cost four times as much as the output produced from it each year.

Just as improvements in labour productivity can be achieved by employing more machinery, so a fall in the capital–output ratio could result from employing more men; neither is, taken by itself, an unambiguous indication of increasing efficiency of the productive process as a whole. Such an indication can only be gained by examining changes in output compared with changes in both capital and labour together, rather than either on its own. If properly calculated and based on good evidence, such a measure examines how well the economy is using the resources available to it.

The measurement of 'total factor productivity' is intended to compare changes in the output of the economy with a weighted average of changes in all the inputs or resources employed; the average is weighted to take account of the fact that the different inputs – land, labour and capital – are not normally of equal importance, and the weights used are the shares which the different resources (or 'factors') receive of national income. The assumptions underlying the whole method can be questioned on theoretical ground, but the technique provides 'a descriptive device, useful for posing matters for study' (Matthews *et al.* 1982: 200).

Table 1.2 shows such a calculation for two broad periods, 1856–73 and 1873–1913. The results suggest that, although the economy continued to improve its efficiency throughout the period, in the sense that it got more and more from the resources which were available to it, this improvement was occurring at a declining rate. There is some evidence, in fact, that this was a continuation of a pattern that had been established earlier in the nineteenth century (Matthews *et al.* 1982: 213). There is clearly here 'matter for study' which is taken up again below.

Two performance indicators have assisted in judging the British economy between 1860 and 1914: growth in real GDP per capita and growth in total factor productivity. But it is important not to become so concerned with growth as to ignore the absolute levels around which that growth was occurring. In other words, performance indicators are needed which describe what it was like to live in late Victorian and Edwardian Britain or, more usefully, how different it was from today. From an enormous range of possibilities, two are particularly useful: movements in average life expectancy and changes in the distribution of income. Like the

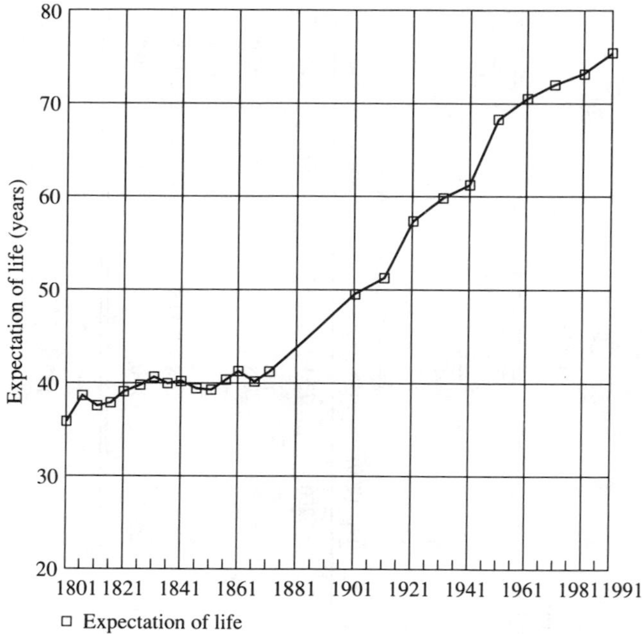

Figure 1.2 Expectation of life at birth, 1801–1991
Note: the estimates are what is known to demographers as 'period' estimates. That is, they represent the average length of life of those people who died at the date shown. This is to be contrasted with 'cohort' estimates, which report the experience of a particular group of people born at a particular time.
Source: See text.

other performance indicators, these have the deficiency of all averages and summary statistics, that they ignore or obscure the variety of experience of different classes, regions and occupations; this point is taken up in the last section of the chapter.

Mortality and nutritional status

Figure 1.2 shows the movement of average life expectancy between 1801 and 1991. It can be seen that life expectancy, which had been static since about 1830, began to rise in the 1860s and at an increasing rate thereafter (see ch. 2). More complex analysis of the distribution of deaths by the age group at which they occurred shows that infant mortality did not begin to fall until the early years of the twentieth century, so that the direct cause of the overall fall after 1860 was improvements in the mortality rate of first

Table 1.3. *Changes in the distribution of the national income, 1880–1913*

	1880					1913				
	Number of incomes		Average income	Total income		Number of incomes		Average income	Total income	
	No. (000)	%	£	Amount (£m)	%	No. (000)	%	£	Amount (£m)	%
Wages	12,300	83·3	37·8	465	41·5	15,200	73·4	50·7	770	35·5
Intermediate incomes (under £160)	1,850	12·5	70·3	130	11·5	4,310	20·8	84·7	365	17·0
Incomes assessed to tax over £160, excluding wage earners	620	4·2	854·8	530	47·0	1·190	5·8	865·5	1,030	47·5
Total	14,770	100·0	76·2	1,125	100·0	20·700	100·0	104·6	2,165	100·0

Source: Bowley (1920: 16) reprinted in Supple (1981: 125).

young and then older adults. The change was not uniform across all parts of the country or all social groups but there was, by 1914, an overall and substantial improvement in this important indicator of social welfare (Mitchison 1977; Anderson 1990). There were more people both because more were born and because those people were richer and lived longer to enjoy – or at least to earn and spend – their increased incomes.

Another indicator of this fact is that the physique of the population changed. Adult heights and weights are greatly affected by what biologists call the nutritional status of infants and children as they grow; that is, by the balance which exists in every human being between energy intakes and requirements. Better food, better housing, less disease, a reduction in the need to undertake hard physical work in childhood, even more love, all allow children to grow taller and more healthy than they would in conditions of deprivation. There is, moreover, a great deal of modern evidence which suggests that the benefits of an improved nutritional status are felt throughout life, that well-nourished children become adults who are healthier and longer-lived than the poorly nourished. It is, therefore, of great interest that there is evidence of a sustained rise in the average height of the British male population (the evidence about females is sparse) during the latter part of the nineteenth and the early part of the twentieth century, after a period in the middle of the nineteenth century when heights fell, apparently under the impact of the urbanisation of Britain and the poor housing and living conditions which it brought (Floud, Wachter and Gregory 1990).

The distribution of the national income

The final performance indicator is that of the distribution of the rewards of the growing economy. Table 1.3 shows the main changes which occurred in the distribution of the national income between 1880 and 1913. It demonstrates the overall rise in money incomes and the growth of numbers of people in the intermediate category of incomes, which approximates to the middle class, but it also shows the very large discrepancy which continued to exist between the incomes of the bulk of the population and those in approximately the top 5 per cent of the income distribution.

Britain between 1860 and 1914 was therefore, on the basis of the four performance indicators which have been used, a rich country, growing richer year by year as its economy made ever more efficient use of the resources which were available to it, although the growth in efficiency was slowing down. Economic growth brought with it improvements in welfare, as evidenced by a rise in life expectancy, but left behind a substantial residue of the population in poverty.

Varieties of experience

Averages are an indispensable means of summarising experience, whether it be economic, cultural or social, but it is always important to remember that around every average is variation or dispersion. Thus, when average life expectancy was discussed, no account was taken of the wide range of experience of different social groups and different areas of the country. Yet that range was wide indeed. In this section, therefore, the balance will be redressed by emphasising diversity.

First, health and death. In general, urban areas were much less healthy places to live than were the rural areas of Britain, as they had been during the eighteenth and early nineteenth centuries, although this did not deter the continual flow of migrants (Williamson 1990a; Baines 1985 and ch. 2 below). But this overall pattern concealed many local variations, such that, as Woods has written (1982: 376): 'There was ... as great a range of mortality experience in England and Wales in the 1860s as there was between that of England and Wales as a whole in the 1840s and the 1960s, namely some 30 years.' The partial spread of sanitary improvements provides part of the explanation, but more important is the wide range of experience of different occupational groups. Anderson (1990: 21–2) has calculated the death rates of men aged twenty-five to forty-four in fifteen different occupations both in 1860–71 and in 1900–2. The healthiest group at both periods was the clergy, so Anderson uses them as a standard; in 1860–71 the average death rate of the male population was 88 per cent higher than that of clergymen, but several occupations – bargees, lightermen, watermen, file makers and chimney sweeps and soot merchants – had mortality rates over 150 per cent higher than those of the clergy.

Moreover, despite rising incomes and living standards, these occupational differentials widened during the later nineteenth century, although all occupations shared in the general reduction in mortality. By 1900–2 fishermen, potters, earthenware workers, glass workers and innkeepers had joined those occupations listed above as having mortality rates 150 per cent higher than the clergy. Despite the fact that the connection between occupation and mortality and, often, the exact agent of death, had long been identified, many workers continued to die from respiratory diseases, cancers and accidents directly related to their work.

High mortality rates were not, however, associated only with the men working in particular trades. They affected also their families and thus can be attributed more generally to the effects of poverty, sometimes exacerbated by pollution and work-related disease. The extent of poverty in late Victorian England came to be seen by many at the end of the nineteenth century as a national scandal, and was much studied. One of the most thorough investigators, Seebohm Rowntree (1901 : 86–7), asserted in 1901 on the basis of extensive investigations that within the population there were two groups living in poverty:

(1) Families whose total earnings are insufficient to obtain the minimum necessaries for the maintenance of merely physical efficiency. Poverty falling under this head may be described as 'primary' poverty.

(2) Families whose total earnings would be sufficient for the maintenance of merely physical efficiency were it not that some portion of it is absorbed by other expenditure, either useful or wasteful. Poverty falling under this head may be described as 'secondary' poverty.

Rowntree estimated that about 13 per cent of the population lived in primary poverty, with a further 14 per cent in secondary poverty, a total of 27 per cent; this figure accords well with the results of contemporary studies of poverty in London and provincial cities (Booth 1889–1903; Hennock 1987: 219–26).

Families living in such conditions would have been stunted in their physical growth, prey to disease and incapable of sustained physical activity or work. Although the effects of ill-health and poverty on physical growth had been known since earlier in the century, the process of recruitment to the army for the South African War from 1899 onwards demonstrated how badly large sections of the working-class population were affected by stunting and other growth deficiencies. Although the average height of the working class population had begun to improve in the 1860s, at the same time as did mortality, and there are some signs of a lessening in the differences in height between social classes, childhood deprivation among large sections of the population remained intense (Floud *et al.* 1990). Moreover, the effects of that deprivation were long-lasting, leading to lower physical efficiency and work productivity in adulthood and ultimately to early death.

Even within single occupations, wages and incomes could vary greatly from one part of the country to another. Ó Gráda demonstrates this clearly for agriculture, but it was true for all but the very small number of occupations, themselves usually centred on one or at most a few areas of the country, in which national wage bargaining took place. Moreover, the Kuznets or trade cycles which are described in chapter 10 had an uneven influence between industries and across regions. Employment was far more precarious in late Victorian Britain than it has come to be in the twentieth century, even if the levels of unemployment in the depths of recession were not very different; the lower levels of capital which were in use and the absence of employment protection allowed managers to vary employment at will. It was, for example, the custom in the engineering trades that even highly skilled workers could leave or be dismissed at any meal break (Floud 1976). Since no assistance was available from the Poor Law to the able-bodied worker and assistance from trade union funds was limited only to some skilled trades, it was no wonder that unemployment was regarded as the best recruiting agent that the army and navy could ever have.

Unemployment to a single man from the working class might mean resort to the recruiting office, but to the married man it brought into sharp relief his responsibility for wife and children. That responsibility had been reinforced by the Poor Law Act of 1834, which sought to replace communal by individual responsibility, but it was further emphasised, throughout the latter part of the nineteenth century, by a growing concentration on the family as the primary social unit and the source of morality and the stability of society. This change in behaviour and attitudes, reinforced by legislation such as the Liberal welfare reforms of the Edwardian era, also served to give increasing emphasis to another fundamental division and source of great variation between different groups and individuals; this was the division between men and women.

It is impossible here to do more than mention issues of the sexual division of labour or of roles within household and family (Davidoff 1990; Joyce 1990). But there is no doubt that this division widened during the nineteenth century in all social classes, as the increasing separation of work from household and the growth of specialised production within a factory environment reduced the likelihood that women and men would work together. For the middle and upper classes and in the latter part of the century, such measures as the Married Women's Property Acts in the 1870s and 1880s gave some women a measure of legal independence, reinforced by tentative moves to make easier divorce or separation. But such measures did little to affect the reality of working-class lives; there, the decreasing opportunities for employment for married women, combined with a birth rate which remained high until the end of the century, produced both economic dependence of women upon men and often its corollary in terms of suffering and sacrifice. There is evidence that, certainly in times of economic stress, expenditure on the food, clothing and health of girls and women was sacrificed to the needs of maintaining the physical strength or even the respectability of males.

Late nineteenth-century Britain was, therefore, an unequal society in a variety of ways, though most were related to the basic, and still very considerable, inequality in income and wealth. Rising real incomes towards the end of the century were experienced throughout the population and did something to relieve the extreme deprivation and malnutrition which had characterised earlier periods; but the relative deprivation remained, reinforced by enormously different standards of housing, clothing, feeding and access to medical care. For the working classes, child labour continued, even if not in the extreme forms controlled by legislation in the first half of the century. Last, to an extent which it is now difficult to imagine, inequality showed itself in the bodies of the rich and the poor. While the upper and middle classes enjoyed the new amenities of bathrooms, the poor struggled with poor and dirty water supplies, outside lavatories and pollution from coal fires and factory effluent. Even in the 1920s, as Davidoff (1990: 123) points out, 'below a certain level, working-class people's bodies, clothes and surroundings were not only shabby but smelled of grease, dust and grime'. Inequalities in income and wealth could be heard, smelled and seen; the average working-class male, child or adult, was several inches shorter than someone of the same age from the middle or upper classes.

Setting standards

This brief account of the growth of the British economy and of its diversity leaves two questions unanswered. First, was the performance of the economy good or bad and, second, why and exactly when was there a slowing in the growth of efficiency as measured by total factor productivity? In answering these questions it is necessary to begin by setting a standard against which the economy can be measured, either in terms of overall growth or in terms of efficiency. That standard must be realistic, in the sense that it is within the bounds of possibility that it could have been attained if men and women at the time had behaved differently.

What standards are appropriate? There is in fact one overall standard – that the economy should have made the best possible use of the resources available to it. At any one time, an economy has an endowment of resources; it has a labour force, educated and trained in a particular way, a capital stock of machines, building and equipment, a stock of land and raw materials and a set of political and economic institutions. Armed with that endowment, it faces demand for its goods and services at home and overseas and its task is to meet that demand by combining its resources in the best possible way, as well as providing for future demands by investing to maintain and improve those resources. The overall counterfactual standard (so called because it is a description of the economy as it did not actually exist and behave but as it hypothetically could have done) is thus easily described in principle, but more difficult to define in practice.

Before trying to do so, consider one problem for the historian. A very simplified form of conventional neo-classical economics – the economic theory currently taught in western developed economies and urged on the rest of the world – teaches that free markets deliver the maximum output by providing the optimum combination of resources. If this is so, then this counterfactual is a tautology when applied to a market economy like that of Britain before 1914; by definition, whatever output was attained must have been the optimum and no decisions could have been taken which would have improved on this situation. So Britain must have performed as well as possible.

To the historian (and to most economists) the situation is more complex. No economies are ever as perfect as theory allows us to imagine: markets are interfered with for political reasons; institutions such as banks, insurance companies and stock exchanges take time to develop and then exert long-term influence; the labour force has endowments of skills and training which cannot immediately adapt to new demands; information flows are complex and costly; the list is endless. For all kinds of reasons, therefore, it is still interesting to postulate the counterfactual and pose the question: could Britain have done better?

In order to answer the question, it must be made more precise. This can be done most easily by turning an absolute standard – doing as well as possible – into a comparative one, of doing as well as anyone else, by which is meant either other nations at the time or the British before or since. In other words, it is essential to seek to answer some or all of the following questions:

(a) Did the output of the British economy increase as rapidly as it had earlier done or as rapidly as other countries were increasing their output?
(b) Did the British economy respond as efficiently as it could have done to such challenges as the development of new technology or the growth of world trade?
(c) Did the British economy make full use of the skills of its citizens?

These questions are certainly not exhaustive, but if they can be answered a start will have been made towards understanding the British economy between 1860 and 1914.

The output of the economy

British output growth, in the sense of per capita growth, was faster between 1880 and 1914 (see Figure 1.1) than during the classical period of British industrialisation before 1860, but slower than the growth of the other major industrial countries. This pattern, of growth slower than that of other countries, has generally persisted to the present day. The evidence for

Table 1.4. *The long-term growth of the British economy, 1700–1973 (annual percentage rates)*

A National product per head	
1700–60	0·31
1760–80	0·01
1780–1801	0·35
1801–31	0·52
B Real GDP per worker	
1831–60	1·1
1856–73	1·32
1873–82	0·90
1882–99	1·43
1899–1913	0·31
C GDP per man-year	
1913–24	0·3
1924–37	1·0
1937–51	1·0
1951–64	2·3
1964–73	2·6

Notes: 1. The concepts underlying these estimates are different, making them not strictly comparable. National product includes income from abroad, which GDP does not. In particular, estimates of output per capita and output per worker (or man-year or man-hour) will differ according to the age and employment structure of the population.
2. All the authors of these estimates emphasise the fragility of the data on which they are based.
Sources: A: Crafts (1985: 45); B: for 1831–60, Feinstein (1981: 141), for 1856–1913, Feinstein (1990c: 337, 344); C: Matthews *et al.* (1982: 31).

these three assertions can be found in Tables 1.4 and 1.5, which are unfortunately not strictly comparable, but give a good indication of broad trends. They suggest also that, within the 1860–1914 period, economic growth slowed towards the end of the period, demonstrating rates of growth between 1899 and 1913 which were lower than has been characteristic of the remainder of the twentieth century.

It is important to note, before discussing the possible causes of these rates of growth, that the picture which they paint is very different from the traditional description of the late Victorian and Edwardian economies, which saw pervasive failure throughout the period. This traditional description was born in the period itself; it is not entirely fanciful to date and ascribe it to the impact on Britain of the Paris Exhibition of 1867, but it was certainly given great impetus by the agricultural depression which

Table 1.5. *Growth of gross domestic product per man-year in the United Kingdom compared with six other industrial countries, 1873–1973 (annual percentage rates)*

	UK	USA	Sweden	France	Germany	Italy	Japan
1873–99	1·2	1·9	1·5	1·3	1·5	0·3	1·1
1899–1913	0·5	1·3	2·1	1·6	1·5	2·5	1·8
1873–1951	0·9	1·7	1·7	1·4	1·3	1·3	1·4
1873–1973	1·2	1·8	1·9	2·0	2·0	2·4	2·6

Notes: more recent research (Feinstein 1990c) has slightly modified one component of the estimates for 1873–1913, by altering the income-based estimates of national output. The estimates above are derived from the 'compromise' estimate of national output, an average of estimates based on income, expenditure and output data. For a criticism of this method, see Solomou and Weale (1991). For the reasons given in these sources, it is likely that the estimates given above slightly underestimate British growth between 1873 and 1913.
Source: Matthews *et al.* (1982: 31, Table 2.5). For detailed sources see notes to that table.

settled over large parts of Britain in the 1870s (ch. 6 below). Both events, one in manufacturing and the other in farming, led to what can best be thought of as a loss of nerve or of confidence in the future of the economy.

Descriptions of the Paris Exhibition brought home to Britain the fact that she was no longer the only industrial nation. At the Great Exhibition in London in 1851 British exhibitors had, it is true, been on their home ground, but they were able to demonstrate that, with the exception of a few pieces of agricultural machinery, British manufacturing industry had hardly any rivals across an enormous range of consumers' and producers' goods. By 1867, by contrast, the growth of manufacturing particularly in the United States but also in France, Germany and other European countries was clearly apparent and, although Britain continued to be the world leader in production and trade, confidence was shaken. During the next decade, the beginning of the period of falling prices for agricultural commodities, which was to persist for the rest of the century, dealt a further blow to confidence and, this time, to the incomes of the landowning and therefore politically important classes.

The intensification of German and American competition during the last quarter of the nineteenth century, which led to a nasty outburst of jingoism directed particularly at the German menace, fortified this lack of confidence and fear of competition. Although there is no sign of a long-term reduction in output either in agriculture or in industry, the period gradually became known to British historians as that of the 'Great

Depression', a title reserved in the United States for the depression of the 1930s (Saul 1969). Even after 1896, the date usually chosen as the end of the depression, there was little cheer, for society and economy entered in the Edwardian years into an era of industrial confrontation. This succession of events led to a questioning of many articles of faith of the early Victorian years, in particular free trade, seen initially as the foundation of Victorian prosperity but latterly as the cause of late Victorian and Edwardian decline. The disillusionment went wider, however, to embrace many aspects of the comfortable society of the middle and upper classes at the end of the nineteenth century (Dangerfield 1936).

The evidence of economic growth demonstrates that much of this concern and lack of confidence was misplaced or exaggerated, although it remains an important political phenomenon. What is undeniable is that the economy was not only growing but changing, and that some of those changes were uncomfortable. This is particularly true of changes in the balance of economic activity between different types of activity and between regions within the country. The substantial changes that took place are indicated by the evidence in Tables 1.6 and 1.7. Not only did agricultural employment decline precipitately, as is described in detail in chapter 6 below, but there was a compensating and substantial growth of a whole range of service occupations, from domestic service to highly skilled professions. Population shifted from rural areas to the towns and, towards the end of the period, the locus of economic activity began to shift towards the midlands and the south-east, in a precursor of changes which have characterised the twentieth century and which diminished the power and importance of the northern manufacturing towns of the industrial revolution. It is particularly noticeable from Table 1.6 that manufacturing employment remained static as a proportion of total employment.

Seen in this light, the fall in the rate of growth of output which apparently occurred between 1899 and 1913 may not seem to have much importance. Although the check to growth was larger than had occurred in 1873–82, when productivity growth was also less than within the preceding cycle, the discrepancy is not large and, as Table 1.5 shows, it was not confined to Britain; the United States experienced an equivalent check, while the third largest economy, Germany, could not improve on the growth record of the earlier period. What is puzzling, however, is that Britain, and indeed these other two countries, should experience a check to productivity growth at all at a time when industrial change and the impact of new technology appears, from other evidence, to have been at its height. This was, after all, the beginning of the age of electricity, of the internal combustion engine and of a whole range of metal-using and processing industries – bicycles, sewing machines, household appliances in the con-

Table 1.6. *Occupational distribution of the working population, 1856–1911 (%)*

			Agriculture	Manufacturing	Services
(A)	Britain	1861	19	39	27
	France	1856	52	22	22
	Germany	1882	46	26	16
	USA	1880	59	18	20
(B)	Britain	1911	9	39	35
	France	1906	43	25	28
	Germany	1907	37	29	22
	USA	1910	31	29	35

Notes: 'Agriculture' includes agriculture, forestry and fishing; 'manufacturing' excludes extractive industries and construction; 'services' includes commerce, finance, transport and communication services.
Sources: Mitchell (1976: 155, 156, 163) for France, Germany, Britain; Bureau of the Census (1976: 138) for USA.

Table 1.7. *Population growth and migration, England and Wales, 1841–1911 (000s)*

	Population 1841 (1)	Population 1911 (2)	Natural increase (3)	Migration (net) (4)	4/3 (%)	2/1
Greater London	2,262	7,315	3,802	+1,251	31.9	3.24
Eight largest northern towns	1,551	5,192	2,747	+893	32·5	3·35
Nine colliery districts	1,320	5,334	3,363	+650	19·3	4·04
Textile towns	1,387	3,182	1,706	+90	5·3	2·30
Rural districts, north	2,426	2,875	2,093	−1,644	−78·6	1·19
Rural districts, south	3,740	4,086	3,209	−2,863	−89·2	1·10
England and Wales	15,914	36,070	21,366	−1,210	−5·7	2·27

Source: Baines (1981) based on Cairncross (1953).

sumer goods sector and machine tools, new types of textile machinery and industrial chemicals among producer goods. The coincidence of a check to growth in the three largest trading nations, Britain, the United States and Germany, suggests the need to enquire into the state of Britain's trade and, more generally, into her overall involvement with the world economy.

Despite or possibly because of the fact that Britain was already, by the beginning of the period, by far the largest exporter of manufactured goods in the world, achieving a share of world exports of 43 per cent in 1881–5 (Matthews *et al.* 1982: 435), British exports continued to grow rapidly throughout the period, both absolutely and as a proportion of British output. Exports defined more widely, of goods and services as a whole, which had been 21.5 per cent of GDP in 1856, rose to 30.1 per cent of GDP in 1913 (Matthews *et al.* 1982: 433). Although imports rose even more rapidly, the balance of payments remained in substantial surplus, helped by increasing earnings from previous foreign investment. The resultant surplus, reinvested abroad, amounted to 4.5 per cent of GDP between 1855 and 1873, rising to 5 per cent of GDP between 1873 and 1913 (Matthews *et al.* 1982: 442). It was this high and, above all, continuing level of foreign investment which allowed the citizens of Britain to become, by 1914, owner of more overseas assets than the citizens of all the other developed economies combined.

Despite this apparent success, there are some features of Britain's involvement with the international economy which may explain why growth faltered slightly at the end of the nineteenth century. First, the rate of growth of exports was lower after 1873 than before; it was 3.6 per cent for goods and services, 3.4 per cent for goods alone, between 1856 and 1873, but 2.6 per cent for goods and services and 2.7 per cent for goods alone from 1873 to 1913 (Matthews *et al.* 1982: 428). Matthews, Feinstein and Odling-Smee (1982: 321, 458) view the growth of export demand as the main proximate determinant of growth in both periods and thus the fall in export demand as the major, if not the only, factor explaining lower growth. They also see falling exports as an important determinant of lower growth in total factor productivity. The fact that export growth, and with it the economy as a whole, faltered at the end of the period, docs not in itself explain why this should have occurred.

Britain and the world economy

There are, essentially, two possible types of explanation; first, that the explanation lies in factors outside Britain, and, second, that it lies within the British economy. Outside Britain, the major factor was the rapid growth of foreign competition, which quickly eroded – though only to 31.8 per cent in 1913 – Britain's share of world exports of manufactured goods (Matthews *et al.* 1982: 435). As the United States, Germany, France and other European countries industrialised, competition intensified in all world markets, even without the additional effects of growing protectionism through the use of tariffs and other barriers. As Matthews, Feinstein and Odling-Smee put it (1982: 453):

for these reasons, a slowdown in the rate of growth of exports was unavoidable. Permanent maintenance of the mid-nineteenth century position was not a possibility. The rapid growth of exports depended in large part on the rapid growth of foreign incomes, and that could only be sustained in the long run by industrialisation, which in turn increased competition in British export markets.

Further effects included a relative deterioration in the terms of trade – the ratio of export to import prices – which had improved substantially in the early part of the period particularly because of the falling prices of agricultural imports; instead, British exporters could not increase their prices, or had to cut them, to meet competitive pressures. This relative deterioration helped to slow down the growth of real wages in the Edwardian period.

The assertion that foreign industrialisation inevitably harmed British export growth was not, of course, accepted by all observers at the time nor by many historians since. Indeed, accounts of British failure are heavily dependent on the view that British entrepreneurs and merchants missed export opportunities, retreated into easy empire markets, marketed badly the wrong goods and failed to learn foreign languages. As is shown in chapters 3, 7 and 8, these accounts are certainly exaggerated. Had they been only half true, and had they applied to a very wide range of British manufacturing, British exports would have fallen much more than they did. As it is, British exports faltered, and with them growth in GDP, but there is little reason to believe that this faltering of exports reflected any structural defects in the British economy which might not, in other circumstances, have been rectified.

What is tantalising, of course, is that the cataclysm of the First World War makes it impossible for us to know what would have happened to Britain's position in world trade and with it British growth if peacetime conditions had continued to prevail after 1913. At that time, British exports were growing strongly and, although both exports and manufacturing output as a whole were dependent on a relatively small range of staple industries, those industries showed few signs of the catastrophes that were to overcome so many of them after 1918.

The efficiency of the economy

If the world economy does not provide the whole answer to the history of the growth of the British economy, then internal factors, and in particular the efficiency of the economy, need to be considered. What was the state of British industry and commerce in the years before 1914? Did the economy and society operate so as to produce the maximum possible output? Was

British industry and indeed British agriculture and mining as efficient as its competitors, as ready to adopt new technologies, as adept at seizing sales as others or as it had been during the earlier years of the nineteenth century? It is questions such as these that have provided the basis for generations of argument, both among economic historians concerned to understand the Victorian and Edwardian economies and among politicians and others anxious to explain the travails of the British economy in the twentieth century.

Earlier sections of this chapter have demonstrated that there are indeed some causes for concern. The growth of labour productivity (output per capita), of output per man-hour and of total factor productivity all faltered towards the end of the period and Britain's share of world trade fell. In addition, imports of a wide range of goods increased as manufacturing industry developed overseas. In some fields, such as machine tools, chemicals and electrical goods, other countries and particularly Germany and the United States appeared to demonstrate greater skills of invention and innovation and Britain increasingly bought their machinery and the goods which they made.

But does such evidence demonstrate systemic inefficiency in the British economy? Evidence of increasing imports by itself certainly does not do so. There is little point in exporting except to import in return (or to build up foreign assets as a basis for future income or purchases) so that rising imports are not by themselves a sign of weakness in an economy unless they rise so much faster than exports that the balance of payments falls into deficit, which did not happen before 1914. Furthermore, the analysis of British agriculture in chapter 6 shows that it is sensible for any country to pursue its comparative advantage, to specialise in the types of produce which it can grow or breed most cheaply relative to other goods and to import those in which foreign countries sensibly specialise. This was the essence of the policy of free trade which was pursued so vigorously by Britain after the 1840s. The analysis of a number of industries in chapter 3 shows that the argument is as applicable there as in agriculture.

The evidence of declining rates of growth of productivity cannot be dealt with so easily, although it is important to remember that the evidence relates to a very short period and the declining rates might well not have persisted. Nevertheless, they did occur and one possible explanation for them is that British industry, agriculture and commerce were faltering in the efficiency with which they carried out their business. The difficulty is to find much direct evidence either that this was so or that, if there is evidence in one sector of the economy or the other, that such faltering was widespread enough to affect the economy as a whole.

Chapters 3, 5 and 6 survey between them the whole of production in the

British economy in the period in question, using different methods and drawing on different and more detailed studies. In recent years, as these chapters show, studies of the period have focussed on the speed of adjustment of sectors of the economy when faced with new circumstances, be they increased foreign competition or a new technology which entrepreneurs and managers must decide whether or not to adopt. In discussing agriculture, the sector which is traditionally slowest to change, chapter 6 shows that not only were there very substantial changes in the patterns of output but the overall speed of response cannot be criticised. Chapters 3 and 5 similarly show for a wide range of manufacturing and service industries that there was substantial change and that entrepreneurs were alive to new opportunities and ready to adopt new technologies when it was profitable to do so. Chapter 4 approaches the same conclusion from a different perspective, showing that employers were ready to collude, at least in general, with powerful unions in the organisation of the workplace, and that this limited innovation and proved ultimately bad for major British industries.

These studies consider behaviour at the level of the individual farmer or firm or, occasionally, of an industry organised with collective bargaining. There may, therefore, have been something in the wider environment within which farmers, firms and industries operated that had the general effect of retarding their ability to change or compete. Changes in the growth of foreign demand have already been considered and it is therefore sensible now to explore whether there were factors on the supply side which retarded British growth.

The distribution and quality of the labour force

An important determinant of economic progress at any one time is the distribution of the labour force between different types of economic activity, together with the agility with which labour responds to economic opportunities. The distribution of labour in the British economy of 1860 differed spectacularly from that found in the economies of the other developed countries. As Table 1.6 shows, a far smaller proportion of her population was engaged in agriculture, reflecting Britain's early industrialisation. The distribution of British jobs continued to alter down to 1914, as the labour force in agriculture shrank still further and the proportion in the tertiary or service sector of the economy grew.

It is particularly significant that, as Table 1.6 shows, and by contrast with the experience in every other developing country, the share of the British labour force engaged in manufacture did not alter during the period. Britain might be 'The Workshop of the World', but it was rapidly becoming the counting-house too. The rise of the tertiary sector reflects a redirection of the British economy and affected both the domestic, non-trading, economy and the sectors engaged in foreign trade. Within the home economy, the distribution of goods became more complex as the growth of national chains such as Liptons and the Home and Colonial Stores replaced the small-scale distribution networks of an earlier period. An obvious sign of the increase in the distributive networks was the growth of the transport and communication sector of the economy, which absorbed 12 per cent of the labour force in 1911, up from 8 per cent fifty years earlier; none of Britain's European competitors had nearly so high a proportion of their labour force so engaged.

The shift, in proportionate terms, from agriculture to the service industries is some evidence that the British population was mobile in its search for jobs and in response to new job opportunities. This is important because, as is described in chapter 5, it is thought that industrialisation is aided by transfers of labour from agriculture, which are clearly easier if the agricultural sector is large. In Britain, much of this transfer had occurred before 1860 but it continued after that date, so rapidly indeed that as many workers were released from agriculture as in France and almost as many as in Germany, despite their much larger agricultural sectors. Even though part of the rise in the proportion of the labour force in services sprang from a decline of women's work in cottage industry, which attracted them instead into domestic service, the rise in other services – banking, shipping and insurance – where Britain had a strong comparative advantage, shows that the labour force was flexible enough to move to new types of activity. The amount of internal and external migration which is discussed in chapter 2 also points in this direction. If these conclusions are correct, then it seems unlikely that any deficiency or faltering in British growth can be ascribed to labour shortages arising from immobility of labour.

It is, however, possible that the growth of the labour force in Britain was deficient in another sense, in that the growth of skills and education did not match that of Britain's competitors nor the demands of new, higher technology, industries and service occupations (Landes 1969: 339–48). In an attempt to introduce measurement into an area rife with anecdote and assertion, Matthews, Feinstein and Odling-Smee have considered changes to the quality of the labour force associated with alterations in its age and sex composition, in the intensity of work associated with changes in hours of work and in education; they were unable to consider changes in health due to changes in nutritional status, an aspect considered in chapter 11 below. An estimate of the combined effect of these changes is given in Table 1.8, where it can be seen that the rate of growth in the quality of the labour input between 1873 and 1913 was greater than between 1856 and 1873.

Table 1.8. *Growth in the quality of the labour input, 1856–1973* (*annual percentage rates*)

	Growth in quality associated with					
	Age, sex, nationality	Work intensity	Education	All such sources	Man-hours	Man-hours adjusted for quality
1856–73	0·2	0·9	0·3	1·4	0·0	1·4
1873–1913	0·3	0·0	0·5	0·8	0·9	1·7
1856–1973	0·2	0·3	0·5	1·0	0·2	1·2

Source: Matthews *et al.* (1982: 113).

While this does not remove the force of charges such as that British higher education, by comparison with German, neglected science and engineering in the late nineteenth century, it reduces the likely impact of such deficiencies on the economy as a whole.

Savings and investment

Apart from labour or 'human capital', the other major resources available to the economy are stocks of raw material and of physical capital. While the labour force is maintained and grows by human reproduction, the stock of capital available to the economy has to be maintained by repair and replacement and increased by the purchase of new equipment. The ability of the economy to incur such expenditure is dependent on the expectations of entrepreneurs, on the fiscal policies of governments and on the willingness of individuals collectively to save and invest resources to maintain and increase productive capacity (rather than to consume them immediately). Such saving and investment must take place continuously if the stock of capital is to be increased or, at the least, maintained and the proportion of the national output which is devoted each year to investment is therefore an indication of the amount of capital which the economy is prepared to supply. The efficiency with which the economy makes use of all its resources is greatly affected by the overall supply of investible funds and by the uses which are made of them.

Table 1.9 shows a calculation of the proportion which capital investment formed of the gross national product of Britain and her main competitors. It is clear that Britain devoted a substantially smaller proportion of her national product to investment in the domestic economy than did any of her major competitors and there is, moreover, little sign of the proportion

Table 1.9. *Capital formation proportions, 1851–1916 (%)*

	Period	GDFCF as % of GDP	GNFCF as % of GNP
UK	1855–1914	9·0	12·8
Germany	1851–1913	19·8	21·1
USA	1869–1913	21·9	22·1
France	1865–1913	20·2	
Italy	1861–1915	12·5	
Japan	1887–1916	10·9	9·7

Notes: GDFCF (GNFCF) = gross domestic (national) fixed capital formation. GDP (GNP) = gross domestic (national) product.
Source: Kuznets (1961: 5).

Table 1.10. *Capital formation proportions for the UK, 1873–1913 (%)*

	GDFCF as % of GNP	Net investment abroad as % of GNP	Total
1873–82	8·2	3·7	11·9
1882–99	6·9	4·4	11·3
1899–1913	7·9	5·4	13·3

Sources: Feinstein (1972: Tables 8 and 37).

rising over the period, as Table 1.10 indicates. If, however, British investment overseas is aggregated with British domestic investment and the whole compared with total investment by other countries, some of the disparity disappears. In other words, as is shown in detail in chapter 7 below, the oddity in Britain's investment performance is not just that savings and investment were relatively low, but also that a substantial proportion of those savings were invested (and increasingly generated) abroad rather than at home; in some years overseas investment exceeded domestic investment.

Detailed investigation of investment flows does not suggest, however, that this unusual pattern harmed the domestic economy. As chapter 7 shows, there is no evidence that overseas investment produced lower returns than did domestic investment, nor that it was riskier; indeed, risk-adjusted returns were probably higher for substantial periods. Conditions varied over time, as is shown in chapters 7, 8 and 9, but there does not seem to have been overall weakness.

Table 1.11. *The components of domestic capital formation, 1851–1914*

		GDFCF	GDFCF excluding residential construction	GDFCF in residential construction	GDFCF in producers' equipment
(A) As % of GDP					
UK	1855–1914	9·0	7·7	1·3	3·2
Germany	1851–1913	19·8	13·8	4·0	5·1
USA	1869–1913	21·9	17·4	4·2	5·3
(B) As % of GDFCF					
UK	1855–1914	100	86	14	36
Germany	1851–1913	100	70	30	26
USA	1869–1913	100	80	20	24

Note: UK: a similar calculation for 1856–1913 from Feinstein (1972: T88–9) gives the proportions as 82:18:42. USA: a similar calculation for 1869–1916 from US Bureau of the Census (1976: Figures 98–124) gives the proportions as 76:24:23.
Source: calculated from Kuznets (1961: 5 and Table 13).

Nor do Tables 1.9 and 1.10 necessarily demonstrate great weakness. Although investment in the domestic economy was lower in Britain than in other countries, this does not prove that investment in domestic industry was lower, since so much of domestic investment is employed in residential housebuilding and, particularly in the nineteenth century, in transport infrastructure. Investment in housebuilding, in addition, follows patterns over time, partially determined by demographic conditions, which differ from those of other parts of the economy as well as being substantially affected by the mobility of the population. It is necessary, in other words, to discover whether the amount of capital available for industry and in particular for industrial equipment was lower in Britain than elsewhere. Table 1.11, therefore, attempts to distinguish between the main components of domestic investment in three countries. It shows that, while the proportion devoted to producers' equipment was lower in Britain than in the United States or Germany, the gap between Britain and her rivals was very much less – of the order of 2 per cent of GNP – than the gap which appears either in Table 1.9 or Table 1.10. In other words, Germany and the United States were devoting much larger proportions of their total investment to building – of houses, factories, public buildings and transport facilities – than was Britain, and it is this component of investment, rather than that in industrial equipment, which mainly accounts for the disparity in Britain's investments. To put it in another way, of the domestic investment which took place in these three countries, Britain devoted a much larger proportion to producers' equipment than did the other countries – for Britain the proportion was 36 per cent, for the United States 24 per cent and for Germany 26 per cent.

What might this difference mean? First, it confirms the evidence shown in Table 1.6, that Britain had a different industrial and commercial structure from other countries, and suggests that she thus had different needs and uses for capital. Britain was first in constructing its infrastructure of houses and factories, roads and railways, canals and ports and, by the end of the nineteenth century, therefore had less need than many other countries to use capital in this way.

Second, turning from the demand to the supply of capital, the evidence of Table 1.11 argues against the view, which has often been propounded, that Britain did not suffer from an overall shortage of capital but rather from its misdirection to overseas rather than domestic projects and away from manufacturing industry within the domestic economy. The favourite culprit for this is the City of London, which was heavily orientated to the finance of large overseas projects such as railways and gold mines, and is thought to have scorned involvement with dirty industry at home (Cottrell 1975). Table 1.11 does not support this view, for it appears that British domestic investment was more heavily orientated towards industry than was the case in Germany or the United States.

It still does not follow, of course, that domestic investment was large enough, or placed well enough, to encourage long-term growth. As to the first, however, Matthews, Feinstein and Odling-Smee conclude cautiously for the whole of their period, including that from 1860 to 1914, that 'It is ... doubtful whether a higher level of investment, due to exogenous causes such as greater availability of finance, would, in the absence of other changes, have made a major difference to the growth rate of GDP over most of the period' (1982: 522). Within the 1860–1914 period, as they point out, there was a sustained rise in investment just before the declining rate of growth of total factor productivity experienced in the Edwardian period. They speculate, therefore, that the investment must have been misplaced but are unwilling to speculate about where it might have been better used. Kennedy (1987), by contrast, believes that faster growth could have been achieved by directing both human and physical capital into newer industries, in particular those which were successful in the United States, but the transformation which he believes to have been desirable would have taken many years and been immensely difficult to achieve.

Summing up, there is no obvious domestic candidate for the role of the cause of slowing productivity in Britain in the early twentieth century, while the reduced growth of world trade still stands as a possible external cause. Arguments for a systemic weakness of the British economy in the late Victorian and Edwardian periods therefore appear to rest on weak ground.

Conclusion

While there is insufficient evidence to conclude that Britain's use of resources was systematically, or over long periods, less efficient than it should have been, had been in the past or was to be in the future, there were nevertheless some obvious problems. Many appeared most obviously after the First World War, so that those who observed them had the benefit of hindsight, but they were nonetheless real. British industry came to be concentrated on a relatively narrow range of so-called staple industries, coal, iron and steel, cotton, shipbuilding and did not develop such a large involvement in a range of new technologies and products. Within the staple industries, there is evidence of collusion between employers and trade unions, aimed at a quiet life rather than at technological advancement. The state, in setting its face – or having its face set by the electorate – against tariffs or other forms of encouragement of industry, left itself without the weapons used by other governments to assist their economies.

As the succeeding chapters show, all these propositions are open to challenge, partly at least because the evidence of incipient decline pales into insignificance beside the achievements of the British economy in the nineteenth century. Much was wrong with that economy, principally in its treatment of the more deprived sections of the labour force and of the community as a whole, but it is difficult to deny its dynamism at home and, through the investments which it made, its contribution to the development of the world economy.

2 Population, migration and regional development, 1870–1939

Dudley Baines

Population growth: the demographic transition model

The most important demographic change of the last quarter of the nineteenth century was the onset of a sustained fall in fertility. Demographers have often used the idea of a 'demographic transition' to explain the event, which has occurred in all western countries. In the demographic transition the population passes through three stages. In the first the rate of population growth is determined mainly by the level of mortality, which is high. In such circumstances fertility has to be high as well if population is not to fall. There is little or no control of the number of births within marriage. In the second stage, economic growth accelerates, leading to public health improvements and better nutrition. Fertility, on the other hand, does not fall in parallel, because the number of children in each family is affected by deep-rooted social institutions – which may take a generation or more to change. As a result the death rate is low but the birth rate remains high: the rate of population growth accelerates. In the third and final stage of the demographic transition fertility finally declines, bringing the growth rate of population down to low levels. A crucial notion in the model is that the fertility decline is caused by 'modernisation'. The factors in such modernisation that one might expect to matter are: an increase in the independence of women; an increase in the proportion of women working outside the home; a fall in infant and child mortality and changes in the costs and benefits of children – including their employment and education.

Population growth: the fall in mortality

Between 1860 and the outbreak of the Second World War the British population roughly doubled (Table 2.1). The doubling was caused, arithmetically speaking, by a sustained fall in the death rate. Population growth was slower than in the first half of the nineteenth century, however, because the birth rate fell, too, and sharply. Deaths per 1,000 of the

Table 2.1. *Population growth in Great Britain, 1861–1939*

	Total population (thousands)	Natural increase since last census	Net overseas migration since last census
1861	23,130		
1871	26,070	3,140 (+13.6%)	−200 (−0·8%)
1881	29,710	3,900 (+14·9%)	−260 (−1·0%)
1891	33,030	4,140 (+13·9%)	−820 (−2·7%)
1901	37,000	4,090 (+12·4%)	−120 (−0·4%)
1911	40,830	4,590 (+12·4%)	−760 (−2·0%)
1921	42,770	2,800 (+6.9%)	−860 (−2·1%)
1931	44,800	2,590 (+6·1%)	−560 (−1·3%)
1939	46,470	1,160 (+2·5%)	+510 (+1·1%)

Source: Carrier and Jeffery (1953: 14); Mitchell and Deane (1962: 12–13, 29–35).

population (the so-called crude death rate) almost halved between the 1860s and the 1930s, falling from 22.6 per 1,000 in 1861–5 to 12.1 per 1,000 in 1935–8. In the same period the crude birth rate fell by more than half, from 35.1 to 15.2. Subtract the two and you have the 'natural' rate of growth (that is, the rate that would occur if there was no migration). The natural rate of growth was less than it was earlier in the nineteenth century. The net migration balance was negative, emigrants exceeding immigrants during every decade except the 1930s (Logan 1950: 135; Mitchell and Deane 1962: 29–35).

Demographers prefer to use measures more sophisticated than the crude birth and death rates, calling the phenomena arrived at 'fertility' and 'mortality'. There are several possible ways of measuring them, but all eliminate the effects of age and sex distribution. That is, the measures relate to the population actually 'at risk', as the demographers say: at risk of dying of tuberculosis at age forty, perhaps, or giving birth to a boy at age twenty-five. As an example, the number of legitimate births can be related to the number of married women at different ages.

A technical point about mortality is that it can be expressed in terms of 'life expectancy' ('*e*' for short) because the average person in a population dying off at a rate *d*, it turns out, can 'expect' on average to live $1/d$ years. If 2 per cent of the people die every year then the average person can expect to live fifty years (which is 1/.02). In other words, it turns out that life expectancy is the reciprocal of mortality. Life expectancy 'at age *N*' is the average life left when a person is *N* years old, and is calculated from the probabilities of surviving from one age to another. Life expectancy at birth

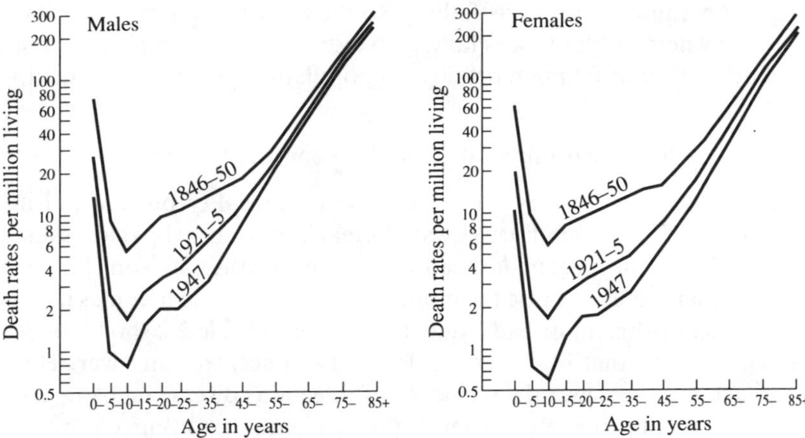

Figure 2.1 Death rates at various ages per million living, England and Wales, 1846–50, 1921–5, 1947 (logarithmic scale)
Source: see text.

is signified by e_0, the zero subscript standing for the beginning of life. In 1861, e_0 in England and Wales was 40.5 years for men and 43.0 years for women. By 1901 it had risen by nearly six years – to 45.3 and 49.4. Life expectancy rose as much in these forty years as it had in the previous century. In the two centuries before that, it had barely risen (Woods 1989: 139). In the twentieth century life expectancy rose still faster. By 1960, e_0 had risen to 68.2 for men and 74.1 for women, twenty-four years more than it had been at the turn of the century. (Another technical point: life expectancy is calculated from the mortality affecting the relevant age group in the year in question, as though that year's mortality was never going to change. Therefore life expectancy does not show what the mortality experience of the 'cohort' of people in question actually, and later, turned out to be. Life expectancy at birth in 1901 would predict that only a half of all women born in 1901 would have been alive in 1950. But since mortality continued to fall, substantially more than half in fact survived to 1950.)

The most affected by the fall in mortality were the young and young adults. Compare for example the mortality levels of the early 1850s (when effective death registration began) with mortality at the end of the Second World War. The mortality of the one to fourteen age groups had fallen by about 90 per cent and that of the fifteen to forty-four age groups by more than 75 per cent (Logan 1950: 169). Infant mortality (deaths under one year) also fell by more than 75 per cent, though the chronology was different. The lowest fall came in the older age groups (see Figure 2.1). (Still another technical point: by the early twentieth century the population was ageing because fertility was falling. So there were fewer people in the age groups where mortality was falling fastest (that is, children), which meant that the effect of falling mortality on population growth was muted.)

Why did mortality fall?: the McKeown controversy

There are many reasons for the decline in mortality but the fall in the incidence of infectious diseases was of great importance. Infectious diseases were the main proximate cause of the deaths of younger people ('proximate' only because the ultimate reason someone becomes ill may be lack of nourishment or bad hygienic practices). Table 2.2 shows all deaths from disease – that is, excluding deaths from accident and war. Holding age structure constant the incidence of infectious disease (cholera and the like) fell to an extremely low level; the incidence of non-infectious disease (heart attacks and the like) only halved. Table 2.2 also confirms that the mortality decline was much faster in the twentieth century. If we divide the period into two – the 1850s to 1901 and 1901 to 1971 – we can see that most of the reduction in deaths from infectious diseases (63 per cent) occurred in the twentieth century and only 37 per cent before 1901. In the non-infectious diseases the contrast is even more striking. Only 10 per cent of the fall in deaths occurred before 1901 and 90 per cent after.

Vital registration was introduced in 1837 and death certification was comprehensive (in England and Wales) by the late 1840s. The vital data were exhaustively examined by McKeown and his collaborators in the 1960s and 1970s. McKeown's explanation of the fall in disease mortality – three-quarters of which was in infectious diseases – was simple. He identified four possible causes: medical treatment, including immunisation and therapy; autonomous declines in the virulence of disease; public health measures including improvements in sewage disposal and water supply; and 'environmental factors', by which he meant the increase in the quantity and quality of food supplies.

In McKeown's analysis, virtually all the reduction in deaths in the second half of the nineteenth century must have been on account of environmental factors. Reductions in deaths from respiratory tuberculosis accounted for 33 per cent of the fall, scarlet fever and diphtheria 12 per cent, cholera and dysentery 12 per cent, typhoid and typhus 17 per cent and smallpox 5 per cent. Deaths from influenza, bronchitis and pneumonia, on the contrary, rose. According to McKeown, medical improvements in the nineteenth century were, except for vaccination against smallpox, virtually worthless. Public health improvements were important, though they can only have affected the water-borne diseases (typhoid and cholera). (There was no cholera outbreak in Britain comparable to the Hamburg epidemic

Table 2.2. *Death rates per 1,000 population, standardised by the age structure of the population in 1901*

	1848–54	1901	1971
From infectious disease	13·0	8·5	0·6
(Respiratory tuberculosis alone	2·9	1·3	nil)
From non-infectious disease	8·9	8·5	4·7
From all diseases	21·8	17·0	5·4

Source: adapted from McKeown (1976: 54).

of 1892, for example.) The fall in scarlet fever is inexplicable except as an autonomous fall in virulence. This leaves the fall in tuberculosis, typhus and several lesser diseases to be explained. Tuberculosis and typhus were not difficult to diagnose and there is no evidence that their autonomous virulence had declined. By default the argument leaves better nutrition – which increased the resistance to disease – as the most important cause of the decline in mortality (McKeown 1976: 54–64, 152–5).

The factors that affected mortality were more complex in the twentieth century but the decline was still dominated by a decline of infectious disease. McKeown's position was that 'medical intervention' remained ineffective almost until the Second World War. For example the sulphonamide ('sulpha') drugs were not used before 1935 and streptomycin (the main treatment for tuberculosis) not before 1947. But these were after the main battle against infectious diseases had been won.

McKeown's views, including the attack on the effectiveness of medicine, have attracted a great deal of controversy. McKeown argued by exclusion. Yet it is clear that the relationship between environmental factors (like better food), the autonomous virulence of disease and the carrying vectors (like lice) is far from simple. Criticism of McKeown came from several directions. The first concerns the 'cause' of death. Nineteenth-century doctors were good at filling in death certificates in persuasive-looking ways, but their diagnostic skills left something to be desired. Even when the diagnosis was accurate the 'cause' of death would only be the proximate cause. For example the reduction in smallpox deaths – which *was* caused by medical intervention – led to more people surviving to die later of tuberculosis (Kearns 1988: 233). The issue here is *morbidity* (the incidence of disease) not mortality. Improvements in medicine or the environment may have significantly increased the general level of health in Britain. But their greatest impact may have been on diseases from which people did not happen to die.

It turns out that treatment, including primitive anaesthetic surgery, *was* reducing mortality from the middle of the nineteenth century, but only gradually. The view that patients were more likely to die if they entered a hospital has been shown to be untrue, for periods as early as the 1850s (Tranter 1985: 73). We must also remember that hospitals may have reduced mortality even when no 'cure' was available. For example, some of the fall in deaths from tuberculosis in the twentieth century must have been a consequence of the building of isolation hospitals, which kept the sick from infecting the healthy.

Even so the impact of hospitals was small, because ordinary people had only limited access to them. In 1880 the number of hospital beds per capita was only one quarter of the number today – when the turnover of beds is much higher. As late as the inter-war period large numbers of people did not ever attend hospitals or clinics (Smith 1979: 256–60). And for a long time general hospitals discriminated against people suffering from infectious diseases, preferring to admit people that they could cure – of broken bones or appendicitis, for example.

McKeown did not explain the 'environmental factors' in detail, but he had food consumption in mind. There are other possible improvements in environment. The steady improvement in housing conditions may have had an important effect, and this was partly because of policy – that is, it was a 'social intervention' (Szreter 1986; Woods and Woodward 1984: 30).

Some recent research leans back towards the McKeown position. Adult height is correlated with 'nutritional status'. Nutritional status is not quite the same thing as nutrition, because it could include the effects of inherited health, infection and public health improvements, for example. It turns out that average height fell in the early decades of the nineteenth century, perhaps because of the unhealthy environment of cities. But then up to the First World War it rose, and continued to do so at a slower rate up to the Second World War. The data support McKeown's general conclusions – assuming that 'nutritional status' as measured by individual heights is a proxy for the standard of living and health of the population (Floud *et al.* 1990: 312–14).

The health improvements were not of course enough to eliminate the differences between rich and poor. Available family budgets for the later nineteenth century, when food accounted for about 60 per cent of expenditure, show that some families had insufficient calorific intake for people to grow normally (Oddy 1976: 322). This is corroborated by descriptions of the health and stature of many children at the time and by the medical inspections of recruiting officers in the First World War. The best estimate is that half of the conscripts of 1916–18 were unfit for front line service – although this did not stop many of them being sent to the Front (Winter 1985: 62).

Despite a continued improvement in health between the wars the serious gap between the health standards of rich and poor remained. As late as 1937–9 mortality, standardised for age and sex, in Lancashire, Northumberland, Durham and South Wales was 29 per cent higher than in south-east England. Britain had welfare services by the late 1930s but they were partial and in the economic depression they were reduced to little more than crisis management. For example, free school meals could be provided but a recent estimate shows that only 2 per cent of the school population managed to obtain them in 1939 (Webster 1985: 214, 229).

It is difficult to draw conclusions about nutrition from evidence about the aggregate supply of food. We know relatively little in quantitative terms about the quality of food that was available to the working-class household, the adequacy of storage and the efficiency of cooking (for an optimistic view see Roberts 1988: 313–14). Nor do we know much about the distribution of food within the working-class household. There is qualitative and some survey evidence about this and it is possible that the breadwinners (that is, the prime-age males) were given a disproportionate share of the food, and especially a large share of the meat. Such a division of the meal may have been rational behaviour from the point of view of the family budget. Alternatively the practice may simply have reflected relative power within the household.

The urban penalty, early and late

The heights and mortality data understate the improvement in health and nutrition because the proportion of the population living in cities was increasing. The disease environment was less favourable in the cities because of the density of population. Hence, as the country became more urbanised life expectancy at birth would have fallen, merely because of urbanisation, had there been no countervailing improvements in health. But in fact, as we have seen, life expectancy rose. What happened was that life expectancy rose faster in the cities, causing the 'urban penalty' at last to fade. For example, in 1861, when expectation of life at birth was forty-one in England and Wales, it was forty-five in the rural areas but only thirty-seven in London. In 1911, on the other hand, life expectancy had risen to fifty-three in England and Wales, fifty-three in the rural areas and fifty-two in London (Friedlander *et al.* 1985: 144; Woods 1985: 650).

The great puzzle: infant mortality and social change

There is a part of the fall in mortality that deserves close and separate study: infants. Some of the fall in urban mortality, for example, came from a fall in infant mortality (that is, deaths of children under a year old) that did not follow the trend of child and adult mortality.

The downturn in infant mortality did not occur until a generation after it occurred at older ages. There was a slight fall in infant mortality in the 1870s and 1880s but in the 1890s infant mortality was as high as it had been in the 1860s (and close to its level in the 1840s) at about 150 per 1,000. The decisive fall came in the early twentieth century and, by the outbreak of the Second World War, it had fallen to 55 or 60 per 1,000.

The implication is that improvements in nutrition and public health were insufficient reasons for the fall in infant mortality. (The difference between the trend in infant deaths and those of young children (ages one to three) is particularly puzzling.) In other words, low levels of infant mortality almost certainly depended on changes in behaviour, for example, in the way that infants were nurtured. Infant life has to be actively fostered – which means, for example, that in the long run the value parents put on babies' lives may have been critical. Unfortunately, if this was the case, we do not know why.

Infant mortality was related both to urbanisation and to income. For example, as late as 1939, infant mortality in East Anglia was 17 per cent below the national average, but 26 per cent above the national average in Northumberland and Durham. And as we would expect, infant deaths were high in the poorest inner city areas. The variance increased in the early twentieth century because infant mortality fell fastest in those regions where it was already low (Lee 1991: 59–61). The greater contrast was in deaths after three months, which would be especially sensitive to the home and nutritional environment (Titmuss 1943: 44–5; Winter 1982: 107). The differentials did not depend simply on income. For example the inner cities were affected both by the 'urban' and the 'poverty' effect. A wealthy family in the city still suffered some from being there. What we do know is that agricultural labourers (who, in general, were poor) lost fewer infants than did better off urban workers and coal miners. We must also remember that infant mortality in both urban *and* rural areas remained in Britain among the lowest in Europe as late as the 1930s. Whatever troubles remained, there had been great progress over pre-industrial rates of death of small babies.

There is a suggestion that the late turning point in infant mortality is a statistical artifact, caused by the large number of deaths from infantile diarrhoea in the exceptionally hot summers of the 1890s (Woods *et al.*

1989). The argument is that infant mortality would have continued to fall had these deaths not occurred. But the argument partly depends on an assumption that the proportion of women who were breast feeding in the 1890s was less than in previous decades. The assumption is crucial because breast feeding partially protected an infant from disease. The alternatives to mother's milk – condensed milk, for example – were neither sterile nor nutritionally adequate. Not surprisingly, data on feeding practices are hard to obtain but it was thought at the time that only 80 per cent of mothers were breast feeding. Unfortunately, since we have no estimates for previous years we cannot be sure how many children had been fed on non-breast milk and semi-solid food in still earlier years, when such food was even more unhealthy. The practice of weaning from breast milk early was common in parts of continental Europe (Knodel and Van de Walle 1986: 406). In other words, Woods effectively supports the view with which we began. The achievement of low levels of infant mortality partly depended on changes in attitudes and behaviour (Woods *et al.* 1989: 114–16; Fildes 1986; Smith 1979: 97).

Some commentators in the early twentieth century were convinced that what they saw as a high level of infant mortality was caused by 'ignorance'. This may indeed have been true, though it is difficult to reconcile with the low level of infant deaths among the rural compared with the urban poor. In any event the conviction lead to a revolutionary change – 'social intervention' in the working-class household in forms such as health visitors. Another early twentieth-century view blamed working-class mothers for working outside the home. The old calumny was resurrected that infant mortality had declined in the Lancashire cotton famine of the 1860s because the unemployed mothers were able to feed their babies properly. In fact there was no relation between married women's participation in the labour force and the death of their infants, not least because a woman out of work would not be able to pass on much nutrition to the child (Dyhouse 1978: 251–2; Roberts 1982: 156–7; Rose 1986: 9).

Another intriguing factor in the fall of infant mortality is the fall in fertility, fewer children per mother. Fertility fell steadily from the 1880s to the Second World War. One way this occurred was by contracting the child-bearing years. On average, mothers were younger when their children were born, with less chance of complications leading to infant deaths. Further, the probability of a child being born second or third in the birth order increased and of being born sixth or seventh decreased, since large families were fewer. First children and very late children have more than average infant mortality, but a second or third child born to a young mother has lower than average mortality.

Did smaller families lead to better standards of infant care? The turning point in fertility came well *before* that in infant mortality, which makes it difficult to connect smaller families with better care. But up to the Second World War, both infant mortality and the number of children per family were in continuous decline. It would seem likely that *both* phenomena were related to some fundamental changes that affected public and private attitudes to children in society as a whole.

The fall in fertility

Fewer deaths meant an increase in the total number of years that the female population was at risk of pregnancy. In early centuries many women had died before they reached the end of their fecund period. Hence, falling mortality should have led to an increase in the number of births.

But births did not in fact rise, because fertility fell. The most convenient way of measuring the fertility of historical populations (the age of mother is rarely known) is to relate the number of births that actually occurred to a theoretical maximum. The highest fertility ever recorded is that of the Hutterites, a North American Anabaptist sect, in 1921–30. Each Hutterite woman could on average expect to bear twelve children. Marital fertility (I_g) is calculated from

$$I_g = \frac{B_l}{\text{Sum of } F_i \text{ times } M_i}$$

where B_l is the number of legitimate births in the period; F_i is the Hutterite fertility schedule, that is, the number of children born to Hutterite mothers aged i; and M_i is the number of married women in the historical population aged i. F_i times M_i is therefore the number of births that would have occurred if the fertility of the mothers in question was the same as that of the Hutterite mothers. These measures were devised by the Princeton Fertility Survey, which was able to chart the course of fertility decline in the provinces (or counties) of most of Europe (Coale and Treadway 1986: 34–5).

Figure 2.2 shows the extent of the decline in fertility in Britain. The early rise in the series can be ignored (it was caused by improving birth registration which was only made compulsory in 1874). Fertility began to fall in the 1870s and sharply so in the 1880s.

The data are good enough to enable us to eliminate several possible causes of the fall. For example, in pre-industrial Britain, fertility had been controlled by the age and frequency of marriage, but from 1851 to the First World War there was virtually no change in the rate or age of marriage.

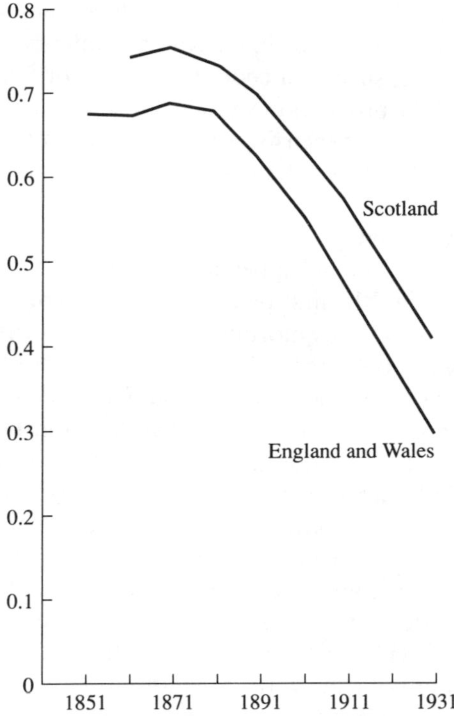

Figure 2.2 The decline in fertility in Britain, 1841–1931.
Note: the chart shows the average number of births at the date shown, compared with Hutterite fertility; the latter at an index value of 1·0 corresponds to twelve children per married woman.
Source: see text.

Between 83 per cent and 88 per cent of women always married, a rather lower proportion than in the 1980s. The female singulate age of marriage was 25.8 ± 0.6 years over the period (Teitelbaum 1984: 98, 100, 117).

The decline in fertility was caused by a fall in the number of children born within marriage. Couples married in the 1870s had on average about six children. Couples married in the 1900s had about five, in the 1930s about two. In other words the fall in fertility was much faster after the First World War than before.

Clearly couples must have been using some form of birth control. This cannot be a sufficient explanation, however, since most couples used the 'safe period' or *coitus interruptus*, methods which had been known for centuries. Induced abortions were fairly common, although illegal. Informed guesses suggest that perhaps 10 per cent of all pregnancies were aborted in the 1930s (Davey 1988: 332; Glass 1940: 51–3). Responses to questions about contraceptive use are also rather problematic but, when asked, only 18 per cent of the 1920–4 marriage cohort – inter-war parents – admitted using an appliance, such as a condom, pessary or diaphragm. Before the First World War the proportion would have been much less, not least because appliances could be expensive or difficult to obtain (Lewis-Faning 1949: 175; Peel 1963). Hence the question becomes not *how* the births were avoided but *why*?

How far does the mortality and fertility history of Britain fit the idea of a 'demographic transition'? The model appears to have had little relevance to what happened in Britain. In the first place, population growth before 'modernisation' was not controlled by mortality but mainly by the age and incidence of marriage. To use the jargon, England's, and indeed most of Europe's, was a 'low pressure' regime (Wrigley and Schofield 1981). The assumption in the demographic transition model that there was no fertility control *within* marriage before 'modernisation' is also incorrect. A distinction has to be made between 'spacing' and 'stopping' behaviour. Nowadays couples stop having children when they reach some target number. Such behaviour was rare before the nineteenth century. But spacing behaviour, in which couples determined *when* children were conceived – for example, after the harvest – was common in many pre-industrial societies (see the evidence for it in vol. 1). In other words the desire to control fertility did not start with 'modernisation'.

The most telling feature of the British fertility transition is that compared with all other European countries the fall in fertility came *late* in Britain's industrialisation. Marital fertility had fallen by 10 per cent in England and Wales by about 1892 and in Scotland by about 1894. The equivalent dates in France, Belgium and Germany were 1827, 1881 and 1888, well before they had reached the British level of 'modernisation' (Coale and Treadway 1986: 39). In fact there is no country having a population more than 50 per cent urban, and where less than 45 per cent work in agriculture, that has not had a substantial fall in fertility – criteria which Britain met in 1850.

There is no evidence that falling infant mortality influenced the desired family size in Britain (one might expect so: it becomes possible to assure oneself of the desired number of children with a smaller number as their deaths become rarer). As we have seen, infant mortality began to decline *after* the fall in fertility had started, not before. The relationship may have been stronger the other way round because, as we have seen, smaller families would *ceteris paribus* lead to lower infant mortality. This seems to have been the case in several other European countries (Van de Walle 1986: 397).

The rapid diffusion of the fertility decline in Britain is also puzzling. The 10 per cent downturn first occurred in 1886 when it affected counties with

8 per cent of the population. By 1891 counties with 50 per cent of the population were affected and by 1903, 90 per cent – a rate of spread with no parallel in Europe. The rapid diffusion suggests that information may have been a key variable. Couples were learning about fertility in other parts of the country. The increase in the number of publications advocating birth control in the 1880s and 1890s may be important here (Banks 1954). But the willingness of couples to discuss the size of their family rather than leaving it to chance may have been more important. In a situation where there was no parity specific birth control at all, opening the question of family size could lead only in one direction.

The fertility decline did not start from a plateau where all classes had identical fertility. But the differences by social class were probably caused by differences in nutrition, maternal health and feeding practices, not so much by deliberate limitation. In the 1870s, the lowest fertility was probably among professional families and the highest among miners and agricultural labourers. It is difficult to say if the fall in fertility was faster for one social class than another. The calculation is complicated by differences in the age of marriage (Anderson 1990: 42; Woods 1987: 288–9). Contemporary fears that the poor would outbreed the middle classes and cause 'national degeneration' were unfounded, though politically powerful.

We should be wary therefore of explanations of the fall in fertility that depend on social capillarity or a demonstration effect. For example, the argument that upper-middle-class families were forced to control births because the costs of 'gentility' – including the wages of good servants and the costs of starting sons in the professions – had risen can only be applied to that group (Banks 1954). Miners did not have servants.

It is also difficult to interpret occupational fertility in the later nineteenth and early twentieth centuries. Most of the data come from cross-section observations. For example, there was a comprehensive Fertility Census in 1911, but the occupations recorded were those in 1911, not those when the children were born; nor do we know the occupations of the mothers. To investigate further we need data on the life cycle. Recent research on textile workers in the late nineteenth century is instructive in this regard. Textile workers had the lowest fertility of any occupation in manufacturing. Textiles also had a high proportion of married women workers, which would predict low fertility. The study examined married women workers in the woollen town of Keighley, Yorkshire. It showed that the married women who remained in textiles were those who happened to have small families. The married women with small families were also more likely to be married to male textile workers. This meant that those with small families were more likely to be returned as 'textile workers' than those with large families. The point is that women who happened to have large families were more likely to leave work. It was low fertility that enabled these women to work not vice versa (Garrett 1990: 137, 149).

The main conclusion about the reasons for the fall in fertility is that we know too little about it. The general issues are, however, fairly clear. Britain changed from a partly rural to an almost entirely urban society. This and similar changes increased the relative cost of children because their work became relatively less valuable. Late in the century education became compulsory. Consumption rose and with it the alternatives to having children. Social factors were also important. People had more information and were more likely to question old-fashioned attitudes towards procreation. Finally the status of women rose, although probably not by much before the First World War. Smaller families were the outcome.

The catalogue sounds rather like the model of the 'new home economics', which has been used to explain the contemporary fertility decline (Becker 1981). The Becker model, however, is inappropriate for the period before the Second World War. In the decline of the 1970s and 1980s, female income, which was rising relatively, was the single most important variable (Ermisch 1979). But in the earlier period, female earnings were low and participation in the labour force (from the 1880s to the First World War) was in fact falling, not as the model requires rising. Only 10.5 per cent of married women were in paid employment in 1911 and as late as 1931 it was only 11.3 per cent (Gales and Marks 1974: 63). Most women were confined to traditional occupations such as domestic service. Few worked in modern industry, even in the 1930s (Savage 1988). A married woman could not gain social or economic independence by restricting her fertility (Tilly *et al.* 1976; Roberts 1982, 1988; Gittins 1982: 184).

The effects of demographic change: dependency, employment, skills

The most important effect of the demographic changes came via changes in age distribution (Figure 2.3). Assuming no migration the age structure of a population changes through the effect of current fertility and mortality on each age group, which itself depends on previous fertility and mortality. The dominant reason for the change in age structure was fertility not mortality. This is because fertility is the only demographic event that affects a single age. A shortfall of births in year 1 will mean a shortfall of ten-year olds in year 10. This can be seen in Figure 2.3, which shows among other things the marked effect of the wars on fertility.

We can see that the shape of the age pyramid began to change between 1891 and 1911. The diamond-shaped age distribution, as in 1851 and 1871,

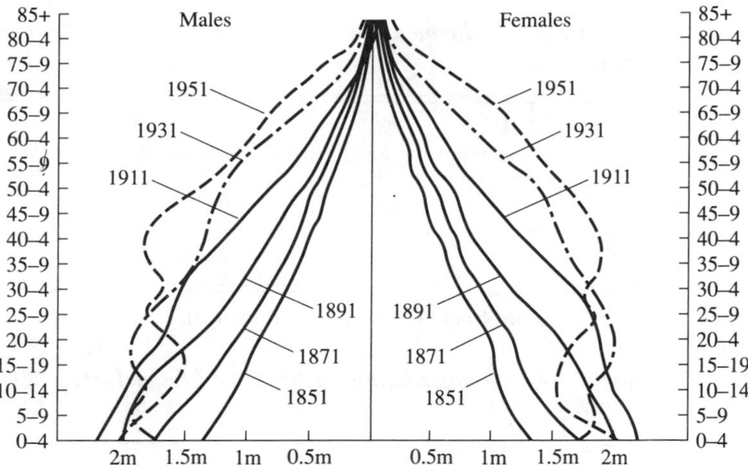

Figure 2.3 The age structure of the British population, 1851–1951
Source: Mitchell and Deane (1962).

is characteristic of countries with high mortality and fertility – that is, with high wastage at each age. Many developing countries in the 1990s have a similarly patterned age distribution but with lower mortality. The slope of the pyramid is steeper. Hence they have faster population growth than Britain, which never exceeded 1.2 per cent a year (though high by nineteenth-century European standards). The characteristic age structure of modern industrial societies starts to appear in 1911. Each age group is a little smaller than the previous one. Population growth is slow. Note the effect of age structure on the number of births. Fertility in Britain was falling from the 1880s, but the effect on the number of births was muted before 1911 because of the large number of young people in the population. The opposite was true of the 1930s. The young adult population was large. But by then the age-specific fertility was so low that it was possible to predict that the population would decline in the long run. This caused consternation in some circles (Charles 1934; Teitelbaum and Winter 1985). In fact the situation was reversed during and after the Second World War. In other words the prediction was based on a *ceteris paribus* other-things-equal assumption which turned out to be wrong.

The rise in the proportion of the population aged fifteen to sixty-four meant that, other things being equal (a large assumption), the number of 'dependants' fell relative to the number of 'producers'. In 1931, 68 per cent of men were aged 15–64 compared with 63 per cent in 1911 and 59 per cent in 1861. In the 1990s the dependency problem is 'age dependence' – a large proportion of older people. In the 1930s the main problem was

Table 2.3. *Employment and the labour force, UK, 1920–38 (000,000s)*

	Working population	Employment	Unemployment
1920	20·7	20·3	0·4
1921	20·1	17·9	2·2
1938	23·6	21·4	2·2

Source: adapted from Feinstein (1976: Table 127).

Table 2.4. *Age distribution of the male labour force, 1901, 1931 and 1951 (%)*

Age group	1901	1931	1951
< 25	32	25	18
25–44	43	41	45
> 45	25	34	37

Notes: children could be counted as 'occupied' at ten years in 1901, at fourteen in 1931 and fifteen in 1951. 3 or 4 per cent of the labour force were over sixty-five at each census.
Source: calculated from Mitchell and Deane (1962: 15–18).

'child-dependence'. Age structure also had welfare implications. For example, old age pensions were introduced at a time (1909) when there were proportionally few old people in the population. There were similar age structure effects in education. Before the First World War the cost of education fell on a relatively small number of 'producers', which was one reason why education was poor. After the war the *number* of children was declining. Schools took fewer new entrants each year, which allowed an improvement in the quantity and quality of education (Lowndes 1937).

Age structure effects meant that the labour force – defined as those looking for work – was increasing in the inter-war period. This contributed to the high level of unemployment. Table 2.3 shows that about 1.8 million jobs were lost in the post-war collapse (1920–1). The jobs lost in the 'staple' industries were never regained. Table 2.3 also shows that 3.5 million jobs were created between the low point of 1921 and 1938, a creditable performance. At the same time, however, the labour force increased by 3.5 million. Hence unemployment in 1938 (2.2 million) was as high as in 1921. It is reasonable to assume that the size of the male labour force was demographically determined. Most adult males were looking for work. (Female participation is more complicated.) Ageing *within* the labour force (Table 2.4) had implications for the stock of human capital. Most skills were learned 'by doing' – that is, at work. An older labour force meant that average skill levels were increasing. Other things equal there was less wastage of younger workers. On the other hand the older labour force may have made retraining more difficult. This may have been important, for example, when the staple industries declined after the First World War.

The reduction in the variance of family size also had important consequences. In a high fertility regime, chance meant that there was great variance in the number of children per marriage. In the 1870s' marriage cohort there were about as many families with ten children, or five children, as there were families with no children (Anderson 1985: 80). The number of children often determined whether the family lived in poverty or not, a factor recognised by social investigators at the time. By the 1930s the variance in family size had declined markedly. For example, 65 per cent of the 1925 marriage cohort had two children or less.

Falling family size also meant, as we have noted, that the average woman's childbearing years were shortened. In the 1870s many women could be bearing children well into their forties, which meant that many still had young children at sixty. By this time their own parents would probably have died. By the inter-war period the situation was quite different. The fall in the number of births had benefited women's health and had made it possible for women to re-enter the paid labour force relatively young (Anderson 1985: 73). A rise in married women's participation depended on demand as well as supply, however, and was not to take effect in peacetime until the 1950s, when there was a shortage of *male* labour.

Emigration had its own demographic effects. Britain lost population by migration in all decades except the 1930s, but the greatest net losses were in the 1880s and 1900s, when the country lost about 820,000 and 760,000 people (Table 2.1). We can estimate that about two-thirds were aged fifteen to thirty-four. This implies a shortfall of about 550,000 young adults in the 1880s and 500,000 in the 1900s, 60 per cent of whom were men. The direct effect of emigration would have been to reduce the growth in the male labour force from 17 per cent to 13 per cent in the 1880s and from 15 per cent to 13 per cent in the 1900s. The losses also reduced the ultimate population size, of course, but not its ultimate age distribution, since emigration removed the potential dependants from the population as well as the potential parents.

The demographic consequences of the First World War

War deaths and emigration affected similar age groups and we might expect a trade-off between them. War deaths in England and Wales were 634,000 (722,000 in the UK), which was 6.8 per cent of males aged fifteen to thirty-nine in 1911. The twenty to twenty-four age group was depleted by 16.1 per cent and the twenty-five to twenty-nine age group by 9.9 per cent (Winter 1988: 82). The 'lost generation' was much debated in the 1920s. It was supposed to have affected the marriage chances of the 'excess' women. In fact the demographic effect of the war was surprisingly small. The most important change was probably the permanent birth deficit of some 670,000 (Winter 1985: 253). But, in the light of post-war unemployment it is difficult to see population size per se as a problem in the period. The effect of the war on civilian health was largely neutral. Infant and adult mortality continued to fall (Winter 1988: 14), as was to be expected. The war had positive and negative effects on civilians. It led to full employment, the narrowing of skill differentials and (eventually) price controls and rationing – all of which disproportionately benefited poorer people. But the war also had a serious effect on the housing stock, to the detriment of the less well-off.

The age structure effects of the war were muted because the war interrupted a period of heavy emigration. Net outflow was probably of the order of 150,000 per year in the three years before 1914 but only 75,000 per year in 1920–1. In other words, it is likely that if there had been no war, emigration would have been higher. Nor were the marriage chances of a generation of women ruined. The number of widows increased, of course, but the likelihood of a woman being married was higher in 1921 than it had been in 1911 in every age group except one (thirty to thirty-four). Before the war around 15 per cent of women had never married. After the war this fell to 10 per cent. There was no reason for the British to adopt the French post-war pattern, where men married younger and women older. France (where in any event there was no cushion of emigration) lost in the war proportionately more than twice as many men as Britain (Wall 1988: 68, 72). There was in fact no 'lost generation' in Britain. The literary prominence of the loss arose from class, not from the aggregate statistics: deaths of officers had been exceptionally high.

Migration

The third of the main demographic phenomena – migration – differs from mortality and fertility. For obvious reasons, migration is more difficult to define than simple life and death; and therefore it is more difficult to measure. Secondly, migration is selective. People normally *choose* to migrate.

Migration models

Migration is normally explained in one of two complementary ways, by 'push–pull' and by information flow. In the 'push–pull' formulation migration depends on the difference between the income which an individual can expect to earn if he or she remains where they are and the expected income in a new environment. ('Income' may be defined widely, of course, to include all the attractions of home and abroad.) If migration were determined entirely by 'push–pull', then migrants would come from the poorest regions. The migration decision may also be thought of as an investment decision, which implies that the returns to migration will be higher the younger the individual. Hence, young adults would be (and in fact are) more likely to migrate.

The model of information flow stems from the idea of uncertainty. Obviously, all migration depends on a degree of information, but because good information about, say, wages, prices, employment and transport reduces uncertainty, the more information that is available the higher the migration rate. The model implies that the poorest regions would not necessarily have had the highest outmigration rates. On the contrary, since information was likely to increase and transport improve as economic development occurs we might expect more migrants to have come from the regions that were at the centre of economic change, rather than from the periphery.

We must remember, however, that migrants may not need information about more than one destination. This is the main reason for the phenomenon called 'chain migration', which explains, among other things, the existence of immigrant ghettos. It was in fact rare for the British who went overseas to live in ghettos. In English-speaking countries the British were more similar to the native population than they were to other immigrants.

The two models have been applied to both internal migration and emigration. But there are differences. Internal migrants obviously found information easier to obtain. (A young woman from Wiltshire could find a post as a domestic servant in London through personal contacts.) It was easier to move within the country than to emigrate. It is also possible, as we shall see, that internal migration and emigration were functionally related.

Table 2.5. *Destinations of British emigrants (outward bound passengers) other than Europe, 1853–1930 (000s and %)*

	USA	Canada	Australia/NZ	All
1853–1900	3,117 (55·9)	735 (13·2)	1,133 (20·3)	5,571 (100)
1900–30	1,528 (27·1)	2,122 (37·7)	970 (17·1)	5,638 (100)
Entire period:				
1853–1930	4,645 (41·4)	2,857 (25·5)	2,103 (18·7)	11,209 (100)

Note: outward passenger movement was only 236,000 in 1931–8.
Source: calculated from Carrier and Jeffery (1953: 95–7).

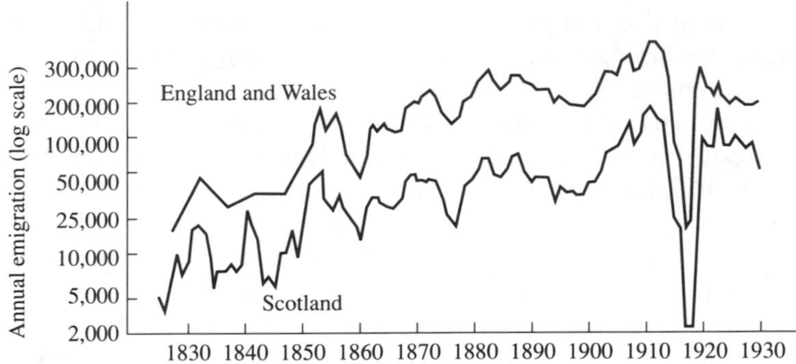

Figure 2.4 Emigration (outward passenger movement) from Britain, 1825–1930
Source: see text.

Emigration

About 20 per cent of all European emigrants between 1815 and 1930 came from Britain. Only three European countries had higher emigration rates over the long haul (Ireland, Italy, and Norway; see Baines 1991: 9–11). In the nineteenth century the main destination of British emigrants was the United States, but Canada became the most important destination in the twentieth. Australia was the other important destination (Table 2.5).

Emigration from Britain was discontinuous and the same discontinuities occurred in other European countries, suggesting the same causation (Figure 2.4). We now know that the discontinuities were mainly caused by fluctuations in the economies of the United States, Canada and the rest of the destinations. The implication is that emigrants had access to information about economic conditions abroad. The information came from letters and, increasingly, from the experience of previous emigrants who had returned. Returned migration rates to Britain were high from the 1870s, which was the first decade when emigrants were able to travel by steamship. It has recently been estimated that at least 40 per cent of British emigrants returned (Baines 1985: 128–35).

Until quite recently it was assumed that British emigration could be entirely explained by the 'push–pull' model – that is, by the problems of the countryside and to a lesser extent by the problems of redundant industries, including the decline of some craft skills (Jones 1973). In other words the emigrants were assumed to have come from areas of the country lagging behind in the process of economic change. Cornwall is a notorious example. The county had the highest emigration rates in England (1861–1900), apparently related to its dependence on agriculture and the collapse of its only industry – copper and tin mining (Baines 1985: 159; Rowe 1953: 326, 378). If the 'push–pull' explanation is correct the majority of emigrants would have come from counties with problems comparable to those of Cornwall. And emigration from Britain should have fallen as the country became more urban and industrial.

In fact, as Figure 2.4 shows, the trend of emigration rates rose to the First World War. Serious doubts about the provenance of British emigrants were first raised in a classic article by Charlotte Erickson. Using data which enumerated the passengers on ships entering US ports she showed *inter alia* that, by the 1880s, British emigrants were close to a sample of the British population. They were predominantly urban and predominantly unskilled. And when emigration was high the proportion of urban workers increased (Erickson 1972: 370). In other words, British emigration was more likely to conform to the information flow model. Baines was able to show that over the period 1861–1900 a third of English and Welsh emigrants had been born in London, Lancashire or the west midlands and another third had been born in the other counties with large urban populations. He was also able to show that relatively few of the urban emigrants were people who had previously moved to the towns from a rural area. The phenomenon, called 'stage-migration', seems to have been common in Scandinavia, but not in Britain. The majority of the English and Welsh emigrants had been both born and brought up in an urban environment. That is to say, emigrants were more likely to come from the centre of economic change than from the periphery, in accord with the information model (Baines 1985: 145–7, 254, 264–5).

The urban character of British emigration may have been related to the high rate of return to Britain, which was the highest to any European country over a comparable period. That is, British emigration moved into a high return phase in advance of other European countries. It was to be expected. Britain industrialised earlier and had better transport links with the 'regions of recent settlement'. In some cases the labour markets in New York and London may have overlapped. To return to our original formulation, this is another way of saying that the information flow to Britain was superior.

The urban character of British emigration also raises doubts about the so-called 'Atlantic economy'. In one important version of the idea it proposes that British and American development was complementary and characterised by alternating decades of investment and emigration. In one phase, British investment in the USA and emigration to the USA were high. In the second phase British overseas investment was low but domestic investment was high. Since investment in housebuilding could be seen as the alternative to overseas investment the British building cycle was the obverse of the overseas investment cycle. The migration implications are that in one phase migrants went overseas (as in the 1880s) and in another phase to the British cities (as in the 1890s) (Thomas 1954: 124–5, 128, 1972: 45–54). For this analysis to be correct the bulk of the emigrants would have to have come from the countryside. Such we now know was not the case. In fact a recent study of the period 1861–1900 found no systematic relationship between internal migration from the countryside and rural emigration (Baines 1985: 246–9).

Emigration after the First World War

Only a minority of British emigrants before the First World War travelled with an official subsidy. Subsidies were used to encourage emigrants towards empire destinations, which were very distant (especially Australia) or that were relatively undeveloped (parts of Canada). It is more likely that subsidies diverted emigrants from the USA to the empire than that they increased the emigration rate from Britain. After the First World War, politically motivated settlement schemes increased – this time, as in the early nineteenth century, partly financed by the British government. Unfortunately the prospects for agricultural settlement in the White Dominions – which was the aim – were not good (Pope 1985). The schemes collapsed in the international depression of the 1930s and for the first time in over 200 years Britain had a positive migration balance.

Internal migration

Although it is notoriously difficult to measure, we can be fairly sure that internal migration rates were high in the nineteenth century. The scraps of evidence that we have suggest that transience was common in the nineteenth century, as it was also in the period before industrialisation

(Anderson 1990: 13). Reasons for moving would include marriage, seasonal employment, the 'tramping' of artisans, housing and the avoidance of creditors and landlords. We could also say that both the housing and labour markets were more open than today and that migrants were less likely to be deterred by the problems of educating children or looking after relatives. The exact volume of movement is difficult to assess. Most of the data used by historians were gathered at a point of time, such as a census enumeration. But point-of-time enumerations show only the effect of a period of migration – how many migrants are present – not the number of intervening moves. Measuring the moves would require a continuous population register or a sophisticated enumeration, as there has been in more recent censuses. The first sophisticated attempt to measure total mobility was in 1948–9, when Britain still had its wartime registration system. The study defined migration as a change of address. It showed that in most parts of the country net migration – the effect of the movement – was only 5 per cent of all moves (Newton and Jeffery 1951). Put another way, 95 per cent of the moves were countervailed by a move in the opposite direction. The large number of countervailing moves implies that areas with small populations will have higher net migration rates than areas with large populations. In other words, net migration rates from (or into) the cities will tend to be lower than net migration rates from the countryside, which is what we observe in the nineteenth century. This difference does not prove that the rural population was more mobile than the urban. It may simply mean that the cities had a higher rate of return.

The fact that total mobility was high gives us an insight into the way the nineteenth-century labour market and the economy worked. But we also need to know whether we can discern patterns of migration from the large amount of apparently random movement. A 2 per cent sample from the 1851 census showed that 54 per cent of the population were living more than 2 km from the place of birth that they had given in their returns. (People living in urban and rural areas were equally likely to be migrants.) But two-thirds of the rural movers had moved less than 26 km compared with less than two-fifths of those who had gone to cities. And only one fifth of migrants to London had come from nearby (Anderson 1990: 8, 11). These and other data show two patterns. A large amount of net migration was short distance but the important labour markets, like London, drew relatively more migrants from long distances.

The most important component of the net migration pattern in the second half of the nineteenth and early twentieth centuries was the continuous outflow from nearly all of the countryside. Rural migrants often moved only towards the nearest town, but superimposed on the short-distance movement was a strong pattern of flows towards a limited

Table 2.6. *Population growth and migration, England and Wales, 1841–1911 (000s)*

	Population 1841	Population 1911	Natural increase	Migration (net)	Migration × 100 / Natural increase	1911 × 100 / 1841
Greater London	2,262	7,315	3,802	+1,251	32·9	324
Eight largest northern towns[a]	1,551	5,192	2,747	+893	32·5	335
Coalfields	1,320	5,334	3,363	+650	19·3	404
Rural areas	6,166	6,961	5,302	−4,507	−85·0	113
England and Wales	15,914	36,070	21,366	−1,210	−5·7	227

Note: [a] Manchester, Liverpool, Birmingham, Leeds, Sheffield, Leicester, Hull, Nottingham.
Source: adapted from Cairncross (1953: 78).

number of the large towns and the heavy industrial areas. London, Leeds, Liverpool, Manchester, Birmingham, Glasgow and the coalfields all had substantial net gains (Table 2.6). On the other hand, the emigrants came from both urban and rural areas, as we just saw. There was also some immigration from overseas, mainly from Ireland, with contributions at the end of the nineteenth century from eastern Europe.

London remained the most important single destination. It gained 1,250,000 migrants net of returns between 1841 and 1911. By the later nineteenth century it had no heavy industry but remained the most important centre of demand. London had offered the greatest range of employment opportunities since the Middle Ages and it is hardly surprising that it continued to attract large numbers of migrants.

The countryside lost a total of more than 4.5 million people between 1841 and 1911. That outmigration was continuous from all the countryside suggests that there was no single cause. It means, for example, that the outmigration could not mainly have been caused by the increase in the import of grain from the 1870s. Migration losses continued both from arable counties, which were badly affected by imports, and from livestock counties, which benefited from imports. Compared with the loss of 4.5 million people between 1841 and 1911 the decline in the agricultural labour force was modest – about 0.75 million (Figure 2.5). The data are imprecise but we can conjecture that less than a half of the outmigrants from the countryside were agricultural workers and their dependants. There was a decline in the demand for labour in nearly all occupations in the countryside coupled, as we have seen, with a high rate of natural increase. The most important proximate reason for migration was probably the increase in specialisation within the economy, caused by improvements in transport, particularly railways. Specialisation increased the demand for labour in the urban/industrial areas but led to the decline of rural industries – lace making, for example, or straw plaiting, glovemaking and furniture manufacture – or of rural services. Studies have confirmed the importance of urban demand in the rate and timing of rural–urban migration (Baines 1985: 239–41, 247–8).

The decline in rural employment affected women more than men and it is not surprising that women were, in the main, more likely to leave the countryside than men, at least by the measure of net migration. The most important destination for young women was domestic service in the cities. The growth of domestic service is an example of the importance of the demand for labour, derived in this case from the growth of middle-class occupations in the cities. If demand was the key to the growth of domestic service we would expect that the position of domestic servants in the labour market was quite strong. This seems to have been the case. The wages of

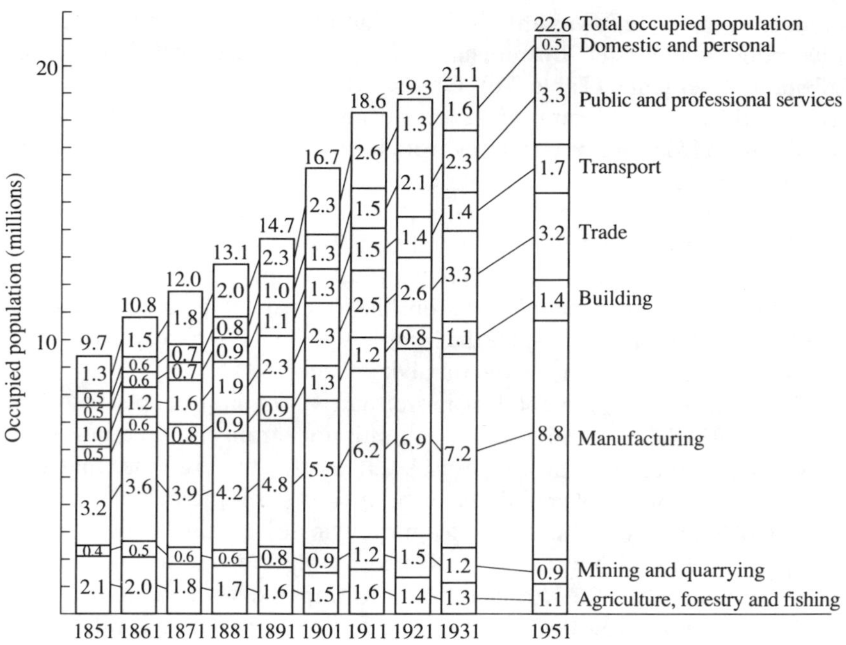

Figure 2.5 The estimated industrial distribution of the British labour force, 1851–1931
Source: adapted from Deane and Cole (1967: 143).

domestic servants rose faster than the national average for most of the period. By 1900 relatively high female migration rates meant that the female surplus in the countryside had been almost exhausted. In 1901, for example, there were 106.8 females per 100 males in England and Wales (men emigrated in disproportionate numbers); but in the rural districts there were only 101 females per 100 males (Saville 1957: 33).

The rate of outmigration from the countryside began to slow in the 1880s and fell markedly in the twentieth century. Towns were spreading into the countryside but there is no simple reason for the decline in rural outmigration. Since migration rates were higher among young people the countryside was ageing by the early twentieth century, but again this fact is insufficient to explain the fall. Age-specific migration rates also fell.

Migration had the effect of reducing the growth rate of the rural population to almost zero (Table 2.6). The population of some areas actually fell – rural Wales and the Borders, southern Scotland and the Highlands. These were areas where marital fertility was high and infant mortality low. On the other hand the cities grew mainly by natural increase rather than by migration. Natural increase accounted for 75 per cent of the growth of the main cities (Table 2.6). Migration into the cities did have an effect on their age structure, but allowing for the effect would reduce the natural growth component only to about 60 per cent. In the colliery districts natural increase accounted for 84 per cent of all growth, or 65 per cent discounting for age structure. Miners had high marital fertility, as we have seen.

Jewish and Irish immigration

About a million Irish immigrants entered Britain (net of returns) between 1841 and 1911, of which 600,000 had arrived by 1861. In the 1850s, the Irish-born were at their all-time peak of 3.5 per cent of the British population. By 1911 the share had fallen to 1.6 per cent, to which might be added the people of Irish extraction. The timing of Irish immigration was related to the famine of 1846–8 but the Irish – sometimes as seasonal workers – had been a part of the British labour market since the early nineteenth century.

Irish immigrants were geographically concentrated. In 1851 about a half of the Irish-born population were living in London, Manchester, Glasgow and Liverpool. This was also true in 1911. In other words the Irish moved to the places where labour demand was high. As we have seen, the main (net) destinations of rural migrants were the same list of large cities. Hence the effect of Irish immigration on the British labour market depends on whether the Irish were paid lower wages than natives and the extent to which they replaced them.

We may assume that Irish immigration did replace rural–urban migrants. In other words, without Irish immigration the movement to the British cities would have been greater. The assertion can be put another way: rural Ireland had in effect become part of the same labour market as rural Britain. Since most of the Irish were unskilled, their effect on the economy would have to be seen in the context of a possible labour shortage in Britain. But throughout the whole period of Irish immigration, British emigration far exceeded Irish immigration. This was true when Irish immigration was at its peak. Estimates suggest that, net of returns, about 600,000 Irish entered between 1841 and 1861 and about 1,000,000 British left (Baines 1985: 48–50, 218).

There is no evidence that the Irish undercut the local wage levels. Nor would we expect it. If the native unskilled workers had no more bargaining power than the Irish it would not be in the interests of employers to pay *them* higher wages. Of course, the Irish entered at the bottom of the labour market – as nearly all unskilled immigrants have to do. And the Irish lived and worked in the centre of towns where there was great pressure on housing. They were visible. But this does not mean that they were paid less than native workers (Lees 1979: 247; Hunt 1973: 298–9).

Jewish immigration, from eastern Europe, had many features in common with Irish, although it was quantitatively much less important. Probably 120,000 entered before the First World War, especially in 1882–1905. The Jews were even more geographically concentrated than the Irish, three-quarters in London by 1911. Unlike the Irish, their most important occupation was, in effect, a new industry – mass-produced clothing. Their apparent poverty was also visible, although in the Jewish case it was partly because there were economic advantages in the extreme concentration of the East End clothing industry in which they were concentrated (Gartner 1960).

One can ask: why was immigration into Britain not higher? After all, it was the most important industrial economy in the world. The simple answer is that the growth rate of the economy, and, hence, the demand for labour, was not high enough. Britain cannot be compared with the USA which had continuous immigration, nor with Germany, which had net immigration from the 1890s. Both had higher growth rates of GNP and urbanisation. On the other hand, Britain would have been a reasonable destination for many other Europeans. But most of the early chains of information which made emigration possible led across the Atlantic.

Regional variations in employment

The growth of heavy industry was concentrated on the coalfields because coal was the dominant power source. On the other hand, much of the growth of commercial services was concentrated in cities that were remote from the coalfields, notably in London where 36 per cent of the increase (1851–1911) occurred. By 1900, industries and occupations in Britain were probably more localised than at any time before or since (A. J. Brown 1972)

In the nineteenth century there were wide regional differentials in the wages paid for the same job. Some reflected different capital–output ratios (and hence, productivity) in the different regions. But in the nineteenth century wages differed even in occupations where there was no mechanisation or where technology in the regions was the same. Table 2.7 shows the wide variance in the wages of agricultural labourers; the wages of agricultural labourers are a good proxy for unskilled wages in general. The most important fact is that wages were highest close to the cities. This was not compensation for higher urban prices. Wages in real terms were in fact higher in cities because living costs in cities, except for rents, were

Table 2.7. *Wages of agricultural labourers, 1867–1907 (per week)*

	1867–70			1907		
	(s	d)	(a)	(s	d)	(a)
London and Home Counties	16	6	115	18	7	102
Primarily industrial						
South Wales	12	8	88	18	2	100
Lancashire, Cheshire, Yorkshire/West Riding	17	1	119	19	7	107
East and west midlands	14	1	98	18	5	101
Central Scotland	14	4	100	20	4	111
Northumberland/Durham	18	9	131	21	6	118
Primarily rural						
South-west England	12	5	87	16	10	92
South-east England	14	5	101	16	5	90
Lincoln, East and West Ridings	17	1	119	18	10	103
Cumberland/Westmorland	18	6	129	19	2	105
Rural Wales	13	0	91	17	8	97
Southern Scotland	15	0	105	19	4	106
Highlands of Scotland	13	2	92	17	7	96
Britain (unweighted mean)	14	4	100	18	2	100

(a) = index relative to GB mean.
Source: based on Hunt (1973: 127–96).

normally lower than in the countryside. In the absence of strong unions and government interference, wage differentials in the nineteenth century must have reflected differentials in the demand for and supply of labour. This in turn must have depended on demand for products.

The table shows, however, that regional differentials in the wages of unskilled workers narrowed in the nineteenth century. The narrowing of regional wage differentials must have been largely a consequence of migration – that is, it could not have happened without migration. (The brief flowering of agricultural trade unions in the 1870s may also have had some effect (Boyer and Hatton 1990).) We have seen that much of the growing industry in the nineteenth century could be located in a limited number of areas. In theory, some industry could have been relocated to take advantage of low rural wages; but obviously it did not in fact happen. It is also probable that rural workers were less adaptable than urban. On the other hand the migration of rural workers to the cities probably made them more adaptable and, hence, more mobile within the urban labour market. Migration also increased the level of rural wages. If labour had not left the land, agricultural productivity would have fallen.

The growth of national bargaining in the First World War and the ability of trade unions to enforce it led to further reductions in regional wage differentials. But the existence of high unemployment in the inter-war period complicates matters. Because of the growth of trade union power and unemployment insurance, quite high wage levels could coexist with high unemployment in some industries. This did not happen in the nineteenth century. By the inter-war period regional incomes were determined largely by the distribution of industry – whether there was a large or a small number of high wage occupations. In the nineteenth century, by contrast, the variance in regional income was more likely to be determined by the variance in income for the same occupation.

The origins of the regional problem

The labour market after the First World War differed from the period before the war in several important respects. In the first place, recorded unemployment rates were much higher. The variance in regional unemployment rates was also greater and, significantly, the differences persisted until after the outbreak of the Second World War. Participation rates showed the same pattern. The more prosperous regions tended to have more workers per family. Hence the regions where there was high unemployment had relatively low income and vice versa.

The existence of depressed areas in the inter-war period raises many questions. These include: was the economy *as a whole* able to create full employment? That is, was the problem in fact regional? And why did the labour not move away from unemployment? The issues are discussed in detail in volume 3, but something needs to be said here.

The relation between regions may be seen as similar in some respects to the relation between countries. Regions 'exported' goods to other regions (and overseas), in exchange for 'imports'. Services (many of which could not be exported) developed around the 'export' industries of each region. In the inter-war period, however, several of the regions depended on a narrow range of industries and had relatively few people employed in services. The more prosperous regions had a more diversified industrial structure. And the less prosperous regions became less diversified, that is, they failed to attract new investment. Virtually all the new employment in the period was created in the south-east and midlands – the majority in services (Law 1980: 88–9). The point is that regions with the great (overseas) export industries of the nineteenth century – textiles, shipbuilding, coal mining and heavy engineering – were heavily specialised in those industries. Regional income was hostage to their ability to export. Hence, when exports declined there was a severe squeeze on regional incomes. In other words, in the nineteenth century, when the staple industries were at the forefront of the British economy, they were not attracting enough other industries and services around them – industries that would have protected South Wales, Clydeside, the north-east, and the north-west from the collapse of exports after the First World War.

Table 2.8 compares the growth in employment 1841–1911 in Greater London and in two of the important 'staple industry' regions, Lancashire (textiles, coal, engineering) and Clydeside (shipbuilding, engineering). Both Lancashire and Clydeside were depressed after the war. The analysis of nineteenth-century employment data presents difficulties but the main trends are clear. Even in the period when these regions should have had the greatest advantage, employment growth in Greater London was faster. Total employment rose by about 317 per cent in London compared with 235 per cent in Lancashire and only 169 per cent on Clydeside. Put another way, in the heyday of the staple industries, a third of all new employment was created in Greater London (Lee 1979).

These data are surprising because both Lancashire and Clydeside were high income regions (Table 2.7). The workers in the staple industries had the highest incomes in the country, which when spent should have encouraged the growth of services and consumer industries. What seems to have happened is that a larger proportion of their income was spent on 'imports' – for example, from London – than the Londoners spent on 'imports' from the other regions. In other words the employment multiplier was larger in London: expenditure 'leaked' out of South Wales or the north-east. This meant that the London economy diversified much faster than the regional economies, which returns us to the question of what determined the location of industry.

A distinction is often made in economics between 'absolute' and 'comparative' advantage. Since coal was the dominant power source the regions with large coal deposits had an absolute advantage in coal and a comparative advantage in the heavy industries. London, with a few other areas, had a comparative advantage in other (mainly consumer) industries and particularly in services (national and international), an extremely important component of economic growth during the twentieth century (Lee 1986). There was no overwhelming reason for consumer industries and services to be located in London (that is, no absolute advantage); yet it was more profitable to do so because so many similar industries and services were already there. (The concept of external economies is important here.) And London was still the seat of government, the most important port and the home of the richest people. In other words the

Table 2.8. *Employment growth in Greater London, Lancashire and Clydeside, 1841–1911 (000s)*

	Greater London	Lancashire	Clydeside
Males			
1841	432	479	256
1911	1,735	1,539	716
Increase	1,303 (302%)	1,060 (221%)	460 (180%)
Females			
1841	203	218	109
1911	913	792	263
Increase	710 (50%)	574 (263%)	154 (141%)
All			
1841	635	697	365
1911	2,648	2,331	979
Increase	2,013 (317%)	1,634 (235%)	614 (169%)

Note: 'Greater London' = London proper and Middlesex; 'Clydeside' = Strathclyde.
Source: calculated from Lee (1979).

effect of industrialisation was to reduce the dominance of London in the economy but not to replace it with the dominance of anywhere else. After the First World War the relative decline of international trade reduced the absolute advantage of the regions. The pull of London (now including parts of the south-east) became even greater. Changes in the cost and quality of transport were important. After the First World War the motor vehicle increased the flexibility of transport, which made it possible for the new consumer industries to be located anywhere. In theory this could have led to a wider geographical distribution of industry. But in a country as small as Britain it meant that the new industries could be located where the greatest comparative advantage now lay. It was not on the coalfields.

Was labour more mobile before the First World War than after?

That the differences in regional unemployment rates persisted through the inter-war period has led to a suggestion that labour may have been relatively immobile. The argument goes that in the nineteenth century there were few institutional barriers to mobility. Hence there was little variance in regional unemployment rates, as workers moved from high to low unemployment regions and forced their way into the bottom of the labour market by accepting low wages. But after the war the housing market, it is said, became less free, trade unions became stronger and, most important, the coverage of the unemployment scheme was massively increased. These factors would all tend to decrease mobility.

Is it true? The commonest measure of net migration is to sum the net gains or losses in the individual areas. By this measure, mobility after the war was less than in some decades in the late nineteenth century, and mobility after the Second World War was even less. But as we have seen, crude migration rates are difficult to interpret, because they measure only a fraction of the number of moves. It is possible that after the First World War the observed migration was a lower proportion of the migration that actually occurred. The reason for suspecting this is that both emigration and rural–urban migration were more important before the war than after. Both emigration and rural–urban migration have a high proportion of lifetime moves, and lifetime moves are the only ones counted by the net migration method, since all return moves mask a move in the opposite direction. It also seems likely that intra-regional (and intra-county) migration was higher after the war. And, finally, a larger proportion of the labour force lived in one area and worked in another. None of these movements are picked up by the net migration method. In other words, the evidence of lower mobility is doubtful, and perhaps seriously misleading.

It is also inappropriate to use regional unemployment rates to judge whether the labour force was mobile or immobile. The relevant variable should be the number of *vacancies* in each region – the number of jobs that were on offer. We do know that there was a great deal of movement – for example, of South Wales miners to the new motor industry in Oxford (Daniel 1940; Makower *et al.* 1938, 1939, 1940; Thomas 1937). We do not know if additional migrants would have found additional jobs. In fact the majority of new jobs in the south-east were taken by people from within the region. The labour supply was abundant, partly because of the exceptional number of school leavers (the demographic reasons for this phenomenon were discussed above). In other words, it is difficult to say that labour was immobile if no part of the country had a tight labour market. People may have been perfectly willing and able to move, but there would be no point in moving if vacancies were few. Unemployment rates in the regions would only fall when the number of jobs created in the economy *as a whole* exceeded the number of people searching for them.

3 Entrepreneurship, 1870–1914

Sidney Pollard

Introduction

In historical as well as in theoretic writing about modern economies, the entrepreneur is often taken for granted. He seems to arouse interest only if things go wrong, and a scapegoat for failure has to be found. In these volumes, not untypically, the entrepreneur has a chapter to himself only for the period 1870–1914, when the faltering in British growth and the dimming of mid-Victorian economic success required an explanation.

The economic theory of entrepreneurship

Much of the literature on entrepreneurship is concerned to differentiate it from management. The dividing line is indeed not clear, particularly in smaller firms typical of the nineteenth century, where owner-entrepreneurs may also have had to manage, but as a general rule we may say that the broader, strategic decisions about a firm belong to the 'entrepreneur', who need not be an individual but may be a board or a group of people, while the tactical decisions in carrying out the strategy are the tasks of management. Thus if a firm, an industry or a whole country shows signs of failure, which as a preliminary definition may be taken to mean failure to make the most of the available economic opportunities, the blame may in the first instance be laid at the door of the entrepreneur. It is he who should have acted differently.

Neoclassical as well as classical British economic theory notoriously ignores the entrepreneur. The world of such theories is populated by eager firms (or their owners and controllers) who take the best chance the market offers them; if they do not, others will take their place and they will go under. Firms, and the people running them, are in a sense substitutable for each other: given the same stimulus, it is assumed, then they all, or at least the successful ones among them, would act in exactly the same predictable way.

But, against the views of the predominant tradition, there is an alternative, going back to the French economist J. B. Say and in a way even to the eighteenth-century author Richard Cantillon (Hebert and Link 1988; Casson 1982; Geary 1990) which places considerable emphasis on the role of the entrepreneur in economic growth and in the efficient conduct of economic affairs. His chief function, according to Say, was to organise the firm and make the main decisions on the use of factors of production to meet the market. 'The entrepreneur was the impresario, the creative force, the initiator of the economic cycle. He it was who conceived the end, found the means, bore the burden of risk, and paid out the other factors of production' (Perkin 1969: 222). In a modern paraphrase, he 'unites all means of production' and pays out their income, including his own profit. His is the 'art of superintendence and administration'. Entrepreneurs are the people responsible for the 'initiation, maintenance and aggrandisement of profit-oriented business institutions' (Cole 1946: 3, and 1968: 106), 'allocating the resources for the business as a whole' (Alford 1977: 116). In detail, this would mean determining the objective of the business, developing its organisation, securing financial resources and effective technical equipment, developing and meeting the markets and maintaining good relations with the public authorities and with society at large; interestingly enough, selling skills are not specially emphasised (Mathias 1957; Payne 1974: 14) and relations with the firm's own workforce do not get a direct mention in this list (Cole 1946: 6).

In the course of time, the elements of risk taking and decision making in a world of future uncertainty were added, to which might also be assigned the question of the ownership of resources put at risk. Entrepreneurial investment and other decisions have to be made well ahead of supplying the market to recoup the outlay in a future which could not be predicted with certainty.

With Schumpeter, the role of the entrepreneur took on a different dimension altogether. The Schumpeterian entrepreneur had the task of innovation, of introducing something new. It might be in the technique of production, in the nature of the product, the organisation of the firm or the market, purchasing or financing. Entrepreneurial profit was thus the difference between the income of the innovating entrepreneur and the income of the others, until such time as they had copied him.

Entrepreneurship in the Schumpeterian theory therefore involved being different, engaging in deviant behaviour, trusting one's own judgement against that of the herd, upsetting and reorganising existing structures, making worthless some of the old invested capital or some of the old transmitted skills. It involved creative destruction, within a competitive environment. It was above all the action of the individual, not the class as a whole, and it was the mainspring of progress and growth in the world's capitalist economies (Schumpeter 1947; Redlich 1952–3; Gerschenkron 1953–4).

Some modern economists have tried to incorporate something of the role of the innovative individual in a theoretical framework that does not entirely jettison the neoclassical impersonal market. Thus one approach might be to note that the 'market' does not move automatically towards equilibrium, but only does so because decisions are made by individual firms to react and to be alert to opportunities provided by temporary disequilibrium positions. On that basis, the entrepreneur, while still reactive and acting as an individual, would tend to create equilibrium rather than, as with Schumpeter, disequilibrium. He brings together different plans, conceived by different firms, via the market (Kirzner 1973, 1989; Hebert and Link 1988). Another approach would be an evolutionary theory of economic growth, in which firms are continually on the move reacting to stimuli, while engaged in search and selection for possible solutions. Firms react to the profit stimulus, working within a market, but it is recognised that they dispose over different resources and equipment, and may reach different individual solutions (Nelson and Winter 1974).

It is possible to summarise these various entrepreneurial tasks by reverting to the traditional definition of the achievement of profit maximisation, which in its more sophisticated form would be expressed in terms of maximising the present value of the enterprise, as the discounted value of future profits (Sandberg 1981: 102). Unfortunately, this leaves open the question of the time span over which returns were to be maximised. It is, moreover, too vague to act as a guide through the maze of incompatible definitions.

Yardsticks for Victorian entrepreneurs

Clearly, if British entrepreneurs are to be made responsible for the allegedly poor national economic performance in the period 1870–1914, as measured by the slowing down of growth and the decline in the British share of world markets, the charge against them would have to be based on something like the Schumpeterian definition, a failure to innovate or to adopt rapidly the innovations pioneered abroad – unless, indeed, it were held that the market had ceased to function altogether in Britain, which no one has suggested as yet. To be sure, the ideal entrepreneur has seldom been found in large numbers, and even contemporary Germany and the USA had their record of failure: Germany, for example, failing to develop a motor car industry on what was largely a German invention; the USA for her poor showing in coal-tar dyes and in shipbuilding, and for failing to adopt the idea of radio when offered to it, among others (Sandberg 1981: 100, 112). For Britain, however, it was alleged that there was substantial, widespread failure, especially failure to innovate. 'The opinion that by the late nineteenth century British entrepreneurs, taken as a whole, were less dynamic, less adaptable and less efficient than their counterparts abroad or their forerunners at home is now a commonplace', it was said in the 1960s; 'there is ample evidence, in both contemporary and recent literature, to suggest that British businessmen were weighted down by complacency, conservatism and antiquated methods from the 1870s onwards' (Aldcroft and Richardson 1969: 113, 142).

The issue has, however, remained controversial. The substantial literature alleging failure on the part of the entrepreneur, beginning with the now classical contributions by Landes (1969), Levine (1967) and Aldcroft (1964) – Chandler even speaks of Britain as a 'late industrializer' in the so-called second industrial revolution of the later nineteenth century (1990: 295) – is matched by an equally substantial literature exonerating him (McCloskey and Sandberg 1971; Wilson 1965: Chaloner 1983–4).

It is also by no means agreed exactly how the failure is to be measured. Overall macro-economic statistics provide no clear verdict. There is no doubt that the rate of British economic growth slowed down at some time after 1870, though the exact turning point is hotly debated; there is also no doubt that some other countries, notably the USA and Germany, were growing at a faster rate. Nevertheless, slower growth is no adequate proof of poor entrepreneurship; there may be many other reasons for it (McCloskey 1970).

The facts relating to economic growth are discussed elsewhere in this volume, so that they need only to be referred to briefly here. For one thing, comparison is usually made only with the two countries named; over all others Britain still maintained a commanding lead. Even then, only the United States had reached an output and an income higher than the British by 1913. Germany, the oft-quoted rival, was, on a per capita basis, still one third or one quarter below the British level, depending on the method of calculation. Even in manufactured exports, perhaps the most telling index used by contemporaries, a substantial British lead remained, especially when the smaller population of the United Kingdom is taken into account. After all the alarms and dire prophecies of contemporary critics (Hoffman 1933; Ashley 1902), British manufactured exports enjoyed a remarkable spurt in the immediate years before the outbreak of the First World War (Pollard 1989: ch. 1; Greasley 1986). It would not be difficult to find good reasons for the higher per capita incomes in North America, the only area ahead of the British in absolute terms, nor could it be expected that Britain would continue forever to dominate world manufacturing production and remain at the technical frontier as she did in the 1850s and 1860s. The catching-up process would necessarily mean that others would grow faster, at least in percentage terms. Whether the comparatively slower growth betokened more than this, the beginning of a decline which put the economy below the level which might have been achieved, cannot be determined from the available statistics. At the same time, if there were indeed failures, or patches of failures, weaknesses in entrepreneurship cannot be ruled out. For present purposes, entrepreneurship will therefore be taken to mean making use of all available opportunities, and failure to do so would be proof of failed entrepreneurship, in view of the entrepreneur's own goals.

Non-entrepreneurial sources of 'failure'

Let us begin by examining some other explanations, besides poor entrepreneurship, for the poor economic performance in macro terms. Resource endowment may be one possibility. Though Britain had plenty of coal, the best seams had been worked out earlier and coal was now less accessible than in other countries (McCloskey 1971b: 292–5); a similar story might be told of iron ore, and there were few other resources compared, say, with the United States. At the same time, compared with most continental countries, coal was cheap, and the wasteful use of energy, the failure to use the latest fuel-saving technology in Britain, might thus have a perfectly rational explanation.

Another, more complex, reason might be the particular nature of the market facing the British producer, and its growth rate. Population growth was slower than in the countries cited in comparison, and since Britain started at a higher level of incomes than continental countries at least, the possibilities of growth were more restricted in that way also. Slower overall demand growth might be expected to lead to slower adoption of new technologies (Habakkuk 1962; Temin 1966). It was also widely believed that the British market was less democratic than the American, demanding more differentiation to meet the wishes of different social strata, and less willing therefore to accept standardised, mass-produced articles. As far as exports were concerned, these were additionally adapted to the specific needs and wishes of the customers in the many colonial and overseas countries, again precluding mass-production methods (Payne 1974: 55–6) – though it should be noted that this weakness of pandering to the whims of overseas buyers was contradicted by another widespread accusation made against British entrepreneurs, to the effect that they failed to take the wishes of foreign customers into account, maintaining a 'take it or leave it' attitude.

A further possible cause put forward for the poor showing of British industrial progress in this period was the structure of the British and, particularly, the London capital market. On the one hand, it was said, British banks traditionally did not make long-term investments in industrial firms, unlike the banks in some other countries, notably Germany, and industrial firms therefore lost not only a relatively easy access to capital, but also the advice and expertise which German 'universal' banks were able to supply to their favoured customers. On the other hand, private investors were persuaded, largely by the predilection of brokers, merchant bankers and others, to invest abroad if they tried to do better than home gilt-edged securities, rather than in home productive industry. The issue is highly controversial and by no means settled as yet (McCloskey 1970; Kennedy 1976, 1987; Michie 1988; Pollard 1985), but there is no doubt that while savings in Britain as a proportion of incomes were comparable with those in the USA, Germany and other advanced countries, a far larger share of them went abroad, so that a far smaller share was left to finance home productive industry.

More serious, perhaps, was the problem of the survival of much out-of-date capital which its owners were unwilling to scrap as it had been written off and thus carried no balance-sheet costs, whereas without that burden, they would have had to invest in up-to-date equipment. This problem is connected with the problem of the so-called 'interrelatedness'. As an example, it might have paid to build new, larger and more efficient railway wagons, but only if the railway companies had been willing at the time to widen their tunnels: in the widely dispersed traditional ownership pattern of Britain, it was seldom possible to get all the necessary participants together when a major innovation had to be carried through. Against this, however, it has been argued that it cannot be a disadvantage to start with owning more capital rather than less (Kindleberger 1961). Much has been said on both sides of the argument, which is but one aspect of the thesis of the alleged disadvantages of the 'early start', pointing to the out-of-date relics of Britain's earlier phase of industrialisation; but the debate is to some extent misplaced. The real problems of the country with the early start, whose technology was appropriate to an earlier phase but had become a hindrance after a certain time, were often locational: shipyards built too high up the rivers for the ever larger ships that had to be launched, steel works surrounded too closely by their workers' houses, preventing their expansion, coal pits sunk too closely together for modern underground technology.

A further cause of the slow adoption of particular new techniques from abroad might be differences in relative factor prices. In particular, labour, and especially skilled labour, was much cheaper in Britain than in the

USA, so that it would sometimes not pay to substitute capital for it in Britain, while it might have paid to do so in the USA (Harley 1974; Aldcroft 1966). There was also the frequently cited obstruction by labour, and above all by the organised trade unions, to technical innovation, either by outright objections, as in some of the cutlery tool trades, by glass makers and printers, or, more commonly, by combining acceptance of the new equipment with demands which made its installation unprofitable (Levine 1967: ch. 5).

Lastly, the relative slowdown of British economic growth might have been caused by the action or inaction of government. Policies detrimental or unhelpful to economic growth have been held to include the inadequate provision of education, particularly facilities for education in science and technology as well as in research; maintaining free trade in a world of rising protectionist barriers; factory and other protective legislation; and specific decisions such as those affecting tramways in 1870, electric power supply in 1882, the notorious 'Red Flag Act' and the patent law until its reform in 1907 (Michie 1988).

Clearly, several of these causes could obtain simultaneously, and might well reinforce each other, to contribute to the retardation of the British economy at a time when others were still on an unhampered earlier or different phase of growth. More important for our purposes: these are all alternatives to the accusation of entrepreneurial failure. To the extent that these, or any of them, operated, entrepreneurs are exonerated: it would then turn out that they reacted correctly to the signals, and it was not their fault if the signals were set to encourage 'wrong' decisions. Only in the case of faulty education, itself no doubt a responsibility of government, might it be said that some blame remained with the entrepreneurs, as it was their poor education or inadequate scientific knowledge which induced them to fail to spot the 'right' course of action. Yet in all other countries, including the United States, education has been accepted to be a governmental rather than an entrepreneurial function. Indeed, it might well be true that it was British firms – and, as chapter 4 argues, British skilled labour – which have provided much of the technical education themselves, that elsewhere was provided by public authorities.

Betting on the wrong horses? Alleged technical failure

In the face of all these adverse factors, much of the literature is nevertheless certain that in addition it was the failure of the entrepreneurs, or at any rate entrepreneurial weaknesses, which have to be rated as significant, and possibly as the determinant causes of the relative loss of position of the

British economy, and above all of British industry, in the years to 1914. There were essentially four types of weaknesses that have been named.

The most commonly quoted, and potentially the most fatal, was the alleged reluctance to accept technological innovation: where Britain had fallen behind most obviously, and where it was difficult to blame anything other than poor entrepreneurship, it was said, was in the acceptance and installation of up-to-date technical methods and equipment. In the possible scale of grading for entrepreneurship, from enterprising to imitative to hesitant to sluggish (Cole 1968), it was in the field of technical innovation that the British entrepreneur was given the poorest marks. His slowness was the less excusable since there was no shortage of technical inventive talent: 'The British could invent but were reluctant to innovate' (Lloyd-Jones 1987: 325). Among the most significant British inventions left to others to exploit on a broad front were the Gilchrist-Thomas basic steel-making process, the electric furnace, the continuous rolling mill, and engines driven by furnace gas (Landes 1965).

Much of the later discussion, as indeed the larger part of the literature on Victorian entrepreneurship, does indeed concern itself with such failures in detail. In that debate, the historian, using whatever method comes to hand, such as contemporary criticisms, the achievements of firms abroad and the ultimate installation of the modern equipment in Britain later or 'too late', as well as recalculating costs and expected returns, sets out to prove (or disprove) that British entrepreneurs should have installed some technology or other earlier than they did.

This is clearly a most hazardous undertaking in principle. Even if we could reconstruct all the cost factors, fixed and circulating, even if we could re-estimate the possible markets, and even if we could be sure what the ultimate aims of the entrepreneur were (and they might not have included the maximisation of British output or the British growth rate) we cannot properly judge the entrepreneurial decisions of the day without taking into account the outlook for the future, which is known to us but was hidden from the decision maker. Was he on a rising or falling trade cycle curve – and for how long? What were other firms going to do? Was there an even more efficient technology waiting in the wings, about to be introduced, that would make the immediate investment obsolete before it had a chance to recoup its costs? It is indeed puzzling that entrepreneurs in so many different industries in Britain should all tend to make the same 'mistakes' while their confrères abroad should tend in a different direction. But, even if others turned out to be 'correct', it is not clear that the betting on the wrong horse in the technology stakes was necessarily a sign of faulty entrepreneurship, or even of faulty information, for many successful ventures were based on false premises yet turned out to be right. Moreover, the fact that a technical innovation proved to be successful later is no proof that it would have been successful had it been introduced sooner.

These considerations apply to all aspects of entrepreneurial failure, not merely to technology. As for technical adaptation, there is one element which might possibly be subject to some sort of fairly neutral numerical check; namely the speed of reaction to changed circumstances. In one attempt to carry out such a calculation, Phillips set out to compare how Britain in 1862–1907, and Germany in 1852–1911, reacted to relative price changes of capital and labour by making corresponding changes in the capital/labour ratio. The assumptions behind this econometric exercise were rather heroic and it may be doubted how far a single measure can adequately represent the greatly differing reactions of the different industries and different sectors of the economy, but so far as they go, they show British adaptation to market signals to have been good after 1892, though poor beforehand for the economy as a whole; the changeover from poor to good for coal alone, for which a separate calculation was made, came rather later, in 1897. This would seem to contradict much of the critique which fastens on the Edwardian years as the period of failure. The German performance improved similarly over that period, though it was better in the earlier phase than the British (Phillips 1989). The further questions – how far British entrepreneurs should have limited themselves to accept (or fail to accept) the techniques developed abroad, and how far they should have developed their own appropriate to their relative costs – could, however, not be settled by retrospective calculations of this kind.

Organisational failure

Next to technical innovation, it is in the organisation of his business that the British entrepreneur has had to suffer much adverse criticism. Although the legislation of the 1850s had made the formation of joint-stock companies cheap and straightforward, such organisation, involving large quantities of outside capital and ultimately the loss of control by a single family and the transformation into a 'managerial' company, in which control passed to salaried officials, was slow to develop in Britain outside a few sectors, such as steel making and insurance and banking. Even where they changed over to joint stock, the original family owners generally tried to maintain their undiminished control.

The creation of large firms as an organisational form was also slow in Britain: firms remained small as well as family-controlled. A number of significant mergers took place around the turn of the century, creating a few giant firms, particularly in textiles and in chemicals (such as United Alkali). Most of these were formed to keep up prices rather than to streamline production and make it more efficient. Their constituent units remained fairly independent, and overall management, insofar as it existed at all, was clumsy and incompetent. Very few of the mergers turned out to be successful from the point of view of their owners, or experienced much growth. Typically also the mergers took place among the makers of consumer goods rather than of capital goods as in the USA and Germany (Payne 1967; Chandler 1976; Kocka and Siegrist 1979). Against this, however, it is interesting to note that modern research has found that it is frequently not the largest, but one of the smaller firms that starts an innovation (Kennedy and Thirlwall 1972: 59).

The most devastating criticism of British company structure has come from Chandler. According to him, British entrepreneurs failed to carry through the three-pronged investment which he had discovered to have been the recipe for success in the 'second industrial revolution' of the late nineteenth century, namely investment in manufacturing, in marketing and in management in a number of the decisive new capital-intensive industries. Even if British firms were large enough from the point of view of the technical optimum, their marketing did not grow to its full economic potential, while their management teams remained small, less clearly defined and too often family-dominated. Such examples of good organisation that existed were not only smaller than the American equivalent, but were also found in consumer goods and in the older staple industries only: in brewing, textiles, publishing and printing, shipbuilding and the older branches of engineering, and not in the new high-technology industries as in the USA (Chandler 1990). It may well be doubted, however, if the American organisational model, even if appropriate for a large, fairly homogeneous and rapidly expanding home market, should have been the pattern adopted for a smaller, more diversified and fairly stable home market coupled to a highly volatile and unpredictable export market. In the establishment of overseas branches to form multinational concerns, British entrepreneurs led the world at that time (Nicholas 1982).

The marketing of British goods, especially abroad, has also come in for much criticism. The critical views are based, in part, on the assumption that it was the failure of exports to keep up their earlier rate of growth which caused the slowdown in the economy as a whole and that the weaknesses in the export sector, in turn, were caused by poor marketing. The agency form of selling, in particular, instead of the firm's own branch which only the largest firms could afford, took much of the blame for the less than optimal selling results (Payne 1974). But in part this view was based on a series of devastating consular reports which received wide publicity, and which contrasted the alleged skilful and aggressive selling of other nations, particularly the German, with the lethargic and inept performance of the British. The consuls, however, it is recognised today, mostly had axes to grind, and their reports were not unbiased; some modern research, on the contrary, points to the skilful selling and dispatch abroad of British goods right to the end of our period (Headrick 1981; Nicholas 1984). As noted above, the opposite accusation that too many sizes and shapes were produced for efficiency does also tend to contradict this particular criticism of poor marketing.

An alternative version of organisational weakness emphasising institutional factors points to the inability of British entrepreneurs to alter or escape from market structures and frameworks which hampered progress: rather, they tended to take them for granted and adapt to them, as a second best solution. As a typical example, it has been held that in such industries as cotton textiles and engineering, where skilled labour was sensibly allowed to dictate the details of the labour process in the works earlier in the nineteenth century, the managers or entrepreneurs were later unable or unwilling to enforce the kind of management structures which would have allowed more rapid adaptation to modern methods (Payne 1990; Elbaum and Lazonick 1986).

Why 'failure'? Sociological explanations and their weaknesses

What could have caused such formidable and dangerous faults in British entrepreneurs in the later Victorian and the Edwardian age, presuming them to exist? Individual failures are always easy to understand, but how did a whole segment of society, the heirs, moreover, of entrepreneurs who had pioneered industrialisation and had made their country the leading industrial nation right up to the beginning of this phase of alleged decline, come to fail to match up to its opportunities?

Three types or bundles of answers are possible. One would be sheer incompetence and ignorance on the part of the entrepreneurs. This would imply that they did indeed try to do the 'right' thing, but could not manage it. Or they could have had a conservatism of outlook, coupled with (and difficult to distinguish from) maintaining alternative goals, which had shifted from maximising incomes or output or power to a quiet life or interests outside business. Or it could be maintained that there was a successful performance on the part of the entrepreneurs from their point of view, which, however, conflicted with the goals of overall economic growth or international success of the economy in general, a conflict between private and social interest.

The idea of sheer stupidity, on a national scale, has not found many supporters. For one thing, firms did, on the whole, continue to make quite satisfactory profits by the methods they used, and this, indeed, frequently formed part of the accusation. One possible pointer in that direction would be the notion that in some sectors, at least, the more enterprising emigrated, which may lead to the conclusion that the entrepreneurial population that was left had less than its fair share of talent (Hannah 1976a: 11).

There is, however, the more widespread and more plausible suggestion that British entrepreneurs were deficient in technical education and therefore unable to recognise the value of an innovation when they were presented with one (Kindleberger 1961: 291; Payne 1990: 44). If true, this would make entrepreneurs at least partly responsible for the slower growth, though the deficient educational provisions themselves, as noted above, would ultimately have to be laid at the door of government.

More plausible, though less precise, is the second type of alleged weakness, a generally conservative attitude to all change and improvement. The British manufacturer, it was said, 'was inclined to be suspicious of novelty' while Germany had institutionalised innovation (Landes 1969: 352); there was to be found in Britain the 'conservative blend' of 'sheer inertia, excessive confidence and complacency' (Levine 1967: 68, 69); and there had been built up a classic network of 'vested interests, established positions, and the customary relations among firms and between employers and employees' (Abramovitz 1986: 389).

The wish for a quiet life, for live and let live within a known market of buyers, makers and sellers, is not uncommon, and certainly not the most reprehensible of human attitudes. In an old-established industrial society, which had its own way in the world's markets for a long time, and in which profit rates were acceptable even if not outstanding, such an attitude would not be entirely surprising, and it might continue for quite some time, perhaps several generations, before competitive weakness put the survival of any given firm in question. Large firms, in particular, and those with an established reputation, may go on for a long time even with poor management and entrepreneurship before their substance is eaten up. There is also the tendency for individuals and for firms which have become rich and dominant on the basis of a technology they master, to be reluctant to turn to something new, in which they would enjoy no particular advantages. Under threat from newcomers they will attempt to modernise and improve the old, rather than sail out into the uncharted seas of the new, and it is indeed common for a doomed technology to show a last efflorescence of substantial improvements just before it is overwhelmed by something inherently stronger. A typical example was the Leblanc process to which British chemical firms clung and which they perfected in later Victorian times despite the evident superiority of the Solvay process (Lindert and Trace 1971).

Whether this attitude was indeed present in Britain to a greater degree than in other countries, some of which also had by that time a long industrial tradition behind them, and whether the firms guilty of this attitude were sufficiently important to affect the national growth rate, would be extremely difficult to establish. Individual examples may easily be found, as may examples of the opposite type of old firms alert to new technologies, of which the Wills tobacco firm furnishes a well-known example (Alford 1973). Their significance or typicality cannot be established by simple enumeration.

There is also the well-known 'third-generation' syndrome, of firms being built up by the strong and energetic men of one generation, kept going by the next and then ruined by the neglect of the third. It is partly an economic phenomenon, the third generation in a family firm being less inclined to reinvest its profits than a 'managerial firm', though the argument has been disputed (Kindleberger 1964; Florence 1953). More commonly it is seen as a sociological phenomenon: men brought up to the luxury of a rich manufacturer's home, and possibly educated at a public school where aristocratic rather than commercial values were inculcated, were more inclined to take it easy in the works, and possibly despise them altogether, seeking to spend their time more enjoyably on the hunting field, in the club or in politics. Examples of such great ruined family businesses such as Marshall's in flax spinning, Greg's in cotton spinning and Napier's in engineering are not lacking (Rimmer 1960; Rose 1986; Wilson and Reader 1958). Yet the evidence is by no means clear on the point. There was, in fact, a substantial turnover of firms – relatively very few survived into the third generation within the same family. Conversely, most of the key firms in the later Victorian period were in only their first or second generation of family ownership. It should also be noted that some of the most spectacular examples of third-generation decline occurred in the 1850s and 1860s, a period held up by the later Victorian critics as a phase of the high noon of success. It is, moreover, often forgotten that Victorian families were large, and the proprietors of a family firm would have a fair number of sons and nephews from whom to select those to be groomed for active partnership. The upbringing within the firm of the selected few was by no means the worst possible training in most industries of the day (Payne 1974; Barker 1976). The big expansion of the public schools and their attraction for the sons of the industrial middle classes occurred after 1860, not before, so that those who controlled the fortunes of industry in the period 1870–1914 mostly lacked the benefits (or it may be handicaps) that such education there have given them (Ward 1967). Individual failures could be matched by such successful large family firms as Pilkington Brothers, Huntley & Palmer, Crosse & Blackwell, J. & J. Colman and Harland & Wolff (Payne 1967).

As for the aristocratic embrace, it was an old story: much the same was said of the merchants and manufacturers of the heroic days of the industrial revolution, and indeed of the German manufacturers in the decades to 1914 (McKendrick 1986; James 1990; Pollard 1990). They all aimed for a gentlemanly life as the reward for commercial success, to adopt aristocratic ideals while increasingly looking down on the pursuit of profit, confirming the lowly social status of business and leaving the market place for an estate in the country as soon as they had accumulated enough riches in trade and industry, the oft-lamented 'haemorrhage of talent' (Habakkuk 1962: 190–1). Meanwhile the 'cult of the amateur' (Levine 1967: 70) or of the 'practical man' (Coleman 1973) was said to lead them to despise scientific and technical knowledge as well.

The notion that the cultural environment of late Victorian Britain was unusually inimical to manufacturing enterprise, dominated as it was by pre-industrial ideas and by the landed classes and their hangers-on who kept them alive, was given a considerable lease of life by an influential book written by an American observer and published in 1981 (Wiener 1981). It was no wonder, according to Wiener's view, that enterprise declined and economic success evaporated: society held industry and urban life in low esteem, and the best spirits were persuaded to enter the professions, government service or other occupations rather than to soil their hands with productive industry.

Wiener's approach, which can be found also in other parts of the critical literature, begins with the cultural environment. It is indeed not difficult to find poets and novelists, even philosophers and politicians, who exalted the rustic virtues, the untroubled life of the village and the gentlemanly pursuits that go with the possession of a country house or at least a cottage in the country, deriding on the other hand the hustle and bustle of commercial city life. The Englishman's town house, be it ever so small, attempted to imitate the rustic dwelling, and trees and gardens became ubiquitous features in the suburbs of British cities. Given this cultural bias, so runs the next step in the argument, it was bound to affect the views of businessmen. The entrepreneur who grew up in such an environment would be an easy victim of the tough, unsentimental entrepreneur of the first generation from Germany and the USA.

Plausible though it sounds at first sight, the line of argument has found little support among economic historians. It has been rejected at several levels. For one thing, the influences of the traditions of the industrial provinces have been much under-rated: England had more than a single culture, and in the provincial and middle-class world a success in business was by no means despised (Dellheim 1985). Moreover, there was in Britain, as elsewhere, a well-established tradition of accepting older forms while filling them with new content: the dignities which society had to bestow might well appear in medieval aristocratic clothing, but might contain a modern industrial substance nonetheless.

Secondly, rustic nostalgia was no innovation of the later Victorians: it was found in earlier decades as well. The Lake Poets were the contemporaries of the industrial revolution, the classic age of rampant industrialism, not of an allegedly soft late Victorianism. Moreover, poetic and literary romanticism was to be found at least as strongly marked in Germany – without, apparently, diminishing the successful ruthlessness of the contemporary German entrepreneur (James 1990).

Thirdly, it is possible to take issue with the apparent purity of the aristocratic ideal. British aristocrats, more perhaps than their continental equivalents, were as keen to make money as were Lancashire cotton spinners, though they made it by leasing land for agriculture or collieries, by developing towns and by milking the railways that ran through their estates, and, if need be, by becoming 'something in the City' rather than by manufacturing industry.

The British educational system has had to take much of the blame for the alleged weaknesses of British entrepreneurship. In the public schools, to which successful and aspiring businessmen sent their sons, aristocratic values predominated, including the emphasis on classical as distinct from practical or applied studies, and a disdain for business, the market and the supposedly selfish and competitive spirit necessary for commercial success. Yet these schools were not to be accounted as entirely negative influences. If they diverted some industrialists' sons from business to the professions or to politics, they prepared not a few, as recent research has shown, including many younger sons, for careers in the market place at home or within the empire (Robbins 1990; Rubinstein 1990). Even the highly regarded professions for which they prepared their boys were not uninterested in commercial success, while personal leadership, the team spirit, loyalty to a small group and having the courage of one's convictions were not without value for ongoing business leaders. Certainly, the *Gymnasium*, which held a similar elitist position in contemporary Germany, did far less for future business entrepreneurs, without, it would seem, slowing German economic growth.

At the tertiary level, British educational provisions were similarly unfavourably compared with the *Technische Hochschulen* in Germany and the practical drift taken in American universities. But this criticism not only ignores the chairs in engineering and similar subjects in the older British universities, at a time when their German counterparts firmly resisted such innovation; it also ignores the foundation of the civic universities – Leeds, Sheffield, Manchester and the like – most of which were essentially technical universities. And Imperial College (founded 1907) was in no way inferior to the much-admired institute in Charlottenburg (Berlin). Moreover, there was nowhere else in Europe an equivalent range of evening classes, local technical colleges and London Polytechnics, nor was there the highly developed City and Guilds examination system for technical subjects found in Britain. Critics of British provisions tended to be unduly impressed by the formalised, dovetailed and public authority-run continental education system. They overlooked the merits of the British voluntary and demand-oriented education, with its largely practical emphasis – which was, in turn, admired on the Continent (Sanderson 1988; Pollard 1989; Floud 1984).

The third cause for entrepreneurial 'failure' was the possible divergence of individual and social interests. Entrepreneurs were competent enough, it is said, and achieved what they set out to do. But what they set out to do, as it happened, did not go in the direction in which the country as a whole wished to move.

One variant was the alleged short-term view taken by British entrepreneurs compared with those abroad. In the short term, for example, it would pay to run on antiquated machinery which would save expenditure on capital account and might allow the installation of an even later model later on: in the long run, however, an industry consistently pursuing this policy would drop behind in its capacity for technical up-to-dateness. German entrepreneurs were said to show a much higher 'technological rationality' than the British in going for investment in new technology which might not pay at once, but would benefit the business in the longer run (Landes 1969: 354; Alford 1977; Harvey 1979: 6). Conversely, it might be said that some entrepreneurial action was mistaken in terms of self-interest, but ensured national progress. Thus Ferranti, in his early years, had to suffer many disappointments, while his experiments were undoubtedly socially beneficial (Sandberg 1981: 102). All in all, however, the divergence between successful entrepreneurship and the interests of national economic progress does not seem to have been a major factor in the period under discussion.

Each of these many and varied possible causes of entrepreneurial failure in the later Victorian and Edwardian age is on the face of it reasonable and plausible. No doubt there were many incompetents; no doubt some technical ignoramuses were in charge of high-technology firms; no doubt some families without talent and without engagement ran old-established firms into the ground; and surely some talented people were driven abroad in despair over poor prospects at home. Yet it may be doubted whether a collection of such mishaps could explain an unwarranted slowing down, a 'failure' in that particular phase of British history. We are, after all, not dealing with a society with a built-in bias, social, political or religious, against entrepreneurs; we are dealing with the leading industrial nation, the nation which had introduced modern industrialism into the world, the feared competitor in all the world's markets, the nation which, according to some, had sold its soul to Mammon earlier than any other. Is it conceivable for such a rapid turn-round of entrepreneurial talent to have taken place right across all the major industrial sectors?

The spur of competition

The assumption must surely be, on the contrary, that in a commercial society like Victorian England, within a highly mobile and rapidly changing social structure, against a background of political democratisation and laissez-faire economic philosophy, the failure of anyone to make the most of his opportunities would lead very quickly to his replacement by someone with more talent or more initiative. The challenger might come from within the same firm, either replacing the reluctant chief, or at least by-passing him while leaving him nominally in place. The challenger might also come from outside the firm, but within the industry, or indeed be an outsider altogether. It is, moreover, wrong to see decision making in a typical firm as a Napoleonic command from a single individual. Many decisions are in fact programmed by the cumulative advice and the technical possibilities reported from different levels in a firm, which frequently leave but few real choices to the lone entrepreneur at the top (Alford 1976), whose quality may thus be of less significance than is often thought.

Moreover, if poor entrepreneurship does lead to the decline or demise of a firm, this would normally mean that another expands to occupy its place. The penalties of decline and fall for the badly led firm and its replacement by the better-led enterprise is, after all, the normal mechanism of economic progress and adjustment to changed circumstances. Poor entrepreneurship as a cause of industrial decline must mean that all the entrepreneurs in a whole industry failed to seize their opportunities, surely a most unlikely eventuality. The larger the number of firms, the more unlikely such an outcome. If it should nevertheless happen, there may be one of two results: either their products become costlier, or of poorer quality, than they should be, and the rest of society suffers as consumers; or, they are swept away by foreign competition. In the open, free-trade economy of Victorian Britain the second possibility was far more likely than the first. Such a threat from abroad served to concentrate the minds of lax entrepreneurs and spur them to take the initiative – as in the bicycle industry in the early years of this century. If a whole industry is swept aside because of failing entrepreneurship, resources would be freed for other, expanding sectors.

For entrepreneurship to affect the economy as a whole in a significant way, it would have to fail all along the line – a truly heroic assumption for a country which maintained a large lead in Europe and showed healthily expanding exports throughout the whole period. Put differently the British performance in those years was too good for such a sweeping deterioration to have affected the whole of the British actual and potential entrepreneurial class.

It is theoretically conceivable that reasonable returns and even some expansion might occur with entrepreneurs who yet performed far worse than they should have done. This could be either because the country possessed some natural monopoly or at the least better natural resources than other countries or it could be because of the difficulty of entry for newcomers.

Britain was indeed provided with better coal resources than most other countries, but they were not uniquely superior and, since the best and most easily worked seams had been worked out, other countries were beginning to overtake her even in that resource. As for ease of entry, it was part of the indictment of the British entrepreneur that firms were too small, and organisation poor: such faults do not create barriers against newcomers. More significantly, as the sole free-trade country among the larger industrialised nations, the chances of keeping out foreign imports were far smaller than elsewhere. Again it was on the contrary this fear of foreign competition which was said to have been one reason for the poor British record in making costly investments in new technology, as for example in iron and steel making.

The world of British industry was an open, highly competitive world. Entrepreneurial failure would imply the simultaneous failure of thousands of individuals in positions of authority in industry, plus the failure of some thousands more who were eagerly waiting to take their places if they failed. Such a development would surely strain credulity beyond reason. If wholesale 'failure' of this kind had occurred, its cause would not have to be sought in individual failures multiplied by several thousand, but in some exogenous circumstances affecting all at the same time, and we are back at such other explanations of 'failure' as government action, or trade union obstructionism rather than massed individual shortcomings.

But did all industries and their entrepreneurs fail simultaneously? It is time to look at some individual examples.

Industries: iron and steel

Possibly the most widely debated entrepreneurial performance related to the iron and steel industry. This was so, in part because of its strategic position in the technical growth phase of those years, which had made it a kind of status symbol among the industrial nations, in part because of the spectacular rise of the German and American output and the equally spectacular decline of the British share of world production, and in part possibly also because the output was fairly homogeneous and could easily be measured. From 44 per cent of world production of steel in 1870–4 (the share for pig-iron was even higher) the British share fell steadily to a bare 11 per cent in 1910–14; in terms of steel tonnage produced, Britain was overtaken by the USA in 1886 and by Germany in 1893, among the earliest such signs of British deceleration. In terms of per capita output, however, the British performance was less decisively inferior: the USA overtook Britain in 1899 and Germany only in 1907. As far as exports were concerned, Germany pulled ahead of Britain only in 1910, the USA not at all. The industry's efficiency can be measured, though only crudely, by tonnage output of the men employed in it. On that measure the Americans were indeed ahead at 760 tons per man year in 1913, while Britain with her 440 tons was well within the European range of 470 tons for Belgium and 400 tons for Germany.

It is evident that a small island with only limited resources of rather inferior ores could not go on forever producing almost half the world's output of iron or steel; that share had to drop. But need that share have dropped quite so drastically, and were the entrepreneurs responsible? How, even given the statistical information, does one establish entrepreneurial failure? Critics, then and now, fastened on the alleged tardiness in adopting new technology and the forms of organisation appropriate to it: 'for the lack of receptiveness toward the new cost-reducing techniques, for the failure to employ professional engineers, and for the unfavourable structure of the industry, the British entrepreneur must be blamed ... the British entrepreneur, to judge by his behaviour, was unlike his German and American counterparts' (Orsagh 1960–1: 230). Enumerated among the alleged failures was the slow adoption of larger sizes for blast furnaces and steel furnaces, though these brought considerable economies; the failure to adopt mechanical handling equipment; the slow spread of the Gilchrist-Thomas basic process; the failure to adopt the American system of 'fast driving' which raised output, though it required earlier capital replacement; and, finally, the failure to site a major works on the Lincolnshire ore field.

To all these charges, however, reasonable answers may be found

(McCloskey 1973). British markets were concentrated on plates rather than on the rails which foreign steel works had as their leading output, and for these, the open-hearth process was more suitable than the Bessemer method used abroad, and, in turn, this showed far fewer advantages of scale. The nature of British ore and the relative costs of imports of high-grade ore were other reasons for differences in blast furnace practice, while the failure to develop the Lincolnshire ore could be explained by transport costs as well as by chemical problems which were solved only in the 1930s. It has even been calculated that, using the measure of the difference between pig-iron (that is, input) prices and steel prices, America was far behind Britain in efficiency at the beginning of the period and had caught up only towards its end (McCloskey 1971b, 1973; Allen 1979; Wengenroth 1986).

The debate is partly lost in technicalities which the layman will find difficult to penetrate. What is undeniable is that after 1900 there were some modern works in Britain which could be compared with the best abroad. Foreign methods were known, and ignorance or technical incompetence could not have been the reason for holding back in iron and steel, nor could all entrepreneurs in the industry be said to have failed.

Industries: shipbuilding and other engineering

In the case of shipbuilding, the position is clear: Britain produced, even by the end of the period, some three-fifths of the world's tonnage, and the proportion was higher if only the better-class ships, and ships built without subsidy, were included: clearly, no failure here. Yet curiously enough, the industry delayed considerably in installing modern techniques, including electric and pneumatic drive, modern cranes and gantries and covered berth – though in foreign yards these may have contributed to higher costs, rather than greater efficiency (Pollard 1957). Here was a textbook example of technical improvement installed abroad which was economically misguided, though it might have laid the foundation for progress in the long run.

The performance in the rest of the engineering industry is far more difficult to assess, not least because a number of quite different industrial sectors existed under that general heading, which showed widely differing results on world markets. The 'American system of manufacture', involving the fabrication of parts to a fair degree of accuracy so that they became interchangeable and could be assembled by unskilled labour, was slow to be adopted in such branches as clock making and small arms production, but was installed quickly in the bicycle industry. In machine tools the British performance was mixed, and in part far behind the best that the USA and Germany could offer. Relatively poor or mixed results were noted also in agricultural machinery. Against this, Britain still led the world in the making of textile machinery, in steam engine making, and in marine engineering, as well as being well able to keep up with the best abroad in the building of steam locomotives (Saul 1967).

Some of these differences are explicable in terms of different demand or supply conditions. Thus the plentiful skilled labour force available in Britain compared with North America made for greater reliance on manual, rather than machine production and finishing. It also allowed machine builders to market rather more general machines, which customers then adapted to their own requirements, whereas in America specialised machines were designed within the engineering industry itself. Furthermore, British engineering works tended to offer a much larger variety of products than the more specialised American makers. Such firms as Alfred Herbert, Platt Brothers, Charles Parsons and Vickers could stand comparison with the best abroad: no lack of entrepreneurship in specific cases, whatever general averages might indicate (Floud 1976; Trebilcock 1977).

In electrical engineering, however, the British record was less satisfactory. The failure of the British to keep up with the latest technology and to turn to mass production was underlined in that the firms of any size that did exist had been founded by Americans or Germans: Siemens, for example. Even so, Britain held a leading position in the manufacture of cables, and her exports of electrical goods considerably exceeded her imports, the balance in her favour continuing to grow in the years to 1914. Voices were not lacking which blamed the adverse government legislation, particularly the Act of 1882, for a loss of momentum in the 1880s that could not be made good later. The great variety of voltages and other specifications maintained by local authority suppliers jealous of their independence is said to have held back the move towards standardisation and the mass production of parts. It might be noted, however, that British entrepreneurs were quicker than others to see the possibilities of radio.

Lancashire in decline: the cotton industry

Next to iron and steel it was the cotton industry which attracted the most adverse comment as regards the quality of its entrepreneurship. Again, it was not so much the statistically measurable results which prompted the critics, since these showed no evident signs of failure. Thus, the number of spindles had increased by 50 per cent between 1875 and 1913 and the number of cotton looms by almost 75 per cent in the same years. Since cotton, unlike mass-produced steel, was long past its primary stage of technical development, its rate of expansion was of a different order, though not to be despised. As a proportion of the world's spindleage, Britain still in 1913 held about 39 per cent. Her share of the world's cloth output was lower, but at 20 per cent was still ahead of that of any other industrialised country.

In 1913, 74 per cent of the yarn spun in Britain was exported, either as yarn or as finished cotton cloth. The British cotton industry was therefore overwhelmingly an export industry in a highly competitive world market in which the older European industrialised economies and now countries at earlier stages of development, such as Japan or India, had a share. Nevertheless, Lancashire maintained itself without subsidies or protection at home. It was true that the British share of world production and exports had shrunk since 1870, but no one could have expected one country to maintain a share of 44 per cent of the world's cotton textile output forever. It is also true that British exports had been driven from some European markets and had continued to grow by supplying the less developed world, above all India. Altogether, however, production and exports were still rising year by year. British yarn exports were mostly of the finer counts, which others could not yet produce; her exports of finished cloth were mostly of coarser quality, supplied to the poorer and less developed countries. Both these markets clearly required a high degree of marketing skills.

It might have been thought that this was, taking it all in all, a not discreditable performance, given that cotton was an old-established industry in which the British share could only decline, and which newly industrialising countries would tend to tackle first. Nevertheless, there was criticism of entrepreneurship, beginning in the 1920s and continuing down to the present day. One cause of concern was the slow rise in productivity. As far as can be ascertained overall productivity per man-hour had been rising slowly up to about 1890, but thereafter, according to one influential critical account (Jones 1933), labour productivity stagnated. This gave rise, once more, to the accusation – which could not be statistically proved but seemed plausible enough – that the entrepreneurs of Lancashire were dilatory in introducing improved technology, the benefits of which had already been proved in the United States. In particular, the British firms were said to have 'failed' to adopt the ring spindle and the Northrop automatic loom.

In spinning the position by 1913 had become truly remarkable. The American cotton-spinning industry and then that of practically every other country in the world had moved over to ring spinning; only Britain remained predominantly in the older mule-spinning technology: of 55.7 million spindles in Britain in 1913, only 10.4 million were ring spindles, leaving 45.2 million, or 81 per cent, the older mules. The fact is even odder when it is considered that a large proportion of the world's ring spindles had been made in Britain and exported. The technology was certainly known there.

It has been possible, however, to find causes other than sheer bad entrepreneurship for this British technical 'backwardness' (Sandberg 1974). For one thing, mules required skilled labour, freely available in Britain but not elsewhere, while rings could get by on lesser skill: it was significant that the only other countries to prefer mules at the time, though less markedly than Britain, were France and Switzerland, which also had a pool of traditional skilled labour in the industry. Against this, ring spindles needed longer staple cotton, a serious cost element for Britain, though less so for the United States. Ring-spun yarn is also not a perfect substitute for mule yarn: the latter was more suitable for the finer counts demanded by many British markets. The locational structure of the Lancashire industry also made a difference. Since its weaving area was not as in other countries situated close to the spinning area, but some distance from it, transport costs mattered, and since mule yarn, carried on paper cops, cost less to transport than ring yarn on bobbins (which were expensive devices made out of wood, and had to be returned), this gave a further edge to the mule. Finally, it has been argued that the Brooklands Agreement concluded between employers and unions in the cotton industry in 1893 acted as a brake on innovation. With piece rates firmly fixed for spinners, labour-saving innovations would not reduce labour costs but would add to capital costs. The businessmen had therefore no incentive to install rings, and could do better by saving on material, above all by using the notorious 'bad cotton', placing greater burdens on the non-unionised piecers. It was thus good economic logic and not technological conservatism which might be held responsible for the survival of the 'stubborn mule' (Lazonick 1981a; Mass and Lazonick 1990; Sandberg 1974). It might on the other hand be held that entrepreneurs might be considered to be at fault for not moving spinning and weaving closer together, and for not being capable of renegotiating the Brooklands Agreement, if such practices stood in the way of genuine progress.

In the case of the automatic loom, Britain was not alone in showing a lag in its application, since other European countries did not do much better. In comparison with the United States the progress was abysmal; whereas by 1914 the Northrop accounted for 40 per cent of the looms in the USA, it had reached only a negligible 2 per cent in Britain. Here also, good economic causes might be cited in place of entrepreneurial failure: the

Northrop worked best with ring yarn, it was most economical with long runs of simple cloth, and one of its main advantages was that it saved skilled labour: all of these fitted it well for the USA and badly for Lancashire, where the additional capital cost would not have been counterbalanced by adequate savings. Moreover, British workers refused to supervise the larger number of looms which had now become possible and which alone made the automatic loom worth while (Sandberg 1974).

Curiously enough, the other major textile industry, the production of woollens and worsteds, came in for far less criticism than cotton in the years to 1914 (Jenkins and Malin 1990). Its growth rate, to be sure, was rather faster, output doubling between the early 1870s and the years before the First World War; productivity also increased, but the export record was much poorer than that of the cotton industry. Although export losses could be largely accounted for by rising tariff barriers abroad, there was, nevertheless, one major entrepreneurial failure to record. This was the loss of much of Bradford's worsted trade to the French, who foresaw more quickly and reacted more flexibly to the changeover to softer wools from the 1860s onward. Fashions must always remain guess-work, but in this case Yorkshire clearly guessed wrongly. There has also been some criticism of British designs in the woollen trade (Jenkins and Ponting 1982). The early adoption of artificial fibres by Courtaulds and their successful development to a merchantable commodity before 1914 form, by contrast, one of the success stories of British entrepreneurship (Coleman 1969).

Coal mining

The third sector which, besides steel and cotton, has been subjected to sustained criticism for its alleged technical backwardness, was coal mining. To the relative backwardness in installing mechanised transport and lifting equipment and in the use of electricity underground, there were said to have to be added two major failings: firms were too small, the pits were too close together to be efficient while entrepreneurs refused to amalgamate, and the installation of mechanical cutting equipment was demonstrably much slower than in the USA, though continental Europe did no better than Britain in that respect. By 1913, 51 per cent of coal output was cut by machine in the USA against only 8 per cent in Britain as a whole, though Scotland showed an exceptional 22 per cent. At the same time, British coal output had been rising exceptionally fast, more than doubling between the early 1870s and the years before 1914, and so had exports, amounting still to no less than 85 per cent of world coal exports, much of this, however, for bunkers for British ships overseas. Productivity per man had been falling since 1883–4 overall, and usually from some time in the 1880s in most coal districts in turn, though it was recognised that the main cause for this was not declining efficiency as such but the need to work less accessible or inferior seams.

In the case of coal mining it is particularly difficult to judge entrepreneurial performance from information of this kind. Geological conditions differ not only as between Britain and the USA, but also from district to district in Britain, and almost from colliery to colliery. Whether cutting machines pay or not depends on those conditions, as well as on the stage of efficiency reached by the machinery itself. One measure, horse power per worker, seems not to have been inferior to the USA, though output per man-shift was considerably lower (McCloskey 1971b, 1981; Church 1986). It could be said that labour was plentiful, particularly in slumps, and coal prices could easily be raised in booms, so that coal masters had little incentive to invest in modernising their plant. There were great differences in efficiency among the nearly 1,800 collieries and enormous differences in regional working practices. While the majority of pits had falling output per man-shift, many were still on a rising curve. No doubt there were numerous collieries which survived despite poor entrepreneurship because of their favourable geology (Taylor 1961; Greasley 1990; Dintenfass 1988).

The new industries, failing and succeeding

Among the newer industries, motor cars and bicycles showed very different results. There was no shortage of brilliant engineering talent among the early motor car manufacturers before 1914, including Lanchester, Maudslay and Napier, nor was there a dearth of entrepreneurship. Herbert Austin and the later Lord Nuffield were clearly thrusting, dynamic inventor-entrepreneurs. No one in Britain, however, matched the skill of Henry Ford in breaking through to mass production sufficient to capture new layers of demand. Instead, British cars were made in small quantities, for a narrow luxury market, as indeed they were all over Europe. In the case of bicycles, however, Britain took an early lead, which she later recaptured after a period of American and German success, using mass-production methods to ensure both cheapness and quality. Several successful firms shared in this boom (Harrison 1969).

Among the newer industries, chemicals contain the most frequently noted 'failures'. In absolute terms the chemical industry in Britain grew faster in output and exports than most other industries, but what is normally understood by 'chemicals' is a group of quite separate industries, in some of which Britain maintained a strong position while in others her industrialists had fallen badly behind. In coal-tar dyes (though a British discovery) and associated products, like explosives and pharmaceuticals as well as photographic products, Germany took an unassailable lead, Britain's output being a mere fraction of world production. Since the raw materials were plentiful in Britain and the German success was due to her chemists and entrepreneurs, it might be felt that there was a decided failure here, both of technical education and of entrepreneurship. Worse still was the case of the Solvay ammonia-soda process, clearly superior to the older Leblanc process of alkali production, yet neglected by British firms while the rest of the advanced world changed over. Brunner Mond, a firm founded by immigrants, did adopt the newer process, but most other British firms stuck to their traditional method, and attempted to hold up their declining market share by combining in one near-monopoly firm, United Alkali. This case probably represents the best-documented entrepreneurial failure of the period, since it can be shown that even on the information available in the 1880s it should have been obvious that the Solvay process was preferable (Lindert and Trace 1971).

In other chemical fields the British performance was distinctly better. Altogether, the German and American output of chemical products per head in 1913 was about 25 per cent above the British, while in exports the German lead was even smaller, at 12.74 marks as against the British 11.75 marks per head. Belgian exports per head were about double that rate, and American about a quarter. The commercialisation of Anglo-Persian Oil on the other hand was an example of outstanding entrepreneurship (Ferrier 1976). In the manufacture of soap as well as of rubber tyres, British entrepreneurs were among the world leaders.

The making of soap, though in one sense an old industry, could be considered part of the new expanding sector of mass-produced consumer goods. These are often neglected in the literature, possibly because they are not to be found among the 'classical' early industries, and they are also frequently neglected in the production statistics, or valued by their inputs only, thus omitting a significant field of activity of British entrepreneurs. Crosfield's for technology, and William Lever for marketing and organisational innovation, may be matched by others who developed or installed new techniques, or expanded on the basis of branded and packaged goods (Musson 1965; Wilson 1954).

Among drugs there were Beecham's pills and the whole range of products developed by Jesse Boot for his retailing empire; there were cigarettes, in the mass production of which the British just beat the Americans; and in food, Huntley & Palmer biscuits and Brown & Polson cornflour as well as Bird's custard were typical examples. Quite remarkable was the rise of highly successful chocolate firms, including those of Cadbury, Rowntree and Fry, whose Quaker origins led to reliable quality and to considerable innovations in the management and welfare provision for their staff (Alford 1973; Chapman 1974; Wilson 1954 and 1965).

Quite astonishing was also the development of the newspaper press for mass reading. The innovational entrepreneurship of such pioneers as the later Lord Northcliffe included writing, editing and printing for an entirely different market from that for which the expensive and stodgy press of mid-Victorian years had catered, and some aggressive and inventive marketing. To sell newspapers on a mass basis, branch retailing of firms such as W. H. Smith was called into being by pioneering entrepreneurship. The creation of new forms of retailing, by the formation of department stores and above all by the chain stores in food, drugs, footwear, tobacco and other fields, was in fact among the most successful and innovative achievements of the later Victorian and Edwardian entrepreneur. It was in the service sector that some of the largest firms were to be found (Wardley 1991; ch. 5).

One remarkable event was the rise of the cooperative store movement, which developed in our period from insignificant beginnings to supplying over 10 per cent of the national consumption of a range of foods. Though the stores and their wholesale societies (CWS in England and Wales, SCWS in Scotland) and their associated factories were run by professional managers, their 'entrepreneurs' consisted of unpaid committees of working men – among the pioneers of departmental and chain store trading, as they were to be the pioneers of self-service after the Second World War (Cole 1944). Another group of frequently neglected entrepreneurs was made up of (generally) middle-class town aldermen and councillors (Hennock 1973), who provided water and gas among other supplies to British citizens well ahead of most other countries. The service sector will not be further enlarged upon here, since it and the even more successful sectors of banking, shipping, and insurance are treated in another chapter (ch. 5; see also Trebilcock 1986). In the assessment of Victorian entrepreneurship as a whole, however, it must not be, as it usually is, forgotten.

Striking a balance

It will have become clear that there was no representative Victorian 'entrepreneur', and that it is hazardous to offer generalisations covering all of those who might lay claim to the title. In many areas there were considerable numbers of vigorous, innovative, aggressive, risk-taking, pioneering entrepreneurs; in others, at least individual achievements rescued the British from the taunt of technological conservatism; but there were some areas also, and of course numerous individual firms, in which entrepreneurial performance was disappointing, the failure of entrepreneurship only too obvious. Where so many successes were registered, where an economy still kept a leading place among the nations despite the arrival of vigorous, and partly much better endowed young competitors, there can be no question of total failure – or even of a hostile environment, a cultural weakness or an industrial decline as a whole.

We can go a little beyond such conclusions. For it is evident that entrepreneurial performance, particularly in an international comparison, was much better among services and among consumer goods, and again among the higher qualities, than among the older staples. This is not altogether surprising. Some of the staples were those which newly industrialising economies could tackle first: they were also among the products which found a ready market in other parts of the world. By contrast, the services and higher quality consumer goods were marketable only in a wealthy society with higher incomes and a long tradition of urban living and industrial production. Similarly the widening availability of spare incomes, beyond sheer necessities for survival, created a demand for chocolates, newspapers, cosmetics, bicycles – and even holidays, the provision of which called forth its own form of entrepreneurship in seaside resorts (Ashworth 1966). That entrepreneurs concentrated on such growing sectors of the economy is no failure; it could rightly be deemed 'a manifestation of entrepreneurial perspicacity' (Payne 1978: 211). By contrast, staple products like pig-iron and steel might well be left to newly arrived economies, with their lower labour costs.

It was precisely for that reason that the failures in areas which ought to have gone well in rising mass consumer societies like the British, called for the most severe criticism. Dyes and drugs, scientific instruments and optical glass, the weak spots, were not among the most vital of products, and in electrical engineering, the other sector of backwardness, the British performance was less definite. The heart searching at the time and the criticism since then arose from the conviction that these were industries of the future, in which a leading economy ought to have shown outstanding entrepreneurial success.

In short, some failures there undoubtedly were, but they were surely not characteristic of the period as a whole. The entrepreneurs who had got to the top in late Victorian and Edwardian Britain could hold their own with the very best abroad.

4 Employment relations in manufacturing and international competition

William Lazonick

Introduction: the worker and the 'British disease'

During the decades after the Second World War, British industrial workers acquired a reputation for being altogether 'bloody-minded'. They were said to engage in restrictive practices – a refusal to work up to their productive potential – as they sought to control the relation between the work that they performed and the pay that they received. Some observers even alleged that workers spent their time inventing new restrictive practices so that they could make 'concessions' to employers to forgo 'customary' work rules in exchange for higher pay and more employment security (see, for example, McKersie *et al.* 1972).

While shop-floor employees were trying to enforce their versions of 'custom and practice' in their workplaces, national unions sought to exert collective power, sometimes through parliamentary means and sometimes through strikes, to protect the employment security and living standards of their members. The ability of workers to exercise power in the workplace, the industrial sphere and the political arena made it plausible to blame the labour movement for Britain's faltering economic performance in the 1960s and 1970s. For some, including the government of Margaret Thatcher in the 1980s, the power of the British labour movement amounted to nothing less than the 'British disease' (Bassett 1986: ch. 2; Maynard 1988: chs. 6–7). For example, Michael Edwardes, the managing director of BL (formerly British Leyland) in the late 1970s and early 1980s, recounted how at a meeting with BL senior executives in 1981 the economic adviser to Thatcher, Alan Walters, launched the theory that the closure of BL, whether as a result of a strike or in cold blood, could have a positive effect on the British economy within six months (1983: 216–17). The short-term impact on regions such as the west midlands and on the balance of payments might soon be offset, according to Walters, by the beneficial effect of the shock of closures on trades union and employee attitudes across the country. Restrictive practices would be swept away, pay increases would be held down and a more rapid improvement in Britain's competitiveness would thus be achieved through the closure of BL than by any other means available to the government.

In historical perspective, blaming the British worker for the nation's relatively poor competitive performance since the 1960s seems simplistic. Such an explanation fails to ask why and how British workers gained so much bargaining power over the conditions of work and pay that they could impede the growth of the economy. Well into the twentieth century, after all, Britain was a dominant economic power. Why should British workers and their unions be any more or less disruptive to the process of economic growth than workers and unions in nations such as the United States, France, Germany, Sweden, Italy, Canada, and Japan – advanced capitalist countries that are Britain's main competitors for global manufacturing markets?

Indeed, some studies of labour–management relations in the other countries have argued that trade unions often promote productivity (for the case of the United States, see Freeman and Medoff 1984; for the case of Japan, see Koike 1988). Why should British unions do just the opposite? In historical perspective, can it be assumed that the power of British workers has always been a barrier to economic progress? If not, when and why did the exercise of power by workers become a problem for British economic performance?

To provide answers one needs to inquire into the historical evolution of British shop-floor relations from the last decades of the nineteenth century in the manufacturing industries directly subject to international competition. Skilled workers made a crucial contribution to British economic performance in the last half of the nineteenth century. 'Craft' organisation, and the industrial relations structures for which it provided the foundation, augmented both the skill and effort that British workers were able and willing to supply to the production processes in which they laboured.

The rise of international competition altered the ability of British employers to abide by the traditional bargains over the relation between work and pay – bargains that had been the essence of the cooperative employment relations that had been critical to superior British performance in the last half of the nineteenth century. In the short run, employers and skilled workers continued to cooperate within the framework of the traditional bargains in order to adapt to the pressures of foreign competition. In the long run, however, as the pressure of competition from technologically dynamic foreign rivals became too great, conflicts erupted between employers and skilled employees, with adverse impacts on economic performance.

In explaining how British employment relations became an impediment to superior economic performance, one must stress the rise of foreign competition and the limits inherent in the skills and machine technologies that Britain used. The root cause of Britain's inferior economic performance was the failure of British enterprises to invest in modern managerial structures that could plan and coordinate shop-floor work.

The British labour force before the First World War

Although manufacturing remains important to the overall performance of the British economy today, it was more important earlier in the century. British manufacturers and the workers they employed found themselves under increasing competitive pressures from the 1890s, but it would only be in the inter-war years that dramatic changes in the occupational structure would begin. In 1911 the occupational structure was much the same as that which had been in place when Britain dominated global competition in the 1870s and 1880s (see the census data for earlier years in Mitchell and Jones 1971: 60).

Table 4.1 shows that in 1911 over 38 per cent of the British labour force were engaged in the manufacturing sector (namely, all the categories listed consecutively in Table 4.1 from metal manufacture and machinery through food, drink and tobacco). All such sectors were subject to direct international competition, whereas occupational categories like building and construction and gas, water and electricity supply were not. The percentage occupied in manufacturing plus mining and quarrying (another industrial sector that exported to global markets) was 45 per cent. Another 14 per cent of the British labour force, mainly women, were occupied in domestic and other service. The other major employers of labour were transportation (9 per cent), agriculture (8 per cent) and building (6 per cent). By way of contrast, fifty years later manufacturing occupied only 22 per cent of the working population, and manufacturing plus mining under 25 per cent (Mitchell and Jones 1971: 36).

Price and Bain (1988: 164) have estimated that in 1911 7 per cent of the occupied population were employers and proprietors, another 19 per cent were non-manual workers, and the remaining 74 per cent were manual workers. Fifty years later, employers and proprietors had dropped to under 5 per cent of the occupied population, but non-manual workers almost doubled their share, to 36 per cent, and the manual workers' share dropped to 59 per cent. By 1981, just under 48 per cent of the occupied population of Britain were manual workers.

While manufacturing employed a high proportion of women (45 per cent) in 1911, 70 per cent of female manufacturing workers (and 32 per cent of all occupied females) were concentrated in textiles and clothing. Another 40 per cent of the female labour force were engaged in domestic service. Of

Table 4.1. *Occupational distribution of the British labour force, 1911*

Occupational sector	Number male (000s)	Number female (000s)	Percentage of labour force	Percentage male
Public administration	271	50	1·7	84
Armed Forces	221	0	1·2	100
Professions and services	413	383	4·3	52
Domestic and personal	456	2,127	14·1	17
Commercial	739	157	4·9	82
Transport and communications	1,571	38	8·8	97
Agriculture	1,436	60	8·2	96
Fishing	53	0	0·3	100
Mining	1,202	8	6·6	99
Building	1,140	5	6·3	99
Metal manufacture and machinery	1,795	128	10·5	93
Woodwork	287	35	1·8	89
Bricks, cement, pottery, glass	145	42	1·0	77
Chemicals	155	46	1·1	77
Leather	90	32	0·7	73
Paper, print	253	144	2·2	63
Textiles	639	870	8·2	42
Clothing	432	825	6·9	34
Food, drink, tobacco	806	308	6·1	72
Gas, water, electricity	86	0	0·5	100
All others	741	98	4·6	88
Total	12,931	5,356	100.0	70

Source: Mitchell and Jones (1971 : 60).

the manufacturing sectors, metal manufacture and machinery as well as woodworking and furniture – preserves of craft labour – were the most heavily male dominated.

In 1911, women represented 30 per cent of the total occupied population and 31 per cent of all manual workers. Figure 4.1 illustrates that men had a much greater commitment than women to continuous employment in the paid labour force. Many married women stayed in the paid labour force out of economic necessity, the prevailing ideology being that a woman's place is in the home. To make the gender-based division of labour possible the male workers needed to earn a wage sufficient to support a family (see Humphries 1977). During the inter-war period the share of women in total employment remained at about 30 per cent (Price and Bain 1988: 166).

Table 4.2. *Relative wages of selected workers by pay level, 1886–1926 (highest wage in each year = 100)*

	1886	1913	1920	1926
High pay				
Bricklayers (building)	79	83	72	80
Coalgetter (coal mining)	79	100	100	89
Mule spinners (cotton)	82	89	95	87
Turners (engineering)	75	82	73	70
Engine drivers (railways)	100	92	76	100
Medium pay				
Painters (building)	72	74	71	80
Putters and fillers (coal mining)	62	73	79	65
Grinders (cotton)	54	63	71	64
Machinemen (engineering)	56	66	65	49
Guards (railways)	69	66	62	75
Low pay				
Labourers (building)	49	55	62	62
Labourers (coal mining)	54	65	73	60
Female weavers (cotton)	46	47	53	49
Labourers (engineering)	45	46	53	46
Goods porters (railways)	51	48	54	56

Source: Rowe (1928: 42).

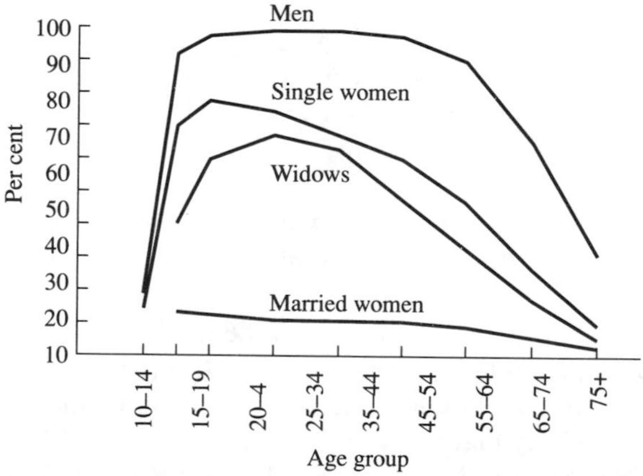

Figure 4.1 Rates of participation in the labour force, 1911 (England and Wales)
Source: calculated by Baines (1981) from the *Census of Population*, 1911.

Indeed, the labour force participation rate of women – the percentage of women who worked for pay – actually fell slightly from 35 per cent in 1911 to 34 per cent in 1931 and to less than 33 per cent in 1951 (Price and Bain 1988: 168). Only thereafter did the labour force participation rate of women begin its steady rise, reaching over 45 per cent by 1981.

Among the industrial labour force the men most able to earn enough to support a family were those who, by some type of apprenticeship systems, had acquired specialised craft skills. Table 4.2, derived from a compilation made by J. W. F. Rowe in 1928, shows the relative earnings of selected categories of workers in five major sectors in 1886, 1913, 1920 and 1926, with a value of 100 assigned to the highest paid category of worker in each year. The movement of coalgetters (or hewers) to the top of the pay scale among the selected categories in 1913 and 1920 reflects a combination of the enhanced power of the unions and a strong demand for their labour in the years around the First World War rather than an upward movement in their productivity. So too in the case of the mule spinners (see Benson 1982; White 1982; Clegg *et al.* 1964: chs. 3 and 11; Clegg 1985: chs. 2 and 3). By way of contrast, as we shall see, mechanisation and redivision of labour combined with weak craft unionism constrained pay gains by the turners – the labour elite of mechanical engineering – despite rising productivity (Zeitlin 1983). Depending largely on the degree of mechanisation and the pressure of international competition, each industry had its own unique history of industrial relations.

In setting out the wage rates of the various categories of workers from which Table 4.2 is derived, Rowe (1928: 42) labelled the high-paid workers 'skilled', the medium-paid 'semi-skilled', and the low-paid 'unskilled'. But by any account, the cotton weavers, male or female, were at least 'semi-skilled', as Rowe (1928: 31–3) himself noted. Yet even male weavers received wages that were low in comparison with semi-skilled workers in other industries. The low wage was not from a lack of union organisation: before the First World War the cotton weavers had the second largest union in Britain. Rather the cause was the even split of weaving between men and women. Many women continued to work as weavers after marriage, thus contributing to family income. As a result, male weavers in Lancashire did not have to earn a 'family wage' to have access to a 'family income'. Although the payments per unit of output (piece rates) specified in the wage lists that governed earnings in Lancashire did not discriminate against women, on average female weavers earned less than male weavers because on average they tended fewer looms, and hence generated less output per unit of time (see Wood 1910; Lazonick 1986).

Table 4.3 shows how the wages of the high-paid workers varied in relation to the medium-paid and lower-paid workers. From 1886 to 1926

Table 4.3. *Relative pay of selected workers by industry, 1886–1926*

	1886	1913	1920	1926
High pay/medium pay				
Building	1·09	1·12	1·01	1·00
Coal mining	1·20	1·36	1·27	1·38
Cotton	1·53	1·41	1·35	1·35
Engineering	1·33	1·26	1·11	1·18
Railways	1·44	1·40	1·22	1·33
High pay/low pay				
Building	1·62	1·51	1·15	1·30
Coal mining	1·37	1·53	1·36	1·48
Cotton	1·79	1·91	1·78	1·78
Engineering	1·68	1·77	1·38	1·53
Railways	1·97	1·93	1·42	1·80

Source: Rowe (1928: 42).

mule spinners along with the railway engine drivers did best relative to other workers in their own industries. In all five industries the rapid wage inflation after the First World War compressed relative wages. The less skilled workers gained the benefits of union organisation (see, for example, Hyman 1971).

The organisation of the less skilled had begun in 1889, with the rise of general unionism, but before the First World War it was still the elite craft workers – known as the aristocracy of labour – who were best organised to protect their conditions of work and pay (see Hobsbawm 1964: ch. 10). In 1910 by far the largest union was the Miners Federation, with almost 600,000 members, while the next largest were those of the weavers (112,000 members) and engineers (100,000 members), all comparatively skilled. As Table 4.4 shows, after a stagnant period in the first half of the 1900s, union membership rose steadily, especially in the First World War, and then exploded during the tight labour market conditions of the immediate post-war years, only to fall dramatically with the coming of depressed economic conditions. The vast majority of union members were men; a small increase in the proportion of female union members occurred during the First World War and its aftermath. The density of male union membership (that is, the proportion of prospective male union members who were actually in unions) doubled between 1905 and 1915, and then doubled again by 1919. Male union density fell off during the 1920s and the first half of the 1930s. Setting aside the extraordinary number of working days lost

Table 4.4. *Union membership, density and work stoppages, 1893–1939*

Year	Union members (000s)	Percentage male	Density, males (%)	Density, females (%)	Work stoppages	Working days lost (000s)
1893	1,559	na	na	na	509	30,440
1894	1,530	na	na	na	903	9,510
1895	1,504	na	na	na	728	5,700
1896	1,608	91	14	3	906	3,560
1897	1,731	92	15	3	848	10,330
1898	1,752	92	15	3	695	15,260
1899	1,911	92	16	3	710	2,500
1900	2,022	92	17	3	633	3,090
1901	2,025	93	17	3	631	4,130
1902	2,013	92	16	3	432	3,440
1903	1,994	92	16	3	380	2,320
1904	1,967	92	16	3	346	1,460
1905	1,997	91	16	4	349	2,370
1906	2,210	91	17	4	479	3,020
1907	2,513	90	19	5	585	2,150
1908	2,483	90	19	5	389	10,790
1909	2,477	89	18	5	422	2,690
1910	2,565	89	19	5	521	9,870
1911	3,139	89	23	6	872	10,160
1912	3,416	89	24	7	834	40,890
1913	4,135	90	30	8	1,459	9,800
1914	4,145	90	30	8	972	9,880
1915	4,359	89	31	9	672	2,950
1916	4,644	87	32	11	532	2,450
1917	5,499	84	36	16	730	5,650
1918	6,533	82	42	22	1,165	5,880
1919	7,926	83	62	24	1,352	34,970
1920	8,347	84	55	24	1,607	26,570
1921	6,632	85	44	18	763	85,870
1922	5,625	85	39	16	576	19,850
1923	5,429	85	37	15	628	10,670
1924	5,544	85	38	15	710	8,420
1925	5,506	85	37	15	603	7,950
1926	5,219	84	35	14	323	162,230
1927	4,919	84	32	14	308	1,170
1928	4,806	84	31	14	302	1,390
1929	4,858	84	31	14	431	8,290
1930	4,841	84	31	13	422	4,400
1931	4,624	84	29	13	420	6,980
1932	4,443	83	28	12	389	6,490
1933	4,389	83	27	12	357	1,070
1934	4,570	84	29	12	471	960
1935	4,867	84	31	12	553	1,960
1936	5,295	85	33	13	818	1,830
1937	5,842	85	37	14	1,129	3,410
1938	6,063	85	38	15	875	1,330
1939	6,274	84	39	16	940	1,360

Sources: membership: Mitchell and Jones (1971: 68); density: Price and Bain (1988: 68); stoppages and days lost: Pelling (1976: 293–5).

during the General Strike of 1926, the most working days lost were to strikes when the unions were coming into their strength, in the boom periods centring on 1912 and 1920 (Cronin 1982).

How, then, did the workers and their organisations influence the economic performance of the British economy? And did the employment relations into which the workers entered have a different impact on British economic performance in Britain's period of dominance than later? We focus here on those machine-based industries – iron and steel, mechanical engineering, shipbuilding and cotton textiles – central to Britain's rise to international economic leadership, and on the new industries of the twentieth century, such as car manufacturing, that made heavy use of mechanical technologies.

Skill and effort in the 'workshop of the world'

In the early 1880s Britain's share of world exports of manufactures was 43 per cent, vastly greater than the 6 per cent of the United States and the 16 per cent of Germany. By 1913 Britain's share had dropped to 32 per cent, whereas the share of the United States had increased to 14 per cent and that of Germany to 25 per cent (Matthews *et al.* 1982: 435). Even in relative decline, British industry still supplied almost one third of the world's manufactured exports.

Chief among such exports was cotton yarn and cloth, which constituted 36 per cent of all British exports in 1870 and 24 per cent in 1910. Other major British manufactured exports were woollen yarn and cloth and iron and steel products. In 1910 machinery represented almost 7 per cent of all exports (up from less than 2 per cent in 1870), while coal and coke represented almost 9 per cent of all exports in 1910 (up from less than 3 per cent in 1870). During the inter-war years, iron and steel and textiles remained important exports, but by 1950 machinery and vehicles, the new industries, had become Britain's leading export sectors (Mitchell and Jones 1971: 304–6).

The production of goods to be sold both at home and abroad required particular combinations of physical resources (structures, machines, materials) and human resources (workers, technicians, managers). Such combinations of inputs are called simply 'technologies', and a restructuring of the physical and human resources to generate a given product or to generate a new product is called a technological change. In an economic system based on the employment of wage labour an employer pays workers wages to induce them to contribute their skills – their abilities to provide useful labour services – to the operation of those technologies in which the enterprise has already invested.

The ensuing relation between the employer and the worker cannot be considered a mere market transaction – the impersonal exchange of a specified wage for specified labour services. The employment relation invariably entails attempts by both employers and workers to exercise power over the quantity of labour services supplied – what is generally called 'effort' – and the amount of wages paid (see Lazonick 1990). Workers want to be paid well for their effort, and may through individual and collective actions seek to limit the effort they give per hour and to increase the wages received in return. At the same time the employer wants to reduce unit costs, and prefers therefore to get high levels of effort and output in exchange for a given wage. The effort supplied by the worker affects unit labour costs, of course, but also the utilisation of plant and equipment and unit capital costs: a worker strolling between machines instead of running will use the machines less efficiently. Any analysis of the contribution of labour to economic performance must allow for the relative power inherent in relations between employers and workers to control the relation between effort and pay.

The analysis of employment relations and economic performance dates back to the nineteenth-century writings of Karl Marx (1867(1977)). Marx placed the evolution of employment relations at the centre of his analysis of British capitalist development. In Marx's view, that the capitalist employer controlled the physical means of production gave the employer power to extract more effort from the worker for a given wage. As long as workers had specialised skills to supply to the production process they could resist the attempts by employers to 'intensify their labour' – that is, to extract more effort per unit of time. But according to Marx, with the advent of machine technologies that rendered the specialised skills superfluous the worker became an easily replaceable input into production. In making the worker 'an appendage to the machine', as Marx (1867 (1977: 799)) put it, the capitalist was able to increase the intensity of labour to the maximum possible, while paying the worker the low wage for unskilled labour.

Subsequent historical research has offered a different perspective on employment relations. Notwithstanding the mechanisation of production in the nineteenth century the skills of key groups of shop-floor workers remained central to the technologies that permitted Britain to become an industrial giant (Samuel 1977), and indeed remained important well into the twentieth century (Harley 1974; More 1980). Marx overemphasised the degree to which the mechanical technologies in which British capitalists invested superseded the need for complementary skilled labour. Contemporaries marvelled at the new machines, but the technologies were still far from being fully automated. They required skilled labour to keep them in motion and thereby to enable high volumes of output to be generated on the shop floor.

Marx also overestimated the power of British capitalists to control the shop floor. Employers relied heavily on experienced shop-floor workers to manage the recruitment, training and utilisation of junior workers and to keep up the pace of work. The control over the management of production gave the experienced workers power in dealing with their employers, called 'craft control' (Zeitlin 1985; Lazonick 1990: ch. 6).

The foundation of craft control was not the power of unions. Rather the origins of craft control can be found in the willingness of British employers to leave the control of work organisation on the shop floor. The authority and responsibility to manage the shop-floor organisation of work in turn provided a basis for key groups of workers to form powerful trade unions that, through collective bargaining over the conditions of work and pay, consolidated craft control (Burgess 1975; Harrison and Zeitlin 1985; Lazonick 1990: ch. 3). The key groups of workers became known collectively as 'the aristocracy of labour' (Hobsbawm 1964 and 1984). They included such workers as turners and fitters in mechanical engineering, boilermakers in shipbuilding, puddlers in iron manufacture, mule spinners in cotton textiles, and hewers in coal mining.

The persistence of craft control and the consequent power of craft unions depended on the regional concentration of industry, the degree of industrial fragmentation among employers and the pace of skill-displacing technological change. All of the three factors were inextricably linked in the evolution of British industry, and created a uniquely British system of industrial relations.

A prime impetus to regional concentration of industry was the practice of senior workers recruiting new workers locally at an early age and employing them as assistants or apprentices receiving on-the-job training. The junior workers expected to find future employment as senior workers in the crafts and districts in which they were trained. In the cotton industry a piecer would hope to be promoted to the position of minder on self-acting spinning mules, while a tenter who assisted in weaving hoped one day to be granted his or her own complement of power looms (Lazonick and Mass 1984). In the iron and steel industry, again, the underhands provided a source of potential skilled workers (Elbaum and Wilkinson 1979). In the coal-mining districts of Durham and Northumberland, haulers looked forward to becoming hewers, at much higher pay (Daunton 1981). In some of the mechanical engineering industries (such as shipbuilding), formal apprenticeship systems were widespread (Pollard and Robertson 1979: chs. 7–8; Lorenz and Wilkinson 1986; Lorenz 1991: ch. 3).

To be sure, some young men took their training acquired in their home districts and migrated to other districts or, more typically, abroad. But most who acquired highly specialised on-the-job training remained ready to take up employment in the industrial districts and specific trades where they had grown up. The prime incentive for junior workers to remain put was the prospect of promotion into the aristocracy of labour.

As a result of the training and incentive systems the supplies of labour with particular skills reproduced themselves, and indeed tended to grow, in the industrial districts in which those skills were already in heavy demand. The concentration of particular types of workers in particular industrial districts itself reinforced the tendency toward regional specialisation of industry. New firms tended to locate in the same regions, where labour with the requisite skills was already abundant.

As a consequence the industries became increasingly concentrated in particular localities (Hudson 1989). Employers got access to large supplies of skilled labour. They could take advantage of proximity to suppliers and distributors to smooth the flow of work-in-progress. British industry became characteristically 'disintegrated', that is, split into different firms through the vertically related stages of purchasing, production and marketing. Given the localised concentration of industry, new businesses were able to specialise in a narrow range of activities, relying on specialised firms to supply them with inputs and on still other specialised firms to purchase their outputs. As more firms set up as specialists the suppliers and buyers for intermediate products became all the more readily available, thus reinforcing the trend to vertical specialisation. The specialisation had an important cost: British managers did not get experience in managing the large, integrated firms of the future. Therefore firms tended to confine themselves to single-plant operations – which made it easier for new firms to enter, and hence increased further the extent of horizontal and vertical fragmentation of industry.

The narrow product and process strategies of British industrial enterprises reinforced both their willingness and their need to rely on craft control in their production processes. In contrast to the organisation-building that characterised managerial capitalism in Germany and the United States, such relatively small, specialised firms did not need to invest in managerial structures. Hence the British firms could not achieve what have come to be called internal economies of scale and scope (Chandler 1990).

In the evolution of managerial capitalism in the United States, for example, the assertion of managerial control over shop-floor production activities was generally a final step in the development of a firm's capabilities to plan and coordinate its various business activities. The managers actually managed. The relatively underdeveloped organisational capabilities that characterised most British industrial firms gave such employers no choice but to rely on craft control to coordinate the organisation of shop-floor work. Before the 1890s the ready availability of skilled labour made British firms quite willing to countenance the persistence of craft control.

Nevertheless, even as they accepted craft control as a normal mode of productive organisation, British employers would have preferred that craft control not be translated into union power. The 1830s and 1840s saw major conflicts in the cotton textile industry over the right of workers to engage in collective bargaining. As late as 1854 the cotton manufacturers of Preston locked out their workers rather than recognise the union (Dutton and King 1981). The newly formed Amalgamated Society of Engineers suffered a major defeat in the lockout of 1852 (Burgess 1975: 23–4). In the iron industry, union organisation was nearly obliterated in the late 1860s after a series of industrial conflicts (Elbaum and Wilkinson 1979: 285).

The confrontations between employers and their workers did not, however, usher in a non-union era. The cohesion of workers was increased by their geographic concentration. On the employers' side, meanwhile, the 'great Victorian boom' of the third quarter of the nineteenth century undermined the incentive and ability of British firms to fight unionisation (Burgess 1975: ch. 1). Eager to generate output for sale while there were profits to be made, employers became receptive to sharing power with workers' organisations.

The 1852 lockout in mechanical engineering is a case in point. The official reason that the engineering firms gave for locking out the workers was to end their opposition to systematic overtime and piece rates. But for many employers the ultimate goal of the lockout was to eliminate the recently founded Amalgamated Society of Engineers as an effective bargaining agent. After three months of lockout the engineering employers emerged victorious. Impecunious workers signed declarations that they would give up union membership as a condition for being allowed to come back to work (Burgess 1975: ch. 2).

Yet despite the apparent defeat of worker organisation in mechanical engineering in 1852, over the following two decades the Amalgamated Society of Engineers emerged as the epitome of the 'New Model' union, that is, a union that entered into cooperative bargaining with employers, gaining job security and higher wages for an emerging aristocracy of labour (Cole 1962). For as in other British industries during the Victorian boom, engineering employers found that it was better to win the cooperation of workers by bargaining than to risk the loss of revenues from labour conflict. Across the staple industries in which Britain ruled the world the foundations for negotiating collective bargains were customary work practices and earnings norms, some of which had been embodied in wage lists issued by employers in the non-union era (Huberman 1992). The period that proved to be the apex of British industrial dominance saw the consolidation of craft control.

The employers' acceptance of collective bargaining in turn opened the way for political transformations that served to reinforce the power of unions to preserve craft control. In the eyes of the British political elite of the 1860s and 1870s the advent of cooperative industrial relations under the aegis of business-minded union leaders transformed craft workers from uncontrollable subversives into responsible citizens. One result was the 1867 extension of the right to vote to the better-paid of the workers. With the acceptance of workers as responsible members of the political community in the 1870s came changes in labour law that facilitated the accumulation of strike funds by unions and the staging of strikes (Pelling 1976: ch. 4; Hunt 1981: ch. 8). To build its electoral strength the Liberal Party (which was strongly influenced by the interests of industrial capitalists) entered into a political alliance with working-class leaders. The alliance endured from the 1870s until 1901, when the infamous Taff Vale decision convinced most workers that they had to seek independent political representation (Saville 1960).

From the late 1860s through the late 1880s the employers and workers in various manufacturing industries sought formal systems of wage determination, permitting both sides to share the gains of the good times and the burdens of the bad (Porter 1970). The cotton industry, for example, saw the institutionalisation of their wage lists. By the 1880s the major source of conflict in the industry was the adjustment of earnings over the ups and downs of the business cycles. In iron and steel, hosiery, footwear and coal mining 'conciliation boards' were set up to settle disputes. Iron workers and coal miners agreed to 'sliding scales,' which adjusted wages over the course of the business cycle according to changes in the selling prices of the iron or the coal (Clegg *et al.* 1964: 15–23). In mechanical engineering, in which employers were continually seeking to substitute unskilled workers for skilled workers, the Amalgamated Society of Engineers was able to establish and enforce standard district rates. In shipbuilding the skilled workers – and in particular the platers, riveters and caulkers, collectively known as boilermakers – were highly organised by the 1870s. But because the shipbuilding industry was subject to severe ups and downs the workers had only limited success in engaging in collective bargaining (McClelland and Reid 1985).

The growth of union influence and the spread of collective bargaining through the 1880s enabled experienced workers to consolidate their positions of craft control on the shop floor. Even the weavers of coarse cotton goods, whose skills were much more easily replicable than those of, say, puddlers, boilermakers, fitters or mule spinners, were able to maintain customary divisions of labour and manning ratios as the bases for collective bargaining (Hopwood 1969: ch. 17; Fowler and Fowler 1984).

Employment relations and foreign competition

Until the 1890s the reliance on craft control improved the international competitiveness of British industry. On-the-job training from an early age (children started factory work in their early teens) generated an abundant supply of workers whose skills had evolved specifically to complement the newest machinery. In coal mining, for example, which was barely mechanised before the First World War and in which employment almost tripled from 1870 to the First World War, reaching 1.1 million in 1913, output depended almost entirely on accumulations of human strength and skill (Daunton 1981).

But, as indicated earlier, the achievement of high levels of productive efficiency is not merely a matter of the accumulation of skill. Through its day-to-day, and even minute-to-minute, application to the production process, skill must be transformed into effort. As a result the contribution of workers to superior economic performance depends on their attitudes. Workers will only expend high levels of effort in the production process if they expect to receive what they consider to be a 'fair share' in the consequent returns. In industries in which, as was generally the case in late nineteenth-century Britain, individual firms had small market shares, employers were too subject to intense competitive pressures to be able to make credible promises to workers that their shares would be 'fair'. Workers required the power of collective organisation to feel confident that they would have some bargaining power. By giving workers the assurance that their expectations for rewards would be met, collective organisation made workers more willing to contribute high levels of effort to production.

Craft control helped to elicit high levels of effort from senior workers, and from junior workers whose future employment prospects depended on how well they helped senior workers. The prospect of eventual promotion to a senior position encouraged junior workers to contribute high levels of effort despite low wages. The chances for junior workers to be promoted were greater when the industry was growing. But promotion was not absolutely assured.

From the late 1880s, however, the rise of foreign competition, combined with the availability of large supplies of low-paid but capable junior workers who had been trained on the job, created incentives for employers to attack craft control. The employers looked for ways to cut costs by using cheaper labour. Some industrialists even campaigned to cease collective bargaining altogether in order to restore to themselves the 'power to manage'. The engineering employers, as in the early 1850s, were in the forefront. Colonel Dyer, president of the Engineering Employers' Federation (EEF) put it thus in a letter to the *Times* on the eve of the 1897–8 engineering lockout: the employers in his organisation were determined 'to obtain the freedom to manage their own affairs which had proved to be so beneficial to the American manufacturer as to enable them to compete ... in what was formerly an English monopoly' (quoted in Pelling 1976: 112). Colonel Dyer held up Carnegie Steel, which had rid itself of unions in 1892, as an example of how to regain the power to manage. The Carnegie victory of 1892 was indeed the beginning of a non-union era in American industry that would last until the unionisation of mass-production workers during the 1930s (Brody 1980: ch. 1).

Faced by low wages well into manhood the younger workers became more susceptible to black-leg tactics on the one hand and to new forms of industrial unionism on the other. The threat to the privileged positions of the labour aristocrats became particularly apparent in the wake of the 'New Unionism' of the 1880s (Hobsbawm 1964: ch. 10).

Another threat to craft control came from the wave of skill-displacing technologies of the late nineteenth century, most of them emanating from the United States (Rosenberg 1976: chs. 1 and 2; Hounshell 1984; Thomson 1989). As a whole British industry was laggard in adopting the new technologies (though see ch. 3). The abundance of skilled labour and the successes of craft control had convinced many firms to stick with, and even make more investments in, the traditional technologies. Nevertheless, the diffusion of new technologies in Britain varied from industry to industry. In boot and shoe manufacture the rapid adoption of new technologies resulted in the serious erosion, if not obliteration, of craft control (Clegg *et al.* 1964: 24–6). In the mechanical engineering industries, new technologies were by the 1880s and 1890s creating opportunities for substituting unskilled for skilled men (Zeitlin 1983; McKinlay and Zeitlin 1989). In cotton textiles the adoption of ring spinning permitted the employment of low-paid female operatives instead of high-paid male operatives on the mule spindles. Yet even when substantial numbers of ring frames were adopted, in the decade prior to the First World War, mule-spinning factories remained the norm and the craft control of the operative mule spinners was as solid as ever. In cotton weaving the highly productive automatic loom barely entered the British industry before the First World War, and even in those firms where it was introduced the utilisation of the new technology – especially the number of machines per weaver – quickly became an issue of collective bargaining (Sandberg 1974; Lazonick and Mass 1984). In coal mining, mechanised coal cutting remained rare before the First World War, but, as Daunton (1981) has shown, differences across coal-mining districts in the hierarchical and technical divisions of labour had different implications for craft control. Toward the end of the nineteenth century, in short, the labour aristocrats began to feel pressure from above and below.

The persistence of craft control

The cotton textile industry was central to British economic development. In 1900 the industry employed over 3 per cent of the British labour force and contributed over 26 per cent of the value of all British exports. Moreover, in the decades before the First World War the number of firms in the industry expanded by 14 per cent and both the numbers of spindles and looms by almost 25 per cent (Jones 1933: 275–7; Sandberg 1974). In the post-First World War period, however, the cotton textile industry experienced a rapid and, as it turned out, permanent decline. During the inter-war years the British cotton textile industry lost its lower quality markets to Indian and Japanese competition, and in the decades after the Second World War it lost its higher quality markets to competitors in western Europe and the United States (Sandberg 1974; Lazonick 1986; Mass and Lazonick 1990).

But in the product markets for the coarsest cotton goods, competitive pressures of Indian production were already being felt in the 1880s. The loss of markets to India lay behind the major confrontation in 1891 over 'bad spinning' – the attempt to cut costs by using lower cost cotton. The conflict prompted Lancashire's spinning mill owners and managers to form the Federation of Master Cotton Spinners' Associations, with a militant faction advocating that the employers use their new-found unity to renounce the wage lists. The dominant faction in the employers' federation argued, however, that orderly relations with the minders constituted the industry's most valuable asset (Macara 1923; see also McIvor 1988). Moderation prevailed, in the form of the 1893 Brooklands Agreement creating formal procedures for cyclical adjustments in earnings and the resolution of shop-floor grievances. In the absence of any concerted attempt by employers to transform the shop-floor division of labour, mule spinners were able to use a combination of coercion and concessions to keep their junior workers in line. All the essential features of work organisation in mule spinning remained intact, and indeed were to persist into the 1950s.

In weaving, too, the rise of international competition did little to alter the traditional division of labour. The Uniform List of 1892 covering all cotton-weaving districts remained in force into the second half of the twentieth century. In 1935 the List, revised to take into account the high levels of unemployment, was made statutory by Act of Parliament. In the 1930s the cloth manufacturers made some attempts to increase the number of power looms per weaver above the standard four. On the whole, however, they were not successful. As in spinning, traditional modes of work organisation continued to characterise the weaving section of the cotton textile industry.

In the iron and steel industry, Britain lost its dominant position in the late nineteenth and early twentieth centuries. In 1870 Britain produced 50 per cent of world tonnage of pig-iron and 43 per cent of steel. By 1913 the United States was producing 40 per cent of world tonnage of iron and steel, and Britain only 10 per cent. After controlling about three-quarters of world exports of iron and steel around 1870, the British industry still accounted for over one third in 1913. But by 1913 Germany had surpassed Britain as the world's leading exporter. Despite this fall from hegemony the British iron and steel industry expanded steadily in the late nineteenth and early twentieth centuries, from an average annual output of 1.8 million tons in the period 1880–1904 to 7.0 million in 1910–14 (McCloskey 1973; Elbaum 1986: 51, 57).

On the eve of the First World War, British iron and steel continued to maintain international competitive advantage in higher quality sheet and tinplate markets. At home the industry was serving the still dominant British shipbuilding industry, which alone took 30 per cent of the nation's steel output in 1910–12. Like the cotton textile industry, British steel suffered from excess capacity in the 1920s. Although the industry experienced a recovery in the late 1930s, its fragmented structure of industrial organisation so obstructed the rationalisation and re-equipment of the industry that by the 1950s nationalisation had become a necessary, if not sufficient, condition for its technological renewal and ultimate survival (Elbaum 1986; Tolliday 1986a).

Rising iron and steel output made for harmonious labour relations. After a series of industrial conflicts in the 1860s employers and employees joined together to set up boards of arbitration and conciliation to negotiate the standard tonnage rates. Through the 1870s the skilled workers were generally contractors who employed underhands on fixed time-wages. The boards also negotiated sliding scales for tonnage rates to adjust for cyclical variations in the selling price of manufactured iron (Elbaum and Wilkinson 1979; see also Vichniac 1987).

Skilled iron and steel workers saw their earnings grow, because their bargaining power enabled them to maintain tonnage rate levels even as, largely through technical change, productivity increased. Left behind at first were the underhands, paid time-wages and possessing little bargaining power to extract higher wages from the senior workers who employed them. But unlike the piecers in cotton spinning, who were never able to organise independently of their worker bosses, from the 1880s the underhands formed their own unions and were increasingly successful in putting an end to the contracting system. They were able to negotiate their own tonnage rates directly with employers.

The breakdown of contracting did not spell an end to craft control, however. Even as underhands gained the right to bargain directly with employers, work organisation on the shop floor remained essentially unchanged. Indeed, with various classes of underhands now trying to control their particular occupations, craft control became even more entrenched and collective bargaining even more fragmented by type of job. Such was the overall balance of power between workers and employers in the iron and steel industry, moreover, that the first national sliding-scale agreement negotiated in 1905 endured until 1940 (Wilkinson 1977). Despite conflict during the depressed conditions of the 1920s, in iron and steel, as in cotton textiles, collective agreements concerning work and pay became 'laws' of employment relations that employers dared not challenge.

In sharp contrast, therefore, to the experiences of workers during the non-union era in the US iron and steel industry, British iron and steel workers continued to exercise substantial control over the relation between effort supplied and pay received. In particular, bargains for particular types of work that applied across all firms enabled workers to capture large shares of productivity gains.

The workers' power to capture productivity increases deterred the more financially solvent and potentially aggressive firms from making high fixed-cost investments in new technologies. The relatively low earnings of workers in low productivity plants facilitated the survival of firms that sought to rely on existing plant and equipment. The persistence – and indeed the spread – of craft bargaining reinforced the fragmented structures of industrial organisation in deterring investment in best-practice steel technologies (Elbaum 1986; and for another view McCloskey 1973).

In British iron and steel, as in cotton textiles, therefore, the existence of firms too weak to exercise control over external market forces, let alone over their own internal organisation, discouraged the industry from making investments in new technologies. Confronted by the new international competition from the late nineteenth century, employers in the staple industries sought the cooperation of their workers in the attempts to cut costs on the traditional organisational structures and technologies.

A willingness to share power with workers did not, however, characterise all the manufacturing industries. In the engineering industries – building textile machinery, steam engines, boilers, locomotives, iron ships and agricultural implements – employers united in the late 1890s. In a number of important dimensions the engineering lockout of 1897–8 replicated the attack on engineering workers in 1852. Both lockouts took place during the upswing of the trade cycle, as employers and workers sought to establish their claims to shares of productivity gains. The workers' demands were the same: an end to 'systematic' overtime, elimination of piece-rate payments and a ban on the use of 'illegal' men. In both lockouts the Amalgamated Society of Engineers (ASE), founded in 1850, represented the skilled workers, primarily the turners who shaped metal parts and the fitters who fitted the parts into the machines (Burgess 1975: ch. 1).

The ASE opposed systematic overtime because it increased unemployment among their members during periods of slack trade. In cotton there was 'short-time working', maximising the number of workers who could share in available wages while preventing the growth of an industrial reserve army pitting the unemployed against the employed. Engineering firms, however, preferred to hire fewer workers for longer hours, in order to employ only those workers whom they considered to be the best. The division between the employed and unemployed aided employers in the reduction of wages and the extraction of more effort from the workforce.

The ASE opposed piece-rate systems, too, not as a matter of principle but because in practice engineering employers had the power to use piece rates to divide and conquer the workers on the shop floor. In the conflict of 1852 the ASE had objected in particular to the 'piece-master system', the practice of subcontracting work to a skilled worker supervising gangs of workers paid time-wages. Unlike the mule spinners and skilled iron workers, whose unions preserved internal subcontracting and piece rates, engineering workers found that the piece-master system enabled a small proportion of skilled workers to strike individual bargains with employers and thereby gain the right to supervise gangs of other workers. The piece masters would employ less experienced workers, whom the displaced skilled workers deemed to be 'illegal men'. But even when skilled fitters and turners were employed they found themselves in the same subordinate position as piecers in cotton spinning.

The skilled engineering workers in fact faced much dimmer prospects than did the piecers. Each senior mule spinner – called a 'minder' – generally employed one 'big' piecer, who was in line to be promoted to minder status when he entered manhood, whereas the piece masters employed many skilled adult males, with no orderly line of promotion to piece-master status. In cotton textiles the minder-piecer system provided the shop-floor foundation for the rise and consolidation of union power and collective bargaining after the 1840s, whereas in engineering the piece-master system served only to break down the solidarity among skilled workers.

With employment conditions buoyant and technology relatively stable in the third quarter of the nineteenth century, skilled engineering workers had little reason to complain about systematic overtime and the use of illegal men. By the early 1890s the ASE had become the largest single union in Britain, with the skilled fitters and turners making up most of its membership of over 70,000 (Hyman 1985: 105). But by the 1890s the cooperative relations between the ASE and engineering employers were eroding rapidly – again under competitive pressure from America and Germany. In 1880 Britain had 63 per cent of world exports of capital goods, but by 1899 this share had fallen to 44 per cent. Making the greatest gains was the United States, whose share rose from 6 per cent in 1880 to 23 per cent in 1899, with American strengths lying in machine tools, agricultural machinery, locomotives and sewing machines. For the British economy itself the rise of US competition in both machine tools and machinery was, by the late 1890s, being characterised as 'the American invasion' (Saul 1960a).

Under the pressure of international competition, British engineering employers began to challenge the structures of work organisation and the levels of pay that had been put in place during the earlier decades of economic prosperity and industrial harmony. As in the 1840s, so in the 1890s the introduction of skill-displacing machine tools led employers to hire less skilled and less expensive labour in place of ASE members. At the same time the pressure of the new competition prompted employers to disavow existing arrangements for giving workers shares in the value that their labour helped to produce. Once again in the mid-1890s, ASE opposition to systematic overtime, piece rates and illegal men came to the fore. Despite its size and entrenched position as a New Model union the ASE was vulnerable because its membership included only about half of the fitters and turners in the engineering industry. There was in engineering, moreover, an ample supply of less skilled, adult male workers whose employment was independent of the fitters and turners, and who, unlike workers who had served apprenticeships, had no avenues of eventual entry into the ranks of the skilled. The semi-skilled workers were willing and able to operate the new machine tools, and displace the fitters and turners (Zeitlin 1983).

As had typically been the case with British working-class movements of the nineteenth century the ASE sought to unify and build its national membership during the 1890s by campaigning for a shorter workday (in this case, eight hours). In 1896 the engineering employers reacted by forming the Engineering Employers' Federation (EEF). As the introduction into British industry of American machine tools quickened in the last half of the 1890s (particularly during the boom in bicycle manufacture that permitted the use of mass-production methods), employers renewed the assault on craft control that they had failed to carry through almost a half century before.

Like the defeat of the workers in the 1852 lockout, the 1897–8 lockout ended with ASE members going back to work on the employers' terms. Indeed, if one reads the 'Terms of Settlement' that the ASE executive was forced to sign to put an end to the lockout, one gets the distinct impression that engineering employers had put an end to craft control – that they had gained 'the power to manage' (Zeitlin 1983).

Yet the defeat of the ASE was only partial, particularly when compared with the eradication of collective bargaining in the metal-working industries of the United States in the early decades of this century. The very insistence by the EEF that the ASE sign the Terms of Settlement reveals that British engineering employers accepted collective bargaining as an unavoidable fact of industrial life. In the United States, employers insisted on, and won, the right to manage. In Britain, employers had to be content to struggle over, as they themselves put it, the power to manage, the right of British employers to manage having been irrevocably lost sometime and somewhere in the last half of the nineteenth century (Wigham 1973).

As it turned out, even the power to manage was severely circumscribed in British engineering firms after the turn of the century by the tendency of employers to continue to rely on experienced workers to coordinate the shop-floor division of labour and the transformation of inputs into outputs. Between the end of the lockout in 1898 and the First World War, British engineering employers did invest in more automatic machine tools, and they did employ less expensive labour to perform many tasks. The problem is that, unlike their American counterparts, most British firms failed to make the investments in managerial structures that, in conjunction with the new mass-production technologies, were needed to take the control of work off the shop floor. Like employers in the cotton textile and iron and steel industries, British engineering firms chose the low-cost strategy of relying on shop-floor workers to run their production. In 1914 some 60 per cent of the labour force in firms that belonged to the EEF was classified as 'skilled' – a classification that may have been more an indication of the persistence of craft control than of the persistence of difficult-to-replicate craft skills (Zeitlin 1983: 35).

The clearest manifestation of persistent craft control was the growing importance of the shop steward – a workers' representative drawn from the ranks of the operatives, with whom employers negotiated particular piece rates for the performance of particular, narrowly defined tasks (Hinton 1973). The shop steward's knowledge of production and his standing among his fellow workers became a critical link in the attempts by the engineering firms to introduce piece rates. Shop stewards began to play important roles in coordinating the organisation and flow of work on the shop floor. From 1909, shop-floor control and plant-level bargaining became the basis for a resurgence of labour militancy. It led to the replacement of the old ASE executive, who had sought to help employers enforce the Terms of Settlement. In 1913, the same year that the cotton spinners withdrew from the Brooklands Agreement negotiated in 1893, the ASE unilaterally rejected the Terms of Settlement (Zeitlin 1983: 44). Craft militancy among engineering workers gained momentum during the First World War, in part to ensure that 'dilution' from the influx of women would not remain permanent (Reid 1985; Downs 1987).

In 1914 the ASE had 170,000 members, up from fewer than 100,000 in 1897. By 1918 membership was close to 300,000; and by 1920, under the newly formed Amalgamated Engineering Union (AEU), about 450,000. Membership in the employers' organisation, the EEF, also grew, from 714 firms in 1914 to 1,468 in 1918 and 2,600 in 1921 (Zeitlin 1983: 47). But the very number of member firms in the EEF in the 1920s reflected a degree of industrial fragmentation.

In 1922 the EEF, in yet another attempt to regain the power to manage, locked out the workers, and once again the workers were forced to return on the employers' terms. As in the aftermath of the signing of the 1898 Terms of Settlement, engineering employers used their victory to continue the shift from time-wages to payment by results. In 1886 only 6 per cent of fitters and turners and 11 per cent of machinists in British engineering had been on piece work; by 1906 the numbers had climbed to 33 per cent and 47 per cent, with most of the increase apparently coming after the defeat of the workers in 1898. In 1914, 31 per cent of all engineering workers were paid by the piece; and in 1918, 41 per cent. By 1927 piece workers were 49 per cent of all engineering workers (Lewchuk 1987: 109). British engineering employers continued to rely on the manipulation of piece rates to elicit effort from workers. They did not take the path of the other capitalist economies, such as the United States, Germany and Japan, in building managerial structures that could exercise direct control over the shop floor.

The legacy of craft control

During the 1920s and 1930s, in the newer and expanding engineering industries such as motor vehicles and electrical equipment, British firms invested in mass-production machinery, permitting them to shift from skilled to semi-skilled workers. Because unions were not entrenched in the newer engineering industries, the EEF victory of 1922 virtually ended formal collective bargaining, thus ushering in a non-union era throughout the inter-war years. Yet, in sharp contrast to mass production in the United States, substantial control over the organisation of work and the determination of the relation between effort and pay remained with workers on the shop floor (Lewchuk 1987: ch. 9; Tolliday 1985 and 1986b).

Through multinational investments in Britain the American mode of shop-floor management was to some extent transported across the Atlantic. Most notably, the Ford Motor Company, which began operations in Britain in 1911, invested in managerial capabilities to plan and coordinate the flow of work on the shop floor. Ford chose to pay its workers time-wages. In Britain, as in the United States, Ford used a high-wage policy, coupled with close supervision, to gain the cooperation of its shop-floor workers (Lewchuk 1987: ch. 8; Tolliday 1991).

But as Lewchuk (1987) has demonstrated in his comparative study of the British and American motor vehicle industries, the British mass producers chose not to invest in managerial structures. Instead they relied extensively on payment by results to elicit effort. Stressing the critical organisational difference between the American and British systems of automobile production, Lewchuk has argued:

> The majority of British motor vehicle workers in the 1930s could not be classified as skilled workers. In fact the production techniques used were surprisingly similar to those found in many American factories. New types of machinery and the emergence of volume production drastically reduced the skill required from individual workers. The most striking contrast between the American and British system was the limited extent to which British management had been able to exert direct control over labour effort norms and the limited extent to which management had claimed responsibility for organising the work place. Labour retained a significant say over the setting of effort norms and the organisation of work, while management controlled the process by which piece-rate prices were set, allowing them to control the ratio of wages to effort. (Lewchuk 1987: 185)

During the 1930s, when the major car producers were making large profits, motor vehicle workers received wages that were toward the high end of the earnings scale of engineering workers, with piece workers in the automobile industry doing especially well (Lewchuk 1987: 94; Jolly 1988: 102). With the level of piece-rate incentives under managerial control, workers had to supply enough effort to earn a decent wage but not so much as to provoke cuts in the piece rates. To avoid frequent rate-cutting that would have prompted workers to engage in restricting output (that is, keeping effort, and hence output, levels deliberately low in order to keep piece rates high), employers implemented premium bonus systems. Yet, without close supervision or significant managerial coordination of the flow of work between vertically related production activities, the supply of effort remained under the control of workers.

So that workers could not bargain over the piece rates the non-union engineering firms tended to avoid group incentives, preferring instead to enter into informal piece-rate bargains with individual workers for particular tasks (Lewchuk 1987: ch. 8; Zeitlin 1983: 39–40). A *de facto* division of labour emerged on the shop floor. The shop-floor workers were induced by piece rates to keep the flow of work proceeding apace from one part of the plant to another (the system was called 'induction'; Lewchuk 1987: 142). British managers were content to leave the coordination of the flow of work-in-progress to the workers.

In an industry such as motor vehicles, informal bargaining based on shop stewards had generally preceded formal union recognition, precisely because employers preferred bargaining with individual workers and their shop stewards to the collective power of a union (Purcell and Sisson 1983: 101; Batstone 1984: 99). In the 1940s and 1950s, as in the inter-war period, workplace bargaining was left in the hands of lower level managers – rate-fixers and first-line supervisors – and within the firm the shop-floor bargaining took place independently of high-level planning.

During the full employment decades of the 1950s and 1960s the mass-production metal-working industries became increasingly unionised. But in the absence of managerial planning and coordination of production activities, 'custom and practice' became the foundations for workplace bargaining. The shop stewards had considerable leverage in interpreting the customs and practices of the workplaces that they knew so well – and about which enterprise managers above the first-line supervisory level know so little (W. Brown 1972). As argued by the authors of a well-known study of labour relations in the car industry in the mid-1960s:

> In a sense the leading stewards are performing a managerial function, of grievance settlement, welfare arrangement and human adjustment, and the steward system's acceptance by managements (and thus in turn the facility with which the stewards themselves can satisfy their members' demands and needs) has developed partly because of the increasing effectiveness – and certainly economy – with which this role is fulfilled. (Turner *et al.* 1967: 214)

Elsewhere one of the authors of the study ascribed even more profound managerial functions to the shop stewards, arguing that 'the shop steward organisation ... aimed, ultimately, to keep men at work and to control – even discipline – union members'. He continued: The 'senior shop stewards were involved in the enforcement of collective agreements, and concerned with the implementation (even planning) and co-ordination of many details of production – such as transfers of men around the factory the scheduling of overtime or short-time working, and the recruitment and training of labour' (Clack 1967: 97–8).

Given the absence of personnel management in major British firms the shop stewards were critical for maintaining labour peace and eliciting effort. In the 1950s the shop stewards were particularly prominent in the metal-working industries, and in the 1960s and 1970s the model spread across all unionised sectors (Terry 1983; Batstone 1984: 79–82). Reliance on shop stewards enabled British industrialists to continue to avoid investments in personnel management, while creating a coherent, if informal, system of employment relations.

Economically, the peculiarly British system of workplace bargaining benefited both employers and workers as long as existing technologies and workplace practices could generate sufficient productivity to enable British firms to compete. But already by the early 1960s, as German and then Japanese, Swedish, French and Italian manufacturers joined the Americans in competing for world markets, British industry found itself in an increasingly competitive international environment. A response required investments in high-throughput technologies, which in turn required significant – and in most cases dramatic – alterations in shop-floor 'custom and practice' to generate returns on the investments. But reliance on payment by results and 'informal' shop-floor bargaining were resulting in upward 'wage drift' – that is, the power of workers to capture the gains from productivity growth for themselves (Marsh and Coker 1963). The results were inflationary pressures in the British economy and an erosion of profits for British manufacturing industry (Armstrong and Glyn 1986: 55).

Many observers of Britain's inferior performance in manufacturing have been quick to point the finger at labour. What they are observing is the legacy of craft control. But in long-run perspective, craft control has persisted in Britain because British firms chose not to build managerial structures. By contrast, the Japanese since the early twentieth century have pursued a strategy of investing in the skills of managers as much as shop-floor workers, and American firms have pursued a strategy of investing at least in the skills of managers (Lazonick 1990: chs. 7–10, 1991: ch. 1).

In contrast to both of these strategies (in the late twentieth century it is the Japanese who are showing the best results), British employers chose simply to leave skills on the shop floor, giving workers control over the utilisation of the firm's investments. Even in the absence of unions, and in the presence of unions often in conflict with formal bargaining agreements, British employers came to rely on shop stewards. Attempts to reform the informal system in the aftermath of the famous Donovan Report of 1968 ended by increasing the power of shop stewards (Terry 1977; Batstone 1984: 183).

A century ago, craft control played a productive role in making Britain an industrial power. Even, in the twentieth century, with the rise of managerial capitalism abroad, it was possible for a time for British industry to compete in international markets, in part because it had access to an abundance of industrial skills without having to make high fixed-cost investments in them. Over time, however, organisational and technological innovation abroad raised productivity to levels that rendered the British strategy competitive only if workers supplied more effort for lower pay. In reaction to attempts to erode their standard of living, British workers sought to protect craft control. Given the strategy of avoiding investments in managerial structures that British firms had been pursuing for decades, the firms were ill-prepared to take the control of work off the shop floor.

The Thatcherite attack on the trade union movement in the 1980s succeeded in diminishing the ranks of union membership in manufacturing and the ability of unions to stage effective strikes (Bassett 1986; MacInnes 1987). But in the absence of positive measures to encourage the building of managerial structures to plan and coordinate the productive transformation on the shop floor, British firms have tended to continue their reliance on shop-steward organisation. As Peter Nolan (1989: 118) argued in a critique of the so-called 'productivity miracle' during the Thatcher years:

> The (survey and case study) evidence seems to point to labour intensification as a key element in recent productivity gains ... The progressive weakening of labour, both collective and individual, has helped entrench the legacy of the past. Firms have sought short-term gains, through a series of step-by-step adaptations, which have left untouched basic structural weaknesses. (Nolan 1989: 118)

In an age of global competition, it is perhaps not enough to overturn the shop stewards. To put in place the organisational capabilities that global manufacturing competition in the late twentieth century requires, the firms and the nation must make large investments in the capabilities of their employees – whether managers or workers.

5 The service industries

Clive Lee

Services and growth: theories

The service industries have been treated with a mixture of disdain and neglect by historians and economists. The historians, schooled in a tradition that perceives the factory as the cause and vehicle of modern economic growth, have defined services as symbolic of pre-industrial backwardness, either an irrelevance or an obstacle to development. The economists have tended to accept Adam Smith's distinction between manufacturing as productive labour and employment in services as unproductive labour:

> Thus the labour of a manufacturer adds, generally to the value of the materials which he works upon, that of his own maintenance, and that of his master's profit. The labour of a menial servant, on the contrary, adds to the value of nothing ... His services generally perish in the very instant of their performance, and seldom leave any trace or value behind them for which an equal quantity of service could afterwards be procured. (Smith 1776: 430)

Smith's classification was embodied in the Marxian tradition and formalised in the material balance system of national income accounting. More recently a variety of models have either ignored services or cast them in a role inimical to growth. Ironically, since the service sector has become very large in all modern economies, fear that its expansion could stifle growth has attracted considerable scholarly attention to the sector.

One of the most prominent, and representative, of such models was devised by the economist Nicholas Kaldor. It comprises three inter-related propositions and identifies the links between growth, productivity and structural change. According to Kaldor's thesis the rate of growth of national product is determined by the growth of output in manufacturing. Labour productivity in manufacturing is simply a function of the growth of output, achieved through economies of scale ('Verdoorn's Law'). Since manufacturing alone generates growth and productivity, its expansion will attract labour away from less productive sectors, like services. Such a structural change will increase labour productivity in services by drawing off under-utilised labour, and enhance the productivity of the workers transferred to manufacturing. Industrial growth is thus the prime catalyst for economic growth, its own expansion being determined mainly by export demand. Services play an entirely passive role. Concentration of resources in services therefore will inhibit growth. Kaldor's model was originally devised to explain Britain's modest growth in the 1950s and 1960s and the supposed threat posed by an overgrown service sector. His views were influential enough to lead to the introduction of the selective employment tax, which sought to stimulate the transfer of labour from services to manufacturing (Kaldor 1966; Thirlwall 1983).

An even less optimistic scenario was imagined by the economist William Baumol (1967). Baumol's model divides the economy into commodity production and services, commodity production being technologically progressive and services only sporadically so. Wages in the commodity sector are linked to productivity. But growth generates increases in income which stimulate, alas, the demand for services. Wages in services follow those set in commodity production, of course, and the increasing demand for services will therefore tend to push the cost of services up. Unless demand for services is highly elastic in relation to prices and incomes, the quantity and in all likelihood the quality of service provision will decline. For services provided by the public sector the increasing costs will pose a choice between an increase in taxation or a reduction in services. That the growth rate of productivity in manufacturing is higher than in services will mean that relatively greater increases in service sector labour are required to achieve growth. Labour will move steadily from manufacturing to services, reducing the growth of aggregate productivity. Further growth will be restricted to the rate of expansion of the labour force. A static labour force implies zero growth. Thus growth can be undermined as services draw labour away from manufacturing, thereby reducing productivity, and create an outcome which is the converse of that proposed in Kaldor's model although consistent with the legislation he inspired. The historical question is whether the Kaldor and Baumol models are even approximately true.

Growth and change

The classification of services is controversial. Construction, which was included in one of the earliest attempts to define the tertiary sector, clearly does not constitute a service (Clark 1957). Utilities such as gas, water and electricity are often included as a borderline case, but the fact that they produce a measurable commodity suggests they should be excluded. Other classifications have excluded transport from services on the grounds that such activities are closely related to manufacturing and because they use capital intensively (Fuchs 1968). Yet utilities and transport unquestionably provide a service rather than a commodity.

The International Standard Industrial Classification identifies four groups of services: (a) wholesale and retail trade, hotels and restaurants; (b) transport, storage and communication; (c) finance, real estate, insurance and business services; (d) community, social and personal services (Petit 1986: 11). The major categories adopted in the British Census of Population are: (a) transport and communications; (b) distribution; (c) insurance and banking; (d) the professions; (e) miscellaneous services, such as hotels, restaurants and domestic service; (f) public administration and defence (Lee 1979). A more ambitious classification divides services by function: (a) business services – accounting, research and development, advertising, engineering, employment agencies; (b) household services – hotels and restaurants, personal care, leisure, repairs; (c) collective services – health, education, government, defence, non-profit organisations; (d) intermediate services – trade, transport, communications, insurance and finance (Petit 1986: 12).

Other definitions have sought to distinguish between producer and consumer service, and between non-durable services, such as a visit to the theatre, and semi-durable services yielding utility over a longer period, such as legal advice. A recent and popular distinction has been made between marketed services, purchased directly from the supplier in the market, and non-marketed services, provided by the state or local authority on behalf of tax payers.

Some of these definitions have counterparts in Hill's ambitious scheme (1977) in which the principal division is between services affecting commodities, like transport, storage, cleaning and repairing, and services affecting persons, such as health treatment, hairdressing, transport and restaurant services. These two groups can be sub-divided into permanent and transitory, reversible and irreversible services, and those effecting physical or mental changes. His scheme also distinguishes between public services and other services. Pure public services are distinctive because individuals cannot be identified as consuming them so that no distinction can be made between consumers and non-consumers. All residents must be assumed to be passive consumers of police protection and similar indivisible services.

In practice the categorisation is determined by the form of available data. It is not possible to estimate accurately the volume of knowledge supplied to a pupil by his teacher, nor the amount of advice given by a doctor to his patient. Various proxies and indicators have to be used, such as hours of instruction per pupil, which often and crucially are unable to gauge the quality of the service. The output of the police is even more difficult to measure, since the output manifests itself in the non-occurrence of events, such as theft and assault. If the services are measured by inputs, as is conventionally done, the resultant output level precludes any evaluation of resource allocation.

There are two principal methods of estimating service industry output. The expenditure approach takes the final purchase value for each service and commodity, subsuming all intermediate goods and services (Feinstein 1972: 206). The production approach seeks to measure value added to give the aggregate contribution of each industry to GDP. Feinstein used forty-nine indicators of service production for the distributive trades, over twenty for transport, and over twenty for the professions (Feinstein 1972: 209–10). But in some cases the service output can only be derived from employment data, adjusted for productivity increase. Maddison has strenuously attacked the expenditure approach as netting out service inputs into manufactures. He estimated the contribution of services to the GDP of the United Kingdom in 1975 at 42.7 per cent by the expenditure approach and 60.5 per cent by the production approach (Maddison 1983: 37).

The most comprehensive, detailed and reliable indicator of size and change in services is the employment data contained in the decennial Census of Population. The source is not without difficulties. Until 1871 retired persons were included under their previous occupation, the unemployed were never properly identified and omitted, women were often included under the occupation of their husbands, and no distinction was made between full-time and part-time employment. Categorisation was less than totally reliable, many workers being returned under the general heading of 'clerk' or 'labourer', although employment classifications were based on industrial rather than occupational groups.

Some employment categories were artificially augmented by practices such as including as members of the medical profession the manufacturers of false teeth and dental apparatus, while some draughtsmen and house decorators managed to have themselves entered as artists. Changes in business practice have also induced spurious changes in service industry employment. Accountants, lawyers, and other professional workers appear as such when directly employed by the title of their calling, while those employed by manufacturers appear as the producers of the particular commodity. In the twentieth century, multinational corporations have frequently changed between the direct employment of such professionals and purchasing such services from outside their organisation, thus creating apparent shifts in employment structure.

Table 5.1. *Output growth rates, 1861–1951* (*per cent per year*)

	1861–71	1871–81	1881–91	1891–1901	1901–11	1924–37	1937–51
Agriculture	0·24	−0·52	0·59	−0·63	0·38	1·08	1·74
Industry	2·98	2·20	1·67	2·54	1·13	3·13	1·90
Transport/communications	3·20	2·69	2·67	2·54	2·43	1·47	2·46
Distribution	2·81	2·19	1·95	2·10	1·52	1·78	−0·07
Insurance/banking	13.62	6·38	5·12	5·30	5·51	1·53	0·68
Professions	2·24	3·61	2·65	2·49	2·40	1·34	1·67
Miscellaneous services	1·90	1·93	1·83	0·80	1·62	1·59	−1·38
Public administration	0·08	1·45	2·24	3·78	1·22	1·32	3·44
GDP	2·07	1·79	1·73	1·98	1·46	2·20	1·26

Source: Feinstein (1972: Tables 8, 53); data for benchmark years are three-year averages. Estimates prior to 1920 include Southern Ireland.

Few statistical series are available in a format which allows a clear division to be made between non-durable and semi-durable services or between consumer and producer services. Lawyers, accountants, bankers and most other professional workers provide their services for both private consumers and corporate producers, and the allocation of their efforts between them is impossible to determine or aggregate. The distinction between marketed and non-marketed services is easier, of course, since the government provides most of the non-marketed services (with the exception of registered charities such as the Salvation Army).

The principal indicators of growth and change should thus be accepted as good general indicators, based on the best estimates currently available but subject to some uncertainty of detail.

The growth rates for output (Table 5.1) indicate that four of the six service industry groups remained consistently above the GDP growth rate throughout the half century before the First World War, while miscellaneous services and public administration fluctuated around that average. No data permit an estimate for the period of the 1914–18 war. Service industry output growth fell below the national average during the inter-war years and exhibited both substantial increases and absolute decline in the Second World War, as the economy adjusted to wartime requirements.

Growth of labour in services (Table 5.2) was generally above the national average before the First World War and, with the exception of transport, remained so during the inter-war years. As with output, labour input in 1937–51 showed wide divergencies between services: transport, public administration (including defence) and the professions grew rapidly.

Service sector employment in Britain increased from 2.7 million jobs in 1851 to almost 10.4 million a century later. The figures probably underestimate the size of the Victorian service sector, and thus rather overestimate the shift towards service industry employment. Yet for what they are worth the figures say that population and total employment in Britain grew at a rate of 0.86 per cent annually over the century and employment in services grew at an average of 1.36 per cent. Therefore the share of services in total employment increased markedly, from 28.8 per cent in 1851 to 49.0 per cent by 1931 (it fell back to 46.9 per cent in 1951, war matériel being commodities, not services).

Most services enjoyed unbroken expansion, some at a high rate of growth from a small base, like financial services and the professions. The most radical change was recorded in the miscellaneous services group, mainly domestic service. Employment in domestic service grew rapidly in Victorian times, but collapsed in the first half of the twentieth century (Table 5.3): 'Upstairs/Downstairs' is a pre-1914 world.

Table 5.2. *Labour input growth rates, 1861–1951 (per cent per year)*

	1861–71	1871–81	1881–91	1891–1901	1901–11	1924–37	1937–51
Agriculture	−2·66	−0·86	−0·80	−0·82	−0·08	−1·15	0·45
Industry	−0·44	0·83	1·19	1·22	0·93	1·34	0·90
Transport/communication	1·05	1·25	2·62	2·71	0·86	0·65	0·51
Distribution	0·62	2·16	2·39	1·95	2·14	2·57	−2·25
Insurance/banking	5·57	5·73	4·67	3·15	4·36	1·86	−0·82
Professions	0·03	3·12	1·28	1·84	1·43	1·76	3·46
Miscellaneous services	0·15	0·87	0·95	0·41	0·64	2·14	−5·54
Public administration	−2·15	0·91	1·84	4·82	−0·46	1·77	4·27
Total	−0·78	0·70	1·04	1·15	0·88	1·45	0·05

Sources: Feinstein (1972: Tables 59, 50); Matthews *et al.* (1982: 566–7); data composition as for Table 5.1. Labour input is measured by the number of employed persons weighted by the average number of hours worked in a year. The average number of hours worked per year declined from 3,185 in 1856 to 2,753 in 1913 and 2,071 in 1951.

Table 5.3. *Employment in domestic service, 1851–1951 (000s)*

	Males	Females
1851	108	870
1861	119	1,097
1871	136	1,324
1881	226	1,363
1891	265	1,551
1901	249	1,333
1911	295	1,403
1921	78	1,271
1931	271	1,258
1951	101	398

Source: data disaggregated from Lee (1979); includes indoor and outdoor domestic service. The majority of males were outdoor servants employed as grooms, coachmen, gardeners or gamekeepers. Female servants worked primarily indoors as housekeepers, housemaids, cooks, nurses or laundrymaids.

Table 5.4. *Employment in services, 1851–1951 (per 10,000 population)*

	1851	1871	1891	1911a	1911b	1931	1951
Food	192	199	233	277	—	—	—
Transport/communication	204	235	343	362	398	342	349
Distribution	41	43	46	55	410	614	547
Insurance/banking	3	11	22	45	59	87	89
Professions	127	134	158	179	179	200	312
Miscellaneous services	664	756	720	707	707	600	479
Public administration	66	93	90	135	107	231	349
Total	1,297	1,471	1,612	1,760	1,860	2,074	2,125

Source: Lee (1979); food processing and distribution has been included in the pre-1914 series because it was comprised largely of distributive workers. The large increase in distribution in the final three columns reflects both better identification of those employed in this industry as well as a growing separation of processing and distribution in industries like food and drink.

Female employment was affected by the decline in domestic service to a much greater extent than male, with some compensation for women in the growth of jobs in the professions, public services and distribution. Overall the growth of service industry employment favoured men. In 1851 males and females comprised almost equal numbers of service industry workers; by 1951 males enjoyed a majority of almost three to two. Yet looking at it from the other side, women were more dependent on service industry

Table 5.5. *Regional employment in services, 1871–1931 (per 10,000 population)*

	1871	1871	1901	1901	1931	1931
South-east	1,966	133·7	2,315	133·3	2,718	131·1
East Anglia	1,382	94·0	1,667	96·0	1,980	95·5
South-west	1,600	108·8	1,863	107·3	2,240	108·0
West midlands	1,238	84·2	1,422	81·9	1,570	75·7
East midlands	1,245	84·6	1,401	80·7	1,613	77·8
North-west	1,389	94·4	1,607	92·5	1,874	90·4
Yorkshire/Humberside	1,135	77·2	1,385	79·7	1,654	79·8
North	1,212	82·4	1,359	78·2	1,579	76·1
Wales	1,252	85·1	1,432	82·4	1,606	77·4
Scotland	1,132	77·0	1,474	84·9	2,046	98·7
Great Britain	1,471	100·0	1,737	100·0	2,074	100·0

Source: Lee (1979); figures in cols. 2, 4, 6 show regional employment rates as percentages of national average.

work. In 1931, 61.9 per cent of working women were in services, as against 43.4 per cent of the men.

The service industries were heavily concentrated in the south-east, which contained 35.2 per cent of all service employment in 1851 – when it had only 24.5 per cent of the national population. By 1951 the south-east had 38.1 per cent of service industry employment and 30.8 per cent of population. East Anglia and the south-west were also structurally oriented towards services – the south as a whole accounted for about half of employment in the service industries, as compared with 40 per cent of population (Lee 1979). The share of regional employment in services in the south-east was 10 per cent above the share in the economy as a whole. The south-east region acquired almost 40 per cent of the new jobs added to the service sector in Britain between 1851 and 1951.

In contrast the regions of the English north and midlands, with the exception of the north-west, remained far below the average, as did Wales. Between 1871 and 1931 the pattern appears to have changed little, though Scotland gained. The trend of services was tied, of course, to differences in regional development.

Consumer services

The most obvious demand for services is direct purchases by individual consumers which, in turn, depend on their annual income, their wealth and their stock of income-earning assets. During 1856–1913 gross domestic product per head grew at an average rate of 1.1 per cent annually, increasing to 1.8 per cent between 1924 and 1937 (GDP actually declined between 1913 and 1924 (Matthews *et al.* 1982: 498)). Both income and wealth were unevenly distributed, especially wealth. In 1911–13, the top 5 per cent of wealth holders enjoyed 87 per cent of the national total; the figure was still 74 per cent in 1950. For income the share of the top 5 per cent was smaller, but still reached 40 per cent of the national total in 1913 and 24 per cent in 1950 (Lee 1986: 147).

Considerable attention has been paid to the notion that services have a higher income elasticity of demand than commodities, which is said to explain their growth as income grows. Evidence in support of the proposition, however, is mixed. Recent evidence suggests that there is not much difference between services and commodities on this score (Kravis *et al.* 1983: 199–201). Estimates for a cross-section of countries in the late nineteenth century suggest a similar conclusion, with income elasticities for both commodities and services ranging from 1.0 to 1.4 (Lee 1990a: Table 5).

Aggregate consumption expenditure, at constant prices, doubled between 1870 and 1914 at an annual growth rate of 1.7 per cent, 1.8 per cent between 1924 and 1937. The two world wars saw diminished consumer spending: after 1915 the pre-war level was not restored until 1927, and the 1939 level was not regained until 1946, dipping to a low in 1943 (Feinstein 1972: Table 5). Otherwise consumer spending increased steadily.

A recent estimate of consumer spending in 1900 concludes that 21.2 per cent of expenditure went directly on services, the principal categories identified being transport, domestic service, medical treatment and entertainment (Feinstein 1991: 158). The division between working-class spending and that of the middle- and upper-income groups was markedly different in size and composition. About three-quarters of total spending on services came from the middle and upper earners, who spent about one third of their incomes on services. The working class allocated less than 10 per cent of its total spending to services, although it did spend heavily on life assurance and funeral expenses. Estimates for consumer spending in the first half of the twentieth century suggest modest alterations. The share of consumer spending on direct purchases of services ranged from 20 to 25 per cent of the total; expenditure on public transport grew steadily while that on domestic service, as we have noted, fell (Feinstein 1972: Table 25).

The inequality in wealth and income distribution was important for the growth of domestic service. Servants were not cheap. A household manual written in 1845 indicated that an income of £100 a year was required to allow the employment of a single maid – the average working man at the time would be earning perhaps Mr Macawber's £20 a year. And Mrs

Beeton's famous *Book of Household Management*, published in 1861, set £150–200 a year as the minimum income needed to employ servants. The majority of middle-class incomes were less than £300 per year at the time. A survey conducted in London in 1894 found that 27 per cent of households that employed servants had only one, while 35 per cent had only two (McBride 1976: 50). Male servants were twice as expensive as females, so that a family income had to reach £600 to provide a butler or footman. Furthermore, board and lodging comprised a substantial part of the cost of keeping servants, and actually exceeded the cost of wages, accounting for half the total outlay in employing a man and two-thirds in employing a woman.

The employment of domestic servants reached a peak about the First World War, although the decline in employment suffered in the war was partly offset in the 1920s. The sharp fall in domestic service in the Second World War was much greater and was not reversed (Table 5.3). The historian of the industry has depicted the crucial change, so far as the middle classes were concerned, as the replacement during the first two decades of the twentieth century of the live-in servant by day-workers. Middle-class dissatisfaction with the live-in system, a growing preference for exclusiveness within the home, and bad servant/master relationships meant that the maid gave way to the charlady, an older and more reliable daily visitor. The declining middle-class birth rate assisted later by reducing the need for help with the daily routine. Alternative work opportunities for young women – as school teachers, shop assistants and clerical workers – provided other sources of income and an acceptable bridge between childhood and marriage. Washing machines and Hoovers at first increased the productivity of servants and in the end substituted for them.

Feinstein's recent estimates for consumer spending at the turn of the century do not include working-class expenditure on domestic service. Financial services were necessary for all social and economic conditions. The wealthiest benefited from the expertise of their stockbrokers in investing their funds. The growing range of insurances to protect against the effects of fire, death, illness and road accidents also reflected the demands of growing affluence, as did the growth of building societies in their aim to promote home ownership. The increase in affluence was clearly demonstrated in the growth of industrial insurance, modest-value policies designed for working men and offering cover against the inability to work through illness or retirement. The Prudential was eminent in the business and by the 1880s had over seven million policies in force with a combined value of £66 million. The policies also covered funeral expenses, so large a demand that by 1930 premium payments exceeded the contributions of workers and employers to national health insurance and the state pension scheme. Prior to 1914 most policies paid a benefit on the death of the person insured, and the premiums were collected door to door by agents known as 'penny-a-week death hunters'. Rising real incomes, and falling child mortality, encouraged a shift from the 1880s to endowment policies which matured at the end of a specified period of time (Johnson 1985: 14, 32).

Growing affluence allowed the accumulation of savings, albeit on a modest scale. Depositors in the Post Office Savings Bank and the Trustees Savings Bank increased from 2.5 million in 1870 to 14 million by 1939 while the average balance per depositor (corrected for inflation) rose by 39 per cent. The membership of building societies increased substantially, especially in the inter-war years, when favourable interest rates and tax-free interest proved attractive. Loan capital grew from £24.5 million in 1924 to £155.7 million in 1938. Membership of cooperative societies increased from something over 600,000 in the early 1880s to reach nearly 3,000,000 by 1913 and over 8,000,000 by 1938 (Johnson 1985: 89–90, 119–23).

The growth of affluence and consumer spending was manifest in the growth in leisure activities. Holiday savings clubs in the Lancashire cotton towns flourished in the late nineteenth century, enabling workers to accumulate for a few days at Blackpool. Clubs in Oldham paid out over £1,000 each in the 200 recorded in 1906, and the list was incomplete (Walton 1981: 254). The seaside trip, made possible by the railway, enabled temperance and religious organisations to transport their members away from the traditional temptations of fairground and public house.

Professional sport attracted increasing crowds. By the turn of the century an important county cricket match could attract 20,000 spectators, and race meetings often drew 10,000 or 15,000, and upwards of 80,000 for Bank Holidays. In 1888–9 the first Football League season was watched by 602,000. By 1913–14 the first division games were watched by nearly 9 million people a year (overwhelmingly men) and by 1937–8 the aggregate attendance at the four divisions of the Football League exceeded 28 million (Vamplew 1988: 63). Professional sport was closely linked with other entertainments like gambling and drinking. Bookmakers and publicans were prominent in the organisation of race meetings in London in the 1860s, and the publicans became prominent amongst the directors of football clubs. By the 1930s, gambling on football results was attracting far more income than attendance at the matches, some £800,000 per week being spent on the football pools, compared to a mere £48,000 on gate money. In 1935–6 the management committee of the Football League tried to stamp out the practice by refusing to release the whereabouts of fixtures until a few days before they were played. After much internal dissent within the League the 'Pools War' was lost (Inglis 1988: 145ff). No such scruples affected horse racing, and legal betting on the tote generated a turnover of £9 million in 1938 (Vamplew 1976: 227).

The growth of spending on entertainment was closely related to the development of transport, especially railways and later urban tramways and bus services. The railway transformed horse racing by enabling horses to compete outside traditional local circuits. The 1850s witnessed the appearance of meetings attracting horses from all parts of the country. Crowds increased, brought by special trains to race-courses like Sandown Park and Newbury, both of which relied heavily on London for spectators. Golf courses like Gleneagles and Turnberry, with their attendant hotels, were also creations of the railway. So too, again, was the seaside holiday trade which enabled towns like Blackpool and Southend to increase their population tenfold in the half century before 1914. All the original tram routes established in Leeds in the 1870s terminated at public houses. Transport development was also intimately linked to the emergence of urban concentrations and the transformation this wrought on distribution: street markets and itinerant vendors had to compete with specialised shops, department stores and multiple branch stores.

The strong link between demand for consumer services and income was manifest in the regions. The high level of service provision per head of population in the south-east seems to have been matched by high per capita incomes. The income taxes paid are one indicator. In 1879–80 the income tax indicated an average per capita in the south-east of £22.49 while the other regions ranged from £10.66 to £16.43 (Lee 1984: 149). Statistical analysis showed a relation 1861–1911 between service industries and regional income per head (Lee 1984: 144–6). During the inter-war years the south-east boomed in services: over half the new firms created were located there (Foreman-Peck 1985: 416–19).

Producer services

Producer services are supplied as intermediate inputs in production or as an adjunct to the provision of other services. Obvious examples are transport and distribution. A variety of definitions have been offered to distinguish producer from consumer services. O'Brien includes in the producer category all financial and banking services, half of those engaged in the professions, transport and commerce, and half of non-military government personnel. According to this scheme, 48 per cent of those employed in services in Britain in 1911 would have been classed as providing producer services (O'Brien 1983: 81). Katouzian does not quantify his categories, but includes banking and finance, transport and wholesale and retail trade (Katouzian 1970: 366). He excludes 'old' services such as domestic service and 'new' services like education and entertainment.

The most obvious producer service was financial services. Until the 1830s government borrowing was the main source of demand for capital, but the expansion of the railways required borrowing on an unprecedented scale, sufficient to create stock exchanges in Liverpool and Manchester. By the 1880s the investment in railways at home and abroad accounted for 40 per cent of nominal share values on the London stock exchange. Railways with gas and electricity, docks and tramways and telegraph and telephone systems were the bulk of the massive increase in overseas investment in the second half of the century. The two world wars caused a redirection and an increase in borrowing: the government's share of total investment stood at 32.7 per cent in 1918 and 55.8 per cent in 1945. Between the wars large companies such as Imperial Chemical, Morris, Ford, Bowater and Beecham sought funds from the capital market. There was thus a sustained and growing demand for investment possibly supplemented by the pressures of accumulated funds seeking an outlet (Edelstein 1982; ch. 7).

Oldham became the main centre for cotton industry stock flotations, Sheffield for iron companies, while the bicycle share boom was handled in Birmingham. Banks, brokers, building societies and especially insurance companies were important institutional investors. By 1913 the assets of British insurance companies exceeded £500 million. While their principal business lay in underwriting insurance risks, the premiums in their trust provided great opportunities to generate additional income. In 1913 the investments of United Kingdom insurance companies included £181 million in debentures and other stocks and shares, £118 million in British and overseas government securities and £114 million on mortgages, the remainder being placed in loans and property (Supple 1970: 332). The range of investments was considerable. Standard Life Assurance had substantial holdings in Canadian land and municipal securities, together with shares in shipbuilding, mining and local government at home. Most companies held government stock and railway shares. By 1914 Prudential Assurance had become the largest shareholder in the Bank of England, the major holder of railway securities and ground rents, the owner of more than half a square mile of the metropolis, and a major owner of freehold property in the rest of the country (Lee 1986: 58–9). Even low interest rates in the 1930s did not prevent the Royal Exchange Assurance from covering dividend payments with income from interest in almost every inter-war year. Indeed, the company's investments increased from £6 million in 1913 to £23 million in 1938, the bulk of them in securities on the London stock exchange. Government stocks, in particular, were a significant component in the increased investment, stimulated initially by the war (Supple 1970: 461–2).

Transport was, of course, a crucial service to producers. Railway goods receipts exceeded passenger receipts from the early 1850s onwards, and a major component of the freight was coal, accounting for over half the volume of freight traffic. The North Eastern Railway obtained 30 to 40 per cent of its annual income from mineral traffic in the half century before 1914 (Irving 1976: 292). The railways, however, did not hold a monopoly. Coastal shipping played a major role in coal and ironstone, and in 1900 more coal was supplied to London by sea than by railway, partly because of the increasing demands of gasworks on the Thames.

Since mineral traffic generated about one fifth of all railway receipts by the early twentieth century, the depression suffered by heavy industry in the inter-war years had serious effects on the railways. The volume of coal freight traffic fell steadily, from 225.6 million tons in 1913 to 188.1 million tons in 1937. The north-east was particularly hard hit. The volume of mineral freight carried by rail in the region in 1938 was only 69 per cent of the 1924 level. During the 1930s the London and North Eastern Railway Company generated only 60 per cent of its pre-war revenue.

Public sector services

The growth of consumer and producer services in response to population increase, rising per capita incomes, changing consumer preferences and economic advance was determined by market forces. But the growth of the public sector, which provides mainly services rather than commodities, was not.

During the past century, many economies have experienced a marked increase in government provision of health, education, social welfare, police and defence, together with the administrative structures needed to organise it. The share of government expenditure in GDP increased in the United Kingdom from 9.9 per cent in 1880 to 13.3 per cent in 1913 and 28.8 per cent in 1938, similar to that in other western European economies. In recent decades the share has risen to nearly 50 per cent (Maddison 1984: 57).

In constant prices British government expenditure increased from £61 million in 1850 to £265 million in 1900 and £849 million in 1938, rising from the 1890s on as a share of national income (Veverka 1963: 114). At the beginning of the century, most of the tax revenue came from local rates and taxes on goods, such as beer. The growth in spending during the following half century depended on national insurance contributions, payments to state health schemes and above all the tax on incomes.

Public spending changed a good deal in the late nineteenth century. Local authority expenditure grew more quickly than did central government, its share increasing from 22 per cent in 1840 to 50 per cent in 1910. The share of expenditure allocated to defence and the national debt fell relatively, from 65 per cent to 34 per cent of the total. Most impressively, spending on social services, together with economic and environmental services, increased from 18 to 52 per cent (Veverka 1963: 119).

During 1910–51 all levels of expenditure increased dramatically. Social services maintained their relative position, rising £658 million, almost matched by spending on goods and services. While spending on defence and the national debt maintained its share of expenditure at 34–6 per cent, in absolute terms it increased by £403 million. The national debt is a transfer payment (one pays now to bondholders for weapons acquired long ago, transferring money from tax payers to the bondholders), and so transfers rose by £468 million. The central government's expenditures became correspondingly large. Administration costs, it may be noted, accounted for a declining share of expenditure, reaching their peak as early as 1890.

Since consumers do not pay for non-marketed services in direct proportion to their consumption of them, the quality and quantity of service provided may not match exactly with the demand preferences of those consumers. Decisions on the supply side are taken by various officers of the state. This has stimulated much debate about why and how public services are provided, including much criticism of the inefficiency of this allocation mechanism.

A number of theories can be marshalled to explain the growth of public spending. The theory of institutional change suggests that government activity might increase if private markets are not well developed. The 'public choice' theory explains the increase as a response to vested interests. And the classical theory of economic welfare claims that government activity can be justified on grounds that its benefits are indivisible and must therefore be provided for everyone (like the police force or a public park), or if income redistribution is considered desirable.

The growth of the education system would be an example (Davis and North 1971: 27–9, 257). In an ideal world the optimum level of public provision of education would be that at which the sum of each citizen's marginal valuation of the service was equal to the aggregate marginal cost of providing it. The essence of the problem is that in a democracy there is likely to exist an asymmetry between consumption and payment. Those who pay lower taxes, or who are exempt, will be more inclined to vote for an expensive provision of public services than those who pay high taxes. Those who bear the brunt of the costs may find themselves outvoted and saddled with obligations far greater than they would wish. Much of the most acrimonious debate has thus centred on the appropriate level of provision, or a perceived over-provision, rather than upon the acceptability of any provision at all (Gramlich 1985: 276).

Why does government grow? Voters may not be clear about the fiscal intentions of the candidates seeking their support, as indeed might the candidates themselves. Interest groups may form pacts to secure specific subsidies. The bureaucrats themselves may wish to increase public provision in order to augment their departmental interests and their own careers in an environment which lacks the achievement indicator of profitability. Cost-minimising strategies, or even cost control, may not be an important constraint. Public services appear to be demand led by the preferences of voters who do not have to bear the full costs of their choices, by politicians who secure election through making extravagant promises, and by bureaucrats whose careers prosper with the expansion of the operations they manage.

The century after 1850 witnessed a massive extension of the British franchise, transforming a small property-based electorate into one which included all adult males and, in the present century, all adults. The number of votes cast in elections increased from 744,000 in 1852 to 5,235,000 in 1910 and 21,997,000 in 1935 (Mitchell 1988: 795). There can be little doubt that the increase in the electorate was to the benefit of the less prosperous members of society who might be expected to support increased public expenditure. The growth of the Labour Party, with its prime commitment to improve general welfare, was crucial.

A rather similar thesis is contained in Wagner's Law, arguing that the growth of public expenditure is the result of increasing welfare obligations assumed by the state in response to social progress. The maintenance of law and order is required to allow the economy to function effectively, which necessitates greater centralised administrative control. Further, the increasing complexity of the economy and the social fragmentation caused by development increases friction between interest groups, so that intervention is needed. State intervention is thus required to stabilise the economy under the stress of growth.

Such forces were involved in the growth of elementary education. The number of children attending inspected day schools at primary level in Britain increased from 282,000 in 1851 to 6,105,000 in 1913 (Mitchell 1988: 798–800); a slump in fertility caused a later fall. Legislative obligations were imposed on local authorities by parliamentary Act in 1870: school boards were empowered to provide elementary schools, funded from the local rates, as a supplement to church and private schools. Compulsory education was introduced in the following decade. Expenditure for school buildings, teacher training to maintain certificated staff at an established ratio of eighty-five pupils per teacher, and salaries fell mainly on the rates. In 1902 public education was fully absorbed into the local authority system and school boards were abolished. Local sources were never able to meet the full cost of elementary education; from the 1830s the central government provided supplementary grants, especially for school buildings. By the time of the Royal Commission on Education of 1858 the grant authorised twenty-five years earlier had increased fortyfold, and the Treasury indicated its anxiety about the drain on resources. Such concern probably underlay the value-for-money practice introduced in the 1860s. The salaries paid to teachers became partly dependent on the rate of pupil attendance and the performance of the students in an annual examination, foreshadowing the 11-Plus exams of the mid-twentieth century.

In 1918 the award of specific grants was replaced by a percentage supplement to local expenditures, which in turn had to be approved by central government. The new administrative structure enabled the Treasury to effect stringent economies. The Board of Education issued instructions that no expenditure could be undertaken by a local authority until both the proposal and the estimated costs had been approved. In the 1930s education spending was reduced by increasing school fees, by replacing free scholarships by places subject to an incomes test on the parents and by a 10 per cent cut in teachers' salaries. Central government was still needed to sustain the system financially. In 1919 the central grant comprised 54.7 per cent of the total expenditure on schools of £53 million. By 1949–50 the expenditure had increased to £230 million and the grant to 63.0 per cent (Lawrence 1972: 138).

The wars of the twentieth century made massive demands on the state. It has been argued, in an extension of the Wagner thesis, that wars made big government popular.

> Both citizens and government may hold divergent views about the desirable size of public expenditure and the possible level of government taxation. This divergence can be adjusted by social disturbances which destroy established conceptions and produce a displacement effect. People will accept, in a period of crisis, tax levels and methods of raising revenue that in quieter times they would have thought intolerable, and this acceptance remains when the disturbance itself has disappeared. (Peacock and Wiseman 1961: 27)

The wars revealed wretched social conditions – the poor health of recruits was shocking – and roused public opinion to acceptance of social action. The First World War starkly revealed the limitations of the hospital service and cost the War Office almost £1 million in payments to voluntary hospitals. But the system remained dependent on relief funds, payments by patients, contributing schemes, insurance schemes, tax relief on payments to charities and pressure on insurance companies to pay hospitals for the treatment of road accident cases. By 1939 the service was little better than it had been twenty-five years earlier (Abel-Smith 1964: 281–3, 325–6).

One of the central issues regarding public service provision is the conflict of interest between economic efficiency and the quality of service. The issue was debated strenuously in the 1870s between the Treasury and the senior officials of the Post Office, a state monopoly. The Treasury pressed for attention to profitability, but the Post Office demurred, on the grounds that it was obliged to provide a service in localities where a profit could never be realised, that Admiralty and Foreign Office interests determined the detail of contracts with shipping companies and that revenue was constrained by the control of prices by the state – so that it could neither increase prices nor cut costs. The Select Committee on Revenue Department Estimates produced a suitable equivocal judgement:

> Your Committee are fully alive to the fact that in all its branches the General Post Office cannot from time to time escape the necessity of unremunerative outlay. But this consideration appears to them to constitute an additional reason for keeping in mind the necessity of working in the main upon business principles, and with a view to a profit on the transaction of each year. (quoted in Daunton 1985: 324–7)

High and low wages in services

The popular image of services as domestic service or shopkeeping has encouraged the notion that services entail low skill and low pay. Although some services fit the image, the full range of service industries varies greatly. In accord with popular notions, Routh's analysis of the industrial and occupational structure of employment in 1951 showed that over 70 per cent of those employed in the miscellaneous services group were either semi-skilled or unskilled, as were over 50 per cent of those employed in transport and communications, distribution and public administration. Average wages in such occupations fell below those of other groups during the first half of the twentieth century (Routh 1980: 4, 41, 120). But at the other extreme, 57 per cent of those employed in the professions were placed in social groups 1A and 1B (the top), compared to 6 per cent in the workforce as a whole, while 85 per cent of those in financial services were placed in social groups 2 and 3, compared to 20 per cent in the entire workforce. Average earnings in these groups were substantially above the national average. Service employment structure and pay, therefore, was strongly represented at both extremes. Recent estimates for the Victorian age confirm the pattern. Average earnings for wage earners, excluding self-employed and salaried personnel, indicated that most service industries came above the average, including manufacturing, with the police and dock workers amongst the highest paid. But female domestic employment and some jobs in transport came at the bottom of the income distribution (Feinstein 1990b: 603). The distribution of average earnings in the main industrial groups in the inter-war period showed a similar variation, with financial, professional and public administration coming amongst the highest annual earnings, but distribution and miscellaneous services exceeding only agricultural earnings (Chapman and Knight 1953: 28).

The competitive structure of service industries

A similar polarisation towards the extremes is found in the size of service activities. Some services, like lawyers or barbers, are provided personally. But a survey of the fifty largest employers in 1907 and 1935 contained service companies among the biggest. The General Post Office dwarfed all other single employers, having three times the employees of the second largest employer in 1907 – the London and North West Railway, with 212,000 employees, another service provider. By 1935 the Post Office still retained its position, just, despite the railway amalgamations of the 1920s, which created the London, Midland and Scottish Railway Company, some 200,000 employees strong. Apart from the Post Office, large-scale employment was dominated by railway companies. Both in 1907 and 1935 service companies accounted for the bulk of employment in the fifty largest companies, 63.2 per cent and 58.5 per cent. By 1935 the service businesses appearing in the group were more diversified than in 1907, and included distributive firms such as the Co-operative Wholesale Society, Woolworth & Co. and Home and Colonial Stores, and financial companies such as Lloyds Bank, Midland Bank and Prudential Assurance (Jeremy 1991: 96–103).

The pre-eminence of services amongst the very largest businesses is equally apparent when capital rather than employment is taken as the measure. Wardley found that thirty-eight of the fifty largest firms in 1904 and twenty-six in 1934, in terms of the market value of capital, were services. Railway companies and financial institutions were most prominent. By this standard the ten largest firms in 1904 were all railway companies. Together the twenty-two railway companies accounted for 71.7 per cent of the market value of the top fifty companies in 1904, compared with 41 per cent of employment in 1907; all service companies accounted for fully 84.9 per cent. By the 1930s the concentration was diminished, with the appearance of large manufacturers such as Imperial Chemical, Imperial Tobacco and Courtaulds. But railways still accounted for 30 per cent of market valuation among the very large firms, and services together accounted for more than half (Wardley 1991: 278–9).

Not surprisingly, the service companies included some with the highest capital–labour ratios, particularly railways and financial houses. Prior to the First World War few manufacturing firms enjoyed either the size of capital input or the capital–labour ratio of the very large service companies. By the 1930s only the financial institutions stood out in this way, and the railways, following the amalgamations of the 1920s, had reduced their capital–labour ratios.

The diversity in scale of operation, capital and labour intensity of service industry production was mirrored in the variety of competitive markets. At one extreme, some distributive services such as street markets must have conformed quite closely to the ideal form of perfect competition. At the other extreme, the Post Office held a monopoly over the distribution of mail and, from the 1860s, in telegraph services. The power of the Post Office to act as a profit-maximising monopolist was inhibited by the public service orientation of its managers and by the conflicting pressures imposed by its political masters. The telegraph system was nationalised with popular approval, the private companies having been criticised for providing a service which was geographically limited, expensive and inaccurate (by contrast, the telegraph remained private in the United States). State monopoly brought a marked increase in the number of telegraph stations and volume of business, but its operation and effectiveness were constrained by the bureaucratic and political pressures laid on the Post Office (Foreman-Peck 1989: 98–9).

Oligopoly is a more common market structure than either perfect competition or monopoly. The railways operated in such a framework, since few major centres of population were not served by two or more companies and coastal shipping provided competition for important freight, like coal (Cain 1988: 105). In the early 1870s and again in the 1900s, amalgamations between railway companies were proposed to improve profitability. In the 1870s opposition from customers and government prevented amalgamations. The companies responded by ending price competition in favour of service competition. Construction of new lines and price cutting gave way to proliferation of services and train-mileage, and the proliferation of ancillary services achieved in docks, steamboats and hotels (Cain 1988: 115–16). In the years before the First World War customer opposition through parliamentary lobbying again prevented the restructuring sought by the railway companies, postponing it for a decade.

A more unusual form of market appeared in professional sport. The leagues allowed team competition, but not the domination of any one team. Success depended on balanced play. Attendances are big when the outcome is uncertain. Yet it was difficult to control the desire of each team to dominate, buying up the best players (Sloane 1971: 121ff).

County cricket exhibited balanced competition. Only three of the currently competing major counties were admitted in the present century, Northamptonshire (1905), Glamorgan (1921) and Durham (1992). The strategy against external competition, instigated by Lancashire and Yorkshire league cricket, was to ban any player who refused to play for his county if requested. Residential requirements were applied to players to stop them moving freely between counties. The proposal in 1937 to allow the immediate transfer of players released by their original county club was an attempt to bolster some of the weaker teams (Schofield 1982: 337ff).

In sharp contrast the Scottish Football League adopted a strategy of devil-take-the-hindmost. There was no maximum wage, no restrictions on player recruitment, and no barriers to transfers. The best players soon gravitated to the most successful clubs. Payment was reputed to be better in the Rangers reserve team than in Partick Thistle's first team. Nor was there any restriction on entry. The first competitive season of the Scottish League 1891–2 had a single division of twelve teams. By 1938–9 there were thirty-eight teams competing in two divisions. The enduring supremacy of two clubs, Rangers and Celtic, was established before 1914 (Vamplew 1982: 549ff).

The productivity of services

The estimation of productivity from historical data comprises a difficult balance between uncertain data, basic assumptions and statistical calculation. Not surprisingly, it gives rise to considerable dispute and debate. The simplest measure is labour productivity. There are a number of benchmark indicators for service industry labour productivity in the nineteenth century (Gemmell and Wardley 1990: 306; Lee 1990a: Table 3). These suggest that the level of labour productivity in services was higher than in manufacturing or agriculture, and that the superiority was not peculiar to the British economy. Similar analyses for France in 1896 and Japan in 1905 also indicate high labour productivity in services, and especially in transport (Carré *et al.* 1976: 88, 518; Okhawa *et al.* 1979: 282, 310). In the United States between 1839 and 1899 relatively high labour productivity was enjoyed by transport and communication, distribution, finance and the professions (Gallman and Weiss 1969: 300–3).

The rate of growth of labour productivity in services was rather modest in the half century before 1914, so that the gap between services and manufactures narrowed. This too was experienced by other high income economies. The slowing rate of labour productivity was common to most services, the exception being the rather erratic performance of financial services (Table 5.6). Other estimates have also found lower growth of labour productivity in services than manufacturing (Gemmell and Wardley 1990: 308; Feinstein 1990c: 339). In the inter-war period, with the single exception of transport, all services experienced absolute falls in labour productivity (Table 5.6).

Estimates for capital productivity in services are even less secure than those for labour, because of the difficulty in estimating the capital stock. Gemmell and Wardley have ventured such an estimate, suggesting lower capital productivity in services than manufacturing but an increase throughout the second half of the nineteenth century (Gemmell and Wardley 1990: 306, 308). Viewed as 'total' productivity the increasing productivity of capital would tend to offset some of the loss on the labour side. The combined productivity growth of labour and capital, each weighted by its share of national product, is the fullest measure. The most recent estimates of total factor productivity for the Victorian age confirm the relatively slow productivity growth in services as compared to manufactures (Gemmell and Wardley 1990: 308; Millward 1990: 425).

It has been suggested, however, that the conventional method of estimating service sector productivity contains an inherent downward bias. In the absence of output data, growth of labour in services has often been used as a proxy: labour hours of a domestic servant are taken as the 'product' of the domestic service, chargeable hours by a lawyer are again the product of that service. The proxy is adequate for judging how large services bulk in the economy. But it means, of course, that the increase in labour productivity is, by definition, zero: output grows at the same rate of input if one takes the input to be the measure of the output. Total factor productivity growth in these parts of services (railways and other industries with natural measures of output are not affected) can only be capital productivity weighted by its share in national product. As Millward put it:

> Since capital productivity is equal to output divided by capital stock and since output is proxied by labour then the official approach basically equates productivity growth with the rise of labour intensive technique. In fact over the long term for other sectors of the British economy it is capital productivity rather than labour productivity which has tended to be zero. (Millward 1990: 426)

On the alternative assumption that productivity in the non-marketed sector will be a function of capital intensity of technique, Millward adopts on the contrary the growth of *capital* as the proxy for output growth. His procedure is certainly plausible and has the effect of modestly increasing productivity in public and professional services particularly in the inter-

Table 5.6. *Labour productivity growth rates, 1861–1951* (*per cent per year*)

	1861–71	1871–81	1881–91	1891–1901	1901–11	1924–37	1937–51
Agriculture	2·90	0·34	1·39	0·19	0·46	2·23	1·29
Industry	3·42	1·37	0·48	1·32	0·20	1·79	1·00
Transport/communications	2·15	1·44	0·05	−0·17	1·57	0·82	1·95
Distribution	2·19	0·03	−0·44	−0·29	−0·62	−0·79	2·18
Insurance/banking	8·05	0·65	0·45	2·15	1·15	−0·33	1·50
Professions	2·21	0·49	1·37	0·65	0·97	−0·42	−1·79
Miscellaneous services	1·75	1·06	0·88	0·39	0·98	−0·55	4·16
Public administration	2·23	0·54	0·40	−1·04	1·68	−0·45	−0·83
Total	2·85	1·09	0·69	0·83	0·58	0·75	1·21

Note: productivity growth rates derived from Tables 5.1 and 5.2.

war years. This, in turn, increases the estimate for service sector productivity by 0.07–0.15 per cent annually in the Victorian age, and in the inter-war years revises a rate of decline of 0.10 per cent annually into a growth rate of 0.14 per cent (Millward 1990: 425–7). Such is altogether plausible, it being strange to think of a sector regressing in its technique.

The various productivity estimates tend to confirm each other in three aspects. In the middle of the nineteenth century the service industries generally enjoyed relatively high labour productivity levels when compared with manufacturing and agriculture. The high value added in financial and professional services and the capital intensity of the railways were responsible. Secondly, the productivity performance in services in the latter part of the nineteenth century exhibited continuing improvement but at a lower rate than manufacturing which, therefore, closed the productivity gap between the sectors. Finally, in the inter-war years productivity performance in services was poor, in contrast to the strong performance in manufacturing. In terms of labour productivity almost all services experienced a decline between the wars, so that by the late 1930s their productivity levels compared poorly with their counterparts in the United States (Rostas 1948a: 83–93, 238–48). In railways and telecommunications both labour productivity and total productivity in the United States were at least three times that of their British equivalent (ch. 15).

Several studies have analysed the productivity performance of the railways in Victorian Britain. Recent total factor productivity estimates suggest an annual rate of increase of 1 per cent between 1870 and 1910, with increased coal consumption and a growing workforce as the retarding influences (Foreman-Peck 1991b: 81) – though it was in fact faster travel that increased coal consumption and required higher manning levels for safety. Much of the pressure for greater frequency of service and higher standards of punctuality came from both customers and the government. As a result many railway services operated well below capacity in the later decades of the century. Productivity suffered. Furthermore, government legislation prevented railway companies from increasing their tariffs to cover additional costs (Irving 1976: 277). Operating practices are said to have been a major obstacle to improvement. It is claimed that small coal wagons kept operating costs high, since they had a low proportion of paying load to gross wagon weight. The wagons were usually owned not by the railway companies but by their customers, such as coal mines, who were disinclined to buy new cars without compensation in lower freight rates (recent work has suggested that the small cars may have been rational after all, as a cheap distribution system in the face of expensive hay and a dense rail network). When one company, the North Eastern Railway, restructured its freight operations in progressive fashion after 1900, it was able to achieve an 87 per cent increase in earnings per freight train-mile in the following decade (Irving 1978: 62–3).

In the Post Office, net revenue increased relative to expenditure from the 1840s until the 1880s. Thereafter, while costs of transport fell relative to net revenue the costs of labour increased substantially and profit rates fell. Greater financial control over wage costs in the inter-war years made some improvement (Daunton 1985: 330). Certainly before the war the Post Office workers enjoyed a 'lenient application of the laws of supply and demand': money wages increased at five times the rate of the national average, while the substitution of permanent for part-time staff, the separation of telegraph from counter work, increased costs of supervision, and the creation of a highly paid grade of first class duties all increased costs and offset the economies of scale obtained by the expansion of business (Daunton 1985: 232–4).

These weak productivity performances reflect a variety of influences including political pressure, feeble cost control under the protection of state monopoly and failure to exploit or sustain economies of scale. But why then was productivity performance in services far worse between the wars? It has been suggested in explanation that high unemployment crowded labour into services, and that services tend to absorb labour during depressions and keep it underemployed (ch. 15; Millward 1990: 428).

The service industries certainly did increase their labour between 1924 and 1938, accounting for over 76 per cent of the total increase of 3 million jobs (Chapman and Knight 1953: 18). In insurance and banking the average salary fell from £419 to £328 between 1920 and 1938, so that while employment increased by one third the total bill for salaries rose only slightly (Chapman and Knight 1953: 154). Similarly in distribution the increase in employment of 37.5 per cent was accompanied by falling rates of pay, so that the increase in aggregate wages was 24.9 per cent and in total salaries 13.2 per cent (Chapman and Knight 1953: 149). While the number of domestic servants increased by over 400,000, the total bill for their services fell by almost 10 per cent (Chapman and Knight 1953: 218).

But not all the increase in service industry employment can be attributed to the desperation of unemployment. As we have seen, most of the service jobs were created in the south-east, where per capita incomes were higher and unemployment lower than elsewhere (Lee 1986: 258; Foreman-Peck 1985: 419). Services were part of the consumer boom of the 1930s in the metropolitan hinterland.

Services and growth

In the second half of the nineteenth century services accounted for half the growth in national income, and for about one third in the inter-war decades. Services contributed about 75 per cent of the total increase of employment in the century after 1850 (Lee 1986: 12, 14).

The growth models discussed at the beginning imply that such growth boded ill for the economy. Kaldor's thesis is that growth is industry-led and that only manufacturing is able to achieve substantial productivity increases. But the links between service sector growth and GDP are no less impressive, and services have also demonstrated a capability to generate impressive productivity gains (Lee 1990b: Tables 1, 3). The third strand of Kaldor's model, that manufacturing will attract labour away from services, is clearly false before 1950. Service sector employment growth prior to the First World War came primarily from expansion of the workforce through population increase, and in the inter-war years from a pool of unemployed workers: it hardly took labour away from manufacturing. British economic history supports only a highly modified version of the Kaldor model.

The poor productivity performance in services between the wars together with the substantial increase in employment seems to offer support, on the other hand, to the Baumol hypothesis. But again there is no evidence of substantial shifts of labour into services at the expense of industry. Certainly productivity performance in services was disappointing. But it needs to be seen in the context of the high productivity levels which obtained in services from the beginning. While eroded by the faster growth of productivity in manufacturing, the differential advantage of services was not eliminated. Estimates for value added per person in 1949 found an average of £492 in services compared to £449 in goods. Only public administration and defence, amongst the services, came below manufacturing, while financial services were far ahead of all other sectors, with a value added of £655 (McMahon and Worswick 1969: 142). The poor productivity performance of services in the late nineteenth and early twentieth centuries was rooted in the events of the time, but was not an eternal constant, to be built into grim forecasts of the end of growth. As indicated in the mid-Victorian productivity achievement and the resumption of productivity advance after 1945, services can be a leading sector (vol. 3, ch. 11). The Baumol thesis fails.

The relationship of services to each other and to the rest of the economy is complex and seldom stationary. Services like transport and distribution were obviously stimulated by the growth of industry. But the growth of services such as professional sport generated a demand for commodities, from stadia and equipment to jerseys and other clothing. One Birmingham manufacturer prospered in the late Victorian era by selling upwards of 50,000 footballs a year. Golf and tennis generated a sufficiently large demand for equipment to warrant factory production (Vamplew 1988: 55). Related services which benefited included the football pool industry which, in turn, generated massive business for the Post Office, the sporting press and the railway. Nor has the pattern of substitution been simple. It has included 'the substitution of a commodity for a commodity (meat for bread [with cheaper ocean transport]), or of a service for a service (an expensive restaurant meal for a cheap one), or of a service for a commodity (restaurant food for home-cooked food), or of a commodity for a service (ready-to-serve food for household help)' (Kravis *et al.* 1983: 197). The major substitution prior to 1939 was almost certainly the replacement of a service (domestic service) by a commodity (the fridge and the gas cooker).

The service industries made a substantive contribution to British economic growth before 1850 (Lee 1986: 10). Since the Second World War the service sector has enjoyed explosive growth in many advanced economies. In the intervening century, services contributed to the growth and productivity of the British economy. The view that services are optional, unproductive, stagnant and low wage needs historical revision.

6 British agriculture, 1860–1914

Cormac Ó Gráda

Introduction

During the industrial revolution productivity growth in the agricultural sector was impressive (see vol. 1, ch. 5). The growth was founded on a combination of institutional changes (e.g. enclosure) and process innovations (such as the diffusion of fodder crops and better breeds of livestock). During the 'second agricultural revolution' (*c.* 1820–60), agriculture's productivity was boosted further, as farmers took advantage of artificial grasses and manures, clay-pipe drainage, and farm mechanisation (Thompson 1968). The increasingly capital-intensive 'high farming' of these decades took place largely in the context of a land tenure system which outlasted the period surveyed here: in 1914 almost nine-tenths of both holdings and cultivated area were rented by farmers from landlords (Ministry of Agriculture, Fisheries and Food 1968).

Though firm estimates are unavailable, agricultural output may have doubled between 1800 and 1860 (Deane and Cole 1962: 170). Between 1816 and 1914, however, output failed to register any sustained increase, while agriculture's share in the gross national product of Great Britain dropped from about 20 per cent to less than 7 per cent (Feinstein 1972: Tables 4 and 60). This need not signify 'decline' in any pejorative sense, since the change could have resulted simply from greater specialisation in international trade. Indeed, though Britain had long been an importer of food-stuffs such as cheese from Holland and live cattle and grain from Ireland, her dependence on food imports grew rapidly after mid-century. The opening up of the vast American prairies for grain production, improvements in long-distance transport technology both on land and on sea, and the massive increase in the output of dairy products in parts of the European Continent, were important developments for the British economy. Moreover, the substantial rise in imports during these years – a fourfold increase in wheat, a fivefold increase in butter imports, for example – was accompanied by a sharp drop in the relative price of food-stuffs.

Table 6.1. *The trend in agricultural output and incomes, 1862–1914*

Period	1862	1878	1896	1905	1913
(1) Agricultural output	101·0	104·9	101·0	98·0	100·0
(2) Agricultural prices	116·0	110·0	72·0	82·0	99·0
(3) Cost of living	111·0	110·0	83·0	92·0	102·0
(4) Working population	100·0	84·4	76·6	74·6	73·0
(5) Average real income	100·0	117·8	108·4	110·9	129·8
(6) Class shares					
a. landlords	22·0	24·0	27·0	19·0	18·0
b. workers	35·0	37·0	38·0	37·0	33·0
c. farmers	43·0	39·0	35·0	44·0	49·0
(7) Agricultural wages (1911 = 100)	76·8	85·3	88·3	96·5	105·6

Sources: output, Feinstein (1972: Table 118); prices, Mitchell and Deane (1962: 472–3, 343–5); labour force, Feinstein (1972: Table 131), with the following adjustment: 50,000 was added to Feinstein's total for 1862 to allow for seasonal labour inputs, 30,000 in 1878, 20,000 in 1896 and 10,000 in 1905; class shares from Bellerby (1968: 268), Feinstein (1972: Table 60); agricultural wages, Feinstein (1990b) for 1880, 1896, 1905 and 1913 and Mitchell (1988: 158) for 1862. Average real income from agriculture for 1862 was set equal to 100.

Nevertheless, the period is often regarded as one of agricultural 'decline' in a less trivial sense. As R. E. Prothero (Lord Ernle) wrote in 1912, 'Since 1862 the tide of agricultural prosperity ceased to flow: after 1874 it turned, and rapidly ebbed' (Ernle 1912: 377). Since he wrote, the widening gap between agricultural and non-agricultural incomes has been a recurring theme. A relative fall in landlord incomes at the time is understandable, since (following Ricardo) rent levels might be expected to bear the main brunt of free trade; however, similar trends in farmers' and farm workers' incomes, if substantiated, need to be explained. The alleged failure of British agriculture to respond to the challenge of foreign competition and the opportunities presented by the shifting patterns of consumer demand is the explanation most often given.

Despite auspicious beginnings it would seem that 'high farming' along lines advocated by Alderman Mechi or the journalist James Caird was not enough. As Kindleberger (1964: 243) put it,

> it was left for Denmark, the Netherlands and New Zealand to provide the bacon, eggs, ham and cheese in which the British worker and middle class member chose to take such a large proportion of their increased productivity. These countries did transform under the pressure of British demand. The question is why it was they and not the more strategically placed British agriculture?

By and large, the farmer and the landlord have been given low marks for adaptability and initiative in the mid- and late-Victorian era.

Income and productivity

But did rural incomes fall behind? A variety of evidence, ranging from cartoons in *Punch* to doleful data on bankrupt farmers, would suggest a decline even in absolute terms from the early 1870s to the end of the century. One survey, which relies heavily on such information, dwells at length on the 'deteriorating economic and social position' of the landed proprietors, and the 'falling' income of farmers, while conceding that labourers did not fare so badly (Perry 1974: 91, 92, 126). The evidence presented to the Royal Commission on the Depressed Condition of Agricultural Interests (1880–2), the Royal Commission on the Agricultural Depression (1894–7) and the Royal Tariff Commission (1905) is almost uniformly pessimistic. Reliable data on the overall movement in incomes, needed to clinch the issue, are scarce, however, and not easy to construct. Table 6.1 attempts merely to provide a very approximate guide, using business cycle peaks, to the course of incomes adjusted for the change in the cost of living between the early 1860s and the First World War. Since per capita income equals

$$\frac{\text{(output in current price terms)}}{\text{(numbers employed in agriculture)} \times \text{(consumer price index)}}$$

calculation of the standard-of-living index in row 5 of Table 6.1 is straightforward.

The figures do indeed imply that the 1878–1905 period was depressed as regards incomes. This is in line with more impressionistic accounts. The period includes 1878–81, years of dismally bad harvests and low prices, when agricultural prices reached a low point. But Table 6.1 also suggests that mean income rose by almost one third over the half century. True, average real income is somewhat elusive, bound to conceal interesting variations across regions and classes. Regional differences, which have received increasing attention in recent years from historians, are discussed briefly below. Meanwhile estimates of factor shares in agriculture in Table 6.1, combined with census information on occupational structure, permit some broad generalisations on the incomes of farmers, farm workers and landed proprietors over the five decades. The tripartite division offers a useful means of presenting data. For example, the number of farmers in Britain fell from 312,000 in 1861 to 280,000 in 1911 (Orwin and Whetham

1964: 342); Table 6.1, then, assumes that farmers' income rose on average by

$$\frac{\text{(1913 output)} \times \text{(farmers' share)/(farmers in 1911)}}{\text{(1862 output)} \times \text{(farmers' share)/(farmers in 1861)}}$$

$$\text{that is,} \quad \frac{(100) \times (0.49/280{,}000)}{(101) \times (0.43/312{,}000)} = 1.26$$

or by 26 per cent. Adjusting for the fall in agricultural prices relative to the cost of living reduces this to 17 per cent. By the same token, since the number of landed proprietors hardly changed, their average income from the land fell by about 30 per cent between 1880–2 and 1900–2, while the huge decline in the farm proletariat – from 1.4 million in 1861 to 0.9–1.0 million in 1911 – assured those remaining on the land an average increase in incomes of almost one half. That increase had been achieved by the mid-1890s, however.

The outcome suggests that growth in average real incomes in agriculture did not quite match that of the rest of the economy (compare Feinstein 1972: Tables 188 and 131). However, a relative decline in per capita average income does not necessarily imply that resources were misallocated to agriculture; efficiency requires, in economic theory, the equalisation between sectors of the economy of marginal returns, not of average returns which are measured by average real incomes. In addition, Table 6.1 suggests that there was a sharp rise in output per worker, which is often taken as a sign of increased efficiency. Labour productivity alone, however, may be a misleading guide to economic performance; the movement in total factor productivity, if it can be measured, provides a better guide to overall 'progress' or 'decline'. Total factor productivity may be defined as a ratio of output to inputs, the latter weighted by their respective shares of output. As explained in chapter 1, its measurement is fraught with difficulties, both conceptual and practical. Yet an increase in its size over time may be interpreted, though loosely, as a move towards greater efficiency in resource use, provided that all inputs are included and properly weighted and measured. Accurate measurement is often impossible, but the direction of the bias may be controlled.

In the present context, since agriculture is on trial for sluggish response, the input measures should, if anything, favour the null hypothesis of 'not guilty'. For this reason the indices have not been adjusted to allow for improvements in quality. The results, which are presented in Table 6.2, suggest an average annual productivity growth rate of 0.4 per cent between the 1860s and the 1910s (compare Matthews *et al.* 1982: Table 8.3). This is not far short of the rates reported for 1700–1850 in volume 1, chapter 5. In

Table 6.2. *Total factor productivity change in British agriculture, 1871–1911*

	Inputs			Factor shares				TFP
Year	Land (1)	Labour (2)	Capital (3)	Land (4)	Labour (5)	Capital (6)	Output (7)	(1870–2 = 100) (8)
1862	100	100·0	100·0	23	64	13	101·0	100·0
1878	100	84·4	105·0	24	62	14	104·9	110·3
1896	100	76·6	96·0	23	64	13	101·0	119·2
1905	100	74·6	95·0	19	69	12	98·0	119·5
1913	100	73·0	96·0	18	70	12	100·0	124·0

Sources: labour (col. 2), as in Table 6.1; capital (col. 3), Bellerby and Boreham (1953), adjusted for use by Statist-Sauerbeck overall index in Mitchell and Deane (1962: 474–5); factor shares, Bellerby (1968: 264). For the share of labour (col. 5), the shares of wages and farmers' and relatives' incentive incomes were added together.

comparative terms, 0.4 per cent is less impressive. For instance, productivity growth rates up to 1 per cent have been reported for Japanese and American agriculture in the pre-First World War period (D. André, cited in Dumke 1988: 29; Kendrick 1961: 362–4). The British data are admittedly less precise, but refinement would probably reduce estimated British productivity growth. In addition the estimate for agriculture is also considerably below that for the economy as a whole over the period. Labour productivity also grew less rapidly than in several other countries for whom data exist. Such results might be taken as evidence that this was indeed a period of relative 'decline' in British farming. But it does not explain the decline. There are several possible explanations.

The farmer: supply responsiveness

British farmers, landlords and labourers have all been blamed, though not with equal conviction, for British agriculture's allegedly weak performance. Farmers and landed proprietors may have forgone income in order to remain within agriculture at a time of adversity (Bellerby 1956). Alternatively, agriculturalists may have generated a low output simply because they shifted inadequately into those farm commodities yielding the best returns at any one time. Though the case for sluggish response, for the presumed 'appalling obstinacy of the British farmer', is seldom cogently made, examples of behaviour which at first sight imply low allocative ability are numerous. R. H. Rew guessed that the refusal of livestock farmers to use a newly developed mechanism for weighing livestock cost them as much as £7 million in 1888 alone (Perry 1974: 64), but this is ludicrous: £7 million was 6 per cent of agricultural output in that dismal year, and the farmers' loss in any case was presumably somebody else's gain. In the same vein the *Daily News* complained in 1879 that 'as to the ability of the English farmer to take out of the hand of foreigners the trade in butter, no one doubts that they might have kept in the country most part of the £10,000,000 which was paid for imported butter in 1878'. Other more mundane examples illustrate the alleged delay in switching resources to 'safer and more promising openings' such as horticulture and dairying, in using the advantages of agricultural cooperation in production and marketing and in applying cost-saving process innovations.

The list of seeming error and inertia is impressive. Nevertheless, to argue by anecdote is a gambit to be indulged in as a last resort, particularly since the documentation is not all negative, and some of it is open to different interpretations. Presumably, farmer intelligence was distributed among the farm population around some average, as among the population as a whole: if so, individual examples might come from the upper or lower extremes of the distribution.

The agricultural and price statistics of the period, supported by background data on technical and institutional factors, permit a different approach. A broader focus raises its own problems, however. How slow is sluggish? 'The British farmer', we are told, 'does not act precipitately, but gradually alters his method over long periods of time' (Wrightson 1890: 281). Yes, but where is the dividing line between caution, impetuosity and sheer pigheadedness? A comparative approach to the problem may help, drawing on evidence from other countries. But before turning to direct measures of supply response, examine briefly the change in the composition of agricultural output over the period.

Table 6.3 presents a picture of a substantial shift in the composition of output between the 1870s and 1900s. Most notable are the decline in the relative importance of grain and the increase in milk production. Moreover, the figures conceal further shifts within these sectors. Thus both oats and barley acreages overtook that under wheat, while within dairying butter and cheese gave way more and more to the production of liquid milk.

The fall in the acreage under grain, which probably began before 1860 (Kain and Prince 1985: 173–4), is perhaps the best known aspect of British agricultural transformation during this period. In retrospect the transformation of dairying, though less emphasised by economic historians, seems equally radical. It too took place against a background of increasing intrusion from foreign producers, from continental Europe at first and from New Zealand after 1880. At a rough guess, between the 1860s and the

Table 6.3. *Gross agricultural output of Great Britain, 1870–6 and 1904–10*

	1870–6		1904–10	
	£m	(%)	£m	(%)
Crops	80·9	(41·4)	44·2	(28·5)
Animal products	114·3	(58·6)	111·0	(71·5)
Total	195·2	(100·0)	155·2	(100·0)
Some individual items				
Wheat	26·6	(13·6)	8·4	(5·4)
All grains	49·8	(25·5)	20·1	(13·0)
Beef	34·8	(17·8)	29·4	(18·9)
Milk	27·0	(13·8)	36·5	(23·5)

Sources: Ojala (1952: 210–11); Ojala's calculations for the United Kingdom have been adjusted by using (with slight corrections) the estimates for Ireland presented in Irish Agricultural Output 1908 (Dublin, 1912) and Solow (1971: 17).

Table 6.4. *Elasticities of supply of British agricultural products, 1874–1914*

Crops	Short-run elasticity	Long-run elasticity
Wheat	0·63	1·11
Barley	0·35	0·76
Oats	0·26	1·63

Notes and sources: the structure estimated was that used by Fisher and Temin (1970). Data from Mitchell and Deane (1962: 78–9, 488–9). For a somewhat different approach, though giving similar results, see Olson and Harris (1959).

First World War British butter and cheese production declined by 40 per cent. The rise in imports of dairy products shocked jingoistic contemporaries, and the notion grew – and persisted – that British dairying 'failed' in its struggle (Haggard 1911: 248–76; Kindleberger 1964: 243).

In reality, though, for most British farmers specialisation in liquid milk production made perfect sense under free trade conditions. Liquid milk output more than quadrupled and milk consumption per capita doubled (Taylor 1976, 1987). Transport costs and the problem of quick spoilage ensured that British producers had the home market to themselves, while farmers who were suitably located could make almost twice as much from their liquid milk, sold fresh, as from butter. Not surprisingly it was only in remote areas, removed both from the railway network and centres of consumption, that farmers persisted with cheese and butter production on a large scale. By 1914 the bulk of British butter and cheese production was confined to the south-west of England and Wales. Nearer London and Manchester the proportion of dairy produce being sold in liquid form reached nine-tenths; in Wales it only slightly exceeded one half. The regional variation reflected locational constraints rather than differences in commercial acumen. Indeed, in the worst-endowed parts of the periphery, just as in parts of Ireland, not only were farmers in no position to get the high prices for liquid milk; the advantages of the centrifugal cream separator, available in theory from the 1880s, eluded them as well (Hall 1913: 325–7; Taylor 1987).

Table 6.3 suggests that the British farmer of the late Victorian and Edwardian years was no exception to the rule that farmers as a group respond positively to market forces. Still, since what is at stake is an inadequate rather than a zero response to prices, a more exact notion of price responsiveness is required. Examine therefore the supply elasticity – the response of supply to a change in price – of one category of agricultural output, cereals, in more detail. Cereals, 'the besetting temptation of British agriculture' according to Brodrick (1881: 296), are chosen because they have been the focus of much previous writing and – as we have seen above – contributed significantly to agricultural output. Reliable acreage and price data are available from the early 1870s (J. T. Coppock 1956) and can be used to obtain the supply elasticities shown above for Great Britain over the period 1874–1914 (see Table 6.4).

The results show, for example, that on average a 1 per cent fall in the price of wheat produced a fall of 0.63 per cent in output in the short run, and of 1.11 per cent in the long run: if such elasticities seem 'small', they nevertheless are on a par with elasticities calculated for nineteenth-century agriculture elsewhere. It seems unfair, then, on this evidence to blame the British farmer for cereal 'over-production'. Indeed, because there were important cost-saving innovations in cereal production during these decades, the response of farmers to changes in relative prices (the figures estimated here) must have been less than their response to changes in net revenue per unit output. If, as frequently suggested, cereal farmers were likely to be the least responsive group, that creates a strong presumption that response in other sections within British agriculture was 'adequate' at the time.

The farmer and technical change: the reaping machine

Even if farmers were producing the right crops, perhaps they were not using the best methods, and in particular the best machinery. The mechanisation of British agriculture began before our period. Mid-century farming manuals, such as Henry Stephens' *Book of the Farm* or J. C. Morton's *Cyclopaedia of Agriculture*, contain descriptions of much of the machinery in use thirty or even fifty years later (Thompson 1968: 5–6). Yet the post-1860 period saw the widespread diffusion and refinement of a few machines that had shown earlier promise. The failures included the steam plough, the successes the threshing machine, the horse hoe and the chaff machine (Collins 1972; Mutch 1981).

The American reapers exhibited at the Crystal Palace Exhibition of 1851 were a great attraction, but British farmers were slow to adopt the new techniques at harvest time. While mechanisation of reaping in the American Midwest proceeded quite rapidly from the mid-1850s, in Britain the 1850s and 1860s saw only modest diffusion. Almost four-fifths of American small grain acreage was being cut mechanically by 1869–70, while in 1874 the proportion in Great Britain was still less than half (David 1975: 236). Was the delay simply another instance of British farmers' lethargy? The timing of the reaper's diffusion is a puzzle which still awaits an agreed explanation. A number of competing hypotheses have been put forward, but none has been generally accepted; the paucity and uncertainty of evidence on the temporal and spatial diffusion of machines and grain acreages, and on the regional differences in the wages of harvest labourers, leaves much room for argument.

It seems unlikely that either the organised hostility of agricultural labourers or the paternalism of farmers, who might have retained labourers when it was no longer strictly economic to do so, were significant factors in preventing diffusion. The most obvious explanation is that the speed of diffusion was a response to the relative costs and prices of the old and new methods. The reaper was a classic example of labour-saving machinery (Wilson 1864: 149; McConnell 1906: 237), and it has been suggested that the state of the labour market was an important determinant of reaper diffusion. Until mid-century and later the British farm population, with considerable help from Irish seasonal migrants, was adequate to cope with harvest demands at low wages. Given the fixed cost involved in buying a reaper, diffusion was delayed by the relative cheapness of farm labour (Habakkuk 1962: 199).

But the price of harvest labour relative to capital does not suffice to explain the speed of diffusion. Another possibility is that the smaller farmer, for whom buying a reaper would have meant incurring a higher fixed cost per acre of grain, might have been less likely to adopt the new technique. This consideration has prompted the use of the concept of 'threshold acreage' (David 1975: 195–217). Income-maximising farmers with an acreage above the threshold would buy a reaper, while others would cling to traditional methods. According to the threshold interpretation the size distribution of farms is a crucial determinant of the spread of mechanisation.

Thirdly, it has been argued that the farming landscape in Britain was an added consideration: smaller fields, the use of open furrows for drainage, and blade-breaking stones meant in practice an additional fixed-cost element in preparing arable land for the reaper. 'Mechanisation of the corn harvest would have been a profitable undertaking on a great part of Britain's cereal acreage even at the beginning of the 1850s supposing only that the more serious among the terrain problems ... could have been first removed' (David 1975: 244). In other words, the use of the machine required the use of a complementary third factor – proper terrain – whose improvement was more expensive in Britain than in America.

That does not exhaust the list of possibilities. A fourth was the change in the productivity of reaping machines themselves over time. So long as harvesting techniques remained constrained by hand-tool methods the scope for productivity increase was limited. But as soon as cutting became what Marx called 'the mechanism of an implement', this was no longer so. Though the machines on show at the Crystal Palace had tremendous curiosity value, they were unwieldy for British use, liable to break down under British conditions, and difficult to service (Mutch 1981: 128). They were intended for the American prairies, which were often flat, had few hedges and fences and whose crops were much lighter sown and grown. But after 1851 refinements continued apace both in Britain and in the United States. Almost 300 reaper patents were taken out in Britain alone in 1850–70, and competition between manufacturers was intense. Fourteen years after the Exhibition an observer could state of earlier superseded reaper models that 'they now rot in corners, looking in comparison to modern reapers like skeletons of the Mammoth and the Mastodon among recent animals'. Moreover, though the reliability and performance of the machines improved, price did not increase between 1851 and 1914. Finally, the diffusion of the reaper (and other farm machinery) may have been delayed for fear of the ensuing unemployment. Machinery introduced near the peak of the trade cycle could produce technological unemployment (E. J. T. Collins 1989).

Which of these interpretations best fit the available evidence? Though many instances might be cited of intelligent farmers retaining elderly or unproductive workers, it may be assumed that self-interest undoubtedly dominated in this sphere as elsewhere. Returning to the threshold model, there is only limited evidence for a market in reaper hiring and the informal sharing of reapers. Even if reaper hiring existed, the smaller farmer may still have been less in a position to switch techniques, since there could also have been a threshold – though a lower one – for hiring. But the threshold argument must face the evidence that in mid-century most of Britain's small grains were grown on acreages exceeding the average utilisation of early reaping machines, if not their cutting capacity. The size distribution of farms is fundamental, since we are less interested in the number of farmers adopting the reaper than in the total grain acreage cut by a machine in a season. David (1975: 30–1) has suggested fifty acres as the average annual use per reaper in 1850–70, so the threshold model's main relevance is limited to grain acreages under fifty. But a farmer with fields below fifty acres would probably not use the reaper in any case, and a farmer with more acres, say seventy, might be expected to use a combination of a reaper and hand labour.

The threshold model may thus help to explain the diffusion lags in Ross and Cromarty or Inverness, where the average cereal acreage was about seven acres in the early 1870s; it is certainly of less help in the case of the midlands or East Anglia, where the average in mid-century probably approached fifty. Indeed, it is arguable that the model's potential coverage extends to only a quarter or even a fifth of Britain's grain acreage at the time, since the vast bulk of the crops were being grown on large farms: large farms exceeded the threshold. For example, average farm size in Hertfordshire in 1870 was eighty-one acres, and eighty-one per cent of the land was on farms exceeding 100 acres. The average size of those large holdings was over 250 acres.

Contemporary cost comparisons of hand and machine methods – of which there are several – must be treated with caution. A number of them, however, such as Jacob Wilson's careful and detailed study of the early 1860s, imply that the reaper was then a marginal proposition even in areas where harvest wages were relatively high. According to Wilson's calculations for Midlothian in Scotland the saving per acre on labour was about 5s. But the average acreage cut in a season by Wilson's sample of 160 machines was less than fifty, and depreciation on a £30–£40 machine with a five-year life – considered usual at the time – would thus have accounted for about 3s per acre. Nor does this take into account the extra outgoings on horses and oil associated with the new technique, items which might easily account for a few shillings per acre. Problems of terrain apart, then, Wilson's data are consistent with slow diffusion being the sensible option for Britain (Wilson 1864). The available figures therefore make the coexistence of hand-tools and machines quite plausible. When emigration and urban employment reduced the supply of seasonal workers, in the 1860s – parliamentary returns suggest a 20 per cent rise in weekly earnings by task work in the 1860s – mechanical reapers became increasingly viable.

Improvements in the machines themselves provided an added spur. The earlier McCormick model was pulled by one horse, which also had to carry the driver, while another worker raked the cut crop from the machine as he walked alongside. The model exhibited in England in 1851 had a second seat, but was still very heavy, and tough on the horses. In the late 1850s 'the attainment of a completely effective reaping machine [was] an object yet to be sought for' (Slight and Scott Burn 1858: 343). Yet within a few years several companies were producing a working model which could be operated by one man, delivering a cut crop in sheaves.

Modifying the reaper was also a substitute for changing the landscape. Smaller and lighter machines were developed, which could more easily negotiate the furrows and enclosures which created problems for the earliest reapers. The late 1870s finally witnessed the introduction of a successful reaper-and-binder, the last word in the horse-drawn technology. By the end of our period the cost of harvesting on all but the most intractable fields was 4s to 6s per acre, while hand methods would have cost three to four times as much (Wrightson 1906: 99–106). Labour abundance was no longer relevant, and the vast bulk of the grain was mechanically harvested.

The reaper-and-binder, unlike its predecessors, would have paid even at the wage level of the 1850s. In the event, its arrival on the scene at the onset of the collapse in corn prices was a godsend to hard-pressed farmers. It lessened the blow of the price slump, and limited the reduction in corn acreage, making it viable to grow wheat at 30s a quarter, 'though no one will grow rich at the job' (McConnell 1906: 238). In sum, the pace of reaper diffusion is no argument against the British farmer: at an aggregate level, it would seem to have followed economic logic.

The landowners

The distribution of landed property in nineteenth-century Britain was notoriously uneven. Using official data, Bateman estimated that less than 1700 'peers' and 'great landowners' owned two-fifths of the total area of England and Wales in the 1870s (Brodrick 1881: 152–87). Yet relatively few people within British agriculture thought of a radical redistribution of landed wealth as a formula for radical recovery and progress. Such a plan was firmly ruled out by Gladstone in the 1870s. Almost twenty years later a disillusioned member of the Royal Commission of 1894–7 found that body's majority report 'vigorous and uncompromising only in its defence of the existing land system' (Gladstone 1879; Channing 1897: i). There was no revolution in landed property at the time. The proportions of land under tenancy and owner-occupancy hardly changed.

Nevertheless, criticism of landlords after the middle of the century was widespread, though more restrained than in neighbouring Ireland.

Landlords were charged with giving tenants no security of tenure and, on top of that, of refusing them compensation for unexhausted improvements the tenants had made. The landlords were also blamed for unreasonably delaying rent reductions, and for refusing tenants permission to convert arable land to pasture when tillage became unremunerative. In such ways the landlords were thought to be responsible for failing to give tenants 'a fair field' in their struggle against foreign competition.

While anecdotes can be found to support the criticisms, their overall importance has almost certainly been exaggerated. Reluctance to permit the conversion of tilled fields to grass, and to reduce rent claims, was normally short-lived. It would have been unreasonable to expect that expectations about future prices would adjust overnight after decades of relative price buoyancy: indeed, neither landlord nor tenant thought at the outset that the fall in prices would last. But surviving estate accounts suggest that most of the decline in 'rent received' was rather quickly reflected in the 'rent demanded' column (Rhee 1949). Even where cuts were delayed, there was usually a liberal attitude to arrears. While a small minority of landlords in the areas of the Celtic fringe – Wales and Scotland – still evicted for political reasons, such behaviour was atavistic by late nineteenth-century British standards, and it was almost unheard of for a landlord to evict for non-payment of rent during a crisis year. The absence of litigation about 'tumbled-down' land, and of convincing statistical evidence, make it unlikely that landlords prevented tenants from adjusting land use in response to the changes in relative prices.

It is true that conflicting claims about rents from interested parties, in newspapers and in oral evidence to Royal Commissions, pose a problem of interpretation. What is most significant, though, is the existence 'in nearly every county [of] a competition for farms' as late as the mid-1890s (Parliamentary Papers 1897: XV, 213). Such excess demand implies either very foolhardy tenants or, which seems more likely, attractive rent levels. A pro-tenant Royal Commissioner, in desperation, rationalised that 'with most commodities, the supply tends to equal the demand: but the area of land in Great Britain is limited, and the number of land occupiers being recruited from so many sources is practically unlimited' (Parliamentary Papers 1897: XV, 213). The dubious economics cannot conceal the apologetic nature of the argument.

In addition, although most tenants in Britain were on yearly tenancies by 1860, there is little evidence that lack of security in practice prevented them from improving their holdings (Thompson 1968: 76–7). Tenants were very rarely ejected. 'Tenant rights', formal and informal, were widespread at the time, and seem to have adjusted as economic conditions dictated. As free agents, tenants with cause for concern at lack of security could have insisted on special terms in their contracts; no evidence has been adduced for such pressure, nor, indeed, for any correlation between 'security' and the tenant outlays on the land. The replies to the questionnaire prepared by Assistant Commissioner Little for the Royal Commission of 1880–2 imply that the farmers in the south of England who complained loudest about insecurity were no more reluctant to spend considerable sums annually on lime and fertiliser than those who had tenant right written into their covenants (Parliamentary Papers 1882: XV, 200–27). The same source suggests that despite legal changes, tenancies typically stayed for several decades within the same family. Finally, there is no sign that the land system materially hindered the development of fruit farming and market gardening at the time, even though these involved considerable fixed outlays on the part of the tenant.

The traditional view, long associated in particular with Arthur Young and James Caird, that long leases were essential if tenants were to improve the land, does not therefore fit the facts of nineteenth-century agriculture. Tenancy-at-will provided greater flexibility in the face of fluctuating prices; indeed, the widespread use of long leases would have made adjustment during the price fall itself more costly. On the other hand, whether tenancy-at-will promoted efficiency by keeping tenants on their toes is not clear, since the sanction of eviction was hardly ever applied. Individual proprietors, furthermore, had nothing to fear from a system such as tenant right in its English form, whereby farmers simply recouped the value of their fixed investments in the land.

In many of its aspects, therefore, landlordism did not act as a brake on agricultural adjustment. The story does not end there. Landlord control of the Royal Agricultural Society (founded in 1838) has been blamed for diverting it for a time from the business of farming to that of entertaining landed peers and squires with social events and pointless sporting competitions. Again, landlord economies in the area of landlord improvement have been blamed for exacerbating the crisis after the late 1870s: 'Successful adaptation ... required from the landowner a certain level of expenditure, both on land and on farm buildings ... [since] increased livestock numbers usually implied heavier expenditure on new buildings to house them, especially if the farmer concentrated on stall- or yard-feeding' (Goddard 1988: 64–77; Perren 1970: 37). An alternative interpretation has it that landlords, caught in a futile attempt at bailing out hard-hit tenants, were simply throwing good money after bad. This would be in the spirit of allegations about landlord investment during the decades of 'high farming' and earlier, it being argued that much of their investment before the Depression never paid, and resulted in an over-capitalised agriculture (Chambers and Mingay 1966: 175–7). If indeed

Table 6.5. *The size distribution of British farms, 1885–1915 (%)*

Year	< 5	5–50	50–100	100–300	> 300
1885	28·5	42·0	11·7	14·4	3·5
1895	22·7	43·3	12·8	15·6	3·6
1905	21·5	45·5	29·4		3·4
1915	21·3	45·5	13·1	16·2	3·3

Source: Ministry of Agriculture, Fisheries and Food (1968: 19, 22).

landowners channelled into agriculture funds that would have yielded a higher return in other sectors of the economy at the time, their action would have represented a subsidy to farmers, and reduced the flight of farmers from the land. But a recent analysis of estate evidence suggests that at least in the important case of drain building landlords were well rewarded for their considerable outlays (Phillips 1989).

The tripartite division of landlord, farmer and labourer was associated with farms that were large by European standards (see Table 6.5). Although large farms were the envy of European observers in an earlier era, some argued that, managed by men who never got their hands dirty, their existence made adjustment tougher and output smaller in the era under review: 'England has too many farms too big for men prepared to use their hands and too small for men prepared to use their heads' (cited in Offer 1989: 107). A good deal of modern research suggests that both labour and total factor productivity is higher on smaller farms (e.g. Berry and Cline 1979).

The labourers

Between 1860 and 1914, Britain's farm population dropped by about a quarter, and the number of labourers by a third. The fall was accompanied, as already explained, by an increase in earnings of over a half; it also brought a marked decline in inter-regional wage variation. The county data that form the basis for the calculations reported in Table 6.6 indicate no sustained reduction in the regional spread of nominal wages (measured by their coefficient of variation) before the 1860s, but significant narrowing later.

Wage payments to labourers differed considerably between counties in mid-century, as the Scottish agricultural expert James Caird noted on his famous tour (1852: 510–19). Caird was surprised to find regular weekly wages for agricultural workers as low as 7s in Wiltshire and Gloucestershire, half what a labourer might earn in Lancashire or the West Riding.

Table 6.6. *Regional wage variation, 1790s–1890s*

	1767–70	1794–5	1833–45	1867–70	1898
England and Scotland (*n* = 75)					
Mean		91·2	119·4	173·8	208·0
S		19·8	16·4	24·5	21·7
CV		0·217	0·137	0·141	0·104
England only (*n* = 42)					
Mean	86·4	104·0	126·6	180·3	205·8
S	11·4	13·6	15·8	24·8	21·0
CV	0·132	0·131	0·125	0·137	0·102

Source: derived from Hunt (1986: 965–6). 'S' is the standard deviation, 'CV' the coefficient of variation (i.e. 'S' divided by the mean).

To some extent the gap may have been offset by the greater prevalence of task-work in the low-wage areas during the summer months, but this is debatable; the semi-official returns collected in 1860 and 1870 suggest a strong positive correlation between regular wage- and task-work rates. Caird's explanation for the phenomenon was the low mobility of rural workers, an argument supported by Clapham, though in less prosaic language: 'the men of Surrey may be pictured moving easily over their suburban sands; those of Essex, stuck beyond East London in deep clays or hidden in the folds of their north-western chalk,' and so on for Buckinghamshire and Oxfordshire (1938: 89–90). Those taking a less idyllic view of social relations in the countryside would argue that the ignorance of their labourers left farmers in an enviable monopsony position, which the farmers exploited to the full (see e.g. Parliamentary Papers 1893–4: XXXVI, 17).

An alternative interpretation for the wage variation is that statistics such as Caird's reflect genuine productivity differences from county to county. This was sometimes suggested by contemporary observers, in the spirit of 'a Lancashire workman at half-a-crown [30d] a day is not dearer than most Welsh labourers at a shilling [12d]'. This is difficult to prove, given the variety of work carried out by farm workers. Harvest earnings arguably provide a possible clue, since the scytheman's work was similarly carried out in different areas. Reports that it cost only 7s 6d to mow an acre of wheat in the North Riding in 1860, while it cost 12s in Surrey may seem strong support for the Caird–Clapham view that there were persistent imperfections in the labour market. In fact the story is less simple, since crop yields as a rule were higher in Surrey, and thus demanded more work (David 1970; Clark 1991). The crude test of the Caird–Clapham hypothesis

Table 6.7. *Reapers' wages and implied reaping rates, 1850 and 1860*

	Number of observations	Winter wage (bushels of wheat per day)	Reaping (bushels of wheat per man-day)
Southern England, 1860	54	0·27	8·2
Southern England, 1850	109	0·24	8·6
Northern England and Scotland, 1860	17	0·34	12·6
Northern England and Scotland, 1850	32	0·29	10·6
Ireland, 1860	20	0·18	5·6

Source: Clark (1991).

Table 6.8. *The age structure of agricultural workers, 1871–1911*

	1871	1891	1911
Percentage of male agricultural workers aged over 45	31·7	30·1	30·7
Percentage of all males over ten years also aged over 45	25·6	24·2	28·9
Median age of agricultural workers	28.6	27.8	28.8
Median age of all males over ten	27·6	27·3	29·3

Source: Census Reports of Great Britain.

suggested by Table 6.7 – the comparison of day wages (measured in wheat purchasing power) and reaping rates – suggests that much of the gap in day wages is explained in terms of productivity differences.

In emphasising the productivity argument, Wilson Fox argued that the men of the north of England constituted 'a finer race, physically and intellectually, than the Southerner ... because good feeding for generations has done much for them in body and in brain' (1903: 168–9). There is, indeed, evidence that labourers in low-wage areas in the south may have been earning less than the minimum amount needed to keep themselves and their families at full physical efficiency, even as late as the 1910s (Heath 1874: chs. 1 and 2; Rowntree and Kendall 1913). It does not follow, however, that it would have profited farmers to pay such workers more, a point sometimes urged by reformers. The farmers were probably being maximisers in paying the workers less than a 'living wage' (Pigou 1913b), because the effort supplied by labour may have been inelastic with respect to the wage rate. Still, Caird's distinction between a northern high-wage and a southern low-wage area had some relevance even on the eve of the First World War (Hunt 1986).

The release of labour into the industrial sector is one of agriculture's contributions to economic development. In nineteenth-century Britain, though, the flight from the land gave rise to shrill complaints and polemics from interested parties. It was frequently suggested that agriculture after the depression was the refuge of aged and inferior workmen. The point is familiar in other contexts: those with initiative and drive leave, and employers must manage with a lazier, older and duller workforce. Contemporaries such as Rider Haggard saw this trend as one of the reasons for agricultural decline: in more polemical vein, he and others argued that it represented a long-term security risk, since agricultural labourers had traditionally been the best soldiers in the realm. But those labourers who remained on the land must not be blamed for the farmers' and landlords' problems simply on the basis of anecdotal evidence from their bosses. The census data shown in Table 6.8 lend no support, for example, to the view that the labourers were an ageing class over the period. Moreover, if the literacy of agricultural workers is a relevant input to agriculture, then British workers of the 1910s were far better endowed with it than those of half a century earlier. The proportion of the farm labour force able to read and write grew from about two-thirds in mid-century to well over 95 per cent on the eve of the First World War.

Supply and demand factors both contributed to the reduction in the rural proletariat from 1.4 million in 1860 to less than 1 million in 1914. On the demand side the relative importance of mechanisation and the shift from tillage to pasture are difficult to gauge, because of poor data on machine diffusion and the labour requirements of machines of different vintages. Nevertheless, two labour-saving developments stand out. The reaping machine in its reaper-and-binder version saved two to three worker days per acre over traditional methods, meaning several hundred thousand harvest workers at full diffusion. Most immediately affected were Irish and urban seasonal harvesters, but the machine also undoubtedly allowed the farmers to reallocate work and therefore reduce their regular workforce (McConnell 1906: 237–9). The threshing machine, which came into its own after mid-century, may have involved even greater savings. While a man with a flail might manage six to nine bushels daily with difficulty, the contemporary threshing machine increased his output four or fivefold (Collins 1972; Fenton 1976: 79–93). If one assumes that half the grain in Britain was still being threshed manually in 1860, then mechanisation of threshing would account for the loss of winter work for as many as 200,000 workers. Thus these two innovations alone could explain one half of the decline in the labour force. This finding emphasises the extraordinary labour intensity of traditional British agriculture and its hand-tool technology. By comparison the 'tumbling down' of arable land was less important: accepting the rule-of-thumb calculations of contemporaries, the conversion of 3 million acres between 1880 and 1914 could have meant 100,000 less jobs. But there is no clear correlation in the county data between decline in acreage under grain and decline in the agricultural labour force; fruit growing and dairying, which came to the rescue in some of the arable areas, could be more labour intensive than grain growing.

Regional aspects

Ownership

The ownership of land was concentrated in very few hands throughout this period. Merely 1688 peers (the number is amusingly significant) owned over two-fifths of all the land in England, and concentration was greater still north of the border. Bedfordshire, divided between seventeen owners, and Sutherland, nine-tenths of which was owned by the Duke of Sutherland, stand out. Ownership was most widely spread in the Home Counties and East Anglia, and in north-west England, where the yeoman had survived (Rubinstein 1986b: 158; Ministry of Agriculture, Fisheries and Food 1968: 19, 22). Farm size, too, was subject to considerable regional variation. Small farms predominated in the Highlands and Islands of Scotland, but farms over fifty acres predominated in lowland counties such as Ayr and Berwick. England and Wales were subject to regional contrasts too. Thus while farms of less than fifty acres dominated in the West Riding, Derby or Carnarvon, well over one half of all farms in counties such as Essex and Devon exceeded fifty acres.

Specialisation

Agricultural practice and specialisation differed markedly between regions and within Great Britain. While comfortable farmers in the Lothians and East Anglia discussed the virtues of steam ploughing, liquid manure or the cost of labour, one might still find in the Highlands or Western Isles of Scotland 'the smaller and poorer crofters ... [with] their families sitting around the fire ... a whole winter picking the corn from the straw and chaff', or hacking away at stony soils with *caschroms* (McDonald 1872: 18). Yet such practices, even if the objects of outsiders' derision, were a sensible answer – short of emigration – to a miserable land–labour ratio.

Farm output too was subject to marked regional variation (Overton 1986). The southern and eastern counties, for example, were the main cereal-producing area throughout the period; the south-west had most orchards; Lancashire and Cheshire specialised most intensely in dairying. Since the price slump after the mid-1870s was confined largely, though by no means entirely, to grain prices, it is not surprising that a minority of the Royal Commissioners of 1894–7 felt obliged to point out that 'the depression has been and still is far more serious in the southern and eastern counties of the United Kingdom'. One fair indication of spatial spread is the fall in assessments of land value. In ten counties – Berkshire, Cambridge, Essex, Huntingdon, Kent, Norfolk, Northampton, Oxford, Suffolk, Wiltshire – assessments declined by over 30 per cent between 1879–80 and 1894–5, while in Cheshire and in Cornwall the decline was less than 10 per cent over the same period (Parliamentary Papers 1897: XV, 10).

When wheat prices fell, farmers in the south and east reduced their acreage more slowly than elsewhere, and much of the reallocation that did take place was through 'tumbling down', that is, disinvestment in the land, or through using it for other cereal crops. As a result the ten most depressed counties listed above accounted for 31 per cent of the wheat acreage in Great Britain in 1874, and 40 per cent in 1913. But one should not conclude that the south-eastern farmer was simply more set in his farming ways than his northern or Scottish counterparts. The stiff clay soils of the main corn counties were costly to switch to other uses, and the lower rainfall in the south-east, while good for grain, also limited the growth of grass. Nor was the slower shift out of grain in the south and east due entirely to greater adjustment costs. Since the decline in wheat acreage was accompanied by an increase in the average yield per acre, and by a tendency, though slight, for the dispersion in yields to narrow, it would seem that those counties which reduced acreage most were marginal wheat producers. So even if adjustment costs had been zero it is likely that acreage decline would have been less in the south-east.

Price trends and improving communications also affected the pattern of regional specialisation in livestock (Whetham 1979). Before steam navigation, most British cattle were brought to market by drovers, but the steamship and railway meant that animals could be sent direct to consumption points, quickly and without loss of condition. The change allowed some areas, previously too isolated, to concentrate on beef fattening (Perren 1978: ch. 2). Fattening gave way to dairying in those areas where the latter was an economic proposition, as in the south of England, though less so in Scotland and Wales (Orwin and Whetham

1964: 137, 358). Pig numbers increased by about 15 per cent between the late 1860s and the First World War, but the increase was again subject to marked regional variation. The pig population grew most in dairying and potato- and fruit-growing counties, where feed was relatively cheap and increasing in supply, but decreased markedly in most of Scotland, Wales and the English midlands. The result was an increase in the coefficient of variation of pig numbers across counties from 0.98 in 1869–70 to 1.16 in 1909–10 – or from 0.57 to 0.71 for English counties alone. This is best interpreted as a move towards increasing specialisation by British farmers, as local markets merged into one national market.

Adjustment outside the south-east was less traumatic because soils were more adaptable. Indeed, it is likely that some mixed farming and dairying areas were better off on account of the decline in prices. The cost of the grain they fed to animals fell. Free trade and cheaper long-distance transport paradoxically improved their competitive position. Fletcher has argued that in Lancashire milk producers could buy maize and oilcake for a third less at the end of the century than thirty years earlier, while the prices of their output, milk, hardly dropped at all. The same can be said for poultry and pig farmers (Fletcher 1961).

Factor movements

What of factor movements between regions? Though precision here is impossible, emigration from rural areas almost wiped out the natural increase: in England alone, the population of England more than doubled between 1841 and 1911, but that of rural areas rose by only 13 per cent (Baines 1985: 215–17). Farm labour accounted for much of this migration. The migration of farmers was less important. The British system of land tenure, at least in theory, encouraged an active land market and thereby mobility. A rent-maximising landlord would let to the group of tenants – presumably a shifting group – offering the highest prospective return on his property. But in practice this did not generate much farmer mobility, particularly between regions. The post-1880 period marked the real beginning in Britain of a long-range migration of farmers within the agricultural sector. The migration was largely from the north and west to the south and east: contemporaries noted especially the influx into Essex and Suffolk from Scotland. The farmers moved largely because they were prepared to accept a lower return on their labour and capital than their southern and eastern counterparts. 'They and their families', reported Assistant Commissioner Wilson Fox to the Royal Commission of 1894–7, 'work immensely hard. The Scotch women certainly undertake work which no Suffolk woman would dream of doing', while the men 'practically take the position of working foremen or bailiffs, being up in the morning when their men arrive and occupied with work connected with the farm after they leave at night' (Parliamentary Papers 1895: XVI, 67–8).

Free trade: agriculture and the consumer

Before mid-century Britain's livestock sector was protected by transport technology from intense foreign competition. There was then a marked rise in imports of sheep and cattle, coupled with a shift towards distant sources of supply such as Argentina and New Zealand, and towards dead meat (chilled and frozen) over live animals (see Figures 6.1–6.4 and Perren 1978). The price of meat declined, but the rise in meat imports did not prompt the same clamour for protection as did that in corn.

Free trade in corn

In 1848, soon after the repeal of the Corn Laws, the free trade campaigner John Bright reminded his fellow members of the House of Commons that 'the industry of this great and growing population has escaped from the pressure of that screw, which, through the medium of the Corn Laws, you had laid upon the necessaries of life' (Bright 1869: 428). Yet the relative prosperity of the 'high farming' decades, evidence that the acreage under corn held its own for a time (Kain and Prince 1985: 173–4), and especially the buoyancy of corn prices, has led some to the conclusion that Corn Law repeal was of less economic than political import. Thus Kitson Clark has argued that 'the attack on the Corn Laws should not be considered for a moment as a clear demonstration of economic truth, nor even as a passionate statement of economic opinion, but more as an outpouring of social opinion, using a symbol or a myth as a catalyst' (1951: 3). The argument may be true, but the usual evidence for it is inconclusive. It neglects the unprecedented increase in corn imports that took place during the 1850s and 1860s, a rise which the uncertainties of the 'sliding scale' and the attendant risks for corn exporters before repeal would almost certainly have made impossible. Indeed, in the decade before repeal, imports of corn accounted for only a twelfth of total consumption, while by 1869/71 they were almost half. The assertion that the price of corn would have been the same, repeal or no repeal, is therefore false. The benefit to consumers, it is true, became more visible after 1879, when corn prices began to fall markedly. By 1888–92 domestic production of wheat had fallen to two-fifths of consumption requirements: on the eve of the First World War the proportion was slightly over one fifth.

Supply and demand curves offer a simple method of estimating the static gains and losses to British consumers and producers of free trade in corn,

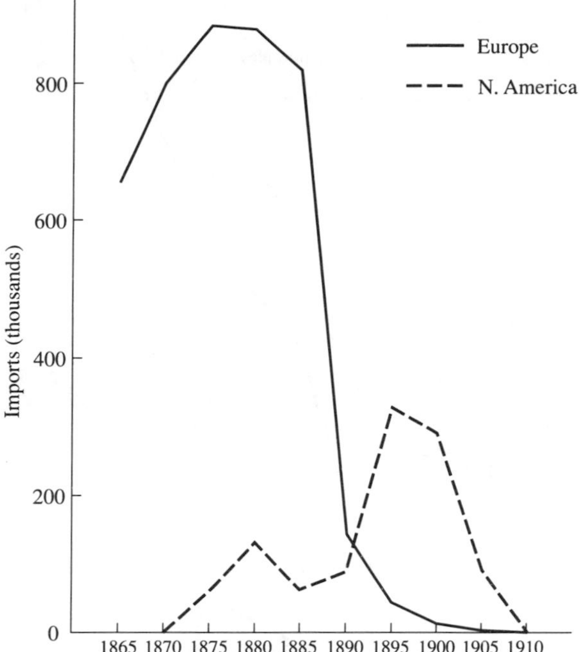

Figure 6.1 British sheep imports, 1865/9–1910/13
Source: Perren (1978: 131, 164, 213–14).

and in particular wheat. The corn market before repeal can be represented as a result of a tariff imposed on the world price of corn, pushing the British price up, encouraging British farmers to supply more, and (incidentally) encouraging British consumers to demand less. This was the entire point of the tariff: to enrich agriculture at the expense of the rest of the nation.

In Figure 6.5 the enrichment of agriculture is measured by the shaded area, the rental income lost by repeal. Point A is the actual domestic output of wheat and its price after repeal. In 1888–92, for instance, it was a quantity of 7.4 million quarters (of eight bushels each) selling for about 32s a quarter. Point C cannot be observed from the historical data; it is the counterfactual output and price, that is, the output and price that would have been observed had a tariff (of 18s) brought the 1888–92 price back up to its pre-repeal level of about 50s a quarter. We could estimate C if we knew the slope of the line from A to C. We do not know it, but we can make a reasonable guess (in the light of the results given above) that it was roughly the slope corresponding to unit elasticity – in other words, that the supply curve was roughly a ray through A and the origin 0. In such a case domestic output would, under a tariff, go up in proportion to the rise in

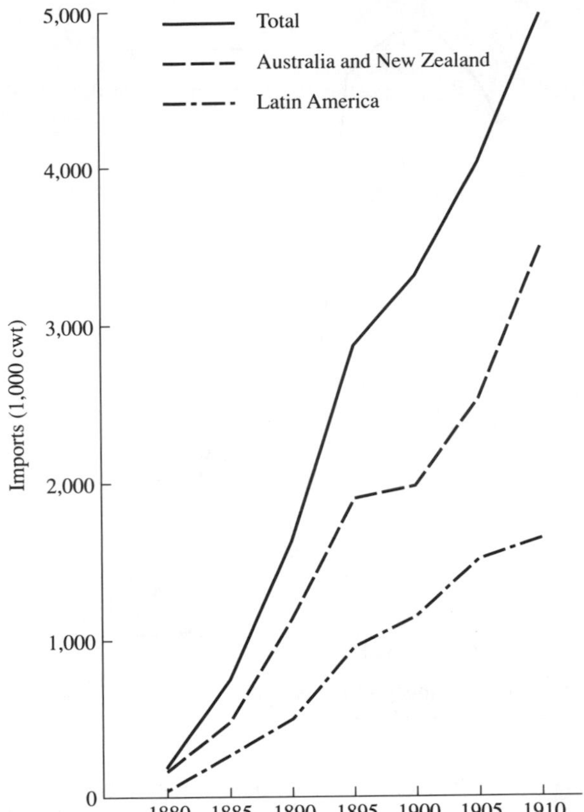

Figure 6.2 British mutton and lamb imports, 1880/5–1910/13
Source: as for Figure 6.1.

price, namely, in the proportion of 50 to 32. The actual domestic output of 7.4 million quarters of wheat would therefore have been 7.4 multiplied by 50/32, or 11.6 million quarters. Let us assume that the world price was uninfluenced by British demand; since even in the 1880s British imports consumed only a fraction of world production, this is not so far-fetched. Now it is a simple exercise to find the area of the trapezoid: its height (18s per quarter) multiplied by the average of its lengths (7.4 and 11.6 million quarters), or

$$(18s\ \text{per qr}) \times [(7.4 + 11.6)/(2)\ \text{m qrs}] = 171\ \text{million s}$$

or £8.55 millions. This figure is some 5 per cent or so of all agricultural income in 1888–92, or less than 1 per cent of national income. What producers gained, consumers lost, at least approximately – the other large

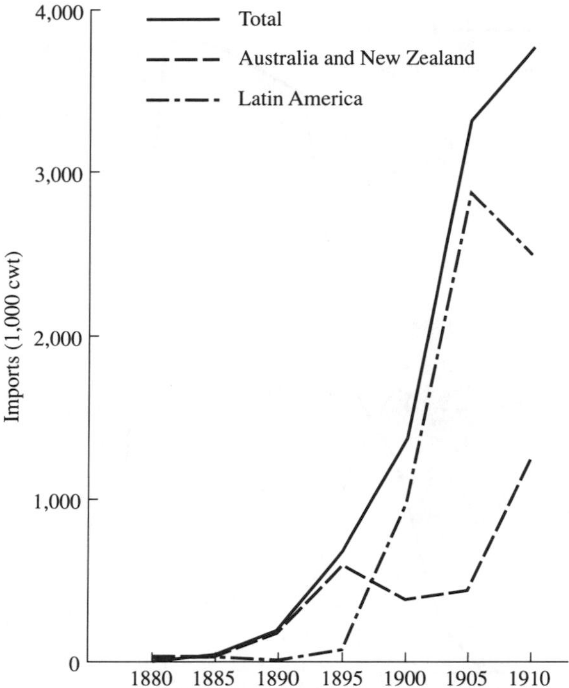

Figure 6.3 British beef imports, 1880/5–1910/13
Source: as for Figure 6.1.

element of the consumers' loss was the government's revenue on this account which would have been offset by lower taxes imposed on consumers at some other juncture. Curiously, the farmers' and landlords' campaign for an import duty of 5 per cent in the 1890s and 1900s (Fussell 1983) mirrored closely the implied transfer to agricultural producers prior to repeal (for corroboration, Williamson 1990b).

Food imports

The transfer from consumers to producers was not the only issue in commercial policy, especially in the early years of the twentieth century. The United Kingdom became increasingly dependent on food imports after repeal. While repeal itself and population growth was largely responsible for this, the role of technical developments in transport and storage should not be forgotten. Half the price reduction in American wheat was due to lower freight charges, while new cold storage and refrigeration techniques allowed the importation of frozen meat and New Zealand butter from the early 1880s on. By 1910–14 consumers relied on

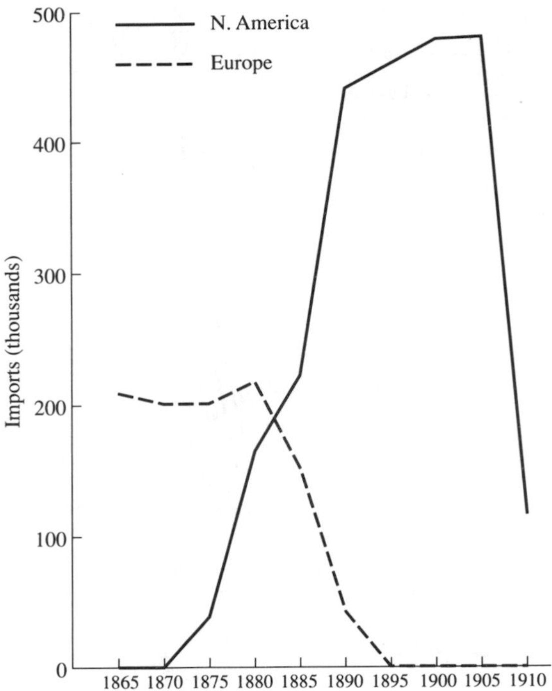

Figure 6.4 British cattle imports, 1865/9–1910/13
Source: as for Figure 6.1.

imports for the greater part of their bread, butter, cheese and fruit, as well as 40 per cent of their meat and a third of their eggs. Not surprisingly agricultural protectionists increasingly returned to home truths in the style of Adam Smith about defence being of more importance than opulence. They warned against the dangers of 'a hostile combination of European nations' starving Great Britain into submission, arguing in effect that the gains from free trade were rapidly diminishing as the probability of open conflict increased. The cost of such an insurance policy of self-sufficiency in grain, however, would have been substantial. And the silliness of such a policy – plain to all except some farm lobbyists – was underlined by a member of Parliament who pointed out that self-sufficiency for insurance amounted to assuming that Britain 'was going to be at war with all the nations of the world for ever'. Government policy was to rely instead on a strong navy to meet any potential blockade, and on the substitution possibilities within the economy itself to increase domestic food supplies in the short run, if necessary. This policy was vindicated when war came in 1914 (Offer 1989: part 3).

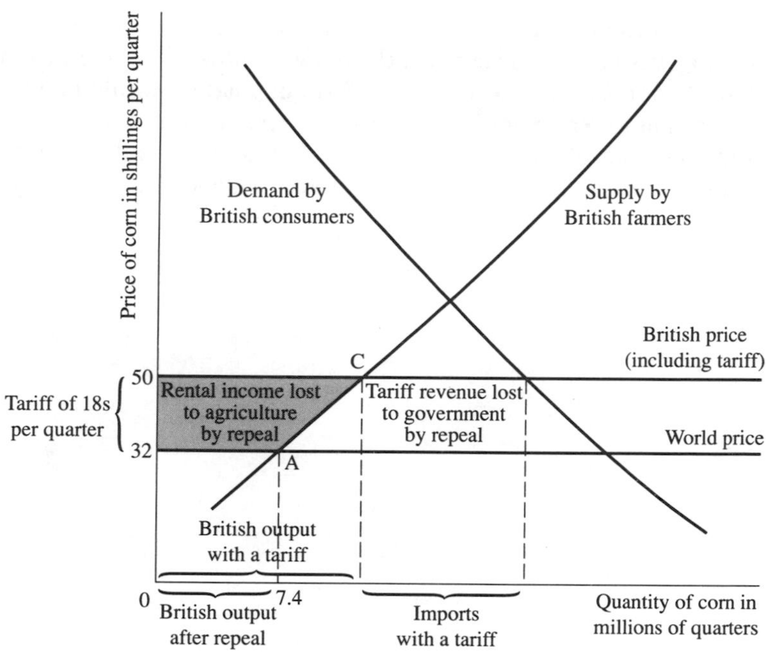

Figure 6.5 The effects of free trade in corn

Conclusion

By 1914, Great Britain was relying on imports for more than half its food. Its agricultural labour force, which peaked in 1861 or thereabouts, declined almost continuously after then, as did agriculture's share in GNP. No other country experienced such a transformation during the nineteenth century. The change was naturally not without trauma: for farmers who relied on cereals for most of their income these were trying decades. For them there was indeed a 'Great Depression' in farm incomes, though for others the picture was less bleak. Moreover, British agriculture did not perform famously in the face of foreign competition, judged at least by its relatively sluggish productivity growth. We have suggested that slow responses within agriculture itself were less to blame for 'decline' than the gradualness with which the farm population reconciled itself to a reduction in numbers. Between 1860 and 1914 the number of farmers dropped by 10 per cent, but virtually all the drop had occurred before 1881. Evidently for every farmer who died or moved out of agriculture, there was a son – or a Scotsman – to replace him. Contemporaries argued that many farmers 'were dipped too deep to move', while others remained on in the hope of getting 'a reasonable amount of their capital back' (Bellerby 1956: 65). A more important reason surely is that the psychic income element in British farming was large, and stemmed the outward flow before the First World War. A more substantial fall in the farm population would undoubtedly have meant lower domestic agricultural output, and some of the marginal land going out of cultivation. On the other land, it would have meant a more efficient use of resources, and therefore a higher productivity growth.

7 Foreign investment and accumulation, 1860–1914

Michael Edelstein

Introduction

Great Britain's immense export of capital is among the most important events of the late nineteenth century. Rising in the 1850s and 1860s, the flow of net foreign investment averaged about a third of the nation's annual accumulations from 1870 to 1914. As a result of the annual flows the stock of net overseas assets grew from around 7 per cent of the stock of net national wealth in 1850 to around 14 per cent in 1870 and then to around 32 per cent in 1913. Never before or since has one nation committed so much of its national income and savings to capital formation abroad.

To some observers the immense capital export went abroad because of the high profitability of railroad and other social overhead investments in the emerging primary product economies of North America, South America and Australasia. Others have argued that the capital export was a result of weaknesses in the domestic British economy. In one variant domestic investment demand weakened due to a pause or slowdown in British productivity growth – a productivity climacteric – and, because Britons continued to save despite slowing domestic investment demand, funds moved abroad by default. Another variant argues that the British distribution of income and wealth led to tendencies to oversave, with the excess carried off abroad. Institutional factors are also said to have influenced the capital export.

If there is controversy about the reasons for the immense capital export, there is also controversy concerning its effects. On the positive side it is often argued that the capital exports paid a higher private rate of return than domestic investment and, given a secularly low unemployment rate, it thus augmented British incomes more strongly than alternative domestic investments. Furthermore, by helping to lower the costs of overseas transport and extending the margin of cultivation and mineral extraction into hitherto inaccessible but highly productive soils and deposits, British capital exports helped to lower the cost of British imports of food and raw materials.

Sceptics, however, have argued that the capital export may have had a number of pernicious effects. First, some have argued that in fact the realised return from investment abroad was lower than at home, on account of widespread defaults by spendthrift overseas governments and railway executives. Second, it is sometimes argued that the distribution of British incomes was more sharply skewed by directing British savings abroad. Had these funds remained at home they would have helped to augment the stock of domestic housing and other urban social overhead projects, which would have more widely benefited the British populace than the uses to which the overseas profits were employed. Finally, modern studies of technical progress have found that an important source of productivity growth stems from the accumulated experience of production, often termed 'learning-by-doing'. If, as seems to be the case, British capital exports tended to increase the demand for the products of the older export industries, it might be argued that to some degree the newer segments of the British capital goods industry were inadvertently starved of demand during their infant and later learning years, with consequent effects on the growth rate of British per capita incomes.

The pattern of foreign investment

Rates

Net long-term lending by Great Britain is thought to have made its first significant peacetime appearance in the 1820s (Cottrell 1975). In the seventeenth and eighteenth centuries joint-stock trading and colonising companies, interloping merchants and the individual owners of West and East Indian plantations gathered a certain amount of long-term funds for ships, warehouses, plantations and slaves. Wealthy Britons also held a certain amount of interest-bearing debt of various European governments. For most of the eighteenth century it is likely that these outflows of long-term capital were roughly balanced by inflows of Dutch and other foreign funds. Recent research has suggested that Britain became a small net creditor on international account in the late eighteenth century (Feinstein 1988b: 164). This secularly low level of international lending continued after the Napoleonic Wars, net foreign investment averaging 1 or 1.5 per cent of gross national product from 1811 to 1850 (Table 7.1). In the 1850s, however, the rate rose to 2.1 per cent and in the 1860s rose again to 2.8 per cent. From 1870 to 1914 the average rate was 4.3 per cent. Clearly, there was a major shift in the nature of British capital accumulation in the third quarter of the nineteenth century.

A second feature of British overseas investment in the late nineteenth

Table 7.1. *UK rates of savings and investment, 1830–1914 (%)*

Period	GNA/ GNP	GDFI/ GNP	II/ GNP	NFI/ GNP	GPS/ GNP	GS/ GNP	E/ GNP	PH/ GNP	PO/ GNP	Yr	OA/ GNW	OA/ NNW
1830–9	7·83	6·56	0·36	0·91								
1835–44	8·57	7·37	0·29	0·91								
1840–9	9·84	8·38	0·70	0·76								
1845–54	10·96	9·15	0·90	0·92						1850	6·02	7·04
1850–9	10·08	7·42	0·60	2·05								
1855–64	10·68	7·22	0·92	2·55			48·94	48·49	2·57	1860	8·91	10·57
1860–9	11·44	7·55	1·08	2·81			47·69	49·27	3·05			
1865–74	13·90	8·04	1·18	4·67			47·02	49·23	3·76	1870	11·90	14·16
1870–9	13·31	9·12	0·20	4·00	12·31	1·00	47·69	47·65	4·66			
1875–84	12·16	8·66	0·51	2·99	11·16	1·00	49·07	45·63	5·29	1880	14·83	17·74
1880–9	13·17	7·03	1·42	4·72	12·17	1·00	49·17	44·84	5·99			
1885–94	12·42	6·61	0·87	4·94	11·42	1·00	50·34	42·95	6·70	1890	21·05	25·46
1890–9	12·02	7·61	1·04	3·37	11·02	1·00	51·05	42·38	6·57			
1895–1904	11·76	9·12	0·67	1·97	11·76	0·00	50·93	42·85	6·22	1900	22·65	27·84
1900–9	12·61	8·75	0·19	3·66	12·61	0·00	50·70	42·54	6·76			
1905–14	14·13	7·20	0·42	6·51	13·13	1·00	50·15	42·05	7·80	1910	26·23	32·12

Note: GNP = gross domestic product at market prices plus net property income from abroad; GNA = gross national savings = gross national investment; GDFI = gross domestic fixed investment; II = change in inventories; NFI = net foreign investment; GPS = gross private savings (= GNA − GS); GS = government savings; E = income from employment; PH = income from home property (= GNP − E − PO); PO = net property income from abroad; OA = stock of overseas assets; GNW = gross national wealth, including domestic reproducible assets, land and overseas assets; NNW = net national wealth (GNW less depreciation on domestic reproducible assets).
Sources: the sources for domestic investment, foreign investment, public and private saving and gross national product are Mitchell (1988: 831–3), Feinstein (1988b: 462–3), Imlah (1958: 70–5) and Edelstein (1982: 315–23). The factor income ratios derive from Mitchell (1988: 828–9) and the wealth stocks from Feinstein (1988b: 464–5). Platt (1986) argues the overseas wealth stock estimates presented here are too high but his methodology involves some serious flaws (see Feinstein 1990b).

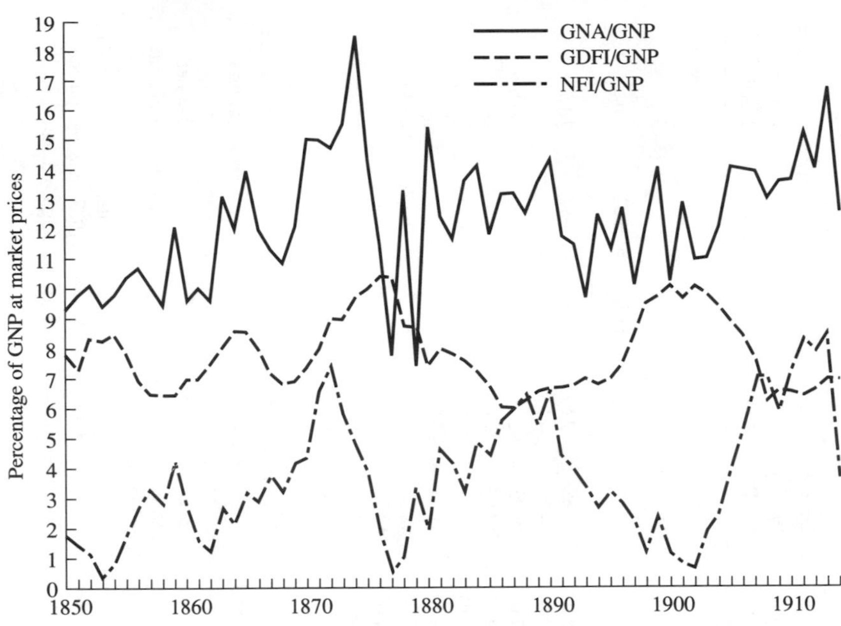

Figure 7.1 British savings and investment rates, 1850–1914

and early twentieth centuries was its volatility. As Figure 7.1 illustrates, the volatility was set in a repeating pattern of long cycles lasting between sixteen and twenty-four years. From troughs of 1.3 per cent of GNP in 1862, 0.6 per cent in 1877 and 0.8 per cent in 1901, the overseas investment rate went to peaks of 7.5 per cent in 1872, 6.6 per cent in 1890 and 8.5 per cent in 1913. Up to the early 1870s the broad fluctuations in the overseas investment rate roughly paralleled the fluctuations in the domestic investment rate, but thereafter the long movements in overseas and home investment moved inversely.

Direction

In the early 1850s about half the stock of UK overseas wealth was in European-issued securities and other assets – that is, bonds rather than direct ownership of foreign companies. A quarter of the loans made in bonds went to the United States, a sixth to Latin America and the rest to the empire (Jenks 1927: 64, 413, 425–6). Over the next ten years or so India and the Dominions replaced Europe as the dominant hosts of the British capital export. From 1865 to 1914 fully 34 per cent of the £4,082 million pounds of new securities for overseas investment issued in Britain went to North America, 17 per cent to South America, 14 per cent to Asia, 13 per cent to Europe, 11 per cent to Australasia and 11 per cent to Africa (Simon 1967: 23). Of the total stock of overseas securities held in 1913 computed at par (face) value (Feis 1930: 23) the largest national or colonial debtors were the United States (20.0 per cent), Canada and Newfoundland (13.7 per cent), India and Ceylon (10.0 per cent), South Africa (9.8 per cent), Australia (9.4 per cent), Argentina (8.5 per cent) and Brazil (3.9 per cent). The proportion of new issues going to the British empire, 1865–1914, was around 40 per cent and showed little variation over these fifty years (Simon 1967: 24, 28). Of the £2,400 million sent to the trans-European regions, 1865–1914, 68 per cent went to the regions of recent settlement, regions with a disproportionate demand for infrastructure and social overhead capital (Simon 1967: 25).

Direct versus portfolio investment

Before the nineteenth century and after 1945 most British overseas assets took the form of direct investments in overseas structures, land, plant, equipment and inventories by British businesses. Between those dates the bulk of British overseas placements took the form of British purchases of portfolio investment (Cottrell 1975; Edelstein 1982; Dunning 1983; Wilkins 1988). Overseas investment is called portfolio investment when the assets purchased are either the IOUs of governments or the equity and IOUs of private companies in which Britons own less than 30 per cent of the equity interest ('equity' means ownership, as in common stocks). When Britons own more than 30 per cent of the equity interest in an overseas private company their holdings of the company's stocks and bonds are termed direct investment. The distinction between portfolio and direct investment represents an attempt to mark off degrees of control which British wealth owners exercised over the use and management of their savings placed abroad. With 30 per cent or more equity ownership, the reasoning goes, British owners were able to control the use and management of their savings, whereas with portfolio investments the control is assumed to rest elsewhere.

In the years between 1850 and 1914 the proportions of portfolio and direct investment are not known with certainty. Recent research, however, suggests that the proportion of portfolio investment was probably in the range of 70–80 per cent of the total (Cottrell 1975: 11; Stone 1977: 696; Svedberg 1978: 769; Edelstein 1982: 33–7; Dunning 1983: 85). Svedberg's research indicates that in 1913–14 some 40 to 56 per cent of British investment in the low per capita income regions (Africa, Asia, Latin America) was portfolio in character. But these regions only absorbed a third of the 1913 stock of British overseas investment (Feis 1930: 23).

Portfolio investment was proportionately most important (around 85 per cent of the total) in the high per capita income regions (Europe, United States, the Dominions) where 64 per cent of UK overseas investment was placed (Feis 1930: 23).

Control, however, is a more complicated issue than the demarcation of portfolio from direct investment suggests. It was often the case that when Britons held 30 per cent or more of an overseas business' equity the ownership was dispersed among a large number of private individuals rather than concentrated in the hands of a few British owners or a large British business. No unity of control could be exercised. Furthermore the British-held equity and debentures of an overseas business were often held by quite different individuals or corporations. Britons, for example, owned an active and controlling equity interest in a number of Argentine railways but debenture ownership was dispersed and unorganised. British equity interest was also quite significant in Canadian railways but control was largely in the hands of Canadian managers, not the dispersed owners of Canadian equity and debentures in Britain (Patterson 1976: 16–7). British investors in US railways continually complained of their inability to influence the management of their equity interest, whether or not they were above or below 30 per cent equity ownership.

Away from railroads and other social overhead investments, foreign direct investment typically involved significant control by British investors. The principal categories of direct investment were the free-standing company and the multinational enterprise. Recent research by Wilkins (1988, 1989), a pioneering investigator of multinational enterprise, identified the free-standing company as a separate and important class of investment, particularly for Britain. The free-standing company characteristically had a small British head office and British capital, with nearly all of the company's assets committed abroad, in the style of the Belgian company in Conrad's *Heart of Darkness*. The companies had some difficulty managing their far-flung assets. Examples include Ceylonese tea plantations, American cattle farms, mining operations around the world, US textile operations. While other nineteenth-century countries making foreign direct investments might have used the free-standing company form, Wilkins thinks the British were its most active employers. The form kept British control. The few companies that survived to become major British overseas investments, such as Burmah Oil, were likely to have increased central control through a big managerial team.

The multinational enterprise differed from the free-standing company in that the multinational enterprise typically began as a domestic company with substantial production and assets in Britain: the typical case is Lever Brothers. British multinationals were usually found in the production of consumer goods and heavy engineering equipment (Chandler 1980; Nicholas 1982). Many British firms which invested abroad had technical or marketing strengths and began their overseas investment by creating a selling organisation or acquiring raw materials (Nicholas 1982: 616). In this sense their development was similar to the enlarging American corporations of the 1870s and 1880s, which grew through enormous batch production, forward and backward integration and mass marketing. But given the size of the UK market, the limits of its resource base, and its historic and massive trading relations, enlarging was more likely to be played out with a stronger overseas emphasis than in the US case. Furthermore, with tariffs in the United States, Europe, Canada and elsewhere rising from the 1880s onward, moving to overseas branches provided a means to continue to reap profits from behind tariff walls.

Yet there remains the question of why British overseas investment in the nineteenth and early twentieth centuries was predominantly portfolio (and even when direct most commonly with wide dispersal of the ownership). The explanation probably lies in the nature and size of the real capital purchased with British funds. Between 1865 and 1914 almost 70 per cent of British new security issues went into social overhead capital (railways, docks, tramways, telegraphs and telephones, gas and electric works) and 12 per cent went into extractive industries (agriculture and mining; Simon 1967). Very little, 4 per cent, went into manufacturing. Social overhead capital is lumpy; that is, the initial size necessary to give service, let alone to make a profit, is very large relative to the resources of either wealthy individuals or businesses. Consequently, social overhead capital has rarely been financed from the personal resources of a few individuals or businesses. The typical borrower for social overhead capital in modern times has been either a government or a large joint-stock company. Indeed, the institutions of joint-stock organisation and public issue of securities were created in the early seventeenth century, at least in part, as a private solution to the problem of the size and risk of social overhead projects and the resources of individual wealth holders (see vol. 1, ch. 12.) In the mid-nineteenth century the principal overseas borrowers for social overhead capital projects were either governments or mixed government–private enterprises (Simon 1967). During the second half of the nineteenth century, however, the trend was toward placements in wholly private, limited liability companies, probably reaching over 50 per cent of social overhead borrowings by 1914.

Short bursts

Except for the United States, British investment in particular countries or colonies between 1865 and 1914 tended to be concentrated in short bursts. Thus the greater part of British investment in Australia occurred in the 1880s and early 1890s, in Canada after 1900, in South Africa in the early 1900s and in Europe in the early 1870s and just before the First World War. Hall (1963) attributed this spurt-like involvement of British capital to the flexibility of British investors, shifting their aim with the appearance of new opportunities. Unquestionably the British investor was flexible, but the nature of the opportunities was also important. To some extent the 'one-shot' pattern of British overseas investment reflected the lumpiness of the social overhead needs of the regions of recent settlement, their initially limited savings resources and their immature capital markets. In a small country recently settled a large backlog of lumpy social overhead capital projects might have to accumulate before the return was sufficiently great to draw attention to the need for special funding arrangements. Going overseas for some of the entrepreneurship and capital might then be thought of as the cheapest means of arranging for such lumpy projects, leading to a spurt of foreign investment. Later economic development either did not generate as many lumpy social overhead projects or local savings and capital markets were now able to handle the lumps that did appear.

American borrowing from Britain was also variable, but it was always important. Given the size and pace of the aggregate movements in the US economy and its expansion into unsettled territory until the end of the nineteenth century, the continuous flow of British capital is not surprising. The major use of British funds was either for lumpy social overhead capital projects in the newly settled regions – above all the railways – or the purchase of new issues of the older US regions, thereby allowing Americans to purchase the frontier issues.

The causes of foreign investment

Hypotheses

In the late nineteenth and early twentieth centuries there were two streams of thought concerning why overseas investment had surged to such heights. One stream relied upon classical economic thought and saw the money flowing abroad because the rate of return on European capital had reached some sort of diminishing returns. By the late nineteenth century, many observers were aware that technical progress in transportation, manufacturing and agriculture might limit or prevent a fall in rates of return, but either the rate of invention or diffusion of new technologies did not provide enough profitable opportunities or there were still more resource, transportation and industrial investment projects with high returns abroad. Capital moved abroad because of a difference in marginal rates of return. The dispute is whether the funds were pushed out by fading domestic returns or pulled out by eruptively high overseas returns.

The second stream of thought is best represented by J. A. Hobson's work (1902). Hobson held that because too little of Britain's national income was allocated to wage earners, who did most of the nation's consumption, and too much income was allocated to property owners, who did most of the nation's savings, there was a strong tendency for a prosperous Britain to generate too little consumption and too much savings. The crucial assumption was that property owners saved irrespective of the rates of return they received. Given this invariance to rates of return and a tendency to generate too much savings, funds were inevitably pushed abroad searching for any use. Thus Hobson saw the rise in the rate of net overseas investment as an indication of inadequate domestic aggregate demand.

In sum the literature suggested that there were two possible reasons for funds being pushed out of Britain, namely, fading domestic returns or surplus savings. And it suggested a single reason for funds being pulled from abroad, newly high overseas returns.

The 1850s and 1860s

As already noted the rate of net foreign investment first jumped to significant levels in the 1850s and 1860s. It would appear that the flows were pulled abroad by newly high overseas returns rather than pushed by fading domestic returns or an excess of British savings, invariant to rates of return. Many places were growing fast and needed social overhead capital – but had small local savings and immature capital markets. In Australia the gold discoveries provided a strong field for British capital exports. After the Mutiny of 1857 the British wished to extend the Indian railway system, the better to move troops and emergency food-stuffs. Indian government guarantees of dividend and interest payments on railway equity and bonds were offered to draw British funds. With American cotton exports disrupted by the Civil War, railway lines to the cotton-producing regions of India briefly became a lucrative venture. According to Habakkuk (1940) some 40 per cent of the 1850–75 surge in overseas investment went to the British empire. Europe also offered a field for railway investments. But the widest field was the United States. With nearly half the world's track mileage to begin with, the US system tripled in size in the 1850s and then doubled in the 1860s. Great Britain's railway system was also expanding in the 1850s and 1860s, doubling the length of track. Some evidence suggests that the 1850–69 British expansion was into lines generating less profit than the earlier railway investments of the 1840s (Pollins 1957–8) but industry-wide averages of the return on real and financial railway capital show no sign of any downward movement (Broadbridge 1970; Hawke 1970). Thus it seems likely that if the surge of foreign investment in the 1850s and 1860s was motivated by a disequilibrating gap between overseas and home returns, the gap was created by newly high returns abroad rather than fading returns at home.

Another reason why the expansion of overseas investment from the early 1850s to the early 1870s might be attributed to pull factors is the similar pattern of behaviour across the Channel. These decades were among the strongest for French economic growth during the nineteenth century (Caron 1979: 11–13; Crafts 1984a: 51) and in France as in Britain the proportion of income devoted to foreign investment jumped significantly (Cameron 1961). Like the British overseas investments, the principal use of the French capital export was railway and other social overhead projects. Unlike the British the major receivers were European and Middle Eastern.

1870–1914: the role of return and risk

Having risen in the 1850s and 1860s, the ratio of British net foreign investment to GNP rose still higher after 1870, to an average of around 4.3 per cent, 1870–1914. As Table 7.1 and Figure 7.1 make plain, British foreign investment was highly variable during these years. British overseas lending surged twice, in the early 1880s, peaking in 1890, and another in the early 1900s, peaking in 1913. Again the principal use of the funds was railway and other social overhead capital. Geographically the chief borrowers were the regions of recent European settlement, the United States, Canada, Australia, New Zealand and Argentina. As earlier, the proportion going to the empire was steady at about 40 per cent. What balance of push and pull forces was responsible for the massive capital outflow of these years?

First, it must be asked whether overseas portfolio returns were greater than those available at home and, if so, when. If the capital market is reasonably competitive, differences among expected rates of return from one investment to another should not appear unless there are differences in the market's evaluation of their relative riskiness. Thus the only way one can examine whether there were differences in portfolio rates of return is to tabulate the historical record of capital gains and losses, dividends and interest payments, and then compute indices of realised returns. A recent study examined a sample of 566 home and overseas, first and second class, equity, preference and debenture securities (Edelstein 1982: chs. 5 and 6). The sample included issues from every sector of the capital market except overseas mining and foreign governments.

On comparable types of assets, 1870–1913, overseas portfolio investments yielded a higher return than domestic portfolio investments. The most important sector involved in overseas investment was the railway industry (Table 7.2). Except in the case of eastern European railway equity which attracted new British capital only in the early 1870s, overseas railways paid a higher realised return than domestic railway issues. The pattern also held in every other category of portfolio investment where comparison is possible: government, municipals, other social overhead investments and banking. When the entire sample of 566 securities including assets issued by domestic manufacturing and commercial companies is aggregated into weighted home and overseas return indices, overseas placements still offered a superior return to home issues (Table 7.3, column 1). On average, 1870–1913, overseas first and second class investments yielded a return of 5.72 per cent per year while home first and second class investments offered a return of 4.60 per cent. When evidence on returns to overseas mining (Frankel 1967) and foreign government debentures (Cairncross 1953) is taken into consideration, it appears that the average gap was probably somewhat larger.

But the higher return abroad may have been a reward for undertaking more risky investment. One can measure risk first by examining the amount of variation around the mean return on home or foreign assets, to see if returns varied more abroad. They did not; the variation was roughly equal at home and abroad. In addition, the return on foreign assets was less closely correlated with the rate of return on all assets than was the return on home assets (Edelstein 1982: 139). Overseas returns, in other words, were slightly less affected than home returns by the unavoidable risks of major economic disruptions and political events. In short, whatever measure of relative risk is used, it does not appear that foreign assets were significantly more risky than home assets.

What accounts, then, for the gap in risk-adjusted returns? The most plausible hypothesis is that overseas regions tended to generate greater amounts of profitable resource, transportation, industrial and marketing opportunities, which periodically led to higher returns abroad than at home. That is, the places were newer, like the American West.

Contemporary observers of the British economy were concerned to know whether the absolute level of British rates of return was declining. If

Table 7.2. *Realised rates of return to home and overseas railway securities, 1870–1913 (%)*

Region	Equity	Debentures
United Kingdom	4·33	3·74
Eastern Europe	2·58	5·33
Western Europe	6·31	5·28
India	4·97	3·65
United States	8·41	6·03
Latin America	8·43	5·33

Source: Edelstein (1982).

Table 7.3. *Realised rates of return, aggregate indices, selected sub-periods, 1870–1913 (%)*

	1870–1913	1870–6	1877–86	1887–96	1897–1909	1910–13
(*A*) *Domestic*						
(1) Equity	6·37	11·94	7·19	8·93	0·92	6·64
(2) Preference	4·84	9·08	5·70	6·10	1·85	3·25
(3) Debentures	3·21	4·36	4·12	4·92	1·40	1·84
(4) Total	4·60	7·62	5·37	6·42	1·35	3·60
(*B*) *Non-domestic*						
(1) Equity	8·28	7·34	13·27	5·34	9·54	1·37
(2) Debentures	4·92	6·29	6·40	5·16	3·82	1·90
(3) Total	5·72	6·60	8·06	5·23	5·20	1·79
(*C*) *Non-domestic minus domestic*						
(1) Equity	1·91	−4·60	6·08	−3·59	8·62	−5·27
(2) Debentures	1·71	1·93	2·28	0·24	2·42	0·06
(3) Total	1·12	−1·02	2·69	−1·19	3·85	−1·81
(*D*) *Market*						
	4·90	7·72	6·51	5·92	2·97	2·84

Source: Edelstein (1982).

one wants to know why capital flowed overseas, the more appropriate question is whether the gap between home and overseas returns was steady, increasing, or had some other pattern. The evidence of the first and second class securities is that the trend of *both* home and overseas realised returns was downward from 1870 to 1913. A far more prominent feature, however, was an inverse long swing in which one or the other dominated. These alternating periods of home and overseas dominance have the following dating:

1870–76	Home (weak)
1877–86	Overseas
1887–96	Home
1897–1909	Overseas
1910–1913	Home

In the long view it would appear that realised rates of return tended to anticipate the periods of home and overseas investment given in Figure 7.1. Early information of opportunities resulted in winnings which in turn stimulated the demand for physical capital and the issue of new long-term securities. Table 7.3 gives the aggregate indices of home and overseas returns during the alternating periods of home and overseas dominance.

Overseas returns dominated their periods of ascendancy more strongly than domestic returns dominated theirs, yielding the overall edge in favour of overseas returns. The years 1897 to 1909 was the strongest and longest such period. Latin American and United States railway, social overhead and banking securities were particularly strong. And nearly all sectors of the portfolio at home manifested low returns. In the previous period of overseas dominance, 1877–86, returns to home equity in textiles, drink, mechanical equipment, chemicals and communications held up well. Returns to mechanical equipment and textiles were probably responding to some extent to the direct and indirect effects of the period's large overseas investments, while the remaining groupings represented relatively new and highly profitable industries that continued to yield high returns despite the general focus of investment on overseas projects. In the 1897–1909 period of overseas dominance, by contrast, no listed domestic industry showed healthy returns, and in fact home railways, canals, docks, tramways and omnibuses lost money for their investors.

1870–1914: the role of domestic savings pressures

The mere fact that overseas returns exceeded home returns at various points in the period from 1870 to 1913 does not mean that Hobson's push forces were not also present. It could be that there were gluts of private savings from British households and corporations but the gluts were not large enough to satisfy all foreign investment demand and reduce overseas returns to the level of home returns. What evidence is there that the forces of return, income and wealth tended to deliver too much savings? Was Hobson right?

One method of examining this question is to ask whether econometric estimates of the likely amount of British savings for the years 1870–1913 predict more British savings at foreign investment upturns than actually took place. A recent study of British savings behaviour, 1870–1914, shows that estimates of the likely amount of savings (based on relationships of savings to its determinants of income and interest rates) were much higher than the actual amount of total investment in two periods, 1877–9 and 1902–4 (Edelstein 1982: 185). An examination of Figure 7.1 reveals that both periods were the last years of a home investment boom and the first years of a strong foreign investment boom. The implication is that at least in its initial stages a boom in foreign investment was the result of a tendency for Great Britain to generate too much savings during the peaks of home booms. This is Hobson's observation, though not explained the way he proposed.

Another secular phenomenon which may have affected UK saving rates towards the end of this period was the shifting age structure of the UK population. With lengthening life expectation and declining birth rates from the 1870s the age structure of the UK population shifted strongly (Mitchell 1988: 5–7; see also ch. 2). The proportion of the population fourteen or younger was 35–6 per cent from 1851 to 1891 but then dropped across the 1890s and 1900s to 30.8 per cent in 1911. The proportion aged 65 or older rose slightly. Thus the total share of these dependent age cohorts fell from 39.9 per cent in 1891 to 36.1 per cent in 1911. Equally significant, the share of the population in the prime savings years, forty-five to sixty-four years old, averaged around 14.4 per cent, 1851–91, but then rose to 14.9 per cent in 1901 and 16.1 per cent in 1911.

Modern demographic and savings research suggests that life-cycle needs would cause saving rates to rise when the share of dependants fell and when the share of adults in the years of maximal saving rose. Whether the increased savings resulting from a reduced proportion of children was for the children's future education expenses, *inter vivos* gifts to the children to start businesses, or parental semi- or full retirement in old age is not known. With the increasing wealth and professionalisation of the middle and upper middle classes in the late nineteenth century, more educational investment and business seed-money was necessary to reproduce the class status of the parents in the children.

Furthermore, as the wealth of the Victorian middle classes and upper classes increased, more and more middle- and upper-class families could and did choose to retire from the workforce in older age, thereby requiring increased savings in their working years. It is likely that their years of maximal savings for retirement occurred after the period of household formation and child rearing but before diminished physical capacity reduced their incomes, that is, roughly the years from the savers' mid-40s to their mid-60s.

With regard to the working classes, it is fairly certain that before the appearance of state-funded, old-age pensions the working-class elderly laboured until death or infirmity cut them down. Still, diminished physical capacity or illness in old age might require support from their children or dissavings. The fragments of evidence suggest that the working class saved for spells of unemployment, not for old age. Interestingly, when state-funded pensions for the working class became available in the late 1900s the pensions appear to have raised working-class savings rates rather than displacing them (Johnson 1984).

1870–1914: some econometric evidence

Although these data on relative rates of return and aggregate British saving pressures are suggestive, it might be argued that each overseas region contained peculiarities in both its offerings of securities to Britain and the reasons Britons bought them. One can test the forces of push and pull in several ways. One widely applied method regresses indicators of annual variation in UK and an overseas region's investment opportunities on an indicator of the inter-country flow of capital between them. Descriptive statistics (incremental r-squares, beta coefficients) are then utilised to judge which nation's indicators statistically accounted for the largest portion of the annual variation in the inter-country capital flow.

The two studies of the flow of British funds to the US strongly suggest a capital movement which was dominated by the push of domestic British forces (Williamson 1964; Edelstein 1982: ch. 4). This domination was stronger in the early decades of the 1870–1913 period than it was towards the end. British investors could not find bonds at home that resembled American bonds – high return and medium risk. The investors were rich and wanted to take a flier. The result was a push. In the Australian and Canadian studies British variables dominated the annual fluctuations in their capital inflows from Britain by a small edge (Bloomfield 1968: 37–8; Patterson 1976: 35). By contrast, annual fluctuations in Argentina's capital imports were probably more strongly influenced by Argentine than UK indicators (Ford 1971; Edelstein 1982: 103). It would thus appear that the massive capital outflow from 1870 to 1913 was determined by both pull and push forces. It is also likely that the push forces were stronger in the last decades either through the diminished returns to domestic investment or through a secularly increasing savings rate.

1870–1914: institutional and legal factors

Institutional and legal factors may have pushed capital abroad. Many observers have felt that London, though the central capital market of the nation, tended to ignore domestic industry, especially the small and medium-sized firms, favouring overseas governments and enterprise (Kindleberger 1964; Landes 1969; Cottrell 1980; Kennedy 1987). It seems curious that a central capital market which was so flexible with respect to overseas regions could fail to see new industries and opportunities for profitable intermediation close to home. It is therefore sensible to ask whether in fact domestic industry had a significant unsatisfied demand for funds from London.

Probably it did not. First, in the mid-nineteenth century the older industries of Britain had strong internal sources of funding and easy access to local, provincial financing. In the late nineteenth century the firms in some older sectors began to enlarge in the face of the scale requirements of new technologies, or in pursuit of monopoly (Davis 1966; Hannah 1976b; Cottrell 1980: ch. 6). The expanding firms found it easy to raise external funding, from the 1880s onwards issuing stocks, preference shares and bonds. The new issues were offered locally, though often in London as well (the larger the new issue the more likely a reliance on London: Cottrell 1980: ch. 6; Michie 1987: chs. 1 and 4).

Second, virtually all of the newer industries, such as automobiles, artificial fibres, bicycles, telegraphs and telephones, found elastic supplies of venture capital either from local or London sources (Aldcroft 1968b). Two new sectors which may have had some difficulty raising funds in the domestic securities market were electrical supply and electrical equipment manufacturers. New firms involved in electrical supply found funding quickly in the early 1880s, but provincial and London capital markets were less welcoming thereafter. The evidence suggests, nonetheless, that the problem was not the structure of financial intermediation but rather that electrical supply firms faced obstruction from local and central government politics and regulation, and these obstructions dampened capital market enthusiasm (Hughes 1988: ch. 9). Some delay and outright denial of access to urban markets was due to municipal governments favouring existing private and public gas suppliers. In addition, legislation and the late nineteenth-century municipalisation movement threatened private investors with expropriation. Lastly, when alternating-current technologies appeared in the late 1880s, electrical supply firms were held to expensive small scales of operation by laws that gave each local government the right to have its own electrical generating plant. Likewise, electrical equipment manufacturers also had little trouble in finding initial finance. Their trouble was the limited market set by the stunted growth of the electrical supply system.

Automobile investment in the UK appears to have lagged the United States, France and some other European countries. The problem, however, was again legislative restraint, not British capital markets. Legislation passed in the 1860s required a man carrying a red flag to walk in front of an automobile, warning pedestrians and horse-powered transport, and limited the automobile to a maximum speed of two miles per hour. When the law was modified in 1896 the automobile manufacturers received immediate attention from provincial and London financial intermediaries and wealth (Lewchuk 1987: 138, 157; Michie 1988: 518–26). Again, initial British research on artificial silk (viscose) was backed by two private limited liability companies whose shares were held by British and German manufacturers. Courtaulds used £100,000 from its conversion to a public company to purchase the relevant patents, an investment which paid extremely handsomely (Cottrell 1980: 188).

With regard to the supply of finance it is well to point out that direct testing for investor bias in the pricing of capital market assets suggests that if there was a bias it was small and did not always operate in favour of overseas assets (McCloskey 1970; Edelstein 1982: 65–71).

Nevertheless, Britain did not have an institution which is widely considered important to the rapid advance of the German and US economies in the period. The large investment bank was capable of nursing large industrial firms from cradle to adulthood, complete with short- and long-term financing, engineering and accounting advice, and entrepreneurship. According to Kennedy (1987) the fundamental problem was that information about British industrial firms, particularly new ventures, was largely held within the firm by the principal owners. The wider public therefore was ill-prepared to support industry's external financing needs. Some sort of financial intermediary, Kennedy posits, was necessary to collect and analyse such information, fashion a financing package for new projects and offer financial instruments to the public which would diversify the high risks of these new ventures for the often quite conservative investing public. In Germany the financial intermediary that performed the function from the mid-nineteenth century onward was the large investment bank. Similar financial intermediaries became involved in US industrial and financial affairs in the late 1890s.

From the early nineteenth century the British banks developed good information concerning their industrial clients and used it to provide a mix of short- and some longer-term financing. But as British firm sizes rose after mid-century the banks lending long to the larger industrial firms put themselves and their depositors at some risk. After the banking crises of the 1870s the banks apparently left the field of long-term lending to industrial firms (Cottrell 1980: ch. 7; M. Collins 1989, 1990b). The amalgamation of banks created institutions big enough to handle large enterprises comfortably, but it appears that they offered long-term financing assistance on a limited scale before the First World War (Cottrell 1980: ch. 7). With the banks less involved, new British ventures had to rely more heavily upon the hodgepodge of provincial and London new issue firms and specialists which first appeared in the limited liability booms of the 1860s and 1870s. In the provinces, new issues were most often handled by lawyers but sometimes by accountants or specialised company promoters. The latter specialists were usually based in the larger capital markets of Glasgow, Manchester and London, generally appearing when the new issues were large, warranting non-local participation. Kennedy argues that there were only a few honest company promoters (e.g. Chadwicks, Ellerman, O'Hagan) and, in any case, they offered little or no aftercare for the firms and sectors which they had assisted at birth. The honest company promoters certainly made money so the question becomes why were they so few and why was aftercare so limited.

One important reason is that the problems of British industry were different from those of German or American industry. Davis (1966) found that British industry showed little tendency to change its location or sectoral distribution, and only a few sectors displayed significant economies of scale. This meant that industrial investment spending put less stress (demands for new facilities or lumpy firm and sectoral funding needs) on the British financial system than was the case in Germany or the US. Thus the existing British constellation of short- and long-term financial services was quite adequate and investment banks would not have been very profitable.

It is also notable that the new vertically integrated firms appearing in the US in the 1870s and 1880s, Swift and Armour in meat packing, Rockefeller in kerosene refining and supply, McCormick in reaping, Singer in sewing machines and Duke in tobacco, all relied upon local (i.e. provincial) capital markets and internal profits to get to their immense scales, not the New York capital market. Until the merger movement in the late 1890s, American new ventures faced virtually the same hodgepodge of personal and local capital market structures and services as did the British. Certainly Cleveland, Cincinnati, Chicago and the like were wealthy towns but so too were Manchester, Liverpool, Birmingham and the like. Nor could one argue that good information about industrial companies was more widely distributed locally or nationally in the US in these decades than in the UK. Investment banking's involvement with American industry begins in the late 1890s with the merger movement, a movement whose major effect was probably a significant increase in the degree of monopoly. Indeed, it is widely held that the efficiency gains from the unrationalised mergers of the 1895–1907 era were often quite limited (Chandler 1977; A. P. O'Brien 1988). What seems to explain the investment banking assistance for industry in both the US and Germany was the prospect of monopoly profits, importantly buttressed by protective tariffs. With free trade and a very high degree of competition, Britain was infertile territory for investment banking.

It is also well to point out that the constellation of long-term British financing facilities for industry was not static. The 1880s saw increasing use of preference and debenture new issues by industrial firms, clearly tailored to attract conservative investors. Perhaps there was some connection between the innovative use of preference and debenture shares and the fact that the banking sector lessened its involvement with longer-term financing after the banking crises of the 1870s. Furthermore the diffusion of telegraph and telephone facilities vastly improved the communication between provincial and central capital markets, giving greater depth to the nation's markets for outstanding securities, thereby offering safer prospects for new issues and venture capitalists (Michie 1987: chs. 1 and 4).

Investment banking was a well-known European institutional innovation by the mid-nineteenth century. Continental investment banks were quite willing to set up branches or new banks in other countries (Cameron 1961; Crisp 1967). Kennedy found several unsuccessful British attempts to start investment banks in the 1860s and 1870s. In describing the boom conditions in the domestic new issues of the 1890s, Michie notes several experienced émigré firms promoting new issues of both provincial and London enterprises. Given the availability of the continental model and the inability for the model to take root in Britain, together with the vigorous new issue markets in the provinces and London and the limited number of domestic company specialists in the central capital markets, it seems fair to conclude that there was simply no demand for domestic investment banking of the continental variety. If British financial institutions and wealth paid attention to overseas opportunities, it was the demand for financing which called the tune, not biassed capital markets.

Another aspect of the institutional framework for investment was the set of regulations on the purchase of assets by trustees (Keynes 1924). Most trusts gave specific directions on what investments should be purchased. In 1886 the *Economist* noted that municipal stocks, colonial bonds, English railway debenture and guaranteed stock, Indian guaranteed railway equity and even the better American railway bonds and equity were the securities in highest demand for these purposes. If, however, there were no specific instructions in the trust, the trustee was limited by statute. Up to 1889 the list consisted of Consols, Bank of England and East India stock and mortgages of freehold and copyhold estates in England and Wales. The list was enlarged by the Trustee Acts of 1889 and 1893 to include the stocks of English corporations and guaranteed Indian railways, the debentures of British and guaranteed Indian railways and a number of other securities.

The Colonial Stock Act of 1900 extended the list to registered and inscribed stocks of colonial governments. As Cairncross (1953) notes, however, the list was rather long to support a claim of special bias (cf. McCloskey 1970). The securities which were added to the list in the 1900 Act were already favourites for the vast majority of accounts where there were specific directions. Again, if these regulations did produce a bias, it was certainly very small (Davis and Huttenback 1986: 173; see also below).

The consequences of foreign investment

The role of defaults

What were the consequences of the massive capital overflow? Economic theory does not suggest that overseas investment by private investors will necessarily lead to increases in the welfare of the investing nation (Pearce and Rowan 1966). Even if the private realised rate of return is greater abroad, taking into account defaults and bankruptcies, there are several factors which may make the social rate of return differ from the private rate of return.

At one time it was argued that one advantage of home over overseas portfolio investment was that if there was default or bankruptcy, then the domestically located machinery and plant would remain in the UK (Keynes 1924). The argument, however, has a number of ambiguities. The ultimate receivers of a bankrupt overseas firm might be British citizens. Alternatively, consider a domestic firm which entered a new home market, found the profit too small, and ended in bankruptcy. Is this firm's specialised capital equipment convertible to other uses? Rather than undertake an examination of each case of default and bankruptcy, it seems sensible simply to ask whether the loss from overseas default and bankruptcy was so much higher than the loss at home that it outweighed the differential in rates of return.

Something like £1 billion was lost through domestic company bankruptcy, 1870–1913 (Edelstein 1982: 129–30). Domestic portfolio capital fell from around 67 per cent of UK-held long-term negotiable capital in 1870 to 55 per cent in 1913. Assuming the average was 61 per cent, net losses from overseas investment would have to be £640 million for overseas and domestic portfolio holdings to have been equally risky. The gross nominal value of defaulted government issues in the 1870s was around £60 million (Cairncross 1953), but at least 50 per cent of this was recovered. From 1880 to 1913 the worst overseas government defaults occurred during the early 1890s, when various Argentine government bodies defaulted on £40 million of debentures, but most of this amount was recovered by the mid-1900s. Thus, £50 million appears to be a plausible upper-bound estimate of the net losses from overseas government defaults, 1870–1913. Some £450 million was lost on overseas companies if it is assumed that the overseas rate of net insolvency was the same as that at home. Combined with the £50 million of government defaults the total lost overseas appears to be around £500 million, substantially short of the £640 million amount which would make the risks of overseas and domestic portfolio capital equivalent.

It is likely that the rate of net insolvency of overseas companies was somewhat higher than that at home because the overseas company portfolio contained more firms in risky extractive industries, but this rate would have had to be much higher before the losses from overseas and home default and bankruptcy would have become equal. In short the differential between overseas and domestic private rates of return seems to have been substantially unaffected by home and overseas financial failure.

Terms of trade

Consider the various factors involved in the balance of the social rate of return. One is the terms of trade. From 1870 to 1913 the terms of trade – the ratio of British export to net retained import prices – gently rose, by about 0.1 per cent per year (Imlah 1958). The sources of the change were various, but few would question the importance of social overhead and extractive capital formation abroad. In places like Australia, Argentina, Brazil, Canada and Mexico where the alternatives of water and road transport were missing the railway made a significant contribution to reducing the cost of transport from the interior regions to the coast. In the United States the gains were relatively smaller due to the excellent alternative of river and canal transport, but still were substantial. A substantial amount of hitherto inaccessible but higher productive soils and mineral resources became the cheapest sources of the world's agricultural and mineral goods. So the price of imports to Britain fell, bettering the terms of trade.

It is difficult to judge how much of the change in the British terms of trade was due to the capital exports for such projects. Technical change in agriculture and mining was partly responsible. Furthermore, in the absence of capital inflows from Britain the social overhead and extractive industry capital stock of the US, Australia and Canada would not have been smaller by the size of the actual British capital export. The capital import into these countries occurred because local savings supplies were relatively small and local capital markets were relatively immature. Borrowing from Britain represented a cheaper solution than relying on domestic resources, but not the only solution. While British funds to the smaller economies were often a high percentage of total local saving for a short period, they were never the only source of local savings. In the absence of British funds the local rates of return – for example on the profitable Latin American and United States railways – would have been somewhat higher, encouraging more local savings and financial intermediation services. Nevertheless in some of the smaller economies overseas, such as Canada and Argentina, British funds mattered a great deal; if British capital had remained at home, their development would have been slower and later, which would have affected the speed at which the British terms of trade fell. It is difficult to calculate how much of the movement in the terms of trade was due to this irreducible contribution of British capital export. But a broad swath of British society benefited from the relationship in the form of cheap grains, meat, and industrial products dependent on overseas raw materials (compare ch. 6).

Another potential effect of a pattern of capital export which is focussed on a particular region is that it may depress returns on British wealth which has previously been accumulated in that region, assuming all else held constant. The spurt-like character of British investment in most regions of the globes tended to minimise the problem, even if the evidence of declining returns in Table 7.3 suggests that it could not be totally avoided. Of course, a similar pattern of incremental investment pursued at home might, all else held constant, lower rates of return on the existing stock of domestic capital. But there is one critical difference. When rates of return fall as a result of an incremental investment, it may in turn lead to a fall in the share of national income accruing to capital and a rise in labour's share. If the incremental investment and consequent fall in returns takes place abroad, *overseas* labour benefits; if it occurs at home, domestic labour benefits. To complicate matters further, suppose that in the absence of incremental British capital exports, other foreigners replaced British investors or overseas locals saved more, thereby driving down the overseas rate of return. In this case the existing British investments abroad would decline in value. If returns on the incremental investment were greater abroad than at home then Britain as a nation might lose more by not adding to their overseas holdings than by adding to them.

All these hypotheses are quite legitimately open to both theoretical and factual challenge. For example, it is quite likely that investment in the undeveloped regions of recent settlement proceeded for a long time before returns diminished (setting aside the problem of all other things, particularly technology, not remaining constant). Yet both home and overseas returns did fall. So the issue is whether the good effects on the terms of trade exceeded the bad effects of a declining return abroad, when there is the possibility that other foreign overseas investment or savings might have expanded somewhat in the absence of British capital exports.

We have seen that there was a persistent, risk-adjusted gap between overseas and home returns in favour of foreign investments. Except in Canada, Argentina and a few of the smaller colonies, British contributions were small relative to local savings (Green and Urquhart 1976). It seems likely therefore that the good effects on the terms of trade outweighed the bad effect of diminishing returns. If this is so the social rate of return to overseas investment would still be larger, not smaller, than the private return.

Home investment and growth effects

The allocation of British savings between home and overseas outlets was largely a private affair in the nineteenth and early twentieth centuries, each investor balancing ambitions of return and risk. The capital market did not evaluate the social benefits of a project; indeed, due to information costs and other phenomena the capital market does not perfectly evaluate even the private returns. For example, housing typically pays a low return spread over a long period. If investors tended to be risk averse and myopic the private rate of return on housing would have been lower than the social return and in consequence private markets would not have built enough housing. If foreign investment had been restricted, and if, as suggested earlier, British property owners had continued to save, the fall in the rate of return would have lowered the rate of British total investment but there still would have been more domestic investment than actually obtained. It is, however, difficult to know what form that increased domestic investment would have taken; given the rentier character of much foreign investment the funds seeking steady income and security of principal might have moved to mortgages on urban property. It is an open question, however, whether the social gains from more housing would have counterbalanced the effects which overseas investment had on the terms of trade and on the purchasing power of labour over food and other imported necessities.

Perhaps more controversial is the question of whether any significant part of a counterfactually restricted flow of British foreign investment would have gone to domestic industry, especially the new industries of the late nineteenth century, or to domestic human capital formation, especially technical education. First, since few new industries in Britain complained about capital shortage, one wonders where and how much the counterfactual funding would have taken hold? Furthermore, the cost of financial capital was not a serious consideration for the expansion of British educational plant and equipment at the secondary or university levels.

The closest industrial competitors with Great Britain were in western Europe and the US. Their social structures for encouraging technical change were quite different from the UK. Infant industries were protected by general tariffs; industry in general was often thought to be infant relative to the UK. Scientific and technical education on the secondary level in Europe and in the universities in the US and Europe were widely supported by regional and national businesses and governments, in some places explicitly to challenge British technical competence. These same nations had developed strong traditions of universal primary education, fundamental to the production of a large corps of secondary and tertiary educated technologists and scientists. Britain probably fell behind its closest industrial competitors in secondary school science education in the late nineteenth century and university technical education and research clearly lagged in the 1870s and 1880s (Pollard 1989: ch. 3). These developments were significant because in the latter half of the nineteenth century the applicable scientific knowledge involved in electricity, chemistry, load-bearing, etc., became substantially greater and more complex. Formal education in basic science and technical applications from professors engaged in mixtures of university and private research were becoming the standard method for generating technical personnel and ideas for industry.

In sum, restrictions or overseas capital embargoes were not the prevailing method for encouraging domestic, scientifically based industry; tariffs and publicly supported general and technical education were. British private and social rates of return to industry might have diverged but it is unlikely that substantial sums were needed or would have found their way into the new, science-based, industries of the late nineteenth and early twentieth centuries with an overseas capital embargo. Such a policy would not have been sufficiently focussed to obtain the desired result. Had Britain wanted to alter its industrial direction, infant-industry tariffs and publicly supported secondary and tertiary technical education and research would have more certainly altered the private rates of return towards their social rates; these were the policies used successfully in the US and Europe and the ones closest to consideration in Britain.

8 Imperialism: cost and benefit

Michael Edelstein

The growth of the British empire

The expansion of British investment abroad from 1860 to 1914 was paralleled by expansions of trade, migration, culture and political sovereignty. Of the earth's land area, 10 per cent was added to the British empire. By 1914, with nearly a quarter of the earth's population and land mass the empire was the largest the world had known. The amounts of new territory taken in each half of the hundred years between 1815 and 1914 were roughly equal; many historians have given the last quarter of the nineteenth century the title, 'the age of high imperialism' but this overemphasises the extent of the territory acquired in that period. If there is a case to be made for singling out the period from the early 1880s to the early 1900s, that case must be that the acquisitions of these years were motivated by factors which were substantially different from those operating in the earlier part of the century (Wehler 1970; Hopkins 1973; Fieldhouse 1973).

The following factors are thought by some historians to have changed the nature of imperialism in the fourth quarter of the nineteenth century: the altered balance of European power following the Franco-Prussian War of 1870; the higher tariff levels emerging in the rapidly industrialising nations such as France, Germany and the US after the mid-1870s; the possible slowing of investment opportunities at home and the fear of reductions in opportunities in other industrial and independent nations; the problems of integrating a newly emergent and vocal urban working class into national political life; and finally the faltering political economies of the independent African regions which were involved in important trading relations with coastal European trading settlements. Some have argued persuasively that the value of the colony, the strength of its politics, the readiness of local rulers to collaborate with British purposes, the ability of the local society to undergo economic change and the extent to which domestic British and international politics allowed Britain a free hand had all operated in the earlier extension of empire rule in the nineteenth century

(Gallagher and Robinson 1953; Louis 1976). Similarly, at various times in the nineteenth century, Britain brought its political power to bear on a number of independent nations. This is often termed 'informal' imperialism, although a good deal of controversy surrounds just where such power was employed, how often and to what end (Gallagher and Robinson 1953; Platt 1973; Fieldhouse 1973; Louis 1976).

There are two aspects of these extensions of British political power which are of interest to British economic historians. First, there is the question of what role economic forces at home and abroad played in the extension of formal and informal empire. Second, there is the question of the economic benefits and costs of formal and informal empire. To some degree these two questions are separable; what caused extension of empire might have nothing to do with the consequences. For example, one motive of Britain's informal imperialism in China was the high profit expectations of Lancashire and overseas British merchants who saw the potential of the immense Chinese market; it is doubtful, however, whether the excess of benefits over costs ever approached these expectations. Conversely there were several territories which were acquired for substantially non-economic reasons but which yielded a large economic reward. Since these questions are to some degree separable the remainder of this chapter is concerned with the realised return to formal and informal empire; the motives for imperialism have been widely discussed (Cain 1980; Cain and Hopkins 1980, 1986, 1987).

The gains from the empire: measuring standards

By what standard should the gains from formal and informal empire be measured? One might, for example, sum up the net amounts of profits and wages shipped home to Britain, the net transfer of government monies to Britain, and divide this sum by the total of public and private capital placed abroad. The result would be the 'social' return from possessing, for example, India at a particular moment in time or over a specified period. The same sum of net private and public transfers home might be divided by British GNP, thereby making it possible to compare the possession of India with that of other types of British incomes. Either method, however, implicitly assumes that, in the absence of British imperialism, there would have been no economic entity called India from which Britons might have derived an economic return. Britain did very well in its economic relations with the United States without much, if any, employment of formal or 'informal' imperialism after the Treaty of Ghent ending the Anglo-American War of 1812–14. The Treaty restored the equal *status quo ante bellum* with regard to the trade and impressment issues but, more significantly for the future, it provided for joint Anglo-American commissions with equal weight for each nation to determine disputed boundary issues. To some undefined degree, a similar pattern of settlement and economic opportunities would have occurred in Australia, Canada, and some other parts of the British empire even if Britain had not ruled them.

To determine the gains from empire or imperialism, one must first define the 'non-empire' or 'non-imperialist' economy with which the 'empire' or 'imperialist' economy is to be compared. Lenin (1915) avoided this issue by arguing that imperialism was a stage of capitalism, thus making possible the interpretation that the world of the late nineteenth century could not present examples of 'non-imperialist' economic and political relations. It seems likely, however, that Lenin would not have characterised Britain's actual relations with Germany, for example, as imperialist. There was a sufficient balance of power between Britain and Germany to prevent any abuse of political sovereignty or inter-regional economic exploitation whether through a negotiated treaty or any other economic relationship. This reasoning suggests a second way of measuring the gains from imperialism.

If the state of political and economic relations between Britain and Germany (or France or the US) provides an example of 'non-imperialist' economic and political relations, then the gains to Britain from ruling India (for example) can be measured as the amount by which Britain benefited from its economic relationship with India minus the benefits she would have gained if Britain had not ruled India but merely traded with India as she did with Germany, France or the US. To be specific, as a direct consequence of British rule in India all Indian railway equipment in the nineteenth century had to be purchased from Britain. The gain or loss from this exertion of political power was not the profit from all British equipment sales, only that portion specifically due to the Raj purchase requirement or any other colonial policy affecting trade. Some railway equipment probably would have come from British factories even without the regulation. But like the first standard of 'non-imperialism' this one also has a hidden and somewhat artificial assumption. That assumption is that roughly the same economic opportunities would have been available in the colonised regions without British formal and informal imperialism. This counterfactual is artificial because if Britain had not meandered and fought its way into its nineteenth-century empire, it is likely that there would have been fewer regions of the globe involved in the world economy. Furthermore, other European powers might have filled the vacuum, and then imposed extra costs on Britain.

In the following discussion of the gains from empire, two standards of 'non-imperialism' will be employed. They will be termed, respectively, the 'marginal non-imperialist' standard, and the 'strong non-imperialist' standard. The 'marginal non-imperialist' standard assumes that the empire had the actual economic development that it underwent in the nineteenth and early twentieth centuries, but that at the moment of measurement of the gains it acquired the political independence and power of the US, Germany or France in its economic and political relations with Britain. This 'marginal non-imperialist' standard underestimates the British gains from empire because it overestimates the degree of economic development which would have taken place if there had never been a British empire; it does, however, measure the benefit of not relinquishing control of the territories at that particular moment. The 'strong non-imperialist' standard will assume that the countries of the empire were independent from British rule throughout modern economic history with consequent effects on their involvement in the world economy and their political power vis-à-vis Britain.

There is a further issue, not considered here, that of the benefit to the countries of the empire. Britain's net gain from empire does not imply that India, Malaya, Nigeria, Canada and the rest had a net loss from membership in the empire. For example, Britain may have been able through manipulation of trade, investment or other government policies to extract a net gain from India. Yet it is possible that the civic order imposed on India by British rule gave India economic advantages which would not have occurred in the absence of empire. Alternatively, the policies of the British Raj may have delayed an Indian industrialisation even as Britain may have lost due to the burdens of defence or other expenses. A separate calculation is required for each colony to assess whether it gained or lost from membership of the empire, independent of whether Britain gained or lost.

The gains from trade with the empire

Some theory

In matters of international trade, political sovereignty over the empire gave Great Britain two powerful policy levers: colonial tariffs and the regulations guiding the purchase of supplies for colonial government and mixed government–private enterprise projects. Both presented opportunities to favour domestic producers. Were they employed and with what gain or loss to Great Britain?

If we use the 'marginal non-imperialist' standard it is immediately evident that Britain gained from her empire. Tariff levels imposed by France, Germany or the United States were substantially higher than those of the colonies, even the white-settler colonies which were increasing the degree of their political autonomy across this period and imposing protective tariffs against heated opposition in the British Parliament.

If one wishes, however, to demonstrate the full power of domestic British interests the Indian case is revealing (Harnetty 1972). The British Indian government was short of funds due to expenditures connected with the Indian Mutiny of 1857 and wished to enlarge its tax base. The proposed method was to increase tariffs by a small amount. The duty would cover all imports, including cotton yarn and cloth. Lancashire cotton interests mobilised to put pressure on London to defeat the Indian government's proposal. The threat to their interests was clear; an infant Indian cotton textile industry of perhaps a half-dozen firms had recently appeared. Although Manchester interests were quite prepared to allow the proposed tariff to remain on other imports, they felt an exception should be made for British yarn and cloth. In the event, despite pleas from the Indian government, Manchester interests were successful and the British Raj financed the deficit by issuing debentures.

The trade flows in railway equipment are another example of the supposed gains from imperialism. Nearly all the Indian railway equipment was ordered from Great Britain in the nineteenth century. Legally, there was no choice because the British Indian government stipulated this pattern of purchase. But, given that many of the entrepreneurs guiding the construction and maintenance of the Indian railway system were Scots who wanted Scottish and English materials, the near-zero tariffs were probably more important than the stipulation. The pattern of Canadian railway purchases was also overwhelmingly British until the appearance of their first tariffs (Saul 1960b). At this point, as in a number of other Canadian industrial branches, a substantial resident Canadian industry appeared. The Indian railway system was larger than the Canadian until just before the First World War. Furthermore, as evidenced by the Indian cotton textile, jute and iron industries, Indian and British entrepreneurship, engineering and capital were not lacking in late nineteenth- and early twentieth-century India. It must, therefore, be concluded that here also free trade rather than direct regulation was the source of Britain's advantage.

The marginal standard

In exploring the size of this advantage in general, let us make the assumption that the relatively low tariff of the white-settler colonies was due to British rule. There is good reason to doubt the full force of this assumption; colonial parliamentary debate suggests that British politics and policies were not often involved directly in their tariff decisions. Still, the tariff levels of these white-settler colonies certainly gave political expression to the closer economic links between the manufacturing metropolitan country and the primary product economies overseas than was the case for countries outside the empire. Further, it will initially be assumed that the supply of British output is quite elastic, so that the actual level of British output was determined by demand forces and any shift in demand would have low costs. Obviously, these assumptions are questionable. For that reason the numbers which follow are to be taken as conjectures of direction and order, not precise magnitudes.

Assume that the colonial tariff rate was zero, while the 'non-imperial' rate was 20 per cent in 1870 and 40 per cent in 1913. These latter rates are close to the average tariff imposed by the United States at these two dates (Davis *et al.* 1969). British commodity and services exports were 30.3 per cent and 33.0 per cent of GNP at these two dates. The shares of commodity exports to the colonies in total British exports were 26 per cent *c.* 1870 and 36 per cent *c.* 1913. Assuming that the colonies bought the same shares of invisible service exports (an underestimate in all likelihood), colonial purchases of commodity and service exports represented 7.9 per cent (i.e. 26 per cent of 30.3 per cent) of GNP in 1870 and 11.9 per cent of GNP in 1913.

What percentage of GNP would have been lost if Britain had faced 'non-imperialist' tariff levels in its colonies? Assuming that Canada, India and others had exactly the same level of economic development as actually prevailed at these dates, the only hypothesised difference is the tariff-raising power they would have had if they became as independent as, for example, the US.

Wright's studies (1971, 1974) of nineteenth-century cotton markets suggest that the price elasticity of British demand for colonial products was probably below unity, say 0.75, and that the price elasticity of colonial demand for British goods was somewhat above unity, say 1.5 (see also Hatton 1990). If we assume first that the home and colonial marginal propensities to import were equal to 0.2, secondly that (as noted above) Britain's supply curves were highly elastic and thirdly that the imposed tariff levels would have been 20 percentage points and 40 percentage points higher than the existing tariff levels of 1870 and 1913 respectively, then we can calculate the gain to Great Britain from the actual state of near-free trade with the colonies. On the basis of these assumptions, it was 1.6 per cent of GNP in 1870 and 4.9 per cent of GNP in 1913. (Let Ecc and Ebb = the price elasticities of colonial demand for British products and of British demand for colonial products; Cc and Cb = the marginal propensities to import of the colonies and of Britain; qX = the share of British exports to the colonies in British GNP; dt = the change in tariffs; and dW

= the percentage change in British GNP due to the tariff change. Then, from Pearce (1970: 171), dW = qX[(Ecc + Cc)/(1 + Ecc + Cc + Ebb)]dt.)

Enhanced political autonomy for the white-settler colonies (Canada, Australia, New Zealand and South Africa) meant that the gap between their tariffs and the 'non-imperial' tariff was smaller than 40 per cent in 1913. About 45 per cent of Britain's colonial exports in 1913 went to the Dominions; if it is assumed that their average tariff was 20 per cent (an overestimate) then the gain to Great Britain from 'freer' trade with the Dominions and other possessions becomes 3.8 per cent of GNP in 1913.

The strong standard

If we now use the 'strong non-imperialist' standard it must be argued that if the empire territories had remained independent of empire rule, they would not have participated in the international economy to the same extent. One example is India where it is likely that the British Raj brought a more peaceful, unified, and commercially oriented political economy than would have been the case in its absence (Morris 1963; Mukerjee 1972). As a guess, let us assume that Britain's trade with India and the other, non-Dominion regions would have been 25 per cent of its existing level in 1870 and 1913 if there had never been British rule. (West African purchases of British goods quadrupled between 1870 and 1913 at the same time that British rule spread from a few enclaves to significant territorial sovereignty.)

To what degree would the economic development of the white-settler areas have been similarly inhibited by the absence of British rule? The US experience might be thought instructive because the US was also founded by British migrants who had a common core of political, cultural and economic institutions. Still, the US industrialised much earlier than the white-settler colonies of the nineteenth century, and had earlier and much stronger income and population growth. One alternative standard might be the pattern of growth and development in Argentina. Although the political and cultural traditions of Argentina were different from those of the British white-settler colonies, Argentina entered the international economy at about the same time as the future Dominions and had a very similar pattern of economic development. Argentina grew through extensive development of land and mineral resources, using largely British funds to build its railway and other social overhead capital. Argentina's consumption of British exports per capita was about 70 per cent of the average for the white-settler colonies, so let it be assumed that British exports to the white-settler colonies would have been 70 per cent of their actual level if these colonies had been independent.

Summing the 75 per cent reduction to British exports to the non-Dominion colonies and the 30 per cent reduction to British exports in the Dominion regions (weighted by their respective shares in British colonial exports), British colonial exports in 1870 and 1913 would have been 45 per cent of their actual levels under this 'strong non-imperialist' standard of the gains from empire. (The shares of white-settler and non-white-settler colonies in British exports to the colonies were approximately 45 per cent and 55 per cent, respectively. With their 'strong' non-empire levels hypothetically reduced to 0.7 and 0.25, respectively, of their actual levels, British exports to both types of colonies would have been = 45 per cent (0.7) + 55 per cent (0.25) = 45.25 per cent of actual levels.)

The 'strong' gain is the difference between the actual British empire exports and this hypothetical 45 per cent level in the absence of empire. British exports of goods and services to the empire were approximately 7.9 per cent and 11.9 per cent of GNP in 1870 and 1913; therefore the 'strong' gain from empire was 4.3 per cent (i.e. 55 per cent of 7.9 per cent) of GNP in 1870 and 6.5 per cent of GNP in 1913 (Table 8.1).

The gains from investment in the empire

The marginal standard: analysis

Would the amount of Britain's investment in its colonies or its returns have differed from the actual amounts in 1870 and 1913 if we assume that the colonies were as integrated into the world economy as they in fact were, and as independent as the US, France and Germany, that is, the 'marginal non-imperialist' standard. First, it seems fairly certain that both Dominion and non-Dominion regions would have had many social overhead and primary product capital projects worthy of local and international financial interest. Furthermore, it is likely that their governments (assumed independent) would have participated in the financing of the social overhead capital projects. From 1850 to 1871 the government of the United States regularly gave land grants to help attract domestic and overseas investors to the equity and debenture issues of US private railway companies; the same policy was pursued in Canada and Argentina. In France, Germany, Russia and, indeed, throughout Europe, the nineteenth-century railway network was constructed partly at state expense (financed with government debentures) and partly privately (the interest on railway company debentures guaranteed by the state). Government subsidies and government guarantees of internationally marketed, private railway debt instruments were standard financing modes for the independent nations of Latin America and Asia. It is therefore likely that under the 'marginal non-imperialist' standard similar types of debt instruments would have

Table 8.1. *Some conjectures on the gains from imperialism, 1870 and 1913 (% of GNP)*

	Standard of 'non-imperialism'			
	'Marginal': same level of economic development: US, German, French standard of international economic development		'Strong': independent nineteenth-century political and economic policy	
	1870	1913	1870	1913
Exports of commodities and services	+1·6	+3·8	+4·30	+6·50
Overseas investment	−0·20	−0·94	+0·31	+0·45
Net government transfers				
a. direct assistance	−0·06	+0·11	−0·06	+0·11
b. defence	−0·04 to −1·01	−0·23 to −1·40	−0·04 to −1·01	−0·23 to −1·40
Total	+0·33 to +1·30	+1·57 to +2·74	+3·54 to +4·51	+5·66 to +6·83

Source: see text.

been issued to finance social overhead investment projects and, given the lumpiness of this sort of investment, these securities would have been internationally marketed like those of places like the US and Argentina.

The question of the gains from imperialism ('marginal non-imperialist' standard) now becomes how much of this debt would have been funded in Britain and at what cost to the (hypothetically independent) borrowers. There can be little question that the British capital market treated empire borrowers differently from foreign borrowers. Davis and Huttenback (1986: 171–4) recently examined the yields on 944 domestic, colonial and foreign government securities issued in Britain from 1882 to 1912. Employing regression analysis, Davis and Huttenback attempted to estimate the interest rate differentials among six political-economic groupings: domestic British governmental units, colonies with responsible governments (i.e. the white-settler Dominions), colonies with dependent governments, India, foreign governments in developed economies and foreign governments in underdeveloped economies. Given the Consol rate, the amount of the issue and its average maturity, in one regression test covering the entire data set, Indian government interest rates were 0.64

percentage points above the UK municipal government rate, dependent colonial governments were 0.84 percentage points above, responsible colonial government issues were 1.14 above, independent developed countries were 2.04 above and underdeveloped independent countries 4.26 percentage points above. (In a test of the impact of the above described Colonial Stock Act among empire issues, Davis and Huttenback (1986: 173) found that post-1900 average yields for empire government issues declined relative to pre-1900 yields by only 0.16 percentage points.)

Recasting Edelstein's sample of first and second class securities into domestic, colonial and foreign groupings, Davis and Huttenback found that the average realised return per annum, 1870–1913, on UK railway debentures was 3.77 per cent, colonial railways, 4.48 per cent and foreign railways, 5.72 per cent (Davis and Huttenback 1986: 81). A similar rank order characterised domestic, colonial and foreign railway equities and non-railway social overhead equity. In sum, government and railway securities issued by Dominion and non-Dominion colonies were typically financed at lower interest rates than independent foreign nations at similar levels of economic development.

Some portion of the explanation for the lower colonial government derives from parliamentary loan guarantees. Even stronger, Indian government bonds carried the full backing of the British government and were listed in the official rosters of the London stock exchange with 'British funds'. Parliamentary loan guarantees were used for the debt issues of the white-settler colonies with responsible government through the 1870s but little thereafter. Before 1900 debt issued by the governments of the dependent empire nearly always came with some sort of London guarantee. With the passage of the Crown Colonies Loan Act of 1899 and the Colonial Stock Act of 1900, unguaranteed issues from the governments of the dependent empire began to appear. Throughout the late nineteenth and early twentieth centuries most debt issues of the dependent empire were very carefully scrutinised by the Colonial Office. The monies raised were almost always used for pre-designated projects and projects were expected to generate income which would defray the interest and amortisation expenses of the debt.

But, even when London backing and oversight were absent from colonial government issues (e.g. colonial municipal debt), the British capital market charged lower interest rates than comparable securities from independent nations at similar levels of economic development. Private colonial railway issues usually involved colonial government support but no more than Argentine or US private railway issues and these colonial securities also showed lower issue yields and realised returns. The strong inference is that colonial status, apart from the direct guarantees, lowered whatever risk there was in an overseas investment and that investors were therefore willing to accept a lower return. In some colonies, particularly the newer ones, British rule and law directly reduced the potential losses from default and bankruptcy. In others, risk and uncertainty were reduced by the justice which was expected from colonists of British extraction.

The marginal standard: measurement

It is thus clear that membership in the British empire involved a more favourable interest rate on the financing supplied by Britain to both the responsible and the dependent empire. Attempting to measure the extent of the subsidy, Davis and Huttenback use their regression equation for government yields to estimate how much the colonies would have paid if they were forced to pay interest at rates similar to foreign governments. In this exercise the colonies with responsible government (synonymous with Dominion status by 1914) are treated as if they were foreign governments with developed economies and the colonies with dependent governments (non-white-settler, non-Dominion) are treated as foreign governments with underdeveloped economies. It is further assumed that these governments, now hypothetically independent, still borrowed as much as they did as colonies. Davis and Huttenback thus provide a highly useful estimate of the value of the implicit interest subsidy paid by Britain to the members of the British empire.

This subsidy constitutes a cost of imperialism to the British under the 'marginal' standard of non-imperialist behaviour. If the colonies are assumed to attain the independent power status of the US, France, etc., in 1870 or 1913, this cost would disappear because the ex-colonial regions would pay interest rates something like Davis and Huttenback's hypothesised market rates. The subsidy to colonial government borrowers, *c.* 1870, was about £0.5 million or 0.05 per cent of 1870 GNP and, *c.* 1914, £9.2 million or 0.36 per cent of 1914 GNP (Davis and Huttenback 1986: 176).

As Davis and Huttenback note, these estimates do not entirely capture this cost of empire. First, as already noted, private railways in the colonies were charged a lower interest rate by Britain than foreign private borrowers at similar levels of development. The lower colonial yields were not due to the presence of guarantees or other subsidies from the colonial government, because private foreign railway borrowers received similar support from their governments. It would be highly useful to have a regression analysis of private railway yields similar to Davis and Huttenback's for government securities. Failing such an estimate, it might be noted that colonial railway borrowing was three times that of colonial government borrowing *c.* 1870 and about 1.6 times, *c*. 1914 (Edelstein 1982: 48). If it is assumed that the private railways received similar subsidies at the margin and a similar ratio of private railway borrowing between colonies of responsible and dependent government, the total subsidy (government and railway securities), *c*. 1870, becomes 0.20 per cent of 1870 GNP and *c*. 1914, 0.94 per cent of 1914 GNP, entered with a negative sign in Table 8.1 to denote that it was a cost of empire, not a gain.

These estimates of the total government and railway subsidy are, however, quite crude. First, the yield differentials between colonial and foreign railway borrowers of similar levels of development were probably smaller than for government borrowers; it would appear that British lenders thought empire reduced the risks of government securities more than railway issues (Edelstein 1982: 123, 125). Second, according to Davis and Huttenback, responsible governments borrowed 3.22 as much as dependent governments while their private railway borrowed 2.11 as much. The first factor would tend to lower the total subsidy and the second raise it.

There are other difficulties. The subsidy to empire borrowers may have had wider effects. With the colonial imprimatur, colonial government and railway borrowers were placed in lower-risk categories by the British lenders, but it is possible that some domestic and foreign 'safe' borrowers were thereby displaced or perhaps higher interest rates prevailed in the 'safe' sector of the capital market. Furthermore, the reduced presence of colonial government and railway borrowers from the riskier sectors of the capital market may have meant that more funds were available for riskier domestic and foreign borrowers and perhaps at lower interest rates. If we make the bold but plausible assumption that for given use (e.g. tramways), domestic borrowers were always treated as less risky than foreigners, it is likely that foreigners were the most affected by the colonial subsidy. Foreign borrowers were the most displaced in the 'safe' market due to the subsidy, perhaps paying a higher interest rate as well, and they were likely to be the ones who most benefited in the market for risky securities. What direction these wider effects would have had, and how large they would have been, is difficult to evaluate. It is plausible that these two, general equilibrium, readjustments just cited more or less cancelled out each other, so that the wider effects were small, but clearly more research is warranted.

The strong standard

Finally, the Davis and Huttenback estimates only contend with the 'price' effects of the subsidy, not the quantity effects. In the absence of the direct and indirect subsidies of empire status, there probably would have been less borrowing, especially from the poorest regions of the empire. Hypothetically freed from colonial rule in 1870 or 1913, it is doubtful that a freed Nigeria, India, Malaya, etc., would have been able to attract the same attention from the London or any other capital market. In the Davis and Huttenback calculation of the subsidy, these regions pay a higher interest rate but borrow the same amount. If they counterfactually borrowed less because of higher interest rates or other effects, the implicit subsidy is less than the Davis and Huttenback calculation. How much less is difficult to hazard; again more research is warranted.

Turning to the 'strong non-imperialist' standard, the issue becomes how much British investment would have taken place without empire rule in the nineteenth and twentieth centuries. With regard to the white-settler colonies, it seems plausible to assume that British investment per head in Canada, Australia, New Zealand and South Africa would have been closer to the Argentine per capita investment. The required rate of return, however, probably would have been higher to compensate for the greater risk of foreign political pressures and court systems. British investment per head in Argentina was approximately 70 per cent of what it was in Canada, Australia, New Zealand, and South Africa but the realised rate of return on Argentine (and US) securities was about a third higher than on the Dominion securities. Thus, it seems likely that whatever income for Britons would have been lost from a drop in the quantity of investment in the white-settler colonies, under these rough assumptions it would have been made up through a higher rate of return.

It seems safe, though, to suggest that under the 'strong non-imperialist' standard there would have been less investment income from India and the remainder of the non-Dominion empire. Plausible political and economic analogies to India without empire rule in the nineteenth century might be the experience of China, Turkey and Japan. Clearly, there was some amount of 'informal' imperialism in these regions affecting their openness to foreigners (McLean 1976; Cain 1980; Cain and Hopkins 1980, 1986, 1987). It is therefore quite generous to assume that the non-white-settler colonies would have had British investments one fifth their actual £140 and £480 million levels in 1870 and 1913. The realised rate of return was approximately 4 per cent on colonial investments, 1870–1913, but in order to draw funds into these hypothesised independent regions, the required rate of return would probably have had at least to double to compensate for the perceived increased risk. If we reduce the non-Dominion colonial investments by 80 per cent and assume an 8 per cent return, the gain to Great Britain from empire investments based on a 'strong non-imperialist' standard was 0.3 per cent of GNP in 1870 and 0.5 per cent of GNP in 1913 (Table 8.1). (The stock of British portfolio capital in non-Dominion colonies was £140 million in 1870 (Hall 1963) and £480 million in 1913 (Saul 1960b). British GNP was £1,081 million in 1870 and £2,542 in 1913 (Feinstein 1972: Tables 8 and 9). The change in British GNP from the assumed lowered rate of investment in non-Dominion colonial areas in 1870 would thus be [(0.04)(140)–(0.08)(0.2)(140)]/1081 = 0.0031 and in 1913, [(0.04)(480)–(0.08)(0.2)(480)]/2542 = 0.0045.)

Net government transfers to and from the empire

Monetary transfers

Throughout the late nineteenth and early twentieth centuries a fundamental tenet of Colonial Office oversight was that colonial governments were to find sufficient local tax and other revenue sources to finance current (non-capital) expenditures. Most colonies came close to this in normal times, relying upon direct assistance from London principally when a major military campaign or natural disaster caused fiscal stress. India, however, was a different matter. Not only was India self-supporting but Indian troops and funds were regularly used for empire military actions in Africa and Asia. According to Mukerjee (1972), some £0.4 million *c.* 1870 and, employing his methods, £4 million *c.* 1913 were transferred to Britain for (a) unjustified debt service for wars which an independent India would not have undertaken, (b) military expenditures for campaigns in Africa and Asia and (c) civil charges for empire operations outside India. These Indian transfers, however, must be matched against the direct assistance to other colonial governments from London government under unusual fiscal stresses. Such direct assistance averaged perhaps £1 million *c.* 1870 (Feinstein 1972) and £1.3 million *c.* 1913 (Kesner 1981: 34–43). Both the British outflows and inflows from India would disappear under either a 'marginal' or 'strong non-imperialist' standard.

A second form of colonial expense was the shipping and cable subsidies to maintain mail and telegraphic communication within the empire (Davis and Huttenback 1986: 181). Since other advanced nations subsidised their shipping and cable companies for mail and telegraphic benefits, or would have, in the absence of British services, we have to assume that these expenses would remain under either standard of imperialism.

Transfers in kind: defence

A third form of budgetary assistance provided by the British empire was an 'in kind' transfer, national defence. One of the central arguments of Davis and Huttenback's recent volume on the political economy of imperialism

Table 8.2. *Average annual defence expenditures, 1860–1912 (£ per capita)*

United Kingdom	1·14
UK colonies	
responsible governments	0·12
dependent governments	0·04
India	0·10
princely states	0·03
special princely states	0·03
Foreign developed nations	0·46
Foreign underdeveloped nations	0·18

is that none of the colonies, with or without responsible government, paid for anything like a reasonable defence establishment. The data shown in Table 8.2 illustrate their hypothesis (Davis and Huttenback 1986:161). The colonies with responsible government (the white-settler colonies) appear to have paid around a quarter of what foreign developed nations spent on defence, and the dependent colonial governments and the princely states paid about a fifth of what foreign underdeveloped nations expended. India, as we have already noted, paid more, but it too expended about half of what foreign underdeveloped nations spent. Davis and Huttenback's estimates also show Britain's defence spending per capita was double the rate of France and Germany, suggesting that Britain was buying two defence establishments, one for home defence and one for its empire.

Two problems are evident in the Davis and Huttenback defence expenditure comparisons. First, a substantial part of the difference between the defence expenditures of foreign underdeveloped countries and the empire's dependent colonies appears to be due to the fact that the empire had separate police forces whereas in many foreign underdeveloped countries the military served this function (Davis and Huttenback 1986: 164). Second, a recent critique by Offer (forthcoming) presents evidence that Davis and Huttenback missed certain secret French and German military and naval expenditures. Given these substantially higher estimates of French and German per capita defence costs it seems plausible to surmise that more of Britain's expenditures were meant for home island security and less were devoted to empire defence. As Offer argues elsewhere (1989: 215–318), Britain's strategic planners viewed the nation's food and raw material imports as an important part of home island security and felt that these resources required extensive naval and military protection. British naval and military forces stationed overseas thus served both home and colonial security purposes.

On the 'marginal non-imperialist' standard the portion of the British defence establishment and its expense devoted to colonial security would hypothetically disappear. According to Davis and Huttenback's data this overseas military establishment cost £10.9 million, *c.* 1870, and £30.3 million, *c.* 1909, or 1.0 per cent and 1.4 per cent of UK GNP. (Averaging Davis and Huttenback's data (1986: 164) for 1860–9 and 1870–9, total British defence costs were approximately £0.70 per capita, *c.* 1870, of which £0.35 per capita was for imperial defence, that is, 50 per cent of total British defence costs. Average annual total defence costs, 1905–12, were £1.58 per capita, of which £0.68 per capita was for imperial defence, 43 per cent of total British defence costs. These figures include the Mediterranean fleet in home defence costs. Given that other major European powers maintained Mediterranean fleets, assuming Britain would maintain one in the absence of an overseas empire appears plausible. The total defence budget in 1870 was £21.1 million and £73.5 million in 1913 (Mitchell 1988: 588). Thus, the empire expense was 0.50 × £21.1 million in 1870 and 0.43 × £73.5 million in 1913. British GNP was £1,081 million and £2,542 million in 1870 and 1913, respectively (Feinstein 1972: Tables 8 and 9).)

However, because this assumes that all of the forces committed abroad are for empire defence it must be considered an upper-bound of the defence subsidy to the empire. A lower empire defence subsidy would result if part of the overseas military and naval expenses is credited to keeping shipping lanes open for essential food and raw material imports for Britain's home defence.

Assume that all of the difference between the defence expenditures of the independent underdeveloped countries and India and the dependent colonies was due to differences in accounting for police functions. Second, assume that the Dominions would have spent per capita the amount that the US spent if they, hypothetically, were to have become independent in 1870 or 1913 and the difference represents the British subsidy for their defence. The US appears to have spent approximately double per capita the Dominion rate (United States: United States 1975: Series A7, Y458–9; Australia: Maddock and McLean 1987: 353, 359; Canada: Urquhart and Buckley 1965: Series A1, G26). The resulting hypothetical increment for the Dominions would be approximately £0.5 million in 1870 and £5.0 million in 1913, or 0.04 per cent of 1870 GNP and 0.23 per cent of 1913 GNP. (Davis and Huttenback (1986: 28, 161) give per capita defence expenditures and population for the Dominions. Multiplying these figures yields about £0.5 million *c.* 1870 and £5.0 million *c.* 1913. The text assumes the Dominions would increase their defence expenditures by the same amount if counterfactually independent. British GNP was £1,081 million and £2,542 million in 1870 and 1913, respectively (Feinstein 1972: Tables

8 and 9).) Table 8.1 displays these upper- and lower-bound estimates of these subsidies as costs of empire.

On the 'strong non-imperialist' standard, a similar assumption seems equally plausible. Part of Britain's military expenditures involved a naval presence which guarded British shipping lanes from predatory states and privateers. Given their level of commercial development in the late nineteenth and early twentieth centuries, the hypothetically freed regions of the British empire ('marginal non-imperialist' standard) might be expected to continue to maintain order in their adjacent trade routes. The 'strong non-imperialist' standard counterfactually assumes that the empire never came into being, hence a trading (empire-less) Britain would have had to spend something to make the waters off Asia, Africa and the Americas safe for commercial activity in the eighteenth and nineteenth centuries. How much naval expense would have been necessary? France and the United States, with lower naval expenditures than the UK, made their presence felt when privateers were a problem in the nineteenth-century Mediterranean and elsewhere. Since France and Germany, two substantial European commercial and naval powers, had considerably larger defence expenses than the typical developed countries, and British *home* defence was similarly expensive, it seems likely the cost of imperialism was similar under both standards of 'non-imperialism' (see also P. K. O'Brien 1988).

Summary of the economics of empire

The net gain, 1870–1913

These rough calculations, summarised in Table 8.1, suggest three important features of the economics of empire. First, the empire meant more for the economic well being of Great Britain in 1913 than it did in 1870. This trend was largely due to the increased proportion of British commodity and service exports which were marketed in the empire.

Second, if we employ the 'marginal non-imperialism' standard the gains to Britain from her empire do not appear to have been very large. The ability to manipulate the international trade, investment and fiscal policies of the developed colonial economies appears to have yielded perhaps 1 per cent *c.* 1870 and 2 per cent in 1913. Whatever the trade and investment advantages, they were moderated by the direct and indirect subsidies to empire. In addition, the trade calculation assumed that the relatively low tariffs of the white-settler colonies were due to British rule. Colonial parliamentary debates suggest that this assumption must be modified. If, for example, it is totally dropped, the trade gains from the 'marginal' standards are halved. Needless to say, the fact that the nation as a whole did not gain much according to this standard does not mean that certain sectors of the British economy did not benefit from freer trade with the empire. The cotton trades, shipping, overseas insurance and banking, and railway equipment manufacturers are good examples but they are not alone. In other words, private rates of return may have been higher than the social rate of return.

Third, Britain probably received a significant return if we use the 'strong non-imperialism' standard. This is best viewed as an estimate of the return on the role which empire played in enlarging the extent of the nineteenth-century world economy. Furthermore, because the gains from 'informal' empire have been largely ignored, it is likely that the gains from imperialism in Table 8.1 are understated. Argentina, which was used as an example of a 'non-imperialist' economy, was subject to the pressures of Britain and other imperial powers at various points in the nineteenth and early twentieth centuries.

The size of the gains reported in Table 8.1, however, must be examined in the light of our earlier assumption that supply curves were elastic and hence British output was set by the level of demand. To assume elastic supply curves means that if there had been no empire the domestic labour and capital resources employed in empire-induced activities would have either never participated in the economy or, through lower population growth rates, never come into existence. Alternatively, it might be assumed that some portion of the labour and capital involved in empire-induced activities would have been employed in other economic activities, albeit less productive. Unfortunately, it is quite difficult to measure accurately how much of the labour and capital resources involved in empire-induced activities would have been employed elsewhere in the economy. It is possible, however, to specify a range of possibilities. If, on the one hand, all factors of production were employed elsewhere and the only change was a drop in their rate of return by 1 percentage point, after forty-four years without the empire-induced growth British GNP would have been lower by around 1 per cent. If, on the other hand, it is assumed that the resources involved in the empire-induced economic activity had remained unused (or never come into existence) and the pace of technical change is proportionately lowered as well, British GNP would have been lower by somewhat more than 5 per cent after forty-four years.

How can we tell whether this range of proportions is large or small? One way is to compare the gains from empire with the gains from various forms of technical progress. Hawke's study of the diffusion of the railway in Great Britain indicates that in 1860, after thirty-five years of the railway, GNP was at most 10 per cent higher than it would have been without the railway (Hawke 1970). Since it is likely that the railway was the most important single technological innovation of the nineteenth century, the empire does not appear to have been as important as is sometimes thought. Still, the empire made a significant contribution to the growth in the income and output of Great Britain in the nineteenth and early twentieth centuries. Chapter 1 suggested that between 1870 and 1914 the forces of innovation and economies of scale were exerting a diminishing effect on growth. By contrast the contribution of the empire was increasing.

The First World War

Finally, in September of 1914 Britain entered into a European war of immense carnage and cost. The empire came quickly to the defence of Britain and in key battles towards the end carried an especially heavy combat role. How does the empire's contribution to the First World War fit in a cost-benefit calculus of the late Pax Britannica. First, it is best to think of the contribution of empire to the First World War as quite separate from its contribution during the relatively peaceful years of the nineteenth and early twentieth centuries. During the latter period, economic goals were important motivators for individual and social life. But for the survival of an autonomous national life, 1914–18, governments and peoples were willing to throw immense human and other resources into battle with little reference to economic considerations. Thus the distinct motivational structure means any calculation of wartime costs answers different questions.

The empire was not settled to provide a reserve army for home defence. Furthermore, in the early months of the First World War the high rates of voluntary enlistment in the Dominions were quite surprising to the British government and people (Offer 1989: 313–16). The protection of food and raw material exports from the empire was part of Britain's pre-war military plans but so too was the independent United States (Offer 1989: 215–317). Eventually the United States joined the Allied military effort for reasons which probably would have drawn the Dominions into combat if they had been independent, that is, their cultural links with Britain and the German submarine campaign which was aimed at choking off Britain's food and raw material imports. Thus, perhaps only the quick troop and financial support from the Dominions and the colonies might be thought the irreducible contribution of empire to the First World War.

On the 'marginal standard' of non-imperialism, it thus seems plausible to treat the actual empire contribution to the First World War as an upper-bound of what Britain would have had to provide without empire. Great Britain spent £44.029 billion on the First World War; the empire spent £4.494 billion (Bogart 1921:105). Thus, Great Britain's direct expenditures might have been 10.2 per cent higher without empire support. From 1915 to 1918 British military expenditures absorbed 25–30 per cent of British GNP (Mitchell 1988: 833). Thus, an upper-bound estimate of the benefit of empire might be 10.2 per cent of this share, that is 2.5–3.0 per cent of GNP. More significantly, Britain lost 744,000 persons in military uniform while the empire lost 225,000 (Mendershausen 1943: 361). British wartime deaths might therefore have been 30.2 per cent higher in the absence of empire support. How one translates this sacrifice into an annualised cost is too difficult to attempt here. In any event, by the 'marginal standard' of non-imperialism, the distinct wartime benefits of empire overshadow the gains calculated for the peaceful empire *c.* 1913 (Table 8.1) and probably would still do so even if we hazard what a hypothetically freed empire would have contributed if the United States' later entry is used as a standard. With regard to the 'strong' standard of non-imperialism, the growth of the British empire across the modern era bulks so large in the origins of the First World War as to make calculation implausible.

9 Money in the economy, 1870–1939

Forrest Capie and Geoffrey Wood

Introduction

The late nineteenth century and the early twentieth saw striking developments in the financial sector in Britain, and in the monetary system within which the financial sector operated.

At the start Britain had a large number of banks (in January 1870 there were 387), some of them operating nationwide. The numbers soon began to fall, and by the First World War the system was dominated by a few large banks – the 'clearing banks', as they were known. The change occurred through a variety of processes – voluntary amalgamation, amalgamation in the face of failure, take overs hostile and friendly, outright failure and occasional simple withdrawal from the industry.

The timing of events in the monetary system was almost the opposite: peace followed by turmoil. The years 1870 to 1914 were years of relative monetary tranquillity, the heyday of the classical gold standard. Britain was on the standard and more and more countries were joining it. Being on the gold standard was regarded as economically prudent, and, indeed, as the discussions before Austria joined in 1892 make clear (see Yeager 1984), essential for belonging to the civilised community of nations. As Schumpeter (1954) observed, it was 'a symbol of sound practice and badge of honour and decency'. There were, of course, fluctuations in the rate of growth of the supply of gold, and fluctuations in the demand for it as new nations joined the standard. But so far as Britain was concerned the only alteration in the system 1870–1914 was the open acceptance by the Bank of England of the role of lender of last resort.

After 1914 all changed, and for the worse. The gold standard was suspended. Prices rose dramatically during the war. The Armistice brought boom and then monetary stringency, until the gold standard was resumed at the pre-war parity in 1925. Britain finally abandoned the gold standard in 1931. Floating exchange rates, and domestic monetary autonomy unconstrained by any commodity base, characterised the years down to the Second World War.

Money under the gold standard

What is possible under the gold standard? Suppose first of all that the standard was simply a fixed exchange rate system – set aside that it was based on the commodity called 'gold'. If exchange rates were fixed, money would move *after* changes in (real or nominal) income, but would not precede them. The explanation is straightforward. Assume the monetary authorities expand the money supply. Since there is no concern about exchange risk, money flows abroad to obtain a higher interest rate there, and the monetary expansion promptly ceases (in fact some of the monetary expansion will remain; the proportion will depend on the share of the originating country in the world economy). Conversely, consider an expansion of *real* income in a country, increasing the amount of money demanded. By various channels, including a rise in interest rates in view of the initial excess demand for money, money is attracted into the economy until the excess demand is eliminated and interest rates are again the same world-wide. In such a setting, then, money can *follow* fluctuations in real income, but cannot lead them.

It must, however, be emphasised that money following income does not mean that money is unimportant for income. The argument is made by Friedman and Schwartz (1982: 325 fn 14). They wrote:

> In a fixed exchange rate régime the quantity of money is endogenous, and cannot be determined, except for brief periods, by the monetary authorities. Monetary policy cannot affect the quantity of money except temporarily; nonetheless changes in the quantity of money, however produced, will affect income. Indeed, it is precisely because they do that a gold standard or other fixed exchange rate régime is self-adjusting... The exchange rate régime does not affect the existence of a 'causal' link from money to income; it affects the forces determining the quantity of money and thereby whether the situation is one of largely unidirectional influence from money to income or of simultaneous determination and interaction.

The full force of the argument can be understood by moving from a fixed exchange rate to a gold standard. In such a system the money supply in Britain could expand (more than temporarily) for *two* reasons: income expansion in Britain, producing a monetary inflow as described above; or a gold discovery (outside Britain). The newly mined gold is spent on goods, services and assets, and thus finds its way into circulation in every country of the world. Some gold flows into Britain, and produces its usual effects. And so in this case the money flow precedes changes rather than follows them. Even if the money flow followed rather than initiated a change, it may have subsequent effects; for the ratio of nominal money to income will be higher if the money flows than if it does not, which in turn will have consequences.

To these two possible relationships between money and income a third must be added. It occurs if the economy is sufficiently large that monetary fluctuations originating within it, although spilling over to the rest of the world, nevertheless affect that country's money stock by having a significant effect on the *world's* money stock. Of course, Britain was not a gold producer, so the last possibility seems to be ruled out. But the British banking system evolved so as to support a larger and larger money stock on an unchanged gold base. Further, the British economy bulked large in the world, giving some reason to suppose that the Bank of England could influence the world distribution of gold. Whether it actually could and did remains to be seen.

Money demand before the First World War

The connection between income and money is well summarised in the British demand for money, a thoroughly studied function. Friedman and Schwartz (1982) include 1870–1914 as part of a longer study. Others have examined the demand for money 1870–1914 itself (Capie and Rodrik-Bali 1983; Mills and Wood 1988; and Klovland 1987). The crucial statistic is the money supply, the thing to be demanded, estimates of which have recently been revised (Capie and Webber 1985: 9–51). Three conclusions stand out. First, the demand function is stable. A change in income, the price level or the interest rate each has the same effect in all years; and at any given level of the variables the amount of money demanded is the same, regardless of when the observations occur. Second, the income elasticity of demand is very close to unity: a 1 per cent rise in income, other things equal, causes a 1 per cent rise in the quantity of money demanded. Third, the demand is best expressed as a demand for real balances, which is to say that the price-level elasticity of demand for money was also unity. A 1 per cent fall in prices causes a 1 per cent fall in the demand for money. In short, one can interpret changes in the ratio of nominal money to nominal income as producing excess supply of or excess demand for money.

Money, prices and the Great Depression

A widely held view of the British economy in the last quarter of the nineteenth century is that it experienced 'depression'. Other countries were emerging as competing industrial powers, and agriculture suffered as the American Midwest was opened up. The data, however, do not provide much support for 'depression'. Some students of the period claim there was at least a 'climacteric,' but the timing alleged differs widely. For example, D. J. Coppock (1956) places it in the 1870s, while Phelps Brown and Handfield Jones (1952) set it in the 1890s and McCloskey (1970) in the 1900s, if at all. Matthews, Feinstein and Odling-Smee (1982) present a picture of slow and steady deceleration of growth from 2.5 per cent per year in the 1850s to around 1 per cent per year in the 1900s. Still later Crafts, Leybourne and Mills (1989a and b) find only a slight fall in trend growth over the period 1870–1913, and no evidence at all of a climacteric in the 1870s (the evidence has been refined further by Feinstein 1990b). The years 1873–96 were not a sustained period of depression.

Why, then, were there so many reports of depression by contemporaries and later historians (Saul 1969)? The reports were not confined to Britain. Histories of almost all the developed and some of the developing world claim the period as 'depression'. The answer is that prices fell. Prices drifted down world-wide from 1873 to 1896. British wholesale prices fell by 39 per cent from 1873 to 1896, and then rose by 40 per cent to 1914; and Feinstein's GDP deflator, broader based with less emphasis on agriculture, fell by 20 per cent and then rose by 17.6 per cent.

There are two contrasting explanations of the fall. One is real. Prices fell, it is said, because the extension of arable farming in the New World and the revolution in transport drove agricultural prices down; similarly, technological change was bringing down the price of manufactured goods. Such events, however, would cause a change only in relative prices: agricultural and manufactured prices would fall; but without something driving down prices as a whole the prices of, say, services and rents would rise (their relative prices were going up, not down).

The second explanation is monetary. Prices were lowered by a scarcity of money relative to output in the first half of the period, and the opposite in the second. Money in Britain grew by 33 per cent in the downswing 1873–96 while real output grew by 53 per cent; in the upswing 1896–1914, in contrast, the money stock grew by 40 per cent and real output by 36 per cent. The different patterns of money growth were produced by a combination of rapid economic development world-wide and the main industrial countries joining the gold standard. The demand for gold increased, and there was no rise in supply until the gold discoveries in the early and mid-1890s in Australia, South Africa and the Klondike (Rockoff 1984 and Barro 1984 argue that the discoveries were in fact induced by the earlier rise in demand).

The monetary explanation is consistent with the behaviour of wholesale prices in relation to the GDP deflator in Britain; and it is also consistent with the international character of the price decline. More elaborate empirical work (Capie *et al.* 1991; Mills and Wood 1992) lends further support. The authors constructed a statistical model of money, prices, output and interest rates. The conclusion was that output in Britain influenced money, and that money and output both influenced prices, but that money had no effect on output. Recognising, of course, the dangers of using such delicate techniques on the data of these years (see Wood 1984) the results nevertheless support the interpretation of the period as one of price decline, not real output depression, produced by the demonstrable shortage of money relative to output (Cagan 1965). The shortage was reflected in the popular pressure at the time for an increase in the money supply (in the United States through the coinage of silver).

There was undoubtedly a depression in agriculture (see ch. 6). The prices of agricultural goods fell on average by 42 per cent – in other words a substantial relative price decline against the general index. But the 'Great Depression' from the 1870s to the 1890s was a two-part phenomenon: overall prices fell and agricultural prices fell further. The first was a monetary phenomenon, the second a real one produced by changing supply conditions in agriculture.

The business cycle

If there is a relationship between money and real output it exists only in the short run. In the long run money is neutral with respect to output. It affects only the price level. But in the short run there is at least the possibility that excess money stimulates output growth, or conversely that monetary stringency brings about a contraction in real economic activity. Different approaches to this question are found in, for example, the work of Friedman and Schwartz (1963) and of Lucas (1972, reprinted 1981).

In Friedman and Schwartz the source of cycles is the slippage between the 'monetary base' (gold or other moneys that can be used as reserves in the vault) and 'money', money being all means of payment including cheques. It is the tendency to overshoot that produces a cycle. Any discrepancy between desired and actual money balances results in excess spending, stimulating output.

The discrepancy does not appear if markets clear perfectly, as they do in the new classical models (nor does it occur if the interest rate takes all the slack, as it does in Keynesian models). For the new classicals (among them Lucas) the cycle comes about from a confusion on the producer's part between relative and general prices. A small change in price can bring about a large change in output, reinforced perhaps by the difference between transitory and permanent changes in price (Brunner and Meltzer 1989). A change in the general price level that was mistaken by the producer for a change in the price of his own product, and also thought to be a transitory change, would set cyclical forces in motion.

Friedman and Schwartz found that there was a link between money and real output for the United States in their classic study of 1963. Their cautious conclusion was that changes in the money stock conformed to the *major* movements in the business cycle chronology, with a long lead. The statistical evidence they presented was supported by detailed study of particular historical episodes.

But no such analysis of the British experience has been carried out. There were fluctuations in the British economy long before industrialisation. In the eighteenth century and before, spilling into the early nineteenth century, harvests have been taken as the initiators of the cycle (Rostow 1948; Ashton 1955). But for the nineteenth century the dominant explanation has been exports, as for example for 1790–1850 by Gayer, Rostow and Schwartz (1953) and for 1870–1914 by Ford (1963).

The export model leaves little room for money. Ford (1981) stated that 'monetary influences were not a significant internal cyclical factor in the United Kingdom'. Pre-Keynesian writers such as Hawtrey (1913) on the contrary regarded the cycle as 'a purely monetary phenomenon' and there have been some recent studies that have brought money into the picture. Walters (1969) for instance found that the monetary model outperformed the Keynesian model over the years 1880–1914. And Eichengreen (1983) found that for the late Victorian period the fluctuations in the monetary base were the single most important determinant of the trade cycle.

Recently it has been possible to examine the relationship more rigorously. In addition to Feinstein's output data, new monetary data became available (Capie and Webber 1985). When the techniques of Friedman and Schwartz were replicated for Britain, however, no strong conclusions were possible. The links between money with output were ambiguous. Further, using an approach of Barro (1987) to investigate specifically the response to unanticipated as against anticipated changes in monetary series, no useful results were found (Capie 1990). With the help of the latest time series techniques it was possible to carry out a more detailed examination (Capie and Mills 1990). The techniques allow a more reliable decomposition of the observed monetary and output series into the unobserved trend and the cyclical component. It is then possible to test the relationship between the two cyclical series. But again in the British case the results showed that the causal link between money and output was weak and ambiguous.

Why the contrast with the strong findings for the United States? The most obvious difference is that output and money were less volatile in Britain than in America. Recall that Friedman and Schwartz stressed that money caused output changes only at major turning points. If there were no comparable major turning points in Britain (as the evidence suggests) then neither should there be the strong money/output link. Britain experienced no major banking crises between 1870 and 1913. This undoubtedly contributed to the less volatile monetary series. The sound banking structure, with large banks with head offices in London and branches scattered across the whole country, appears to have allowed diversified portfolios for each bank. In the United States, by contrast, banks were confined by law to one state, and were therefore undiversified, vulnerable to local shocks. Banks failed readily and panics often followed (Bernanke 1983 suggests that the American failures produced recession through the contraction of credit in the area served by the bank, a local effect impossible in Britain). And the Bank of England acted as a lender of last resort, at a time when the United States had no central bank at all.

Interest rates

Figure 9.1 shows two interest rates, a short-term rate on bank bills and a long-term rate on Consols ('consolidated government stock': that is, government bonds with no fixed redemption date). They are adjusted for Goschen's conversion of 1888 (Harley 1976). In 1888 the Chancellor of the Exchequer, Goschen, sought to take advantage of low and falling rates of interest in order to reduce the rate of interest paid on the national debt (that is, the bonds of the government). From 1889 to 1903 Goschen's conversion scheme lowered the nominal rate of interest on Consols to 2.75 per cent per year (£2 15s) and thereafter to 2.5 per cent (£2 10s). Harley (1976) argues that it is incorrect, however, to assume that these were the true yields on the Consols. The markets had fully discounted the 3 per cent Consols in anticipation of a conversion. And the new Goschen Consols could not be considered as long-term securities and therefore it was incorrect to calculate their yield by dividing 2.75 per cent by the price of the Consol. Furthermore, in the mid-1890s the market expected the low short-term rates to rise, resulting in a higher yield for longer-term maturities. The series allows for Harley's corrections.

Note the sluggish movements in the long-term rate. The interest rate in the ordinary sense is a merely *nominal* rate – which is to say, it is the rate of return before any adjustment for inflation. The nominal rate therefore has two components. It is the 'real' rate plus the expected rate of inflation (or, what is relevant for the period before 1896, minus the expected rate of deflation). An interest rate of 2 per cent per year would actually be worth 4.6 per cent per year if prices were falling, as they were from 1873 to 1896, at 2.6 per cent per year on average: a £100 investment would earn 2 per cent from the bond and 2.6 per cent from being able to buy more with each

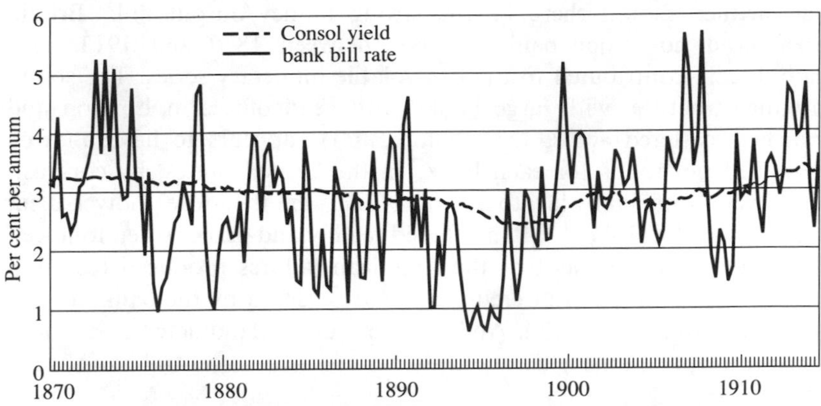

Figure 9.1 UK Consol yield and bank bill rate, 1870–1915
Source: Capie and Webber (1985).

pound sterling, for a total 'real' return of 4.6 per cent. Dividing the nominal interest rate into these two components is important because different forces affect them. The real part is determined by the balance of supply and demand between saving and investment; the inflation part is determined by expected inflation.

The money supply did not grow exactly as demand required. Therefore the price of holding money – the nominal interest rate – had to fluctuate, to induce the changed supplies to be held. But notice the stability of the long-term rate. The monetary fluctuations would have fed through to the long rate only if they led to expectations of inflation or disinflation. They did not do so – because they were expected to be transitory. It was sensible, albeit perhaps not rational in the technical sense, to form expectations from past inflation experience. The stability of the long rate relative to the short is therefore a product of the money supply regime, under which sustained inflation had been modest in pace and very slow to change.

The above argument requires that the real rate also be stable. It apparently was. The observed stability of the nominal rate would require an implausible offset in expectations if the underlying real rate was in fact moving around. Friedman and Schwartz (1982; summarised in Schwartz (1982) and Mills and Wood (1992)) have by quite different statistical techniques found that the real rate was stable. The observed stability of the long rate relative to the short rate should be interpreted as the result of the stability of inflationary expectations.

Notice also in the figure that the long-term rates were low. Here too the distinction between real and nominal rates is crucial. Over the first part of the period (1873–96) the price level fell as we have seen at 2.6 per cent per year on average; and over the second part (1896–1913) it rose 2.24 per cent per year on average. (The inflation was gradual by later standards: even in the stable 1950s it was 4 per cent per year, in the 1960s 5 per cent, in the 1970s fully 15 per cent and in the 1980s 6.5 per cent.) The low level of the long rate as compared with rates typical recently was, therefore, a second product of the money supply regime.

And note finally that the rise and fall of the long-term interest rate paralleled the fall and rise of prices. The fact is known (from Keynes 1930) as the Gibson Paradox, after the writer who first drew attention to it. It is 'paradoxical' because a change in the price level should leave interest rates unchanged, being a mere change in the unit of account.

Keynes and the Swedish economist Knut Wicksell saw nominal rates as being pulled down by a decline in real rates in the first half of the period – the notion of a Great Depression again – and then rising after 1896 with the boom of investment world-wide. Prices followed, they argued, because market rates lagged the decline and produced monetary stringency. But we have seen that there is little evidence of a decline in the real rate. And the Keynes–Wicksell arguments suppose that monetary stringency was produced by interest rates contracting bank lending; as argued above (and in Capie and Webber 1985) it was in fact produced by a relative shortage of gold.

The American economist Irving Fisher (1867–1947) argued that inflationary expectations would adjust, with a lag, to actual inflation. In consequence the deflation of 1873–96 would produce a gradual realisation that inflation was going to continue, and a gradual lowering of nominal interest rates to reflect the expectation. In 1896 the financial markets expected deflation to continue. They were wrong, but it took a similarly long lag for them to realise it: during which realisation the nominal interest rates gradually rose. Friedman and Schwartz (1982) note that the Gibson pattern disappeared when inflation rates had become so volatile that it was unreasonable to forecast inflation by simple extrapolation, slowly adjusting.

In short, the peculiarities of the late nineteenth century in the matter of money were the product of a peculiarly stable monetary environment (reinforced, it may be, by the way gold production responded (Barsky and Summers 1988)).

Financial intermediation

The bulk of all financial intermediation, taking the savings of depositors and transforming it into investment, was done by the banking system. A useful framework for examining the contribution of the banking system is one that places it in the money supply process alongside the monetary authorities and the public. The simplest expression of this is:

$$M = mB$$

where m is the money multiplier, B is the monetary base (the gold in a strict gold standard, for example), and M is the money stock. The money multiplier can be shown as:

$$\frac{C/D+1}{R/D+C/D}$$

The public, who decide how much currency (C) to hold in relation to deposits (D), can influence the size of the money stock if they change the ratio. Equally the banks, who decide how much cash reserves (R) to hold in relation to their deposit liabilities (namely, as cover for the chequing accounts they owe to the public), can also influence it. When they feel the need to raise the cover they dampen down the total money stock. This way of examining the money supply emphasises that there are three parties influencing the total money stock – the monetary authorities (who set B), the banks, and the public.

There were no legal restrictions on the reserve/deposit ratio, and the variation from bank to bank could be quite considerable. Indeed the idea of a reserve ratio had not yet been articulated at the beginning of the period, though obviously banks worked with some idea of requisite cover or they went out of business. The first consciously stated reserve ratio appears to have been self-imposed by the Lincoln Bank in 1872; in the course of the next twenty years or so most English banks had come to employ an announced minimum ratio. Contemporary estimates of the size of the ratio lend support to our own estimates. According to one survey of seventy-five non-clearing banks the ratio of reserves to deposits ranged from 9 to 17 per cent. Twelve London clearing banks ranged from 10.4 to 16.8 per cent. Our own estimates for the system as a whole show that it fluctuated between 8.5 per cent and 12.5 per cent (with a mean of 10.4 per cent and standard deviation of 1.1 per cent; Capie and Webber 1985).

After some initial erratic behaviour in the 1870s, the reserve to deposit ratio (R/D) trended upward. That is to say, the banks held a rising quantity of reserves in relation to deposits. The rise held down the growth of the money supply. The growth of the reserve/deposit ratio is on the face of things perplexing. A jump in the proportion of reserves is generally associated with fears of instability or financial uncertainty. It was not a jump, however, but a slow and steady growth. Furthermore, small banks should hold higher reserves than large banks, since the large banks acquire

Table 9.1. *The proximate determinants of changes in the UK money supply, 1870–1913*

Fraction of the change in £M3 attributable to	1870–1913	1880–1913	1870–9	1880–96	1897–1913
B	0·692	0·72	1·16	0·32	1·21
C/D	0·38	0·35	0·16	0·5	0·24
R/D	−0·084	−0·039	−0·315	+0·15	−0·43
Interaction	+0·012	−0·03	0·00	0·03	−0·02

Source: Capie and Rodrik-Bali (1983). B = 'high-powered money' (the base); C/D = the currency–deposit ratio; and R/D = the reserve–deposit ratio.

a certain soundness by their size. But if this were the case the trend in R/D would have been *downwards*, since small banks shrank as a proportion of total bank population.

The solution to the puzzle may be as follows: small banks in fact held smaller reserves than large banks. Turner (1972) found that the lowest ratios of all were amongst the non-clearers. The private banks were not obliged to publish their accounts. As more and more banks published accounts there was therefore an increase in the ratio: the need to publish in itself provided a pressure to keep a higher ratio of reserves. And the move to publish coincided in time with the Baring crisis of 1890, when it became accepted that the banks should hold a higher ratio.

Friedman and Schwartz (1963) used a method of determining the contribution of each proximate determinant of the money supply for the US. Table 9.1 gives the results of our application of the method to the UK, giving the fraction of monetary change produced by each of the determinants between the beginning and the end of the period.

The sub-periods selected are chosen to allow comparisons with other studies. Over the period as a whole it was high-powered money (the base, B) that explained by far the greatest part of the change in M3 – some 70 per cent. As already shown, R/D was acting to reduce the monetary expansion; C/D was acting in the other direction, and was considerably stronger taken over the whole period. In the sub-periods 1870–9, 1880–96 and for 1880–1913 the respective contribution of each of these factors was more or less the same. For the period 1897–1913 the monetary base is the most powerful explanation, R/D is strong, and C/D has lost a little of its importance. In summary, whichever way we look at it the monetary base is the prime determinant of money supply in the period. Table 9.1 shows the effect over a variety of sub-periods.

Table 9.2. *Banks and bank branches, 1870–1920*

	London banks		Provincial banks		All United Kingdom banks		Bank branches per 10,000 of population
	A	B	A	B	A	B	
1870	56	84	299	1,093	386	2,728	0·87
1880	65	109	258	1,396	358	3,454	1·0
1890	65	149	200	1,795	303	4,347	1·16
1900	39	134	108	1,875	188	5,922	1.44
1910	27	36	47	1,516	112	7,564	1·68
1920	29	31	21	949	75	9,668	2·08

Note: columns A = number of banks; columns B = number of branches.
Source: Capie and Webber (1985).

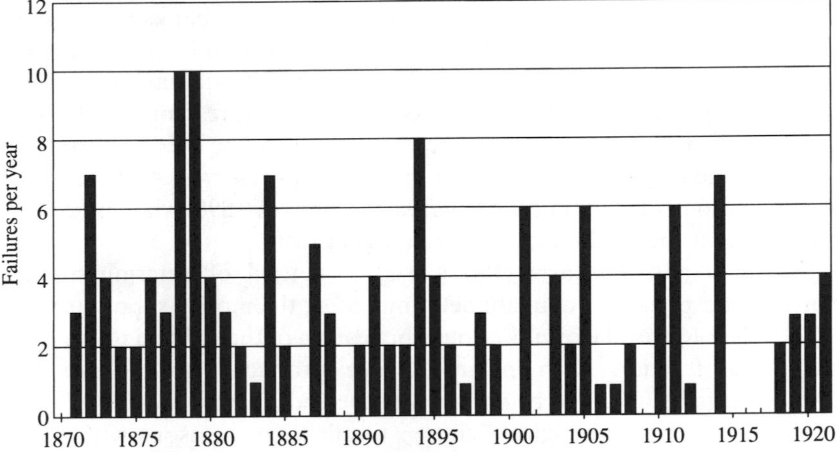

Figure 9.2 UK bank failures, 1870–1921
Source: Capie and Webber (1985).

What catches the eye is the growth and changing structure of the banking system. By 1870 British banking had already begun to resemble its modern form, with a number of commercial banks the largest of which had many branches across the country. Table 9.2 shows how the form developed over the next fifty years. As early as 1870 there were 2,728 bank offices in the country (0.87 offices per 10,000 of the population). Although the total number of banks in all categories fell fairly steadily throughout the period there were still over 100 banks in 1914 and there were around

8,000 bank offices at that point (1.63 per 10,000 of the population). The fall in the total number of banks was in part the result of an advantage of large size, associated as it was with greater reserves, security and prestige; hence the accelerating mergers of the 1890s. But the pattern was older. Any one bank, usually with headquarters in London, had loans and sources of funds in most if not all parts of the country covering the whole spectrum of industry, agriculture and services. The branch pattern, as we have noted, meant that if a branch (or even several branches) were in trouble in an area adversely affected by a fall in demand for its product the resources of the bank could readily be diverted to ease the pressure.

Many banks in Britain continued without branches, and there were fairly frequent bank failures (Figure 9.2) and corresponding entry to the places left open. But failures, as has been noted, did not result in runs. They were accepted as part of the normal pattern of business enterprise. The City of Glasgow Bank failure in 1878 is a case in point. Although a considerable bank, it was badly managed and corrupt. It was allowed to fail, which caused difficulties for other banks. Yet there was no run on banks in general, no banking panic, no financial crisis, no significant rise in C/D or R/D ratios, those indicators of caution.

The banks and industry

A considerable literature contrasts 'banking' and 'market' orientated economies. Large European banks, for instance, are said to have helped industry develop, while British banks are said to have failed in this role. A long list of allegations has been made against the banks: that London-based deposit banks were averse to industrial finance; that amalgamation contributed by increasing the extent of 'London' practices; that British banks held portfolios radically different from their continental counterparts, being biassed to liquid assets.

The indictment comes with an explanation: the banks, it is said, grew up in the industrial revolution, when their function was to provide short-term credit for small businesses. The alleged aversion to long-term commitments seems to be instanced by the experience of the 1860s, when several investment banks were formed on the continental model but then spectacularly crashed, in the Overend Gurney crisis of 1866. Liquidity conscious banks with short-term loans and safe readily saleable investments seemed to become the norm from 1870 onward.

But an indictment is not a conviction. We know little in fact about the relationship between banks and industry, and more research needs to be done before the banking industry can be convicted of failure to serve industry's needs. It is quite possible, for example, that industry demanded little finance from the banks: other financial institutions, such as the active British stock market, provided the required capital (Collins 1990a).

Financial crises and the lender of last resort

A financial crisis threatens the stability of the entire system, and causes therefore a collapse in the stock of money, as people and banks rush for liquidity. Such events should be distinguished from 'financial distress' or 'pseudo crises' (Schwartz 1986), which may threaten someone's wealth but do not threaten the prosperity of the entire economy. The United States undoubtedly experienced a genuine financial crisis in worsening waves from 1929 to 1933. By contrast, the City of Glasgow Bank failure in 1878 caused shareholders to suffer loss, but without threat to the banking system as a whole.

Branch banking was one insurance against crisis. The other was the attitude and action of the Bank of England, as lender of last resort – which is to say, the bank of banks, issuing money when the banks ran out. On 10 May 1866 Overend, Gurney & Co. shut down. The market was nervous, and panic broke out the next day. There was an immense demand for cash, and the Bank, for fear of breaking the legal limit on the amount of paper money it could issue, hesitated. The Bank Charter Act was then suspended, allowing an expansion of paper money unbacked by gold, and more cash was forthcoming: the Bank bought Consols with the new cash on the open market, putting cash into the hands of the investors seeking it. The panic ended abruptly, for people knew they could get cash. Although a small drain of notes continued for about a week the crisis ended without the Bank in the end having to issue more paper money than the suspended law allowed (Batchelor 1986).

Similar behaviour by the Bank in the still earlier crisis of 1825 was described by Jeremiah Harman, a director of the Bank:

> We lent it by every possible means and in modes we have never adopted before; we took in stock on security, we purchased Exchequer bills, we not only discounted outright, but we made advances on the deposit of bills of exchange to an immense amount, in short by every possible means consistent with the safety of the Bank, and we were not on some occasions over nice. Seeing the dreadful state in which the public were, we rendered every assistance in our power. (quoted in Bagehot 1873: 73)

The crisis of 1825, too, ended within days.

The Victorian essayist and editor of the *Economist* Walter Bagehot is often credited with convincing the Bank of England of the need to act as lender of last resort. That was plainly unnecessary. What he in fact did was to urge it to commit itself in advance to doing so (see Rockoff 1986).

This, he argued, would eliminate the fear that cash could not be obtained and so would prevent crises from arising in the first place. As Meltzer (1986: 33) puts it, Bagehot's 'main recommendation is that the Bank should announce in advance that, although it is privately owned, it accepts the responsibility of a bank of issue to protect the money stock'.

It is difficult to distinguish between the Bank's pre-commitment to the lending in a crisis and the branched structure of the banking system as the cause of the absence of banking crises in Britain. Both may have contributed; perhaps either would have been sufficient.

An instance is the so-called Baring crisis. The Baring bank got into difficulties in 1890, as a result of involvement in Argentina. The flow of remittance from Argentina stopped. The Bank of England organised a rescue – a lifeboat. Against the thinking of the Chancellor of the Exchequer, Goschen, who was reluctant to provide government assistance lest Baring prove to be insolvent, the Bank decided that the problem was one of illiquidity. It persuaded other banks to agree, on the basis of a report concluding that Baring was fundamentally sound but needed some £10 million in liquidity. Baring was liquidated and there was a modest rise in the demand for cash. The bank was reconstituted as a limited liability company with a new chairman and the Argentinian debt written off (which is to say accepted as a loss). Although both the Bank of England and the rest of the City were very active there was no crisis. Note that there was not a classic lender-of-last-resort operation – one was not needed.

Another illuminating crisis was that of 1914 (Seabourne 1986). The problem had two aspects. The prospect of imminent war caused plunging stock prices and a failure of remittance from overseas. A rush for liquidity began and the banks called in their loans to the stock exchange (which dealt in stock certificates) and the discount market (which dealt in bills), further weakening the stock exchange and driving the discount market to the Bank of England. Fortunately all this occurred just before a bank holiday – which was extended. Assistance was provided to the stock market under a scheme proposed by the clearing banks, and the Bank of England gave assistance to the discount market. There may have been a subsequent inflation (see below; and Goodhart 1986) but it was to some extent intertwined with the exigencies of war finance, not the crisis. Again the episode exemplifies the problem of explaining UK financial stability in these years. The consequences of large well-diversified banks are inextricable from those of having a pre-committed lender of last resort.

War finance

The First World War was to last much longer, and to cost more in lives and other resources, than anyone expected. There was therefore no advance planning to raise funds for the war on the scale required.

Governments can raise funds by three means – taxation, borrowing and inflation. The last of these is possible under a fixed exchange rate system only if all countries inflate. During the First World War Britain, as was conventional at times of war, suspended the gold standard. Sterling floated, interest rates were raised to defend it, and a variety of exchange controls were adopted (Pollard 1983). The floating of sterling meant that all three sources of finance were available. This is not to imply that inflation was necessarily a deliberate policy choice, but when it happened it helped the government's finances: the government issued paper money that depreciated in value.

In August 1914 the stock of government debt stood at just over £700 million; by August 1919 it had risen to roughly £7,500 million. Over the same period the monetary base (M0: gold, currency and other promises by the Bank of England to pay) grew by around 119 per cent and broad money M3 (including chequing and savings deposits) by around 114 per cent. There was also a fiduciary issue of currency notes (that is, paper money unbacked by gold) totalling £320 million in issue by the end of the war. Prices therefore rose from 100 in 1913 to 211 in 1919. In the last year of peace, tax revenue from income and other taxes (except inflation) was £198 million. In the last year of war it was £889 million. National income in wartime is peculiar, much of it being waste by the standards of peacetime. A large but short-lived boom occurred after the war. Table 9.3 below makes two comparisons, setting bounds (upper for the war years, lower for the first year of peace) on the true ratio. The ratios are to be compared with the values in 1913.

In November 1914 the income tax and super tax rates were doubled to 2s 4d (12 per cent) and 1s (5 per cent) and duties on beer and tea were raised. It was not enough. Tax rates were raised again during the second half of 1915 and still again later – income tax by a further 40 per cent and super tax to 2s 6d and then to 5s in 1916–17 and 6s in 1918–19. The exemption limit was reduced from £160 to £130 in 1915 (£100 was the rough equivalent of £1,500 in purchasing power of 1990). Indirect taxation continued to rely primarily on its traditional bases of alcohol and tobacco. Customs, excise, estate, land and house duties rose from £115.8 million in 1913 to £169.2 million in 1916–17 and £208.8 million in 1919–20. On an index basis there was a rise from 100 to 114.7 followed by a fall to 94.80. There was also a profits tax (Kirkaldy 1921; Morgan 1952).

Table 9.3. *Revenue and debt in the First World War, 1913–20*

Year	Total revenue (£bn)	GNP (£bn)	National debt (£bn)	Rev./GNP	Debt/GNP
1913	0·198	2·322	0·6	0·0853	0·258
1914	0·227	2·347	1·105	0·0967	0·471
1915	0·337	2·676	2·133	0·1259	0·797
1916	0·573	3·176	4·011	0·1804	1·263
1917	0·707	3·951	5·872	0·1789	1·486
1918	0·889	4·77	7·435	0·1864	1·559
1919	1·34	4·992	7·832	0·2684	1·569
1920	1·426	5·688	7·585	0·2507	1·334

Sources: Liesner (1989); Capie and Webber (1985).

All this was not nearly enough to finance the war. So the government borrowed, as it had done in time of war for two centuries, at high rates. In November 1914 £350 million of 3.5 per cent bonds were issued at a price of £95 against a face value of £100, repayable in 1925–8. An unlimited loan was announced in June 1915 of 4.5 per cent bonds issued at par. By March 1916 £900 million had been raised. Conversion rights – into 3.5 per cent war bonds 1925–8, 2.5 per cent Consols and 2.75 per cent and 2.5 per cent annuities were attached. By 1917 only £100 million of the first type of bonds were outstanding. The third and last big issue of war loan offered two types of security, a 5 per cent bond (issued at 95) repayable 1929–47 and a 4 per cent bond repayable 1929–42, free of income but not of super tax. Then in 1917 the government began issuing war bonds in a steady stream. Floating debt (that is, short-term debt) also rose substantially. In March 1919 the total of Treasury Bills and Ways and Means Advances had reached £1,400 million, as compared with £16 million just before the outbreak of the war.

Inflation and the 1914 crisis

As was remarked above, one symptom of the 1914 panic was an 'internal drain' – a run to cash by UK residents. Provision of currency notes was therefore an essential part of the scheme to deal with the panic. But was the injection too large or too prolonged? Goodhart (1986) suggests that it was both, and that it contributed substantially to wartime inflation. The monetary base certainly expanded very fast over the first few months of the war.

While the initial injection of notes was certainly desirable, it is far from clear it was desirable for it to remain. The financial panic was expected to end fairly quickly, and indeed did so. Why, then, was the cash injection allowed to remain in the system? It may have been deliberate – a resort to the inflation tax because nothing else could be levied so quickly. In any event, a substantial part (approaching one half) of the wartime monetary expansion took place by November 1914, three months into a war that was to last four years. The monetary base then fell back below the November 1914 level for a year and a half. The monetary expansion was certainly triggered by the 1914 panic – but it is likely that it went on too long. Just why it did remains obscure.

Money in the economy: 1918–39

After the war, from 1919 to April 1925, sterling floated, with the objectives of returning eventually to gold at the pre-war parity. From 1925 to September 1931 Britain was back on gold. From the end of September 1931 to 1939 there was a managed float; the Exchange Equalisation Account (EEA) was established in 1932. The question is what the effect of all this was on money.

In the first, floating period, so long as there was no intervention in the foreign exchanges the stock of money was entirely determined by domestic factors. This is, of course, in sharp contrast with the gold standard. To get back to gold, however, money was kept tight. Figure 9.3 shows growth in the money base; Figure 9.4 shows the nominal price of dollars in terms of sterling, the £/$ ratio; Figure 9.5 shows Bank Rate, the bill rate, and the Consol yield. The policy was 'successful', in that sterling managed to attain its old parity.

Exchange rates, being prices determined in asset markets, can move much more quickly than national price levels. Consequently there can be a gap between the *nominal* and the *real* exchange rate. The nominal rate is that quoted on the exchanges; the real exchange rate is the nominal rate adjusted for actual changes in the price level, relative to some base. For example, suppose the nominal rate of the pound against the dollar in the exchange market depreciated by 10 per cent during some year. If the two national price levels did not change there would also be a 10 per cent real depreciation. But if the British price level had in the meantime risen by 10 per cent the real rate would not have changed at all; for the price of British relative to American goods would not have changed.

Figure 9.4 shows the behaviour of sterling in *real* terms and the nominal exchange rate against the dollar (for a detailed discussion of the real series see Dimsdale (1981a)). It can be seen that there was a real appreciation of sterling, from 94.7 to 111.1 (17 per cent), between 1921 and 1926. Of course the calculations are uncertain; but it would be hard to argue that there was

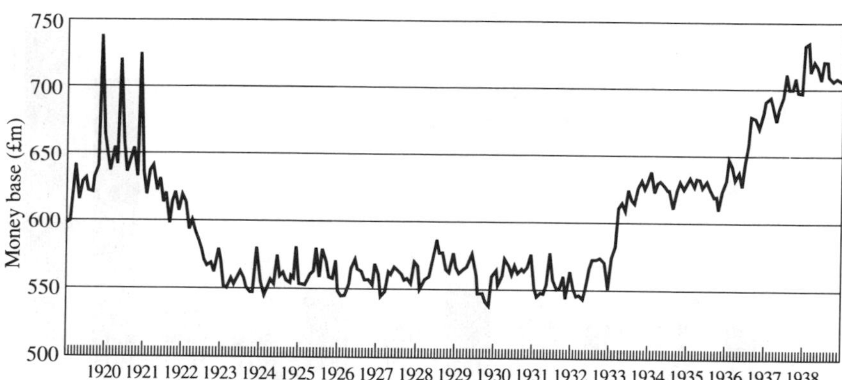

Figure 9.3 UK money base, 1919–39
Source: Capie and Webber (1985).

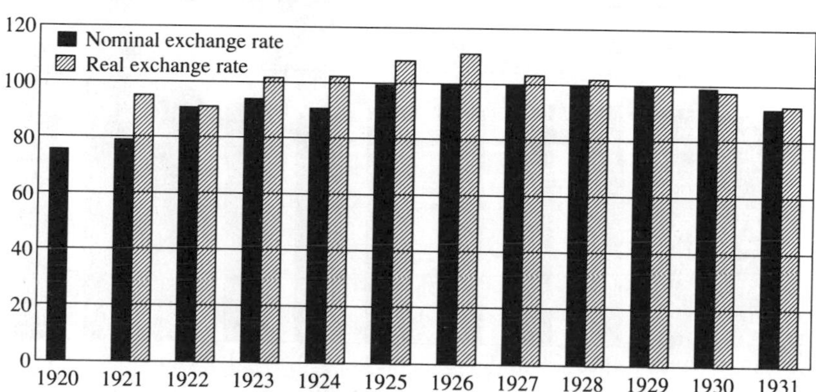

Figure 9.4 Real and nominal exchange rate, 1920–31
Source: Dimsdale (1981b).

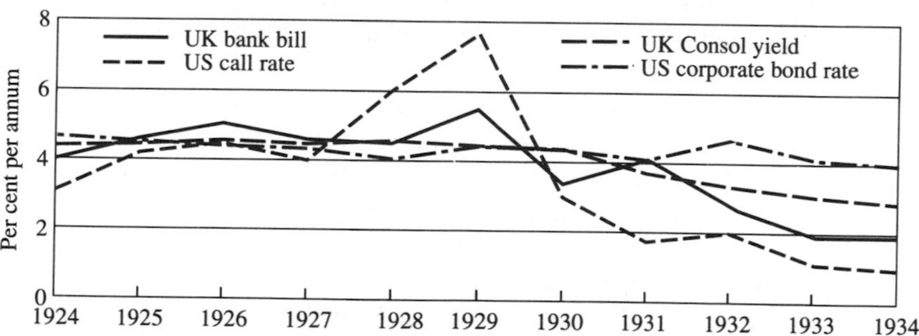

Figure 9.5 UK and US interest rates, 1924–34
Sources: Capie and Webber (1985) for UK, Friedman and Schwartz (1982) for US.

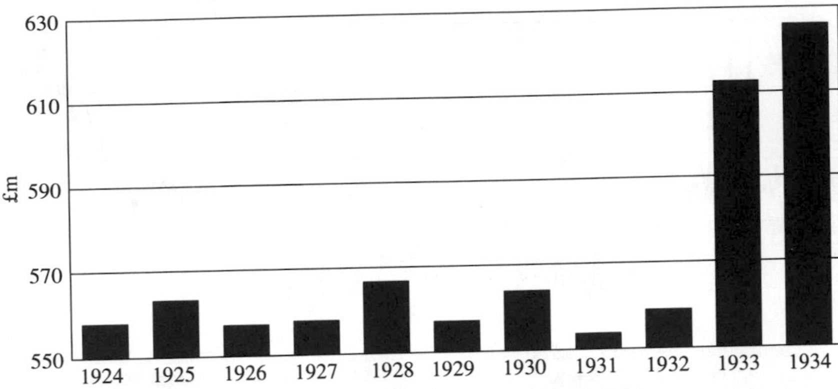

Figure 9.6 UK monetary aggregate (M0), 1924–34
Source: Capie and Webber (1985).

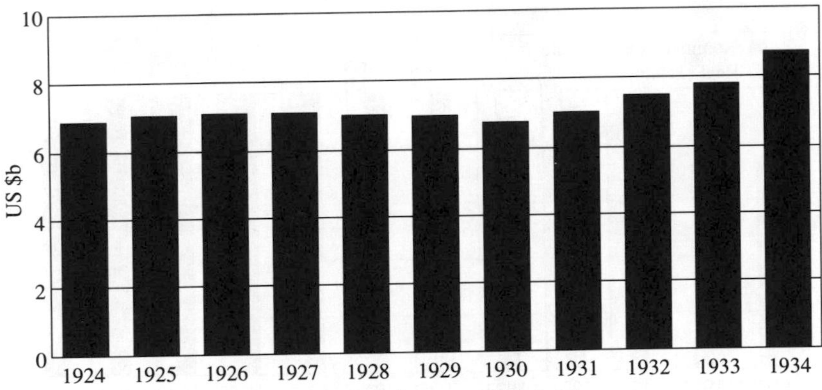

Figure 9.7 US high-powered money, 1924–34
Source: Friedman and Schwartz (1982).

no real appreciation at all. It produced a squeeze felt particularly by the traded goods sector and therefore helps explain the boom in house building and the recession in traditional exports.

During the late 1920s the influences on the money stock were once again primarily external. Britain was linked again to the United States through a now-fixed exchange rate. Figure 9.5 shows the extent of the linkage in UK and US short and long rates. Figures 9.6 and 9.7 show the behaviour of monetary aggregates. The US monetary collapse of 1930 can be seen vividly, but Britain dodged it by going off gold.

The years down to the Second World War were years of 'managed float'. The authorities intervened on the exchanges to dampen fluctuations in the rate, but not to keep it artificially high or low. External influences on the economy, therefore, were felt entirely in the rate of exchange.

Inter-war background

The British economy emerged from the war in a condition vastly altered. Wartime disruption led foreigners to substitute their own for Britain's goods, and Britain being a particularly open economy, dependent on trade, it was therefore exposed to current account deficits. Before 1914 the visible trade deficit was amply offset by earnings on invisibles – not least the interest earned on foreign securities. During the war Britain had been obliged to run down her holdings of foreign assets, and the consequent loss of wealth was a weakening factor; shipping services, too, were reduced with the contraction in trade, and other invisibles were similarly affected adversely. The deficit on current account made it harder to drive the pound back to its pre-war parity.

More strictly domestic was a problem that derived directly from the war effort, the huge quantity of government debt. In 1913 government debt was approximately £600m – that is, around 35 per cent of national income. After the war it was approximately £8,000m – that is, more than 200 per cent of national income. (The ratio was similar after the Napoleonic Wars and again after the Second World War; much higher, it should be noted, than the ratios that have recently alarmed the United States.) The burden which servicing the debt placed on the Exchequer was substantial, particularly since the debt had been issued in wartime at historically high interest rates.

The monetary and macro-economic variables

Figure 9.8 shows the movement of the main monetary and macro-economic variables in the economy in the inter-war years. There was considerable economic growth, with prices tending to fall at first, then rise. Across the whole period real GNP grew by on average over 2 per cent per annum – perfectly healthy by British historical standards. The monetary variables did not grow as fast as output and thus overall prices fell. In accord with the quantity equation, the real output growth of 2 per cent per annum was matched by monetary growth of 1 per cent per annum and a price fall on average of 1 per cent per annum. It was again the case that the money multipliers were relatively stable and that the monetary base provided most of the explanation for the way 'broad money' moved.

The currency/deposit ratio (a measure among other things of the caution of bank customers) exhibits a pronounced cyclical pattern. It rises from 1922 to 1926 then falls to a trough in 1931–2 before turning up and rising for the rest of the decade. The range, however, is not great, lying between 12.5 and 16 per cent. The stability dispels any notion of a British

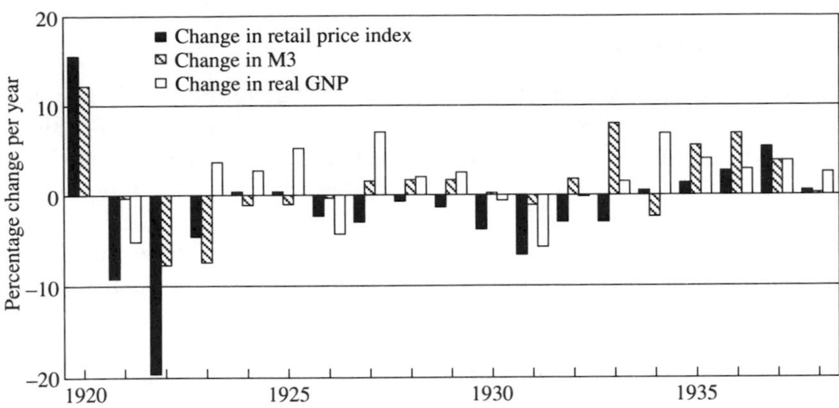

Figure 9.8 Annual changes in the retail price index, M3 and real GNP, 1920–39
Source: Capie and Webber (1985).

financial crisis in 1931. The competing forces of financial sophistication (the tendency to get out of money and into financial assets) and monetisation (the extension of the monetary economy by increasing use of money) were probably weak and certainly more or less equal. The widespread belief that low points in the currency/deposit ratio coincide with peaks in the business cycle and vice versa is derived in the main from US data, bank panics there beginning close to the business cycle peaks (Gorton 1988). But Britain in the inter-war years shows no such relationship (nor did it from 1870 to 1914), since it had no panics. A sharp rise in the ratio did occur in 1931, though never to panic levels – in view of the fears about liquidity spreading through Europe at the time the surprise would have been if people had not attempted to get out of bank deposits and into currency. But the fear was dispelled quickly and the ratio quickly reverted to normal. The threats of war in the late 1930s were more potent in this respect than the collapse of the international monetary system in 1931.

The reserve/deposit ratio (under the control, recall, of bankers, and reflecting their attitudes) showed very little variation across the whole period, and averaged 11 per cent. Even through the depression years in Britain 1929–32 there is nothing exciting to report – itself a startling fact in comparison with events in Germany and the United States. The ratio jumps in 1933, readily explained by the huge inflow of funds from abroad, drawn by the attractiveness of sterling (the dollar was devaluing; cf. McCloskey and Zecher 1984). After the link with gold was severed in September 1931 the pound depreciated by 24 per cent in three months, and in 1932 it still looked cheap to foreigners. The Exchange Equalisation

Account, established in 1932, was unable to sterilise these inflows completely and they therefore found their way into the banks. Bank reserves remained high partly because the Bank of England, alarmed by world banking failures in the early 1930s, pressed bankers to keep them high. There is no evidence of what used to be asserted, namely, that in the 1920s when a tight money policy was being pursued it was offset by the banks lowering their reserve/deposit ratios. The famous Macmillan Committee (1931) stressed the need for the banks to maintain fixed cash ratios.

Banking

Some of the bigger bank mergers took place during the First World War. Ever-bigger banks seemed reasonable in view of German competition – Germany being notorious for enormous investment banks – a point made especially by the Chairman of Midland Bank. Before the First World War there were no legal constraints on mergers. The heavily concentrated system that resulted by 1918 persisted through the inter-war years and beyond: in 1919 the five largest clearing banks held around 80 per cent of current account deposits in England and Wales. They were prevented from further mergers only by the Treasury's opposition.

In the late nineteenth century, bank profits had been healthy and grew steadily, though the greater fluctuations in interest rates between the wars resulted in somewhat more pronounced fluctuations. Even in the depression of 1929–32 no losses were reported by the commercial banks, at the same time that thousands upon thousands of banks around the world were collapsing. The British banks remained highly liquid and very cautious in investment. After the highly liquid assets of cash and Treasury bills, the banks invested largely in UK government securities. The only illiquid part of the balance sheet were so-called 'advances', that is, short loans to businesses and individuals: fixed period loans, overdrafts and commercial bills. Thus the banks continued their role of offering short term credit to industry.

The Macmillan Committee (J.M. Keynes was a major influence on it) wanted the banks to behave more like German investment banks, lending long to industry allegedly 'starved' of such funds. The British banks defended themselves by pointing out that around 50 per cent of their assets were tied up in loans of one kind or another to industry, a high degree of commitment to industry, leaving industry free to seek somewhat longer loans elsewhere. As Collins (1990a) puts it, 'in effect [the banks] claimed they were prepared to meet all legitimate demands for credit from industrial and other customers within the established guide lines governing the granting of such loans'. The 'starving' of British industry of long-term finance from banks continues to fascinate historians; yet industry floated loans in the City and locally with ease. Collins argues, however, that the banks did exercise some oligopoly power to constrain the advances to the private sector. Strict price-fixing ruled; a minimum rate of 5 per cent was set for advances for any customer, no matter how good.

Boom and slump

Immediately after the war there was a considerable boom and then a dramatic end to the boom and the deepest and steepest of economic recessions in British economic history, that of 1920–1. The usual story is that during the war the public built up liquidity, since there were few consumer goods available and non-war investment was low. At the end of the war the liquidity was released for consumption. The authorities could have dampened spending as a precaution against overheating, but the political climate (a war-weary populace, revolution in Russia and elsewhere and the need to placate potentially rebellious returning troops) impelled them to permit easy conditions.

Money was important. The monetary base rose sharply between the third quarter of 1918 and the second quarter of 1920 – from £540 million to £671 million, 25 per cent in eighteen months. In the next quarter it sharply contracted. Short-term interest rates had in fact been moving up from late 1919, well in advance of the downturn. The movement in interest rates may not have been strictly a policy choice but rather the result of a struggle between Whitehall and Threadneedle Street. The Treasury favoured low interest rates, the better to refinance the war debt; the Bank favoured high interest rates, the better to re-establish sterling at the pre-war parity. The Bank won. The Bank was concerned to choke off inflation, and was also keen to regain the control over rediscount policy that it had surrendered in wartime. The role of money in producing the 1920–1 slump should not, however, be exaggerated. The slump was particularly severe in industries which expanded massively in the war, and again in the 1919–20 inflation, known generally as 'the restocking boom', making up for war damage. Such industry could scarcely escape sharp contraction with the coming of peace.

The return to gold

Britain returned to the gold standard, at the pre-war parity, in 1925. The exchange rate against the dollar was then once again $4.86/£. The decision has been widely regarded as having been taken without much thought, and is blamed for the persistent unemployment in Britain during the 1920s. Winston Churchill, Chancellor of the Exchequer at the time the decision was taken, came to regard it as the greatest mistake of his life (Grigg 1948). But recent work shows that the decision was not taken unthinkingly and that it is far from clear that the return did harm.

Britain took the lead and other countries followed. Therefore had Britain chosen another rate the likelihood is that the other countries would have set their rates in proportion: so it is doubtful that choosing, say, $4.40/£ – a 10 per cent lower figure, which is what has been contemplated in retrospect – would have made much difference for Britain's international position. Furthermore, the decision to return seemed well founded in experience. Countries which had operated without the restraint of gold had undergone after the war wild swings in both output and prices – the examples of Germany and Austria, with price levels increasing by factors of literally millions, were on the minds of policy makers. And perceptions of how the standard had worked before 1914 were important. Britain had been on the gold standard, at the historic price of sterling for gold, with an interregnum from 1797 to 1819, since 1717 (Ashton 1955). The years immediately before 1914 were the cumulation of a long and most satisfactory experience. Output fluctuated moderately about a rising level; short-term price movements were, and were seen to be, transitory and insignificant (note in evidence the behaviour of Consol yields); and world trade grew steadily. All of this may have been purely *associated* with gold – there may have been no causal connection. But such a long association was persuasive, and not unreasonably so (Sayers 1960a). Finally, as a great trading power – perhaps not quite so great as was assumed in 1925, but important nonetheless – Britain, it was thought, could stabilise the conditions of world trade, to its own long-term benefit in larger exports and cheaper imports, by leading a re-establishment of gold.

From 1919 the government had resolved to return eventually to gold at the old parity (useful narratives of the period are Aldcroft 1970 and Pollard 1983). By January 1924, the pound was at $4.26, and thereafter it rose steadily towards the pre-war parity. This was convenient, and was still another argument for fixing the parity at its old value. The Gold and Silver Export Embargo Act (1920) expired in 1925, so a decision on exchange rate policy had in any case to be taken. The return at the old parity was announced by Winston Churchill in his budget speech of April 1925.

The decision, in other words, was not precipitate or irrational. The British delegation to the Genoa Conference of 1922, for example, had urged a world-wide return to gold. The Association of Clearing Banks and the Federation of British Industry supported the move. Criticism did not develop until the summer, when John Maynard Keynes published *The*

Economic Consequences of Mr Churchill, but even then the criticism was of the rate chosen, not the return to gold itself. On the basis of purchasing power parity calculations – that is, how much British prices had moved relative to other prices since 1914 – Keynes argued that sterling was 10 per cent overvalued. 10 per cent is well within the inevitable margin of error in such calculations; and subsequent authors have produced different figures. Gregory (1957) produced a much lower figure, while Redmond (1982) on an effective rate basis (that is, allowing for the importance of particular currencies in British trade) produced an overvaluation of 25 per cent.

This last calculation could, of course, not have been carried out at the time; the data did not exist, and the concept was not well articulated. But setting that aside, does it confirm Churchill's subsequent regret? It is far from clear that it does. There are both analytical and empirical arguments on the other side. In a striking anticipation of concepts subsequently made much use of by economists – credibility and the money supply regime – Kiddy, editor of the 'Bankers Magazine', argued at the time that to change the parity would wreck the standard; it would remove the guarantee of stability. It is a point of some substance. And by 1929, four years after the 'wrong' parity, many industries were exporting more than at their 1913 peak; the industries still in difficulties by 1929 had anyway shown signs of weakness before the war, because of a changed structural pattern of comparative advantage.

Causes of depression

Money played at best only a minor role in the economic depression of 1929–32. The main evidence on the role of money in economic cycles is found in Friedman and Schwartz's study of the US (1963). Their conclusions were that money was a prime factor in bringing about *major* cyclical downturns. The main point is that the British depression of 1929–32 was not major. Over the three years output fell by a mere 6 per cent, trivial in relation to the US (35 per cent) or even many European countries, especially Germany. The slump of 1921 had been worse in Britain.

Stock market prices did fall from late 1929 onwards and in 1933 reached a low point of some 30 per cent below their peak of 1929 (again, no disaster by American standards). While a case can be made that the stock market had real effects through a variety of channels the case is not strong. For one thing British consumption and investment both held up through 1930. More importantly, holdings of securities by individuals, even indirectly through pension schemes, were on a small scale at this time. Deflating nominal wealth by prices would reveal little change in real wealth.

The late 1920s, however, show monetary stringency. Money growth and prices were relatively flat from 1924 onwards. In the last quarter of 1928 money base fell, and it fell in three of the four quarters of 1929. The broader definition of money, M3, was also falling in late 1928 and fell in every month in the first half of 1929. Short-term interest rates were rising, consistent with this indication of monetary stringency. The Treasury bill rate was drifting upwards from 4.1 per cent in late 1928 and rose through 1929 to 6.1 per cent. Bank Rate was seen as the clearest indicator of the monetary authorities' intentions and it rose steadily from late 1928 when it was 4.5 per cent to 6.5 per cent in September 1929, and this when prices were flat and with price expectations more or less flat, too. But this is not the stuff of major depressions. Our judgement is that factors other than the money supply, most obviously the collapse in exports as world trade fell, were of far greater importance.

The 1931 crisis

In 1931, after a change of government, Britain left gold. This was not as before simply a wartime suspension, an event allowed and, to the extent that war is normal, normal under the rules of the gold standard. Was it the result of the parity chosen in 1925? Or was there some other influence?

Problems with the parity emerged in 1930, when gold losses resumed (having abated since 1928). Although both France and the USA supported the pound, in the sense that their central banks were willing to buy and sell pounds at the official rate, French opinion was that the UK's unbalanced budget was the source of the problem. True, the budget was in deficit. But a large part of the deficit was merely cyclical, and therefore transitory. Unemployment in 1931 was 21 per cent of the insured workforce, equivalent on the current definition to an unemployment rate of around 16 per cent. Unemployment relief contributed substantially to the deficit. The underlying budgetary position was not unsustainable, in the sense of being both structural (that is, not a product of the cyclical position) and so large as to be incapable of being financed except by money creation (Sargent and Wallace 1981). What of the *actual* budgetary position? A case can be constructed for arguing that it did cause problems. A deficit financed by bonds could raise interest rates, which would reduce the demand for money. The resulting excess supply of money could produce a once-for-all depreciation. But bond yields were not rising throughout 1925–31; and short rates only started to rise *after* the exchange rate came under pressure. Furthermore, the supposed chain of events would require an implausibly high sensitivity of money demand to interest rates.

Excess money produced by over-rapid supply growth can also be ruled

Table 9.4. *Money and prices from 1920 to 1932*

Year	Money supply M3 (£m)	Annual change in M3 (proportional)	Retail price index	Annual change in RPI (proportional)
1920	2,890	0·12	244	0·16
1921	2,880	0·00	222	−0·09
1922	2,660	−0·08	179	−0·19
1923	2,470	−0·07	171	−0·04
1924	2,450	−0·01	172	0·01
1925	2,430	−0·01	173	0·01
1926	2,420	0·00	169	−0·02
1927	2,460	0·02	164	−0·03
1928	2,500	0·02	163	−0·01
1929	2,540	0·02	161	−0·01
1930	2,550	0·00	155	−0·04
1931	2,520	−0·01	145	−0·06
1932	2,570	0·02	141	−0·03

out. Table 9.4 shows both money and prices from 1920 to 1932; they give no hint of excess supply. Can overvaluation therefore be blamed? The evidence is not compelling. Some export industries were depressed – but as noted above they had been depressed before 1914, and were only sustained by the closing off of foreign competition by the war. Moggridge (1972) focusses on the invisible account, which deteriorated as interest rates fell at home and world trade slowed abroad (reducing Britain's large receipts from shipping and financial services). These no doubt combined to produce weakness.

The weakness was made fatal for the gold pound of 1717, however, by a world-wide scramble for liquidity, having little or nothing to do with British policy. It swept through Europe following the collapse of Kredit Anstalt in May 1931 and in Germany throughout the summer of that year (Kindleberger 1986). At the same time the Macmillan Report revealed Britain's short-term liabilities to be even greater than previously thought: merely knowing the precarious balance sheet was enough to make it a factor. Balances were withdrawn from London, funds were drained from the Bank, and, in the wake of the Invergordon mutiny on 15 September (the sailors refused a pay cut), Britain left gold, on 21 September 1931.

Britain's position *was* weak; but it was the kind of weakness that could reverse given time, a kind that had been ridden out before. There were *real* structural adjustments to be made to the pattern of production, which an exchange rate could not prevent. The government deficit and the revelations of a weak liquidity position for the nation required borrowing from abroad. Instead the French gobbled up British gold. What happened in 1931 was not a vindication of claims that 1925 had been catastrophic: it was largely the result of the French failing to play by the rules of the old game.

Economic recovery

Yet leaving gold was not undesirable. Being off gold meant that Britain did not import the subsequent US monetary squeeze. In fact, the economy recovered smartly. The economic upswing in Britain from mid-1932 was amongst the strongest ever experienced. Many explanations have been offered as to how it started and was sustained and in these accounts money has featured strongly. The 1930s are known as the decade of 'cheap money'. In late 1932 the Bank Rate was lowered to 2 per cent and it stayed unchanged until the eve of war. All other short-term interest rates reflected the easy money conditions of the time. One line of argument is that the government brought about a reduction in interest rates in mid-1932 by carrying out a great conversion of the national debt, from the high-interest bonds coming due from the war to low-interest bonds suitable to the conditions of the time (Kaldor 1985). Since government cannot by decree reduce long-term interest rates the argument is somehow incomplete. The conversion operation was to offer a new dated stock with a coupon rate of 3.5 per cent in exchange for the 5 per cent war loan stock of 1917 of which over £2,000 million was outstanding (in 1932 some 27 per cent of the total national debt). Through a combination of propaganda, cajoling major holders of war loan stock, offering financial incentives and by other means the authorities were able *in the favourable contemporary conditions* to effect the conversion (Capie *et al.* 1986).

The principal condition was indeed the abandonment of the gold standard, freeing Britain from concern about attracting funds from abroad. With prices flat or rising only slightly, real interest rates fell. As to whether or not one views the departure from the gold standard as a policy decision or a *fait accompli* given the state of Britain's reserves there is no unambiguous position. But that only matters if the question is the role of the government. We are interested here in the role of money rather than the means by which monetary magnitudes came to be what they were. In any case, interest rates around the world were falling. British interest rates could fall rather than being used in defence of the exchange rate. The conversion of the national debt to low interest rates – seen as a result rather than a cause of monetary conditions – eased the government's budgetary burden and at the same time fostered expectations of improving monetary conditions. All these developments helped to bring down and hold down money rates of interest. And in any event real interest rates stayed low. They undoubtedly encouraged investment. Interest rates were low at a time when the nation needed such encouragement. Real rates in the long run are not the product of monetary conditions (Mills and Wood 1988). Money was not therefore central to the recovery, but doubtless it was accommodating.

Preface to war: 1937–8

The British economy experienced a strong cyclical upswing in the 1930s and reached a peak late in 1937. It then entered a short but quite sharp contractionary phase, reaching a low point late in 1938. Had war not been on the horizon the contraction might well have been deeper and longer. Industrial output fell by over 10 per cent in a twelve-month period in 1937–8, comparable to the first year of the 1929–32 depression. Strangely, prices were rising sharply in the months leading up to September 1937 and yet unemployment was still substantial.

The US underwent a similar cyclical experience and Friedman and Schwartz (1963) place the blame at the door of the Federal Reserve Bank (the American central bank). But most contemporary commentators did not list monetary stringency among the causes of the 1937 recession in Britain (Capie and Collins 1980). There was no sharp contraction in the most important bank variables, and more apparent to contemporaries the short-term rates of interest remained low (and with prices rising somewhat, real rates were surely lower). Long rates had been drifting upwards from mid-1935 but short rates remained low. The authorities pursued a 'cheap money' policy, and there is a clear and steep rise in the monetary base in 1936 and 1937. The rise in long rates in 1937 has been attributed to the commercial banks running down holdings of long-term securities in order to maintain cash reserves and to sustain high levels of advances. There was, too, the growing expectation of war, and the shift to a war footing that it augured.

Conclusions

It appears from the British experience, then, that money is important for real output only in *major* economic fluctuations. Institutions were crucial to the contrast in monetary stability between Britain and the rest of the world, especially the United States. Britain was served well by its clearing banks and even, in most times, by its devotion to gold. Finally, prices moved proportionately with the difference between money and the growth in real income. In the long run the quantity theory held.

10 Economic fluctuations, 1870–1913

Solomos Solomou

Introduction

The business cycle is the up-and-down of the economy. When we think of present-day business cycles we think of very short-run variations in unemployment, aggregate output and inflation. The business cycles of 1870–1914, however, do not look the same, and in particular look longer. The fluctuations in investment after 1945, for example, averaged five years in duration, a marked contrast to the twenty-year investment cycles of the pre-1914 period. One can ask: how variable was the macro-economy during the period 1870–1914 relative to other periods? The question is of particular interest because it was a long era of fixed exchange rates. Thus, a comparison of the pre-1914 era with the inter-war era involves a comparison of a rules-based policy regime (guided by the rules of the gold standard) and a discretionary policy regime of flexible and devalued exchange rates (cf. chs. 9, 12 and 13).

Definitions and data

When engineers speak of 'cycles' they are thinking of regular recurring waves such as the sine curve. Economists sometimes prefer the word 'fluctuations' rather than 'cycles' to describe the upswings and downswings of an economy, because of the highly irregular nature of the putative 'cycles'. The fluctuations cannot have the perfect regularity of a pendulum's swing, since the regularity would imply foreknowledge of events and therefore opportunities for profit that would in fact eliminate the fluctuations. As W. C. Mitchell, an American student of business cycles, put it in the 1920s, 'If we could foresee the business cycle there would be none.' When we speak of a nine-year 'cycle' in the economy of the nineteenth century we may in fact mean anything between seven and eleven years. Zarnowitz (1985) uses the following working definition: 'Business cycles represent expansions and contractions that consist of recurrent serially-correlated and cross-correlated movement in many economic variables.' What is required for the definition to hold is that a variable depends on its own past values (serial correlation) and is correlated with other economic variables (cross correlation).

Much of the existing historical research on business cycles makes the assumption that an economic variable such as national income or industrial production can be decomposed into three parts: trend, cycle and a residual of random influences. If such a simple perspective were wholly valid all one would have to do to identify the cycle would be to fit a long-run trend to the data and then take the pattern of absolute or relative deviations about the trend. But the procedure makes strong economic and econometric assumptions, which may be misleading if wrongly assumed to be true. For example, one of the assumptions used to make this decomposition is that economies follow a 'trend-stationary' path, which means that the economy is supposed to be fluctuating around a constant long-run rate of growth. Many econometric studies have shown that accepting the assumption when it is false will lead to errors of interpretation.

A bigger problem is the reliability of the data available. Feinstein (1972) has provided a system of national accounts comparable to the post-war period. But the data for the pre-1913 era are far less reliable than post-war data, though the reliability improves with time. The data on national income before 1914 are the fruit of a century of quantitative research, but they contain pitfalls for the study of cycles. Some of the output data, for example, were constructed by linear interpolation and by extrapolation from the known to the unknown (such as the output of the service sector); some series have been produced on the assumption that there exists a cycle in the data imposed *a priori* by the historian constructing them (the Lewis series of industrial production, for example, imposed nine-year cycles in many of the component series). Other series have been constructed from related, or 'proxy', data which may generate a cycle of the wrong size in amplitude and possibly even in duration. For example, much of the industrial production index has been constructed from trade data without adjustment for traders' stock-building. The adjustment would smooth the index.

Accounting implies that with ideal data the national income can be measured in three equivalent ways: from how much people earn (income), from how much they spend (expenditure) and from how much they produce (product). Although the three estimates attempt to measure the same variable at different points of the circular flow of the economy, there are in fact discrepancies between them (Feinstein 1972; Feinstein *et al.* 1982; Solomou 1987). As can be seen from Figure 10.1 the residual error between the income and expenditure estimates follows a time path with a distinctive time pattern, not a random one.

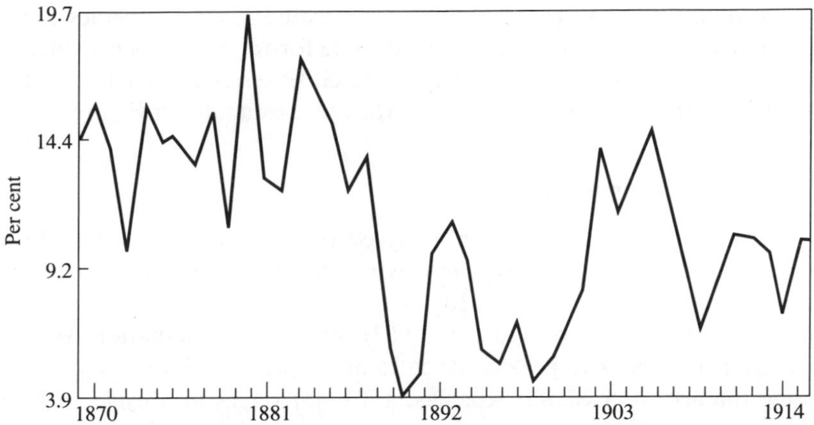

Figure 10.1 The residual error of GDP, 1870–1914
Source: see text.

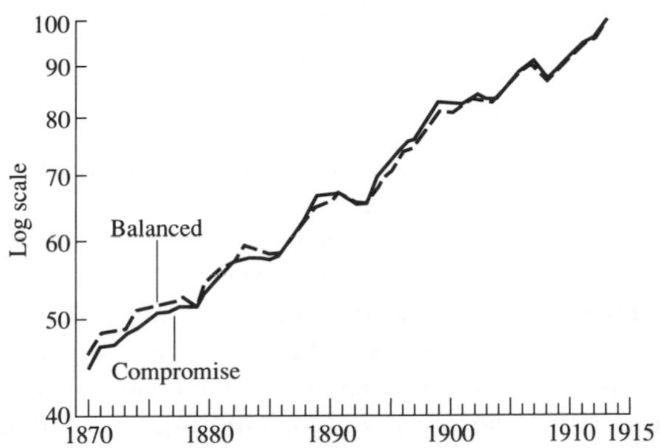

Figure 10.2 Compromise and balanced GDP, 1870–1914
Source: Solomou and Weale (1991).

The way the quantitative literature in economic history has coped with the problem so far has been to use the compromise estimate of GDP (an average of income, expenditure and output indicators). Such a mechanical solution is not adequate: the component series are of different reliabilities, the reliabilities change over time, and the quantity estimate of the income series is derived by deflating nominal income with the GDP deflator, which is itself derived from the expenditure accounts. Thus the three measures are not independent of each other. An improvement in the data is provided by the technique of balancing proposed by Stone, Champernowne and Meade (1942) and developed further by Byron (1978) and Weale (1988). The technique balances the discrepancies in the national income accounts using the accounting constraints and the disaggregated reliability values of the component parts. A balanced GDP estimate for the period is provided in Solomou and Weale (1991), the aggregate GDP series analysed here. The series is plotted, together with the compromise estimate, in Figure 10.2.

Describing business cycles

Three different cycles have been analysed by economic historians of the period: the trade cycle, the Kuznets swing and the Kondratieff wave. The trade cycle, also known as the Juglar cycle (named after Clément Juglar (1819–1905), who discovered it in 1862), refers to a fluctuation with an average period peak to peak of seven to nine years; the Kuznets (or long) swing (named after Simon Kuznets, 1901–85) refers to a cycle with an average period of sixteen to twenty-two years; and the Kondratieff wave is supposed to have an average periodicity of fifty to sixty years. Thus, from the Kondratieff wave perspective the whole era of 1870–1914 represents one long wave in economic evolution.

The Juglar trade cycle

A number of studies have argued that the Juglar is the dominant cycle influencing the UK economy over the period (Aldcroft and Fearon 1972; Rostow 1948; Crafts *et al.* 1989a). The path of UK industrial production (see Figure 10.3) gives some support to the idea.

Aggregate industrial production attained peaks in 1873, 1882, 1889, 1899, 1907 and 1913. The average peak to peak cycle is eight years. But Lewis' series, as noted, was constructed using indicator variables and methods of extrapolation and interpolation, imposing a cycle of nine years on *a priori* grounds (Lewis 1978). The cycle is imposed on iron and steel products, commercial building, clothing, printing and chemicals, which account for over 28 per cent of Lewis' total industrial production index and 35 per cent of the manufacturing and construction index. Thus the index, whatever its uses for analysis of longer trends, can provide only limited independent information for describing the business cycle. Considering only the path of industries where the cycle is not imposed on *a priori* grounds yields mixed results. As has now been documented, the construction sector followed longer-term fluctuations of twenty years (Thomas 1973); coal mining showed variations in trend without any discernible short cycle; the only industries showing a significant short cycle were iron and steel, shipbuilding and textile finishing, which account for a total of 10.9 per cent of the total industrial production index. All these were heavily dependent on export performance.

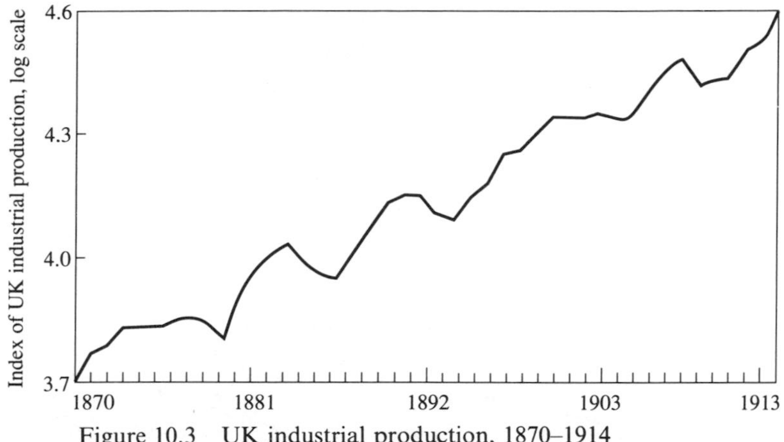

Figure 10.3 UK industrial production, 1870–1914

The path of other time series of the period reinforces the conclusion: investment followed a longer-term fluctuation of twenty-three years (Cairncross 1953); agricultural production followed a long swing of twenty years (Solomou 1986). Such evidence suggests that UK business cycles cannot simply be described as following a generalised Juglar pattern. Hicks (1982a) argued that the more regular Juglar cycle was a feature of the earlier, 1825–75 period. During 1875–1914 the business cycle became far more irregular. Feinstein is currently revising Lewis' industrial production index; the revised data should settle the issue.

The Kuznets swing

The Kuznets swing refers to a variation in economic growth that is longer than the Juglar trade cycle but shorter than the Kondratieff wave. The swings observed are variations either in levels or in rates of growth, depending upon the variables being analysed. The actual length of the swings varies with different studies, but something between fourteen to twenty-two years is representative. The relevance of Kuznets swings to understanding the cyclical path of the UK is clear from a study of the path of domestic investment (see Figure 10.4).

A Kuznets swing in the level of the original series stands out. Kuznets swings can also be observed in the level and growth of agricultural production, construction output, migration, the sectoral terms of trade and the trade balance (Solomou 1987; Lewis 1978; Thomas 1973; Cairncross 1953; Rowthorn and Solomou 1991).

Is the Kuznets swing observed in the macro-economy? Until recently it has been held that it was not (Friedman and Schwartz 1982; Matthews

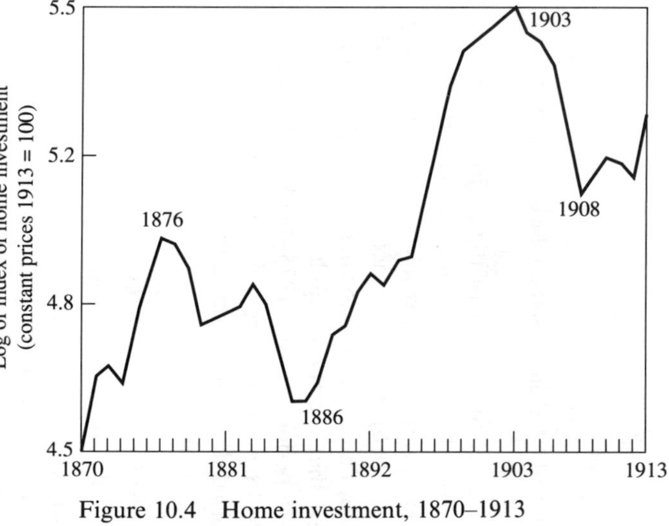

Figure 10.4 Home investment, 1870–1913

Table 10.1. *Balanced GDP peak to peak growth rates, 1874–1913 (per cent per year)*

	Growth rates	Inter-period change
1874–83	1·68	—
1883–9	1·55	−0·13
1889–99	2·19	0·64
1899–1907	1·35	−0·84
1907–13	1·72	0·37

Source: Solomou and Weale (1991).

1959), but the conclusion no longer seems valid. Feinstein, Matthews and Odling-Smee (1982) have shown that a long swing phasing of British economic performance is useful for understanding macro-economic performance during 1870–1913. Solomou (1987) has shown that a significant long swing pattern is observed in both the income and expenditure estimates of GDP throughout 1870–1914. The swings are out of phase and therefore the compromise estimate of GDP simply averages them into statistical insignificance. The balanced estimate of GDP (Solomou and Weale 1991) shows that an irregular long swing may be relevant for the macro-economy. Table 10.1 reports the peak to peak growth measures for the balanced-estimate GDP. The variations suggest that the economy underwent one and one half swings between 1874 and 1913.

The Kuznets swing was not uniform in all sectors and activities. The swings in construction, for example, were of a different phasing than those of agriculture. The strongest statement that the evidence allows is that a block of variables – domestic investment, overseas investment, migration and construction – followed a similar long swing, allowing for lags.

The Kondratieff wave

In some of the earlier literature the Kondratieff wave was used as a framework for understanding epochs such as the 'Great Depression' of 1873–96 and the Edwardian inflation of 1899–1913 (Kondratieff 1935; Schumpeter 1939). But recent economic historians have found it difficult to use the Kondratieff wave as a framework for analysing this period. The economic history of the period 1873–96 is written in terms of the '*Myth* of the Great Depression' (Saul 1969). Macro-economic variables (such as output, investment and industrial production) have not followed the long wave, even over longer periods (Kleinknecht 1987; Van Duijn 1983;

Solomou 1987). The only variables that followed the path of alternating long periods of rapid and retarded growth are volumes of exports and price of wholesale goods (Lewis 1978; Solomou 1987). Particular shocks, not a systematic cycle, would seem the best explanation. We are left with two cycles: the Juglar and the Kuznets.

Explanatory frameworks

The causes of business cycles can be viewed two ways: from 'propagation' or from 'impulse'. The propagation perspective sees cycles as arising from inside the economic system. For example, certain parameters of a Keynesian multiplier-accelerator model can generate recurring cycles, as Paul Samuelson proved in the early 1940s. The impulse perspective, by contrast, views cycles as arising from external shocks to the economy. Even random shocks are capable of generating regular-looking cycles, because each shock imposes an adjustment path on the economic system (Slutsky 1937). The shocks may be, among other things, technological change, climatic variability or shifts in policy regimes.

The two approaches are not mutually exclusive. A propagation mechanism, for example, is needed to convert random shocks into business cycles. Similarly, economists who emphasise the propagation perspective recognise that shocks determine the specific historical details of particular cycles and, thus, can account for why one cycle may be longer than another or why one depression is more severe than another. It has therefore proven difficult to decide whether economic cycles are best understood by emphasising the propagation or the impulse.

Exports

The Juglar has been attributed, for one thing, to export shocks (Ford 1981; Hatton 1990). During 1870–1914 the export ratio of goods and services as a proportion of GDP averaged about 23 per cent (Matthews *et al.* 1982: 442). With such a high share of GDP one would expect export shocks, caused partly by exogenous international influences, to be an important determinant of domestic fluctuations. Ford (1963) has argued that the proximate cause of income fluctuation was merchandise exports. In shipbuilding, iron and steel and textile finishing industries, highly dependent on exports, the hypothesis is very reasonable. Further, it is not necessary for the shock in exports to follow a regular cycle in order to generate a quite regular one at home. A bumper harvest abroad, to give an example, may confuse business people – since they do not know if the shock is permanent or transitory (as the economic jargon has it). Business people may then make inappropriate decisions that commit them to a cycle

Table 10.2. *Peak to peak growth rates for the volume of exports, 1866–1913* (*rate of growth per year*)

	Growth rate (per cent per year)	Inter-period change (change in percent per year)
1866–72	6·12	—
1872–81	2·43	−3·69
1881–9	2·33	−0·10
1889–99	1·19	−1·14
1899–1907	3·99	+2·80
1907–13	2·79	−1·20

Source: Feinstein (1972).

of boom and bust more regular than the impulse. A transitory increase in exports may lead to an expansion of investment which will not be warranted in the future. The shocks themselves are not improbable: Britain traded a good deal with poor countries, inside and outside the empire; banks and farming were subject to panic and the weather would make for unstable demands.

The role of exports in generating the Kuznets swing is more difficult to document. Table 10.2 presents the peak to peak growth rate of the volume of British exports between 1866 and 1913. The evidence suggests that exports did not follow a long swing pattern. The retardation of exports observed in the 1870s relative to the mid-Victorian period persisted throughout 1872–99. This was then followed by long-term improvement in export growth during the Edwardian period. Thus for most of the period the variations in export growth are much more long term than expected in a Kuznets swing. Exports could nonetheless have been important over some sub-periods. For example, the significant retardation of exports in the 1870s is likely to have acted as a depressing effect on output and investment in the domestic economy. But the production structure adjusted to meet the needs of rising domestic demand for services in the 1880s and 1890s. The long-term retardation of exports did not have a long-term depressing effect on the macro-economy. True, during the Edwardian period the rapid growth of exports was partly a result of depressed conditions in the home economy: steelmakers and the like sought vent for their surpluses abroad. Some of the literature has also argued that the growth of exports in the period reinforced a demand structure favouring the old staple industries, generating a depressed path of productivity growth (Kennedy 1987; contrast McCloskey 1970, 1981). But on the whole the connection between exports and production must be considered weak.

Investment

The multiplier-accelerator theory claims that variations of investment are important in explaining business cycles (Matthews 1959). But aggregate investment followed a long swing, twenty-three years in fact (Cairncross 1953; Solomou 1987), not a short nine-year cycle. Investment therefore is unlikely to have been very important in explaining the Juglar. Investment does help explain the long swings. Thomas (1954) argued that domestic investment levels were above trend in the high-growth phase and below trend in the low-growth phase. He viewed the 1870s and the 1890s as high growth and the 1880s and 1900s as low growth.

The level of investment is not simply proportional to the rate of growth of output. The *rate of change* of investment is more informative. Output and investment exhibited long swings, but investment lagged output. From 1876 investment followed output down; similarly investment fell from 1902, following the retardation of output growth from 1899 on.

The literature has explained investment swings as a response to international migration (Thomas 1954). The large outward migration of the 1880s and 1900s are said to have resulted in a large reduction of population-sensitive investment at home. But an analysis of the sectoral variations of the British capital stock illustrates the problems with accepting such an explanation. Investments in houses, electricity, gas and water are most obviously sensitive to population. Defining a peak year in the capital stock as a transition year from above trend to below trend growth, Table 10.3 divides the peak to peak swings in the rate of growth of capital into sectors.

The results suggest that the population-sensitive investments accounted for a variable part of the inter-swing changes – explaining 20.1 per cent of the inter-swing variation during 1862–96 (calculated from the right column as 17.0 + 3.1), 40.5 per cent during 1878–1905 (that is, 26.6 + 13.9) and 37.4 per cent during 1896–1913 (28.0 + 9.4). The evidence does not indicate that population-sensitive investments dominated the swings throughout the period. In particular, the population-sensitive category accounted for a low proportion of the downswing during 1878–96. Agricultural investment accounted for 21 per cent of the downswing during 1878–96, suggesting that structural change in the economy, partly accelerated by international competition, was as important as the change in population. What is also clear from Table 10.3 is that the notion of a long swing driven by demographic–economic interactions is more relevant to the 1890s and the Edwardian period than to the 1870s and the 1880s.

Table 10.3. *A sectoral analysis of the peak to peak phases in the British gross capital stock, 1862–1913*

	(1) Share in stock of capital	(2) Annual rate of growth in cycle	(3) Contribution ((1) × (2))	(4) Change in contribution	(5) As per cent of change, swing to swing
Population-sensitive dwellings					
1862	0·258				
1878	0·241	0·0199	0·00513		
1896	0·239	0·0163	0·00392	−0·00121	17·0
1905	0·240	0·0250	0·00597	+0·00205	26·6
1913	0·237	0·0135	0·00325	−0·00272	28·0
Gas, electricity and water					
1862	0·0207				
1878	0·0281	0·0429	0·00089		
1896	0·0361	0·0310	0·00087	−0·0002	3·1
1905	0·0470	0·0539	0·00195	+0·0011	13·9
1913	0·0498	0·0221	0·00104	−0·0009	9·4
Not population-sensitive					
Building and works (excluding dwellings)					
1862	0·559				
1878	0·531	0·0207	0·01160		
1896	0·514	0·0151	0·00800	−0·0036	51·1
1905	0·495	0·0204	0·01049	+0·0025	32·2
1913	0·480	0·0112	0·00555	−0·0049	50·8
Plant, equipment, vehicles and ships					
1862	0·183				
1878	0·227	0·0377	0·00686		
1896	0·247	0·0217	0·00492	−0·0019	27·5
1905	0·266	0·0327	0·00807	+0·0032	40·7
1913	0·283	0·0227	0·00604	−0·0020	20·9
Agriculture					
1862	0·181				
1878	0·128	+0·0034	+0·00051		
1896	0·098	−0·0088	−0.00096	−0·00146	20·9
1905	0·072	−0·0040	−0·00032	+0·00064	8·2
1913	0·062	−0·0023	−0·00015	+0·00017	−1·8

Source: Solomou (1987: 105).

Table 10.4. *Peak to peak growth rates in broad money, 1873–1913 (percentage growth rate per year)*

	Capie and Webber	Friedman and Schwartz
1873–82	0·19	0·41
1882–9	1·51	1·59
1889–99	2·98	2·81
1899–1907	0·93	1·29
1907–13	2·34	2·61

Sources: Capie and Webber (1985); Friedman and Schwartz (1982).

Monetary factors

The role of money in generating business cycles was a theme emphasised in many pre-Keynesian cyclical theories (and see ch. 9). In recent years the idea that unanticipated monetary shocks can generate real fluctuations has seen a revival (Lucas 1972; Barro 1981). The basic idea is that a random monetary shock fools rational agents into changing their real behaviour with respect to work and leisure, consumption and investment. Since gathering information has a cost, maximising individuals do not acquire all information instantaneously; thus, absolute price changes are likely to be mistaken for relative price changes, and to have real effects. Hence, monetary shocks are likely to have at least temporary (cyclical) effects.

Although such models of business cycles were popular in the 1970s it is now recognised that their ability to explain British and American business cycles in the twentieth century is weak (Gordon 1986; Kydland and Prescott 1982). How well do monetary variations explain pre-1914 business cycle behaviour? The existing literature provides us with mixed results: Aldcroft and Fearon (1972) conclude that the influence of monetary factors varied from cycle to cycle, making it difficult to draw general conclusions; Ford (1981) argues that money supply accommodated itself to changes in activity rather than causing it (and compare McCloskey and Zecher 1976); even Friedman and Schwartz (1982) concluded that UK money supply variations did not influence real performance. The results are consistent with the descriptive evidence presented above, namely, that the better story is one of sector by sector shocks.

The peak to peak growth rates of Friedman and Schwartz's and Capie and Webber's money stocks are reported in Table 10.4. The series show a similar pattern – a long-term stepping up of nominal monetary growth during 1889–99 relative to the period 1873–89, and a retardation during

1899–1907. Taking the growth behaviour of the balanced GDP series as representative of aggregate long swings there appears to be a similarity between long-term monetary growth and output growth. GDP growth is low between 1874 and 1889 as is nominal money supply growth; GDP growth reaches a peak in the 1890s, as does nominal monetary growth; GDP growth reached its lowest point in the cycle of 1899–1907, a period when nominal M3 growth was significantly retarded; both growth rates pick up again in 1907–13. Friedman and Schwartz (1982) were too hasty in rejecting a connection between money and growth (they used the wrong national income series).

The connection could come by way of unanticipated inflation. If all price variations were perfectly anticipated then real variables would be left unaffected by inflation. But if the variation of prices was not correctly predicted by economic agents (this would be particularly likely during adjustment periods towards a new price level, such as the 1870s and 1890s) monetary variations could have real effects.

Another connection, as explained in chapter 9, is the interest rate. Irving Fisher argued long ago that the expected real rate of interest can be thought of as the nominal rate of interest minus the expected price change. In the 1870s, with falling aggregate prices real interest rates would be expected to rise, unless the market for loanable funds has perfect foresight and adjusts market interest rates down by the same proportion as the rate of deflation. Hence, in periods of unexpected deflation the real cost of borrowing is expected to increase and vice versa for periods of unexpected inflation.

A direct test for this hypothesis would require a complete macro-model of the economy. A rough test can be attempted by looking at trends in interest rates, prices and real interest rates (after the event). The relevant trends are presented in Table 10.5. During 1873–82 market interest rates in Britain were remarkably stable, despite deflation averaging 2 per cent per year. Rates adjusted downwards in the 1880s when the rate of deflation slowed, suggesting a degree of lagged adjustment. In the 1890s, however, interest rates continued moving down, despite the reversal of prices, profitability and investment. Thus for much of the 1890s the low real interest rate generated favourable investment opportunities (Harley 1977). When price trends were at length perceived to be permanent, the money interest rates adjusted upwards, as did real rates.

A third possible connection between money and long swings is variations in real money balances. To the extent that world prices were being determined by non-monetary factors, differences could occur between monetary and price variation over time, implying large shifts in the growth of real money balances. In Britain real money balances grew slowly during

Table 10.5. *Market interest rates and ex-post-real interest rates, averaged over five cycles, 1873–1913*

	Nominal interest rates			Real interest rates	
	Short (three-month bills)	Long (Consols)	Annual change in price level	Short (nominal minus price change)	Long
1873–82	2·938	3·113	−1·678	4·616	4·791
1882–9	2·650	2·953	−0·919	3·569	3·872
1889–99	2·232	2·471	0·000	2·232	2·471
1899–1907	3·373	2·754	0·872	2·500	1·882
1907–13	3·102	3·130	0·887	2·150	2·243

Source: Friedman and Schwartz (1982).

the Edwardian era relative to the 1873–99 period. During 1899–1907 the growth rate of real money balances was practically stagnant. Such changes could act to constrain the growth path, with an adverse wealth effect on consumption (Pigou 1943; Matthews *et al.* 1982).

Fourth, the co-movement of money supply growth and aggregate output growth could also be accounted for by an endogenous money supply. Money would be an effect, not a cause. In periods of reduced output growth less money will be demanded for transactions purposes, leading to an endogenous fall in money supply growth (McCloskey and Zecher 1976). To test the hypothesis would require more evidence on the behaviour of money demand.

Climatic shocks

One of the oldest explanations of cycles is the sunspot theory of Jevons (1884): 'after some further careful inquiry, I am perfectly convinced that these decennial crises do depend upon meteorological variations of like period, which again depend, in all probability, upon cosmical variations of which we have evidence in the frequency of sun-spots, auroras, and magnetic perturbations' (Jevons 1884: 235). Modern economists have argued that such an inference is so mistaken as to be not worth pursuing. Aldcroft and Fearon (1972), for example, concluded that harvest fluctuations were not important to understanding business cycle behaviour after 1846, considering the coming of free trade in agricultural goods and the decline in the relative importance of domestic agriculture. Such generalisations, however, are difficult to uphold. Although the agricultural sector

Figure 10.5 British agricultural production, 1855–1914

declined in importance after the mid-nineteenth century, the decline was not steady (Feinstein *et al.* 1982); thus, climatic effects on agriculture could still have had cyclical effects on the macro-economy. Agriculture was not the only weather-sensitive sector in the economy; construction activity was also affected by the weather (Russo 1966). Another source of influence could be climatic effects on world agricultural supplies and thus on the inter-sectoral terms of trade.

As can be seen from Figure 10.5 agricultural production saw large annual and longer-term variations. In order to isolate the more regular cyclical component of agricultural production a so-called 'Kalman filter' technique was employed (it is a statistical device for isolating the trend, cycle and irregular components of a time series). The long-run level of agricultural production follows a trend, the Kalman filter isolating a cycle around the trend. Figure 10.6 shows that the cycle of agricultural production is a twenty-year cycle out of phase with the macro-economy for much of the time: agricultural output saw a downswing in the 1890s when the macro-economy was booming and an upswing in the Edwardian period when the economy was in a downswing. Such evidence makes it at least conceivable that the agricultural production cycle was being determined, at least partly, by exogenous climatic variables.

Both rainfall and temperature would be important, though not independent of each other. Their effect on agriculture is not additive in any simple way. What is needed is an index of agricultural drought that relates these two inputs. Agricultural drought would be determined by rainfall, evaporation and the timing of the rainfall. Thus the average soil moisture

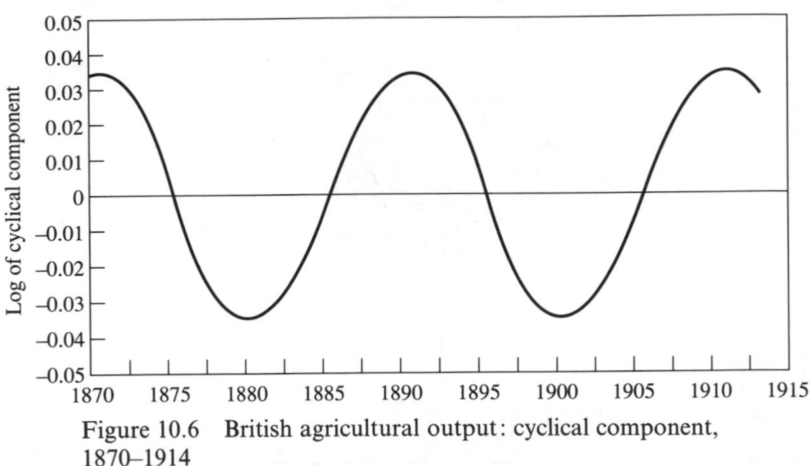

Figure 10.6 British agricultural output: cyclical component, 1870–1914

content over the growing season (May–August) can be used as an index of drought severity or the opposite (too much moisture in the soil) (Rodda *et al.* 1976).

Using homogeneous series for precipitation and evapotranspiration at Kew Gardens in London, Wigley and Atkinson (1977) have constructed a record of soil moisture deficits back to 1698. This series is employed as a proxy for weather conditions influencing agricultural production. The data reported in Table 10.6 are constructed in such a way that a high value represents drought conditions (as in 1891–1902) and a low value represents excessive moisture content in the soil (as in 1875–81). Solomou (1986) showed that during the period 1870–1914 the annual growth rates of agricultural production were closely related to the growth rates of deficits in soil moisture. Climatic conditions also followed a long swing pattern similar to the long swing phases of agricultural output. Table 10.6 shows that soil moisture deficits were extreme (high or low) in both phases of low agricultural production: during the 1870s soil moisture deficits were exceptionally low, reflecting the heavy rainfall of those years and below average temperatures. In the 1890s the deficit values rose reflecting high temperatures and low rainfall. The periods 1866–75, 1881–91 and 1902–9 were closer to the long-run mean values.

The structure of the UK economy in the 1870s and 1880s would have left it vulnerable to climatic shocks. In 1868 Britain still produced 80 per cent of domestic food consumption. Although the 1870s witnessed an increase in imports of agricultural commodities relative to domestic agricultural output, between 1873 and 1881 the sectoral terms of trade were moving in favour of agriculture and the international terms of trade were moving against the UK. Therefore both imports and domestic supplies of food

Table 10.6. *Weather variation over the peak to peak phases of agricultural production, 1866–1909*

Period	Average for specified period	Standard deviation	Average for specified period minus average for 1855–1909
(*A*) *Temperatures during growing season*			
1866–75	14·361	0·673	+0·2600
1875–81	13·949	0·780	−0·1524
1881–91	13·789	0·581	−0·3119
1891–1902	14·224	0·823	+0·1232
1902–9	13·684	0·650	−0·4173
(*B*) *Rainfall during growing season*			
1866–75	91·310	23·720	−9·9700
1875–81	122·740	29·045	+21·460
1881–91	104·050	22·589	+2·7655
1891–1902	95·708	17·699	−5·5717
1902–9	103·130	16·427	+1·8450
(*C*) *Mean soil moisture deficits during growing season*			
1866–75	88·070	17·784	+8·1560
1875–81	61·257	39·169	−18·657
1881–91	72·655	22·763	−7·2595
1891–1902	95·792	18·283	+15·878
1902–9	72·375	31·391	−7·5390

Notes: (*A*) In degrees Celsius.
(*B*) Expressed as a per cent of the rainfall for the 'standard period' 1881–1915.
(*C*) Expressed as an index, where a high value represents a drought and vice versa.
Source: see text.

were being purchased at a rising relative cost. Moreover, the real wage was affected by the terms of trade, which would depress aggregate demand (Lewis 1978).

A regression of GDP growth on agricultural production growth between 1870–90 and 1891–1913 illustrates the changing role of agriculture in the macro-economy. During 1870–90 the annual variations in agricultural production, which were partly determined by climatic conditions, had a significant effect on aggregate GDP growth and were closely correlated with GDP growth. During 1891–1913 variations in agricultural production were not correlated with aggregate GDP growth. In examining sectoral growth over the long swing between 1873 and 1913 Feinstein, Matthews and Odling-Smee (1982) found that the agricultural sector accounted for the largest part of the retardation in total factor productivity in the 1870s and of the rise in the 1880s (it was not important to the retardation of the Edwardian period).

The evidence does not support Jevons' sunspot theory of economic cycles. It does suggest, however, that climatic shocks were still important to the fluctuations of agricultural production during 1870–1914.

Conclusions

The era 1870–1914 manifests a diversity of cyclical paths quite different from other times. The Juglar cycle characterises the behaviour of some industries; Kuznets swings are observed for a block of variables, including the macro-economic variables of GDP and investment; a separate agricultural long swing is also influencing the economy. The evidence shows the importance of taking an historical approach to the business cycle. One- or two-variable macro-economic models of business cycles are clearly inadequate to explain such complexities. Future research should be conducted at a more disaggregated level of analysis, with rigorous attention to the errors in the historical data.

11 Living standards, 1870–1914

Mary MacKinnon

Britain's economic pre-eminence in the world economy began to be challenged in the late Victorian era, though in terms of income per capita her citizens were, and would remain, by far the richest in Europe until the First World War (Crafts 1985: 54). What were the living standards of the British population at the time? How much, and why, did they improve between 1870 and 1914? Answers to the questions are important for a wide range of historical issues. For example, part of any explanation for emigration from the British Isles must rely on living conditions in the sending region. Similarly, there are links between social and political unrest and general living standards, and the social tensions of the Edwardian era are often attributed to a stagnation of real incomes (Thomson 1950: 196–202). Unless we have a sound understanding of the underlying economic phenomena, it is of little use to try to develop explanations which depend on them.

Definitions

The first, and perhaps the most general, question one might ask about living standards in the later nineteenth century is 'How well off was the average person?' Before addressing such a question, definitions of 'well off' or 'standard of living' and 'the average person' must be agreed upon. It is also necessary to decide when to be interested in the 'average person' and whether the same definition of the standard of living is always appropriate. Some evidence about late nineteenth-century living standards is available for the population as a whole, while other evidence is relevant to the experience of a narrower group. The emphasis here will be on working-class living standards, with the working class defined as roughly the bottom two-thirds of the population. It is anything but a homogeneous group, including everyone from beggars and vagrants to skilled workmen and clerks. The cut-off at the bottom two-thirds is based on Rowntree's claim that one third of all households were wealthy enough to keep servants. In his classic study of York he estimated two thirds of the population to be working class (Rowntree 1901: 14, 26). Sometimes evidence is available for the United Kingdom as a whole. Other information is available only for parts of the UK, most often England and Wales.

It is not possible to measure all the factors which affect an individual's standard of living. Benefits from greater measured consumption may be offset by deterioration in other, unmeasured, conditions. The chapter on urbanisation (vol. 1, ch. 15) gives one example. During the nineteenth century income levels in urban areas were higher than in rural areas, but urban areas were crowded and dirty, and therefore had higher death rates from infectious diseases. The higher mortality rate at least in part offsets the effect of higher income – so that one cannot immediately argue from higher income levels that the town worker was substantially better off than the rural worker.

For the late nineteenth and early twentieth centuries we can at least roughly measure many more of the variables which enter utility than for the late eighteenth and early nineteenth centuries (the period of the classic debate over the standard of living; vol. 1, ch. 14). A growing understanding of statistics is a feature of the period. Government departments were keeping more records because they were trying to chart the progress of the economy and researchers were collecting and analysing information. The work of the turn of the century social scientists, such as Bowley (1937) and Wood (1909), Booth (1889–1903) and Rowntree (1901), has been an invaluable source for economic historians.

Incomes say what consumption possibilities were and how they changed over time. One of the most often used measures of income is national income per capita. Since the construction of national accounts and population estimates have been two major activities of economic historians and demographers, fairly robust estimates of national income per capita are available for most western nations for the late nineteenth century. If one is interested in international comparisons, then, such statistics are immediately appealing. As every introductory course in economics stresses, however, national income measures only market transactions. Some goods and services were produced at home. By ignoring them, national income underestimates consumption possibilities.

Estimates of national income include income from all market sources, with labour income, property income and investment income being the three most important. Roughly 55 per cent of income accrued to labour, 45 per cent to property and investment (Matthews *et al.* 1982: 164). Most property and investment income accrued to the very wealthy. Therefore any attempt to estimate the income of the 'ordinary' person, using national income, will overestimate the income of the non-wealthy. The extent of the overestimate may not be constant over time, since the benefits of economic growth are often unevenly distributed to the different factors of production. From 1870 to 1900, for example, labour's share of national income was nearly constant, but in the early twentieth century, labour's share of income rose (Feinstein 1990c: 344).

An average, such as income per capita, tells nothing about the shape of the distribution. It is possible to have an income distribution in which most people have incomes close to the average. If so, the average is a good approximation to the level of income 'most' people have. It is also possible, and indeed more common, to have an income distribution which is very unequal. Extremely high incomes to a few very rich individuals counterbalance low incomes to a larger group in the population. In this case a fairly small proportion of the population will have incomes close to the average. While there is an extensive debate about how much, if at all, the distribution of income changed in late nineteenth-century Britain, inequality was far greater before the First World War than after the Second World War (Rubinstein 1986a: 55–78). For the modern period, therefore, national income per capita is a rather better estimate of ordinary incomes than it was in the nineteenth century.

Another common method of measuring living standards is to use estimates of wages or earnings. As noted above, labour income was a little more than half of all national income, and most people in the bottom two-thirds of the income distribution derived their income entirely from labour income. Estimates of hourly or weekly wages are available for agricultural labourers and for a wide variety of urban occupations, particularly those employing adult men. Information on actual earnings is less common. Earnings data reflect the importance of short-time working, overtime pay and occasional bonuses. They also take into account changes in hours worked over time. Average weekly hours dropped substantially at the outset, from sixty-five to fifty-six, and then stayed constant until the First World War (Matthews *et al.* 1982: 65). Looking simply at hourly wages therefore overestimates the increase in annual earnings, because hourly wages were usually raised when standard hours were cut. Given that unemployment is notoriously difficult to measure in the period (Garside 1981), it is only possible to adjust estimates of annual earnings for unemployment for a limited range of occupations.

Taking an average of wages across regions or occupations may in some instances mislead us, and so may averaging earnings over a month or a year. Short-term job contracts were the norm for nineteenth-century workers, and workers were severely constrained in their ability to borrow. They did borrow, but effective interest rates charged for buying on credit or pawning, and certainly for borrowing from moneylenders, were very high (Johnson 1985: 144–92). Even where we can determine unemployment levels and their effect on earnings, the resulting estimate of average income ignores the difficulty workers faced in smoothing their consumption over periods of employment and unemployment.

From the early 1870s to the mid-1890s, prices generally trended downwards, and from then until 1914 they rose (Mitchell 1988: 722–8). For estimates of incomes, wages or earnings for different dates to be comparable, 'nominal' values must be converted to 'real' values. At the simplest level, a doubling of nominal income implies no change in real income if the price level also doubles. Economists measure changes in the average level of prices by weighting each price by its 'importance'. Cost of living indices weight the price of each good relative to its expenditure share in a typical consumer's consumption bundle.

Over time, consumption bundles change. As income rises, the proportion of income spent on necessities, such as bread or potatoes, falls. As new goods are introduced and are widely used, they become part of regular consumption patterns. When the relative prices of goods change, consumers substitute away from the items which have become more expensive, and towards those which have become cheaper. Thus the choice of the consumption bundle on which to base a price index can have a substantial impact on the measured aggregate change in prices, at any rate if prices of important commodities in the budget change by different amounts.

Earnings data are available for individuals, while consumption decisions are generally made by families. Family consumption depends on how many workers there were per family, and how much female and juvenile workers earned relative to adult males. Survey evidence suggests that the earners were typically the best-fed members of the family; for example, fathers ate much more meat and fish than mothers or young children (Pember Reeves 1913: 113–45). If it was generally true, we would expect to find relatively higher standards of consumption for men than for women and children.

In principle, there are empirical and conceptual difficulties in measuring the standard of living, and this is just as true of the modern era as it is of the late nineteenth century. In practice, the size of, and reasons for, discrepancies between different measures can be determined, so that the range of possibilities can be defined. Historians can measure certain components of welfare other than income. Mortality statistics are readily available, and there is some evidence about the incidence and duration of illness. Economic historians have begun to analyse data on heights as another measure of health. As a population becomes better nourished and the incidence of disease drops, average height increases. Before the First World War, as still today, differences in children's heights varied by social background. In Glasgow in 1914, children at school in the best working-class areas were about two inches taller than schoolchildren from the poorest districts (Floud *et al.* 1990: 238). For the very poor, evidence about the incidence of pauperism can also be a useful supplement to income estimates. So long as one can control for changes in Poor Law policy – making it more or less difficult for the poor to receive assistance – the proportion of the population in receipt of poor relief will be an indicator of the extent of destitution.

Average consumption of some goods, particularly food, can be measured directly. Some indicators of housing quality, such as the number of persons per room, are also available from surveys and censuses, and these give an idea of changes in housing conditions. Since we want to measure income to determine what consumption possibilities were, collecting consumption data might appear to be a more reliable and immediate way of approaching the question. In fact, similar problems arise whether one is measuring income or consumption. It is impossible to measure the consumption of all goods and services and we rarely know exactly what proportion of a good was consumed by the working class. For some ordinary items, such as staple foods like bread or beer, it is plausible to assume that by 1870 the top one third of earners were consuming as much as they wanted, so that increases in per capita consumption were probably concentrated among the working classes. For most other goods and services, however – holidays, to give one example – consumption almost certainly rose for all income groups.

If consumption of a particular good rose when its price fell (or because the price of a substitute rose), one must be careful to attribute at least part of the increase in consumption to the substitution caused by the change in prices – not to higher income. The relative prices of both tea and sugar – superior goods for nineteenth-century working-class consumers – fell substantially in the late nineteenth century, and consumption increased sharply (see Table 11.6 below). Therefore not all of the increased consumption indicates an improvement in welfare.

Quite apart from changes in prices and incomes, changes in tastes and the availability of new goods explain some consumption trends. The late nineteenth century saw the development of mass markets for many standard consumer items. Brand names such as Oxo, Lipton, Rowntree and Pears date from the period. Technological changes allowed for more production of packaged and processed foods, and retailing and advertising boomed (Fraser 1981: 134–46).

Income and earnings

Table 11.1 shows estimates of income per capita in several European nations for 1870, 1890 and 1910. All are expressed in terms of 1970 US$. Clearly, incomes in the United Kingdom were higher than on the Continent. While from 1870 to 1890 income per capita in the UK rose at roughly the same rate as in several other countries, income growth slowed down in the UK after 1890, so that the gap between British and continental incomes decreased somewhat by 1910.

Income gains for the hypothetical average worker resulted from a combination of increased wages within occupations, shifts in the composition of the labour force towards higher wage occupation and population shifts away from low-wage regions. Early on, at least in aggregate, there is no doubt that working-class incomes rose swiftly. After 1900, however, progress slowed, and it has sometimes been argued that average real wages actually fell in the decade before the First World War.

When the demand for labour increases, wages will rise unless the supply of labour is perfectly elastic. Therefore we expect to see the largest wage gains in occupations and regions where the demand for labour increased the most, and where the supply of labour was growing slowly, and not much affected by increases in the wage rate.

If the demand for a good or service is rising, one expects the demand for the workers who produce it to be rising as well. Changes in relative wages between occupations and industries therefore often depend on shifts in the composition of output. Increases in the amount of capital per worker are also important in explaining increases in earnings, since with more capital, each worker produces more output. For skilled occupations the supply of labour is typically fairly inelastic, because few workers are capable of doing the work. For unskilled occupations, by contrast, the supply of labour is normally very elastic – a small increase in the wage rate will draw in large numbers of workers, especially if wages rise for only a few occupations.

There is considerable controversy about how quickly real wages grew before 1850. Crafts estimates that between 1780 and 1850 the average real wage rose by 0.8 per cent per annum (Crafts 1985: 103). According to Feinstein's most recent estimates the average real wage rose by 1.58 per cent per annum between 1882 and 1899, but by only 0.29 per cent per annum from 1899 to 1913 (Feinstein 1990c: 344).

Why did real wages grow roughly twice as fast in the 1880s and 1890s as in the classic industrial revolution period, and then drop to a lower rate after the turn of the century? Output per worker shot up in the late Victorian era, in large part because of improvements in the quality and quantity of capital (including human capital). At the same time, labour

Table 11.1. *European per capita incomes, 1870–1910 (1970 US$)*

	1870	1890	1910
United Kingdom	904	1,130	1,302
Belgium	738	932	1,110
Denmark	563	708	1,050
Germany	579	729	958
France	567	668	883
Sweden	351	469	763
Norway	441	548	706
Italy	467	466	548

Source: Crafts (1984a: 54).

force growth was fairly modest. In earlier times, by contrast, economic growth had been concentrated in relatively few sectors of the economy, and population growth was very rapid (and at least until the 1820s, there was little change in the capital stock per worker; Crafts 1985: 76). It is entirely plausible, therefore, that aggregate income growth was greater in the last third than the first third of the nineteenth century.

The debate about the causes of slower economic growth at the end of our period, and whether and how it affected real wages, has raged for seventy years, and is too broad to be adequately covered here (see chs. 1–4). Definitionally, if productivity growth was low after 1900, as it appears to have been, the demand for labour would increase more slowly (Feinstein 1990c).

Wages paid are the result of formal or informal bargaining. If workers and employers misperceive the size and permanence of changes in price levels the wage rates they accept will yield unexpected changes in real wages. Inflation or deflation rates were rarely more than 1 or 2 per cent per year, and the lack of official statistics made it hard to detect the small deviations. If price changes were small enough to be noticed only after persisting for several years, the pattern of wages can be explained in part as a lagged response. Prices trended downwards until the mid-1890s, and upwards from then on. Money wages increased more rapidly in the 1900s than in the 1880s and 1890s, which suggests that contemporaries became aware of inflation after 1900 (Feinstein 1990c: 344–5) – but this does not prove the absence of the 'money illusion' making wages lag behind price increases.

Feinstein's recent estimate of aggregate real wages presents a rather different picture of the growth of workers' incomes between 1880 and 1913 than does the previously widely used index, which Bowley compiled

Table 11.2. *Estimates of nominal and real wage changes, 1873–1913 (annual percentage growth rates)*

	1873–82	1882–99	1899–1913
Bowley			
Money wages	−0·98	1.01	0·76
Cost of living	−2·01	−1·01	1·23
Real wages	1·03	2·03	−0·46
Feinstein			
Money wages within sectors	0·61	0·95	
Money wages between sectors	0·31	0·30	
Cost of living	−0·66	0·97	
Real wages	1·58	0·29	
Real employment income per worker (includes salaried workers)	1·71	0·58	

Source: Feinstein (1990c: 330, 344).

Table 11.3. *Working-class cost of living indices, 1870–1913 (1900 = 100)*

	1 Bowley	2 Feinstein	3 Feinstein Food	4 Gazeley Low income workers[a]
1870	119	113·1	125·3	
1875	121	114·8	126·7	
1880	114	108·7	120·5	
1885	99	100·2	104·1	99·7[b]
1890	97	98·3	100·2	97·6
1895	90	93·7	91·8	92·1
1900	100	100·0	100·0	100·0
1905	100	100·7	101·0	100·4
1910	105	106·0	107·2	104·7
1913	111	110·0	112·9	

[a] Family expenditure < 300d per week.
[b] 1886.
Sources: column 1: Bowley (1937: 121–2); columns 2 and 3: Feinstein (1991: 170–1); column 4: Gazeley (1989: 215).

between 1910 and 1920 (Table 11.2) (Feinstein 1990b: 597). Feinstein's index suggests more gradual earnings gains between 1880 and 1900 than does Bowley's. After 1900, however, the Feinstein index continues to rise, while Bowley concluded that real wages were falling. Bowley's nominal wage index has several peaks and troughs representing temporary wage movements which are not evident in Feinstein's nominal series.

Bowley's nominal wage index is based on a few major sectors of the economy, with a strong emphasis on agriculture, building and export oriented industries such as coal mining, engineering and shipbuilding, and textiles. Feinstein has revised the earnings estimates for several of the constituent series Bowley used and has added series for many other sectors of the economy, particularly service occupations. Bowley's series covered about half of all wage earners; Feinstein's includes about 85 per cent. The difference between the two measures depends largely on the broadening of occupational coverage, not on revisions to the earnings estimates for the series included in both indices. Feinstein's revisions are plausible because the economic slowdown of the post-1900 period was concentrated in building and export oriented industries. One would expect to see more sustained growth of earnings in sheltered sectors of the economy.

Bowley's cost of living index has also been re-evaluated in recent years (Table 11.3). Feinstein has used new sources to measure price trends for some components of the cost of living, expanded the range of goods and services included and changed the expenditure weights for different categories of consumption. The differences between Bowley's and Feinstein's cost of living indices arise mainly because Feinstein is able to estimate price series for several categories of consumption which Bowley omitted. Bowley's index depends almost entirely on expenditures for food, rent, clothing and fuel. About 30 per cent of Feinstein's index is made up of items not included by Bowley. In particular, he assigns an expenditure weight of 18 per cent to alcohol and tobacco. He also adds expenditure on furniture and furnishings, travel and some services. These additions have a substantial impact on estimates of the cost of living, because the prices of goods in the 30 per cent are nearly constant from 1870 to 1910. By contrast, the 70 per cent of Feinstein's index which overlaps with Bowley's shows a decline of about 30 per cent between the mid-1870s and the mid-1890s, and an increase of about 15 per cent by 1910 (using the starting year of each period as the base). Feinstein argues, therefore, that the price decline to the 1890s was smaller than previously assumed, with the price increase thereafter also being more gradual (Feinstein 1991: 174).

Gazeley (1989) has examined Bowley's cost of living index for the period after 1885 to check how sensitive it is to changes in the price series and expenditure weights used. His aggregate results are similar to Feinstein's, and he demonstrates that cost of living indices are not much affected by the use of expenditure weights appropriate to different groups within the working class. A comparison of columns 2 and 4 of Table 11.3 shows that the cost of living index for the poor (families spending less than 25s a week

Table 11.4. *Wage earners in the United Kingdom, selected sectors, 1881 and 1911, and average annual full-employment earnings, 1911*

	Wage earners (000s)		Average earnings per year (£)
	1881	1911	1911
Agriculture	1,870	1,540	39·0
Mining	565	1,135	83·2
Building	735	920	71·7
Engineering	755	1,465	73·9
Cotton textiles	520	620	50·2
Clothing and footwear	915	975	41·1
Manufacturing	3,985	5,440	56·7
Transport	935	1,595	61·3
Distribution	655	1,240	67·5
Domestic service (females)	1,720	1,855	44·8
Domestic service (males)	245	435	74.3
Total	12,270	15,880	58.6

Source: Feinstein (1990b: 603–4).

in 1890–1) is almost the same as an index weighted by the expenditure patterns of an average working-class family (spending 46s a week in 1900).

Average wages rose both because wages increased within sectors and because workers shifted towards higher wage sectors of the economy. Roughly a quarter of the rise in average money earnings was due to changes in the composition of the wage-earning labour force between sectors (Feinstein 1990b: 607). Changes in the distribution of jobs would account for a higher proportion of earnings gains if salaried workers (such as teachers, nurses and clerks) were included in the earnings index. The size of the salaried workforce increased dramatically, more than doubling between 1881 and 1911, while the wage-earning labour force increased by only about 30 per cent (Feinstein 1990b: 602; see also ch. 5). It is customary to think of salary earners as middle class and wage earners as working class, but many clerks and teachers had incomes similar to those of skilled manual workers.

High-wage, and rising-wage, sectors expanded most quickly, while low-wage sectors lost workers (see Tables 11.4 and 11.5). Coal-mining is a sector where sustained high demand for output raised wages significantly. The number of coal-miners more than doubled between 1881 and 1911. While for all wage-earners (including inter-sectoral shifts), money wages rose roughly 40 per cent between 1880 and 1913, miners (most of whom were coal miners) experienced wage increases of almost 90 per cent.

Table 11.5. *Indices of average full-time money earnings, selected sectors, 1880–1913 (1911 = 100)*

	1880	1890	1900	1913
Agriculture	85·3	86·5	93·6	105·6
Mining	59·1	90·4	98·5	110·3
Building	87·0	81·7	100·0	103·5
Engineering	74·5	84·5	93·7	104·1
Cotton textiles	75·1	81·7	90·9	103·2
Clothing	89·6	92·2	95·5	100·9
Boots and shoes	97·7	90·0	95·1	103·3
Manufacturing	76·0	87·7	92·9	105·0
Transport	82·1	85·3	94·0	107·0
Distribution	81·6	79·9	90·0	101·9
Domestic service	80·4	80·7	87·3	104·3
Average earnings, all sectors	74·8	80·7	91·2	105·5

Source: Feinstein (1990b: 608–10, 612).

Agricultural labourers were always amongst the lowest-paid workers in the country, and their wages increased relatively slowly between 1880 and 1913 – less than 25 per cent. There were about 20 per cent fewer agricultural labourers in the UK in 1911 than in 1881. While building workers earned only about 20 per cent more at the end of the period than at the beginning, the number of workers in the industry rose by roughly 25 per cent (Feinstein 1990b: 603). This is a case of an industry where wages were growing slowly, but began at a relatively high level, so there was an incentive for workers to stay in the sector.

If Feinstein's estimates are accepted the contrast between wage growth before and after 1900 is smaller than has traditionally been believed. Average real wages were not falling in the Edwardian era. Average full-time earnings of wage earners, for a constant distribution of the labour force, rose by about the same amount as the cost of living. The combined effect of movements of the wage-earning labour force between sectors, and the growth of the salaried labour force, raised real wages gradually.

Changes in the composition of the workforce are an important explanation for aggregate improvements in wages. Unless it is easy to change occupations, however, the beneficial effects of changes in the distribution of occupations are irrelevant for many individuals. Especially for older workers all that matters is earnings growth within occupations. The children of workers in low-wage jobs were often able to enter higher-wage occupations or move to a higher-wage region; their parents were more likely to be trapped. Restrictions on the availability of credit also trapped many children. Very poor families could not afford to keep their children in school long enough for them to acquire the literacy and numeracy required for clerical jobs. Similarly, such parents needed to set their children to work in jobs which paid the highest wages in the short term. A dead-end job, as a messenger or an errand boy, offered little or no training, and few prospects for adult employment, but paid a higher wage than an apprenticeship (Freeman 1912). Considerations such as these show why one cannot use an average as a guide to the earnings of all types of workers.

Economists stress the importance of equilibrating forces in reducing or eliminating differentials. As noted above, workers moved from low- to higher-wage jobs whenever possible. They also moved from low- to higher-wage regions. It was rare for regions to experience emigration greater than the rate of natural increase, but all low-wage regions saw a substantial proportion of each generation move to wealthier parts of the British Isles, or abroad (see ch. 13). Regional variations in earnings, however, remained substantial until the First World War (Hunt 1973; Boyer and Hatton 1991). Earnings of secondary workers tended to follow the same regional patterns as those of adult males, so that family income showed much the same regional variation as did wages for adult males. Urban wages were highest in Scotland, northern England and especially in London (although living costs were also highest in London), lowest in southern England (Hunt 1986). Perhaps surprisingly, given that Irish agricultural wages were lower than English wages, skilled workers in Dublin earned almost as much as London workers, although unskilled workers earned much less (O'Rourke 1991). Either the forces causing regional wage differentials were persistent, or the tendencies towards equilibration of wages were relatively weak.

So far, no allowance has been made for the effects of unemployment or short-time working on earnings. Economic historians do not yet know enough about unemployment and underemployment in the late nineteenth century to make adjustments. Earnings estimates for individual years would change substantially if we could do so, because unemployment rates fluctuated considerably. In industries such as iron and steel the probability of employment was closely tied to the overall level of economic activity. For workers in such sectors the annual earnings varied more over the business cycle than calculations assuming full-employment indicate (Barnsby 1971; Hall 1981).

The main source of information on unemployment comes from trade union returns, which mostly tell us about the experience of skilled workers in building and export industries. The trade union data show unemployment rates in times of slump of 9 to 11 per cent, compared to 1 to 2 per cent in booms. The extent and timing of unemployment varied across the labour force. While in some occupations most unemployment was cyclical, in others, such as dock labour, chronic underemployment was the rule, and earnings were always well below notional full-time levels. On the other hand, long-term comparisons of average earnings, or of earnings within a particular occupation, will be altered only if average levels of unemployment changed over time. So long as average unemployment over each business cycle is roughly constant the rate of growth of earnings will be correctly measured.

Consumption and health

So far, we have considered how much wages rose between 1870 and 1914, but have not looked at what working-class earners purchased and consumed. It is easier to learn about working-class living standards at the turn of the century than in the 1870s because many detailed budget studies of working-class incomes and expenditure patterns were undertaken at the time. Researchers collected and studied records of the income and expenditure of selected working-class families. They were particularly interested in the persistence of poverty. After some thirty to fifty years of fairly rapid economic growth, they wanted to find out how many working-class families were poor, and why they were poor.

The studies of working-class consumption are important not only for the information they gathered, but also for their contributions towards defining poverty. Rowntree's definition of 'primary poverty' has been extremely influential. He defined a family to be living in primary poverty if their current income was less than the amount required to maintain 'physical efficiency'. Food, which was about 50 per cent of expenditure for average working-class families, and closer to 60 per cent for very poor families, received Rowntree's most careful attention. He tried to determine the caloric requirements required to retain health and fitness, and established a hypothetical diet, based on, but less generous than, actual workhouse diets. Bread, porridge and gruel featured prominently in his dietaries, and boiled bacon was the only meat allowed. He argued that it was the minimum feasible diet working-class families could live on. Actual diets of low-income families generally allowed for a little more variety, but yielded less than the 3,500 or 3,000 calories per adult male or female that Rowntree considered necessary. Allowances for other categories of expenditure (such as rent, clothing, fuel and cleaning supplies), by contrast, were based on actual expenditures, or the opinions of housewives about the minimum feasible expenditure. The hypothetical family could purchase only necessities. 'The children must have no pocket money for dolls, marbles, or sweets. The father must smoke no tobacco, and must drink no beer. The mother must never buy any pretty clothes for herself or for her children' (Rowntree 1901: 134). For 1899, Rowntree estimated that a single person could live on 7s 0d a week, a couple with one child on 14s 6d, and a family of six on 26s.

Rowntree considered a larger group of the working class to be living in 'secondary poverty', which is a very different way of defining poverty. Families living in secondary poverty were also spending their incomes so that they did not maintain physical efficiency. However, these families had current incomes which would have been adequate to keep them out of primary poverty, if none of their income had been used for other expenditure, 'either useful or wasteful' (Rowntree 1901: 148). For example, purchasing alcohol, or repaying debts contracted during a period of unemployment or illness, could both cause a family to suffer from secondary poverty. To estimate the proportion of the population living in secondary poverty, Rowntree relied on observation of households where there was 'obvious want and squalor'.

Rowntree's 1899 study of York indicated that over 40 per cent of the wage-earning class (close to 30 per cent of the total population) lived in poverty. About two-thirds of the poor were living in secondary poverty (Rowntree 1901: 150–1). Before the First World War, similar studies were conducted in several other cities. Not surprisingly, the extent of poverty differed depending on the industrial and occupational structure of the labour force, but all suggest that Rowntree's findings for York were typical (Bowley and Burnett-Hurst 1915). Using contemporary standards of need, about 30 per cent of the population did not spend enough on necessities to maintain physical efficiency.

The extent of poverty varied systematically across age groups. Rowntree identified a poverty life cycle, with three phases where an individual was likely to be below the poverty line – childhood, as a parent with several young children and in old age. While about 30 per cent of the population were poor at any time, more lived in poverty for part of their life. The highest rates of poverty were for children. Although poverty among the elderly generated much concern in the late nineteenth century, and the introduction of non-contributory old-age pensions in 1908 was one of the most important pieces of social legislation of the pre-war period, the poverty rate for the over sixty-fives was slightly lower than for all adults fifteen to sixty-four.

For a substantial group of the very poor, then, any improvement in living standards which took place between 1870 and 1900 still left them malnourished, and living in housing injurious to their health. For the rest of the population, however, the gains were considerable. Table 11.6 shows

Table 11.6. *Estimated weekly per capita consumption, selected foods, 1860–1913*

	1860	1880	1900	1909–13	1913
Wheat (lb)	6·2	6·6		6·4	
Flour (lb)			4·0		4·3
Meat and bacon (lb)	1·8	1·8	2·4	2·5	2·2
Eggs			2·2		2·2
Fresh milk (pt)	1·75	2·2	2·8	3·2	2·9
Butter (oz)	2·7	4·0	4·6	4·8	4·8
Margarine (oz)			1·4		2·4
Cheese (oz)	1·9	2·6	2·7	2·2	2·4
Potatoes (lb)	6·8	5·7	3·2	4·0	3·8
Tea (oz)	0·8	1·4	1·9	2·1	2·1
Sugar (lb)	0·7	1·2	1·3	1·4	1·3
Beer (pt)	4·4	4·7	4·9		4·3
Spirits (oz)	3·1	3·3	3·4		2·1

Note: estimates are for the population as a whole and are for the United Kingdom. The estimates for beer and spirits are for 1870, not 1860.
Sources: 1860, 1880, 1909–13 (except for beer and spirits), Mackenzie (1921: 224); 1900, 1913, and beer and spirits, Prest and Adams (1954).

that per capita consumption of milk, meat, butter, sugar and tea rose substantially in the later nineteenth century, while potato consumption actually fell.

Food prices fell throughout the later nineteenth century (column 3 of Table 11.3), and fell by more than the aggregate cost of living, which encouraged consumers to purchase more food. As chapter 6 explains, imported food became a major part of the British diet. By modern standards, diets were still stodgy, with high consumption of bread and potatoes, and low consumption of meat, milk products and fruits and vegetables. Compared to the 1860s, however, there had been substantial increases in the consumption of these superior foods (Burnett 1979: 203).

People were eating more of what they liked, but it was not necessarily better for them, as indicated, for example, by large increases in the use of sugar and salt. Technological change in food production brought both costs and benefits in terms of the quality of food, with flour an important example of the changes. Consumers had long desired white bread. The introduction of roller milling in the 1870s and 1880s allowed the wheat germ to be separated from the flour. It meant that roller-milled flour was whiter and had better baking qualities than stone-milled flour. Bakers had little incentive to adulterate roller-milled flour with alum because it was already white (Burnett 1979: 140, 265). Without wheat germ, however, flour has little nutritional value.

Working-class Edwardians ate a greater variety of food than did their counterparts in the 1870s, but they drank less. As noted above, the inclusion of alcohol in a working-class cost of living index affects aggregate price trends because workers spent a substantial amount on drink, and unlike food, alcohol prices stayed nearly constant from 1870 to 1909. Table 11.6 shows a peak of alcohol consumption per capita around 1900, but consumption levels were highest in the mid-1870s. In terms of alcohol consumption per adult (the proportion of children in the population dropped over the period), consumption from 1880 to 1900 was close to the 1870 level, and dropped substantially in the early 1900s. Rising real wages and the limited range of goods that workers could afford help to explain the increase in consumption in the 1870s (Dingle 1976). Thereafter, as other prices fell, the range of alternative purchases widened and temperance campaigns gained force, alcohol consumption levelled off. The sharp drop in consumption after the turn of the century may partly be due to the slowing of real income growth, as well as to the cumulative impact of the increased range of consumption possibilities (including leisure activities) and the temperance movement.

The crudest overall measure of housing density indicates some improvement between 1871 and 1911, with persons per dwelling in England and Wales falling from about 5.3 to 5.0. Late nineteenth-century Scotland showed a similar trend, but with slightly lower levels (Barnes 1923: 340, 413). The official late Victorian definition of overcrowding was two adults per room, with children aged one to nine counted as half an adult. By this standard, in 1891 11.2 per cent of the population of England and Wales lived in overcrowded conditions, but by 1911 only 7.8 per cent. Housing conditions, however, especially in urban areas, were extremely diverse. For example, in 1901, 1 per cent of dwellings in Leicester were overcrowded, compared to 35 per cent in Gateshead (Burnett 1978: 143).

Generally, rapidly growing cities or towns had the worst housing conditions. Conditions could be made worse by urban improvement schemes, since the demolition of slums for railways, schools and higher-quality housing for the working class tended to reduce the available housing stock. Until cheap public transport was available the workers had a strong incentive to live near their work, which again raised rents and encouraged high population densities. In London transport facilities did not expand enough to allow substantial decentralisation of working-class housing until the 1890s (Jones 1971: 322). From the mid-1870s the local authorities could exercise substantial control over housing and sanitary standards, raising the quality of new construction. Bye-laws regulated such

Table 11.7. *Death rates 1870–1914 (per 1,000 people of that description; per 1,000 live births for infants)*

	Infants (under 1 yr)		Males		Females	
	England and Wales	Scotland	Child 5–9	Adult 45–54	Child 5–9	Adult 45–54
1870–4	154	125	7·5	19·9	7·0	15·7
1875–9	145	120	6·4	20·3	6·0	15·8
1880–4	142	119	6·1	19·3	5·9	15·1
1885–9	142	119	4·9	18·9	4·9	14·8
1890–4	149	126	4·7	20·2	4·7	15·4
1895–9	158	130	4·1	18·1	4·2	14·2
1900–4	143	122	3·8	17·8	3·9	13·6
1905–9	121	114	3·4	15·9	3·5	12·3
1910–14	109	109	3·2	14·7	3·3	11·3

Source: Mitchell (1988: 57, 58, 60–4).

matters as the width of streets, the size of windows, the location of privies and the height of ceilings (Burnett 1978). Of course, new housing only gradually replaces old housing, so that the impact on the total housing stock was gradual. To the extent that higher standards required lower housing densities and higher construction costs, new dwellings tended to be priced beyond the means of poorer working-class families.

Death rates for children and teenagers (but not infants) fell by more than 50 per cent between the 1860s and the First World War (see Table 11.7). The mortality of young adults also declined sharply, although it began about ten years after child mortality started to drop. Death rates for those above their mid-forties, however, did not begin to decline until the end of the century, and infant mortality remained high until the beginning of the twentieth century. Reductions in deaths from a small group of infectious diseases – tuberculosis, cholera, typhus, typhoid, and scarlet fever – were responsible for most of the late nineteenth-century decline. Chapter 2 discusses the reasons for the mortality decline.

Death rates, or the associated measure of life expectancy, are one of the most fundamental measures of human well being. One can argue, however, that in an era of falling death rates the members of each cohort underestimate their improved life expectation because they use the experience of their parents' generation as a guide to their own probable longevity, and therefore do not fully take the improvement into account. One must also consider the extent to which lower death rates are an effect of higher incomes – as a result of better nutrition, housing and health care

– rather than the result of truly exogenous events, such as declining virulence of contagious diseases, or medical breakthroughs not related to increased income. If people live longer because they are better fed, their welfare improves, but we must not treat the increased life expectancy as a separate improvement (Usher 1980: 247–52).

The length of life is one measure of well being; health status is another. If most of the added years of life are spent in illness ('morbidity', is the demographic term), then one's welfare is increased less than if they are typically years of good health. The extent of ill-health also matters when considering the ability of workers to support themselves when not employed. The more time one is incapacitated, the more important it is to be able to draw on savings or insurance, obtain credit or receive charitable assistance.

One might initially expect that as death rates fell, morbidity rates would also have fallen. This, however, did not happen, at least if the morbidity rate is defined as the number of weeks of illness per year. We cannot measure morbidity rates for the population as a whole, but there is a large body of data about the sick claims paid by friendly societies. Workers in fairly regular employment typically belonged to a friendly society, which provided some benefits to paid-up members in cases of death, incapacity or illness. Since most of the workers covered were men, less is known about the experience of working women, and little about women not in the labour force. Friendly society members were probably healthier than the adult population at large, but trends in illness should be the same as for the general population (Riley 1989: 167). Among the friendly society members, morbidity rates were highest for workers in dangerous occupations, especially miners (Snow 1913: 469). High wages for miners should therefore in part be considered to be compensation for higher risks of accident and illness. Morbidity is largely a self-defined condition. How people decide when they are sick enough not to work will depend to some extent on the income forgone, their level of wealth, the type of work they do and prevailing customs, including medical attitudes. Whether these all changed systematically in the late nineteenth century in favour of taking more sick time is unknown. As death rates fell in the later nineteenth century, the incidence of falling ill (at least among adults) remained roughly constant, but the ill died more slowly, recovered more slowly, or some combination of the two (Riley 1989: 170). At each age, therefore, the total amount of time spent in illness rose. While the life expectancy of a man in his twenties increased by over two years between the 1860s and the 1890s, expected years of good health increased by less than half the increased life expectancy. For older men, expected years of good health dropped slightly while life expectancy remained almost constant (Riley

1991: 181) (these are expectations of life and health to age seventy-one). The reasons for longer periods of illness are not yet well understood. Slower deaths were partly due to improvements in medical care, and to a decrease in the incidence of acute illnesses such as cholera, which killed their victims quickly. Slower recoveries resulted from the fact that with lower death rates more people with relatively weak constitutions survived each illness, and more survived with weakened constitutions. As life expectancies rose, more people lived into old age, where long periods of illness had always been common, which again increased the proportion of the total population sick at any time.

Much was learned about the causes of contagious diseases, and many public health measures, such as the building of sewers, were undertaken to reduce the risk of epidemics (Smith 1985). Although effective treatment was still generally impossible, the medical profession worked to reduce the chances of infection by isolating the sick. Some important medical breakthroughs were made. In the 1870s and 1880s, doctors began to follow the principles of antiseptic surgery (Youngson 1979: 157–208). At a minimum, doctors were less likely to use treatments, such as blood-letting, which were actually dangerous to their patients' health (Smith 1979). The growth of trade unions and friendly societies in the later nineteenth century increased the availability of professional treatment. For the very poor, and for illnesses requiring hospitalisation, charitable and Poor Law assistance were the main source of help. While the possibility of receiving treatment remained limited, Poor Law medical services improved it, and the extent of charitable assistance also increased (Abel-Smith 1964).

Data on heights may also tell us something about changes in the health of the population, particularly the health of children. Contagious diseases were rife, with scarlet fever, measles, diphtheria and smallpox the most serious. During an illness a child's energy is diverted away from growth towards recovery. Poorly nourished children are sick often and recover slowly. The combined effects of poverty and illness meant that poor children grew up to be shorter adults. A recent study of the heights of recruits to the British Armed Forces indicates that average heights rose gradually in the late nineteenth and early twentieth centuries, consistent with all the above evidence about incomes, consumption and mortality. The height increases were modest, however, and greatest for recruits born near the end of the era. Futhermore, recruits in the early 1900s were no taller than their predecessors in the 1820s and 1830s, because soldiers' heights had decreased in the middle third of the century. Only by the beginning of the twentieth century did improvements in nutrition balance off the negative impact of urbanisation on health (Floud *et al.* 1990: 319–20).

If the evidence on heights is accepted as an accurate guide to the nutritional and health status of the working-class population, one arrives at a more pessimistic picture of improvements in working-class living standards than the one given by the indicators discussed above. Height data also helps to confirm the impression that resources were shared unevenly within families. If higher real incomes were mainly spent by adults, children's nutritional levels, and therefore stature, might improve rather little.

Higher recovery rates meant that more children survived illnesses which would previously have killed them. Their survival would tend to reduce average heights, if successive cohorts of young men had experienced longer or more severe episodes of illness as children. To the extent that this is the reason for the decline and then only gradual increase in working-class heights in the nineteenth century, height data cannot be used to support a pessimistic interpretation of the progress of living conditions.

The Poor Law is another source of information about living standards, one which focusses on the experience of the very poor. In England and Wales the destitute could apply for poor relief. They might be offered assistance in their own homes ('outdoor' relief) or in a workhouse ('indoor' relief). Poor Law Guardians, the locally elected officials responsible for the operation of the Poor Law in each area, exercised considerable discretion over the types of applicant to whom they offered outdoor relief. Those applicants not offered outdoor relief could accept the offer of indoor relief. Given that, in respectable working-class neighbourhoods, it was a disgrace to enter the workhouse, and considering the rigid institutional environment of the workhouse, only the poorest of the poor were likely to enter a workhouse.

Detailed and regionally disaggregated records of pauperism were kept. If conditions in workhouses, attitudes towards the receipt of relief and the possibility of receiving outdoor rather than indoor relief had remained constant, then one could readily use the level of pauperism as an indicator of the level of poverty. The implied 'poverty line' would be lower than Rowntree's poverty line, but it would be a constant indicator of the proportion of the population who were unable to subsist without government assistance. In fact there were substantial changes in Poor Law policy. In the 1870s it became more difficult to obtain outdoor relief. In the later years of the century, the workhouses, especially their medical facilities, were improved, and for some groups of paupers (children, the sick and the elderly), the workhouse regime was relaxed (Crowther 1981). Both of these changes tended to increase the number of people entering the workhouse, though it is difficult to derive precise estimates of just how large these effects were.

Table 11.8. *Indoor pauperism, 1870–1909*

	Able-bodied males (as per cent of males aged 25–64)			Able-bodied females (as per cent of females aged 15–64)			Not able-bodied males (as per cent of males aged 65+)			Not able-bodied females (as per cent of females aged 65+)		
	North	South	London	North	South	London	North	South	London	North	South	London
1870–4	0·064	0·151	0·239	0·132	0·230	0·288	3·90	4·48	11·2	2·31	2·01	8·12
1875–9	0·077	0·103	0·170	0·134	0·171	0·194	4·73	4·44	12·7	2·57	2·08	9·22
1880–4	0·092	0·120	0·195	0·146	0·173	0·201	5·13	4·78	14·4	2·76	2·14	9·97
1885–9	0·104	0·130	0·250	0·133	0·150	0·197	5·40	4·75	15·3	2·75	2·07	9·59
1890–4	0·142	0·155	0·338	0·131	0·144	0·224	5·25	4·50	14·9	2·43	2·03	9·09
1895–9	0·178	0·168	0·353	0·141	0·145	0·223	5·71	4·72	15·8	3·08	2·21	9·41
1900	0·202	0·150	0·329	0·150	0·128	0·213	6·00	4·81	16·2	2·89	2·41	9·40
1905–9	0·246	0·206	0·428	0·161	0·153	0·233	6·62	5·19	17·7	2·88	2·41	9·25

Notes: able-bodied paupers include workhouse inmates suffering from acute illnesses. Not able-bodied paupers are mainly elderly or permanently disabled. South: south-eastern, south midland, eastern and south-western census divisions; north: west midland, north midland, north-western, Yorkshire and northern census divisions.
Source: MacKinnon (1984: 286–95).

In London and northern England the rates of male indoor pauperism rose substantially from the mid-1880s, while in the south they were more stable (see Table 11.8).

The rise suggests that conditions in the casual urban economy were deteriorating, while in the still more rural south the decline of agriculture had little harmful effect on the very poor. For the very poor, then, economic conditions in southern England appear to have been improving relative to those in the north and in London.

Men were more affected by these trends than women. Indoor pauperism rates for women were generally steady or declining, which suggests that women were becoming less vulnerable. Declining fertility rates are probably an important explanation for the trend. As the incomes of employed friends and relatives rose, very poor women were perhaps seen as more worthy of support (and useful to their families) than very poor men.

Even if one assumes that changes in expenditure on indoor paupers, and lower availability of outdoor relief, played an important role in producing these results, the differences by region and sex remain striking. Unless 'policy' effects are substantially larger than can be estimated econometrically, the incidence of dire poverty, as measured by residence in a workhouse, did not fall nearly as quickly as average real wages rose (MacKinnon 1986).

We derive a more varied picture of progress in working-class living standards from a consideration of non-income-based measures of economic well being than from estimates of incomes and earnings. Perceptions of the extent of improvement depend on how one weights different aspects of living standards. While indicators of the standard of living of the population at large show unambiguously that living conditions improved substantially between 1870 and 1914, those which reflect mainly the experience of the poorest in society (principally heights and pauperism) suggest that the improvements were more modest.

Emigration and overseas living standards

One of the most striking features of the 1870–1914 period was the high rate of emigration from the British Isles. Outward population flows were at their highest in the 1880s and in the decade before 1914. Baines (1985; see ch. 2) discusses the nature of emigration. The relevant question here is simply how much better off a working-class British subject could expect to be in the United States or in the Dominions than in Britain. Part of the gain, and perhaps the most important part for many migrants, was the greater social and political equality in the countries of immigration. For example, universal male franchise was a reality in the white-settler colonies. Emigrants were more likely to be able to purchase status-enhancing goods, such as a house, than were those who stayed in Britain (Offer 1989: 132–3).

Life expectancy, too, was greater in the colonies. For boys born between 1901 and 1910, life expectancy at birth in England and Wales was 48.5. In Australia, boys born in the same decade had a life expectancy of 55.2 and Canadian life expectancy was close to that of Australia. In all countries, the life expectancy of girls was about four years greater than that of boys (Lancaster 1990: 44; Beaujot and McQuillan 1983: 29). The substantial gaps cannot be attributed solely to income levels. Differences in public health standards, and in the rate of urbanisation, explain part of the contrast between Britain and her colonies, but they are another indicator of the benefits of leaving Britain.

Attempts to compare real wages across countries are more difficult than comparisons within a country. Consumption patterns typically vary more between than within countries. For example, Australian workers at the beginning of the century spent only about a third of their income on food, compared to roughly a half in Britain (Allen 1991). Deflating Australian wages by an Australian consumer price series which used Australian consumption patterns for weights could give quite a different picture of the course of real wages than using British consumption patterns and Australian prices. If one assumes that a prospective British emigrant planned to continue with his existing consumption pattern, then the second approach is appropriate.

British real wages were much lower than real wages in Canada, the United States or Australia. Real wages were exceptionally high in Australia in the boom of the 1880s. While the long stagnation of the 1890s and the 1900s cut income per capita sharply, the depression was concentrated in the agricultural sector, and real wages for urban workers held up well. Canadian real wages at the beginning were below those prevailing in the US and Australia. There was rapid growth in the 1890s, so that by the turn of the century the gap between Canadian and American wages had closed substantially. US wages show a higher degree of inequality between skilled and unskilled wages than in Australia, Canada or Britain. While unskilled American workers earned little more than their British counterparts, skilled manual workers in the US were extremely highly paid (Allen 1991; Shergold 1982).

Some social historians try to down-play the relative wealth of the colonial working classes. They dwell on the insecurity of employment and the dangerous working conditions of resource industries, emphasising the extent of inequality within colonial societies. It is correct for the 'dominion pessimists' (Offer 1989 uses the term to describe works such as Copp

(1974), Piva (1979) and Fitzpatrick (1987)) to point out that Canada and Australia were not working-class paradises. Over certain periods real wages stagnated and inequality was greater than in the post-First World War period, but conditions were indubitably better than in Britain. Some British emigrants no doubt regretted their decision, and indeed many returned to the UK, although it may have been part of their initial plan, rather than a sign of disillusionment. Most of those who emigrated benefited substantially from their move.

Policy responses

Government actions may be a response to underlying changes in the economy. For example, it is sometimes argued that poverty among the elderly was becoming more widespread in the late nineteenth century, which helps to explain the introduction of old age pensions. One can also argue, however, that policy changes occurred not as a result of changes in living conditions but as a result of changed perceptions of living conditions, or as a result of changes in what was considered to be a feasible or desirable policy. It is extremely risky to infer changes in living standards from the type and extent of government action (or inaction).

The late nineteenth century is usually thought of as an era of 'self-help', with the role of the state in redistributing income, promoting equality of opportunity or providing a safety net for the destitute narrowly circumscribed. The innovations in social policy after the turn of the century are sometimes seen as a fundamental break with the past (and a precursor to the welfare state of the post-Second World War period), sometimes as the outgrowth of ideas developed in the nineteenth century.

The Poor Law had long provided the assistance of last resort to the destitute, and it retained this function in the late nineteenth century. As we have seen, the number of paupers relieved outside of workhouses declined, especially in the 1870s, while expenditure on indoor relief per pauper, and the number of paupers in workhouses, rose. Rising incomes are partially responsible for the decline in outdoor pauperism, but a pronounced change in policy, known as 'the crusade against outrelief', was also important. Reformers argued that the indiscriminate granting of outrelief sapped the poor of their self-reliance. During the crusade, outdoor relief to the aged, and to widows with children – two of the main groups of outdoor paupers – was restricted (Thomson 1984; MacKinnon 1987). In the early 1870s about 3.5 per cent of the population were in receipt of outrelief on any day; by the 1890s less than 2 per cent were.

Although from 1870 to the 1890s the government reduced its role in providing outrelief, in some other ways state intervention became more important in the lives of the working classes. The period saw the introduction of compulsory, and later free, elementary education. As noted above, strides were made in improving urban living conditions by clearing slums (although the evicted slum dwellers often had great difficulty in finding new homes) and building sewers. Minimum standards were imposed for new housing. The scope of the Factory Acts was extended, so that at least on paper the conditions of work even in small workshops were subject to government regulation.

In the 1880s and 1890s the actions of the government were limited, but at least the study of social problems, by royal commissions, was widespread. After 1900, governments continued to study, but also introduced welfare reforms, which began to come into effect in the years just before the First World War. Some of the interest in innovation arose from the perception that Britain's relative economic position was slipping. Fears that the working class were suffering 'physical deterioration' were widespread, and the high rejection rates for recruits during the Boer War fuelled the concern. If the working classes were not strong enough to work hard (or to fight for their country), Britain's prospects were bleak. Interventions to improve health, especially of workers and children, could easily be justified on such grounds. Similarly, unemployment was often viewed as a result of the lack of coordination between buyers and sellers of labour. Human resources were wasted, and the employability of workers diminished, when they were employed only sporadically. Labour exchanges, which would improve the matching of jobs and workers, and unemployment insurance, which would reduce the degree of deprivation associated with spells of unemployment, could therefore also be ways of improving the efficiency of the economy (Searle 1971; Harris 1972).

The development of the welfare state is sometimes thought of as the inevitable result of the expansion of the franchise, but the welfare reforms undertaken in Britain in the early twentieth century were not widely supported or advocated by the working class. The kinds of policies introduced depended on the attitudes of politicians and civil servants. Though politicians were concerned about working-class unrest, the changes in social policy were by no means direct responses to working-class demands (Hay 1975).

The welfare reforms of the Liberal governments between 1906 and 1914 touched on many aspects of social policy. All extended the range of government intervention, although the significance of much of the legislation was its pioneering nature, not the level of expenditure. The Poor Law remained in place, but the new measures provided various forms of assistance outside of it, on a non-pauperising basis.

Three of the most important innovations were old age pensions, health insurance and unemployment insurance. Starting in 1909, old age pensions of up to 5s a week were paid to the poor over the age of seventy, who were of good moral character. (Receipt of poor relief was until 1911 one of the main disqualifications from eligibility for the old age pension.) The administration of the old age pension was entirely separate from the Poor Law.

Health insurance benefits were first paid in 1913. Unlike old age pensions, health insurance was a contributory scheme, financed largely by flat rate contributions of workers and employers. Virtually all employees, including domestic servants, were covered. Insured workers were eligible for outpatient care, and for treatment in tuberculosis sanitaria. Illness and disability benefits were also provided. Most types of hospital treatment were not covered, and with the exception of a maternity benefit, dependants were not provided for. Charitable and Poor Law assistance therefore continued to be important sources of health care.

Far more workers were covered by health insurance than by unemployment insurance benefits, also first paid in 1913. Most of the workers contributing to the unemployment insurance fund were skilled, and almost all were male. Benefits were tied to contributions, and unemployed workers had to register at the recently created Labour Exchanges to be eligible for insurance payments (Fraser 1973; Thane 1982). The impact of such measures on working-class living standards before 1914 was modest (Gourvish 1979: 29). Payments were made on a small scale, or were introduced just before the outbreak of war. The redistributive impact of social expenditure payments was small. Both health and unemployment insurance were contributory schemes, and with flat rate contributions, they were regressive taxes.

Conclusions

At the end of the period, a large fraction of the British working class still lived in poverty, but the notional 'average' British working-class family on the eve of the First World War consumed many more goods and services than their hypothetical grandparents in the 1870s, with most of the gains occurring before the turn of the century. Such families consumed more than their counterparts on the Continent, but less than they would have in the US or main settler colonies.

12 The inter-war economy in a European mirror

Barry Eichengreen

Introduction

The quarter of a century that opened with the outbreak of the First World War and closed with the declaration of the Second World War was one of the most turbulent periods in all of modern British economic history. It was perceived by contemporaries and is portrayed by historians as an era of violent discontinuities. The First World War abruptly altered relations between labour and management and between the public and private sectors, and transformed Britain's position in the world economy. It was followed by twenty years of sweeping economic change. The first inter-war decade was dominated by the quest to return to the gold standard at the pre-war parity. It was punctuated by a general strike in 1926 and marred by persistent unemployment and intractable financial difficulties. The 1930s were darkened by the world economic depression. The depression saw the transformation of British international economic policy, from free trade and to protection, from the gold standard to managed money, from multilateralism to closer economic ties with the empire and Commonwealth. The approach of the Second World War was then marked by accelerating economic growth driven by cheap money and rearmament spending.

The period from 1914 through 1939 was one of far-reaching economic change, not merely in Britain, of course, but throughout Europe and the world. Virtually every landmark indicated on the inter-war historian's British road-map – the return to gold in the 1920s, subsequent financial difficulties, the depression of the 1930s and the beginning of recovery – has a counterpart in the inter-war history of other European countries. One wishes for an historian's Michelin Guide, which indicated with one star the aspects of British economic history between the wars that are 'interesting', with two stars events 'recommended', and three stars events 'highly recommended' to scholars seeking to understand what was distinctive about Britain's experience.

The economic consequences of the Great War for Britain

On the eve of the First World War, Great Britain was the world's foremost trading and lending nation. The value of her merchandise imports and exports was nearly a third larger than Germany's and 50 per cent larger than that of the United States. More international trade was invoiced in sterling than in any other currency. Foreign producers and merchants held bank balances in London to settle their accounts with British importers and exporters and with one another. The City was the world's leading financial centre. Half or more of the foreign currency reserves maintained by central banks and governments was held in the form of bank deposits and other assets denominated in sterling (Lindert 1969). From 1911 to 1913 exceptionally large amounts of British capital – on the order of 10 per cent of British GNP – had been lent abroad, the culmination of half a century of large-scale capital export. At approximately £4 billion in 1914, the stock of Britain's overseas investments far exceeded those of other nations and bulked large relative to her annual domestic product (£2.3 billion in 1914).

The Great War was first and foremost a disruption to international trade and finance. Given Britain's exceptional dependence on such transactions, it would not be surprising to find that her economy was disproportionately affected. Yet dramatic changes in Britain's external economic arrangements are not evident. The nation's commitment to free trade and the gold standard survived the war intact. Though the War Office contracted for imported supplies directly rather than relying on British merchants, to the point where it controlled 90 per cent of British imports at war's end, overseas trade quickly reverted to private hands. Admittedly, the McKenna Duties, import taxes imposed in 1915 on luxuries (cars, clocks, musical instruments and the like) taking up cargo space were Britain's first tariffs on imported manufactures in nearly a century; they provided a precedent for the Key Industries Duties imposed in 1921. But the vast majority of imported manufactures still entered duty free.

Though bureaucratic obstacles hindered individuals who wished to convert sterling into gold, the principal provisions of the gold standard remained in place (at least until 1919, when faster decontrol of markets in Britain than abroad forced their temporary suspension). At first the bureaucratic impediments mattered little. The pound strengthened in the opening months of the war, as British investors repatriated funds held abroad. Once shipping tonnage was diverted to military uses and U-boat warfare intensified, exports of manufactures fell off. Imports of grain and war matériel from the United States rose dramatically. By early 1915, sterling began to fall against the dollar. Even then it proved possible to peg sterling at a mere 10 per cent discount against the dollar for the duration of the war.

Trade and investment

The appearance of stability disguised more subtle changes, however. As British producers withdrew from overseas markets, foreign competitors stepped in, American producers in Latin America, Japanese producers in Asia. Having established marketing and distribution networks, the new competitors proved difficult to dislodge. Another enduring legacy was the impact of the conflict on Britain's international financial position. Though war debts were less important for Britain than for the other European Allies (since the government lent on to France and the other Allied powers much of the money it borrowed from the United States), private debts were another matter. A considerable portion of Britain's wartime trade deficit was financed by selling off existing foreign securities. According to Morgan (1952), £285 million of British foreign investments, or roughly 10 per cent of the pre-war total, was liquidated over the course of hostilities. Britain's interest income from abroad therefore declined by 10 per cent following the war, requiring an offsetting improvement in the balance of trade. Given the intensification of American and Japanese competition in Latin America and Asia, the shift would prove difficult to achieve.

Government

Similarly, wartime intervention by government in the home economy had few enduring legacies. In the early stages of the war, public intervention was limited (Checkland 1983). Government asserted its right to control the railways, although it left their day-to-day operation in private hands. Starting in 1917, as shortages of strategic products became increasingly pervasive, it took over the management of firms in sectors as diverse as munitions, coal and flour. By war's end the government marketed about 80 per cent of food consumed at home and controlled most consumer prices. Few of the changes endured, however. By 1920 government had largely withdrawn from intervention in the home economy. By 1922 the entire control apparatus had been dismantled. Wartime schemes to nationalise the railways and electrical power were consumed in the single-minded effort to restore the pre-war status quo.

Wartime destruction of physical capital in Britain was limited to the merchant shipping fleet, in contrast to the situation in France and elsewhere on the Continent, where plant and equipment were extensively damaged. A more serious impact of the war on Britain's productive capacity was the death of more than 600,000 servicemen and the wounding of 1.6 million others, many so seriously that they would never work again. These tragic deaths and disablings had few persistent effects on the economy. Unskilled workers could be replaced by attracting into the labour force women and recent school leavers. Skilled workers could be replaced in a matter of years through apprenticeship and on-the-job training.

Innovation

Yet here again the war had a variety of more subtle effects. Britain has been criticised for failing to adopt modern mass-production methods with the alacrity of Germany and the United States (Chandler 1990). The war sped the transformation. The need to mass produce all forms of military equipment from rifles to airplanes led to 'new methods of doing old jobs, new methods of factory layout, new methods of management and more intensive mechanisation' (Milward 1970: 54). Scientific-management techniques, such as time-and-motion studies, were widely applied for the first time. The need to provide cost information for military contracts compelled many firms to adopt modern accounting practices.

Wartime shortages and imperatives provided, for example, an incentive for the development of new alloys for use in aircraft and tanks. Sheffield steel makers learned how to substitute home ores for high-grade Swedish iron. Machine tools imported from the United States were installed in a variety of industries where they had been unknown. As skilled workers were conscripted, unskilled labour was substituted (a process known as 'dilution'). The installation of automatic machinery allowed assembly lines to be operated by labourers with minimal training and consigned the skilled to the repair and maintenance of equipment. By raising the demand for unskilled relative to skilled labour, these innovations reduced the wage premium commanded by the highly trained. This encouraged the entry into industrial employment of inexperienced workers, notably women and juveniles, ultimately altering the distribution of men and women across occupations. Although the vast majority of manufacturers who hired women to replace conscripted males ultimately turned the jobs back over to demobilised servicemen, some traditionally male jobs in the transport and service sectors (in offices, hotels, shops, buses and railway stations) were transformed permanently into female occupations.

Competition

The war also stimulated changes in competitive conduct and performance. Labour and management practices departed increasingly from the norm of atomistic competition. Manufacturers were encouraged to collaborate rather than to compete. Increasingly they shared technical expertise and information. Collaboration led to the formation of trade associations that enabled domestic producers to lobby more effectively for tariff protection and tax concessions, which became vehicles for restricting output and 'rationalising' production in the 1930s.

Labour

The war simultaneously strengthened the labour movement. The expansion of industry encouraged workers to join trade unions, as did public policy once union leaders began to collaborate with government to discourage strikes and work slowdowns. Trade union membership doubled, from 4 million in 1913 to more than 8 million in 1919. Small unions merged into amalgamations and federations. Industry-wide as opposed to local collective bargaining emerged for the first time. Between the wars, a third to a half of British workers were covered by collective bargaining agreements, a much larger share than before the war. Long wartime hours and shortages of consumer goods induced workers to demand increased leisure after the war, while more effective labour organisation allowed them to achieve shorter hours without a reduction in weekly wages (Broadberry 1990). The average length of the work week declined by 13 per cent immediately after the war (Dowie 1975: 440; Dimsdale 1984: 94). Unions and the Parliamentary Labour Party applied pressure to extend the purview of the recently established unemployment insurance scheme. The Trade Board Act of 1918 widened the scope of a set of labour market institutions, established before the war to set minimum wages and regulate hours and working conditions for 'sweated labour', mainly women and juveniles. It is alleged that because of such anti-competitive institutions the inter-war economy adjusted less smoothly to changing market conditions than had its pre-war predecessor. If so, the roots of the changes lay in the First World War.

Of course, similar changes were evident elsewhere in Europe. The corporatist approach to wartime economic management, emphasising industrial combination, labour organisation and government intervention, was common to the belligerent countries. Every European country suspended the gold standard during or after the war. The liquidation of foreign financial assets and the decline in exports to Asia and the western hemisphere was a Europe-wide, not merely a British, phenomenon. The question therefore is whether these developments had distinctive implications for the British economy.

The performance of the inter-war economy

The growth of the British economy is juxtaposed against that of its continental European counterparts in Figure 12.1. Included are all eight continental countries for which comparable estimates of real GDP are provided by Maddison (1982). Per capita real GDP grew by 1.3 per cent per annum between 1914 and 1944, or at almost exactly the same pace as the eight continental economies (for which the comparable growth rate was 1.4 per cent; 'growth rates' refer to the annual average growth of real GDP per capita; all figures for the Continent are unweighted averages). On its face this supports the claim of authors like Aldcroft (1967) that Britain's inter-war growth performance was entirely respectable. Yet these strikingly similar statistics for Britain and the Continent disguise very different performance in years of war and peace and in the two peacetime decades. The British economy grew more quickly than that of the Continent during the First and Second World Wars but less rapidly during the intervening decades. Its performance compares favourably with the Continent's in the 1930s but not in the 1920s.

Output

British output rose impressively during the First World War, for reasons described above: more people were working; little capital was damaged. In contrast, in countries like France and Germany, where the war was particularly destructive, wartime output fell. Likewise and for similar reasons the British economy again grew more quickly than its continental counterparts during the early stages of the Second World War.

Between 1919 and 1938, on the other hand, the average annual growth rate of the Continent (2.9 per cent) was five times as fast as that for Britain (0.6 per cent). In part the disparity reflects the exceptional severity of the post-war recession in Britain and its absence on the Continent: when calculated for 1922–38 the British growth rate rises to 2.1 per cent, while that of the Continent falls to 2.8 per cent (for this period it is possible to add data for Austria and Belgium; the comparable growth rate for the 'Continental 10' is then 2.6 per cent). Although Britain's growth rate rises within hailing distance of the Continent's, there remains a shortfall to be explained.

Also clear from the figure is that the British economy continued to lose ground to the Continent in the 1920s. Between 1922 and 1929 Britain's growth rate was 2.8 per cent, compared to 4.2 per cent for the Continent. (Again the figure falls only slightly, to 4.1 per cent, when Austria and Belgium are added.) In the 1930s the differential evaporates, because of the

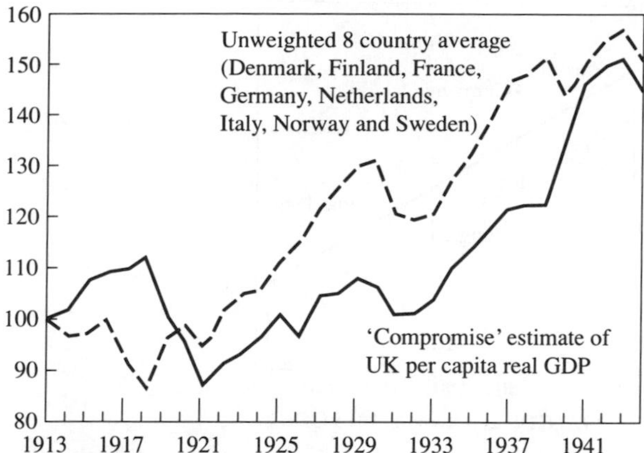

Figure 12.1 Per capita GDP for eight European countries and the UK, 1913–44
Note: 1913 = 100.
Sources: Maddison (1982) and Mitchell (1988).

relatively mild decline in British output in the early stages of the Great Depression: per capita product in Britain expanded by 1.5 per cent between 1930 and 1938, in tandem with that of the Continent (which grew at 1.6 per cent per annum; 1.3 per cent when Belgium and Austria are added).

The legacy of the war

In part the growth performance of Britain and the Continent in the 1920s reflected the legacy of the war. There was considerable scope for economic growth in the first half of the 1920s simply by redeploying resources to peacetime uses. Soldiers could return to productive employment. Resources could be used for building ships rather than sinking them, for producing motor vehicles rather than destroying them. The greater had been wartime destruction of productive capacity, the larger the scope for raising output through repair, reconstruction and reconversion. For Europe in general, every percentage point by which GNP fell between 1913 and 1920 increased the growth rate between 1920 and 1927 by half a percentage point. The estimate comes from a regression using the data depicted in Figure 12.2 (figures in parentheses are *t*-statistics: when they are as high as these are they indicate low uncertainty from sampling variation):

$$GNP_{1927}/GNP_{1920} = \underset{(8.36)}{182.23} - \underset{(2.30)}{0.52}\,[GNP_{1920}/GNP_{1913}]$$

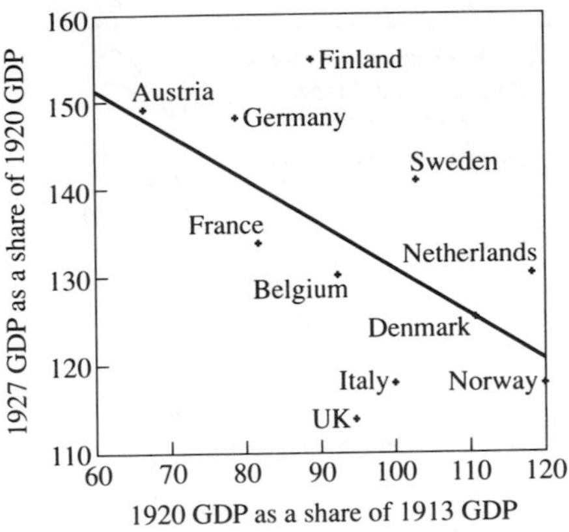

Figure 12.2 Post-war growth and the wartime set-back, 1913, 1920 and 1927
Source: see Appendix.

The regression line is superimposed on Figure 12.2. The data used in this figure are from Maddison (1982). (A technical point: note that errors in measuring GNP in 1920 will produce a negative correlation like that shown only if they are uncorrelated with measurement errors for prior and subsequent years.)

Figure 12.2 shows Britain to have been an outlier. British economic growth between 1920 and 1927 was unusually slow by the standard of what one would have expected from the decline in British GNP between 1913 and 1920 and the performance typical of European countries. Adding a dummy variable for Britain to the equation reported above produces a coefficient of −22.12 with a *t*-statistic of 2.09. The catchup effect is somewhat weaker when 1921 rather than 1920 is used as the base year. But Britain remains a negative outlier (along with, interestingly, Italy). In Belgium, a more typical case, the wartime set-back was the same as in Britain, but the growth of GNP between 1920 and 1927 was nearly four times as fast.

The return to gold

Why did Britain lag? In part, Britain may have suffered more from the wartime loss of export markets to the United States and Japan than did her European counterparts. Most accounts, however, emphasise not the change in market structure but rather government policy, specifically the policy of returning to gold at the pre-war parity. In the two years following the armistice, sterling lost an additional 15 per cent of its value against the dollar, reaching a low of $3.49 in 1921. From there the Bank of England

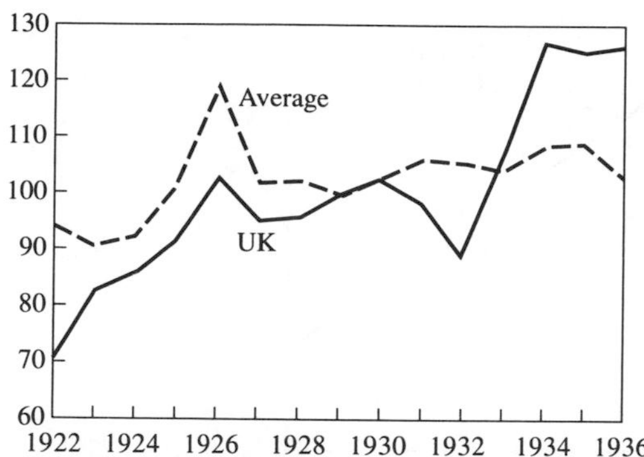

Figure 12.3 The nominal effective exchange rate for Britain and nine European countries, 1922–36
Note: average excludes Germany and Belgium. 1929 = 100.
Source: see Appendix.

and the Treasury applied restrictive monetary and fiscal measures to push the currency back up to its pre-war parity of $4.86, a goal finally achieved in April 1925.

Since other countries pursued the same policy, however, it is not clear how much difference Britain's strategy made. (Broadberry 1984b provides a comparison of Britain with the Scandinavian countries which also restored their pre-war parities at roughly the same time.) Figure 12.3 displays the nominal effective exchange rate for Britain and nine European countries. (Effective exchange rates are computed as trade-weighted bilateral exchange rates, where the exchange rate is expressed as the foreign price of a unit of domestic currency. An increase indicates an appreciation.) Figure 12.3 confirms that sterling appreciated more than other European currencies, measured on an effective basis. Between 1922 and 1936, sterling appreciated by more than 40 per cent, while other European currencies appreciated by only 30 per cent.

The policy allegedly handicapped British exporters. Sterling's appreciation, in the textbook view, was not accompanied by a commensurate fall in domestic prices and costs. Among researchers, in contrast, there no longer exists a consensus on how far or even whether sterling was overvalued (a review of the debate can be found in Alford 1972: 34–6). Moggridge (1969) showed that Keynes' conclusion in 1925 that British prices had risen by 10 per cent relative to American prices between 1913 and 1925 hinged on the price indices used. Other authors suggested that both Keynes' and Moggridge's conclusions might have to be modified when price levels in other countries were considered. Using a variety of price indices and weighting schemes, Redmond (1984) computed real

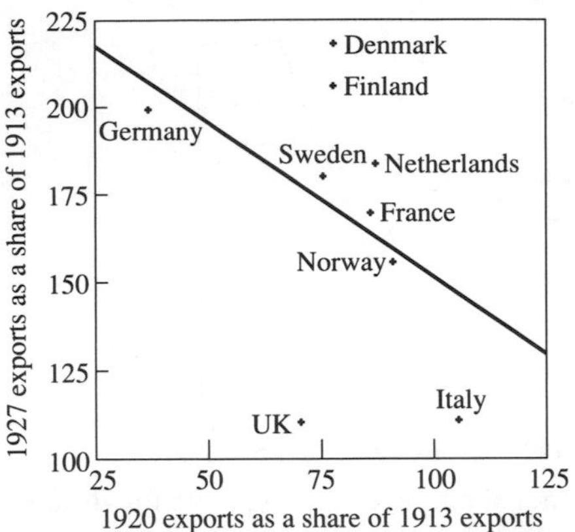

Figure 12.14 Investment as a share of GNP in Britain and Europe, 1920 and 1927
Source: see Appendix.

effective exchange rate indices which generally confirmed that, after expanding the sample of countries and adjusting for exchange rate changes, British prices did rise relative to the prices of Britain's principal trading partners between 1913 and 1925 (by 5 to 10 per cent in the case of wholesale prices, by 15 to 20 per cent in the case of retail prices). In other words, the prices of British exports were pushed up by 5 to 10 per cent relative to the prices elsewhere as a result of restoring the pre-war parity.

Overseas trade

The obvious place to look for the effects of an overvalued currency is in the behaviour of overseas trade. If sterling was overvalued the growth of British exports should have lagged. Figure 12.4 is at least superficially consistent with this view: it shows that where merchandise exports had been most severely disrupted by the war, there was the most scope for their subsequent growth. Once more Britain is an outlier. Her exports grew more slowly between 1920 and 1927 than their wartime set-back and the performance of other European countries would predict. A regression using the data in Figure 12.4 yields the equation (X stands for the exports of each country at the dates indicated):

$$X_{1927} = \underset{(6.07)}{266.25} - \underset{(2.07)}{1.11}\,[X_{1920}/X_{1913}] - \underset{(2.60)}{78.54}\ \text{Britain}$$

But again, before attributing this to the policy of restoring sterling's pre-war parity, it is worth recalling the wartime growth of American and

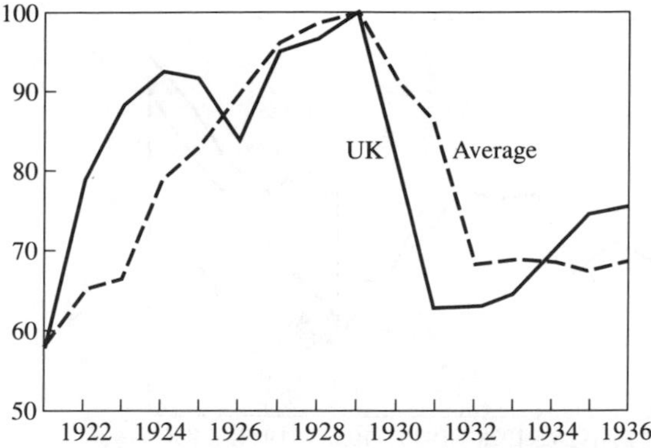

Figure 12.5 Volume of British and European exports, 1921–36
Source: see Appendix.

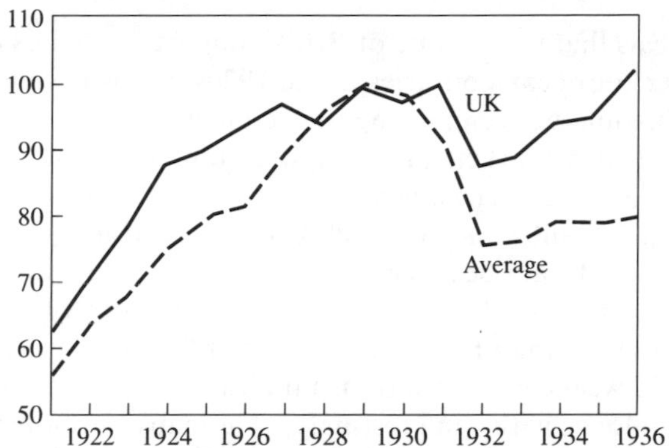

Figure 12.6 Volume of British and European imports, 1921–36
Source: see Appendix.

Japanese competition in Britain's traditional export markets. It may have had a good deal to do with Britain's failure to boost her exports in the peace.

Figures 12.5 and 12.6 paint a more complex picture. Figure 12.5 reveals that the volume of British exports grew more rapidly than those of her European competitors between 1921 and 1924 but more slowly thereafter. Thus there is no evidence that British exports were depressed during the period when sterling was rising from its 1921 low back to its pre-war parity; in contrast, British export performance seems to have deteriorated subsequently, starting around the time the pre-war parity was restored. The decline in British exports in 1926, so prominent in the figure, was caused by the coal strike of that year. But the deceleration of British export growth was already evident at least a year before.

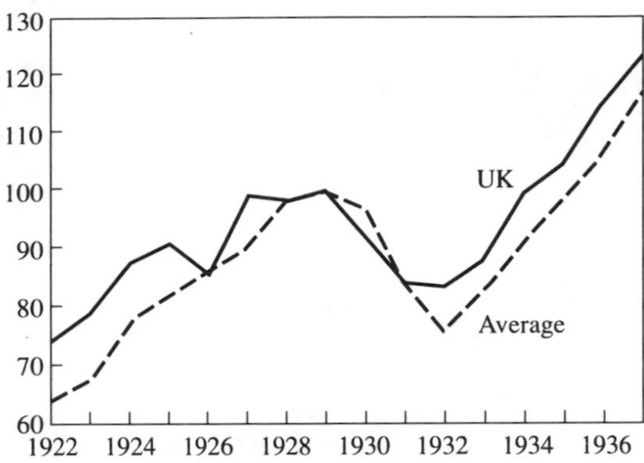

Figure 12.7 Industrial production in Britain and Europe, 1922–37
Source: see Appendix.

Figure 12.6 reveals that the volume of British imports grew less quickly than those of other European countries in the 1920s, not what one would expect if overvaluation was enhancing the competitiveness of foreign producers in the British market. (The import volume indices are constructed to equal 100 in 1929. The index for other Europe is an unweighted average of individual country indices, each benchmarked to 1929 = 100.) That the solid line for Britain begins in 1921 above the dotted line for the rest of Europe indicates that British imports grew less quickly over the period. Using 1921 rather than 1929 as the base year for calculating import growth in the 1920s weakens the relationship although Britain remains a negative outlier (along with, interestingly, Germany). Imports, like exports, grew more rapidly before 1925 than after. If an overvalued exchange rate was the main determinant of import and export trends, as sterling was returned to gold one would expect the growth of import and export volumes to have moved in opposite directions (exports falling, imports rising). In fact the growth of both import and export volumes slowed after 1924, as if other factors, such as changes in output and income growth, were driving both components of the trade balance.

Figure 12.7 supports this supposition. It shows that industrial production, having grown in Britain at the same pace as on the Continent through 1925, rose more slowly thereafter. Again, the coal strike is part of the explanation. But the failure of British industrial production to recover in 1927–8, a period when output elsewhere was expanding rapidly and when Britain had put the labour market disruptions of 1926 behind her, suggests that other factors were at work.

The obvious explanation for the slowdown in British growth after 1924 lies in the restrictive policies pursued by the Bank of England and the

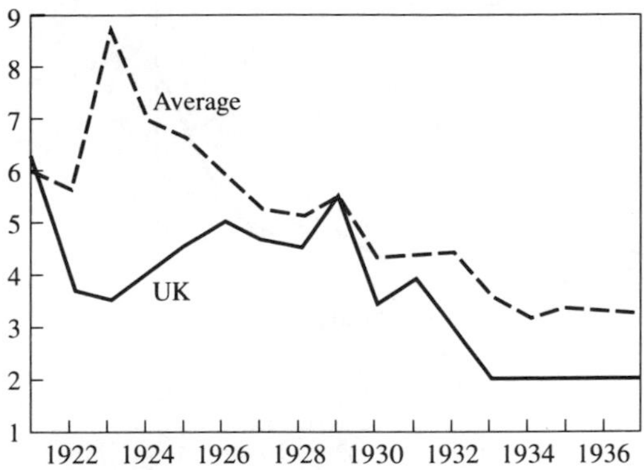

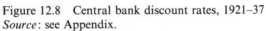

Figure 12.8 Central bank discount rates, 1921–37
Source: see Appendix.

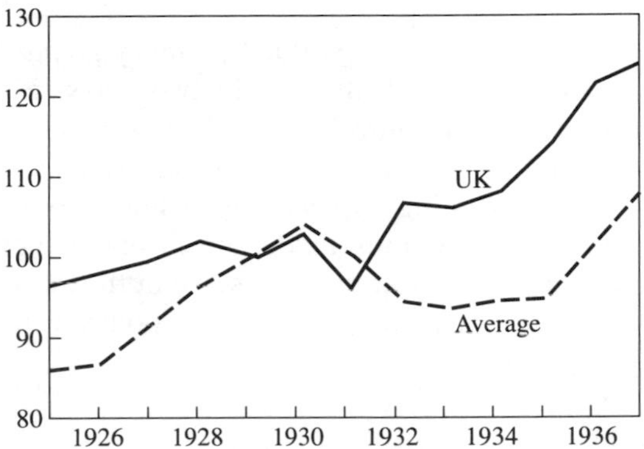

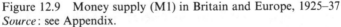

Figure 12.9 Money supply (M1) in Britain and Europe, 1925–37
Source: see Appendix.

Treasury to bring British and foreign prices into line and thereby eliminate the balance of payments problem associated with the return to gold. Figure 12.7 also suggests a restrictive shift in the stance of British policy around 1925. Figure 12.8 shows the tendency for the Bank of England's discount rate (the leading contemporary indicator of the stance of monetary policy) to rise over the period while other central bank discount rates fell. Figure 12.9 confirms that the British money supply grew more slowly than continental money supplies between 1925 and 1929. Figure 12.10 shows the consequent tendency for British prices to fall more quickly than prices on the Continent from 1925 through the end of the decade.

Redmond's (1984) calculations suggest that by 1929 British wholesale prices had finally declined sufficiently to eliminate the 5–10 per cent discrepancy between British and foreign price levels. The question is at

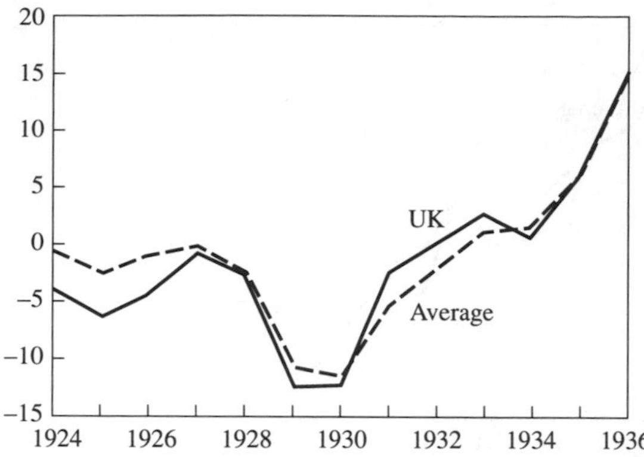

Figure 12.10 Annual average rate of inflation in Britain and Europe, 1924–36
Source: see Appendix.

what cost. Under a gold standard an overvalued currency giving rise to a weak balance of payments can be dealt with in two ways. Either the authorities can allow reserves to flow out, reducing money supply, expenditure and prices until competitive balance is restored; or they can apply measures to compress spending (typically by raising interest rates in order to discourage borrowing by households and firms), achieving the decline in expenditure and prices without the reserve outflows. If money wages fail to match the movement in prices, either policy will depress output and raise unemployment.

Unemployment

Recorded unemployment in Britain hovered above 10 per cent throughout the 1920s (see Figure 12.11). Although the nature of the statistics makes international comparisons problematic, the published figures show British unemployment to have been greater than unemployment elsewhere in Europe through the 1920s, except in 1927. (The rise in unemployment in 1927 on the Continent reflects stabilisation recessions in France and Italy; detailed discussion of the comparability of these unemployment rates appears in Eichengreen and Hatton 1988b.) Casson (1983a), Dimsdale (1984), Matthews (1986b) and many others agree that British unemployment in the 1920s resulted from the failure of wages to keep pace with the downward march of prices. As real wages rose, workers were rationed out of employment. The authors disagree, however, over the underlying cause. Dimsdale argues that the problem originated with exchange rate appreciation and ran from there to downward pressure on prices and wages. Matthews suggests, to the contrary, that the problem originated

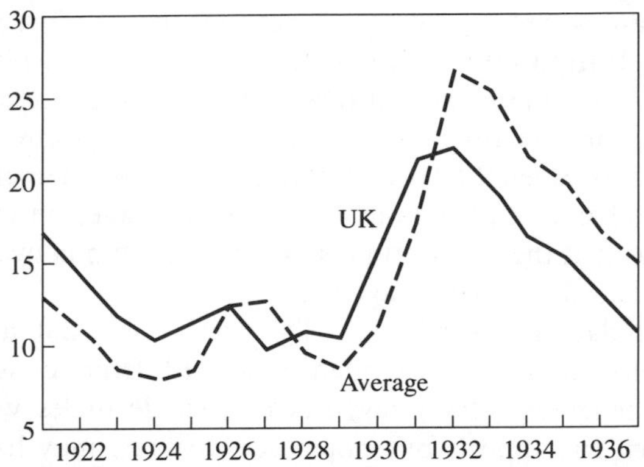

Figure 12.11 Unemployment rate in industry in Britain and Europe, 1921–37
Source: see Appendix.

with upward pressure on wages and ran from there to higher prices and to a higher real exchange rate (a higher ratio of British to exchange rate adjusted foreign prices).

For the argument advanced by Matthews for the 1920s and by others (for example, Beenstock and Warburton 1986) about the 1930s to be correct, there must have existed impediments to wage adjustment. According to the argument made famous by Benjamin and Kochin (1979), the main such impediment was an exceptionally generous unemployment insurance system which subsidised leisure and job search. In the 1920s the ratio of average weekly benefits to average weekly wages hovered around 50 per cent, double the ratio that had prevailed in 1913, when Britain's insurance scheme was established. Benjamin and Kochin showed that the time-series behaviour of average wages, average benefits and employment between 1920 and 1938 is consistent with the hypothesis that a high ratio of benefits to wages substantially increased the level of unemployment in the 1920s. Matthews used similar evidence to argue that the mechanism ran from high benefits to high wages and from there to an overvalued exchange rate and unemployment.

The large literature that arose subsequently to challenge these results is surveyed in chapter 14. The literature has shown that the impact of unemployment benefits on unemployment is extremely difficult to pin down using aggregate data. For example, Ormerod and Worswick (1982) point out that Benjamin and Kochin's finding of a strong positive time-series correlation between the benefit/wage ratio and unemployment rests largely on conditions in 1920, when benefits had not yet been raised to levels typical of the inter-war period, but when unemployment was low for what many historians would regard as independent reasons (the post-war restocking boom). Hatton (1985) shows that the mechanism posited by Benjamin and Kochin – an increase in time spent in search, reflecting the benefit-induced rise in the reservation wage – does not show up in a positive relationship between the ratio of unfilled vacancies to unemployed workers on the one hand and the ratio of benefits to wages on the other. Crafts (1987) shows that there is no time-series relationship between long-term employment and the benefit/wage ratio.

Household level data has shed some light on issues that aggregate statistics have failed to resolve. Evidence derived from a survey of households in Eichengreen (1987) suggests that single males without a spouse and children to support, but not other workers, may have been induced by unemployment benefits to engage in additional search leading to longer spells of unemployment. The accumulated evidence thus points to the conclusion that unemployment benefits made only a marginal contribution to inter-war unemployment.

The slump

The same debate arises in connection with the onset of the 1929 slump. Between 1929 and 1931, although industrial output fell by almost precisely the same amount in Britain and on the Continent, industrial unemployment rose to higher levels in Britain than elsewhere in Europe. More precisely, Figure 12.7 shows that industrial production fell more quickly than on the Continent between 1929 and 1930, but more slowly between 1930 and 1931. Figure 12.1 differs from Figure 12.7 above by the inclusion of Germany, which is omitted from Figure 12.7 because reliable estimates for Germany are not available for the hyper-inflation years 1922–3. The behaviour of exports (Figure 12.5 above) suggests that the early decline of British industrial output reflected the early deterioration of British export markets, such as Australia, Argentina and Brazil. Real wages rose faster in Britain than elsewhere in Europe (see Figure 12.12). The rise did not reflect different price trends in Britain and elsewhere, since deflation proceeded more quickly in Britain in 1929–30 but more slowly in 1930–1 (Figure 12.10). Once again, the dispute is whether the failure of wages to adjust reflected the intrinsically inertial character of British labour markets or the distortions imposed on the market by public policy.

Any differences between Britain and the rest of Europe through 1931 are dwarfed by those which emerged subsequently. After declining rapidly for two years, British industrial production stabilised in 1932, despite continuing to fall at a 10 per cent annual rate elsewhere in Europe. The main factor in the divergence was Britain's abandonment of the gold

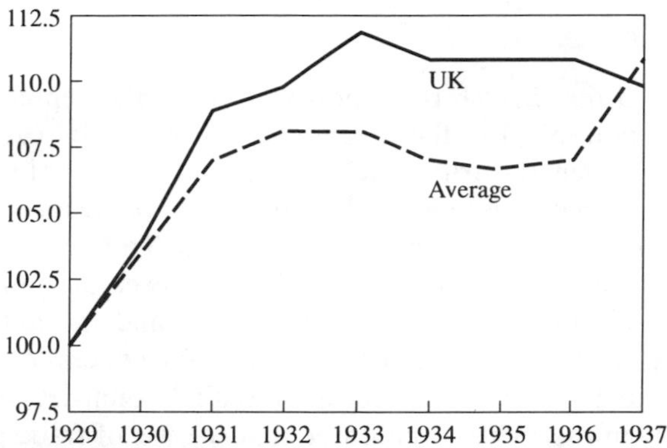

Figure 12.12 Hourly earnings in industry, mines and transport in Britain and Europe, 1929–37
Source: see Appendix.

standard in 1931 and the depreciation of sterling. The Bank of England had fought a losing battle against gold outflows since 1927. In 1931, with the collapse of economic activity world-wide, there was an abrupt decline in the dividends paid by foreign corporations and the interest paid by foreign governments on monies borrowed previously on the London capital market, leading to a deterioration in the invisible component of the British balance of payments (Moggridge 1970). Under normal circumstances, the higher interest rates adopted by the Bank of England would have restored external balance (Cairncross and Eichengreen 1983). But in the summer of 1931, a period of financial crisis in Europe and the United States, confidence was not easily maintained. A run on the Bank of England's reserves forced the suspension of convertibility on 19 September 1931.

By December of the same year, sterling had fallen from £1 = $4.86 to a low of £1 = $3.24. By reducing the prices of British goods on international markets, depreciation switched demand toward the products of domestic industry. Figure 12.5 shows that the volume of British exports stabilised in 1932, coincident with the stabilisation of output, despite continuing to fall on the Continent at an alarming rate. This much is readily explained by the depreciation of sterling in 1931–2. But the tendency for British exports to continue to rise through 1936, despite remaining stagnant on the Continent, is not so easily explained. As Figure 12.3 shows, after depreciating in 1931–2, sterling appreciated sharply in 1933–4, mainly as a result of the depreciation of the American dollar. By 1934, the nominal effective sterling rate had risen significantly relative to the exchange rates of Britain's European competitors.

The tariff

It might be argued that British trade policy, and not the depreciation of sterling, was responsible for these favourable trends. In early 1932, Parliament passed a general tariff, which imposed a 10 per cent import tax, exempting only raw materials, and established an Import Duties Advisory Committee to consider applications for higher rates. To prevent the tariff from disrupting economic relations with the Commonwealth countries, the government met with their representatives in Ottawa and agreed to extend preferential treatment to their exports in return for concessions on the treatment of British goods. The Commonwealth countries recovered relatively quickly in the 1930s. It could be that the use of trade policy to divert British exports toward the Commonwealth thereby stimulated the home economy.

Most authors are sceptical, however, that British trade policy was a major factor in the recovery. Imports, after all, expanded as fast as exports (Figure 12.6). Both import and export volumes recovered, rapidly compared to those on the Continent. Richardson (1967) estimates that the overall influence of the tariff on employment was negligible. Foreman-Peck (1981) estimates that the General Tariff raised British output no more than 3 per cent, a conclusion with which other recent authors such as Broadberry (1986b) and Worswick (1984) generally agree.

Even if the tariff had a minor impact on the level of output, it could still have had a major impact on its composition. Richardson (1967) and Capie (1978) provided detailed analyses of the intersectoral reallocation of resources. Capie computed effective rates of protection (adjusting tariffs on imports of final goods for tariffs on imports of intermediate inputs). He found that the protection was enjoyed by chemicals and motor vehicles, examples of the so-called 'new industries', but also by traditional staple industries such as textiles and apparel. Thus it is not clear that the tariff played a major role in shifting resources into the rapidly expanding new industries, since it subsidised both new industries and old staples. Richardson went further, concluding that the expansion of the new industries was largely unconnected with the tariff, on the grounds that output growth in those sectors was larger than the fall in imports of competing products. Kitson and Solomou (1990) dissented on the grounds that the tariff shifted resources toward sectors characterised by scale economies, thereby giving a powerful boost to output and productivity.

Monetary policy

Some dispute, then, remains over the impact of the tariff. But surely more important was the domestic monetary policy that accompanied currency depreciation. This is the conclusion of many recent authors, such as Worswick (1984) and Dimsdale (1984). Notable dissenters are Beenstock, Capie and Griffiths (1984), who disagree on the grounds that short-term interest rates were not noticeably lower at the beginning of the recovery than they had been before. Worswick (1984) challenges their position on the grounds that they neglect the behaviour of long-term rates and fail to distinguish the high level of rates during the 1931 financial crisis from the lower level of rates during surrounding periods.

It would seem in any case that abandoning the gold standard was the critical precondition for adopting a more accommodating monetary policy. Lower interest rates provided much-needed stimulus for recovery. Bank Rate was lowered to 2 per cent in the summer of 1932 to minimise the appreciation of the floating pound sterling. Having inadvertently discovered the benefits of cheap money, the Bank of England pegged its discount rate at 2 per cent for the remainder of the decade. Long-term interest rates were pushed down, allowing the government to convert the 5 per cent War Loan to a 3.5 per cent stock in the summer of 1932. (Details on British monetary management in the 1930s are provided by Howson 1975.) In contrast, countries still on the gold standard (France, Belgium, Switzerland and the Netherlands among them) were forced to maintain high interest rates to defend their reserves (Figure 12.8).

The different policies had a powerful impact on the course of economic recovery, as Eichengreen and Sachs (1985) have shown. Money supply in Britain was allowed to expand much more quickly than on the Continent until 1936, when the remaining members of the gold bloc finally abandoned convertibility and adopted expansionist monetary policies of their own (Figure 12.9). Hence prices recovered more quickly in Britain than on the Continent between 1931 and 1934 (Figure 12.10).

Other countries that abandoned the gold standard in the early 1930s recovered from the depression in much the same fashion. Indeed, as Figure 12.13 shows, other European countries that devalued early on (Denmark, Norway, Finland, Sweden) or that imposed exchange control (Austria, Germany, Italy) recovered even more quickly than Britain from the 1931 trough. In contrast, the economies of the gold bloc (France, Belgium, the Netherlands, Switzerland) continued to stagnate.

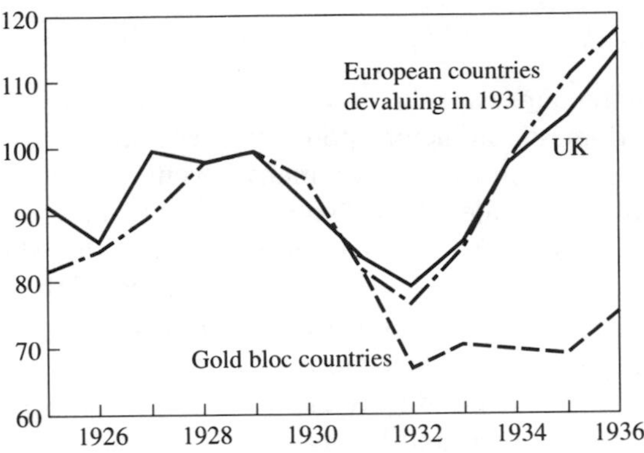

Figure 12.13 Industrial production of gold and non-gold countries, 1925–36
Source: see Appendix.

Housing

Given the source of stimulus, it is not surprising that interest-rate-sensitive categories of spending led the recovery. Prominent among these were residential construction and consumer durables. The housing boom is one of the most notable features of the British economy in the 1930s. House building stabilised in 1931–2, coincident with the initiation of recovery, even while other forms of fixed investment were continuing to fall. The increase in house building accounted for 17 per cent of the increase in GDP between 1932 and 1934. It stimulated output and employment in other sectors through its backward linkages to firms producing bricks, tiles, pipes and other construction materials. House building and associated trades together accounted for 30 per cent of the increase in employment in the first three years of recovery (Worswick 1984).

Average monthly mortgage payments on new homes declined by 9 per cent between 1931 and 1933, reflecting the advent of cheap money (MacIntosh 1951). The building society movement expanded rapidly in the 1930s, increasing the average length of mortgages and providing cheap credit to home buyers, thereby enhancing the capacity of monetary policy to stimulate recovery. This is not to say that monetary policy was solely responsible for the housing boom. Broadberry (1987) found that cheap money accounted for roughly half of the rise in housing investment at the start of the recovery. Rising real incomes and falling construction costs accounted for the rest. Bowden (1988) similarly concluded that the declining relative price of consumer durables (in which the cost of credit presumably played an important part) and rising real incomes both contributed to the growing demand for consumer durables in the thirties.

Fiscal policy

Compared to cheap money, fiscal policy played little role in recovery. Middleton (1985) computed the constant employment budget balance (correcting the actual budget balance for changes induced by the business cycle). Although the actual budget swung from a surplus of 0.4 per cent of GDP in 1929/30 to a deficit of 1.3 per cent of GDP in 1932/3, the constant employment budget surplus grew from 0.4 per cent of GDP in 1929/30 to 3.0 per cent of GDP in 1932/3. The increase in the constant employment surplus was achieved by a combination of tax increases and expenditure cuts. The single largest swing in the full employment surplus occurred in 1931/2, reflecting the extremely restrictive budget adopted in September 1931 in response to the financial crisis. Thus, it is hard to attach much importance to fiscal policy as a factor helping to initiate the recovery.

Budgetary policy remained neutral, and even deflationary, into the second half of the 1930s, raising the question of why the fiscal authorities failed to respond. It is not that the case for counter-cyclical fiscal policy was unknown prior to the publication of Keynes' *General Theory* in 1936; experts had articulated it at the hearings of the Macmillan Committee and the meetings of the Economic Advisory Council in 1930–1, to cite but two representative instances. But serious obstacles stood in the way of its implementation. A £500 million increase in government spending, which Thomas (1976) estimates to have been needed to put back to work even a tenth of persons unemployed in the early 1930s, would have radically transformed a central government budget amounting to less than twice that amount, even if the programme had been spread over five years. (These pessimistic conclusions have not gone unchallenged: see Garside and Hatton 1985 and, for a rejoinder, Glynn and Booth 1985.) Middleton overstates the case when he suggests that such a programme would have required the socialisation of investment and nationalisation of industry, but it still would have represented a radical break with the past.

Defence spending

Only in 1936–7 did the constant employment budget surplus decline significantly. The trend reflected not a conscious shift in economic policy but geopolitical imperatives associated with the approach of the Second World War. British defence spending rose, as a share of GDP, from 2.7 per cent in 1935/6 to 7.7 per cent in 1938/9. Defence spending rose from 13 per cent of central government expenditure in 1935/6 to 19 per cent in 1936/7, 25 per cent in 1937/8 and 32 per cent in 1938/9. In computing the ratios, total government spending is taken on a constant employment basis

(Middleton 1985: 140). A radical break with traditional fiscal policy had finally taken place, and without forcing the socialisation of the British economy of which contemporaries warned. Experience proved that those who had objected to increased public expenditure on the grounds that, because of binding supply constraints, it would give rise to inflation rather than increased employment, had been overpessimistic. Thomas' (1983) analysis of public spending on rearmament suggests that it stimulated output and employment not just in defence-related industries such as iron and steel and engineering but economy-wide. The British rearmament programme created 445,000 jobs in 1935, compared to 2.4 million unemployed persons that year. By 1938, jobs created had risen to 1.5 million. Rearmament thus helped to sustain the recovery and to mitigate the 1937–8 recession.

Unemployment

Modern pessimists take refuge in the stubborn persistence of high unemployment. The number of persons unemployed fell by only 200,000 between 1935 and 1938. (The tiny fall in unemployment was consistent with the large rise in employment described in the last paragraph because of increases in labour force participation. Broadberry (1983) and Beenstock and Warburton (1986) debate whether the increase in the participation rate was a response to the high level of real wages.) The overall unemployment rate, as officially measured, remained in double digits through the end of the decade. The traditional figures are annual average unemployment rates. Feinstein (1972) has adjusted the official unemployment statistics downward better to coincide with the 1931 census benchmark, on the grounds that the census provides a more comprehensive picture of unemployment than the statistics generated by the unemployment insurance system.

The failure of real wages and unemployment to fall more quickly is one of the central paradoxes of British economic performance in the 1930s. Had real wages fallen more rapidly after 1933, employers would have found it profitable to rehire additional workers, and British output would have expanded even more rapidly than it actually did. Crafts' (1989b) explanation for the failure of real wages to fall despite the persistence of double-digit unemployment rests on the emergence of long-term unemployment in the 1930s. In 1929, only one in ten unemployed persons had been out of work for more than a year; by 1937 the ratio had risen to one in four. Why were these unemployed workers unable to bid down wages sufficiently to obtain work? Trade unions, Crafts suggests, set the level of wages as high as was consistent with the employment of their active members. As soon as unemployed workers stopped paying union dues, they no longer figured in the calculations of union leaders, an instance of what has come to be known as the 'insider-outsider approach' to unemployment. Trade Boards, which also intervened in the wage-setting process, may have pursued similar policies. Thus the long-term unemployed soon stopped exerting downward pressure on labour costs.

Why such a large share of the unemployed suffered extended spells out of work has proven difficult to ascertain. Crafts (1987) shows that long-term unemployment was disproportionately concentrated in 'Outer Britain', in the midlands, north, Wales and Scotland. The declining staple industries – coal, steel, textiles and shipbuilding – were all located in Outer Britain. These industries accounted for more than half of all long-term unemployment in the mid-1930s (Thomas 1988). Family ties, relocation costs, rent control on working-class dwellings and local authority housing all may have prevented unemployed workers from migrating to other regions with better employment prospects. In addition to these problems of labour supply, Heim (1984b) suggests that the new industries in London and the south may have preferred not to hire workers with previous experience in the staple trades, where they had acquired inflexible attitudes about work pace and organisation.

Insofar as long-term unemployment hastened the depreciation of job skills, eroded work habits and undermined health – for all three reasons reducing the wages which the unemployed could command – the problems caused by restrictive wage-setting would be made worse. Most of the evidence invoked to substantiate such effects is anecdotal (see for example Pilgrim Trust 1938). Recently, however, Winter (1979) has documented the deterioration of health suffered by workers in the 1930s. Harris (1988) has established a link between unemployment and malnutrition. The findings drive the final nail into the coffin of the benefit-induced unemployment thesis. It is impossible to reconcile the notion that unemployed workers were simply on an extended vacation with evidence that they suffered declining health and their children suffered deteriorating diets as a result of their unemployment.

Thus, an eclectic picture of economic recovery in the 1930s emerges from recent research. The British economy was propelled forward by a series of modest but useful stimuli: by currency depreciation in 1931, by cheap money in 1932–5, and by rearmament spending in 1936–7. Real GNP rose at a respectable 4 per cent annual rate between 1932 and 1937, as fast as on the European Continent. But this expansion remained inadequate to bring unemployment back down to socially acceptable levels. For that, the considerable stimulus to labour demand associated with the Second World War would be required.

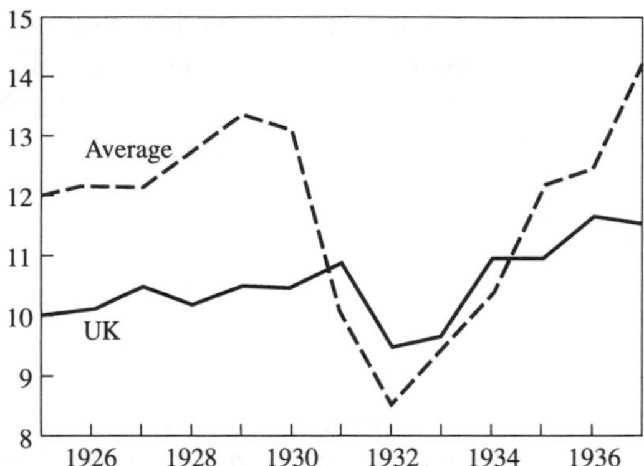

Figure 12.14 Investment as a share of GNP in Britain and Europe, 1925–37
Source: see Appendix.

The post-war legacy

The glass of British economic performance after the Second World War can be seen as half empty or half full. British productivity growth accelerated sharply after the Second World War. It is tempting to characterise the inter-war years as a period of regeneration for British industry which set the stage for the subsequent acceleration. Yet British output and productivity growth persistently lagged behind the growth enjoyed in other European countries in the 1950s and 1960s. The inter-war years can equally well be seen, therefore, as having put in place the shackles that prevented the British economy from keeping pace with its European competitors.

Rosy characterisations of the inter-war period emphasise modernisation, rationalisation, and structural change. Modernisation took the form of new technologies and equipment. In coal mining, for example, Britain nearly closed the gap vis-à-vis the Continent in the 1930s in the proportion of output mechanically cut. The electrical industry expanded its capacity and efficiency through the installation of switchboards, converters and transformers. The shipbuilding industry experimented with welding. The textile industry perfected its capacity to manufacture garments using rayon and other synthetic fibres. Many other examples could be cited (see Buxton and Aldcroft 1979). Investment in plant and equipment was the mechanism that allowed these new techniques and processes to be brought into operation.

From the aggregate statistics it is not obvious that modernisation proceeded as quickly as in other European countries. Figure 12.14 shows the share of GNP devoted to investment in Britain and on the Continent.

The investment share was lower in Britain, except between 1931 and 1934, when investment on the Continent collapsed, on account of the severity of the depression in the gold bloc. Recent research linking the share of national income devoted to investment with the subsequent rate of economic growth suggests that the long-term implications of Britain's low investment rate may have been decidedly negative.

The relatively low level of gross domestic fixed capital formation in inter-war Britain reflects a low level of domestic saving rather than high levels of foreign investment. Net investment abroad was little more than 1 per cent of GNP in the second half of the 1920s; it was consistently negative after 1930 (Feinstein 1972: Table 47). The low level of saving is another peculiar feature of the economy's inter-war performance that does not seem to have been noticed, much less explained. It casts doubt on the notion that the inter-war period was one of regeneration for British industry.

Industrial reorganisation

Some have taken the view that the inter-war years may have comprised a period of regeneration not because new resources were put in place at an exceptional pace but because industries learned how to utilise existing resources more efficiently. Merger allowed British industry to exploit economies of scale. In many important sectors the average plant size was by the end of the 1930s even larger in Britain than in the United States (Rostas 1948a). The closing years of the First World War and the 1920s witnessed an unprecedented wave of amalgamations, the most spectacular example being the creation of ICI, the British chemicals giant, in 1926. Large enterprises appeared for the first time in a variety of industries, including motor vehicles, retailing and electrical engineering (Hannah 1983). The merger movement of the 1920s was reinforced by the rationalisation movement of the 1930s, which concentrated production in the largest, most efficient units. The shipbuilding industry established the National Shipbuilders' Security Ltd to buy up poorly equipped, outdated yards. The British Iron and Steel Federation worked hand in glove, or hand in pocket, with the state to scrap inefficient capacity, to merge complementary firms and to regulate the supply of raw materials. State control went furthest in coal mining, where the Coal Mines Act of 1930 empowered the government to compel amalgamations of competing firms. State involvement reflected the experience of the First World War, when intervention had coincided with considerable productivity growth. The reorganisation of the railways was explicitly designed to secure the efficiency gains that had been enjoyed during the period of wartime government control. Intervention by the Treasury and the Bank of England in the affairs of other sectors was similarly inspired by this experience and by the belief that the economic crisis of the 1930s was an emergency tantamount to war.

Finally, inter-war regeneration could have taken the form of structural change – that is, a shift of resources between sectors. As measured by Matthews, Feinstein and Odling-Smee (1982), whose scale is the dispersion of rates of growth of output across industries, structural change between 1924 and 1937 was twice as fast as it had been between 1900 and 1913. The most prominent aspect of structural change between the wars lies in the contrast between Britain's 'new' and 'old' industries. The decline of the old export staples ultimately stimulated efficiency by freeing resources for more productive uses (Richardson 1965). Output and employment grew much more quickly between 1920 and 1938 in such new industries as motor vehicles, non-ferrous metals, electrical engineering, chemicals, and paper and printing than in traditional export staples.

Yet not all of these developments need be seen in a favourable light. Curiously from the viewpoint of the regeneration hypothesis, labour productivity rose more quickly in several old industries (mechanical engineering, iron and steel, mining) than in several new ones (electrical engineering, chemicals, paper and printing; for details see Aldcroft 1970). Von Tunzelmann (1982) has shown that the new industries were less capital intensive, which may account for their relatively low and slowly growing rates of labour productivity. Structural change, while proceeding more quickly than it had been between 1900 and 1913, still lagged compared to its post-Second World War pace. Inter-war mergers in British industries such as food processing and textiles provided less scope for reaping scale economies than had pre-war mergers in American heavy industries such as iron and steel (Rostas 1948b). In iron and steel, although by 1930 the twenty largest firms controlled 70 per cent of British output, combined steel production was still only one third that of US Steel and about the same as the German Vereinigte Stahlwerke (Hannah 1983: 140). Broadberry (1983) shows that the inter-industry correlation between mergers and productivity growth was actually negative, not positive as the mergers-as-a-response-to-scale-economies hypothesis would predict. Merger, collusion, cartelisation and protection may have insulated British manufacturers from the chill winds of domestic and foreign competition, relieving pressures to cut costs and innovate. Broadberry and Crafts (1990a, 1990d) find that more concentrated British industries had larger productivity gaps vis-à-vis their American counterparts, and suggest that the same may have been true of industries protected by the tariff from foreign competition. Policy, they conclude, permitted the preservation of inefficient firms and practices. Workers and management increasingly turned their attention from building a better mousetrap for the market to obtaining government protection from domestic and foreign competitors.

These are precisely the problems, it is widely believed, that plagued the British economy after the Second World War. If so, it was the public and private sector response to the economic difficulties of the inter-war period that put them in place. Policies for growth in the short run may have had costs in the long run.

Statistical appendix

The data underlying Figures 12.2 and 12.4 come from Maddison (1982). The one exception is GDP figures for Britain; these are Feinstein's revised estimates as reported in Mitchell (1988). Most other data were drawn from League of Nations publications which collected figures published by national statistical offices. All industrial production indices used in this chapter, for example, were taken from the League of Nations' *Monthly Statistical Bulletin* and *Statistical Year-Book*. Data on the volume of merchandise imports and exports were taken from the League's *International Trade and Balance of Payments* and *Memoranda on Balance of Payments and Foreign Trade Balances*. The publications list the value as well as the volume of imports and exports; the ratio of value to volume was the implicit price deflator used to compute the international terms of trade. Wholesale price indices came from the League's *Statistical Year-Book*, while central bank discount rates came from the *Year-Book* and the *Monthly Statistical Bulletin*.

Statistics on the money supply (currency plus demand deposits) were drawn from the League of Nations' *Memorandum on Currency and Banking*. Alternative estimates for Britain constructed subsequently differ primarily in terms of more comprehensive coverage of clearing banks and their deposits (see Capie and Webber 1985).

Contemporary unemployment statistics and estimates of the real producer wage are from Eichengreen and Hatton (1988b).

Estimates of gross national product and its components were not constructed contemporaneously but have been imputed subsequently. The estimates used in this chapter of GNP and of the investment share are drawn from Mitchell (1976), except for French GNP, which is from Clark (1961), and the investment share of GNP for France and Britain, which is from Carré, Dubois and Malinvaud (1976) and Feinstein (1972), respectively.

Since many national statistical offices were only set up in this period, there are significant gaps in the material available to historians. The strategy followed in constructing the figures here was to include only countries for which continuous series could be constructed. The main omissions are Germany and Austria in the early 1920s, for which estimates of economic activity and its components are difficult to reconstruct in the period of hyper-inflation. In many cases two graphs were drawn, one starting in 1921 but omitting Germany and Austria, another starting in 1925 and including them. I have used the first such figure where the early 1920s features prominently in the discussion, the second where the experience of Germany and Austria seems particularly relevant.

The following table denotes with an asterisk countries that are included in each figure.

Appendix table 1.

	Figure number											
	2	4	5	6	7	8	9	10	11	12	13	14
France	*	*	*	*	*	*	*	*	*	*	*	*
Germany	*	*	*	*	*	*	*	*	*	*	*	
Italy	*	*	*	*		*		*	*	*	*	*
Denmark	*	*	*	*	*	*	*	*	*	*	*	*
Norway	*	*	*	*	*	*	*	*	*	*	*	*
Finland	*	*	*	*	*	*				*	*	*
Sweden	*	*	*	*	*	*	*	*	*	*	*	*
Switzerland	*	*	*		*		*		*	*		
Austria	*	*		*		*			*	*	*	
Netherlands	*	*	*	*	*	*	*	*	*	*	*	*
Belgium	*	*	*	*	*	*	*	*	*	*		

13 The macro-economics of the inter-war years

Mark Thomas

Introduction

Macro-economics analyses the economy-wide behaviour of such aggregates as output, employment and prices. Its central tenet is that there are definable and predictable relations between the aggregates – the culmination of a systematic, identifiable process of actions and interactions by micro-economic agents. Its historical interest aside, knowledge of the macro-economics of the inter-war period is vital to an understanding of the origins of today's debates over theory and policy. Before the 1930s, macro-economics as a process of thought was neither fully developed nor well articulated. The ideas and techniques of Keynes, his disciples and opponents shaped the evolution of the subject and continue to frame much of today's policy debates. The current dispute between new Keynesian and new classical economics (Gordon 1990) parallels and in many ways resembles the original debate between 'Mr. Keynes and the Classics' (Hicks 1937).

The longevity of Keynes' ideas is testimony to their intellectual pedigree and to the seriousness with which societies have treated the problems he addressed – the peculiar conditions of inter-war Britain. Indeed, only with the emergence of a new set of problems after 1973 has a fundamental rethinking about the macro-economy emerged. This new thinking has had wide influence, but there remains considerable controversy among economists about the ultimate direction of macro-economic theory. Inevitably, the unease is reflected in the interpretation of inter-war Britain. There remain many areas of continued debate, and it is not yet possible to provide definitive answers to all the questions raised by the inter-war experience.

Growth and fluctuations

The national income, usually measured as real gross domestic product (GDP), is the aggregate used most frequently to summarise an economy's

Figure 13.1 Economic growth, 1900–50

collective performance. The pattern of British national income over the first half of the twentieth century is shown in Figure 13.1.

A clear break in this series is apparent after the end of the First World War. Indeed, it was not until 1934 that Britain again reached the level of national output attained in 1918. The failure to bounce back in the 1920s was deeply disturbing to contemporaries, doubly so since British economic performance languished behind other industrial countries. In retrospect, Britain's output record looks poor indeed. In a league table of nine industrial nations, Britain ranked seventh in output growth between 1913 and 1950 (Feinstein 1988a). In productivity terms, Britain's relative performance does look stronger (third out of six). But this improvement in ranking is a statistical mirage, created by a low rate of investment. Britain's capital stock rose at a very feeble level between 1913 and 1950. Moreover, the failure to maintain aggressive investment in new equipment and techniques between the wars further weakened the economy, by lowering long-run growth potential.

The image of the inter-war years as a wasted generation for the British people does not come, however, from consideration of productivity growth rates. It is hard to invest numbers on real GDP per capita with much powerful emotional imagery. The abiding folk-memory recalls mass unemployment, dole queues, hunger marches. Unemployment was perceived by contemporaries as the dominant social problem of their time, the greatest threat to the stability of the state as well as to the welfare of

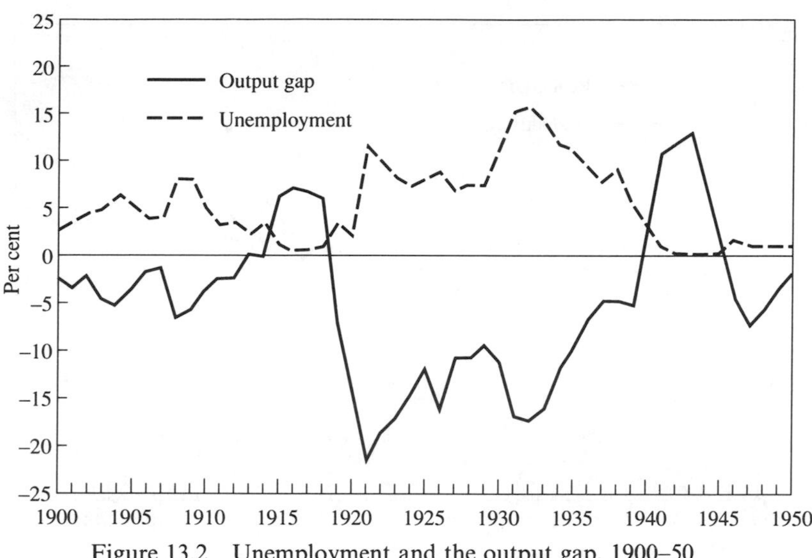

Figure 13.2 Unemployment and the output gap, 1900–50

families and communities. It was both a symbol and an indictment of Britain's inability to adjust to the demands of the post-war world, 'in which the old certainties had slipped away'.

The pattern of unemployment is shown in Figure 13.2. Taking these figures at face value for a moment, it seems clear that the inter-war years were marked by a very high level of joblessness. The average unemployment rate between 1919 and 1938 was 9.3 per cent, compared to 1.4 per cent for the twenty years after 1945, and 4.0 per cent for the twenty years before 1914. These figures are not precisely comparable, especially before and after 1913. The spread of unemployment insurance coverage from a small group of cyclically sensitive unions to almost all workers changed the structure of recorded unemployment, and indeed its very meaning. But, even if there can be no surety in statistical comparisons across the war, most historians accept the unemployment of the twenties as radically different from the experience of the late Victorian and Edwardian years. And looking back from the 1960s (if not from the 1990s), the contrast of the inter-war years is all the more striking.

Unemployment was highly volatile within the inter-war period. The jobless rate was at a peacetime low of 2 per cent in 1920, before a sudden slump sent it to an historic high of 11.3 per cent the following year. Thereafter, the rate stabilised at around 8 per cent for the rest of the 1920s, with small fluctuations around this level. In 1930–1 it climbed rapidly, reaching 15.6 per cent in 1932, before falling gradually back to the 8 per cent mark in 1937. A secondary recession hit the economy in 1937–8, causing unemployment to rise briefly, before the demands of wartime brought it below 5 per cent for the first time in twenty years.

Unemployment represents a valuable index of the failure of an economy to utilise fully its resources. But resources include more than just labour, so many economists prefer a more general measure, based on the output rather than the input side of the production equation. Figure 13.2 provides a simple version of this approach, by plotting the deviations in actual output from its long-run trend (as measured by fitting a logarithmic growth path between 1913 and 1951, two major peak years). The pattern of this 'output gap' is instructive. The total volume of lost output between 1919 and 1938 (as measured by the area between the curve of actual output and the trend line) was almost £300 million, or 12.5 per cent of actual GDP – a level close to the average unemployment rate for the same period. The profile of the output gap broadly parallels the behaviour of the unemployment rate, suggesting that the traditional concerns about the comparability of unemployment statistics across time should not be overplayed. Thus the output gap confirms the two wars as periods of above-average performance (especially the Second World War, with its commitment to the ideal of total warfare), while the periods of depression and recovery are clearly delineated.

But the output gap measure also diverges from the unemployment rate in important ways. Most notably, the depression of 1919–21 is shown to be strikingly sharper than that of 1929–32: output fell to a lower level relative to potential (21 per cent vs 17 per cent), and it fell from a greater height – the British economy in 1929 was already operating well below capacity, while that of 1918–19 was above trend. On an output basis, indeed, the depression of 1931–2 looks no worse than 1926, and considerably less disastrous than 1920–1. The Great Slump is revealed as more of a crisis in employment than in production.

The significance of this divergence is captured in Figure 13.3, which maps out the relationship between unemployment and the output gap (the Okun relation) over the inter-war period. There is a clear and radical shift in the nature of that relationship in the late twenties, with higher unemployment at all levels of output loss. Similar discontinuities show up in other macro-economic variables and relationships at about the same time – in the growth rate of employment and the behaviour of wages (ch. 14 below); in an apparent (albeit minor) shift in the consumption function (Figure 13.6a); in total factor productivity (Figure 13.1); and most evidently in the relationship between inflation and unemployment (the Phillips curve, Figure 13.5c). An important and unresolved issue is why the 1920s look so very different from the 1930s.

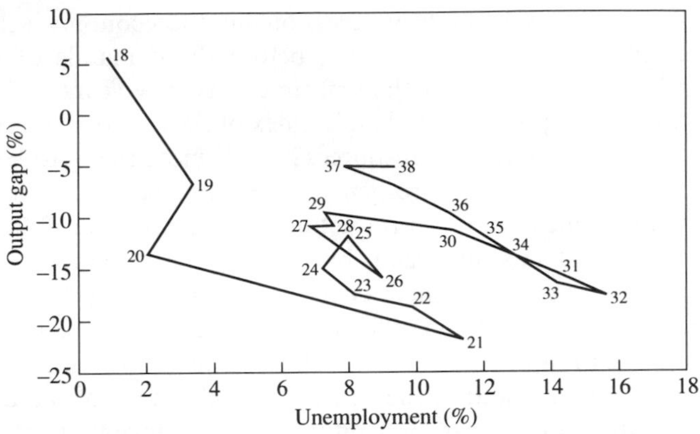

Figure 13.3 Unemployment and the output gap, 1918–38

Aggregate supply–aggregate demand

It is useful to start with a skeletal model to represent changing conditions. The model used is a simple aggregate supply–aggregate demand representation of the domestic economy, adapted to reflect the openness of Britain's economy to international influences. The basic framework is displayed in Figure 13.4. Income (and the deviation from potential output) is marked on the horizontal axis; the vertical axis marks both the price level and the rate of price change (inflation). The dual representation reflects the economist's interest in the monetary as well as the real side of the economy.

The aggregate supply curve is derived from the behaviour of the labour market. The supply and demand for labour determine the real wage and the level of employment (see ch. 14). Employment in turn is the primary determinant of output. In the long run the level of output is independent of the price level – the economy will tend to gravitate towards full employment and output ('the natural rate'), regardless of the level of prices or their rate of change.

The long-run supply curve is vertical. In the short run, however, there are good reasons to believe that output will diverge from its natural rate. In the Keynesian model, this may happen because of frictions and rigidities in the responsiveness of wages to unemployment, or because sticky producer prices inhibit instantaneous market clearing of goods or labour. In the new classical model it may be because information is slow to spread or slow to be assimilated by rational economic agents, leading to inappropriate market behaviour as conditions change, or because of the 'shock of the new', when buyers and sellers do not know how to respond to new circumstances and consequently make mistakes (for an illustration of how awry price expectations were in the United States after 1929, see

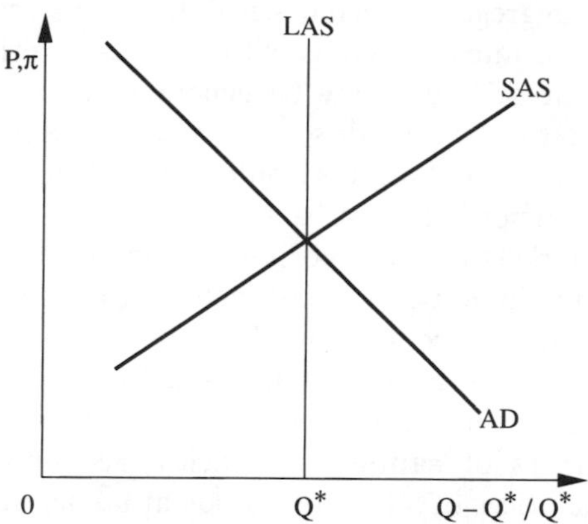

Figure 13.4 A simple model of aggregate supply and aggregate demand

Hamilton 1992). In these situations, the short-run supply curve will be positively rather than vertically sloped.

One complication in the derivation of aggregate supply is the dichotomy between producer and consumer prices. In an open economy the workers buy both domestic and foreign goods; their real wage is thus contingent on price behaviour at home and abroad. These will diverge more the more important non-traded goods and services (such as houses and haircuts) are to British consumers, and the more suspicious are consumers about foreign products (making the products less than perfect substitutes for British-made). The real wage faced by firms, however, is determined only by the price of domestic output. The labour market has thus to accommodate two real wages. Changes in the terms of trade will generate different responses from workers and from employers, causing the aggregate supply curve to change location, and altering the natural level of output and employment.

The aggregate demand curve (AD) represents the reaction of business and consumer spending to changes in the price level. Its negative slope is derived from two propositions: higher prices are associated with higher interest rates (for any given level of the money supply); and higher interest rates suppress spending (since businesses are likely to postpone or abandon investment plans and projects when the opportunity costs of finance rise). More formally, the aggregate demand schedule traces out the levels of price and output at which both the money (asset) and goods markets are in equilibrium. Money market equilibrium is achieved when money supply and money demand are equalised by the interest rate (at any given level of income); the goods market is in equilibrium at the income level and interest rate at which planned expenditures exactly consume aggregate income.

Any movement along the aggregate demand schedule is thus associated with a change in the interest rate, as well as with changes in prices and incomes. Movements of the schedule may be generated by exogenous changes in either the monetary or the goods sector – such as changes in the supply of money, in consumer or business confidence, or in either the government budget or the current account balance.

In an open economy markets are defined internationally rather than domestically. Consequently, domestic prices of factors, goods and assets are contingent on global market conditions. The observation has two significant implications for macro-economic analysis. First, foreign and domestic prices are linked through a system of exchange rates, which determines the relative prices of national currencies. Secondly, world markets will determine the prices of all traded goods at home, unless the domestic economy is large enough to exert influence on global supply or demand.

Exchange rates may be fixed, flexible or managed. All three types of currency regime operated in inter-war Britain. Sterling floated freely against other currencies between 1919 and April 1925; the gold standard, during which the foreign exchange value of the pound was fixed, lasted from April 1925 to September 1931; sterling again floated from September 1931 onwards, mediated after April 1932 by the Exchange Equalisation Account, set up to keep the pound from fluctuating too wildly against other currencies. It is vital to distinguish between these periods when evaluating macro-economic conditions and policies.

Under a free float the exchange rate cushions the domestic economy from real shocks (such as a sudden drop in exports) by adjusting to keep the current account in balance. The mechanism also robs the government of the power to use fiscal policy to stabilise aggregate demand (since higher deficits will be counterbalanced by falling net exports due to exchange appreciation). The central authorities can, however, pursue independent monetary policy, with exchange rate adjustments keeping the currency markets in equilibrium and international capital flows in check. If the government is disturbed by the direction or extent of any exchange rate adjustment it may, of course, intervene by buying or selling currency (a managed float). But such manoeuvres directly alter the home country's monetary base and its money supply. The trade-off between currency management and monetary control is complete with fully fixed exchange rates, which require the central bank to abandon control of the domestic money supply entirely. The transition from flexible to fixed currency markets, in other words, completely alters the macro-economic rules. The causal direction from the money supply to the exchange rate is reversed. Monetary policy becomes impotent, while the economy's immunity to real shocks is removed, and fiscal policy becomes a viable option for the government.

Regardless of the exchange rate system, however, the potential for domestic monetary policy will be restricted in the long run by the global nature of the capital market. The interest parity condition states that, for any small open economy with free capital mobility, as long as economic agents are well informed and rational, domestic monetary authorities will be powerless to set the domestic interest rate at a level other than the prevailing world rate. If they try, capital flows will push the domestic rate back into line. Policy makers are therefore limited to the choice between exchange rate and money supply management. They cannot mandate either dear or cheap money. Only the world money market can do that.

Interest rate parity is an important, if controversial, proposition. If it holds absolutely it compromises several influential interpretations of Britain's inter-war history, notably the Treasury's fostering of economic recovery in the 1930s through a policy of cheap money. It is also symbolic of a larger question. Was Britain a small open economy in the inter-war period, buffeted by international forces, helpless to protect itself? Given the dominance of the United States in the standard macro-economic histories of the industrial (and semi-industrial) world in the inter-war years (summed up in the contemporary phrase, 'America sneezes and Europe catches cold'), it is tempting to see Britain as a prisoner of external circumstance. Yet many historians would resist the argument, preferring to stress the internal origins of many of the difficulties of the 'wasted years', and suggesting that domestic economic policies and institutional reforms could have done much to alleviate the suffering. It was a large debate at the time, and still generates considerable controversy.

The aggregate supply–aggregate demand framework is especially useful in diagnosing the problems of inter-war Britain. Figure 13.5 sets out the equilibrium positions of two measures of price (the GDP deflator and the inflation rate) and two measures of output (the output gap and the unemployment rate). The pictures trace the evolution of price–output combinations for successive years between 1918 and 1938. They produce a largely consistent version of events, although (for reasons discussed above) there are some divergences.

What appears to have happened is as follows. The economy in 1918 was operating in high gear, at full capacity or perhaps even a little above it. The output gap was above trend, and the unemployment level stood at 2 per cent. The economy was subjected to a considerable shock in 1919–20, and it was 1922–3 before the economy had settled back down. The chronology of 1919–23 involved adverse shocks on both supply and demand, causing output to fall, and causing prices to move first up and

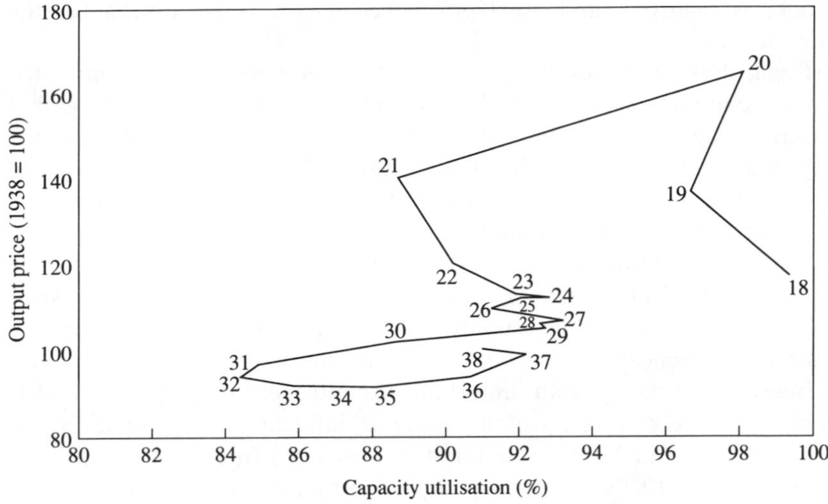

Figure 13.5a Prices and unemployment, 1918–38

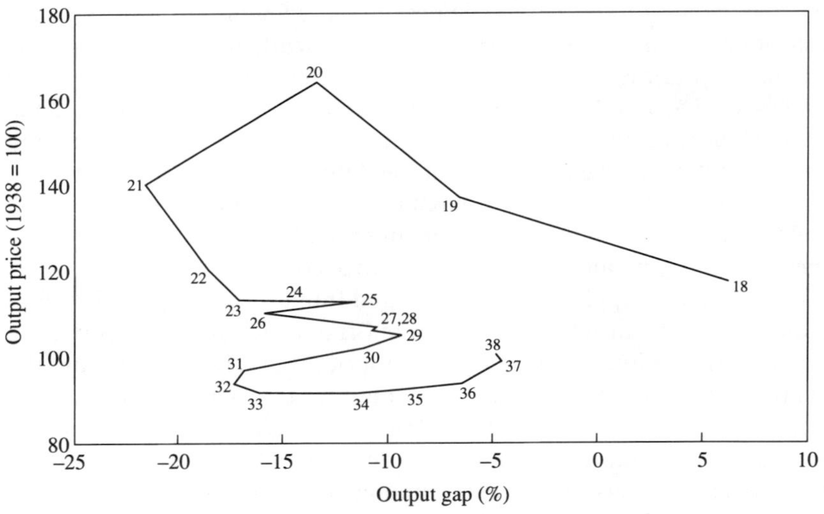

Figure 13.5b The price level and the output gap, 1918–38

then down. The economy then stabilised at a level of unemployment around 8 per cent, and an output gap of about 10 per cent. These values have been interpreted as the natural levels for the 1920s (Broadberry 1986a). There was only limited movement around the equilibrium up to 1929; prices continued to fall, but there was little change in the revealed behaviour of producers or workers. Then in 1929–30 the economy seems to

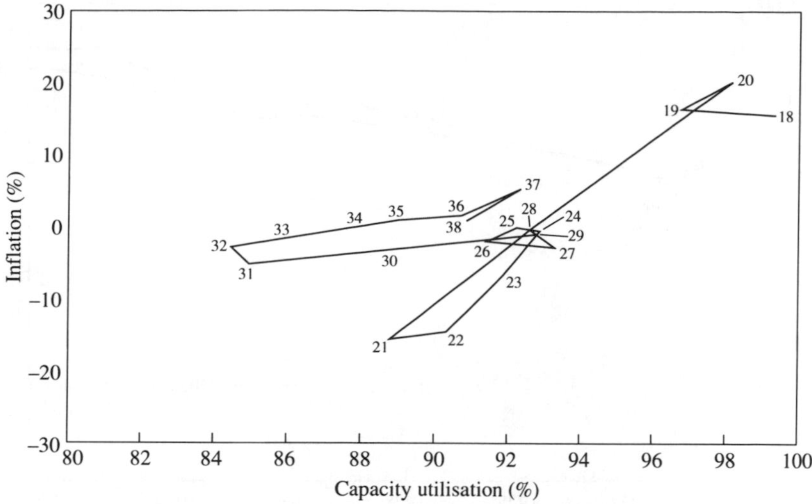

Figure 13.5c Inflation and unemployment, 1918–38

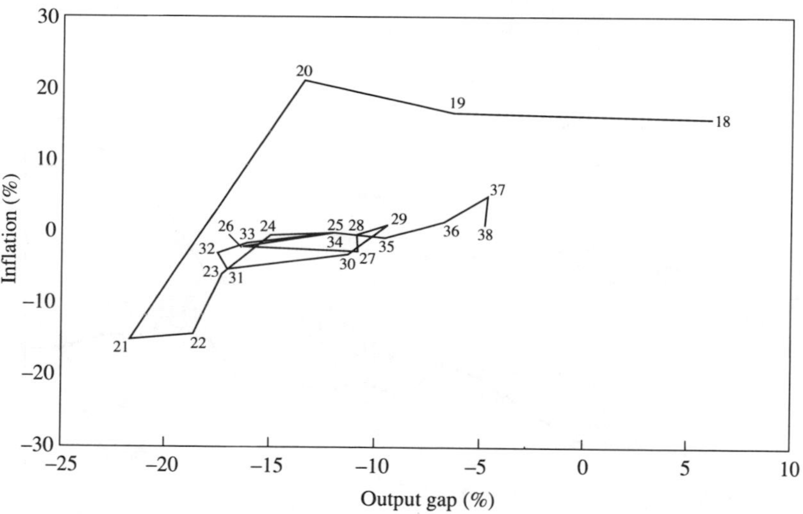

Figure 13.5d Inflation and the output gap, 1918–38

have been struck by a significant shock to aggregate demand, causing prices and output to fall dramatically. The paths of the price–output combinations between 1929 and 1932 are consistent with the economy tracing its way down a (relatively elastic) aggregate supply curve, or with simultaneous shifts in both aggregate supply and aggregate demand, with the latter dominating. And the period of recovery – in which output rose

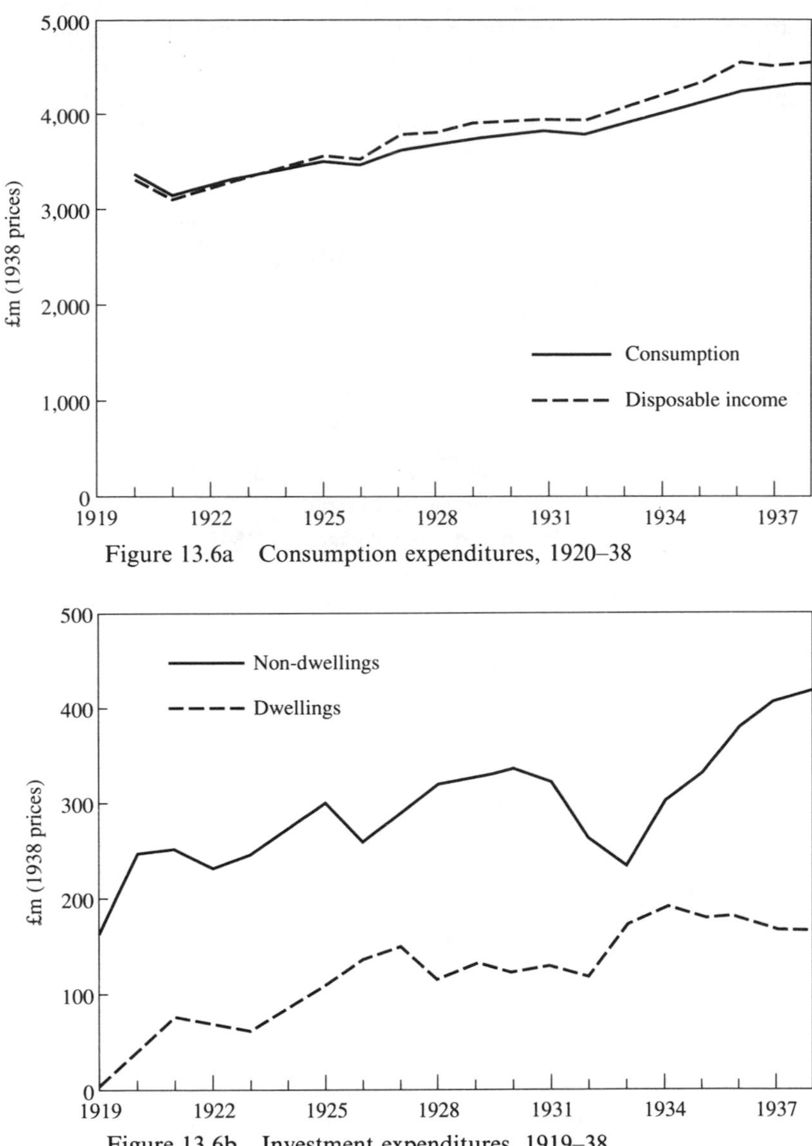

Figure 13.6a Consumption expenditures, 1920–38

Figure 13.6b Investment expenditures, 1919–38

with stable or only slowly rising prices – suggests an inversion of this process, with aggregate demand factors in the ascendancy but with possible reinforcement from the supply side. The macro-economic story of the inter-war period involves both demand and supply factors, operating in different proportions at different times.

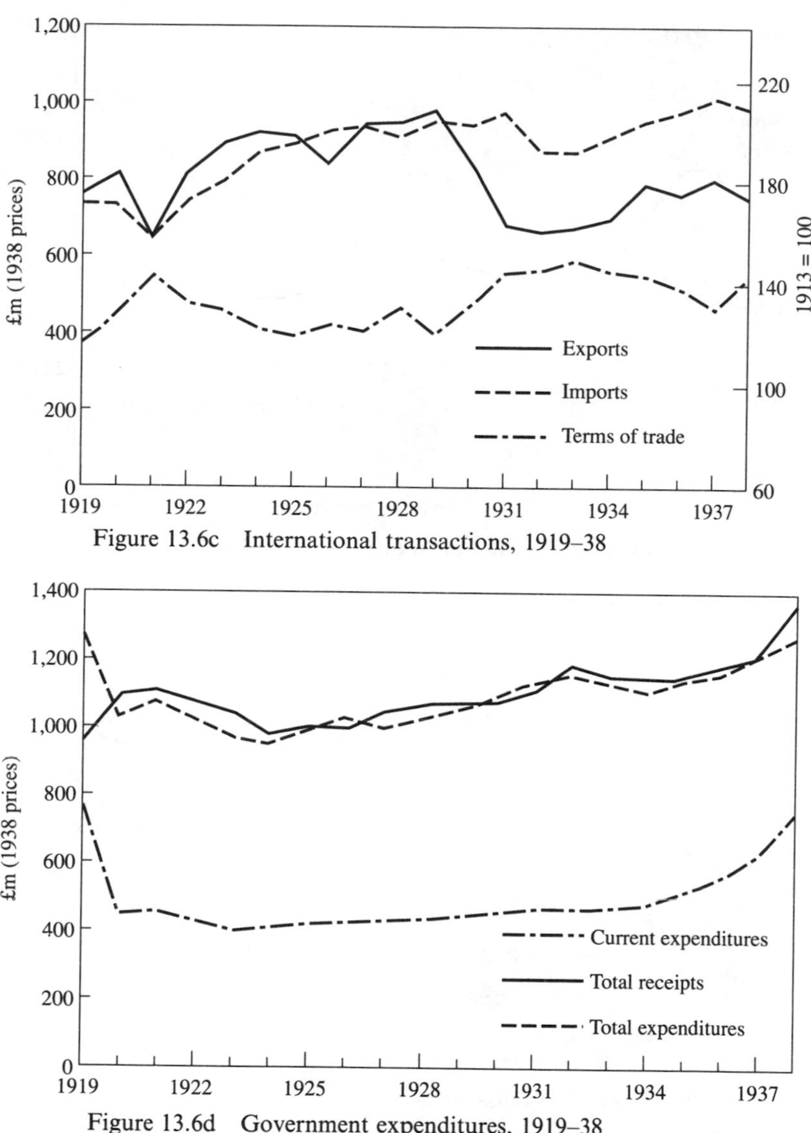

Figure 13.6c International transactions, 1919–38

Figure 13.6d Government expenditures, 1919–38

Before passing to a more thorough analysis of events, it is helpful to examine time-series graphs of the major elements of aggregate demand and supply. Figure 13.6 depicts the components of the expenditure identity of the national income accounts: consumption, investment (distinguishing housing from non-residential capital, but ignoring stock behaviour), government expenditures and the balance of the international accounts

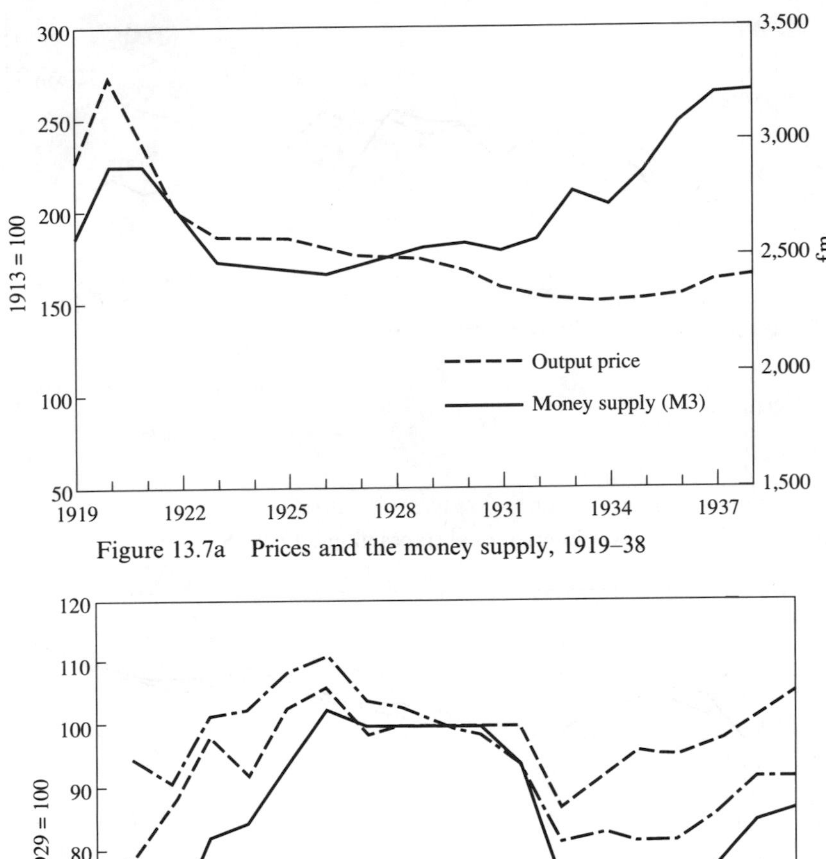

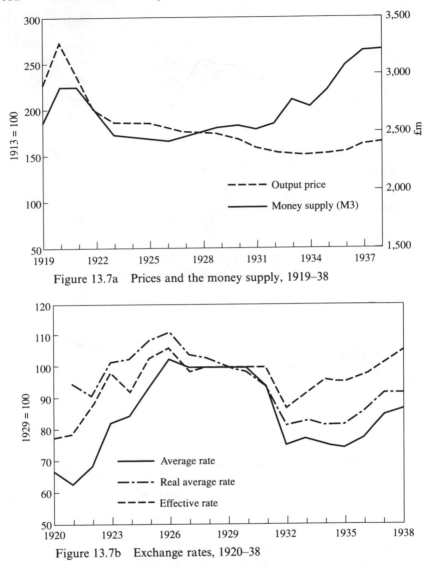

Figure 13.7a Prices and the money supply, 1919–38

Figure 13.7b Exchange rates, 1920–38

(exports less imports). Figure 13.7 gives the key monetary data for the inter-war period: the output price level, the stock of money (M3), nominal interest rates (short and long term), the exchange rate (real effective and real average rates). Finally, Figure 13.8 provides evidence on the behaviour of the major elements in the aggregate supply curve: nominal wages (weekly rates and weekly earnings), real wages (weekly and hourly rates), labour productivity (per worker and per hour) and unit labour costs

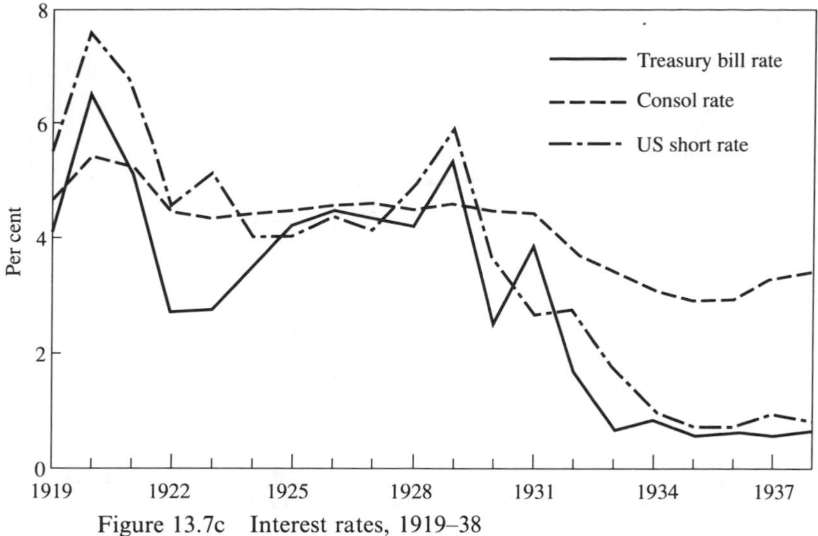

Figure 13.7c Interest rates, 1919–38

(nominal wages divided by real output per worker). With this information in view, it is time to turn to the chronology of events.

1919–21

Britain emerged from the First World War a much weakened force in the international economy. The country had been forced to sell off many of its assets to finance the war effort; resources had been redirected from civilian to military use, and much had been destroyed; the structures of international trade and finance had been irredeemably changed, to Britain's economic and political disadvantage. The economic future had been mortgaged to guarantee military victory.

Long-term problems cast a shadow over the entire inter-war period. But in 1919 the economy was faced with a more immediate concern – the transition from total war. The first months after the Armistice were marked by considerable instability, in prices, profits and production. The build-up of consumer demand during three years of intensifying scarcity of luxuries was unleashed by the end of rationing and the relaxation of price controls. The demand pressures were validated by a government eager to provide a welcome mat of jobs and consumer goods to returning servicemen. Extending the easy credit conditions of the war helped the money supply to surge – M3 rose by 37 per cent between 1918 and 1920. Consumption expenditures (in nominal prices) increased by 46 per cent over the same period. Additional bursts of demand from overseas (nominal exports more than doubled between 1918 and 1920), and from firms eager

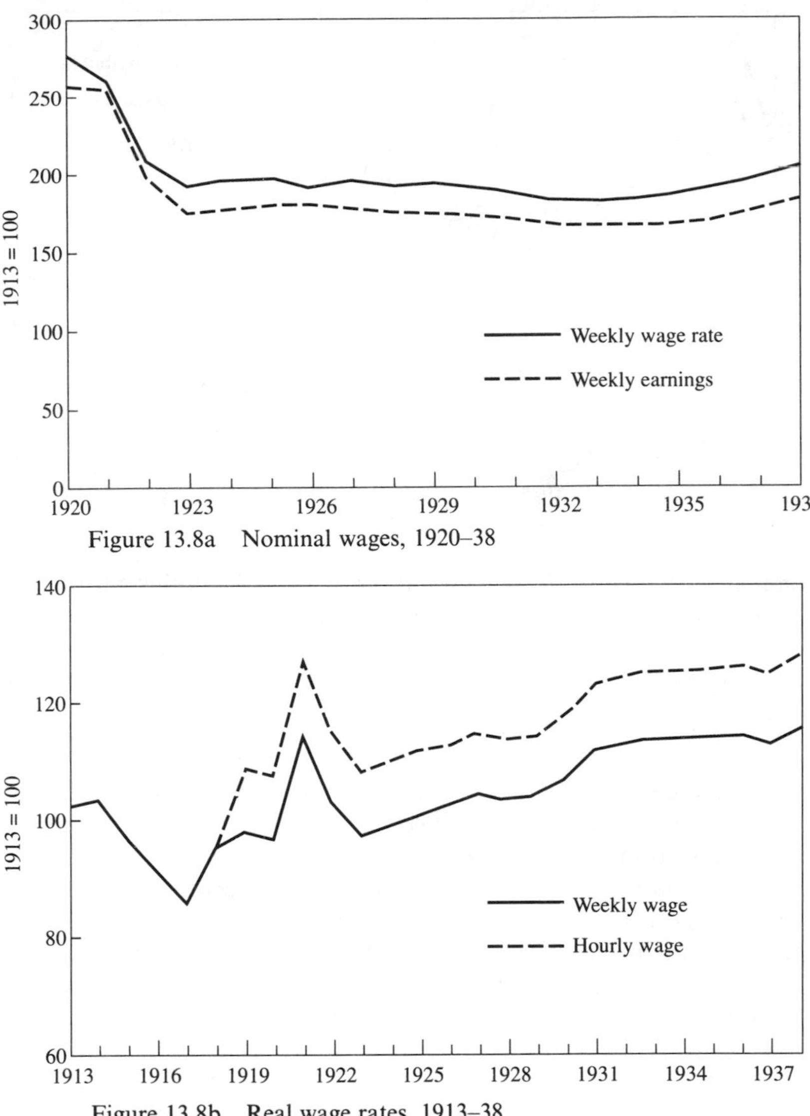

Figure 13.8a Nominal wages, 1920–38

Figure 13.8b Real wage rates, 1913–38

to spend their wartime profits on new plant and machinery, stirred the pot more. The expansion of aggregate demand (marked by the shift from AD_{1918} to AD_{1920} in Figure 13.9) was not, however, met by increased supply. Indeed, quite the reverse. Total output fell between 1918 and 1920 – military orders collapsed, and firms were unable to retool quickly enough to meet the demands of the civilian sector (not least because average

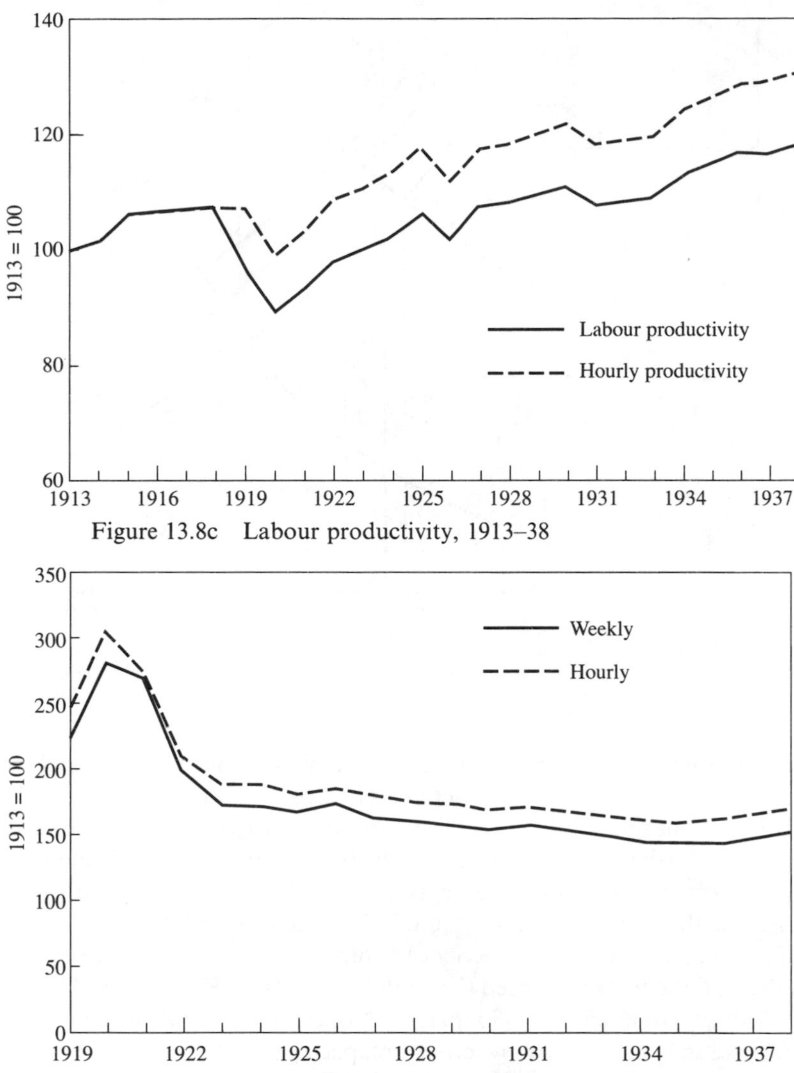

Figure 13.8c Labour productivity, 1913–38

Figure 13.8d Unit labour costs, 1919–38

working hours fell by 10 per cent in the first half of 1919). Aggregate supply contracted (from SAS_{1918} to SAS_{1920} in Figure 13.9); output fell and prices rose. Consumers did make some gains. Real consumption rose by 15 per cent in 1918–20, although real national income fell by almost 23 per cent. Prices, meanwhile, jumped 42 per cent. The years 1919–20 saw a boom of prices, not production.

The nature of the boom had serious consequences for the macro-

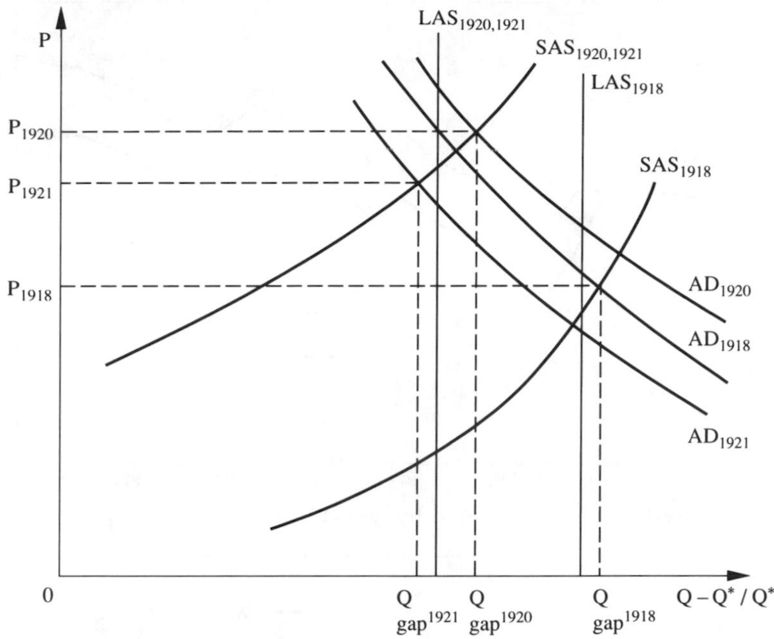

Figure 13.9 A model of aggregate supply and aggregate demand, 1918–21

economy. For some sectors, it represented a missed opportunity, in which accumulated wartime profits were dissipated in an orgy of unwise investments that added little to the economy's growth potential. Speculation was particularly rife in the staple trades: in the cotton sector, in which 80 per cent of production capacity was bought and sold at prices eight times the value of paid-up capital (Balfour Committee 1928: 22); in shipbuilding, in which 'the experienced shipowner sold, the ignorant man bought, and the banks financed the deals' (Macrosty 1927: 71), and where asset values plummeted by 75 per cent once inflationary expectations faded; and in iron and steel, where overcapacity stood at over 30 per cent even in the best years of the 1920s. The fallibility of post-war entrepreneurs should not be exaggerated with hindsight. Textiles and shipbuilding did enjoy a boom in profits and production in 1919–20, and high confidence in Britain's economic future was shared by as sober an authority as *The Economist*. Nonetheless, it is true that investors tended to look to Britain's past for inspiration, and it is also true that expectations were considerably overinflated.

The bubble burst in the early summer of 1920. In the spring, the government initiated monetary contraction to break the hold of price inflation. Wholesale prices peaked in May, and business activity in August (Capie and Collins 1983). Monetary policy triggered the downturn, but did not decree it. A slump was inevitable, given the unreal, speculative and brittle nature of the boom. Certain key sectors (notably textiles, shipbuilding and engineering) were vulnerable to any slowdown in the growth of demand, in view of excessive investment in new (and old) capital in the first flush of the post-war boom, when British firms hoped to dominate world markets *sans* German competition. And there is evidence that business expectations were slipping well before the government's new policy: share prices peaked in January, raw material imports fell from February and new capital issues of the London stock market were at their highest in March. A slowdown in production and profits was apparently anticipated.

The collapse of the post-war boom was felt especially in the export trades, and in the pre-war staples in particular. Export volumes fell by 30 per cent between 1920 and 1921 (Figure 13.6c – and note that exporters in 1921 were already able to sell only 70 per cent of their pre-war volume); what may have been even more injurious to exporters was the price collapse they faced (close to 45 per cent 1920–2), which sent many to bankruptcy. The fall in exports was one part of a serious adverse demand shock to the economy. Households, having satiated much of their pent-up demand, slowed down purchases. Government expenditures were cut by 75 per cent between 1918 and 1920 – largely through the demobilisation of over 3.5 million servicemen in the first eighteen months after Armistice. The decline of public spending may have spelled a long-run gain for the economy, given the return to a more efficient allocation of resources for growth and welfare, but in the short run it undoubtedly presented an added burden of adjustment.

The problem of post-war adjustment was global. The difficulties of transition, however, were intensified at home by a significant supply side shock. As part of the post-war social contract, labour leaders and employers negotiated a substantial reduction in the average working week, from fifty-four to forty-seven hours (Dowie 1975). But there was no compensating reduction in the nominal weekly wage. Indeed, the agreement was being made at a time when nominal wage increases were outstripping producer price inflation. The combined effect of these factors is shown in the rapid leap in the real hourly wage rate in 1919 (Figure 13.8b). Nor was there a sizeable enough increase in average labour productivity to counterbalance higher wages (Figure 13.8c): unit labour costs (hourly basis) increased by 10 per cent between 1919 and 1921 (Figure 13.8d). Employers responded by laying off workers, who had suddenly become much more expensive. Unsurprisingly, the slump of 1921 was particularly felt on the dole queues: prices dropped by 10 per cent in 1920–1, real national income by 5 per cent, while unemployment climbed to 20 per cent.

Indeed, Broadberry (1990) considers the uncompensated drop in hours to have been the most important single determinant of the high unemployment rates of the 1920s. It acted as an adverse supply shock of sustained significance, establishing a new natural rate of 8 per cent (indicated by the shift from LAS_{1918} to LAS_{1920} in Figure 13.9), which stuck throughout the rest of the inter-war years. The real wage data of Figure 13.8b certainly support the hypothesis. While the average weekly real wage fell back to 1919 levels by 1923, the higher hourly wage was maintained. Hours rose in 1926, but only by about 1 per cent. Improvements in labour productivity after 1920 did allow employers to retrieve some of the damage done by the hours reduction. As Figure 13.8d shows, unit labour costs fell continuously from 1921 to 1936. It was equivalent to a series of rightward shifts in the aggregate supply curve, which should have (*ceteris paribus*) increased employment and output. But the gains were too small and too late to reverse the effects of the deal on hours.

1921–9

The twenties were marked by a gradual recovery from the slump of 1920–1, at least until the General Strike of 1926. Insured unemployment fell from its peak of 23 per cent in May 1921 to below 10 per cent by the spring of 1924. It then refused to fall any further, leaving an 'intractable million' on the register (Pigou 1948). The output gap continued to narrow, but further recovery was feeble. The doldrums lasted until 1929.

The standard macro-economic chronology of the 1920s identifies a structural break in 1925, marking the shift from flexible to fixed exchange rates. The approach is a trifle simplistic. The formal reinstatement of the pre-war system may not have been achieved until 1925, but it was a consistent objective of government policy from the moment the Cunliffe Committee reported in December 1919. In Youngson's words, 'the gold standard dictated policy through the 1920s as effectively from the grave as from the throne' (1960: 230).

Ironically, it was the decision to abandon the gold standard in March 1919 that gave the government the instrument – monetary deflation – to plot its resurrection at the pre-war parity of $4.8665. The government's intentions were signalled in April 1920 with a restrictive budget and an increase in Bank Rate to 7 per cent. A policy of deliberate deflation would force British prices down to American levels, and put upward pressure on the sterling–dollar rate. Dear money was therefore maintained throughout the slump of 1920–1, and was only relaxed once inflation appeared to be under control and sterling had appreciated considerably against the dollar. The Bank of England maintained its allegiance to exchange rate targets throughout the 1920s, altering discount rates with a weather eye on sterling balances and the New York money market. Bank Rate was maintained a little above the New York discount rate (with the cooperation of the Federal Reserve Bank of New York), to make sterling more attractive in foreign exchange portfolios. Money was kept as tight as necessary to keep faith with the objective of getting back on to gold and staying there.

But dearer money had its costs and its critics, even within government. High interest costs discourage private investment, and make government borrowing more expensive. The Treasury, conscious of these effects, opposed every move to raise Bank Rate after 1922, despite a shared commitment to the gold standard (Howson 1975). Instead it attempted to ease credit conditions at home by reducing the government's competition for scarce loanable funds. This was at the root of the fiscal austerity that the Treasury maintained throughout the 1920s, most famously by wielding the 'Geddes axe' against government salaries and inessential government expenditures, and by abandoning agricultural price supports. Orthodox economic theory already demanded a commitment to balanced budgets; budget surpluses could be used to retire war-inflated national debt, thereby encouraging employment and growth by freeing funds for private investment. And debt charges could be reduced by converting expensive short-term loans (drawn at the inflationary interest rates of 1915–18) into long-term debt at lower market rates.

Gradually the Bank's policy had the desired effect. The demand for sterling began to recover, and its value appreciated. By the spring of 1922 the pound–dollar rate had recovered from its low point of $3.20 (February 1920) to 91 per cent of 1913 par. Sterling also appreciated significantly against other currencies, Dimsdale's (1981b) weighted average of nine major industrial exchange rates rising by 30 per cent in 1921–3 (see Figure 13.7b). A sustained drop in domestic costs, after American prices stabilised in early 1921, was crucial to the recovery of sterling's value in 1921–2 (although speculation over an imminent return to gold played a role in late 1922). After 1923, interest rate movements and currency speculation largely determined the dollar rate (Morgan 1952; Hodgson 1972; Dimsdale 1981b). The pound fell against the dollar in 1923, but strengthened after June 1924 in anticipation of the return (especially with the October election of a Conservative government committed to gold). In April 1925, two months after the Chamberlain–Bradbury Committee advised that only a small adjustment in relative costs was necessary to ensure a successful return, the Chancellor, Winston Churchill, formally announced that the

Bank of England would sell gold for export without restriction at the 1913 price. The Gold Standard Act was passed a week later.

The Norman conquest of $4.8665

The return to gold was castigated by Keynes as 'a dangerous and unnecessary decision' (1931: 245). He believed that the pound was overvalued at $4.8665, and that the climb in the value of sterling after July 1924 from its true equilibrium level ($4.40) had caused significant loss of competitiveness and jobs in the export sector, halting recovery from the slump of 1921. Moreover, the squeeze on prices that would follow from the return to gold would raise real wages, create unemployment and cause industrial unrest.

Was Keynes right? Certainly the pound appreciated sharply against the dollar in 1924–5 – from $4.32 to $4.85 in ten months – and at a similar rate against other currencies (Dimsdale 1981b; Andrews 1980, as quoted in Broadberry 1986b). And exporters did suffer. After experiencing 12 per cent annual growth since 1921, overseas sales stopped dead in 1924–5. Sterling appreciation did create a significant burden for British firms competing at home and abroad against foreign producers. But the trauma should not be exaggerated. For example, Moggridge's (1972) estimate of 750,000 lost jobs is almost certainly too high, being based on a nominal appreciation of 11 per cent. It is the real exchange rate (the nominal rate corrected for relative price movements) that matters for the real economy. When constructed properly (using GNP deflators or retail prices to measure comparative costs), the real rate shows a much smaller appreciation (about 1–2 per cent in a UK–US comparison, 4–7 per cent against all currencies), implying less of a demand shock. The domestic political reaction to the threat of renewed deflation, notably in the form of the General Strike of 1926, was more devastating to economic performance than the appreciation of sterling, causing unemployment to climb above 14 per cent. But the shock was temporary; by mid-1927 unemployment fell below 9 per cent for the first time since the onset of the slump in 1921.

Investigation of the real exchange rate nonetheless indicates that producers were penalised by an overvalued currency in 1925. Anglo-American comparisons, appropriately made, bear out Keynes' assertion that sterling was too high by about 10 per cent (Dimsdale 1981b). And if we go beyond simple comparisons of the pound–dollar rate the error of Churchill's way seems even greater: Redmond's (1984) calculations of sterling's value against a trade-weighted basket of international currencies suggest a 20–5 per cent overvaluation (retail price basis). Even this figure may be too low, given the relative weakening of the British economy between 1913 and 1925 (implying a lower equilibrium exchange rate against other currencies). Thus British exports were placed at a significant handicap in world markets, and home markets were more vulnerable to foreign competition. In this case, Moggridge's (1969) calculations (based on an overvaluation of 10 per cent) probably understate considerably the losses from the return to gold. A conservative estimate (assuming a 22 per cent overvaluation and a multiplier of 1.2) of job losses would top 1 million, with a corresponding output shortfall of 5 per cent.

Not all economic historians accept the logic of the traditional Keynesian analysis of the return to gold. Matthews (1986b) argues that the real exchange rate (Figure 13.7b) is determined by market forces, especially on the supply side, rather than by policy decisions. The government can set the nominal exchange rate, but the behaviour of the real rate depends on the relative movement of world and domestic prices, which are in turn largely determined by real wage behaviour. Matthews simulates the equilibrium real exchange rate (against the dollar) implied by the behaviour of real wages, output and productivity in the 1920s. He finds that sterling was overvalued relative to equilibrium by no more than one or two percentage points in 1924–5. The return to gold introduced a brief period of disequilibrium in 1926, but during the rest of the 1920s sterling was in fact undervalued compared to the rate predicted by such market 'fundamentals'. If exporters faced a problem in the 1920s, therefore, the responsibility lay with Bevin rather than with Churchill, with wage-setting rather than currency-setting.

The timing of events gives some support for Matthew's argument. The most dramatic surge in the real value of sterling was in 1919–20 (21 per cent), the year of the supply shock to hours, labour productivity, and British competitiveness. Inflationary monetary policy added to sterling's burden (ironically, as Pigou (1948) observed, relaxing the gold standard in 1919 allowed British prices to move much higher than US levels, making the return to gold that much harder). But the major source of the real appreciation in 1919–20 was not internal; it originated in the the rapid nominal depreciation of European and Asian currencies after the Armistice (the lira, yen and Belgian and French francs falling by 35 per cent in nominal terms, and by 26 per cent in real terms). Even though British costs fell relative to those of industrial rivals (by about 7.5 per cent per year 1917–25), sterling was unable to compensate for the competitive disadvantage imposed from abroad. Matthews is correct to assert that domestic prices and wages could have fallen to re-equilibrate sterling at par (by an added 5.2 per cent a year), but it might nonetheless have been simpler to choose a lower market value for sterling, or to allow the pound to float unencumbered by unsuitable policy.

But was it a viable option either not to go back on gold, or to move to a lower dollar rate ($4.40, as Keynes recommended, for instance)? Many historians have suggested not. Market traders and the international financial community expected Britain to renew its commitment to gold. Certainly the policy makers saw the return as one way to recover some of the prestige and influence on world markets lost during the war. Moreover, there were fears that market confidence would swiftly erode if the Bank of England showed weakness by introducing a 'depreciated' currency. On the other hand, it may be argued that the City of London could not retrieve its past status as financial centre to the global economy, whatever the Bank did, and that business confidence would have been best served by the choice of a competitive exchange rate generating orders, profits and employment. It is all very speculative, of course, made more so by the need to imagine what the reactions would have been abroad. Would the French and Belgians have been any less likely to undervalue their currencies if the Bank of England abandoned its commitment to the principle of $4.8665?

It is true that by reverting to the gold standard the British authorities gave up their right to control domestic money. It is also true that Montagu Norman (Governor of the Bank) confessed to the Macmillan Committee that the defence of the pound after 1925 kept interest rates high, suppressing private investment and reducing employment opportunities (though the evidence on British–US short-rates in Figure 13.7c might make us hesitate before believing him). But it is more likely that the stagnation of the British economy after 1925 was caused as much by underlying structural features, originating perhaps even before 1913 (Crafts and Thomas 1986), as by the adherence to the gold standard. The weak performance of the export staples was an abiding problem, with significant regional and locational costs, and it continued after the pound was devalued in 1931; the problems of wage inflexibility were also constants of the macro-economy throughout the post-1923 period. The economic difficulties of the twenties cannot be attributed to gold paranoia alone; there were other, more deep-seated problems involved (chief among them, perhaps, being the supply shock of 1919–20). A more realistic exchange rate might have alleviated the situation, and provided opportunities to escape the doldrums, but it was not a panacea.

The slump 1929–32

The extended doldrums of the 1920s came to an end in mid-1929. The downward trend in unemployment stopped in July, when the insured rate stood at 9.6 per cent; employment in export sensitive trades fell from June, a month after export sales peaked; employment in durable goods production fell from July, and in consumer non-durables the following month; the Board of Trade's industrial production index posted its highest level in the September quarter. The British economy began the slide from doldrums into depression. Industrial production fell by over 5 per cent a year between 1929 and 1931, national income by 3 per cent a year; unemployment rates more than doubled, and a quarter of insured jobs in the export and capital goods sectors were lost (calculated from Feinstein 1972; Capie and Collins 1983).

Yet the slump in economic activity was considerably smaller than that experienced in other countries in the same period (notably the US, but also the European countries analysed in chapter 12 above), and even by Britain during 1920–1. Unemployment did rise to unheralded heights, but the extent of additional job-loss was smaller than elsewhere in the industrial world. The same general pattern emerges from consideration of the output gap, suggesting an important question: why was the British slump comparatively shallow? The question is more puzzling when it is realised that the size of the initial adverse shock, the collapse of exports in 1929–30, was much larger than in most industrial nations.

The shallowness of the British slump is best understood in the context of global events. The global economy after 1929 was beset by price deflation. The world price of manufactures fell by 37 per cent (1929–32), of primary products by 54 per cent (Lewis 1952). Global monetary conditions were to blame. On the supply side, deflationary pressures were put in train by events in the two major holders of monetary gold. From early 1928, massive amounts of gold flowed into Paris to take advantage of high real interest rates and an undervalued currency. France's share of the world gold supply doubled between 1928 and 1932 (Bernanke and James 1991). Under normal circumstances the flow would have been self-correcting, with monetary expansion fuelling French inflation, lowering real interest rates and the value of the franc. The Bank of France, however, prohibited from engaging in open market operations (Eichengreen 1986), was unable to turn the gold into francs. Gold continued to disappear into French vaults unabated. The drain placed considerable pressure on global interest rates, reinforced in turn by the Federal Reserve Board's decision in 1928 to tighten money in the US in order to dampen stock market speculation. Monetary contraction spread globally, New York money rates rising (Figure 13.7c), and US foreign lending all but stopping. Countries that had borrowed heavily in the 1920s lost gold rapidly as their balance of payments deteriorated. Central banks raised discount rates to stem the outflow of reserves, but were powerless to halt the contractionary tide. Monetary stringency on such a global scale was decidedly deflationary. The problem was accentuated in 1929–30 by an increased demand for money in the wake of the US stock market crash in October 1929, which generated a shift in investment portfolios out of equities towards more liquid assets. The net effect was to create a global excess demand for money, and downward pressure on prices. Wholesale prices (reflecting goods traded on world markets) for a sample of twenty countries in Europe, Asia and the Americas fell by 10 per cent in 1929–30, their average GDP deflator (measuring prices of traded and non-traded goods) by 4.5 per cent.

The deflationary trend was transmitted to the British economy through a fall in demand for its exports, as trading partners fought to protect their balances of payments. Real exports fell by 38 per cent between 1929 and 1931 (Figure 13.6c), creating a severe adverse demand shock, more dramatic indeed than in most industrial countries (ch. 12; Figure 13.4). Yet, in contrast with most countries, the shock did not permeate through the economy, creating secondary waves of unemployment and bankruptcies. Investment expenditures slowed, but did not fall until 1931–2; government expenditures continued a slow and steady increase; and consumption outlays were briefly checked in 1932 (in line with the behaviour of disposable income), but otherwise rose steadily. Why were there no secondary shock waves? Why did output not collapse as far or as fast as in the United States, for example?

The answer lies in the comparative stability of the British monetary system (compare ch. 9). In 1930–1 a second wave of deflation further derailed the global economy. The US banking system was decimated twice within six months (October 1930, March 1931), during which over 2,000 banks went under. The year 1931 also saw widespread bank failures in central Europe, France and Belgium (Bernanke and James 1991). The US money supply (measured by M1) fell by 30 per cent (in nominal terms) between 1930 and 1933. Monetary contraction was even greater in Austria and Germany. Global prices (wholesale and GDP) fell by 11 per cent 1930–2. Those countries that experienced the greatest price falls were the hardest hit by unemployment and declining output (Newell and Symons 1988). Nominal inertia in labour and capital markets meant that commodity prices fell faster than factor prices. Real wages and the real interest rate rose sharply (the average real product wage in the twenty country sample rose by 8 per cent between 1929 and 1931), creating layoffs and bankruptcies, unemployment and output loss.

No such trauma hit the UK economy. No great wave of British bank failures occurred 1930–1, and the Bank of England did all in its restricted power to resist monetary stringency. M3 did fall slightly in 1930–1, but not by enough to disrupt domestic economic activity or to destabilise prices. The GDP deflator fell by a scant 1.3 per cent in 1929–30, and by only 5 per cent between 1930 and 1932. Price stability set Britain apart from the rest of the industrial world. How did Britain escape the second wave of deflation? By the simple expedient of abandoning the gold standard. The commitment to fixed exchange rates had ensured that monetary deflation would be passed from one country to another, directly by commodity arbitrage or indirectly as central banks reduced their money supply to protect exchange parity. The severing of this Gordian knot released Britain from the worst of the Great Depression.

The liquidity crisis reached British shores in mid-1931. Evaporating confidence in the stability of both economy and banking system, intensified by fears that the British had overlent to the insolvent German banks, caused a rapid drain on the Bank of England's gold reserves. The Bank was powerless to prevent the rush of events: raising the discount rate and generating loans from abroad merely postponed the inevitable. The Treasury made frantic and unsuccessful attempts to balance the government budget through spending cuts (following the May Committee recommendations) and higher taxes, to encourage foreign lending and take some pressure off domestic money markets, but the gold standard was doomed. The external account was in disequilibrium in the wake of the export crash, and sterling drain could only be stopped by a collapse in domestic incomes (to reduce imports) or by devaluation. In September the new National Government declared the suspension of the gold standard. Within ten days the pound had stabilised at around $3.90.

The government may have had no choice but to leave the gold standard, but it did so at a propitious time. The American money supply fell by 10 per cent between the Wall Street Crash (October 1929) and the gold suspension; in the same period after September 1931, it fell a further 20 per cent (Friedman and Schwartz 1963, Appendix A-1). Had Britain remained on the gold standard, the monetary collapse in the US would have been imported, bringing a second adverse demand shock, with further negative effects on prices, employment and output. Instead the pound was allowed to float down to clear the exchange market of excess supply (although the monetary authorities kept a close eye on its progress). The devaluation largely redressed the fundamental problem of external disequilibrium. Britain was able to stem the haemorrhaging of jobs and confidence, and to halt the depression before much of the rest of the world. Meanwhile the countries that retained allegiance to the gold standard suffered almost ten per cent more deflation (GDP basis) in 1931–3 than those that abandoned the system in 1931.

The greater price falls created dislocation because of significant nominal rigidities, especially in labour markets. The rising real wage created unemployment, both as firms reduced their demand for labour (moving

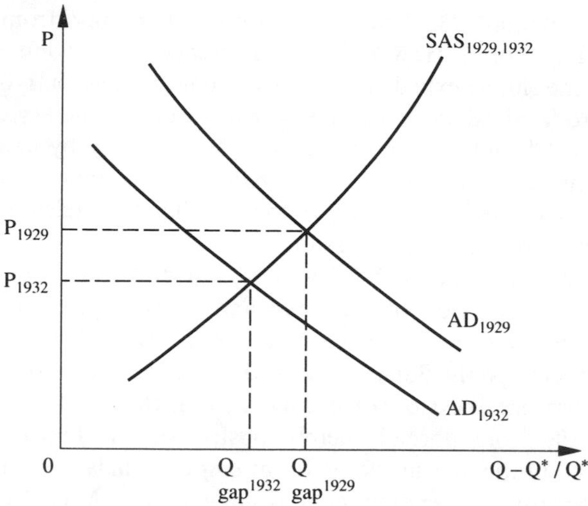

Figure 13.10a A model of aggregate supply and aggregate demand, 1929–32

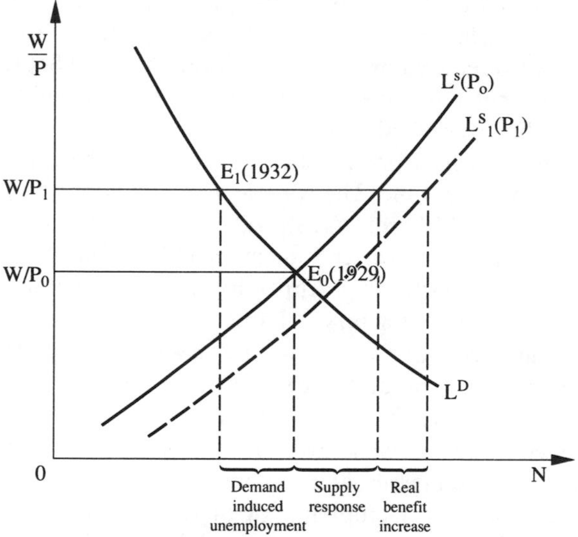

Figure 13.10b A model of the labour market, 1929–32

along the L^D schedule in Figure 13.10b from E_o to E_1), and as labour participation increased as leisure became more expensive (a movement along the labour supply curve from E_o to S_1). The supply reaction was strengthened during the slump by a terms of trade effect emanating from the collapse in world food prices. Workers perceived an even greater increase in real wages, causing the labour supply schedule to shift outwards (from L^S to L^S_1), creating higher measured unemployment. This is orthodox Keynesian analysis. Alternative, 'New Keynesian', models posit that both workers and employers were forced out of equilibrium by the slump in aggregate demand. Prices are determined on a cost-plus (or mark-up) basis. Prices will fall in a slump, either because the mark-up shrinks or because of lower raw material costs, but not by enough to clear the commodity market. The real wage again rises (but by less than in the Keynesian model), and the economy again sees more volatility in employment than in output.

The significance of global price deflation in the genesis of the British crisis of 1929–31 is also recognised by those who do not share the non-market clearing assumptions of the Keynesian models. Thus, Matthews (1986a), in new classical (rational expectations) mode, argues that the deflation of 1929–31 was unanticipated, creating mistakes on the part of wage bargainers, and generating overgenerous real wages that intensified unemployment. That is, the labour supply curve moved left. Similarly, Matthews (1984a), Beenstock, Capie and Griffiths (1984) and Beenstock and Warburton (1991) posit that the availability of generous unemployment benefits in the non-union sector may have provided an effective floor for (nominal) industrial wage rates. The political decision to maintain stable benefits when prices were falling was, consequently, a major source of wage rigidity. The argument shares much with the Keynesians, with its emphasis on deflation and stable nominal wages. The role of benefits, however, should not be exaggerated (cf. ch. 14). They were not the only source of wage rigidity in the inter-war period. And they were probably not the most important during 1929–31, since real benefits (deflated by the GDP price) rose more slowly during the slump than in either doldrums or recovery. Moreover, nominal rigidities were present in all industrial economies between the wars, regardless of the breadth of social insurance programmes (Newell and Symons 1988).

Recovery 1932–8

The period of recovery from the depression may be dated from the autumn of 1932, when most indices of production and consumption posted increases (Capie and Collins 1983). Apart from a brief interruption in late 1937 into 1938 the economy maintained a steady upward path throughout the rest of the 1930s, accelerating as war loomed. By 1939, output had returned to its trend level, although unemployment still remained obdurately high. It was only with the end of the phony war in mid-1940 that (insured) unemployment rates fell below 5 per cent.

It is often argued that the recovery after 1932 was remarkable for its sluggishness. A re-examination of Figure 13.2, however, makes it clear that recovery in output was as fast as in the years after 1921, and was sustained for a longer period. Over the eight years between 1932 and 1940 the extent of 'lost output' was considerably lower than in the similar period after 1921. It is, once again, the behaviour of unemployment that marks out the 1930s as the dismal decade. The visceral images of the Jarrow march, of long lines at the unemployment exchanges, of 'men standing at street corners, with nothing to do, nothing to say' (Mowat 1955: 482), of entire communities desolated by unemployment are images that belong to the thirties, 'the devil's decade'. The nature as well as the volume of unemployment changed with the slump: the period between 1929 and 1932 delineated the transition between a labour market marked by rapid mobility between job and the dole and back again to a labour market with long-term unemployment for a small but significant proportion of the unemployed (ch. 14). In one sense it is the very existence of the long-term unemployed that accounts for the slow recovery of the labour market. These people were, in effect, only nominally in the labour force. Their chances of ever filling another job were very low – they were often trapped in depressed regions and saw little incentive to migrate to richer pastures, perceiving that employers were wary of their work habits and often of their character. Unemployment is 'state-dependent', mathematically speaking: the level and nature of unemployment today is determined by the origins and forms of unemployment yesterday. Hysteresis of this sort – bad luck breeds more bad luck – has good explanatory power for the 1930s.

The pattern of the recovery when mapped out in price-income space (Figure 13.5a) appears much like the depression put into reverse. The image is consistent no matter which measure of capacity utilisation and which price variable is used (even if the speed of the process does vary). The apparent mirror image is reflected in most explanations of recovery. The traditional Keynesian interpretation is that output was demand-determined throughout the period, although the precise balance of demand factors was different after 1932 than before. Dimsdale, Nickell and Horsewood (1989), representing a New Keynesian perspective, see recovery as emanating from rising import prices coupled with a demand boom, the opposite of what shaped the depression. Similarly, Beenstock, Capie and Griffiths (1984), arguing from a new classical position, maintain that real wage moderation after 1932 instigated recovery, just as real wage demands had set off the Great Slump.

Figure 13.5 suggests demand did it (note the flat stretch in the figure). There may have been a supply-side boost from productivity gains (Figures 13.1, 13.8c) that, in combination with stable nominal wages (Figure 13.8a),

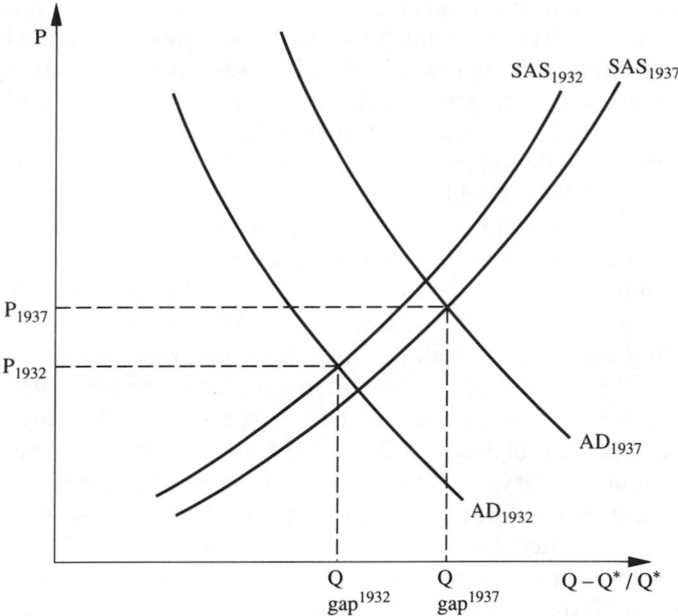

Figure 13.11 A model of aggregate supply and aggregate demand, 1932–7

lowered unit labour costs of production (Figure 13.8d) and quilibrium prices. But this was of secondary importance to the overall shape of recovery. Thus, in Figure 13.11, the shift from AD_{1932} to AD_{1937} dominates the movement of the aggregate supply curve (SAS_{1932} to SAS_{1937}). What were the major sources of increased demand? A review of the main expenditure components of national income (Figures 13.6) indicates that recovery was complex, with different factors dominating at different stages. In particular, the elements that sparked recovery in 1932 need to be distinguished from those that sustained it throughout the 1930s.

Nonetheless, some generalisations can be made. First, recovery was primarily a domestic affair. Exports may have helped trigger recovery – export volumes rose by 24 per cent in the last quarter of 1932 – but such pressure was not maintained consistently in the 1930s. Only 7 per cent of new jobs between 1932 and 1937 were located in export-sensitive industries. The fact is perhaps unsurprising, given the very slow growth rate of manufactured world trade after 1932. Despite improved competitiveness, reflected in the declining real exchange rate after 1932 (Figure 13.7b), British exports in the peak year of 1937 were still lower than in the strike-troubled year of 1926. Secondly, in terms of domestic demand, neither consumption nor government expenditures can account for much. Consumption was passive throughout the 1930s, moving in tandem with personal disposable income. Fiscal policy was net contractionary during early recovery (lowering national income by as much as 4 per cent between 1931/2 and 1933/4); despite an easing of the tax burden in 1934, it was at most mildly reflationary until the eve of the Second World War (Broadberry 1984a; Middleton 1981).

The behaviour of investment and imports provides stronger clues to the ultimate sources of recovery. Import penetration of British markets fell significantly in 1932 (especially in manufactures, in which the import propensity fell from 11.5 per cent in 1926–31 to 8.0 per cent in 1932–7), providing a once-and-for-all boost to domestic producers at the onset of recovery. The most striking aspect of investment in the early 1930s was the housing boom. Expenditure on the construction of dwellings rose by almost 50 per cent between 1932 and 1934. Housing starts were at the very forefront of recovery – building activity rose from November 1932, more or less coincident with the beginnings of the economy-wide upturn. Housing accounted for 17 per cent of the increase in GDP in 1932–4 (compared to 3 per cent of GDP in 1932). After mid-1933, non-residential investment took off (especially in manufacturing and transportation), growing at an average rate of 14 per cent through 1937. Producer durables, employing 11.5 per cent of the insured workforce in April 1933, provided one third of all new jobs over the next four years.

Recovery, like the depression, was global. The broad contours of the cyclical upswing were shared by most industrialised countries, although its precise dynamics, both in timing and in intensity, varied from place to place. We need therefore to look beyond British shores to identify the root causes of recovery. Any global explanation, moreover, needs to make sense of divergent national performance in the 1930s. The most evident divergence is between those countries that abandoned the gold standard in 1931 and those that did not. A simple calculation suggests that staying on gold reduced industrial growth by as much as 17 per cent by 1935 (Bernanke and James 1991). Recovery was stimulated in non-gold countries by a combination of monetary expansion and currency devaluation.

Countries that abandoned the gold standard in late 1931 experienced monetary expansion. Why? Because their domestic monetary authorities were released from the straitjacket of the rules of the game. The gold bloc continued to experience declining money stocks (a cumulative total of 20 per cent in M1 between 1932 and 1936, according to Bernanke and James (1991)); while the money supply stabilised and then slowly grew in the non-gold world. Prices reflected these divergent monetary profiles. Outside the gold bloc, prices stabilised during 1932 and 1933 and then gently increased through 1937. The stability in turn reversed the trend of rising factor prices that had been at the core of the unemployment and bankruptcies of the depression. Real wages fell by 12 per cent during 1932–5 for the countries that abandoned gold in 1931, while rising in the gold bloc by 15 per cent. Monetary expansion further aided recovery by pushing down nominal interest rates world-wide. Cheap money promoted investment. But countries that retained their allegiance to gold were penalised by having to maintain higher interest rates to protect their reserves against raiding by the devaluing countries. The difference between gold bloc and non-gold countries in central bank discount rates amounted to 1.7 per cent by 1935; in view of the different price histories of the two groups, the divergence in real rates was even greater.

The corollary to relaxing the external constraint was currency devaluation. Exchange rates in the non-gold world floated downwards, at least until 1935. Depreciation encouraged output and employment at home by raising the price of imports relative to domestic products. Expenditure switching encouraged increased domestic prices (a movement along the supply curve), which in turn further lowered unemployment by reducing real wages. But the use of devaluation and tariffs (to protect domestic industry and employment) inhibits the potential for export-led recovery in the world economy, unless the extent of monetary reflation is large enough to pump-prime global aggregate demand through lower interest rates. Eichengreen (1992) argues that the competitive devaluations of the early 1930s were indeed 'beggar-thy-neighbour', as was thought at the time, and did retard global recovery. Monetary authorities retained an instinctive distrust of inflation, even after the intense and destructive deflation of 1928–31, and kept monetary reflation on a tight and binding leash.

Britain's recovery fits well with the global pattern. The early decision to leave the gold standard (September 1931); the implementation of a protective tariff (November 1931, February 1932); and continued depreciation of sterling all contributed to what was, by international standards, a rapid and forceful cyclical upswing.

The immediate impact of Britain's departure from the gold standard was sterling depreciation. The pound fell by 30 per cent against the dollar between September and December 1931. The effective devaluation against all exchanges was much smaller (around 13 per cent), since some twenty-five countries with close economic or imperial links to Britain tied their currencies to the pound. The sharp depreciation against the dollar was reversed in 1932, while the pound continued to plummet against the franc. Clearly one needs multilateral calculations to make sense of the foreign exchanges in this period. Two such indices are shown in Figure 13.7b. The effective exchange rate, which measures sterling's value against a broad range of currencies and is most appropriate for analysing balance of payments effects, shows sharp depreciation in 1932, and a gradual appreciation of the pound through the rest of the 1930s. The real average rate, indicating sterling's competitiveness against the major manufacturing nations, shows a continued depreciation through 1933, stability through 1935 and a sharp appreciation in 1935–6. The contrast between these two indices is created by the large weight (80 per cent) given in the average index to gold bloc countries and the US.

Devaluation of sterling gave British manufacturers a competitive edge against their overseas rivals. In the absence of an export boom, the advantage was realised through the substitution of British goods for now-expensive imports. The volume of manufactured imports fell by over 50 per cent between November 1931 and November 1932. The fall of imports undoubtedly gave a boost to domestic producers (a rightward shift of the AD curve). How far it should be attributed to devaluation alone is uncertain, since November 1931 saw the imposition of the Abnormal Importations Act, preparatory to the full introduction of a General Tariff three months later. Note, however, that 75 per cent of the increased wedge between world and domestic manufactured prices (the stimulus to import substitution) created by exchange rates and tariffs in 1931–2 was due to devaluation. Kitson and Solomou (1990) argue that the tariff stimulated output via channels other than relative prices, notably by shifting resources towards sectors (principally the old staples) that embodied increasing returns technology, lowering costs through a higher scale of production. But in the absence of documented evidence of widespread increasing returns, the case for tariffs as a major source of growth after 1932 remains unconvincing.

The other mechanism by which Britain's departure from the gold standard promoted economic recovery was monetary. The traditional story is that as the exchange rate was permitted to float downwards (after September 1931) Britain regained control of its domestic money supply, and the Bank of England proceeded to pursue a policy of cheaper money, converting the national debt to a lower interest band. The policy is said to have created an environment in which interest-elastic investment was stimulated, jump-starting a multiplier-accelerator engine of recovery. It is certainly the case that interest rates (both real and nominal) were lower after 1931 than previously. After a brief period during which the Bank of England, fearful of inflation and wishing to build up foreign exchange reserves (Howson 1975), pushed Bank Rate to 6 per cent, interest rates gradually fell. By June 1932, Bank Rate stood at 2 per cent and the

Treasury bill rate below 1 per cent. Partly to protect sterling, partly to reduce debt charges, partly to encourage recovery, the Bank and the Treasury maintained a policy of cheap money for the rest of the decade.

Challengers to the orthodoxy, invoking the interest parity condition, contend that cheap money was not a domestic policy instrument. Policy makers could not have set domestic interest rates below world levels for long, since capital, searching for the best rate of return, would have flowed out of the British economy until the domestic and world interest rates were brought back into equilibrium. Low interest rates are only possible if world money markets permit. Cheap money may have stimulated investment and promoted recovery, but that was not a result of policy but rather a spillover from the depressed world financial market (ch. 9). Two points may be made. Firstly, on theoretical grounds, interest rate parity is a long-run condition, not necessarily binding in the short run. Secondly, in empirical terms, few countries participated as forcefully or as consistently as Britain. In particular the gold bloc countries maintained considerably higher interest rates to protect exchange reserves and currency values. Britain may have been unable to establish cheap money independent of the global economy, but the decision (voluntary or otherwise) to abandon gold was crucial to the attainment of low interest rates both at home and abroad.

The major beneficiary of cheap money was the housing sector. Low interest rates were not the only factor propelling the boom in residential construction and purchase in 1932–4. Other significant factors include declining building costs, increased real incomes (from improved terms of trade) and especially the active financial intermediation by building societies to offload some of their sizable accumulated assets from the 1920s (Humphries 1987). Some empirical analysis by Broadberry (1986a) suggests that perhaps half the building boom of 1932–3 could be attributed to cheap money. But its role should not be exaggerated. Non-residential investment has been found not to be interest-elastic (Lund and Holden 1968). Cheap money was at best a permissive factor in maintaining recovery after 1933.

The money supply (M3) rose by over 11 per cent during 1932 (Figure 13.7a); after a brief decline in 1933, monetary expansion resumed at 5 per cent a year through 1937. Chapter 9 above suggests that the government had no monetary policy to speak of during the period. The rapid increase in both the monetary base and M3 in 1931–3 was due not to internal policy actions but to an influx of foreign funds attracted by an undervalued sterling. Regardless of its origins, it was bound to have favourable consequences for the path of income and output in the 1930s. Real money balances increased, providing a small stimulus for consumption (through the wealth effect, making individuals feel better off), while profits and equities regained the strength they had lost in the depression, thereby boosting funds and confidence for investment. Indeed, the major stimulus to non-residential investment was the behaviour of corporate profits, which rose dramatically after 1932 (Balogh 1947). Profits, as an essentially passive variable, benefited from improvements in the price-cost structure of British industry, associated with the price-raising impact of devaluation, tariffs and monetary growth, coupled with the continued fall in unit labour costs of production.

A debate has long raged among economic historians as to how far economic recovery in the 1930s was policy-induced. In contrast to an earlier generation of economic historians, who assumed from the post-war period of demand management that government must somehow have been responsible for the rapid growth in the 1930s, the current consensus is that policy made little difference in either direction. Fiscal policy was at best neutral, monetary policy (cheap money) was passive and trade policy was marginal. The one exception to this rule concerns 1935–8, during which rearmament had a clear expansionary impact on the economy, in both depressed and prosperous regions. Even this late in the recovery, as Figure 13.5 shows, the economy was a long way short of its 'natural' level. Rearmament expenditures only became inflationary towards late 1938 and into 1939. The slack in the economy enabled the government to give a boost to aggregate demand without upsetting labour or capital markets. Wages, prices and interest rates do not show much sign of being disturbed by a programme that may have put as many as 1 million people to work by 1938 (Thomas 1983). It is tempting to argue from the example of rearmament that the government missed a golden opportunity to speed up the recovery, and to put back to work large numbers of long-term unemployed by some form of public works programme. Is this a reasonable inference?

Could Lloyd George (and/or Keynes) have done it?

The phrase, famous among economic historians and a perennial in academic conversation and exam papers, originates in the Keynes–Henderson position paper drawn up on the eve of the 1929 election to discuss Lloyd George's proposal to rejuvenate the economy with a £250 million public works programme spread over two years. The authors argued that the programme set out by the old Liberal leader was feasible and desirable. Keynes recommended an easing of credit restrictions, in combination with loan-financed expenditures, to assist private enterprise in promoting growth and employment. The Lloyd George proposal received considerable attention from the Treasury, in particular from a

White Paper that sought to destroy its credibility. As Middleton (1985) notes, the White Paper emphasised the administrative and political barriers to implementing a large-scale public works programme. The traditional version of the 'Treasury view' – that public expenditures crowd out private investment by driving up the interest rate through competition for loanable funds – is a caricature of the Whitehall position. The distrust of the Liberal programme came from the belief that it encouraged projects that would do little to attack the root causes of unemployment (especially the depressed state of the staple industries), and might well raise new problems of its own (in the capital market, and also in the balance of payments, by raising imports at the same time as resources would be bid away from the export sector).

Who was right? Keynes or the Treasury? There is no simple answer. Could a policy of demand management, involving deficit spending out of loans, have achieved full employment in the 1930s? The answer depends crucially on how we think the macro-economy works. In a thoroughly Keynesian analysis of the question, T. Thomas (1981) argues that Lloyd George could *not* have done it. The multiplier from government expenditures to total income was too small (1.44 after twelve years, with an impact multiplier of less than one), largely because of a high propensity to import (thereby transferring the iterative gains from added expenditure to foreign economies). A programme on the scale envisioned by Lloyd George would have made only a temporary dent in unemployment or the output gap. And this in a model that biases the result in favour of fiscal policies, by holding prices and exchange rates constant. Ironically, it is the application of the Liberal programme in a market-clearing, rational expectations model with flexible exchange rates that achieves the most.

Matthews (1986a) argues that the fiscal package would have driven up prices, thus relaxing the primary binding constraint on output and employment – the high level of real benefits. The fall in real benefits and wages would have created a permanent rightward shift in the long-run aggregate supply curve. The natural level of output and employment would have increased, as British workers and British products became more competitive. Matthews, in his simulation of the economy, predicts an immediate gain in employment of 800,000 from Lloyd George's programme, comparable to the short-run gain in Thomas' model (all calculations made for a three-year programme of £250 million). It is in the transition to the longer run that the models' predictions move apart. The expectations-driven model has a declining impact over the longer term as the unanticipated component in the price level is squeezed out by improved information; by the end of ten years, output is simulated to rise by 2 per cent, and employment to fall by 430,000. Since a fundamental parameter has changed in Matthews' system, however, the predicted employment and output gains are permanent. But in the Keynesian model the policy effects last only as long as the policy itself. The multiplier grinds slowly towards its maximum effect, but once the injection of funds stops, only ripple effects continue. Ten years after the onset of a three-year Liberal programme, according to Thomas' model, the added job gain would amount to less than 15,000.

There has been considerable debate over the practical implications of such models. The majority view appears now to be that a fiscally induced expansion could not have broken the back of the depression. Arguing from within the Keynesian framework, and using Thomas' sceptical results, Glynn and Howells (1980) suggest that a demand injection of around 15 per cent of GDP would have been required to bring unemployment down to 3 per cent in 1932–5. They note that the (negative) impact of such a policy on confidence in business circles and in capital and currency markets would have been immense. The likely balance of payments implications were also unfavourable to a Keynesian policy of 'pump-priming', as were the distinctly regional and structural characteristics of the unemployment itself. To this catalogue we should add the formidable problems of coordinating such a programme. Neither the Treasury nor other branches of public administration were equipped to deal with such tasks. Learning would certainly have occurred, which would probably have reduced the efficacy of the programme still further. It is hard to believe that an unsystematic programme of public works could have achieved all that Keynes and Lloyd George hoped.

Yet the dangers of arguing from oversimplified models of the economy can cut both ways. What Lloyd George proposed was not an unsystematic programme of public works, but one designed to improve the infrastructure and general growth potential of the economy by funding increased provision of public (capital) goods, such as telecommunications, electrical supply and roads. Moreover, as the example of rearmament suggests, it was possible to design a regionally sensitive programme of expenditures that could have tackled the legacy of the demise of the staples. And whereas the Treasury was correct to observe that such a policy would not tackle the root causes of the regional problem, it would probably have been on balance best to establish new rules of combat within these regions anyway. There would, undoubtedly, have been a limit to the success of any policy of centralised expansion – Keynes himself recognised that a conscious regional policy was necessary by 1937 (when the insured unemployment rate still stood at 11 per cent). But the limits were surely far from reached in 1933 or 1934. The balance of payments difficulties might have been more serious; the trade problems of the post-war period that gave birth to the 'stop–go' policies of the 1950s and 1960s appear to have been well in place by the early 1930s (Peden 1988). But we should not automatically assume that fiscal policies were self-defeating. The real exchange rate effects of deficit spending could have been neutralised by expansive monetary policy, as originally recommended by Keynes and Henderson. Such a policy would have been inflationary, to be sure, and would have further contributed to the competitiveness problem that lay at the core of Britain's inter-war economic problem. However, as Dimsdale (1981b) and others have observed, the depressed nature of the world economy, and the global commitment to autarkic trade policies, severely restricted the potential for export-led recovery, placing the burden on internal forces. And, to the extent that the 1930s were marked by inflexible wages, global cheap money and depressed primary product markets, inflation-augmented profit margins might have further stimulated domestic reflation by generating more aggressive animal spirits in the private sector.

The conclusion on the potential for pump-priming policies in the 1930s is then a mixed one. On the one hand, there were serious problems of administration, politics and business confidence, on top of the purely economic aspects of the balance of payments and regional factor mobility, that restricted the potential of such a programme. On the other hand, not every problem was insuperable, as the gradual transition to a war economy after 1936 or so reflects. A partial programme of reflation might well have been possible without placing too much strain on the system.

Conclusion

The macro-economic experience of the inter-war years has cast a long shadow. The dominant economic theory of the second half of the twentieth century is grounded in its experiences. The disputes over policy under Mrs Thatcher were fought with the memories and the mythology of the 1930s firmly in mind. The 1930s have come to be regarded by some as a laboratory within which to test hypotheses and models about unemployment and instability in the 1990s. And many of the problems of our own era seem to have developed (or at least first to have been noticed) in the 1920s and 1930s. Mass unemployment; long-term unemployment; the downward rigidity of wages; the negative consequences of overgenerous benefits; the poor record of internal labour mobility; the regional problem; the instability of the British balance of payments; export uncompetitiveness; antiquated industrial structures and equipment: all entered the vocabulary of political economy between 1918 and 1939. The existence of these problems coloured the attitude of economists, politicians and civil servants towards the operation of a market economy. Indeed, the very notion of a fully marketised economy, with all its naiveties as well as its strengths, may have been one of the greatest casualties of the depressed state of the inter-war years. By 1941, attitudes within government were being drawn, probably irresistibly, towards the concept of a managed economy.

14 Unemployment and the labour market in inter-war Britain

Tim Hatton

Introduction

The inter-war period has gone down in history, above all, as an era of mass unemployment. The bitter experience of unemployment, particularly in the 1930s, stimulated the search for new economic remedies and led to a widespread determination that unemployment on that scale should never be allowed to occur again. It was not until the 1980s that unemployment on a similar scale did reappear (see vol. 3, ch. 7). This has led to a re-examination of the inter-war period in the light of more recent experience. As a result, modern theories and techniques have been brought to bear on the historical issues. The central questions are: what went wrong, why and with what effects on those who suffered unemployment?

The annual rate of unemployment for wage and salary earners from 1921 to 1938 is graphed in Figure 14.1. Two things stand out: the major recession of the 1930s which drove the unemployment rate to over 15 per cent, and the persistently high rate of unemployment which prevailed over the whole period. From a macro-economic perspective the questions are: what were the forces which caused fluctuations in unemployment and what prevented the market mechanism from delivering lower average unemployment levels? Micro-economic questions are: why were some people more prone to unemployment than others and what determined the duration of their unemployment? (For a detailed treatment of the relationship between unemployment and public policy see Garside 1990 and for a discussion of unemployment in longer term perspective see Whiteside 1990. To place the British experience of unemployment in an international context, see the introduction to Eichengreen and Hatton 1988a.)

The statistics of unemployment

The recorded level of unemployment depends on how unemployment is defined and measured (Garside 1981). For the inter-war period, most of

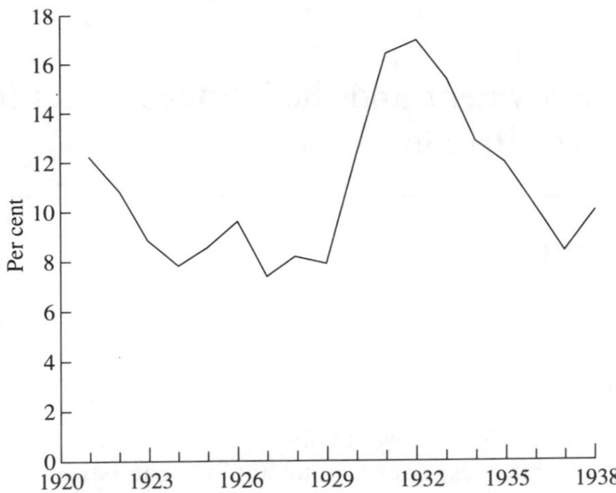

Figure 14.1 Unemployment rate, 1921–38
Source: Feinstein (1972: Table 128).

the available information comes from the joint operation of the labour exchanges (established by an Act of 1909) and the unemployment insurance system (established in 1911). During the inter-war period the insurance system covered about 60 per cent of all employees. On becoming unemployed an insured worker would register at the exchange and at the same time apply for benefit (a small number of uninsured also registered). The rate of unemployment was calculated as the ratio of the number maintaining registration on a particular date to the total number insured under the system. Between 1921 and 1938 the insured unemployment rate measured this way averaged 14.2 per cent. Unemployment was much lower for groups of workers (such as farm workers, domestic servants, certain public employees and white-collar workers) who were outside the system. Among all employees taken together the average unemployment rate (the series graphed in Figure 14.1) was 10.9 per cent. If the whole of the working population is taken as the base (by including groups such as the self-employed) then the average for the period would be 10.0 per cent.

These differences matter because it has sometimes been argued that the insurance figures overstate inter-war unemployment and therefore exaggerate the seriousness of the unemployment problem. Clearly they do, but even a rate of 10 per cent averaged over two decades is still remarkably high. It is difficult to compare this with the pre-First World War experience because the statistics for the earlier period are from the records of trade unions and are concentrated on a narrow range of industries. Between 1895 and 1913 the trade union unemployment rate averaged 4.0 per cent. Since, for the period where they overlap, trade union and insured unemployment rates are similar, it might be argued that the trade union rates also overstate the economy-wide unemployment rate. In any event there seems no reason to depart from the received wisdom that inter-war unemployment was 'between two and three times as severe as before the first World War' (Beveridge 1944: 336). The data for the early post-Second World War period are more comparable since unemployment insurance statistics are used for both. From 1948 to 1965 the unemployment rate for the working population as a whole averaged a mere 1.5 per cent. It was only from the mid-1970s that anything resembling the magnitude of inter-war unemployment reappeared.

Explanations of unemployment

What diagnosis can be offered for the exceptionally high unemployment of the inter-war period? Until a few years ago, most observers would probably have agreed with Beveridge's view, expressed in 1944, that

> The central problem of unemployment between the wars was not what it had seemed to be before the First World War. It was not a problem of cyclical fluctuation reducing demand for a time, or of disorganisation of the labour market wasting men's lives in drifting and waiting. It was a problem of persistent weakness of demand for labour. (1944: 89)

This reflects the predominantly Keynesian approach in which labour demand, determined in turn by the demand for goods and services, is seen as the senior partner. In this view labour supply has little role to play: those unfortunate enough to be unemployed would willingly work at the going wage if only there were jobs for them.

This orthodoxy has been challenged by those who have emphasised the importance of the supply side. The challenge was led in a controversial article by Benjamin and Kochin who argued that: 'the army of the unemployed standing watch at the publication of (Keynes') General Theory was largely a volunteer army' (1979: 474). This, they argued, was due to the high rates of unemployment benefit (relative to wages) offered by the unemployment insurance system and the liberal conditions for eligibility. As a result, a significant proportion of the unemployed spent longer searching for new employment and were more choosy in accepting offers, or were simply content to live on benefits without the burden of having to work. In this view, it was not that too few jobs were available but that too few workers were willing to accept offers of employment. This suggests that, with the exception of sharp cyclical downturns, there was relatively full employment for those who wanted to work despite the high unemployment figures.

There have been other approaches which have attempted to explain or at least contribute to the explanation of persistent unemployment. One theme is that inter-war unemployment was, in some sense, 'structural'. This derives from the fact that unemployment was vastly higher in some industries than in others and in some regions than in others. The difficulty in transferring labour from declining industries and regions to prosperous ones left stranded many of those in localities where the staple industry had collapsed or whose skills were becoming obsolete. To an extent, this is linked with the argument that, given the conditions of demand, the prevailing wage in some sectors was too high. Another line of argument is that, for institutional reasons, wages as a whole were too high. Features of the wage system are held responsible for the failure of the average wage to adjust in a manner which would generate higher employment in aggregate. The newly established system of national wage bargaining, bolstered by strong trade unionism and cushioned by the floor of minimum wages and unemployment benefits is the factor held responsible.

Unemployment and insurance

In their important article, Benjamin and Kochin argued that the benefit system was generous to the point of inducing a substantial amount of unemployment. According to them, the rates of benefit were high enough to provide a genuine alternative to wages. For this to occur, benefits need not have been as high as wages, since the unemployed would also have valued the additional leisure gained from not working. Benefits could be claimed for a period as short as one day provided that that day's unemployment could be linked to a spell of unemployment in the recent past. Once a claim to benefit had been established, benefit could be drawn almost indefinitely, although continuation after several months might be contingent on a means test (particularly from 1931).

The claim that benefits induced unemployment rested principally on the results from an econometric equation estimated on annual observations from 1920 to 1938. In this, the insured unemployment rate depends on the benefit to wage ratio and on the deviation from trend of national income. Thus both the supply-side factor of benefits and the demand-side factor of output fluctuations were given a part in determining the unemployment rate. The benefit to wage ratio was found to have a positive effect. Using this result Benjamin and Kochin estimated that, had the benefit to wage ratio remained at 0.27 (a little over half the average of the series they used), the insured unemployment rate would have averaged between 9.6 and 6.9 per cent over the period 1921 to 1938 rather than the 14.2 per cent observed.

This result has been severely criticised on two grounds. First, the empirical estimate of the effect of the benefit to wage ratio on unemployment is not robust to small changes in specification (Metcalf *et al.* 1982; Ormerod and Worswick 1982). Second, the model itself does not provide an appropriate framework with which to measure the effect of benefits on unemployment (Broadberry 1983; Hatton 1983).

Benjamin and Kochin argued that during the inter-war period benefits were 'on a more generous scale than ever before or since' (1979: 442). The ratio they used was the full weekly benefit rate for an adult male claiming for himself, a wife and two children, relative to an index of average weekly earnings. This gives an average of 0.49 over the whole period with a peak of 0.57 in 1936. This exaggerates the true ratio because some of the unemployed, such as females and young people, received lower rates of benefit than adult males and the unemployed, on average, had fewer than three dependants. If the different rates of benefit are weighted together to reflect the composition of the unemployed the average ratio for the period works out at 0.36 with a peak of 0.41 in 1936. Even this takes no account of the fact that some of the unemployed were ineligible for benefit or received it at a lower rate. If we take the average payment per unemployed worker as the index of benefit and express this as a ratio with the wage then the average is 0.24 over the whole period, reaching 0.33 in 1936. It must be concluded that on any reasonable comparison of benefits and wages, Benjamin and Kochin overestimated the ratio.

This has implications for the argument that benefits were more generous than ever before or since. As Metcalf, Nickell and Floros have shown, the weighted average of benefits relative to wages for 1951 to 1965 was 0.41 and for 1966 to 1976 0.51. The benefit to wage ratio was therefore no higher in the inter-war period than in the early post-war and was significantly lower than in the late 1960s and early 1970s. Given this finding, how can a high benefit to wage ratio in the inter-war period have been responsible for a substantial 'core' of unemployment when, in most of the post-war period, the benefit to wage ratio was at least as high but unemployment was only a small fraction of the inter-war rate? It could be that a given benefit to wage ratio had a bigger effect on unemployment in the inter-war than in the post-war period but so far there has been no convincing argument to explain why this should be so.

When examining benefit to wage ratios, averages can be misleading. The average ratio could be quite low but, if benefits were high relative to wages for a substantial minority, there could nonetheless be a significant effect on unemployment. Contemporaries worried that, for some of the unemployed, benefits received were as high or higher than the wage they could command when working. The Ministry of Labour was prompted to conduct surveys of the unemployed in the late 1930s to investigate the

Table 14.1. *Benefit to wage ratios for claimants to insurance benefits, 1937*

B/W ratio greater than	Men 18–20	Men 21–64	Women 18–20	Women 21–64
1·0	2·6	0·5	3·4	0·9
0·8	6·5	2·0	8·2	4·4
0·6	17·1	11·7	23·1	17·5
0·4	48·0	50·6	78·8	82·8
0·2	97·6	98·8	99·8	100·0
Average B/W	0·38	0·43	0·48	0·5

Source: calculated from *Report of the Unemployment Insurance Statutory Committee* for 1937: 55–9.

issue. As Table 14.1 shows, among insurance benefit recipients, hardly any had benefits in excess of the wage in their last job. Only 2.0 per cent of adult men and 4.4 per cent of adult women had benefits higher than four-fifths of their last wage. Among recipients of Unemployment Assistance, few had benefits in excess of their last wage but a larger proportion had benefits higher than four-fifths of the wage; about 15 per cent of men and 18 per cent of women. (Taken together, these results are similar to those obtained by Atkinson and Micklewright (1985: 173) for the mid-1970s. They found that 12.6 per cent of their sample of unemployed males had benefits in excess of four-fifths of their previous wage.)

Benjamin and Kochin argued that the effects of benefits could be observed in the differences between workers by age and sex. Throughout the period the unemployment rate for females was about two-thirds that for males and for insured juveniles (those aged sixteen and seventeen), only a quarter the adult male rate. Evidence from a household survey of London in 1929 indicates that, among all earners in the survey, benefit to wage ratios were for men aged twenty-one and over 0.48, for women twenty-one and over 0.54, for young men sixteen to twenty 0.41, and for young women 16–20 0.34. It is far from clear from this or other evidence (compare Table 14.1) that there is a systematic relationship between these ratios and unemployment incidence across demographic groups. A similar observation can be made about regional differences in unemployment rates. While it is true that average wage rates were somewhat lower in the depressed regions of the north and west, and therefore benefit to wage ratios were higher, it is hard to believe that the small differences involved could have given rise to the huge differences in unemployment rates which persisted during the period.

Whatever actual benefit to wage ratios were, by themselves they cannot tell us whether or by how much raising the ratio for an individual from, say, 0.3 to 0.5 would increase the chance of that individual being unemployed. The question is basically a micro-economic one. In a recent paper Eichengreen (1987) has attempted to address the issue using data for 3,000 males from a survey of working-class households undertaken in London during 1929–30. The information was obtained from a sample of the surviving records of the New Survey of London Life and Labour which contain detailed information about the employment status, earnings (when in work), age and family circumstances of each individual in the household. Although those who were in employment would not have been receiving benefits, knowledge of each individual's age and the number of dependants together with the prevailing benefit rates can be used to construct the benefit to wage ratio for all earners, whether they were unemployed or not. Using data such as these it is possible to test statistically whether those with higher benefit to wage ratios were more likely to be unemployed, at the same time allowing for the effects on the likelihood of unemployment associated with personal circumstances such as age, marital status, family structure and non-wage income.

Eichengreen analysed the set of adult males from these households, dividing them into two groups: household heads and non-heads. He found no significant impact of the benefit to wage ratio on the likelihood that household heads would be unemployed, but there was a significant effect on unemployment for non-heads. The magnitude of these effects on the overall level of unemployment is somewhat uncertain but Eichengreen suggests that lowering the benefit to wage ratio to 0.27 (0.24 for non-heads) would have reduced the unemployment rate for these individuals taken together from the observed 8.6 per cent to between 6.8 and 7.4 per cent. Thus the effects are more modest than those suggested by Benjamin and Kochin and non-heads seem to have been more susceptible than heads of household. However, since the findings apply only to London, it is necessary to be cautious in generalising from them to the rest of the country. It seems probable that unemployment incidence associated with individual responses is more likely to be revealed in a relatively tight labour market than in one where there is mass unemployment. Hence it appears unlikely that the effects would be greater in one of the depressed regions.

It is worth briefly considering unemployment benefits from another angle, that of income maintenance. After all, the main purpose of the system was to prevent the hardship and deprivation which resulted from joblessness. Inter-war poverty surveys found that unemployment was the most important single cause of poverty. For example, in London in 1929/30, 40 per cent of poor households were in poverty because of

Table 14.2. *Poverty lines and unemployment benefit rates, 1929/30 and 1936 (shillings)*

Household composition	London 1929/30 NSLL standard	London 1929/30 Human needs	London 1929/30 Unemployment benefit	York 1936 1899 standard	York 1936 Human needs	York 1936 Unemployment benefit
Man (alone)	17·7	27·7	17·0	14·6	27·9	17·0
Woman (alone)	16·6	23·9	15·0	13·8	22·7	15·0
Man and woman	25·7	34·9	24·0	19·9	32·8	26·0
Couple + 1 child	32·2	45·4	26·0	24·5	40·3	29·0
Couple + 2 children	38·2	52·8	28·0	29·9	45·0	32·0
Couple + 3 children	44·1	60·3	30·0	36·4	47·9	35·0
Woman + 1 child	21·4	30·9	17·0	18·3	28·0	18·0

Notes and sources: New Survey of London Life and Labour standard taken from Llewellyn-Smith (1930–5: 422); human needs standard from Rowntree (1941: 30) (adjusted to London in 1930 for column 2); 1899 standard from Rowntree (1941: 102). The rents included are the minimum necessary number of rooms to avoid overcrowding. Unemployment benefit rates assume one earner (the man in the case of couples).

unemployment and in Southampton in 1931 (when unemployment was more intense), the share was 66 per cent. Other important causes were old age, sickness, lack of a male breadwinner in the family and large family size. Most of the surveys used a poverty line comparable with that established by Rowntree in 1899 which allowed, in addition to rent, a minimum expenditure on food and clothing (and a few other essentials) necessary merely to maintain physical efficiency. In 1936 Rowntree drew up a new and higher 'human needs' standard which allowed for additional expenditure chiefly on personal and household sundries (Rowntree 1937).

Why, when most of the unemployed received some form of unemployment benefit, was such a large amount of poverty attributable to unemployment? Part of the answer can be found in Table 14.2. This compares the minimum income as defined in the poverty surveys for different family types (in shillings where 20s = £1) with prevailing rates of unemployment benefit. Using the lower poverty line all these households would have been in poverty in London in 1929/30 but, with the exception of those with three or more children, would have escaped poverty in York in 1936. Applying the higher poverty line would leave all the households in poverty in both instances. As a rule during the inter-war period unemployment benefits were close to the bare subsistence poverty lines drawn up before the First World War.

The specific circumstances of individual households varied much more than these examples imply. In London in 1929/30, 58 per cent of households whose principal earner was unemployed were in poverty (on the lower poverty line). In Southampton in 1931 it was 59 per cent. Where a secondary earner was unemployed poverty was less likely. The households least likely to suffer poverty as a result of unemployment were those with more than one earner, with other sources of income, with low rents or with few dependants. Consequently some households with unemployed members were poor even with full benefits while others would not have been poor even without benefits. It can be estimated using surviving records from the London survey that removing unemployment benefits would have raised the percentage of working-class households in poverty from 9.9 to 11.0. Loss of benefits would have meant total destitution for some families but not for others. This provides some justification for the principle of a means test to target limited resources to those most in need. When the means test was implemented in the 1930s, however, it was unevenly applied, and was deeply resented by the unemployed and regarded by most observers as divisive.

There is an important final point about unemployment and poverty. In Table 14.2, for London in 1929/30, a family of four with benefit of 28s and no other resources would have been in desperate poverty. But if the male breadwinner had spent two months unemployed and ten months earning the average wage of 63s, the family would have been comfortably above the human needs poverty line for the year as a whole. Even with six months unemployment the family would have been well above the bare subsistence poverty line. Living for a while with an income which provided only for bare necessities would not have been so serious if resources could be rebuilt when employment was regained. This illustrates the point that those who suffered most were the families of the long-term unemployed. Contemporary investigations such as that of the Pilgrim Trust (1938) graphically exposed the deprivation, demoralisation and squalor associated with long-term unemployment. (For a discussion of the impact of unemployment on health and, in particular, on the physical condition of children see Harris 1988). This reflects a basic policy dilemma: while benefits for the short-term unemployed were often higher than necessary to avert serious need, they were not high enough to provide adequate income maintenance for the long-term unemployed.

The duration and incidence of unemployment

Unemployment rates alone can tell us little about the unemployment process. For example, an annual unemployment rate of 10 per cent could arise from ten workers in every hundred being jobless for a whole year,

Table 14.3. *Composition of the unemployed, 1928–38 (%)*

	Wholly unemployed	Temporarily stopped	Casual workers
1928	69·3	24·6	6·1
1929	72·1	21·5	6·4
1930	68·3	26·7	5·0
1931	73·9	21·8	4·3
1932	75·9	20·4	3·7
1933	78·7	17·6	3·7
1934	79·4	16·6	4·0
1935	81·0	14·9	4·1
1936	81·9	13·8	4·3
1937	82·5	13·2	4·3
1938	76·2	20·2	3·6

Source: Beveridge (1944: 68).

twenty being jobless for six months each, or sixty each with two months of unemployment. In the first case unemployment is a 'stagnant pool' in which the faces change only slowly. At the other extreme it is a 'rushing stream' with individuals flowing in and out rapidly. Which of these characterisations is correct matters both for the assessment of the costs imposed on the unemployed and for understanding the causes of their unemployment. Though it may seem odd at first sight, the inter-war labour market fits both these characterisations in some degree. We will start with the rushing stream and move on to the stagnant pool.

From 1926 the Ministry of Labour distinguished three types of unemployed on the register; the 'wholly unemployed', the 'temporarily stopped' and 'casuals'. The wholly unemployed were those with no job and who were looking for new employment. The temporarily stopped were those who had been laid off by their employers but with a definite promise of re-employment within six weeks. Casuals were those whose normal employment was for a day or a few days at a time, interspersed with occasional or frequent days of unemployment. The best-known example was that of dock labourers who were hired each morning from a crowd at the dock gates. As Table 14.3 shows, casuals were a relatively small minority of the unemployed. The temporarily stopped were a much larger minority; in fact, over the period 1928 to 1938, this category accounted for 19.2 per cent of all unemployment.

The number of temporarily stopped tended to increase at the beginning of a downturn in economic activity but then decreased as a share of all unemployment when, as in the 1930s, the decline became more permanent.

It was also concentrated in certain industries. Among men, in September 1929, over half the temporarily stopped were in mining, metals, engineering and textiles. Among women, nearly 80 per cent were in textiles and clothing. Temporary layoffs and short-time working were characteristic of these industries even before the First World War. In the inter-war period such practices were reinforced by the insurance system (Whiteside and Gillespie 1991). Because short periods of unemployment could be linked together and treated as a continuous spell for benefit purposes, workers repeatedly laid off could claim benefit for every day lost. Such alternating spells of employment and unemployment (often three days of each per week) was a method of work sharing and became known as the 'oxo' system. The 'oxo' system was so called because of the practice at the labour exchange of transcribing details from the insurance books to denote days of employment (O) and unemployment (X), in order to compute entitlement to employment benefit. How far it was perpetuated by unemployment insurance and whether unemployment as a whole would have been lower in the absence of this form of work sharing remains an open question.

The wholly unemployed accounted for the bulk of those unemployed, and were workers whose previous employment had terminated. For the most part, then, these were unemployed workers who were looking for a new vacancy. In fact, the distinction between these and the other groups is not as sharp as the statistics suggest. Among those leaving the register for employment it was estimated that some 33 per cent were returning to their previous employer. In some cases they would have been unemployed for less than six weeks, in other cases more. Doubtless there were also many who, though initially temporarily stopped, were not recalled within six weeks, and subsequently became wholly unemployed.

Some of the available vacancies were notified to the unemployed through the labour exchanges but about four times as many were filled without recourse to the exchanges. The total number of vacancies filled each month can be estimated, indicating that in the 1930s the monthly flow of the wholly unemployed into vacancies averaged 39 per cent of the stock of the wholly unemployed on the register. Though the stock of unemployment was large, so was the flow into vacancies. This means that if all the unemployed had an equal chance of finding a vacancy, that chance would be two in five of finding a job within a month.

Considering that so many of the unemployed found vacancies each month, one might be forgiven for thinking that there must have been a large stock of vacancies waiting to be filled. This was not the case. For the 1920s the average stock can be estimated by making a crude adjustment to the number of unfilled vacancies recorded each week at the labour

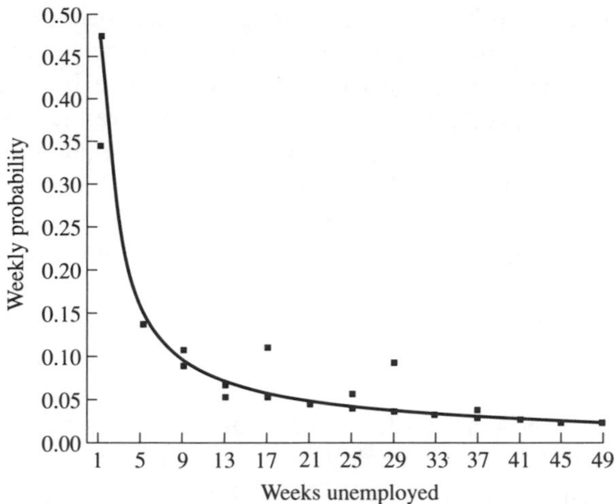

Figure 14.2 The probability of leaving unemployment, 1929

exchanges. This yields the result that there was on average one unfilled vacancy for every eight of the wholly unemployed. This ratio must have worsened in the 1930s though we do not have the data to estimate it. In the light of the depressingly low number of vacancies outstanding, the Ministry of Labour gave up reporting the information in 1929.

Why was the stock of unfilled vacancies so small compared with the monthly flow of workers into jobs? The answer can be found by comparing the weekly number of vacancies notified to the exchanges with the weekly number of vacancies filled by the exchanges. The two series move almost in lockstep. When the volume of vacancies notified rose from one week to the next, vacancies filled increased by almost the same amount. Evidently the new vacancies were taken up immediately; 95 per cent within the same week (Hatton 1985: 268). As a result the number outstanding at any moment was small. This implies that the unemployed queueing at the exchanges were eager to take up the jobs offered; they were not as choosy as some would suggest.

Who were those most fortunate in finding vacancies quickly? In 1929 the Ministry of Labour conducted a special analysis of the numbers of benefit claimants unemployed for different lengths of time. We can use the results to estimate the chance of leaving the register at different unemployment durations, as in Figure 14.2.

Since the points on the graph are approximate, the relationship is best represented by the fitted curve. The curve shows a dramatic decline in the probability of leaving unemployment in the first month on the register, followed by a gentle decline. After a year the weekly probability of leaving

Table 14.4. *The duration of unemployment, 1929–38 (wholly unemployed only)*

	Percentage of unemployed with durations of:		Estimated completed average duration of a spell (weeks)	Estimated uncompleted duration of average unemployed (weeks)
	less than three months	more than one year		
1929	43·7	7·2	—	15·4
1932	40·8	22·0	19·5	34·1
1933	38·9	28·4	17·9	43·6
1934	41·3	29·0	16·6	45·8
1935	41·6	28·5	14·4	45·6
1936	42·9	29·5	13·9	49·1
1937	46·2	28·1	14·2	48·7
1938	48·3	23·2	13·1	39·0

Source: Thomas (1988: 112).

was a mere 0.02; after a year on the register an unemployed worker was likely to go on being unemployed for a very long time.

This pattern has led some to describe the inter-war labour market as 'bifurcated' (Thomas 1988). Those who were most likely to regain employment in any week were those who had spent least time unemployed. It is as if most of those joining the unemployed queue joined it at or near the front. For those near the back the chance of re-employment became increasingly remote. With the sharp rise in layoffs in the early 1930s the chances of re-employment declined for all the unemployed. Consequently those unemployed for a few weeks less frequently escaped. As their unemployment turned from weeks into months their chances of escape declined. It was this that gave rise to what was perhaps the most sombre legacy of the depression: the host of long-term unemployed which persisted into the late 1930s.

From 1932 the Ministry of Labour regularly recorded the unemployment durations of claimants to benefit or assistance in categories of three months up to a year. These statistics form the basis of Table 14.4. The first two columns show that even in the worst years of the 1930s over half the unemployed had been on the register for less than three months. At the other extreme the proportion of long-term unemployed rose to over 20 per cent in 1932 and stayed there until 1938. Crafts (1987: 419) suggests that the available statistics for 1929 underestimate long-term unemployment. This is because, at that time, many of the unemployed who had exhausted their right to unemployment benefits would not have been counted as claimants (though they would have been in the later years). For males alone he estimates that the true proportion of long-term unemployment would have been nearly double the official figure. Taken together, this information can be used to estimate the average completed duration of the typical spell of unemployment. Thomas' estimates reproduced in column 3 of Table 14.4 show that the average length of a spell reached nearly twenty weeks in 1932 before declining to thirteen or fourteen weeks in the late 1930s.

It is important to distinguish between the duration of the typical spell of unemployment and the duration of the typical unemployed worker. Because of the rapid turnover of the short-term unemployed, most spells were short. But because of the sharply diminishing chances of re-employment illustrated in Figure 14.2 the typical unemployed worker would be undergoing a much longer spell. Following Crafts (1987), column 4 of the table shows the average uncompleted duration of those on the register. This was between ten and eleven months for most of the 1930s. Because the unemployed are observed, on average, halfway through a spell of unemployment their average completed durations would have been twice as long. Hence, on a conservative estimate, the average wholly unemployed worker in the 1930s was enduring a spell of unemployment which would last a year and nine months.

Even this figure is likely to underestimate the concentration of unemployment if repeated spells are taken into account. Thus some of those observed as unemployed at a particular date, perhaps with a relatively short duration, had experienced a previous spell of unemployment in the recent past. Of a sample of wholly unemployed applicants for benefit in 1932, the average length of the current spell of unemployment, up to two years, was 23.1 weeks but the average number of weeks spent unemployed over the preceding two years was 53.1.

Structural aspects of unemployment

One of the most prominent features of inter-war unemployment is that it fell very unevenly across different industries and regions. In the staple industries of coal, textiles, iron and steel, shipbuilding and engineering, unemployment rates were two or three times the national average over the period 1923–38. Similarly, across the nine regions distinguished by the Ministry of Labour average rates varied over the same years from close to 8 per cent in London and the south-east to around 22 per cent in the most hard-hit regions of Wales and Northern Ireland. In general, unemployment was substantially higher to the north and west, the 'outer regions', than it was to the south and east, or 'inner Britain'. (The outer regions comprise the five Ministry of Labour divisions: north-east, north-west, Scotland, Wales and Northern Ireland. Inner Britain is the remaining four: London, south-east, south-west and midlands. In 1929 the respective average unemployment percentages for the outer regions and inner Britain were 9.7 and 6.3, in 1932 they were 22.4 and 16.0.)

This has led some observers to argue that, to a large extent, the unemployment problem was a structural problem. Inter-war unemployment, they argue, should be seen more in terms of the problems of specific industries and regions than as a general macro-economic failure. The structural view also implies that policies aimed at moving displaced workers to jobs or jobs to workers would have been more appropriate for alleviating unemployment than the management of aggregate demand (Booth and Glynn 1975).

To a considerable extent, high unemployment industries and high unemployment regions were coincident. The depressed staple industries were chiefly located in the depressed northern and western regions, while the faster-growing light industries and service industries were disproportionately located in the southern and eastern regions. This raises the question of whether the imbalance should be viewed as essentially industrial or regional. A partial answer can be given by calculating the unemployment rate for each region, assuming its industrial composition was the same as the country as a whole but keeping the region's unemployment rates in each industry unchanged. Table 14.5 compares the actual insured unemployment rates for the regions in 1929, 1932 and 1936 with these hypothetical rates.

As would be expected unemployment rates in the high unemployment regions are reduced if weighted by the national industrial composition. But it is surprising how little they are reduced and how little the southern regions are increased. The reason is that, although certain industries exhibited relatively high unemployment in all regions, in each industry unemployment was higher in the outer regions than in inner Britain. Hence there was a significant regional component in the unemployment structure. However, the distinction just made could be misleading if it were interpreted as meaning that the causes of regional imbalances were inherently regional, rather than industrial. To a large extent, the effects of the decline of the great export staples spread throughout the local economies of the outer regions. Workers displaced in one industry sought employment in other industries, adding to the numbers unemployed even in the less depressed industrial sectors. Unemployment was intensified in the depressed regions by the effects on local and regional purchasing power of the decline of major industries which, in turn, affected employment in a wide range of local industries and services.

Table 14.5. *Regional unemployment rates, 1929, 1932, 1936*

Region	1929		1932		1936	
	Actual	Structure constant	Actual	Structure constant	Actual	Structure constant
London	4·7	4·7	12·6	13·5	6·4	6·7
South-east	3·3	3·3	12·0	10·8	5·0	5·6
South-west	6·0	7·7	14·8	16·9	7·1	8·9
Midlands	9·5	8·4	21·2	18·1	8·6	8·1
North-east	12·6	10·8	29·8	24·7	17·5	14·9
North-west	12·8	12·9	26·8	21.0	16·4	16·3
Scotland	10·9	10·2	25·9	23·4	15·8	15·2
Wales	18·1	12·8	37·3	26·4	29·0	20·9
N. Ireland	13·7	9·5	25·9	17·7	19·6	15·3

Note: the structure constant unemployment rates are calculated as $U_r^* = w_{ni} U_{ri}$ where w_{ni} is the labour force weight of each industry in the national average and U_{ri} is the unemployment rate for each industry in region r.
Source: Hatton (1986b: 63).

In the early 1930s the differences in regional unemployment rates clearly evident in the 1920s were increased further. The gap of 8 per cent or so between unemployment rates in the north and the south-east in 1929 became more like 16 per cent in 1932 but by 1936 it had declined almost to its former level. The same pattern can be observed in individual industries; those with the heaviest unemployment in the 1920s suffered an even greater rise in unemployment in the early 1930s but also saw a greater absolute decrease in the recovery of the later 1930s. For example, in the pig-iron industry the unemployment rate rose from 14.4 per cent in 1929 to 43.8 per cent in 1936, falling again to 16.6 per cent in 1936. By contrast in chemicals the unemployment rate at these dates was 6.5 per cent, 17.3 per cent and 9.2 per cent, a less dramatic fall but a less spectacular recovery.

This pattern illustrates the greater cyclical sensitivity of some industries than others, particularly the once great export staples. The pattern in the early 1930s can be seen as an intensification of one of the major causes of unemployment throughout the inter-war period. This was the lack of competitiveness of British exports which was further exacerbated by the shrinkage in total demand. In this respect the so-called structural problem was simply a manifestation of Britain's macro-economic problems, many of which it shared with other countries during the 1930s. To what extent, then, can we say that the economy suffered from structural unemployment when, as the evidence suggests, the causes of high unemployment in particular industries and regions and the causes of high unemployment in general were so closely linked?

The usual argument given by those who stress the problem of structural unemployment is that the decline in demand for labour in many of Britain's traditional industries and industrial regions was permanent. In order to have reached lower levels of aggregate unemployment, labour (and capital) would need to have been reallocated more swiftly to the faster growing, more modern industrial and service sectors already flourishing in the south, east and midlands. These were industries such as electrical engineering, motor vehicles, aircraft, synthetic materials, organic chemicals and a wide variety of services (the importance of services is stressed in chapter 5).

It has sometimes been argued that, during the recovery of the 1930s, these sectors began to face labour shortages even though at the peak of 1937 there were still a million and a half unemployed. A contemporary study investigated the evidence for labour shortages in the rapidly growing London engineering trades in 1936. With the exception of machine shop and tool room workers and for specific electrical work, there was no shortage of labour. Of a sample of 2,500 workers who were placed in employment by the labour exchanges, 54.8 per cent filled vacancies immediately as they arose while another 29.3 per cent filled vacancies which had been outstanding not more than four days (Allen and Thomas 1939). The more skilled the trade, the longer the delay in filling a vacancy tended to be. Yet it could hardly be argued that these lags reflected serious labour shortages. Allen and Thomas reported that, in their sample, for every 100 vacancies notified 187 workers were submitted to employers by the exchanges but only 75 placings were made. As they noted with respect to certain groups of workers, many of these vacancies were filled by direct contact between workers and employers, rather than through the exchanges (1939: 263). Given that this market was one of the tightest in the country, it seems unlikely that the economy as a whole would have reached serious constraints until a considerably higher level of activity had been reached.

Over the inter-war period as a whole, a substantial redistribution of the insured labour force took place. In 1923, inner Britain contained 46.8 per cent of the insured labour force; by 1929 this had risen to 49.1 per cent and by 1938 to 52.3 per cent. These movements closely paralleled the changes in the inner Britain's share of total employment which rose from 47.6 per cent in 1923 to 54.5 per cent in 1938, but were not large enough to reduce the differences in unemployment rates (see chapter 2 for a discussion of migration and labour mobility).

Given that employment prospects were always better in the south and east and in the faster-growing sectors, why did not even more of the unemployed in the depressed region and declining industries move? One factor is that many of the new jobs demanded different skills and working practices. Employers sought to recruit 'new' labour in the form of juveniles, females or workers previously in non-industrial occupations (Heim 1984b). This suggests that industrial experience in one of the declining staple industries was a positive disadvantage. Migrants from the depressed areas often found themselves at the back of the queue for employment elsewhere. As a colliery worker from Crook, Co. Durham, put it 'I know all the people in Crook, and if there was a job here I might get it, in London I'd have no chance' (Pilgrim Trust 1938: 78).

Another factor is that the costs of moving were significant, particularly for men with families and older workers. These and the psychological costs were likely to weigh heavily when job prospects elsewhere were, at best, uncertain. As a consequence, mobility tended to be greater among younger workers and those without families. In 1928 an industrial transference scheme was established to find vacancies for the unemployed in the depressed areas and to help with removal expenses. With the intensification of unemployment in all areas after 1929 many transferees either could not find employment or quickly lost it and returned to their place of origin. The general decline in regional migration during the depths of the depression suggests that, even though the gap between unemployment rates increased, for those at the back of the queue for employment the prospects were almost equally as bleak in all areas.

Labour demand and supply

Enough has been said to indicate that unemployment would have been lower if labour demand had been higher. This raises the important question: what determined labour demand during the inter-war period? Figure 14.3 gives a textbook picture of labour demand and supply. The labour demand curve, De, depends on the real wage defined as the average wage rate divided by the price of firms' output. Its downward slope indicates that the cheaper it is to employ labour, relative to the price of goods, the more labour firms will employ (and the more output they will produce). The labour supply curve, Sa, also depends on the real wage and depicts the size of the total labour force or 'apparent' labour supply. (Note that the demand for labour will depend on the wage rate relative to output prices while labour supply is normally thought to depend on the wage relative to the price of consumption goods. No distinction has been made in the figure between these two different prices.) The labour supply curve is drawn as upward sloping though it need not be so. Because not all those

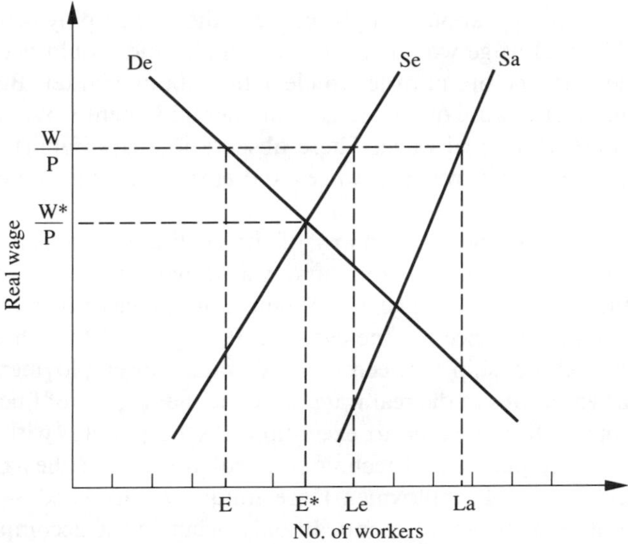

Figure 14.3 Labour demand and supply

numbered in the labour force would be actively seeking work, an 'effective' supply curve is drawn to the left of 'apparent' supply to indicate the number available for work. The way the diagram has been drawn, the prevailing real wage rate is such that there is unemployment. At real wage W/P, firms employ E workers but the number actively seeking work is Le, and the difference Le – E is involuntary unemployment.

The situation crudely depicts the inter-war labour market and it is worth noting some of its implications. First, if the real wage were to fall to W/P* there would be no involuntary unemployment.

This is the situation suggested by Benjamin and Kochin, who instead, would envisage a larger gap between the Se and Sa curves. This would reflect the large numbers who, because of the disincentive effects of unemployment benefits, were not seriously looking for jobs. If instead, the real wage were stuck at W/P leading to involuntary unemployment, it raises the question of why wages did not adjust to clear the labour market – an issue to which we return in the next section.

Second, the degree to which a given decrease in the real wage would generate more employment would depend on the slope of the labour demand curve (or its elasticity). The flatter (or more elastic) was the labour demand curve, the more a change in the real wage would increase or decrease employment. Third, the labour demand curve might also be affected by factors which caused it to shift to the right or left. If there was a leftward shift in the labour demand curve (with no change either in the real wage or in the labour supply curves) then unemployment would increase. The real wage would still be 'too high' and would need to fall even further than before in order to clear the labour market. But in this case the immediate cause of the increase in unemployment would not have been a change in the real wage. These observations are important when considering the debate over real wages and employment in the inter-war period.

During the 1920s and 1930s many of the leading economists believed that the aggregate labour demand curve was downward sloping and that reducing the real wage would generate significant increases in employment (Casson 1983a). Evidence for the early 1920s suggested that there was a clear inverse relationship between the real wage and employment. Some argued that variations in the real wage were the main cause of fluctuations in employment. Keynes was no exception. As he put it: 'with a given organisation, equipment and techniques, real wages and the volume of output (and hence of employment) are uniquely correlated so that in general an increase in employment can only occur to the accompaniment of a decline in the rate of real wages' (1936: 17). Further enquiry in the late 1930s, however, cast doubt on this as a general rule (Dunlop 1938; Keynes 1939).

More recently the debate has been reopened, particularly with regard to the 1930s. Beenstock, Capie and Griffiths have argued that 'Both the recession and the recovery were largely instigated by real wage developments which were concentrated in the manufacturing sector' (1984: 68). A graphical test of this hypothesis is offered in Figure 14.4 which shows, for 1921 to 1938, the relevant real wage and employment measures for all industries and for manufacturing alone. The figure illustrates that, for industry as a whole, while the real wage rose from 1929 to 1932 as employment plummeted, it rose equally fast in the years immediately before the depression. For manufacturing, there is some evidence of a sharper rise in the real wage in 1930–2. Only in the late 1930s is there strong evidence of an inverse relationship between the real wage and employment. This does not mean that the real wage did not influence employment. Rather, it suggests that other influences may have been important, especially at the turning points of 1929 and 1931–2.

Recent studies have attempted to identify the variables determining employment over this period using econometric techniques. The typical approach has been to include as an explanatory variable the real price of raw materials as well as the real wage, and to allow for lags in the effects of these variables on employment. In some cases, 'demand shift' variables are also included to test for the effects of the slump and recovery in goods markets on employment directly (rather than only indirectly by way of the

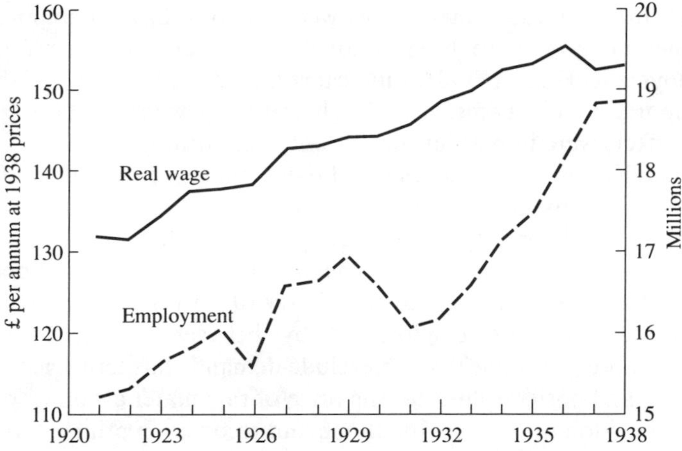

Figure 14.4a The real wage and employment: in aggregate, 1921–38

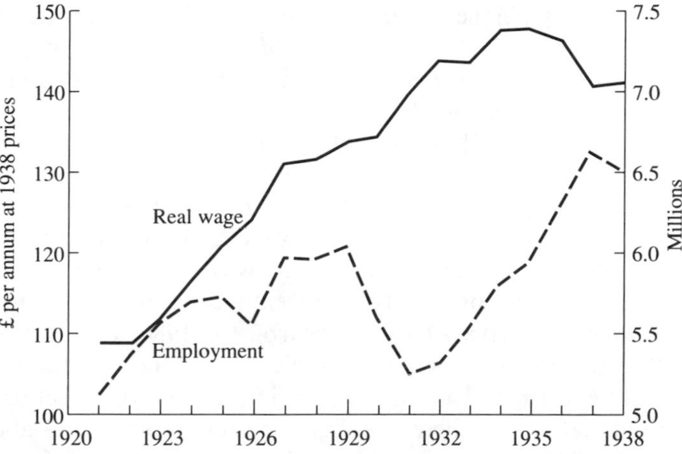

Figure 14.4b The real wage and employment: in manufacturing, 1921–38

Sources: real wage: Dimsdale (1984: 95, 97); employment: Chapman and Knight (1953).

price level and hence the real wage). In his study of annual data, Dimsdale (1984) found that demand shift variables, world trade and the UK money supply were the most important determinants of the slump and recovery in employment. The real wage did have the predicted negative effect on employment with a one year lag. Beenstock and Warburton (1986) found, however, that employment in manufacturing could be explained without the use of demand shift variables. But when analysing total employment, world trade and the money supply were found to have an important role. Further analyses have been conducted on quarterly data for insured employment. Hatton (1988a) indicates that demand shift variables were unimportant while Dimsdale, Nickell and Horsewood (1989) suggest that such effects were important though only temporary.

Though at first sight the results of these studies sometimes conflict, they are not as inconsistent as they seem. Almost all the studies find significant real wage effects on employment. They also find that the effect of a rise in the real wage is to reduce employment with a lag averaging one to two years. In the long run they indicate that a 10 per cent rise in the real wage would have reduced employment by between 2 and 10 per cent. Furthermore, the models which exclude demand shift terms generally find a strong and positive effect for the price of raw materials on employment. The depression saw a dramatic slump and recovery in primary commodity prices suggesting that this is serving as a proxy for the world depression and recovery. Finally, the studies all indicate that the rising real wage alone does not fully explain the slump in employment. There were other variables which contributed at least as much, if not more, to the decline in employment between 1929 and 1932, and which completely dominated in the recovery from 1932 to 1937.

A similar discussion has taken place about changes in the labour force (the Sa curve in Figure 14.3). Was it upward sloping? Did it shift, and if so why? Estimates indicate that there was an upward sloping relationship between the labour force and the real wage faced by workers. The sharp decline in the cost of living relative to wage rates in the early 1930s contributed perhaps one or two percentage points to the rise in the unemployment rate (Beenstock and Warburton 1986: 166; Hatton 1988a: 21) Other factors such as demographic trends and eligibility rules for unemployment benefit had small effects in the opposite direction. It must be stressed that though there was slightly faster growth in the labour force in the early 1930s, fluctuations about the trend were small. It was chiefly the forces affecting employment which were responsible for the bulge in unemployment and its subsequent decline.

Wage determination

The discussion of labour demand and supply points to the need to explain how wage rates were set during the inter-war period. Though the precise magnitudes are uncertain, it is clear that, had real wages been lower, so too would unemployment. If the real wage had drifted down a little more after the early 1920s Britain might not have entered the following decade with an already serious unemployment problem. If rising real wages had been avoided in the early 1930s perhaps the impact of the world depression would not have been so severe. The question is usually seen as one of wage stickiness. Why, given the large numbers unemployed, did not competition for jobs cause the money (and real) wage to be bid down further? In order to answer this question we need to study wage-setting behaviour.

To many contemporaries as well as to more recent observers, the process of wage determination was seen as dominated by institutional forces rather than market forces. They were impressed by the growth in trades union strength. As a proportion of the workforce, membership was double that of the 1900s. More impressive still was the change in collective bargaining from a local or district basis before the war on to a national basis. The basic wage for whole industries or occupations was now negotiated centrally between national representatives of unions and employers. This process had been hastened by the establishment of Joint Industrial Councils during the war following the recommendations of the Whitley Committee in 1917. In addition, in low-wage industries or occupations (where employers and employees were typically not well organised), the Trade Boards set up in 1909 to set minimum wages were strengthened and further extended in 1918. On one estimate, such collective agreements together covered some three-quarters of the labour force (Sells 1939: 50).

The institutional structure of wage bargaining cannot, by itself, explain why wage rates were set in the way that they were. But to some observers, change in the institutional structure was closely bound up with a change in the criteria used in setting wages. For example as early as 1927 the economist A. C. Pigou commented as follows:

> partly through state action and partly through the added strength given to work peoples organisations engaged in wage bargaining by the development of unemployment insurance, wage rates have, over a wide area, been set at a level which is too high ... and the very large percentage of unemployment during the whole of the last six years is due to this new factor in our economic life. (1927: 355)

The reference to unemployment insurance is interesting. It suggests that the prevailing level of benefits may have been used as one of the criteria in wage bargaining. If so, then unemployment benefits could have contributed to persistent unemployment but not because a significant portion of the labour force preferred benefits to wages. Rather, the link would be that trade union leaders needed to worry less about the unemployment consequences of setting too high a wage given that the unemployed at least had some guaranteed subsistence to fall back on. As a result, benefits could have caused unemployment even though those on benefits would have preferred to work at the going wage. There is some evidence of a correlation between the average real wage rate and the average un-

Figure 14.5 Wage rates and the cost of living, 1921–38
Source: Feinstein (1972: Table 140).

employment benefit rate (Matthews 1986a: 54). However, there is very little direct evidence that the level of unemployment benefit was an important criterion in wage setting generally, though it may have influenced the minimum wages set by the Trade Boards.

Undoubtedly of greater importance in the process of nominal wage setting was the price level. As Figure 14.5 illustrates there was a close correspondence between year to year movements in wage rates and the cost of living index. After 1922 these fluctuations were relatively mild, tracing out a gentle curve during the 1930s. During the First World War, many wage rates had been formally indexed to the price level but in most cases this policy was discontinued in the sharp deflation of 1920–1. Nonetheless, there is a strong impression that more account was taken of the cost of living in wage bargaining than before the war (Wright 1985).

Empirical studies have confirmed the close association between annual or quarterly changes in the cost of living and in wage rates which is apparent in Figure 14.5. In the short run, wage rates did not rise or fall by the full amount of the change in the cost of living, but in the longer run a process of 'catching up' took place. As a result, a fall in the price level, such as occurred in the early 1930s would cause the real wage (as viewed by workers) to rise at least temporarily (Broadberry 1986a). Between 1929 and 1933 the cost of living fell by 10 per cent while wage rates fell by 5 per cent. The decline in the cost of living owed much to the sharp fall in world commodity prices, particularly of food and raw materials. These fell more sharply than the prices of domestically produced manufactures and services. Consequently, the purchasing power of those lucky enough to remain in full-time employment rose by more than the real wage faced by employers. The upswing in prices in the later 1930s was more even and, given the lag in wage adjustment, the growth in real wages was attenuated.

What role, if any, did competition for jobs play during this era of high unemployment? There is a long tradition following the pioneering work of Phillips (1958) which suggests that wage increases would be moderated by high unemployment. However, the original studies based on the experience from 1861 onwards indicated that when unemployment was high wage rates declined only slowly. During the inter-war period wage rates appear to have declined by even less than would have been expected on the basis of pre-war experience (Lipsey 1960). One particular puzzle is why wage rates rose so strongly after 1933 despite such high unemployment rates.

It is possible that, in the light of the factors so far discussed, unemployment had ceased to be an effective break on wage increases. Alternatively, some observers have argued that it is important to take account of the composition of unemployment. One argument is that wage adjustment reflected the pressure of demand mainly in the labour markets in the south and east with less weight being given to the high unemployment in the north and west. This amounts to saying that because some part of unemployment was 'structural' (in the sense that it was unevenly distributed), it placed less downward pressure on wage rates than it otherwise would. There is some evidence in favour of this view (Thomas and Stoney 1972), but it is not clear why the high unemployment in the depressed regions failed to put downward pressure on wage rates.

A more compelling argument is that those workers who in the 1930s became part of the host of long-term unemployed exerted very little pressure in the aggregate wage bargain. As we have seen, for the most part, they had become permanently detached from employment. Through the atrophy of skills and motivation they had, at least in the eyes of employers, become rather poor substitutes for those who had remained in steady employment or for those newly entering the labour force. These 'outsiders' did not effectively compete with the 'insiders' for jobs. Firms would have been reluctant to cut wage rates to employ outsiders for fear of losing the more productive insiders. Neither would existing employees or their representatives in collective bargaining be willing to see their wage decrease in order to make it profitable for firms to employ more of the residue of chronically unemployed. The system of collective bargaining did little to alleviate the problem.

It has been argued that the degree of 'corporatism' (meaning the degree of centralisation and of government intervention) embodied in the institutions for determining wage rates influences the amount of wage flexibility that the labour market exhibits in response to shocks. Some economists suggest that wage flexibility is greatest at very low or very high degrees of corporatism (Calmfors and Driffil 1988). Inter-war Britain would seem to fall somewhere in the middle; this suggests a link between the institutional structure for wage negotiation discussed earlier and the process of wage adjustment.

Some evidence for this interpretation has been offered by Crafts (1989b). He found that long-term unemployment exerted weaker downward pressure on wage rates than short-term unemployment. Consequently the downward pressure on wage rates in the 1930s, when long-term unemployment was a significant share of the total, was much weaker than the overall unemployment rate would seem to imply. Given that long-term unemployment was largely concentrated in the depressed outer regions this finding can be reconciled with the notion that these regions had a relatively small impact on wage setting.

In and out of the age of mass unemployment

So far we have concentrated on the period of high unemployment between 1921 and 1938. In 1919 the unemployment rate was only about 4 per cent despite rapid demobilisation of the Armed Forces and in 1940 under the renewed impetus of war it stood at a similar level. How did the economy, and the labour market in particular, slide into mass unemployment in 1919 to 1921 and how did it climb out in 1938 to 1940? The events during these periods have received less attention than they deserve.

Between 1918 and 1922 prices and wages behaved very differently than they did later. During the First World War and immediately after, prices and wage rates increased dramatically until by 1920 they were two and a half times the 1913 level. From 1920 the process was reversed and by 1923 wage rates had dropped by over 30 per cent. These violent fluctuations in wages and prices contrast sharply with the mild fluctuations from 1923 onwards. They were associated with the world-wide post-war boom and subsequent slump as pent-up demand for investment and consumer goods subsided as well as with the stance of government policy which changed from expansion to contraction. Wage rates closely followed movements in the cost of living as had been the practice during the war. Though the formal indexing of wages to prices declined over the immediate post-war years, price changes remained the principal criterion in wage adjustments.

By 1923 average weekly wage rates relative to the cost of living were 3 per cent higher than in 1913. However, the real hourly wage faced by employers had risen by more than 10 per cent. The major reason for this divergence was the sharp decline in weekly hours of work which were reduced by an average of 13 per cent, the bulk of these reductions taking place during the first half of 1919 (Dowie 1975). Typical of the reductions in weekly hours was the engineering industry, where standard hours which were 53.0 in 1913 fell to 47.0, and the cotton industry, where the reduction was from the pre-war level of 55.5 to 48.0.

While workers' organisations negotiated to maintain the real weekly wage, employers faced a sharp rise in their real hourly labour costs. Broadberry (1986a) has argued that this reduced the competitiveness of British industry and aggravated the unemployment effects of the slump in demand. As a result, the recovery after the peak of unemployment in 1921 remained incomplete as Figure 14.1 above illustrated.

One might have expected that wage adjustment would continue gradually to bring the hourly real wage to the full employment level. However, the renewed pressure on British competitiveness and tight monetary policy associated with the return to the gold standard in 1925 cut short the recovery. This was intensified after 1929 by the world depression. Thus in addition to the fall in competitiveness resulting from the cut in working hours, there were two major demand shocks, one in 1920–1 and one in 1929–31 with a demand 'squeeze' in between. After the initial shock each subsequent contractionary impulse made recovery more difficult as the resilience of the labour market declined. By the middle 1930s the economy had settled into what seemed to be a permanently higher unemployment state. Only a strong positive stimulus could bring rapid recovery.

That stimulus came first with rearmament and then with the Second World War itself. Increasingly the unemployed were drawn back into employment as recruitment into the Armed Forces increased and as war-related industries grew. Pockets of unemployment remained in the early stages of the war and many workers still needed to be relocated and retrained. But the total of insured unemployed which had been 2 million in February 1939 fell below 1 million in April 1940 and 0.5 million a year later. The age of mass unemployment had at last been brought to an end.

15 Industry and industrial organisation in the inter-war years

James Foreman-Peck

Introduction

Industrial change in the generation before 1914 had been gradual. New technology, the emergence of new demands and new competition (usually foreign) had made their mark but did not approach the shocks to British business during the First World War and its aftermath. Distorted by the war effort and the subsequent restocking boom, British industry appeared overcommitted to the nineteenth-century export trades (Richardson 1965), especially in coal, iron and steel, cotton and shipbuilding. A rapid response was needed, but during the 1920s structural transformation was slow and fraught with labour difficulties. Such prosperity as was attained was centred in industries like railways, sheltered from foreign competition. Protection abroad and an overvalued exchange rate were the most popular excuses for the troubles at home. At the same time the large gap between the productivity of British and American industry could no longer be ignored.

To cap it off, in 1929 the world depression struck. The depression prompted the formation of an empire economic bloc, redirecting British exports and import demand towards the Commonwealth. The most important effect was to reduce the openness of the economy. Exports and re-exports by 1937 were smaller in current prices than in 1913, even though manufacturing production was higher by two-thirds. Constructing anti-competitive cartels in the home market was accordingly easier.

Manufacturing output expanded from the trough of the depression in 1932 at a remarkable pace. By 1937 activity was 70 per cent higher than five years earlier. Much more than a recovery from the depression, or even a result of substituting home production for imports, the upsurge has been interpreted as being the structural change that the 1920s failed to achieve (Richardson 1967). New industries were at last replacing the old staples. The home market assumed a greater prominence and the 'new' industries catering to it, especially motor vehicles and electric appliances, were far more prosperous than the old export sectors. The recovery of the building industry further boosted domestic demand at the expense of specialisation in international trade.

British industry modernised itself in a manner marked out by its transatlantic cousin. Companies grew larger, with more complex organisational structures and methods of control. They became more science-based, more cost-conscious, and their productivity rose, at least in manufacturing. New industries spread motor cars, washing machines and radios among the middle classes, and showed an increasing concern with marketing and advertising. Persistent unemployment encouraged a second layer of business, small businesses in the service industry, although with low productivity and short life expectation.

The state felt obliged to take a hand in industrial organisation, with varying success, by supplying telephones and buying ships, by regulating the new industries and helping to rationalise the old. British industry was no longer typically on the frontiers of technology. Modernisation and structural change were generally slow relative to America – though the First World War had increased the backlog of technical advances that British firms could take up.

The central concern here is to ask what accounted for the failure to recover nineteenth-century pre-eminence in the years between the wars. Although a number of studies have suggested that there was a pervasive 'British disease', the conclusion remains controversial. Industry might as well be seen as performing adequately under the constraints of resources and markets, at least in the 1930s: after all, output then grew more rapidly than during the heyday of the industrial revolution.

Firms and industries

Assessing and explaining British industrial performance between the world wars requires a theory of the two major institutions of industry, the firm and the market. Both are means of organising people to cooperate in producing goods and services. At the most abstract level one can view relationships within firms and markets as taking place between a principal, who initiates an action, and an agent, who carries out tasks on behalf of the principal. The principal is typically the owner of the firm, but may be the general public, as consumers or as represented by Parliament or by a regulatory body, such as the Board of Trade; an entrepreneur; or a shareholder. The agents may be managers, employees or contractors. A fundamental problem of industrial organisation is how to coordinate relations between the principal and the agent so as to secure compliance with the principal's goals. A company's shareholders, the owners, want managers to do what is best for them. The problem may be divided into three parts; information acquisition, risk-sharing, and avoidance of opportunism.

Firms and markets must acquire information about what products are demanded and what resources are available. By definition the 'entrepreneur' is said to perform the function when the information is novel. When it is a matter of routine it is merely a managerial concern. The time that managers and entrepreneurs are willing to spend on such tasks – and how well therefore they will do for the owners – depends upon their preferences for leisure, which in turn is influenced by the cultures in which their values are formed.

Risk must somehow be shared. The standard distribution of risk in a capitalist firm is between those who have a contractual right to payment – employees, suppliers and bondholders – and those who have a right to the income that remains only after such groups have been paid – the owners, or equity holders. Fluctuations in demand are borne primarily by the owners, the 'residual claimants', as economists put the matter. But the sharing of risk itself affects how eagerly the managers pursue the interests of their stockholders.

And cheating must be avoided. The theoretical way of putting it is to speak of 'divergent interests between principal and agent', giving rise to 'opportunism' or 'moral hazard'. The manager who dissipates his shareholders' capital in projects primarily intended to line his own pocket is behaving opportunistically. So is the lawyer who prolongs the case to get larger fees. 'Moral hazard' has to do with taking advantage of knowledge, the way a farmer might insure a field of corn which he knows is going to fail (supposing the insurance company does not know).

How much the firm does inside itself, and therefore how large firms are, depends upon the costs of using the alternative – namely, the market. A steel firm can buy iron ore on the market or can mine it for itself. The choice of internal or external methods depends on the costs of information acquisition, risk spreading and opportunism (together often called 'transactions costs', the cost of getting things done). The costs varied from industry to industry. In the Lancashire cotton industry the merchant with detailed knowledge of particular foreign markets coordinated through the market. In steel the tendency was for firms to integrate vertically back to the raw materials in a few massive enterprises.

Competitors could be coordinated by price-fixing agreements or by merger. Merger was the American solution, in part because price fixing was illegal under the Sherman Act of 1890. The British, subject to no such legislative constraint, more often chose price agreements (which nonetheless were unenforceable in common law), as in non-ferrous metals, chemicals, electrical cable, the later stages of iron and steel manufacture and shipping. By the late twenties perhaps one fifth of all employees worked in industries covered by such market-rigging agreements. The agreements were defended as a means of avoiding wasting resources, an argument that has recently been given some academic respectability by Telser (1987). Economists more commonly view price rigging with alarm, as a protection for inefficiency. Which view is correct will depend largely on the cost structure of individual industries.

In some sectors, price agreements were unnecessary for attaining stability. The firm known as 'Distillers' dominated whisky production, Imperial Tobacco controlled much of its industry, and J. & P. Coats monopolised sewing cotton. Mergers, though less common in Britain as a means of attaining market dominance and stability than in the United States, were responsible for most of the tendency for British production to be concentrated in the hands of fewer firms (Hannah and Kay 1977). Between 1917 and 1920 United Steel, for example, was created out of the merger of four companies, the aim being 'security', not greater efficiency (Andrews and Brunner 1951).

United Steel wrote down its capital in the aftermath of the so-called Hatry crash and the resulting reorganisation, incidentally giving rise to one of the more radical revaluations in economic history. Clarence Hatry's financial syndicate, Austin Friar Trust, bought the company and at the end of the stock exchange boom the Trust collapsed. United Steel thereby got rid of the burden of excessive debt – held by the Trust, not by the steel company. Tolliday (1987: 158) remarks that 'Hatry was arguably the best thing that ever happened to United Steel; he took its financial sins on his shoulders and, when he was crucified, left it absolved of its financial guilt.'

Competition, in other words, was perceived in the 1920s as a source of uncertainty and instability, cutting returns. On the other hand the best-known merger of the period, Imperial Chemical Industries, created out of four companies in 1926, was intended to gain economies of scale (Reader 1975). Sometimes the large companies were in fact more efficient, though also acquiring market power.

Industry coordination by monopolisation or cartels depends upon ease of industry entry and exit. It takes a long time for an entirely new firm to threaten the big established ones. Cross-entry – entry of big existing firms from other industries – is often quicker.

A monopoly, of course, may not exercise its control in the wider public interest. In his theory of the rise and decline of nations, Mancur Olson assumes it will not, and that in particular monopoly has been important in explaining the slow growth of the British economy. 'Great Britain, the major nation with the longest immunity from dictatorship, invasion and revolution has had in this century a lower rate of growth than other large developed democracies ... It suffers from an institutional sclerosis, that slows its adaptation to changing circumstances and technologies' (Olson 1982: 77–8). Olson implicitly supposes that the longer the time allowed to organise the lower will be the costs of establishing institutions that stop entry. The barriers to entry are profitable for the institutions running them, of course, but will often hamper economic development.

Elbaum and Lazonick's volume (1986) takes another view: transactions costs, they argue, explain the failure of new institutions to emerge (see ch. 4). 'Entrenched institutional structures in ... enterprise and market organisation ... constrained the transformation of Britain's productive system' (Elbaum and Lazonick 1986: 2). Once an industry like cotton textiles had grown to be composed of a large number of small specialised firms, the vested interests prevented a replacement by large, vertically integrated and professionally managed businesses. Instead the industry lost international competitiveness and declined. In the Elbaum and Lazonick view the ability of British industry therefore depended critically upon institutions inherited from the past and upon their transactions costs.

Supply of capital

The British economy already possessed a large and efficient financial sector catering to the needs of industry. That has not exempted capital suppliers from charges of aiding and abetting grievous bodily harm to inter-war British business. The Joint Stock Companies Act of 1856 and subsequent companies' legislation began early to ease the capital constraint upon the family firm or the partnership. Enterprises might borrow capital by issuing bonds and thereby expand faster than retained earnings would allow. But the more they borrowed the higher the risk, since they were incurring contractual obligations to pay interest and repay principal regardless of whether the income was in fact coming in. The position was similar to that of paying labour or suppliers, with the important proviso that the wage obligation could be shed more easily: sacking the workers in a slump. Generally only the owners were willing to bear the risk of the firm, as residual claimants to its income. But before limited liability the owners were liable for all the unsecured debts incurred by the firm's managers. Shareholders therefore were loathe to commit their money to managers whom they did not know or entirely trust.

Even with limited liability there remained in the new, large enterprises of the late nineteenth century a problem of managerial moral hazard. The manager knew the company the way a farmer knows his field, and could exploit his knowledge against the interests of the principals. How were the shareholders to avoid being cheated by management? Voluntary and then compulsory auditing of accounts offered a partial solution. The paid-up capital of joint-stock companies quadrupled between 1885 and 1905, doubling again between 1905 and 1925 ('paid-up' capital is the payment to the firm that stockholders have actually made; they may be liable for more). Firms got bigger, chiefly because company legislation allowed mergers and internal growth. Measured by paid-up capital the railways and the banks provided most of the largest enterprises, but a few manufacturing companies exceeded them. Fraud could still be practised on a vast scale, though, as the collapse of the Hatry empire revealed in 1929.

After 1929 the Companies Act required that accounts be 'true and correct', a novel idea. Many company directors had not conformed with even this minimal requirement. The practice of accumulating undisclosed reserves was widespread. Montagu Norman at the Bank of England had done so and when the pound was floated in 1931 these reserves formed the basis and origin of the Exchange Equalisation Account, devoted to reducing fluctuations in the exchange rate. Since 1926 Lord Kylsant of the Royal Mail Steam Packet Co. had been following the common practice of paying dividends from undisclosed reserves and thereby disguising the true unprofitability of the company. In 1931 Kylsant was convicted under the 1929 Act and imprisoned for using 'untrue and incorrect' accounts in a prospectus.

To raise capital on the London stock exchange a company needed to be large; perhaps £200,000 was the minimum worthwhile new issue. The provincial exchanges were prepared to take issues of one quarter of that amount. They had been a major source of long-term finance for industry before 1914. Birmingham continued to provide a buoyant market for local motor shares – from where London took its valuation – though Manchester during the twenties was the busiest provincial stock exchange. The smaller stock exchanges specialised in secondary markets for shares in enterprises where there was local knowledge: Sheffield concentrated on steels, Newcastle on shipbuilding and shipping, Cardiff on coal and Bristol on tobacco, coal, aircraft and motors (Thomas 1973).

Stock exchange booms in 1919–20 and in 1927–9 caused considerable distortions of the economy. Capital was directed into channels with no long-term possibility of profits. During the post-war boom in Cardiff ships which were fit only for the breakers' yard were often sold to an unsuspecting public. Greyhound racing track and film issues were prominent in the 1927–9 new issue boom, as were gramophone and radio companies and artificial silk issues. Evidence from the years after 1945 suggests that share prices over-react to information both optimistic and pessimistic, so that the market value of a publicly quoted firm is excessively volatile. The market volatility reduces the safe ratio of borrowing to equity for a firm compared with an environment where holders of shares have a long-term commitment to the business and do not intend to trade for immediate gain or avoidance of loss. Firms in an economy dominated by such a stock exchange may therefore pursue more risk-averse investment strategies, favouring known rather than novel technologies, compared with enterprises in economies where banks hold a great part of company shares. Whether the hypothesis explains Britain's relative industrial decline awaits systematic testing.

A second notion of failure in the financial markets is that of the 'Macmillan gap'. The Macmillan Committee Report of 1931 identified a gap in the institutions available for raising long-term capital for industry. Some requirements for funds were too small to be worth a public issue and they feared that promising developments could accordingly be stifled. Inter-war investors differed from those before 1914 in that they more strongly preferred the liquidity of negotiable securities – confidence had been shaken by the upheavals over the war period (Frost 1954). Between 1913 and 1933 the volume of quoted industrial issues expanded far more than can be explained by industrial growth. The Macmillan Committee claimed that small companies could not afford to issue quoted shares and were squeezed by the stronger demand for more liquid assets. (Possibly, too, the availability of British government securities as a result of the war also crowded out less marketable securities. Certainly it was the most radical change in life assurance companies' long-term investment portfolios between 1913 and 1933.)

The evidence for the gap is rather thin. Economic growth was not slower in the inter-war years: the new problem was sustained unemployment. Indeed, the distinctive feature of investment in the 1930s was the redirection of interest to domestic issues, in the absence of traditional overseas investment opportunities. Higher taxation and estate duty, prompting the formation of trusts, reduced the supply of risk capital. A few small merchant banks like Schroders and Charterhouse and some insurance companies such as the Prudential entered the risk capital market for the first time (Balogh 1947; Grant 1937).

Even the older banks contributed some capital. Commercial banks were now major forces in the economy and they sometimes were willing to lend to industry to protect loans whose position had become precarious. Their preference, however, was for safer loans. Barclays Bank in October 1935 lent £56 million for professional and private purposes, within which loans for land and house purchase were the single largest category. 'Productive industry' took £38 million but of that, £12 million was allocated to building. Midland Bank found its loans to Austin and Bolckow Vaughan illiquid in the 1920s and took a hand in company reorganisations. Lloyds similarly supported and influenced a change of managing directors at the Rover motor company as a result of the 1929–32 depression. Small firms in the cotton industry survived with bank assistance (Porter 1974). In general, however, British banks were reluctant to help with industrial reorganisation, which they regarded as obstructing the 'natural selection' of market forces.

Labour

Having secured the supply of capital, management needed to get labour with appropriate skills. In long-established industries such as building, shipbuilding and engineering the apprenticeship was the traditional means. In textiles and clothing it was not. And all across industry the workshop organisation of British industry was increasingly recognised as inadequate to provide a complete training. Evening classes were a traditional way of enhancing labour skills, employers often being willing to pay tuition fees. But full-time technical post-school education was thinly spread. (In Scotland it was more intensive than in England and Wales.) Of the nearly 42,000 full-time students enrolled in universities, a mere one sixth were studying pure science and one tenth technology. Higher technical institutions added another 2,100.

Whether the supply was adequate for industry's needs remains a controversial question, in which misleading international comparisons mingle with conceptual errors. There is little doubt, however, that by 1939 in Germany technical education at all levels was more widely spread among the population than it was in Britain (Barnett 1986: ch. 11). How effective the two systems were on balance is less easy to demonstrate. Qualitative changes are relatively simple to describe. University education virtually replaced apprenticeship as the qualification for elite entry to professional engineering. Employers generally expressed satisfaction with engineering education, although in the later 1930s there were complaints of overspecialisation and inflexibility (Divall 1990).

Had there been an unsatisfied demand for such skilled workers, though, salaries would have shown some tendency to rise and the otherwise considerable range of technical institutions would have increased provision. Skill differentials tended to narrow, consistent with the supply of skilled labour expanding faster than demand. Average salaries for chemists and engineers stayed well below those of general medical practitioners and solicitors at law in 1913–14 and became more so subsequently. But it is not impossible that more technical education would have encouraged industrial change and entrepreneurship. Opportunities might have been identified which were not perceived by shop-trained engineers in Britain. Locke (1984) sees German engineering education as a revolutionary force, providing an autonomous push to German industry (which French and British industry lacked), and resting on the strong research tradition of German universities, inherited by engineers.

Selection of labour was beginning to be put on a more systematic basis. Skilled workers were sometimes given a trade test. A number of firms, of which Rowntree's was the most prominent, used physiological and psychological tests to determine intelligence, reaction time and coordination of hand and eye. Yet managerial labour seems still to have been recruited as much on the basis of status as of suitability. Burmah Oil, for example, took all their potential managers from Cambridge University.

Once recruited the employees needed to be induced not to cheat, opportunistically. Labour effort could flag because the objectives of workers were not wholly similar to those of management or shareholders. Unemployment was one remedial discipline, as Lord Leverhulme noted in 1923: 'We have been combing out inefficient men ... and I am confident this has produced a state of "fear" in the minds of the remainder ... which has been the cause of improved efficiency results achieved today' (Wilson 1954: I, 292). Others, such as William Morris at his Oxford motor vehicle factory, introduced bonus schemes. The Bedaux system, which determined standard outputs without considering rates of pay or the premiums above standard, was increasingly popular with inter-war management (Lewchuk 1987; Littler 1982; Richardson 1954). In coal mining, output determined payment of 40 per cent of workers in the twenties; hewers were paid by this method, and also weavers in textiles. General labourers were on time rates but skilled and semi-skilled workers in manufacturing were typically paid also by results.

For white-collar workers, in whom a substantial amount of on the job training had been invested, management had an over-riding interest in reducing turnover. A cheaper way of inducing loyalty than paying higher salaries was the non-transferable pension. It effectively bonded workers to the firm by making them give up a substantial retirement income if they left the company, or in some other way behaved opportunistically (Hannah 1986).

In principle there was no reason why workers themselves should not have been the residual claimants of the firm's income, the owners of their firm. In practice the risk and trouble proved excessive. The fate of ICI's halfway house, a profit-sharing scheme, is instructive. With the onset of the world depression the employees' shares collapsed in value and many lost their jobs as well as their savings (Reader 1975). In 1924 producers' cooperatives manufactured output worth only £3 million, mainly in clothing. Retail cooperatives, where the consumers were owners, were much more successful, with sales of £264 million and employment of 112,000. Even so, these non-capitalist firms accounted for a small portion of output, revealing by the test of market survival that they were generally less efficient than the capitalist firm.

Top management

Family enterprise had been central to earlier British economic development and remained so in the inter-war years. Pilkingtons, the glass manufacturers established in 1826, and Courtaulds, which invented and developed the artificial fibre rayon, were two of the more prominent family enterprises. The ability of founder entrepreneurs to hand over control to the second generation had been attenuated by the carnage of the First World War. Both the motor manufacturer Herbert Austin and Hugo Hirst of GEC lost their only sons.

Family loyalties were a way of securing managerial compliance with the goals of the organisation as well as tapping sources of capital. On the other hand the family firms have been criticised for conservatism, amateurism and an unwillingness to grow for fear of a loss of family control. Fully 28 per cent of steel company directors were members of owning families in 1935–47, though down from 36 per cent in 1905–25. Chandler (1990) contends that what he calls the British style of 'personal capitalism' led to entrepreneurial failure in a wide range of industries. At the steel companies Dorman Long and Colvilles the families were said to be barriers to managerial reorganisation, but the reverse was true at Richard Thomas and United Steel.

Professionalisation of the very top management made some headway, but accounting rather than engineering skills predominated. In a sample of 436 publicly quoted companies in 1936, 6 per cent of directors were accountants, 2.5 per cent were lawyers and 4 per cent were trained in other technical specialisms (Sargent Florence 1947). These percentages are confirmed by steel management: accountancy was more apparent than technical and production engineering. University graduates were not widely employed as managers in Britain by comparison with other advanced economies.

In the years after the Second World War even management in companies with monopoly power were sometimes represented as being constrained by the capital market from pursuing their own rather than shareholders' interests. Between the world wars the contested takeover remained virtually unknown, probably because of the inadequate information publicly available about firms and because of the narrow dispersion of share-

Table 15.1 *Professional salaries, 1913–37* (£)

	1913–14	1922–4	1935–7
Chemists	314	556	512
Engineers	292	468	na
General medical practitioners	395	756	1,094
Solicitors	568	1,096	1,238

Source: Routh (1980: 63).

holdings in smaller companies. In larger enterprises the sheer size was a barrier for a raider, even if shares were widely held. Thus seven very large firms in 1926 (Imperial Tobacco, Courtaulds, Anglo-Persian Oil, Brunner-Mond, Vickers, Dunlop Rubber and Cunard Steamship) with paid-up capital of £119.6 million, had 385,500 shareholders, and 85 per cent of the holdings were of £500 or less. Even so a shareholder revolt against a lack of dividends shook top management at Rover.

The internal structures of some large firms shifted from a functional organisation towards a multi-divisional form ('M-form') in order to ensure adequate communication took place between those who most needed it. GEC had loosely followed such an approach before the First World War. Managers were given a free hand to develop new products virtually independently of the rest of the company. During the inter-war years the scope for managerial control was extended by the multi-divisional firm, of which ICI was the British exemplar. Tabulating machinery provided rapid accounting information about production; and long-distance telephone connections allowed branches to maintain close contact with head offices, even in other countries (a telephone link with the US opened in 1927). Inter-war management was prone, however, to underestimating the problems of control. Five of the nine largest mergers in the inter-war years failed fairly quickly, and those that survived were not immune from loss of control (Hannah 1974a: 268). ICI's development at Billingham was almost a disaster.

The world depression was a major stimulus to divisionalisation. STC, the telecommunications manufacturer, then employing 5,500, found its profits virtually eliminated in 1931 and negative the following year. The company was therefore reorganised to cope with a smaller volume of business, with provision for later expansion. Three plants were reduced to two and the products were broken up into seven groups, each with an executive head, which were then divided between the two factories. The product executive, with direct access to the managing director, was to control the selling, engineering, manufacturing, inspecting and installation of each product. At each factory, groups were formed to control common functions such as production planning and purchasing. By 1935 STC claimed better coordination, customer care and responsibility. Some 600 employees were lost in 1934 and one quarter of factory space, yet output was maintained and profits rose.

The holding company ('H-form') continued to be popular with British industrialists, but found many critics outside their ranks. Like a cartel under common management, the holding company bore a passing resemblance to the M-form firm in apparently uniting a number of related activities. Typically, however, there was no integration of the activities beyond market-rigging arrangements. In electricity supply the companies belonging to H-form firms were accused of paying an excessive price for generating plant within the organisation. Regulated profits therefore remained low but unregulated profits were boosted by exploiting monopoly power in electricity supply.

For Chandler (1990) the British culture which favoured 'gentlemen' over 'players' grew the bacteria that transmitted the British disease. The symptom was the weakness in business organisation, which in turn, Chandler argues, stemmed from the lack of professional management. The absence of managerial hierarchies was a handicap especially in capital-intensive, technologically advanced, high-throughput industries with product-specific distribution networks: motor vehicles and chemicals, for example. British industry therefore lost international competitiveness in these sectors. Chandler concedes that Britain's smaller, slower-growing national market accounts for backwardness relative to America in certain sectors with economies of scale and of learning, such as motor vehicles, sewing machines and typewriters. But he asserts that British entrepreneurs missed opportunities in electrical equipment, light machinery, metals and chemicals.

Something is amiss with Chandler's argument. If the absence of managerial hierarchies and multi-divisional organisation accounts for Britain's relative backwardness, no major US firm should have risen to prominence in a high throughput sector without a professional management structure. Yet in 1920 Henry Ford's company, still very much his personal empire, dominated the world motor industry with little in the way of managerial hierarchy or multi-divisional organisation. If William Morris had had Henry Ford's home market he may well have headed a firm of similar size. The problem Britain faced in the industries of the 'second industrial revolution' was that she generally lacked rapidly growing mass markets for the products. When the markets were available, as in the urban markets for processed foods such as biscuits, British companies did grow large enough to require professional managers to a much greater extent than elsewhere. Such firms were also internationally competitive. The management structure, in short, may have been a result rather than a cause.

British industry was not inert when it came to political opportunities. National industrial organisations were not merely distributional coalitions in Olson's sense, since they embraced all producers. Founded in 1916 the Federation of British Industries (FBI) attained a membership of 2,480 firms and 157 associations by April 1931, covering employment of perhaps 4 or 5 million. It was not concerned with wages and employment conditions but with political lobbying and supplying specialist information about domestic and foreign markets. The FBI successfully proposed a system of tariffs in 1931 and argued for a reduction in the taxes paid by industry. The National Confederation of Employers' Organisations was formed in 1919 specifically to coordinate employers' organisations dealing with labour matters. It claimed to cover a company employment of 7 million in the early 1930s. The Confederation avoided publicity but was influential in shaping policies on rationalisation, unemployment benefit and public expenditure. Both organisations were concerned not to rock the boat for Conservative and National governments lest they allow in Labour. Only when a Labour government was in power did the FBI and the Confederation cast aside their inhibitions.

Research and development and technical progress

In the development of new technologies British companies had traditionally been restrained. A number of firms such as Burroughs Wellcome, United Alkali and Cadbury had established research and development departments before 1914, but in general research and development was modest, both in sectors such as pharmaceuticals where Britain had been overtaken by other countries and in sectors like telegraphy where she still led. Telcon, which had manufactured most of the world's submarine telegraph cable, only began recruiting qualified chemists and physicists after 1918.

The war focussed business and official minds on British backwardness in advanced technology. Because of the close relation to explosives technology the British deficiency in dyestuffs was regarded with particular concern and led the government to form British Dyestuffs Co., which was in 1926 merged into ICI. In December 1916 the Department of Scientific and Industrial Research was established with the aim among others of encouraging industries to organise their own collective research associations. GEC's research department was formed after the war to avoid continued dependence on Germany for certain technologies, and to exploit the confiscated German Osram lamp works. Tootal's and Courtaulds' laboratories date from 1918. The trend towards more formal research and development was encouraged by the difficulty of combining large-scale production with experimentation on the shop floor. A generation of inventor-entrepreneurs was dying off and their research abilities had to be replaced within now larger firms.

By 1928 some twenty-six industry associations had been founded, but even when combined with other corporate and official research the effort was puny by American standards. In part this was because the US population was three times the size of the UK's, and in part because the US national product per head was perhaps double: a difference in total of six times. The smaller size of firms in the UK probably played a major role as well. And advertising was tax deductible, while research and development was not.

By 1930, 422 firms in Britain spent £1.7 million on research and development. In that year, such expenditure totalled 0.15 per cent to 0.29 per cent of national income, compared with 0.50 per cent in the United States. Formal research and development was concentrated in the electrical and chemical industries, with a few firms – STC, ICI, GEC, Metropolitan-Vickers, and British Thomson-Houston – making most of the effort. The food industry also spent considerable sums (as for example on chocolate with a long shelf life) and in this respect the British industrial ranking differs from that of the United States. The outlays may account for the relative success of British food multinationals abroad and the high propensity to patent.

During the 1930s expenditure on research and development rose substantially in real terms. Some 566 firms spent £5.4 million in 1938, over three times the amount in 1930, although how effective it was remains a matter of conjecture. On occasion research and development could be intended merely to extract concessions in bargaining with other firms, but even such cases may have been socially beneficial (Balfour Committee 1928: I, 318–19; Mowery 1986; Sanderson 1972a; Edgerton 1987).

Profit-oriented research and development was intended to generate ideas that would raise productivity or boost revenue with new or better products. Most innovations take a considerable time to spread, and so technical progress between the wars was largely based upon the diffusion of techniques and products invented before 1914. Bakelite, the most important plastic of the inter-war years, appearing in radio sets and kitchen appliances, was first manufactured in 1910. Courtaulds' dominance of synthetic fibres with rayon was based upon an invention of 1892.

The internal combustion engine, which transformed inter-war transport and contributed to the problems faced by the railways, was already well established before the outbreak of the First World War, and was invented decades earlier. The uses of electricity in the home and on the job were well known before the war. Vacuum cleaners were invented (in the US) between 1901 and 1907, but only in the 1930s were they being manufactured and sold in large numbers in Britain (Corley 1966: 29–35).

Productivity growth therefore depended on the pace at which new techniques spread and on the improvement of the techniques as experience of using them accumulated. Between 1900 and 1938 almost 500 patents for rotary coal cutters were taken out. Over the years between 1913 and 1937, in some regions output per cutter more than doubled (doubling in twenty-six years implies an annual average growth rate of nearly 3 per cent). By 1937 machine cut coal predominated, except in Durham and South Wales. A constraint on adoption of machine cutting was the average seam width: seams were narrow in South Wales (though not in Durham). The coal industry has been criticised for a slow pace of mechanisation, but the machine cutter in coal spread more quickly than did the tractor among American farmers between 1921 and 1957: by some standards the British response was good.

In an expanding industry new techniques should spread more quickly than in a contracting industry, for techniques are embodied in capital and more rapid expansion of capital gives more scope for 'embodying' the new techniques. But the new techniques have to be profitable. One method of appraising the rate of spread of an innovation is to calculate the costs and revenues from micro-data, an approach much used to discuss Victorian economic failure and followed, for example, in evaluating the slow adoption of the motor-ship by British shippers compared with the international pattern in the 1920s. The calculation shows that it would have been more profitable to adopt oil-powered rather than coal-powered ships and that ship owners lost out because of their conservatism (Trace and Henning 1975).

Composition and growth of industrial output

What was the net effect of the industrial application of these factors of production and technology? By 1930 food, drink and tobacco contributed more to national output than mining and quarrying; mechanical and electrical engineering together with motor vehicles were jointly far more important than textiles; paper, printing and stationery accounted for more output than iron and steel; the net output of chemicals was nearly five times that of shipbuilding; public utilities were almost twice the size of

Table 15.2. *Shares of value added in national income, 1930*

Iron and steel	6.1
Mechanical engineering	6.0
Electrical engineering	3.5
Shipbuilding	1.0
Motors and cycles	4.0
Aircraft	0.5
Carriages and wagons	0.3
Non-ferrous metals	1.6
Textiles	9.8
Leather	0.7
Clothing	5.2
Food, drink, tobacco	12.4
Chemicals	4.8
Paper, print, stationery	6.9
Timber	2.1
Clay, building materials	3.0
Miscellaneous factory	2.9
Building and contracting	6.2
Mines and quarries	10.3
Public utilities	11.4
Government departments	1.3

Source: UK *Census of Production*, 1930.

building. The pre-war dominance of the economy by the staple trades had been broken, whether or not the new industries were responsible for the relatively rapid inter-war economic growth (Johnman 1986). No longer was the economy dominated by the old staple trades, as Table 15.2 shows.

The sectoral distribution of the largest firms confirms the redistribution of industrial power since Victorian times. Measured by employment, Unilever topped the manufacturing list in 1935 followed by Guest Keen & Nettlefold, ICI and Vickers. One third of gross capital formation took place in five major growth industries – motor vehicles, chemicals, electricals, rayon and paper. Rapidly growing firms could in any case straddle a number of industries. In 1913 Distillers was only the forty-second largest manufacturing company, concentrating on products based on fermentation, mainly whisky. By diversifying into pharmaceuticals, building materials, antifreeze and synthetic resins, the company grew rapidly, becoming the sixth largest manufacturing company by 1930 (Weir 1989).

Growth of output per head, so far as it can be measured, was respectable across all the census trades. Even the declining industries like cotton spinning, iron and steel (melting rolling and steel sheets) and coal mining increased labour productivity by more than a quarter over the period (an average growth rate of more than 2 per cent a year; Salter 1969). While labour productivity in rubber, cutlery and electricity at least doubled (6.5 per cent per year), in brewing, tin-plate and paint and varnish it stagnated. In Salter's data set the industries with larger output increases showed a strong tendency for higher improvements in labour productivity, greater price reductions and cuts in unit wage costs. Such industries were likely to be 'new' only in the sense of providing new products or absorbing new processes, either of which could appear in a long-established industry. Coal-cutting machines enhanced productivity in the coal industry. In electrical engineering the growth of labour productivity apparently only averaged 0.7 per cent per year and in the drink sector labour productivity actually declined, at a rate of 0.2 per cent per year. Vehicles managed 3.3 per cent (Dowie 1975). The level of aggregation of industries (as well as the accuracy of their output indices) is crucial to such figures (von Tunzelmann 1982: 19). How much productivity growth is attributed to structural change and how much to the growth of an industry depends on the fineness of the disaggregation.

Relative structural change is less subject to this difficulty and therefore the finding that the pace was slower 1924–37 than 1913–24, 1937–51 or 1951–73 is of some significance for assessing the performance of the economy (Matthews *et al.* 1982: 255–7). It should be noted, however, that two of the periods span world wars, which, of course, had large effects on industrial structure. The comparison is therefore biassed against showing the inter-war period as years of rapid structural transformation. But the plight of the old export staple industries throughout these years is evidence that change was not fast enough; it raises the question of what was holding change back.

Industrial structure

During the nineteenth century British industry supplying world markets developed an extensive division of labour. It took the form of vertical specialisation of firms, of delegation of on-the-job training to the workforce through the apprenticeship system, of delegation of the pace of work to the labour force through the setting of piece rates and of union organisation and therefore wage bargaining by craft and by location rather than by industry or by firm. Decision-making units were small because of the extensive use of sub-contracting. Regionalisation and a slow pace of technological change kept transactions costs low and reduced the need for vertical integration or closer managerial control. The question is whether, as the possibilities for automation expanded, such an atomised arrangement failed to adjust, blocking reductions in cost.

That is Lazonick's (1986) claim for the cotton industry. Vertical specialisation meant the spinning mill had a short-run incentive to produce inferior quality yarn and pass the costs of the breakage on to the weaving mill. A weaving mill thinking of automating would be deterred from the investment, because the traditional mule was more adaptable to lower grades of cotton and wider ranges than the more easily automated ring. Weavers and spinners should have found vertical integration profitable under such circumstances, but they generally did not choose to try.

During the inter-war years attempts to raise the number of looms per operative to eight led to industrial conflict and a legalised uniform list, which fixed earnings and discouraged a better arrangement. By 1934 British yarn production had fallen by 40 per cent and cloth production by 55 per cent below 1912 levels. Like Chandler, Lazonick condemns owner-managers as ill-suited for the necessary structural change. Workers won the right to coordinate production activities and British cotton employers lost the incentive to develop modern managerial skills (Lazonick 1986: 45), a claim which Lewchuk (1987) makes also about the motor industry, which was far more successful.

But decentralised structures were not always inappropriate. In shipbuilding they continued to work quite well in the inter-war years, and in motor vehicles the unions had little control of the shop floor. The fragmented structure of shipbuilding only became redundant when factory production was possible, in the 1940s and 1950s. During the 1930s motor vehicle output overtook that of the French industry to become second only to the United States in the world league. There too the 'British system', if such a thing existed, had not yet become redundant. The large role of labour problems in cotton and coal is more consistent with Olson's theory of institutional sclerosis than to a theory of outmoded industrial organisation.

Industrial and competition policy

Public opinion traditionally favoured a large number of small firms, for consumers and economists worried about exploitation by private profit-seeking monopoly in the absence of competitive markets. However, neither the law courts nor the government were convinced of the virtues of competition. The contrast with the US may have emerged because foreign competition was more pervasive in the UK, and fear of monopoly therefore less strong. Germany had long adopted an approach even less favourable to competition, making restrictive practices enforceable at law. Of greater official concern in inter-war Britain was unemployment and overcapacity in industry, neither of which competition appeared capable of eliminating over an acceptable time scale.

An initial post-war interest in monopoly power was reflected in the appointment of the 1919 Committee on Trusts, but the onset of recession quickly altered concerns. Trade associations distributing information and monitoring governmental control had grown during the First World War, amounting to about 500 by 1919. These could easily become means of restraining competition after the war. In this they were supported by a number of pre-war legal decisions, and one of 1925. In *Sorrel* v. *Smith* restrictive practices were judged legal if they were intended to forward the trade and no other wrong was committed. No wider public interest was acknowledged. Cartels and related organisations therefore had a free hand. In 1926 the Tobacco Trade Advisory Committee outlawed retail price cutting by operating a stop list of offending retailers (Alford 1973: 344) and the motor industry did the same. Competition nonetheless could still break out, as in the tobacco coupon war of 1930–3. International trusts also continued to restrict competition. When in 1921 Metrovic found its prices for converting electric locomotives were one quarter higher than those of German industry, negotiations were quickly initiated with the Germans to divide up world markets so as to protect Metrovic's interests (Davenport-Hines 1984: 200). Having resisted for many years, Pilkingtons joined the International Plate Glass Convention in 1929 (Barker 1976).

The formation of British cartels does not support Olson's theory of sclerosis. It was more the unintended consequence of the First World War, which led to a proliferation under government sponsorship of trade bodies that could be adapted to restrictive practices. Professions, too, continued to raise entry barriers in these years. When dentists instituted entry qualifications in 1921, their incomes did not rise, according to Carr-Saunders and Wilson (1933: 462–6). Carr-Saunders and Wilson concluded, without a great deal of statistical support, that although some professions were well paid, there was no reason to suppose that their high pay was a consequence of monopolistic privileges. Later the effects of professional monopoly (the oldest being barristers) became clearer.

State ownership, local or national, was an alternative to an active policy against monopoly. The postal service and telecommunications were owned and operated by central government and local authorities owned and operated a considerable portion of the water, gas and electricity industries and almost all tramways. With the exception of the postal service, state ownership could be and was initially represented as a form of regulation, replacing or competing with badly performing private ownership. State ownership was not subject to the same survival test as cooperatives or most private capitalist enterprise, for typically the nationalised sectors were perpetual monopolies. In the electricity supply industry, where both privately owned and municipally owned generating stations persisted, regulated by the Central Electricity Board and the Electricity Commissioners, the two types of station were about equal in efficiency in 1937. Nor were differences much apparent between enterprises with state and private ownership in the gas industry (Foreman-Peck and Waterson 1985; Millward and Ward 1987). These forms of state ownership were on efficiency grounds, then, successful responses to private monopoly, at least for the time being.

The biggest change of industrial policy introduced during the inter-war years, breaking the tradition of almost a century, was tariff protection. With the exception of one year the motor industry during the 1920s had been protected by a $33\frac{1}{3}$ per cent duty. As an infant industry with scale and learning economies, a protected motor vehicles sector, it could be argued, benefited the economy as a whole. But general protection in 1931/2 was a different matter entirely. It may have been unnecessary besides, in view of the abandonment in 1931 of the fixed exchange rate. The judgement depends upon how the post-1931 exchange rate was determined. If it was pushed too high the domestic industries would suffer. And in fact capital fleeing to Britain from the disorders of the Continent could well have buoyed up the pound, in which case tariff protection may have been justified even for established industries. Under pressure from Commonwealth interests at the 1932 Ottawa Conference Britain conceded general tariff preference in favour of Commonwealth imports. She had been the beneficiary of unilateral Commonwealth preference, most notably in Canada, for many years, and the rising protectionism of the 1930s gave the new concession greater significance.

Industrial policy included attempts at restructuring that were pursued with varying success. Under the 1921 Railway Act about sixty companies were merged into four (Great Western, Southern, London & North Eastern and London, Midland & Scottish). Crosshauling was reduced, and therefore so were operating costs, as experience of unified operation during the war had suggested (the results in productivity, however, were not impressive). Through the Securities Management Trust/Bankers Industrial Development the Bank of England and the commercial banks developed rationalisation especially to prevent the Labour government of 1929–31 assuming that role instead. They devised schemes to re-equip and perhaps merge companies in overcapacity industries. One of their creations, the Lancashire Cotton Corporation, absorbed almost one hundred firms, but within two years showed difficulties in managing the sprawling new entity. A good deal of Bank effort went into steel reorganisation, too. The industry was promised a tariff protection on condition it reorganised. In the end the state sponsored a cartel over which it had little control. The National Shipbuilders' Security scheme, similarly, closed down yards and gave rise to the enraged account by Ellen Wilkinson of Jarrow's plight, *The Town That Was Murdered*.

Coal presented even more complex problems, with the miners pressing for nationalisation after the war and resisting strong downwards pressure on wages from foreign competition. The problems of industrial relations culminated in the General Strike of 1926; the miners remained out after other workers had gone back. The Coal Mines Act of 1930 was intended to introduce a compulsory industry-wide cartel (Kirby 1978; Supple 1988). It would restrict output by assigning production quotas, raise coal prices, and permit a reduction in the working day without wage cuts. The Act foundered on the hostility of the mine owners and there was opposition from the Miners' Federation. From 1937 to 1938 the cartel probably did succeed; amalgamations increased as well (Fine 1990). In 1938 the government nationalised coal royalties, that is, the ownership of the seams. The owners seemed to have impeded rationalisation and mechanisation.

Industrial policy towards the newer industries was more effective. Electricity supply was a crucial element in the modernisation of inter-war industry and households, yet at the end of the First World War Britain lagged well behind Germany and the United States in the electrification. The problem was that (thanks to legislation in the 1880s conferring powers on local authorities to buy up electricity suppliers and to generate by themselves) the industry was fragmented into a large number of excessively small suppliers, each jealously guarding its territory. After a false start with the 1919 Act, the 1926 Act established the Central Electricity Board, empowered to build a national electricity distribution grid and to negotiate contracts with suppliers of electricity to this grid (Hannah 1979; Political and Economic Planning 1935). Built during the world depression, the grid virtually closed the industry's productivity gap with the Americans by 1937, massively increased electricity output and greatly reduced costs. Reorganisation of distribution was less successful, and continued as a source of concern.

In radio broadcasting an Act of 1922 established the British Broadcasting Corporation, like the CEB a non-profit state-sponsored monopoly but not a nationalised industry. The pressure for monopoly came from the Post Office, not as a technological necessity (Coase 1950). But listeners mainly liked what they got from the BBC. Had the service been poor the extraordinary growth in radio sets licensed, from 3 million in 1929 to 6 million in 1933 and 9 million in 1939, would not have taken place (Sturmey 1958).

Military security played a role in policy towards air travel. Subsidised

Table 15.3. *Ratios of total productivity, US as a ratio to GB in three natural monopolies, 1927 and 1937*

	Electricity (a)	Electricity (b)	Railways	Telecommunications
1927	1.98	1.43	2.80	3.37
1937	1.50	1.18	3.57	3.20

Note: (a) includes and (b) excludes US hydro-generated electricity output.
Source: calculated from US *Census of Production* and *Statistical Abstract*; GB *Reports of the Electricity Commissioners*; Aldcroft (1968a); Ministry of Labour *Gazette*.

French competition on the London–Paris route immediately after the war almost eliminated the nascent British industry. To keep a British capability the government subsidised civil aviation throughout most of the inter-war years. State policy towards aircraft manufacturing was highly interventionist. Like other governments, the British government was the big buyer. The Air Ministry maintained a ring of approved firms in order to keep design teams in existence and to stimulate technical progress through competition. The success of the policy may be judged by Britain's success as an exporter of aircraft, until the mid-1930s the largest in the world (Edgerton 1991).

The rearmament programme and the 'shadow factories' of the later 1930s were important; and the government maintained an interest in specific sectors with military potential. Marconi Co., UK, owed to the demands of naval communications its rapid development in the face of the Post Office monopoly before the First World War. The same technology soon was used for finding enemy ships broadcasting from their own radios. During the 1920s Marconi developed shortwave beam (microwave) radio for telephonic communication with the other side of the world. Marconi merged with the cable companies to eliminate competition between the two international communications media (Baker 1970). As the depression of the early 1930s deepened the dominant cable interests slashed the radio research department, dissipating the knowledge which could have maintained a British technological lead. Only rearmament and war reversed the cuts.

Rearmament began seriously with the 'Statement Relating to Defence' of March 1935. Thereafter income tax rates were steadily raised to generate the revenue to cover rapidly growing defence outlays. By mid-1939 complaints of skilled labour shortages were being heard in some areas. The full-employment impact of rearmament seems to have been massive, rising from 444,000 extra jobs in 1935 to 1.48 million in 1938 (Thomas 1983). Thomas calculated that four-fifths of the increase in employment between 1935 and 1938 could be explained by the rearmament drive.

The state as customer influenced industrial structure in the market for civilian goods as well. The spread of motor transport expanded the need for an improved (state) road network. Road building therefore became the archetypal 'public work' to reduce unemployment. But someone had eventually to pay for the construction. The traditional method was through a road licence required of all motor vehicle owners. During the inter-war years the tax was graduated according to the horsepower of the car and therefore discriminated against large vehicles. In practice the tax provided protection for the British motor industry against American car imports, as was demonstrated by the influx of North American imports in 1935 when the rate of tax was reduced. Since the industry produced under conditions of increasing returns the tax-induced expansion of demand for British motor vehicles tended to reduce the unit costs of production of domestic vehicles and to boost the size of the industry.

Comparative industrial productivity

Structural change and policies towards industry should be reflected in productivity performance. Labour productivity in British manufacturing in 1935 was similar to that of Germany (Broadberry and Fremdling 1990). Germany performed better in heavy industries, chemicals, engineering metals; British productivity was higher in food, drink and tobacco.

Productivity was uniformly far behind the United States (Rostas 1948a). In railways and telecommunications the productivity gap between Britain and the United States was already large by the 1870s. For at least forty years before the First World War American railway productivity growth had averaged 2 per cent a year compared with Britain's 1 per cent. But that only accounts for a 50 per cent differential, not the 180 per cent calculated for 1927. Unless an enormous American advantage had suddenly appeared during the First World War the implication must be that there was already a large gap in the 1870s. In telegraphy that was undoubtedly the case. One of the most informed of British observers in that decade noted that New York telegraph operators processed twice as many messages as their London counterparts. Only in finance did British labour productivity match that of the Americans. Broadberry and Crafts (1990b, 1990d) suggest that the tendency to collude, encouraged by the lack of an active competition policy, and to avoid shedding labour in the face of heavy unemployment may be a good part of the explanation.

In fact a productivity comparison of 'natural monopolies' in Britain and in the United States allows us to rule out different degrees of product market competition and collusion in the two countries as explanations. Railways, for example, were big employers in both countries. Railway employment in Britain was 683,000 in 1927 (compared with, say, electricity generation, at 63,000). Labour productivity in British railways fell sharply relative to American productivity and must have adversely affected the performance of the whole economy. The evidence is consistent with the view that British workers in the 1930s were crowded into the service sector (Matthews *et al.* 1982; Foreman-Peck 1985). Since both Britain and America suffered from widespread unemployment it is not obvious why there should have been differential effects.

The calculations are imprecise but the overall picture seems clear. In telecommunications the productivity of labour only slightly improved relative to the US, despite a radical increase in capital enhancing total productivity. In view of the margin of error in the calculation it is possible the British state industry merely held its own against the American. The British telephones did better: they were saddled with a large and declining telegraph sector.

In railways the capital intensity relative to the US remained unchanged but employment increased. Only in British electricity generation was capital used more economically relative to the US, narrowing the gap in total productivity. The case of catching up in electricity generation suggests that scale economies (and natural resource abundance when hydro-electricity is taken into account) played a large part in the British lag behind American productivity. The national grid allowed concentration of generation into a small number of large, efficient stations.

In the tightly regulated electricity industry, then, state-sponsored reorganisation narrowed the productivity gap between the two countries over the period 1927–37; in the wholly state-owned telecommunications industry the gap perhaps slightly closed. But in railways, privately owned, the British productivity lag increased. Overall there seems to have been a tendency to absorb or maintain excess labour in comparison with the United States for reasons which must be cultural, ideological or political.

Services as a whole employed 45 per cent of the British labour force by the First World War, when the sector accounted for 50 per cent of output (see ch. 5). Both labour and total factor productivity growth in services were negative between 1924 and 1937. In some respects the decline is surprising. Improvements in the efficiency of building societies played a major role in financing the building boom of the 1930s; the low interest rates of the period can at the most account for only half the increase in lending (Broadberry 1987; Humphries 1987). Retailing has been identified as the sector into which labour was crowded by deficient demand – yet this was the time of the multiple and the chain store, which increased turnover per employee relative to the corner shop. Hire purchase – a financial service – selling brought consumer durables almost within reach of a mass public. In motor car sales during the 1920s the proportion sold on hire purchase was considerably higher than in the United States and three-quarters of the 400,000 vacuum cleaners sold in 1939 were financed by hire purchase.

In a world economy not too distorted by trade restrictions, industries exporting most are likely to be those in which the economy is relatively more productive. Crafts and Thomas (1986) found that those sectors in British manufacturing used less than average human capital, holding constant physical capital and unskilled labour. United States' exports showed the opposite association. Inclusion of the major export industries of banking, insurance and foreign trade services might affect the British results, but there is other evidence that Britain was competitively disadvantaged in the newer science-based industries. These were the sectors in Britain where subsidiaries of foreign multinationals flourished. In electrical engineering and motors American subsidiaries predominated, although they tended to acquire autonomy in the inter-war years and to 'go native'. Total employment in US multinationals in Britain in 1932 was small, perhaps not much over 66,000, and British direct investment abroad was particularly strong in food, chemicals and electrical engineering (Jones 1988; Nicholas 1991). The presence of chemicals and electrical engineering in the list casts doubt, however, on the thesis of a general British weakness in science-based industry (see Edgerton 1991).

The regional problem

Productivity differences, together with industrial structure, created the regional problem. The old export trades were disproportionately located in 'Outer Britain', Lancashire, the West Riding, the north, Wales, Scotland and Northern Ireland in particular. These areas therefore bore more than their share of the adjustment problems of the inter-war years. Assuming, as did Keynes, that the pound was overvalued by 10 per cent in the 1920s, 3.2 per cent of the jobs in South Wales disappeared through lost exports and 1.9 per cent of the labour force on the Tees and the Clyde was also out of work for the same reason (Jones 1985b). Regions less committed to world markets suffered less attrition.

Between 1924 and 1935 the relative importance of Greater London and Lancashire was reversed. Lancashire produced more than Greater London in 1924 but by the second date Greater London accounted for almost one quarter of national (census trades) output. The industrial structures of

Table 15.4. *Regional labour productivity in industry, 1924 and 1935*

	Regional share of total net output (%)		Net output per employee (£)	
	1924	1935	1924	1935
Greater London	14.50	20.08	262	271
Lancashire	19.50	16.88	204	202
West Riding	11.73	10.94	203	200
The north	6.25	4.91	186	190
Warwick	10.51	12.20	211	221
Rest of England	18.49	19.77	212	227
South Wales	5.21	3.38	200	207
Rest of Wales	0.98	0.75	201	189
West central Scotland	5.32	4.73	205	214
Rest of Scotland	5.35	4.45	208	213
N. Ireland	2.15	1.92	153	143
		Average	£212	£222

Source: UK *Census of Production*, 1930, 1935.

South Wales and some other regions of outer Britain were insufficiently diversified to maintain their shares in the new conditions. The closure of Palmer's the shipbuilders in Jarrow under the National Shipbuilders' scheme pushed Jarrow's unemployment in September 1935 to 72.9 per cent (Wilkinson 1939).

Variation between regions in industrial productivity was enormous. Even excluding Northern Ireland and Greater London, net output per employee ranged from £190 in Northumberland and Durham ('The north' in Table 15.4) to £270 in the west midlands (included in 'Rest of England' in Table 15.4). More prosperous regions specialised in high productivity industries but they also tended to be more productive in all tradable goods industries. Mechanical engineering was comparatively footloose and diverse but building was unable to specialise between regions to anything like the same extent. Building therefore reflected regional factors. There is a positive correlation between total industry and mechanical engineering productivity across the fourteen regions in 1935 ($R^2 = 0.31$ for the whole sample in a simple regression). By contrast there is no association between building and total industry productivity ($R^2 = 0.016$). Coupled with national wage bargaining, such productivity differences reduced the attractiveness of Outer Britain as a location for new industry.

Almost two-fifths of the increase in net output per head between 1924 and 1935 can be accounted for by the regional shifts in output. The conclusion arises from a shift-share analysis of the data of Table 15.4. Where s is the share of a region in net output, Q is output per employee, and hence $\Delta(sQ)$ is the change in value between 1924 and 1935, the national change in labour productivity in the eleven years from 1924 is

$$\Delta(sQ) = s\Delta Q + Q\Delta s + \Delta s\Delta Q$$

The first term is the improvement in labour productivity, holding the regional output shares at 1924 levels (5.42). The second term is the regional shift effect, holding labour productivity at the earlier value (3.90). The third term, the interaction between the change in regional output shares and labour productivity growths, is positive (1.19) because the predominant tendency was for regions expanding their shares also to increase their productivity, and conversely for declining share regions. Some of the 'region specific' effect is a consequence of regional specialisation and is really an industry effect. But not all.

New firms were more likely to be established in the prosperous regions, even allowing for their size and industrial composition, thus reinforcing the imbalance in the longer term (Foreman-Peck 1985). Migration from the poorer regions probably had the same effect. State policy towards the regions (in which policy Montagu Norman at the Bank of England must be included) was designed to deflect political criticism. It was not a scale likely to have a significant impact. Policy created a maximum of 20,000 to 25,000 jobs in 1937 (Heim 1984a).

Conclusion

Inter-war British industrial organisations were obliged to grapple with three types of problems: how to acquire and employ information efficiently, how to cope with and spread risk, and how to secure compliance with the goals of the organisation. By far the most important industrial organisation in this period, measured by output, was the capitalist firm whose quoted shares were owned by a number of individuals and organisations. In these enterprises the risk borne by labour was that of unemployment, while the shareholder accepted the risk of dividend income variation. Increasingly professional management of capitalist firms attempted to make better use of information but in general the lag of indigenous businesses behind best American practice remained substantial. Delay in matching American managerial hierarchies was primarily due to the size of the British market, together with the industrial inheritance of an early start.

Ideological change was little help in securing compliance with the goals of the enterprise. Widespread support for the Labour Party, with its nationalisation commitment, implied an almost equally pervasive antagonism to capitalist institutions. It was in traditional heavy industries both that ideological conflict was most prominent and that Britain's productivity performance was poorest relative to German manufacturing industry. In food, drink and tobacco, a sector not usually marked out by historians, Britain possessed a comparative advantage that most probably stemmed from the extensive market created by early industrialisation.

Olson's (1982) causal explanation of institution formation does not seem to hold up for inter-war British industry. Initial conditions and the economic environment seem to offer more promising explanations. His 'distributional coalitions', local authorities, trade unions, cartels, however, *may* have been an explanation for under-performance. Unfortunately, these intervening variables are substituted out in his formal tests (on other data) and therefore evidence must be sought elsewhere.

More convincing is the institutional costs of an early start to industrialisation, which provided a legacy of vested interests in outmoded structures in some sectors. Commercial banks pursuing conservative policies appear to have tempered the winds of competition for small firms that would otherwise have been extinguished to make way for larger, more professionally managed enterprises.

Governments in this period also typically experienced difficulty in seeing that the goals of established enterprises might not accord with wider social objectives, even though they did not want to support the invisible hand of competition. But they did recognise problems of emerging enterprise in radio broadcasting, electricity, aircraft and air transport. At their most successful, where central coordination was possible, such measures closed the greater part of the productivity gap with the USA.

In competitive industries like motor vehicles, where there were strong economies of scale, matching American performance would have been impossible because a market as extensive as America's was lacking. Had it been possible, the American multinational companies that were to be found in most British advanced manufacturing sectors would have transferred their achievements across the Atlantic.

The greater state and public concern anyway was with old contracting industries that needed rationalising and where unemployment was always a political constraint. Because the declining sectors were geographically concentrated, they gave rise to a severe regional problem. Unfortunately, given labour market institutions, which had not been transformed by trade union defeat in the General Strike, and an unwillingness to commit substantial public expenditure to Outer Britain, there was little that could be done for the regions of high unemployment without raising the national level of economic activity. And that remained an elusive goal.

Unemployment was probably a symptom of the pace of advance of industry as well as a response to the shocks to which the economy was subject. Productivity growth generated by the adoption of improved techniques and organisation reduced labour requirements in progressive sectors. Demand did not grow sufficiently to absorb workers in the appropriate activities, however. The upshot was not only persistent excess supply of labour but the crowding of workers into jobs where their productivity was rather low. So gains in one industry were offset by stagnation in other sectors because of the failure of macro-economic policy.

Chronology

Wade E. Shilts
The University of Iowa

1860s

ECONOMIC AND SOCIAL CONDITIONS

National product of Great Britain (1861, at 1865/85 prices): £565 million.
Export growth rate (1866–72): 6·12 per cent per annum.
Population of Great Britain (1861): 23·1 million.
Life expectancy at birth (1861): 40·5 years (men); 43 years (women).
Net overseas migration (1861–71): 200,000.

1864	Founding of International Working Men's Association.
1866	Collapse of Overend Gurney discount house.

TECHNOLOGY AND IDEAS

1861	Invention of ammonia process of soda making (Solvay, Belgium).
1866	Invention of dynamite (Nobel, Sweden).
1867	Publication of volume I of Marx's *Das Kapital*.

POLITICS, LAW AND PUBLIC POLICY

1860	Cobden–Chevalier Treaty, Gladstone's budget codify principles of free trade.
1864–6	Contagious Diseases Acts.
1865	Death of Palmerston.
1867	Second Great Reform Act. Master and Servant Act.
1869	Disestablishment of Church of Ireland.

INTERNATIONAL EVENTS

1861	Alexander II abolishes serfdom in Russia.
1861–5	American Civil War. Blockade of Southern ports by Union ('cotton famine').
1867	Habsburg empire becomes dual monarchy of Austria-Hungary. Paris Exhibition.
1869	Suez Canal opens.

1870s

ECONOMIC AND SOCIAL CONDITIONS

Output growth rate (constant factor cost, 1873–1913): 1·9 per cent per annum.
Agricultural output (1870–6): £195 million.
Export growth rate (1878–81): 2·43 per cent per annum.
Prices (1873–96): GDP deflator falls by 20 per cent.

1872	Lincoln Bank self-imposes first stated reserve ratio.
1878	Failure of City of Glasgow Bank.
1878–81	Years of bad harvests and low prices.

TECHNOLOGY AND IDEAS

Late 1870s	Introduction of successful reaper-and-binder in agriculture.
1876	Invention of telephone (Bell, United States).
1878	Development of Gilchrist-Thomas open hearth steel-making process.

POLITICS, LAW AND PUBLIC POLICY

1870	First Irish Land Act (compensation for evicted tenants, land purchase loans). Education Act (government assumes responsibility for elementary schools). Married Women's Property Act (removes property-owning disabilities).
1871	Trade Unions Act legalises unions, gives them protection of courts.
1872	Introduction of secret ballot.
1874	Removal of tariffs on sugar.
1875	Unions allowed to picket. Britain acquires controlling interest in Suez Canal.

INTERNATIONAL EVENTS

1870	Third French Republic.
1870–1	Franco-Prussian War.
1871	Suppression of Paris Commune. Creation of German empire.
1878	Congress of Berlin.

1880s

ECONOMIC AND SOCIAL CONDITIONS

National product of Great Britain (1881, at 1865/85 prices): £1,079 million.
Output growth rate (1881–91): 1·73 per cent per annum.
Export growth rate (1881–9): 2·33 per cent per annum.
Population of Great Britain (1881): 29·7 million.
Net overseas migration (1881–91): 820,000.

1882	Peak in industrial production.
1889	London dock strike. Peak in industrial production.

TECHNOLOGY AND IDEAS

1884	Founding of Fabian Society. Invention of steam turbine (Parsons).
1885	Invention of gasoline-powered internal combustion engine (Daimler, Germany).

POLITICS, LAW AND PUBLIC POLICY

1881	Second Irish Land Act. Irish Coercion Act.
1884	Third Reform Act reforming the franchise.
1886	Repeal of Contagious Diseases Act.

INTERNATIONAL EVENTS

1880–1914	Partition of Africa.
1882	Triple Alliance formed between Germany, Austria and Italy.
1886	Gold found in Transvaal.

1890s

ECONOMIC AND SOCIAL CONDITIONS

Export growth rate (1889–99): 1·19 per cent per annum.
Prices (1896–1914): GDP deflator increases by 17·6 per cent.

1893	Brooklands Agreement between employers and unions in cotton industry.
1897–8	Engineering lockout.

TECHNOLOGY AND IDEAS

1895	Invention of wireless telegraphy (Lodge and Marconi).

POLITICS, LAW AND PUBLIC POLICY

1893	Founding of Independent Labour Party.
1899	Crown Colonies Loan Act.
1899–1902	Anglo-Boer War.

INTERNATIONAL EVENTS

1890	United States passes Sherman Anti-Trust Act.
1892	Sergei Witte appointed Finance Minister in Russia.
1898	Spanish-American War. Germany begins naval expansion.
1899	United States proposes Open Door policy in Far East.

1900s

ECONOMIC AND SOCIAL CONDITIONS

Agricultural output (1904–10): £155·2 million per annum.
Export growth rate (1899–1907): 3·99 per cent per annum.
Population of Great Britain (1901): 37 million.
Life expectancy at birth (1901): 45·3 years (men); 49·4 years (women).
Net overseas migration (1901–11): 760,000.

1907	Peak in industrial production.

TECHNOLOGY AND IDEAS

1903	First successful airplane flight (Wright Brothers, United States).
1900	Publication of Freud's *Interpretation of Dreams*.

POLITICS, LAW AND PUBLIC POLICY

1900	Formation of Labour Representation Committee by Trades Union Congress.
1901	Death of Victoria. Accession of Edward VII. House of Lords in Taff Vale decision holds unions liable for the civil wrongs of its agents.
1902	Education Act reforms both primary and secondary education.
1903	Third Irish Land Act.
1903–6	Chamberlain's Campaign for Tariff Reform.
1906	Labour Party returns twenty-nine members in parliamentary election.
1908	Old Age Pensions Plan introduced.
1909	Act establishing Labour Exchanges.

INTERNATIONAL EVENTS

1904	Anglo-French *entente*.
1904–5	Russo-Japanese War.
1905	Revolution in Russia.
1907	Anglo-Russian *entente*.

1910s

ECONOMIC AND SOCIAL CONDITIONS

Output growth rate (1907–13): 1·72 per cent per annum.
Agriculture: approximately 90 per cent of cultivated area is rented. Britain relies on imports for more than half of its food.
Export growth rate (1907–13): 2·79 per cent per annum.

1911–13	Railway and mining strikes.
1913	Peak in industrial production.

1913–19	Trade union membership doubles from 4 to 8 million.
1914	Suspension of gold standard.
1916	Founding of Federation of British Industries.
1919–20	Post-war boom.

TECHNOLOGY AND IDEAS

1910s	Widespread adoption of internal combustion engine.
1919	Publication of Keynes' *Economic Consequences of the Peace*.

POLITICS, LAW AND PUBLIC POLICY

1911	National Insurance Act provides unemployment benefits and health care. Parliament Act establishes five-year elections, curtails power of House of Lords.
1912–14	Irish Home Rule Act passed, but suspended because of war.
1917	Balfour Declaration supporting national home for Jews in Palestine.
1918	Lloyd George coalition government elected in 'coupon' election. Representation of the People Act extends franchise to women aged thirty and over.

INTERNATIONAL EVENTS

1914–18	First World War.
1917	Russian Revolution.
1919	Irish declare independence. Treaty of Versailles. Soviet Communists found Third International (Comintern).

1920s

ECONOMIC AND SOCIAL CONDITIONS

Output rate of growth (constant factor cost, 1924–37): 2·20 per cent per annum.
Population of Great Britain (1921): 42·8 million.
Net overseas migration (1921–31): 560,000.

1920–2	Steep recession.
1921	Major strike by 'Triple Alliance' of miners, dock workers, and railway workers. Alliance broken on 'Black Friday' when dock and railway workers back down.
1925	Britain resumes gold standard at pre-war parity.
1926	General Strike.

POLITICS, LAW AND PUBLIC POLICY

1921	Railway Act merges sixty companies into four. Lloyd George concludes treaty with Sinn Fein for Irish Free State.
1924	Ramsay MacDonald leads first Labour government.

1926	Nationalisation of British Broadcasting Company, National Electricity Grid. Imperial Chemical Industries merger.

INTERNATIONAL EVENTS

1921	Lenin outlines New Economic Policy.
1922	Mussolini takes power in Italy.
1923	Hyperinflation in Weimar Republic.
1924	Dawes Plan.
1928	Stalin issues first Five-Year Plan.
1929	Wall Street crash. Beginning of collectivisation of Soviet agriculture.

1930s

ECONOMIC AND SOCIAL CONDITIONS

Output growth rate (1937–51): 1·26 per cent per annum.
Net immigration (1931–9): 510,000.
Population of Great Britain (1939): 46·5 million.

Early 1930s	International depression. Unemployment in Britain passes 15 per cent.
1931	Britain abandons gold standard.
1932	Parliament passes General Tariff, imposing 10 per cent import tax on all but raw materials.
1932–9	Managed currency float under Exchange Equalisation Account; emergence of sterling area.
1932–7	Upswing in national economic performance.
1937	Recession.

TECHNOLOGY AND IDEAS

1932	Widespread use of vacuum cleaners.
1935	Use of sulphonamide drugs.
1936	Publication of Keynes' *General Theory of Employment, Interest, and Money*.

POLITICS, LAW AND PUBLIC POLICY

1931	MacDonald returned to lead National Government. Macmillan Committee on Finance and Industry.
1932	Ottawa Conference on imperial trade. Oswald Mosley founds British Union of Fascists.
1935	Rearmament begins.
1937	Neville Chamberlain becomes Prime Minister.

INTERNATIONAL EVENTS

1933	Hitler becomes Chancellor of Germany.

1935	Passage of Nuremberg Laws.
1936–9	Spanish Civil War.
1938	Munich Conference and partition of Czechoslovakia.
1939	Nazi–Soviet Pact.
1939–45	Second World War.

NOTE ON SOURCES

Economic and demographic statistics found under 'Economic and social conditions' above were taken from the following sources.

Income/output. National product, 1821–81: Deane and Cole (1967: 282). Rate of growth, 1856–1973: Feinstein (1972: 11, 19), as updated in Matthews *et al.* (1982: 28).

Agriculture. 1870–1910: ch. 6.

Exports. 1866–1913: ch. 10.

Population. 1801–1981: Mitchell (1988: 9).

Life expectancy. 1861–1960: ch. 2.

Net overseas migration: ch. 2.

Prices. 1873–1914: ch. 9.

Peaks in industrial production: ch. 10.

Bibliography

Place of publication is London unless otherwise stated. All references to the *Economic History Review* are to the Second Series, unless otherwise stated.

Abel-Smith, B. 1964. *The Hospitals 1800–1948.*

Abramovitz, M. 1968. The passing of the Kuznets cycle. *Economica* 35: 349–67.

1986. Catching up, forging ahead, and falling behind. *Journal of Economic History* 46: 385–406.

Adams, F. G., and Hickman, B. G., eds. 1983. *Global Econometrics: Essays in Honor of Lawrence R. Klein.* Cambridge, Mass.

Adler, J. H., ed. 1967. *Capital Movements and Economic Development.*

Aldcroft, D. H. 1964. The entrepreneur and the British economy, 1870–1914. *Economic History Review* 17: 113–34.

1966. Technical progress and British enterprise 1875–1914. *Business History* 8: 122–39.

1967. Economic growth in Britain in the interwar years: a reassessment. *Economic History Review* 20: 311–26.

1968a. *British Railways in Transition: Economic Problems of British Railways since 1914.*

ed. 1968b. *The Development of British Industry and Foreign Competition 1875–1914.*

1970. *The Interwar Economy: Britain 1919–1939.*

1977. *From Versailles to Wall Street, 1919–1929.*

Aldcroft, D. H., and Fearon, P., eds. 1969. *Economic Growth in Twentieth-Century Britain.*

eds. 1972. *British Economic Fluctuations, 1790–1939.*

Aldcroft, D. H., and Richardson, H. W. 1969. *The British Economy 1870–1939.*

Alford, B. W. E. 1972. *Depression and Recovery? British Economic Growth 1918–39.*

1973. *W. D. and H. O. Wills and the Development of the U.K. Tobacco Industry 1786–1965.* Oxford.

1976. The Chandler thesis – some general observations. In Hannah 1976a.

1977. Entrepreneurship, business performance and industrial development. *Business History* 19: 116–33.

Allen, R. C. 1979. International competition in iron and steel 1850–1913. *Journal of Economic History* 39: 911–37.

1991. *Real Incomes in the English Speaking World.* University of British Columbia, mimeo.

Allen, R. G. D., and Thomas, B. 1939. The supply of engineering labour under boom conditions. *Economic Journal* 49: 259–74.

Anderson, M. 1971. *Family Structure in Nineteenth Century Lancashire*. Cambridge.

1985. The emergence of the modern life cycle in Britain. *Social History* 10: 69–87.

1990. The social implications of demographic change. In Thompson 1990: vol. II.

Andrews, B. P. A. 1980. The effects of the appreciation of sterling in the 1920s. Unpublished paper.

Andrews, P. W. S., and Brunner, E. 1951. *Capital Development in Steel: A Study of the United Steel Companies Ltd.* Oxford.

Armstrong, P. and Glyn, A. 1986. Accumulation, profits, state spending: data for advanced capitalist countries, 1952–1983. Unpublished data, Oxford Institute of Economics and Statistics, July 1986.

Ashley, W. J. 1902. *The Tariff Problem*.

Ashton, T. S. 1955. *The Eighteenth Century and Economic Fluctuations 1700–1800*. Oxford.

Ashworth, W. 1966. The late Victorian economy. *Economica* 33: 17–33.

Atkinson, A. B., and Micklewright, J. 1985. *Unemployment Benefits and the Duration of Unemployment*. Suntory-Toyota Centre, London School of Economics.

Bagehot, W. 1873. *Lombard Street*.

Bain, G. S., ed. 1983. *Industrial Relations in Britain*. Oxford.

Baines, D. E. 1981. The labour supply and the labour market 1860–1914. In Floud and McCloskey 1981: vol. II.

1985. *Migration in a Mature Economy. Emigration and Internal Migration in England and Wales, 1861–1900*. Cambridge.

1991. *Emigration from Europe, 1815–1930*. Basingstoke.

Baker, W. J. 1970. *A History of the Marconi Company*.

Balfour Committee 1928. Balfour Committee on Industry and Trade: *Further Factors in Industrial and Commercial Efficiency*.

Balogh, T. 1947. *Studies in Financial Organization*. Cambridge.

Banks, J. A. 1954. *Prosperity and Parenthood: A Study of Family Planning among the Victorian Middle Classes*.

Barker, T. C. 1976. A family firm becomes a public company. In Hannah 1976a.

1977. *The Glassmakers. Pilkingtons: The Rise of an International Company 1826–1976*.

Barker, T. C., and Drake, M., eds. 1982. *Population and Society in Britain, 1850–1980*.

Barnes, H. 1923. *Housing: The Facts and the Future*.

Barnett, C. 1986. *The Audit of War: The Illusion and Reality of Britain as a Great Nation*.

Barnsby, G. J. 1971. The standard of living in the Black Country during the nineteenth century. *Economic History Review* 24: 220–39.

Barro, R. J. 1981. *Money, Expectations, and Business Cycles*. New York.

1984. Comments on Rockoff. In Bordo and Schwartz 1984.

1987. *Macroeconomics*.

1989. *Modern Business Cycle Theory*. Cambridge, Mass.

Barsky, R. B., and Summers, L. H. 1988. Gibson's Paradox and the gold standard. *Journal of Political Economy* 96: 528–41.

Bassett, P. 1986. *Strike Free: New Industrial Relations in Britain.*

Batchelor, R. A. 1986. The avoidance of a catastrophe: two nineteenth century banking crises. In Capie and Wood 1986.

Batstone, E. 1984. *Working Order: Workplace Industrial Relations over Two Decades*. Oxford.

Baumol, W. 1967. Macroeconomics of unbalanced growth. *American Economic Review* 57: 415–26.

Beaujot, R., and McQuillan, K. 1983. *Growth and Dualism: The Demographic Development of Canadian Society*. Toronto.

Beaver, M. 1973. Population, infant mortality and milk. *Population Studies* 27: 243–54.

Becker, G. S. 1981. *A Treatise on the Family*. Cambridge, Mass.

Beenstock, M., and Warburton, P. 1986. Wages and unemployment in interwar Britain. *Explorations in Economic History* 23: 153–72.

1991. The market for labour in interwar Britain. *Explorations in Economic History* 28 (July).

Beenstock, M., Capie, F., and Griffiths, B. 1984. Economic recovery in the United Kingdom in the 1930s. *Bank of England Panel Paper* 23: 57–85.

Bellerby, J. R. 1956. *Agriculture and Industry Relative Income.*

1968. Distribution of farm income in the United Kingdom, 1867–1938. In Minchinton 1968.

Bellerby, J. R., and Boreham, A. J. 1953. Farm occupiers' capital in the United Kingdom before 1939. *Farm Economist* 7(b): 257–63.

Benjamin, D., and Kochin, L. 1979. Searching for an explanation of unemployment in interwar Britain. *Journal of Political Economy* 87: 441–78.

Benson, J. 1982. Coalmining. In Wrigley 1982.

ed. 1985. *The Working Class in England 1875–1914.*

Bernanke, B. S. 1983. Non monetary effects of the financial crises in the propagation of the Great Depression. *American Economic Review* 73: 256–76.

Bernanke, B., and James, H. 1991. The gold standard, deflation and financial crisis in the Great Depression: an international comparison. In Hubbard 1991.

Berry, R. A., and Cline, W. R. 1979. *Agrarian Structure and Productivity in Developing Countries*. Baltimore.

Beveridge, W. H. 1944. *Full Employment in a Free Society.*

Bloomfield, A. I. 1968. *Patterns of Fluctuation in International Investment before 1914*. Princeton Studies in International Finance No. 21.

Bogart, E. L. 1921. *War Costs and their Financing. A Study of the Financing of the War and the After-War Problem of Debt and Taxation.*

Booth, A. E., and Glynn, S. 1975. Unemployment in the interwar period: a multiple problem. *Journal of Contemporary History* 10: 611–37.

Booth, C. 1889–1903. *Life and Labour of the People in London.* 17 vols.

Bordo, M., ed. 1989. *Money. History and International Finance: Essays in Honour of Anna J. Schwartz*. Chicago.

Bordo, M., and Schwartz, A. J., eds. 1984. *A Retrospective on the Classical Gold Standard, 1821–1931*. Chicago.

1981. Money and prices in the nineteenth century: was Thomas Tooke right? *Explorations in Economic History* 18: 97–127.

Boulding, K. E., and Murkerjee, T., eds. 1972. *Economic Imperialism*. Ann Arbor.

Bowden, S. M. 1988. The consumer durables revolution in England 1932–1938: a regional analysis. *Explorations in Economic History* 25: 42–59.

Bowley, A. L. 1920. *The Change in the Distribution of the National Income, 1880–1913*. Oxford.

1937. *Wages and Income in the United Kingdom since 1860*. Cambridge.

Bowley, A. L., and Burnett-Hurst, A. R. 1915. *Livelihood and Poverty: A Study in the Economic Conditions of Working-Class Households in Northampton, Warrington, Stanley and Reading*.

Boyer, G. R., and Hatton, T. J. 1990. *Did Joseph Arch Raise Agricultural Wages? Rural Trade Unions and the Labour Market in the Late-Nineteenth Century*. Centre for Economic Policy Research Working Paper 484.

1991. *Regional Labour Market Integration in Britain 1850–1913*. Cornell University, mimeo.

Brandstrom, A., and Tederbrand, L.-G., eds. 1988. *Society, Health and Population during the Demographic Transition*. Stockholm.

Briggs, A., and Saville, J., eds. 1960. *Essays in Labour History*.

eds. 1977. *Essays in Labour History, 1918–1939*.

Bright, J. 1869. *Speeches on Questions of Public Policy by the Right Honourable John Bright, M. P.*, ed. J. E. Thorold Rogers.

Broadberry, S. N. 1983. Unemployment in interwar Britain: a disequilibrium approach. *Oxford Economic Papers* 35 (Supplement): 463–85.

1984a. Fiscal policy in Britain during the 1930s. *Economic History Review* 37: 95–102.

1984b. The north European depression of the 1920s. *Scandinavian Economic History Review* 32: 159–67.

1986a. Aggregate supply in interwar Britain. *Economic Journal* 96: 467–81.

1986b. *The British Economy between the Wars: A Macroeconomic Survey*. Oxford.

1987. Cheap money and the housing boom in interwar Britain: an econometric appraisal. *Manchester School* 87: 378–91.

1990. The emergence of mass unemployment: explaining macroeconomic trends in Britain during the trans-war period. *Economic History Review* 43: 271–82.

Broadberry, S. N., and Crafts, N. F. R. 1990a. Britain's productivity gap in the 1930s: some neglected factors. Unpublished manuscript, University of Warwick.

1990b. Explaining Anglo-American productivity differences in the mid twentieth century. *Oxford Bulletin of Economics and Statistics* 52: 375–402.

1990c. The impact of the depression of the 1930s on the production potential of the United Kingdom. *European Economic Review* 34: 599–607.

1990d. The implications of British macroeconomic policy in the 1930s for long run growth performance. *Rivista di Storia Economica* 7: 1–19.

eds. 1991. *Britain in the World Economy 1870–1939*. Cambridge.

eds. 1992. *Essays in Honour of A. G. Ford*. Cambridge.

Broadberry, S. N., and Fremdling, R. 1990. Comparative productivity in British and German industry. *Oxford Bulletin of Economics and Statistics* 52: 403–22.

Broadbridge, S. 1970. *Studies in Railway Expansion and the Capital Markets in England 1825–1873.*

Brodrick, G. C. 1881. *English Land and English Landlords.*

Brody, D. 1980. *Workers in Industrial America.* New York.

Brookes, B. 1988. *Abortion in Britain, 1900–1967.*

Brown, A. J. 1972. *The Framework of Regional Economics in the United Kingdom.* Cambridge.

Brown, W. 1972. A consideration of custom and practice. *British Journal of Industrial Relations* 10: 42–61.

Brunner, K., and Meltzer, A. H. 1989. *Monetary Economics.* Oxford.

Bureau of the Census. 1976. *The Statistical History of the United States.* New York.

Burgess, K. 1975. *The Origins of British Industrial Relations: The Nineteenth Century Experience.*

Burnett, J. 1978. *A Social History of Housing 1815–1970.* Newton Abbot.

1979. *Plenty and Want: A Social History of Diet in England from 1815 to the Present Day.*

Butlin, N., and Gregory, R. G., eds. 1988. *Recovery from the Depression: Australia and the World Economy in the 1930s.* Cambridge.

Buxton, N. K., and Aldcroft, D. H. 1979. *British Industry between the Wars.* Whitstable.

Byron, R. P. 1978. The estimation of large social account matrices. *Journal of the Royal Statistical Society*, Series A 141: 359–67.

Cagan, P. 1965. *Determinants and Effects of Changes in the Stock of Money 1875–1960.* New York.

Cain, P. J. 1980. *The Economic Foundations of British Expansion Overseas, 1815–1914.*

1988. Railways 1870–1914: the maturity of the private system. In Freeman and Aldcroft 1988.

Cain, P. J., and Hopkins, A. G. 1980. The political economy of British expansion overseas, 1750–1914. *Economic History Review* 33: 463–90.

1986. Gentlemanly capitalism and British expansion overseas I: the old colonial system, 1688–1850. *Economic History Review* 39: 501–25.

1987. Gentlemanly capitalism and British expansion overseas II: new imperialism, 1850–1945. *Economic History Review* 40: 1–27.

Caird, J. 1852. *English Agriculture in 1850–51.*

Cairncross, A. K. 1953. *Home and Foreign Investment, 1870–1913.* Cambridge.

Cairncross, A. K., and Eichengreen, B. 1983. *Sterling in Decline.* Oxford.

Calmfors, L., and Driffil, J. 1988. Bargaining structure, corporatism and macroeconomic performance. *Economic Policy* 6: 7–61.

Cameron, R. 1961. *France and the Economic Development of Europe.* Princeton, N.J.

ed. 1967. *Banking in the Early Stages of Industrialization.* Oxford.

Campbell, B. M. A., and Overton, M., eds. 1991. *Land, Labour, and Livestock: Historical Studies in European Agricultural Productivity.* Manchester.

Capie, F. H. 1978. The British tariff and industrial protection in the 1930s. *Economic History Review* 31: 399–409.

1988. Structure and performance in British banking 1870–1939. In Cottrell and Moggridge 1988.

1990. Money and business cycles in Britain 1870–1913. In Velupellai and Thygesen 1990.
Capie, F. H., and Collins, M. 1980. The extent of British economic recovery in the 1930s. *Economy and History* 23, 1: 40–60.
1983. *The Inter-War British Economy: A Statistical Abstract.* Manchester.
Capie, F. H., and Mills, T. C. 1990. Money and business cycles in the United States 1870 to 1913: a re-examination of Friedman and Schwartz. *Explorations in Economic History* 29, 3: 251–73.
Capie, F. H., and Rodrik-Bali, G. 1983. *Monetary Growth and Determinants in Britain 1870–1913.* Centre for the Study of Monetary History Discussion Paper No. 6, City University Business School.
Capie, F. H. and Webber, A. 1985. *A Monetary History of the United Kingdom 1870–1982*, vol. I: *Data, Sources, Methods.*
Capie, F. H., and Wood, G., eds. 1986. *Financial Crises and the World Banking System.*
eds. 1991. *Unregulated Banking: Chaos or Order.*
Capie, F. H., Mills, T. C., and Wood, G. E. 1986. Debt management and interest rates: the British stock conversion of 1932. *Applied Economics* 18: 1111–20.
1991. Money and price in the Great Depression. In Foreman-Peck 1991a.
Carlson, L., and Terrill, T., eds. 1992. *Labour Markets in the Textile Industries of the World.* Ithaca, N.Y.
Carlsson, G. 1966. The decline of fertility: innovation or adjustment process? *Population Studies* 20: 147–74.
Caron, F. 1979. *An Economic History of Modern France.* New York.
Carré, J.-J., Dubois, P., and Malinvaud, E. 1976. *French Economic Growth.* Oxford.
Carrier, N. H., and Jeffery, J. R. 1953. *External Migration. A Study of the Available Statistics, 1815–1950.*
Carr-Saunders, A. M., and Wilson, P. A. 1933. *The Professions.* Oxford.
Carus-Wilson, E. M., ed. 1962. *Essays in Economic History*, vol. III.
Casson, M. 1982. *The Entrepreneur. An Economic Theory.* Oxford.
1983a. *The Economics of Unemployment: An Historical Perspective.* Oxford.
ed. 1983b. *The Growth of International Business.*
Chaloner, W. H. 1983–4. Was there a decline of the industrial spirit in Britain 1850–1939? *Transactions of the Newcomen Society* 55: 211–17.
Chambers, J. D., and Mingay, G. E. 1966. *The Agricultural Revolution: 1750–1880.*
Chandler, A. D., Jr. 1976. The development of modern management structure in the US and UK. In Hannah 1976a.
1977. *The Visible Hand. The Managerial Revolution in American Business.* Cambridge, Mass.
1980. The growth of the transnational industrial firm in the United States and the United Kingdom: a comparative analysis. *Economic History Review* 33: 396–410.
1986. Technological and organizational underpinnings of modern multinational enterprise: the dynamics of competitive advantage. In Teichova, Levy-Leboyer and Nussbaum 1986.
1990. *Scale and Scope: The Dynamics of Industrial Capitalism.* Cambridge, Mass.
Channing, F. A. 1897. *The Truth about Agricultural Depression.*

Chapman, A. L., and Knight, R. 1953. *Wages and Salaries in the United Kingdom, 1920–1938*. Cambridge.
Chapman, S. D. 1974. *Jesse Boot of Boots the Chemists*.
Charles, E. 1934. *The Twilight of Parenthood*.
Checkland, S. 1983. *British Public Policy 1776–1939*. Cambridge.
Church, R. A. 1986. *The History of the British Coal Industry*, vol. III: *1830–1913: Victorian Pre-eminence*. Oxford.
Clack, G. 1967. *Industrial Relations in a British Car Factory*. Cambridge.
Clapham, J. H. 1938. *An Economic History of Modern Britain*, vol. III: *Machines and National Rivalries, 1887–1914*. Cambridge.
Clark, C. 1957. *The Conditions of Economic Progress*.
1961. *Conditions of Economic Progress*.
Clark, G. 1991. Labour productivity in English agriculture, 1300–1860. In Campbell and Overton 1991.
Clegg, H. A. 1985. *A History of British Trade Unions since 1889*, vol. II: *1911–1933*. Oxford.
Clegg, H. A., Fox, A., and Thompson, A. F. 1964. *A History of British Trade Unions since 1889*, vol. I: *1889–1910*. Oxford.
Coale, A. J., and Treadway, R. 1986. A summary of the changing distribution of overall fertility, marital fertility and the proportion married in the provinces of Europe. In Coale and Watkins 1986.
Coale, A. J., and Watkins, S. C., eds. 1986. *The Decline of Fertility in Europe*. Princeton, N.J.
Coase, R. 1950. *British Broadcasting: A Study in Monopoly*.
Coates, D., Johnston, G., and Bush, R. eds. 1985. *A Socialist Anatomy of Britain*. Cambridge.
Cole, A. H. 1946. An approach to the study of entrepreneurship. *Journal of Economic History Supplement* 6: 1–15.
1968. The stone that the builder rejected. *Tradition* 13: 105–16.
Cole, G. D. H. 1944. *A Century of Co-operation*.
1962. Some notes on British trade unionism in the third quarter of the nineteenth century. In Carus-Wilson 1962.
Coleman, D. C. 1969. *Courtaulds: An Economic and Social History*. 2 vols. Oxford.
1973. Gentlemen and players. *Economic History Review* 26: 92–116.
Collins, B., and Robbins, K., eds. 1990. *British Culture and Economic Decline*.
Collins, E. J. T. 1972. The diffusion of the threshing machine in Britain, 1790–1880. *Tools and Tillage* 2: 16–33.
1989. The 'machinery question' in English agriculture in the nineteenth century. In Grantham and Leonard 1989.
Collins, M. 1989. The banking crisis of 1878. *Economic History Review* 42: 504–27.
1990a. *British Banks and Industrial Finance before 1939*.
English bank lending and the financial crisis of the 1870s. *Business History* 32: 198–224.
Constantine, S. ed. 1990a. *Emigrants and Empire. British Settlement in the Dominions between the Wars*. Manchester.
1990b. Empire migration and imperial harmony. In Constantine 1990a.
Copp, T. 1974. *The Anatomy of Poverty: The Conditions of the Working Class in Montreal, 1897–1921*. Toronto.

Coppock, D. J. 1956. The climacteric of the 1890s: a critical note. *Manchester School* 24: 1–32.

Coppock, J. T. 1956. The statistical assessment of British agriculture. *Agricultural History Review* 4: 4–21 and 66–79.

Corley, T. A. B. 1966. *Domestic Electrical Appliances.*

Cottrell, P. L. 1975. *British Overseas Investment in the Nineteenth Century.*

1980. *Industrial Finance 1830–1914. The Finance and Organization of English Manufacturing Industry.*

Cottrell, P. L., and Moggridge, D., eds. 1988. *Money and Power: Essays in Honour of L. S. Pressnell.*

Crafts, N. F. R. 1978. Average age at first marriage for women in England and Wales: a cross section study. *Population Studies* 32: 21–5.

1984a. Economic growth in France and Britain, 1830–1914: a review of the evidence. *Journal of Economic History* 44: 49–67.

1984b. A time series study of fertility in England and Wales, 1877–1938. *Journal of European Economic History* 13: 571–90.

1985. *British Economic Growth during the Industrial Revolution*. Oxford.

1987. Long-term unemployment in Britain in the 1930s. *Economic History Review* 40: 418–32.

1989a. Duration of marriage, fertility and women's employment opportunities in England and Wales in 1911. *Population Studies* 43: 325–35.

1989b. Long-term unemployment and the wage equation in Britain 1925–1939. *Economica* 56: 247–54.

Crafts, N. F. R., and Mills, T. C. 1991. Economic fluctuations, 1851–1913: a perspective based on growth theory. In Broadberry and Crafts 1991.

Crafts, N. F. R., and Thomas, M. 1986. Comparative advantage in U.K. manufacturing trade 1910–1935. *Economic Journal* 96: 629–45.

Crafts, N. F. R., Leybourne, S. J., and Mills, T. C. 1989a. The climacteric in late Victorian Britain and France: a reappraisal of the evidence. *Journal of Applied Econometrics* 4: 103–17.

1989b. Trends and cycles in British industrial production. *Journal of the Royal Statistical Society*, Series A, 152: 43–60.

Crisp, O. 1967. Russia, 1860–1914. In Cameron 1967.

Cronin, J. E. 1982. Strikes 1870–1914. In Wrigley 1982.

Crowther, M. A. 1981. *The Workhouse System 1834–1929: The History of an English Social Institution.*

Dangerfield, G. 1936. *The Strange Death of Liberal England.*

Daniel, G. H. 1940. Some factors affecting the mobility of Labour. *Oxford Economic Papers* 3: 144–79.

Daunton, M. J. 1981. Down the pit: work in the Great Northern and South Wales coalfields, 1870–1914. *Economic History Review* 34: 278–97.

1985. *Royal Mail: The Post Office since 1840.*

Davenport-Hines, R. 1984. *Dudley Docker: The Life and Times of a Trade Warrior.* Cambridge.

Davey, C. 1988. Birth control in Britain during the inter-war years: evidence from the Stopes correspondence. *Journal of Family History* 13: 329–45.

David, P. A. 1970. Labour productivity in English agriculture, 1850–1914: some quantitative evidence on regional differences. *Economic History Review* 23: 504–19.

1975. *Technical Choice, Innovation and Economic Growth: Essays on American and British Experience in the Nineteenth Century*. Cambridge.

Davidoff, L. 1990. The family in Britain. In Thompson 1990: vol. II.

Davis, L. E. 1966. The capital markets and industrial concentration: the U.S. and the U.K. a comparative study. *Economic History Review* 19: 255–72.

Davis, L. E., and Huttenback, R. A. 1986. *Mammon and the Pursuit of Empire: The Political Economy of British Imperialism, 1860–1912.*

Davis, L. E., and North, D. C. 1971. *Institutional Change and American Economic Growth*. Cambridge.

Davis, L. E., Hughes, J. R. T., and McDougall, D. M. 1969. *American Economic History*. 3rd edn. Homewood, Ill.

Deane, P., and Cole, W. A. 1962. *British Economic Growth, 1688–1959. Trends and Structure*. Cambridge. 2nd edn, 1967.

Dellheim, C. 1985. Notes on industrialism and culture in nineteenth century Britain. *Notebooks in Cultural Analysis* 2: 227–48.

Dennison, S. R. 1939. *Location of Industry and the Depressed Areas*. Oxford.

Dewey, P. 1988. Nutrition and living standards in wartime Britain. In Wall and Winter 1988.

Dimsdale, N. H. 1981a. British monetary policy and the exchange rate 1920–38. In Eltis and Sinclair 1981.

1981b. British monetary policy and the exchange rate 1920–1938. *Oxford Economic Papers* 33: 306–49.

1984. Unemployment and real wages in the inter-war period. *National Institute Economic Review* 110: 94–103.

Dimsdale, N. H., Nickell, S. J., and Horsewood, N. 1989. Real wages and unemployment in Britain during the 1930s. *Economic Journal* 99: 271–92.

Dingle, A. E. 1976. Drink and working-class living standards in Britain, 1870–1914. In Oddy and Miller 1976.

Dintenfass, M. 1988. Entrepreneurial failure reconsidered: the case of the interwar British coal industry. *Business History Review* 62: 1–34.

Divall, C. 1990. A measure of agreement: employers and engineering studies in the universities of England and Wales 1897–1939. *Social Studies of Science* 20: 65–112.

Dowie, J. A. 1968. Growth in the interwar period: some more arithmetic. *Economic History Review* 21: 93–112.

1975. 1919–20 is in need of attention. *Economic History Review* 28: 429–50.

Downs, L. L. 1987. Women in industry, 1914–1939: the employers' perspective. A comparative study of the French and British metalworking industries. PhD dissertation, Columbia University, 1987.

Dumke, R. 1988. Income inequality and industrialization in Germany. *Research in Economic History* 11: 1–47.

Dunlop, J. T. 1938. The movement of real and money wage rates. *Economic Journal* 48: 413–34.

Dunning, J. H., ed. 1966. *International Investment: Selected Readings*. Harmondsworth.

1983. Changes in the level and structure of international production: the last one hundred years. In Casson 1983b.

Dutton, H. I., and King, J. E. 1981. *Ten Percent and No Surrender*. Cambridge.

Dyhouse, C. 1978. Working class mothers and infant mortality in England, 1895–1914. *Journal of Social History* 12: 248–67.

Easterlin, R. 1968. *Population, Labour Force and Long Swings in Economic Growth: The American Experience*. New York.

Edelstein, M. 1982. *Overseas Investment in the Age of High Imperialism. The United Kingdom, 1850–1914*.

Edgerton, D. E. H. 1987. Science and technology in British business history. *Business History* 29: 84–103.

1991. *England and the Aeroplane*.

Edwardes, M. 1983. *Back from the Brink*.

Eichengreen, B. J. 1983. The causes of British business cycles 1833–1913. *Journal of European Economic History* 12: 145–61.

1986. The Bank of France and the sterilization of gold 1926–32. *Explorations in Economic History* 23: 56–84.

1987. Unemployment in interwar Britain: dole or doldrums? *Oxford Economic Papers* 39: 597–623.

1992. *Golden Fetters: The Gold Standard and the Great Depression, 1919–1939*. Oxford.

Eichengreen, B. J., and Hatton, T. J., eds. 1988a. *Interwar Unemployment in International Perspective*. Dordrecht.

1988b. Interwar unemployment in international perspective: an overview. In Eichengreen and Hatton 1988a.

Eichengreen, B. J., and Sachs, J. 1985. Exchange rates and economic recovery in the 1930s. *Journal of Economic History* 45: 925–46.

Einzig, P. 1937. *The Theory of Forward Exchange*.

Elbaum, B. 1986. The steel industry before World War I. In Elbaum and Lazonick 1986.

Elbaum, B., and Lazonick, W., eds. 1986. *The Decline of the British Economy*. Oxford.

Elbaum, B., and Wilkinson, F. 1979. Industrial relations and uneven development: a comparative study of the American and British steel industries. *Cambridge Journal of Economics* 3: 275–303.

Eltis, W., and Sinclair, P., eds. 1981. *The Money Supply and the Exchange Rate*. Oxford.

eds. 1988. *Keynes and Economic Policy: The Relevance of the General Theory after Fifty Years*.

Erickson, C. 1972. Who were the English and Scottish emigrants in the 1880s? In Glass and Revelle 1972.

1980. The English. In Thernstrom 1980.

Ermisch, J. 1979. The relevance of the 'Easterlin hypothesis' and the 'new home economics' to fertility movements in Great Britain. *Population Studies* 33: 39–58.

Ernle, Lord. 1912. *English Farming Past and Present*.

Feinstein, C. H. 1972. *National Income, Expenditure and Output of the United Kingdom 1855–1965*. Cambridge.

1976. *Statistical Tables of National Income, Expenditure and Output in the U.K., 1855–1965*. Cambridge.

1981. Capital accumulation and the industrial revolution. In Floud and McCloskey 1981: I.

1988a. Economic growth since 1870: Britain's economic performance in international perspective. *Oxford Review of Economic Policy* 4: 1–13.

1988b. National statistics, 1760–1920. In Feinstein and Pollard 1988.

1990a. Britain's overseas investments in 1913. *Economic History Review* 43: 288–95.

1990b. New estimates of average earnings in the United Kingdom, 1880–1913. *Economic History Review* 43: 595–632.

1990c. What really happened to real wages?: trends in wages, prices, and productivity in the United Kingdom, 1880–1913. *Economic History Review* 43: 329–55.

1991. A new look at the cost of living 1870–1914. In Foreman-Peck 1991a.

Feinstein, C. H., and Pollard, S., eds. 1988. *Studies in Capital Formation in the United Kingdom 1750–1920*. Oxford.

Feinstein, C. H., Matthews, R. C. O., and Odling-Smee, J. 1982. The timing of the climacteric and its sectoral incidence in the U.K. 1873–1913. In Kindleberger and di Tella 1982.

Feis, H. 1930. *Europe, the World's Banker, 1870–1914*. New Haven, Conn.

Fenton, A. 1976. *Scottish Country Life*. Edinburgh.

Ferrier, R. W. 1976. The early management organisation of British Petroleum and Sir John Cadman. In Hannah 1976a.

Fieldhouse, D. K. 1973. *Economics and Empire, 1830–1914*.

Fildes, V. A. 1986. *Breasts, Bottles and Babies. A History of Infant Feeding*. Edinburgh.

Fine, B. 1990. Economies of scale and a featherbedding cartel? A reconsideration of the interwar British coal industry. *Economic History Review* 43: 438–49.

Fisher, F. M., and Temin, P. 1970. Regional specialization and the supply of wheat in the United States, 1867–1914. *Review of Economics and Statistics* 52: 134–49.

Fitzpatrick, S. 1987. *Rising Damp: Sydney, 1870–1890*. Melbourne.

Fletcher, T. W. 1961. Lancashire livestock farming during the great depression. *Agricultural History Review* 9: 17–42.

Florence, P. S. 1953. *The Logic of British and American Industry*.

Floud, R. C. 1976. *The British Machine Tool Industry, 1850–1914*. Cambridge.

1984. *Technical Education 1850–1914*. Centre for Economic Policy Research Discussion Paper 12, mimeo.

Floud, R. C., and McCloskey, D. N., eds. 1981. *The Economic History of Britain since 1700*. 1st edn. 2 vols. Cambridge.

Floud, R. C., Wachter, K. W., and Gregory, A. 1990. *Height, Health and History. Nutritional Status in the United Kingdom, 1750–1980*. Cambridge.

Ford, A. G. 1963. Notes on the role of exports in British economic fluctuations 1870–1914. *Economic History Review* 16: 328–37.

1971. British investment in Argentina and long swings, 1880–1914. *Journal of Economic History* 31: 650–63.

1981. Trade cycles, 1870–1914. In Floud and McCloskey 1981: II.

Ford, P. 1934. *Work and Wealth in a Modern Port: An Economic Survey of Southampton*.

Foreman-Peck, J. S. 1981. The British tariff and industrial protection in the 1930s: an alternative model. *Economic History Review* 34: 132–9.

1985. Seed-corn or chaff? New firm formation and the performance of the interwar economy. *Economic History Review* 38: 402–22.

1989. Competition, co-operation and nationalisation in the nineteenth-century telegraph system. *Business History* 31: 81–101.

ed. 1991a. *New Perspectives on the Late Victorian Economy: Essays in Quantitative Economic History 1860–1914*. Cambridge.

1991b. Railways and late Victorian economic growth. In Foreman-Peck 1991a.

Foreman-Peck, J. S., and Waterson, M. 1985. The comparative efficiency of public and private enterprise in Britain: electricity generation between the world wars. *Economic Journal Supplement* 95: 83–95.

Fowler, A., and Fowler, L. 1984. *The History of the Nelson Weavers Association*. Burnley.

Frankel, S. H. 1967. *Investment and the Return to Equity Capital in the South African Gold Mining Industry, 1887–1965*. Oxford.

Fraser, D. 1973. *The Evolution of the British Welfare State: A History of Social Policy since the Industrial Revolution*.

Fraser, W. H. 1981. *The Coming of the Mass Market, 1850–1914*.

Freeman, A. 1912. *Boy Life and Labour*.

Freeman, M. J., and Aldcroft, D. H., eds. 1988. *Transport in Victorian Britain*. Manchester.

Freeman, R. B., and Medoff, J. L. 1984. *What Do Unions Do?* New York.

Fremdling, R., and O'Brien, P. K., eds. 1983. *Productivity in the Economies of Europe*. Stuttgart.

Frenkel, J. A., and Johnson, H. G., eds. 1976. *The Monetary Approach to the Balance of Payments*.

Friedlander, D. 1983. Demographic responses and socioeconomic structure: population processes in England and Wales in the nineteenth century. *Demography* 20: 249–72.

Friedlander, D., Schellekens, J., Ben-Moshe, E., and Keysar, A. 1985. Socioeconomic characteristics and life expectancies in nineteenth-century England: a district analysis. *Population Studies* 39: 137–51.

Friedman, M., and Schwartz, A. J. 1963. *A Monetary History of the United States 1867–1960*. Princeton, N.J.

1970. *Monetary Statistics of the United States*. New York.

1982. *Monetary Trends in the United States and in the United Kingdom, 1870–1970*. Chicago.

Frost, R. 1954. The Macmillan gap. *Oxford Economic Papers* 6: 181–201.

Fuchs, V. R. 1968. *The Service Economy*. New York.

ed. 1969. *Production and Productivity in the Service Industries*. New York.

Fussell, G. E. 1983. The tariff commission report. *Agricultural History Review* 30: 137–42.

Gales, K., and Marks, P. H. 1974. Twentieth century trends in the employment of women in England and Wales. *Journal of the Royal Statistical Society*, Series A, 137: 60–74.

Gallagher, J., and Robinson, R. 1953. The imperialism of free trade. *Economic History Review* 6: 1–15.

Gallman, R. E., and Weiss, T. J. 1969. The service industries in the nineteenth century. In Fuchs 1969.

Garrett, E. M. 1990. The trials of labour: motherhood versus employment in a nineteenth century textile centre. *Continuity and Change* 5: 121–54.

Garside, W. R. 1981. *The Measurement of Unemployment: Methods and Sources in Great Britain 1850–1979*. Oxford.

1990. *British Unemployment 1919–1939*. Cambridge.

Garside, W. R., and Hatton, T. J. 1985. Keynesian policy and British unemployment in the 1930s. *Economic History Review* 38: 83–8.

Gartner, L. P. 1960. *The Jewish Immigrant in England, 1870–1914*. Detroit, Mich.

Gayer, A. D., Rostow, W. W., and Schwartz, A. J. 1953. *The Growth and Fluctuations of the British Economy 1790–1850: An Historical Statistical and Theoretical Study of Britain's Economic Development*. Oxford.

Gazeley, I. 1989. The cost of living for urban workers in late Victorian and Edwardian Britain. *Economic History Review* 42: 207–21.

Geary, F. 1990. Accounting for entrepreneurship in late Victorian Britain. *Economic History Review* 43: 283–7.

Gemmell, N., and Wardley, P. 1990. The contribution of services to British economic growth 1856–1913. *Explorations in Economic History* 27: 299–321.

Gerschenkron, A. 1953–4. Social attitudes, entrepreneurship and economic development. *Explorations in Entrepreneurial History* 6: 1–19.

Gittins, D. 1982. *Fair Sex. Family Size and Structure, 1900–39*.

Gladstone, W. E. 1879. *Midlothian Speeches*, Leicester. Reprinted 1971.

Glass, D. V. 1940. *Population Policies and Movements in Europe*. Oxford.

1963–4. Some indicators of differences between urban and rural mortality in England and Wales and Scotland. *Population Studies* 17: 263–7.

Glass, D. V., and Revelle, R., eds. 1972. *Population and Social Change*.

Glynn, S., and Booth, A. 1985. Building counterfactual pyramids. *Economic History Review* 38: 89–94.

Glynn, S., and Howells, P. 1980. Unemployment in the 1930s: a Keynesian solution reconsidered. *Australian Economic History Review* 20: 28–45.

Goodard, N. 1988. *Harvest of Change: The Royal Agricultural Society of England 1838–1988*.

Goodhart, C. A. E. 1986. Comment on Seabourne. In Capie and Wood 1986.

1991. Are central banks necessary? In Capie and Wood 1991.

Gordon, R. 1990. What is new Keynesian economics? *Journal of Economic Literature* 28: 1115–71.

Gordon, R. J., ed. 1986. *The American Business Cycle: Continuity and Change*. Chicago.

Gorton, G. 1988. Banking panics and business cycles. *Oxford Economic Papers* 40: 751–81.

Gospel, H. F., and Littler, C. R., eds. 1983. *Managerial Strategies and Industrial Relations*.

Gourvish, T. R. 1979. The standard of living, 1890–1914. In O'Day 1979.

Gramlich, E. M. 1985. Government services. In Inman 1985.

Grant, A. T. K. 1937. *A Study of the Capital Market in Postwar Britain*.

Grantham, G., and Leonard, C. S., eds. 1989. *Agrarian Organization in the Century of Industrialization: Europe, Russia, and North America*. Greenwich, Conn.

Greasley, D. 1982. The diffusion of machine cutting in the British coal industry 1902–1938. *Explorations in Economic History* 19: 221–45.

1986. British economic growth: the paradox of the 1880s and the timing of the climacteric. *Explorations in Economic History* 23: 416–44.

1990. Fifty years of coal-mining productivity. The record of the British coal-mining industry before 1939. *Journal of Economic History* 50: 877–903.

Green, A., and Urquhart, M. C. 1976. Factor and commodity flows in the international economy of 1870–1914: a multi-country view. *Journal of Economic History* 36: 217–52.

Green, F., ed. 1989. *The Restructuring of the UK Economy*. Hemel Hempstead.

Gregory, T. E. 1957. The Norman conquest reconsidered. *Lloyds Bank Review*.

Grigg, D. 1987. Farm size in England and Wales from early Victorian times to the present. *Agricultural History Review* 35: 179–89.

Grigg, P. J. 1948. *Prejudice and Judgement*. Oxford.

Habakkuk, H. J. 1940. Free trade and commercial expansion, 1853–1870. In Holland Rose *et al.* 1940.

1962. *American and British Technology in the Nineteenth Century*. Cambridge.

Haggard, H. R. 1911. *Rural Denmark and its Lessons*.

Hall, A. A. 1981. Wages, earnings and real earnings in Teesside: a reassessment of the ameliorist interpretation of living standards in Britain 1870–1914. *International Review of Social History* 26: 202–19.

Hall, A. D. 1913. *A Pilgrimage of British Farming 1910–12*.

Hall, A. R. 1963. *The London Capital Market and Australia 1870–1914*. Canberra.

ed. 1968. *The Export of Capital from Britain 1870–1914*.

Halsey, A. H., ed. 1988. *British Social Trends since 1900: A Guide to the Changing Social Structure of Britain*.

Hamilton, J. D. 1992. Was the deflation during the Great Depression anticipated? Evidence from the commodity futures market. *American Economic Review* 82: 157–78.

Hannah, L. 1974a. Managerial innovation and the rise of the large-scale company in interwar Britain. *Economic History Review* 27: 252–70.

1974b. Takeover bids in Britain before 1950. *Business History* 16: 65–77.

ed. 1976a. *Management Strategy and Business Development*.

1976b. *The Rise of the Corporate Economy. The British Experience*.

1979. *Electricity before Nationalization*.

1983. *The Rise of the Corporate Economy*. Baltimore.

1986. *Inventing Retirement: The Development of Occupational Pensions in Britain*. Cambridge.

Hannah, L., and Kay, J. 1977. *Concentration in Modern Industry*.

Harley, C. K. 1974. Skilled labour and the choice of technique in Edwardian industry. *Explorations in Economic History* 11: 391–414.

1976. Goschen's conversion of the national debt and the gold on Consols. *Economic History Review* 34: 101–6.

1977. The interest rate and prices in Britain, 1873–1913: a study of the Gibson Paradox. *Explorations in Economic History* 14: 69–89.

Harnetty, P. 1972. *Imperialism and Free Trade: Lancashire and India in the Mid-Nineteenth Century*. Vancouver.

Harris, B. 1988. Unemployment, insurance and health in interwar Britain. In Eichengreen and Hatton 1988a.

Harris, J. 1972. *Unemployment and Politics 1886–1914*. Oxford.

Harrison, A. E. 1969. The competitiveness of the British cycle industry, 1890–1914. *Economic History Review* 22: 287–303.

Harrison, R., and Zeitlin, J., eds. 1985. *Divisions of Labour: Skilled Workers and Technological Change in Nineteenth Century Britain*. Hemel Hempstead.

Harvey, C. E. 1979. Business history and the problem of entrepreneurship. *Business History* 21: 3–22.

Hatton, T. J. 1983. Unemployment benefits and the macroeconomics of the interwar labour market: a further analysis. *Oxford Economic Papers* 35: 486–505.

1985. The British labour market in the 1920s: a test of the search-turnover approach. *Explorations in Economic History* 22: 257–70.

1986. Structural aspects of unemployment in Britain between the world wars. *Research in Economic History* 10: 55–92.

1988a. A quarterly model of the labour market in interwar Britain. *Oxford Bulletin of Economics and Statistics* 50: 1–26.

1988b. The recovery of the 1930s and economic policy in Britain. In Butlin and Gregory 1988.

1990. The demand for British exports, 1870–1914. *Economic History Review* 43: 576–94.

Hawke, G. R. 1970. *Railways and Economic Growth in England and Wales, 1840–1870*. Oxford.

Hawtrey, R. G. 1913. *Good and Bad Trade: An Enquiry into the Causes of Trade Fluctuations*.

Hay, J. R. 1975. *The Origins of the Liberal Welfare Reforms 1906–1914*.

Hayek, F. A. 1976. *Denationalisation of Money*. Hobart Paper No. 70, Institute of Economic Affairs. Repr. 1990.

Headrick, D. R. 1981. *The Tools of Empire*.

Heath, F. G. 1874. *The English Peasantry*.

Hebert, R. F., and Link, A. N. 1988. *The Entrepreneur*. New York.

Heim, C. E. 1983. Industrial organisation and regional development in inter-war Britain. *Journal of Economic History* 43: 931–52.

1984a. Limits to intervention: the Bank of England and industrial development in the depressed areas. *Economic History Review* 37: 533–50.

1984b. Structural transformation and the demand for new labour in advanced economies: interwar Britain. *Journal of Economic History* 44: 585–95.

Hennock, E. P. 1973. *Fit and Proper Persons*.

1987. The measurement of urban poverty: from the metropolis to the nation, 1880–1920. *Economic History Review* 40: 208–27.

Hicks, J. R. 1937. Mr Keynes and the classics. *Econometrica* 5: 147–59.

1974. Real and monetary factors in economic fluctuations. *Scottish Journal of Political Economy* 21: 205–14.

1982a. Are there economic cycles? In Hicks 1982b.

ed. 1982b. *Money, Interest and Wages, Collected Essays on Economic Theory*, vol. II. Oxford.

Hill, T. P. 1977. On goods and services. *The Review of Income and Wealth* 23: 315–38.

Hinton, J. 1973. *The First Shop Stewards'* Movement.

Hobsbawm, E. J. 1964. *Labouring Men: Studies in the History of Labour.*

1984. *Workers: Worlds of Labour*. New York.

Hobson, J. A. 1902. *Imperialism, a Study.*

Hodgson, J. A. 1972. An analysis of floating exchange rates: the dollar sterling rate 1919–1925. *Southern Economic Journal* 39: 249–57.

Hoffman, R. J. S. 1933. *Great Britain and the German Trade Rivalry, 1875–1914.* Philadelphia.

Holland Rose, J., Newton, A. P., and Benians, E. A., eds. 1940. *The Cambridge History of the British Empire*. Cambridge.

Hollingsworth, T. H. 1970. *Migration. A Study Based on Scottish Experience between 1939 and 1964*. Edinburgh.

Hopkins, A. G. 1973. *An Economic History of West Africa.*

Hopwood, E. 1969. *The Lancashire Weavers' Story*. Manchester.

Horn, L., and Kocka, J., eds. 1979. *Law and the Formation of the Big Enterprises.* Göttingen.

Hounshell, D. 1984. *From the American System to Mass Production, 1800–1932*, Baltimore.

Howson, S. 1975. *Domestic Monetary Management in Britain 1919–1938*. Cambridge.

Hubbard, R. G., ed. 1991. *Financial Crises*. Chicago.

Huberman, M. 1992. The origins of the Bolton and Oldham cotton spinning lists: a case study of efficiency wages. In Carlson and Terrill 1992.

Hudson, P., ed. 1989. *Regions and Industries: A Perspective on the Industrial Revolution in Britain*. Cambridge.

Hughes, T. P. 1988. *Networks of Power. Electrification in Western Society, 1880–1930.*

Humphries, J. 1977. Class struggle and the persistence of the working class family. *Cambridge Journal of Economics* 1: 241–58.

1987. Interwar house building, cheap money and the building societies: the housing boom revisited. *Business History* 29: 325–45.

Hunt, E. H. 1973. *Regional Wage Variations in Britain, 1850–1914*. Oxford.

1981. *British Labour History, 1815–1914*. Atlantic Highlands, N.J.

1986. Industrialization and regional inequality: wages in Britain. *Journal of Economic History* 46: 935–66.

Hyman, R. 1971. *The Workers Union*. Oxford.

1985. Class struggle and the trade union movement. In Coates *et al.* 1985.

Imlah, J. A. H. 1958. *Economic Elements in the Pax Britannica: Studies in British Foreign Trade in the Nineteenth Century*. Cambridge, Mass.

Inglis, S. 1988. *League Football.*

Inman, R. P., ed. 1985. *Managing the Service Economy: Prospects and Problems.* Cambridge.

Irving, R. J. 1976. *The North East Railway Company 1870–1914*. Leicester.

1978. The profitability and performance of British railways 1870–1914. *Economic History Review* 31: 46–66.

James, H. 1990. The German experience and the myth of British exceptionalism. In Collins and Robbins 1990.

Jenkins, D. T., and Malin, J. C. 1990. European competition in woollen cloth. *Business History* 32: 66–86.

Jenkins, D. T., and Ponting, K. G. 1982. *The British Wool Textile Industry 1770–1914*.

Jenks, L. H. 1927. *The Migration of British Capital to 1875*. New York.

Jeremy, D. J. 1991. The hundred largest employers in the United Kingdom, in manufacturing and non-manufacturing industries, in 1907, 1935 and 1955. *Business History* 33: 93–111.

Jevons, W. S. 1884. *Investigations in Currency and Finance*.

Johnman, L. 1986. The largest manufacturing companies of 1935. *Business History* 28: 226–39.

Johnson, P. 1984. Self-help versus state help: old age pensions and personal savings in Great Britain, 1906–1937. *Explorations in Economic History* 21: 329–50.

1985. *Saving and Spending: The Working-Class Economy in Britain 1870–1939*. Oxford.

Jolly, M. 1988. The British motor industry and the labour market during the inter-war period. PhD dissertation, University of Toronto, 1988.

Jones, G. 1988. Foreign multinationals and British industry before 1945. *Economic History Review* 41: 429–53.

Jones, G. S. 1971. *Outcast London: A Study in the Relationship between Classes in Victorian Society*. Oxford.

Jones, G. T. 1933. *Increasing Return*. Cambridge.

Jones, M. A. 1973. The background to emigration from Great Britain in the nineteenth century. *Perspectives in American History* 7: 3–92.

Jones, M. E. F. 1985a. Regional employment multipliers, regional policy and structural change in inter-war Britain. *Explorations in Economic History* 22: 417–39.

1985b. The regional impact of an overvalued pound in the 1920s. *Economic History Review* 38: 393–401.

Jowitt, J. A. and McIvor, A. J., eds. 1988. *Employers and Labour in the English Textile Industries, 1850–1939*.

Joyce, P. 1990. Work. In Thompson 1990: vol. II.

Kain, R., and Prince, H. 1985. *The Tithe Surveys of England and Wales*. Cambridge.

Kaldor, N. 1966. *Causes of the Slow Rate of Economic Growth in the United Kingdom*. Cambridge.

1985. *The Scourge of Monetarism*. Oxford.

Katouzian, M. A. 1970. The development of the service sector: a new approach. *Oxford Economic Papers* 22: 362–82.

Kearns, G. 1988. The urban penalty and the population history of England. In Brandstrom and Tederbrand 1988.

Kendrick, J. W. 1961. *Productivity Trends in the United States*. Princeton.

Kennedy, C., and Thirlwall, A. P. 1972. Technical progress. *Economic Journal* 82: 11–72.

Kennedy, W. P. 1976. Institutional response to economic growth: capital markets in Britain to 1914. In Hannah 1976a.

1982. Economic growth and structural change in the United Kingdom, 1870–1914. *Journal of Economic History* 42: 105–14.

1987. *Industrial Structure, Capital Markets and the Origins of British Economic Decline*. Cambridge.

Kesner, R. M. 1981. *Economic Control and Colonial Development. Crown Colony Financial Management in the Age of Joseph Chamberlain.* Westport, Conn.

Keynes, J. M. 1924. Foreign investment and the national advantage. *The Nation and the Athenaeum* 35: 584–7.

1925. *The Economic Consequences of Mr Churchill.*

1930. *A Treatise on Money.*

1931. *Essays in Persuasion.*

1936. *The General Theory of Employment, Interest and Money.*

1939. Relative movements of real wages and output. *Economic Journal* 49: 34–51.

Kindleberger, C. P. 1961. Obsolescence and technical change. *Bulletin of the Oxford University Institute of Statistics* 23: 231–97.

1964. *Economic Growth in France and Britain.* Cambridge, Mass.

1986. *The World in Depression 1929–1939.* Harmondsworth.

Kindleberger, C. P., and di Tella, G., eds. 1982. *Economics in the Long View: Essays in Honor of W. W. Rostow*. London and Basingstoke.

Kirby, M. W. 1976. *The British Coal-Mining Industry 1870–1946: A Political and Economic History.*

Kirkaldy, A. W. 1921. *British Finance during and after the War 1914–21.*

Kirzner, I. M. 1973. *Competition and Entrepreneurship.* Chicago.

1989. *Discovery, Capitalism and Distributive Justice.* Oxford.

Kitson, M., and Solomou, S. 1990. *Protectionism and Economic Revival: The British Inter-War Economy.* Cambridge.

Kitson Clark, G. 1951. The repeal of the Corn Laws and the politics of the forties. *Economic History Review* 4: 1–13.

Kleinknecht, A. 1987. *Innovation Patterns in Crisis and Prosperity: Schumpeter's Long Cycle Reconsidered.*

Klovland, J. T. 1987. The demand for money in the United Kingdom 1875–1913. *Oxford Bulletin of Economics and Statistics* 49: 251–71.

Knodel, J., and Van de Walle, E. 1986. Lessons from the past: policy implications of historical fertility studies. In Coale and Watkins 1986.

Kocka, J., and Siegrist, H. 1979. The hundred largest German industrial corporations. In Horn and Kocka 1979.

Koike, K. 1988. *Understanding Industrial Relations in Modern Japan.*

Kondratieff, N. D. 1935. The long waves in economic life. *Review of Economic Statistics* 17: 105–15.

Kravis, I. B., Weston, A. W., and Summers, R. 1983. The share of services in economic growth. In Adams and Hickman 1983.

Kuznets, S. 1961. Quantitative aspects of the economic growth of nations VI. Long-term trends in capital formation proportions. *Economic Development and Cultural Change* 9, part 4: 3–124.

Kydland, F. E., and Prescott, E. C. 1982. Time to build and aggregate fluctuation. *Econometrica* 50: 1345–70.

Lamb, H. H. 1982. *Climate, History and the Modern World.*

Lancaster, H. O. 1990. *Expectations of Life: A Study in the Demography, Statistics and History of World Mortality.* New York.

Landes, D. S. 1965. Factor costs and demand. *Business History* 7: 15–33.

1969. *The Unbound Prometheus.* Cambridge.

Langton, J., and Morris, R. J., eds. 1986. *Atlas of Industrializing Britain 1780–1914.*

Law, C. M. 1980. *British Regional Development since World War I.*

Lawrence, B. 1972. *The Administration of Education in Britain.*

Lazonick, W. 1979. Industrial relations and technical change: the case of the self-acting mule. *Cambridge Journal of Economics* 1979: 231–62.

1981a. Factor costs and the diffusion of ring spinning prior to World War I. *Quarterly Journal of Economics* 96: 89–109.

1981b. Production relations, labour productivity, and choice of technique: British and U.S. cotton spinning. *Journal of Economic History* 41: 491–516.

1983. Industrial organisation and technological change: the decline of the British cotton industry. *Business History Review* 57: 195–236.

1986. The cotton industry. In Elbaum and Lazonick 1986.

1990. *Competitive Advantage on the Shop Floor.* Cambridge, Mass.

1991. *Business Organisation and the Myth of the Market Economy.* Cambridge.

Lazonick, W., and Mass, W. 1984. The performance of the British cotton industry, 1870–1913. *Research in Economic History* 9: 1–44.

Lee, C. H. 1979. *British Regional Employment Statistics, 1841–1971.* Cambridge.

1984. The service sector, regional specialisation, and economic growth in the Victorian economy. *Journal of Historical Geography* 10: 139–55.

1986. *The British Economy since 1700: A Macro-Economic Perspective.* Cambridge.

1990a. *Economic Growth, Structural Change, Labour Productivity and Industrialisation 1860–1913.* Department of Economics, University of Aberdeen, discussion paper 90.05.

1990b. *Kaldor's Laws and Economic Growth in Historical Perspective: The Industrial Economies 1880–1973.* Department of Economics, University of Aberdeen, discussion paper 90.04.

1991. Regional inequalities in infant mortality in Britain, 1861–1971: patterns and hypotheses. *Population Studies* 45: 55–65.

Lees, L. H. 1979. *Exiles of Erin. Irish Emigrants in Victorian London.* Ithaca, N.Y.

Lenin, V. I. 1915. *Imperialism, the Highest State of Capitalism.* Moscow.

Levine, A. L. 1967. *Industrial Retardation in Britain 1880–1914.*

Lewchuk, W. 1987. *American Technology and the British Vehicle Industry.* Cambridge.

Lewis, W. A. 1952. World prices, production and trade 1870–1960. *Manchester School* 20: 105–38.

1978. *Growth and Fluctuations 1870–1913.*

Lewis-Faning, E. 1949. *Report of an Enquiry into Family Limitation and its Influence on Human Fertility during the Past 50 Years.*

Liesner, T. 1989. *One Hundred Years of Economic Statistics.*

Lindert, P. 1969. *Key Currencies and Gold 1900–1913*. Princeton Studies in International Finance no. 24.
Lindert, P., and Trace, K. 1971. Yardsticks for Victorian entrepeneurs. In McCloskey 1971a.
Lipsey, R. G. 1960. The relation between unemployment and the rate of change of money wage rates in the United Kingdom, 1862–1957: a further analysis. *Economica* 27: 1–31.
Littler, C. R. 1982. *The Development of the Labour Process in Capitalist Societies*.
Llewellyn-Smith, H., ed. 1930–5. *The New Survey of London Life and Labour*, vols. I–IX.
Lloyd-Jones, R. 1987. Innovation, industrial structure and the long wave: the British economy c. 1873–1814. *Journal of European Economic History* 18: 315–33.
Locke, R. 1984. *The End of Practical Man: Entrepreneurship and Higher Education in Germany, France and Britain 1880–1940*.
Logan, W. P. D. 1950. Mortality in England and Wales from 1848 to 1947. *Population Studies* 4: 132–78.
Lorenz, E. H. 1991. *Economic Decline in Britain: The Shipbuilding Industry, 1890–1970*. Oxford.
Lorenz, E. H., and Wilkinson, F. 1986. The shipbuilding industry, 1880–1965. In Elbaum and Lazonick 1986.
Louis, W. R., ed. 1976. *Imperialism: The Robinson and Gallagher Controversy*. New York.
Lowndes, G. A. D. 1937. *The Silent Social Revolution*. Cambridge.
Lucas, R. E. 1972. *Studies in Business Cycle Theory*. Oxford, Reprinted 1981, Cambridge, Mass.
ed. 1981a. *Studies in Business Cycle Theory*. Cambridge, Mass.
1981b. Understanding business cycles. In Lucas 1981a..
Lund, P. J., and Holden, K. 1968. An econometric study of private sector gross fixed capital formation in the UK 1923–38. *Oxford Economic Papers* 20: 56–73.
Macara, C. 1923. *The New Industrial Era*. 2nd edn. Manchester.
McBride, T. M. 1976. *The Domestic Revolution*.
McClaren, A. 1978. *Birth Control in Nineteenth Century. England.*
McClelland, K., and Reid, A. 1985. Wood, iron, and steel: technology, labour, and trade union organisation in the shipbuilding industry, 1840–1914. In Harrison and Zeitlin 1985.
McCloskey, D. N. 1970. Did Victorian Britain fail? *Economic History Review* 23: 446–59.
ed. 1971a. *Essays on a Mature Economy*.
1971b. International differences in productivity? Coal and steel in America and Britain before World War I. In McCloskey 1971a.
1973. *Economic Maturity and Entrepreneurial Decline: British Iron and Steel, 1870–1913*. Cambridge, Mass.
1981. *Enterprise and Trade in Victorian Britain: Essays in Historical Economics*. Reprinted 1993.
McCloskey, D. N., and Sandberg, L. G. 1971. From damnation to redemption:

judgements on the late Victorian entrepreneur. *Explorations in Economic History* 9: 89–108.

McCloskey, D. N., and Zecher, J. R. 1976. How the gold standard worked. In Frenkel and Johnson 1976.

1984. The success of purchasing power parity. In Bordo and Schwartz 1984.

McConnell, P. 1906. *The Diary of a Working Farmer*.

MacDonald, W. 1872. On the agriculture of Invernessshire. *Transactions of the Royal and Highland Society of Scotland*, 4th series, 4: 1–65.

MacInnes, J. 1987. *Thatcherism at Work*.

MacIntosh, T. 1951. A note on cheap money and the British housing boom. *Economic Journal* 61: 167–73.

McIvor, A. 1988. Cotton employers' organisations and labour relations, 1890–1939. In Jowitt and McIvor 1988.

McKendrick, N. 1986. Gentlemen and players revisited. In McKendrick and Outhwaite 1986.

McKendrick, N., and Outhwaite, R. B., eds. 1986. *Business Life and Public Policy*. Cambridge.

Mackenzie, W. A. 1921. Changes in the standard of living in the United Kingdom, 1860–1914. *Economica* 1: 211–30.

McKeown, T. 1976. *The Modern Rise of Population*.

McKersie, R., Hunter, L., and Sengenberger, W. 1972. *Productivity Bargaining: The American and British Experience*, Washington, D.C.

McKinley, A., and Zeitlin, J. 1989. The meanings of managerial prerogative: industrial relations and the organisation of work in British engineering, 1880–1939. *Business History* 31: 32–47.

MacKinnon, M. 1984. Poverty and policy: the English poor law 1860–1910. Unpublished DPhil thesis, Oxford University.

1986. Poor law policy, unemployment, and pauperism. *Explorations in Economic History* 23: 299–336.

1987. English poor law policy and the crusade against outrelief. *Journal of Economic History* 47: 603–25.

McLean, D. 1976. Finance and informal empire before the first world war. *Economic History Review* 29: 291–305.

McMahon, C. W., and Worswick, G. D. N. 1969. The growth of services in the economy: do they slow down overall expansion? In Aldcroft and Fearon 1969.

Macmillan Report. 1931. *Report of the Committee on Finance and Industry*. Cmd 3897.

Macrosty, H. W. 1927. Inflation and deflation in the United States and the United Kingdom, 1919–1923. *Journal of the Royal Statistical Society* 90: 45–122.

Maddison, A. 1982. *Phases of Capitalist Development*. Cambridge.

1983. A comparison of the levels of GDP per capita in developed and developing countries, 1700–1980. *Journal of Economic History* 43: 27–41.

1984. Origins and impact of the welfare state 1883–1983. *Banca Nazionale del Lavoro Quarterly Review* 37: 55–87.

1987. Growth and slowdown in advanced capitalist economies. *Journal of Economic Literature* 25: 649–98.

Maddock, R., and McLean, I. W., eds. 1987. *The Australian Economy in the Long-Run*. Cambridge.

Makower, H., Marschak, H., and Robinson, H. W. 1938, 1939, 1940. Studies in the mobility of labour. *Oxford Economic Papers* 1: 83–123; 2: 70–97; 4: 39–62.

Mallet, B., and George, C. O. 1929. *British Budgets: Second Series. 1913–1921.*

Manley, G. 1959. Temperature trends in England, 1698–1957. *Archiv für Meterologie Geophysik und Bioklimat* 9: 413–33.

Marsh, A. I., and Coker, E. E. 1963. Shop steward organisation in the engineering industry. *British Journal of Industrial Relations* 1: 176–89.

Marx, K. 1867. *Capital*, vol. 1. Reprinted New York, 1977.

Mass, W., and Lazonick, W. 1990. The British cotton industry and international competitive advantage. *Business History* 23: 9–65.

Mass Observation. 1945. *Britain and her Birth Rate*. A report prepared by Mass Observation for the Advertising Services Guild.

Mathias, P. 1957. The entrepreneur in brewing 1700–1830. *Explorations in Entrepreneurial History* 10: 72–80.

Mathias, P., and Davis, J. A., eds. 1989. *The First Industrial Revolutions*. Oxford.

Mathias, P., and Postan, M. M., eds. 1978. *Cambridge Economic History of Europe*, vol. VII. Cambridge.

Matthews, K. G. P. 1986a. *The Interwar Economy: An Equilibrium Approach*. Aldershot.

1986b. Was sterling overvalued in 1925? *Economic History Review* 39: 572–87.

Matthews, R. C. O. 1959. *The Business Cycle*. Cambridge.

Matthews, R. C. O., Feinstein, C. H., and Odling-Smee, J. C. 1982. *British Economic Growth 1856–1973*. Oxford and Stanford, Calif.

Maynard, G. 1988. *The Economy under Mrs. Thatcher*. Oxford.

Meltzer, A. H. 1986. Comment on Anna Schwartz. In Capie and Wood 1986.

Meltzer, A. H., and Robinson, S. 1989. Stability under the gold standard in practice. In Bordo 1989.

Mendershausen, H. 1943. *The Economics of War*. New York.

Metcalf, D., Nickell, S. J., and Floros, N. 1982. Still searching for an explanation of unemployment in interwar Britain. *Journal of Political Economy* 90: 386–99.

Michie, R. C. 1987. *The London and New York Stock Exchanges, 1850–1914.*

1988. The finance of innovation in late Victorian and Edwardian Britain: possibilities and constraints. *Journal of European Economic History* 17: 491–530.

Middleton, R. 1981. The constant employment budget balance and British budgetary policy 1929–39. *Economic History Review* 34: 266–86.

1985. *Towards the Managed Economy: Keynes, the Treasury and the Fiscal Policy Debate of the 1930s.*

Mills, T. C., and Wood, G. E. 1978. Money–income relationships and the exchange rate régime. *Federal Reserve Bank of St Louis Monthly Review*. 30: 22–9.

1988. Interest rates and the conduct of monetary policy. In Eltis and Sinclair 1988.

1992. Money and interest rates in Britain from 1870 to 1913 in Britain in the international economy, 1870–1939. In Broadberry and Crafts 1992.

Millward, R. 1988. The U.K. services sector: productivity and recession in long-term perspective. *The Service Industries Journal* 8: 263–76.

1990. Productivity in the UK services sector: historical trends 1856–1985 and comparisons with the USA 1950–85. *Oxford Bulletin of Economics and Statistics* 52: 423–36.

Millward, R., and Ward, R. 1987. The costs of public and private gas enterprises in late 19th century Britain. *Oxford Economic Papers* 39: 719–37.

Milward, A. S. 1970. *The Economic Effects of the Two World Wars on Britain.*

Minchinton, W. A., ed. 1968. *Essays in Agrarian History*. Newton Abbot.

Mingay, G. E., ed. 1981. *The Victorian Countryside.*

Ministry of Agriculture, Fisheries and Food. 1968. *A Century of Agricultural Statistics, Great Britain 1866–1966.*

Mitchell, B. R. 1976. *European Historical Statistics 1750–1970*. New York.

1988. *British Historical Statistics*. Cambridge.

Mitchell, B. R., and Deane, P. 1962. *Abstract of British Historical Statistics.* Cambridge.

Mitchell, B. R., and Jones, H. G. 1971. *Second Abstract of British Historical Statistics*. Cambridge.

Mitchison, R. 1977. *British Population Change since 1860.*

Moggridge, D. E. 1969. *The Return to Gold: The Formulation of Economic Policy and its Critics.*

1970. The 1931 financial crisis – a new view. *The Banker* 1970: 832–9.

1972. *British Monetary Policy 1924–1931: The Norman Conquest of $4.86.* Cambridge.

Mommsen, W. J., and Husung, H-G., eds. 1985. *The Development of Trade Unionism in Great Britain and Germany, 1880–1914.*

More, C. 1980. *Skill and the English Working Class, 1870–1914.*

Morgan, E. V. 1952. *Studies in British Financial Policy 1914–1925.*

Morris, M. D. 1963. Towards a re-interpretation of nineteenth century Indian economic history. *Journal of Economic History* 23: 606–18.

Mowat, C. L. 1955. *Britain between the Wars 1918–1940*. Boston, Mass.

Mowery, D. C. 1986. Industrial research 1900–1950. In Elbaum and Lazonick 1986.

Mukerjee, T. 1972. Theory of economic drain: impact of British rule on the Indian economy, 1840–1900. In Boulding and Mukerjee 1972.

Musson, A. E. 1965. *Enterprise in Soap and Chemicals. Joseph Crosfield and Sons Limited 1815–1965*. Manchester.

Mutch, A. 1981. The mechanization of the harvest in south-west Lancashire, 1850–1914. *Agricultural History Review* 29: 125–32.

1983. Farmers organizations and agricultural depression in Lancashire. *Agricultural History Review* 31: 26–36.

Nelson, R. R., and Winter, S. G. 1974. Neoclassical vs. evolutionary theories of economic growth. *Economic Journal* 84: 886–905.

Newell, A., and Symons, J. S. V. 1988. The macroeconomics of the interwar years: international comparisons. In Eichengreen and Hatton 1988a.

Newton, M. P., and Jeffery, J. R. 1951. *Internal Migration*. GRO Studies in Medical and Population Subjects. No. 5.

Nicholas S. J. 1982. British multinational investment before 1939. *Journal of European Economic History* 11: 605–30.

1984. The overseas marketing performance of British industry, 1870–1914. *Economic History Review* 37: 489–506.

1991. The expansion of British multinational companies: testing for managerial failure. In Foreman-Peck 1991a.

Nolan, P. 1989. The productivity miracle?. In Green 1989.

O'Brien, A. P. 1988. Factory size, economies of scale, and the great merger wave of 1898–1902. *Journal of Economic History* 48: 639–49.

O'Brien, P. K. 1983. The analysis and measurement of the service sector economy in European economic history. In Fremdling and O'Brien 1983.

1988. The costs and benefits of British imperialism 1846–1914. *Past and Present* 120: 163–200.

O'Day, A., ed. 1979. *The Edwardian Age: Conflict and Stability 1900–1914*. Hamden, Conn.

Oddy, D. J. 1976. A nutritional analysis of historical evidence: the working class diet. In Oddy and Miller 1976.

1982. The health of the people. In Barker and Drake 1982.

Oddy, D. J., and Miller, D., eds. 1976. *The Making of the Modern British Diet*.

Offer, A. 1989. *The First World War: An Agrarian Interpretation*. Oxford.

Forthcoming. The British empire 1870–1914: a waste of money? *Economic History Review*.

Ojala, E. M. 1952. *Agriculture and Economic Progress*.

Okhawa, K., Shinohara, M., and Meissner, L. 1979. *Patterns of Japanese Economic Development: A Quantitative Appraisal*. New Haven, Conn.

Okochi, A., and Yasuoka, S., eds. 1984. *Family Business in the Era of Industrial Growth*.

Olson, M. 1982. *The Rise and Decline of Nations*. New Haven, Conn.

Olson, M., and Harris, C. C. 1959. Free trade in 'corn': a statistical study of the prices and production of wheat in Great Britain from 1873 to 1914. *Quarterly Journal of Economics* 73: 145–68.

Ormerod, P. A., and Worswick, G. D. N. 1982. Unemployment in interwar Britain. *Journal of Political Economy* 90: 400–9.

O'Rourke, K. 1991. *International Migration and Wage Rates in Twentieth Century Ireland*. Columbia University, mimeo.

Orsagh, T. J. 1960–1. Progress in iron and steel: 1870–1913. *Comparative Studies in Society and History* 3: 216–30.

Orwin, C. S., and Whetham, E. H. 1964. *History of British Agriculture 1846–1914*. Cambridge.

Overton, M. 1986. Agriculture. In Langton and Morris 1986.

Parker, W. N. 1971. From old to new to old in economic history. *Journal of Economic History* 31: 3–14.

Parkin, M., and Sumner, M. T., eds. 1972. *Incomes Policy and Inflation*. Manchester.

Parliamentary Papers. 1882. XV, 1, c. 3375. *Royal Commission on Agriculture. Report by Mr Little: Appendix E.*

1893–4. XXXVI, c. 6894–xiv. *Royal Commission on Labour. The Agricultural Labourer.*

1895. XVI, 311, c. 7755. *Royal Commission on Agriculture. Report by Mr. Wilson Fox.*

1897. XV, 1, c. 7755. *Royal Commission on Agriculture: Final Report.*

Patterson, D. G. 1976. *British Direct Investment in Canada, 1890–1914.* Toronto.

Payne, P. L. 1967. The emergence of the large-scale company in Great Britain. *Economic History Review* 20: 519–42.

1974. *British Entrepreneurship in the Nineteenth Century.* 2nd edn, 1988.

1978. Industrial entrepreneurship and management in Great Britain. In Mathias and Postan 1978.

1984. Family business in Britain. In Okochi and Yasuoka 1984.

1990. Entrepreneurship and British economic decline. In Collins and Robbins 1990.

Peacock, A. T., and Wiseman, J. 1961. *The Growth of Public Expenditure in the United Kingdom.*

Pearce, I. F. 1970. *International Trade.*

Pearce, I. F., and Rowan, D. C. 1966. A framework for research in to the real effects of international capital movements. In Dunning 1966.

Peden, G. C. 1988. *Keynes, the Treasury and British Economic Policy.*

Peel, J. 1963. The manufacturing and retailing of contraceptives in England. *Population Studies* 17: 113–25.

Pelling, H. 1976. *A History of British Trade Unionism.* 3rd edn. Harmondsworth.

Pember Reeves, M. 1913. *Round About a Pound a Week.*

Perkin, H. 1969. *The Origin of Modern English Society, 1780–1880.*

Perren, R. 1970. The landlord and agricultural transformation 1870–1900. *Agricultural History Review* 18: 36–51.

1978. *The Meat Trade in Britain 1840–1914.*

Perry, P. J. 1974. *British Farming in the Great Depression, 1870–1914.* Newton Abbot.

Petit, P. 1986. *Slow Growth and the Service Economy.*

Phelps Brown, E. H., and Handfield Jones, S. J. 1952. The climacteric of the 1890s: a study in the expanding economy. *Oxford Economic Papers* 14: 266–307.

Phillips, A. D. M. 1989. *The Under-Draining of Farmland in England during the Nineteenth Century.* Cambridge.

Phillips, A. W. 1958. The relation between unemployment and the rate of change of money wage rates in the United Kingdom, 1861–1957. *Economica* 25: 283–99.

Phillips, W. H. 1982. Induced innovation and economic performance in late Victorian British industry. *Journal of Economic History* 42: 97–103.

Pigou, A. C., ed. 1913a. *Essays in Applied Economics.*

1913b. A minimum wage for agriculture. In Pigou 1913a.

1927. Wage policy and unemployment. *Economic Journal* 38: 355–68.

1943. The classical stationary state. *Economic Journal* 53: 343–51.

1948. *Aspects of British Economic History 1918–1925.*

Pilgrim Trust, 1938. *Men Without Work.* Cambridge.

Piva, M. J. 1979. *The Condition of the Working Class in Toronto 1900–21.* Ottawa.

Platt, D. C. M. 1973. The national economy and British imperial expansion before 1914. *Journal of Imperial and Commonwealth History* 2: 3–14.

1986. *Britain's Investment Overseas on the Eve of the First World War: The Uses and Abuses of Numbers.*
Political and Economic Planning. 1935. *Report on Electricity Supply.*
Pollard, S. 1957. British and world shipbuilding, 1890–1914. *Journal of Economic History* 17: 426–44.
1978. Labour in Great Britain. In Mathias and Postan 1978.
1983. *The Development of the British Economy.*
1985. Capital exports, 1870–1914 – harmful or beneficial? *Economic History Review* 38: 489–514.
1989. *Britain's Prime and Britain's Decline.*
1990. Reflections on entrepreneurship and culture in European societies. *Transactions of the Royal Historical Society*, 5th ser., 40: 153–73.
Pollard, S., and Robertson, P. 1979. *The British Shipbuilding Industry, 1970–1914.* Cambridge, Mass.
Pollins, H. 1957–8. Railway contractors and the finance of railway development in Britain. *Journal of Transport History* 3: 41–51 and 103–10.
Pope, D. 1985. Some factors inhibiting Australian immigrants in the 1920s. *Australian Economic History Review* 24: 34–52.
Porter, J. H. 1970. Wage bargaining under conciliation agreements, 1860–1914. *Economic History Review* 23: 460–75.
1974. The commercial banks and the financial problems of the English cotton industry. *International Review of the History of Banking* 9: 1–16.
Prais, S. J. 1976. *The Evolution of Giant Firms in Britain.*
Prest, A. R., and Adams, A. A. 1954. *Consumers' Expenditure in the United Kingdom 1900–1919.* Cambridge.
Price, R., and Bain, G. S. 1988. The Labour Force. In Halsey 1988.
Purcell, J., and Sisson, K. 1983. Strategies and practice in the management of industrial relations. In Bain 1983.
Reader, W. 1975. *Imperial Chemical Industries: A History.* Volume II. Oxford.
Redlich, F. 1952–3. The business leader as a daimonic figure. *American Journal of Economics and Sociology* 12: 163–73 and 289–99.
Redmond, J. 1982. *The Norman Conquest of 4.86: Was the Pound Overvalued?* Faculty of Commerce and Social Sciences Discussion Paper No. 9, University of Birmingham.
1984. The sterling overvaluation in 1925: a multilateral approach. *Economic History Review* 37: 520–32.
Reid, A. 1985. Dilution, trade unionism, and the state in Britain during the First World War. In Tolliday and Zeitlin 1985.
Report of the Unemployment Insurance Statutory Committee for 1937, *1938.*
Rhee, A. 1949. *The Rent of Agricultural Land in England and Wales, 1870–1946.* Oxford.
Richardson, H. W. 1965. Over-commitment in Britain before 1930. *Oxford Economic Papers* 17: 237–62.
1967. *Economic Recovery in Britain 1932–39.*
Richardson, J. H. 1954. *An Introduction to the Study of Industrial Relations.*
Riley, J. C. 1989. *Sickness, Recovery and Death: A History and Forecast of Ill Health.* Iowa City, Iowa.

1991. Working health time: a comparison of pre-industrial, industrial, and post-industrial experience in life and health. *Explorations in Economic History* 28: 169–91.

Rimmer, W. G. 1960. *Marshall's of Leeds, Flax Spinners, 1788–1886.*

Robbins, K. 1990. British culture versus British industry. In Collins and Robbins 1990.

Roberts, E. 1982. Working wives and their families. In Barker and Drake 1982.

1988. *Women's Employment, 1840–1940.*

Rockoff, H. 1984. Some evidence on the real price of gold. Its costs of production and commodity prices. In Bordo and Schwartz 1984.

1986. Walter Bagehot and the theory of central banking. In Capie and Wood 1986.

Rodda, J. C., Downing, R. A., and Law, F. M. 1976. *Systematic Hydrology.*

Rose, L. 1986. *The Massacre of the Innocents. Infanticide in Britain, 1800–1939.*

Rose, M. B. 1986. *The Gregs of Quarry Bank Mill.* Cambridge.

Rosenberg, N. 1976. *Perspectives on Technology*. Cambridge.

Rosovsky, H., ed. 1966. *Industrialisation in Two Systems.* New York.

Rostas, L. 1948a. *Comparative Productivity in British and American Industry.* Cambridge.

1948b. *Productivity, Prices and Distribution in Selected British Industries.* Cambridge.

Rostow, W. W. 1948. *British Economy in the Nineteenth Century*. Oxford.

Routh, G. 1980. *Occupation and Pay in Great Britain 1906–79.*

Rowe, J. 1953. *Cornwall in the Age of the Industrial Revolution.*

Rowe, J. W. F. 1928. *Wages in Practice and Theory.*

Rowntree, B. S. 1901. *Poverty: A Study of Town Life.*

1937. *The Human Needs of Labour.* 2nd edn.

1941. *Poverty and Progress: A Second Social Survey of York.*

Rowntree, B. S., and Kendall, M. 1913. *How the Labourer Lives.*

Rowthorn, R. E. and Solomou, S. N. 1991. The macroeconomic effects of overseas investment on the UK balance of trade, 1870–1913. *Economic History Review* 44: 654–64.

Rubinstein, W. D. 1986a. *Wealth and Inequality in Britain.*

1986b. Wealth and the wealthy. In Langton and Morris 1986.

1990. Cultural explanations for Britain's economic decline: how true? In Collins and Robbins 1990.

Russo, J. A., 1966. The impact of weather on the construction industry of the United States. *Bulletin of the American Meteorological Society* 47: 967–72.

Salter, W. E. G. 1969. *Productivity and Technical Change*. 2nd edn. Cambridge.

Samuel, R. 1977. Workshop of the world: steam power and hand technology in mid-Victorian Britain. *History Workshop* 3: 6–72.

Sandberg, L. G. 1974. *Lancashire in Decline*. Columbus, Ohio.

1981. The entrepreneur and technological change. In Floud and McCloskey 1981.

Sanderson, M. 1972a. Research and the firm in British industry 1919–1939. *Science Studies* 2: 107–51.

1972b. *The Universities and British Industry 1850–1970.*

1988. The English civic universities and the 'industrial spirit', 1870–1914. *Historical Research* 61: 90–104.

Sargent, T., and Wallace, N. 1981. Some unpleasant monetarist arithmetic. *Federal Reserve Bank of Minneapolis Quarterly Review* 5.

Sargent Florence, P. 1947. The statistical analysis of joint stock company control. *Journal of the Royal Statistical Society* 110: 1–19.

Saul, S. B. 1960a. The American impact on British industry, 1895–1914. *Business History* 3: 19–38.

1960b. *Studies in British Overseas Trade, 1870–1914*. Liverpool.

1967. The market and the development of the mechanical engineering industry in Britain, 1860–1914. *Economic History Review* 20: 111–30.

1969. *The Myth of the Great Depression, 1873–1896*. London and Basingstoke.

Savage, M. 1988. Trade unions, sex segregation, and the state. Women's employment in new industries in inter-war Britain. *Social History* 13: 209–30.

Saville, J. 1957. *Rural Depopulation in England and Wales, 1851–1951*.

1960. Trade unions and free labour: the background to the Taff Vale decision. In Briggs and Saville 1960.

Sayers, R. S. 1960a. The return to gold. In Sayers 1960b.

1960b. *Studies in the Industrial Revolution*.

Schofield, J. A. 1982. The development of first-class cricket in England: an economic analysis. *Journal of Industrial Economics* 30: 337–60.

Schumpeter, J. A. 1939. *Business Cycles, I & II: A Theoretical, Historical and Statistical Analysis of the Capitalist Process*. New York.

1947. The creative response in economic history. *Journal of Economic History* 7: 149–59.

1954. *History of Economic Analysis*. Oxford.

Schwartz, A. J. 1982. Reflections on the Gold Commission Report. *Journal of Money, Credit and Banking* 4: 538–51.

1986. Real and pseudo financial crises. In Capie and Wood 1986.

Scott, J. W., and Tilly, L. 1975. Women's work and the family in nineteenth century Europe. *Comparative Studies in Society and History* 17: 36–64.

Seabourne, T. 1986. The summer of 1914. In Capie and Wood 1986.

Searle, G. R. 1971. *The Quest for National Efficiency: A Study in British Politics and Political Thought, 1899–1914*. Oxford.

Sells, D. 1939. *British Wages Boards*. Washington, D.C.

Shergold, R. 1982. *Working-Class Life: The 'American Standard' in Comparative Perspective, 1899–1913*. Pittsburgh, Pa.

Simon, M. 1967. The pattern of new British portfolio foreign investment, 1865–1914. In Adler 1967, also in Hall 1968.

1977. *The economics of population growth*. Princeton, N.J.

Slight, J., and Scott Burn, R. 1858. *The Book of Farm Implements and Machines*.

Sloane, P. J. 1971. The economics of professional football: the football club as a utility maximiser. *Scottish Journal of Political Economy* 18: 121–46.

Slutsky, E. 1937. The summation of random causes as the cause of cyclical processes. *Econometrica* 5: 105–46.

Smith, A. 1776. *The Wealth of Nations*.

Smith, F. B. 1979. *The People's Health 1830–1910*. New York.

1985. Health. In Benson 1985.

Snow, E. C. 1913. Some statistical problems suggested by the sickness and mortality data of the large friendly societies. *Journal of the Royal Statistical Society* 76: 445–510.

Solomou, S. N. 1986. The impact of climatic variations on British economic growth, 1856–1913. *Climatic Change* 8: 53–67.

1987. *Phases of Economic Growth, 1850–1973: Kondratieff Waves and Kuznets Swings*. Cambridge.

Solomou, S. N., and Weale, M. R. 1991. Balanced estimates of U.K. GDP, 1870–1913. *Explorations in Economic History* 28: 54–63.

Solow, B. L. 1971. *The Land Question and the Irish Economy 1870–1904*. Cambridge, Mass.

Soloway, R. 1982. *Birth Control and the Population Question in England, 1877–1930*. Chapel Hill, N.C.

Southall, H. 1986. Regional employment patterns among skilled engineers in Britain, 1851–1914. *Journal of Historical Geography* 12: 268–86.

Stevenson, T. H. C. 1920. The fertility of various social classes in England and Wales from the middle of the nineteenth century to 1911. *Journal of the Royal Statistical Society* 83: 401–32.

Stone, I. 1977. British direct and portfolio investment in Latin America before 1914. *Journal of Economic History* 37: 690–722.

Stone, J. R. N., Champernowne, D. G., and Meade, J. E. 1942. The precision of national income estimates. *Review of Economic Studies* 10: 111–25.

Sturmey, R. G. 1958. *The Economic Development of Radio*.

Supple, B. E. 1970. *The Royal Exchange Assurance: A History of British Insurance 1720–1970*. Cambridge.

1981. Income and demand, 1860–1914. In Floud and McCloskey 1981.

1988. The political economy of demoralisation. *Economic History Review* 41: 368–91.

Svedberg, P. 1978. The portfolio-direct composition of private foreign investment in 1914 revisited. *Economic Journal* 80: 763–77.

Szreter, S. 1986. *The Importance of Social Intervention in Britain's Mortality Decline c. 1850–1914: A Re-Interpretation*. Centre for Economic Policy Research Working Paper 121.

Taylor, A. J. 1961. Labour productivity and technological innovation in the British coal industry 1850–1914. *Economic History Review* 14: 48–70.

Taylor, D. 1976. The English dairy industry, 1860–1930. *Economic History Review* 29: 585–601.

1987. Growth and structural change in the English dairy industry, c. 1860–1930. *Agricultural History Review* 35: 47–64.

Teichova, A., Levy-Leboyer, M., and Nussbaum, H., eds. 1986. *Multinational Enterprise in Historical Perspective*. Cambridge.

Teitelbaum, M. S. 1984. *The British Fertility Decline: Demographic Transition in the Crucible of the Industrial Revolution*. Princeton, N.J.

Teitelbaum, M. S., and Winter, J. M. 1985. *The Fear of Population Decline*. Orlando, Fla.

Telser, L. G. 1987. *A Theory of Efficient Cooperation and Competition*. Cambridge.

Temin, P. 1966. The relative decline of the British steel industry, 1880–1913. In Rosovsky 1966.

1990. *The Great Depression*. Cambridge, Mass.

Terry, M. 1977. The inevitable growth of informality. *British Journal of Industrial Relations* 15: 76–90.

1983. Shop steward development and managerial strategies. In Bain 1983.
Thane, P. 1982. *The Foundations of the Welfare State.*
Thernstrom, S. ed. 1980, *The Harvard Encyclopedia of American Ethnic Groups.* Cambridge, Mass.
Thirlwall, A. P. 1983. A plain man's guide to Kaldor's growth laws. *Journal of Post Keynesian Economics* 5: 345–58.
Thomas, B. 1937. Influx of labour into London and the south-east, 1920–36. *Economica* 4: 323–36.
1954. *Migration and Economic Growth. A Study of Great Britain and the Atlantic Economy.* Cambridge. Revised edn, 1973.
1972. *Migration and Urban Development. A Reappraisal of British and American Long Cycles.*
1983. Rearmament and economic recovery in the late 1930s. *Economic History Review* 36: 552–79.
1988. Labour market structure and the nature of unemployment in interwar Britain. In Eichengreen and Hatton 1988a.
Thomas, R. L., and Stoney, P. J. M. 1972. Unemployment dispersion as a determinant of wage inflation in the United Kingdom. In Parkin and Sumner 1972.
Thomas, T. 1976. Aspects of UK maroeconomic policy during the interwar period. Unpublished PhD dissertation, University of Cambridge.
1981. Aggregate demand in the United Kingdom 1918–1945. In Floud and McCloskey 1981.
Thomas, W. A. 1973. *The Provincial Stock Exchanges.*
Thompson, F. M. L. 1968. The second agricultural revolution 1815–1880. *Economic History Review* 21: 62–77.
ed. 1990. *The Cambridge Social History of Britain, 1750–1950.* Cambridge.
Thomson, D. 1950. *England in the Nineteenth Century.*
1984. The decline of social welfare: falling state support for the elderly since early Victorian times. *Ageing and Society* 4: 451–82.
Thomson, R. 1989. *The Path to Mechanized Shoe Production in the United States.* Durham, N.C.
Tilly, L. A., Scott, J. A., and Cohen, M. 1976. Women's work and European fertility patterns. *Journal of Interdisciplinary History* 6: 447–76.
Titmuss, R. M. 1943. *Birth, Poverty and Health.*
Tolliday, S. 1985. Government, employers, and shop floor organisation in the British motor industry, 1939–1969. In Tolliday and Zeitlin 1985.
1986a. Management and labour in Britain, 1896–1939. In Tolliday and Zeitlin 1986.
1986b. Steel and rationalisation policies, 1918–1950. In Elbaum and Lazonick 1986.
1987. *Business, Banking and Politics: The Case of British Steel 1918–1939.* Cambridge, Mass.
1991. Ford and Fordism in postwar Britain: enterprise management and the control of labour, 1937–1987. In Tolliday and Zeitlin 1991.
Tolliday, S., and Zeitlin, J., eds. 1985. *Shop Floor Bargaining and the State: Historical and Comparative Perspectives.* Cambridge.
eds. 1986. *The Automobile Industry and its Workers.* Cambridge.

eds. 1991. *The Power to Manage? Employers and Industrial Relations in Comparative-Historical Perspective.*

Trace, K., and Henning, G. R., 1975. The diffusion of the motor-ship. *Journal of Economic History* 35: 353–85.

Tranter, N. L. 1985. *Population and Society, 1750–1940.*

Trebilcock, C. 1977. *The Vickers Brothers.*

1986. The city, entrepreneurship and insurance. In McKendrick and Outhwaite 1986.

Turner, A. J. 1972. The evolution of reserve ratios in English banking. *National Westminster Bank Quarterly Review* 52–63.

Turner, H. A., Clack, G., and Roberts, B. 1967. *Labour Relations in the Motor Industry.*

United States. 1975. *Historical Statistics of the United States. Colonial Times to 1970.* Washington, D.C.

Urquhart, M. C., and Buckley, K. A. H., eds. 1965. *Historical Statistics of Canada.* Toronto.

Usher, D. 1980. *The Measurement of Economic Growth.* Oxford.

Vamplew, W. 1976. *The Turf: A Social and Economic History of Horse Racing.*

1982. The economics of a sports industry: Scottish gate-money football 1890–1914. *Economic History Review* 35: 549–67.

1988. *Pay up and Play the Game: Professional Sport in Britain 1875–1914.* Cambridge.

Van de Walle, F. 1986. Infant mortality and the European demographic transition. In Coale and Watkins 1986.

Van Duijn, J. J. 1983. *The Long Wave in Economic Life.*

Velupellai, N., and Thygesen, N., eds. 1990. *Business Cycles, Non Linearities, Disequilibria, and Simulations: Readings in Business Cycles Theory.*

Veverka, J. 1963. The growth of government expenditure in the United Kingdom since 1790. *Scottish Journal of Political Economy* 10: 111–27.

Vichniac, J. E. 1987. Union organisation in the French and British iron and steel industries in the late nineteenth century. *Political Power and Social Theory* 6: 321–49.

von Tunzelmann, G. N. 1982. Structural change and leading sectors in British manufacturing 1907–6. In Kindleberger and di Tella 1982.

Wall, R. 1988. English and German families and the First World War, 1914–18. In Wall and Winter 1988.

Wall, R., and Winter, J., eds. 1988. *The Upheaval of War. Family Work and Welfare in Europe, 1914–18.* Cambridge.

Walters, A. A. 1969. *Money in Boom and Slump.* Hobart Paper 44, Institute of Economic Affairs.

Walton, J. K. 1981. The demand for working-class seaside holidays in Victorian England. *Economic History Review* 34: 249–65.

Ward, D. 1967. The public school and industry in Britain after 1870. *Journal of Contemporary History* 2: 37–52.

Wardley, P. 1991. The anatomy of big business: aspects of corporate development in the twentieth century. *Business History* 33: 268–96.

Weale, M. 1988. The reconciliation of values, volumes and prices in the national accounts. *Journal of the Royal Statistical Society*, Series A, 151: 211–22.
Webster, C. 1985. Health, welfare and unemployment during the depression. *Past and Present* 109: 202–30.
Wehler, H. U. 1970. Bismarck's imperialism 1862–90. *Past and Present* 48: 119–55.
Weir, R. E. 1989. Rationalisation and diversification in the Scotch whisky industry 1900–1939: another look at the old and new industries. *Economic History Review* 42: 375–95.
Wengenroth, U. 1986. *Unternehmensstrategien und Technischer Fortschritt*. Göttingen.
Whetham, E. H. 1979. The trade in pedigree livestock 1850–1910. *Agricultural History Review* 27: 47–50.
White, J. L. 1982. Lancashire cotton textiles. In Wrigley 1982.
Whiteside, N. 1990. *Bad Times: Unemployment in British Social and Political History*.
Whiteside, N., and Gillespie, J. A. 1991. Deconstructing unemployment: developments in Britain in the interwar years. *Economic History Review* 44: 665–82.
Wiener, M. J. 1981. *English Culture and the Decline of the Industrial Spirit*. Cambridge.
Wigham, E. 1973. *The Power to Manage: A History of the Engineering Employers' Federation*.
Wigley, T. M. L., and Atkinson, T. C. 1977. Dry years in south east England since 1698. *Nature* 265: 431–4.
Wilkins, M. 1988. The free-standing company, 1870–1914: an important type of British foreign direct investment. *Economic History Review* 41: 259–82.
1989. *The History of Foreign Investment in the United States to 1914*. Cambridge, Mass.
Wilkinson, E. 1939. *The Town That Was Murdered*.
Wilkinson, F. 1977. Collective bargaining in the steel industry in the 1920s. In Briggs and Saville 1977.
Williamson, J. G. 1964. *American Growth and the Balance of Payments 1820–1913*. Chapel Hill, N.C.
1990a. *Coping with City Growth*. Cambridge.
1990b. The impact of the corn laws just prior to repeal. *Explorations in Economic History* 27: 123–56.
Wilson, C. 1954. *The History of Unilever: A Study of Economic Growth and Social Change*. 2 vols.
1965. Economy and society in late Victorian Britain. *Economic History Review* 18: 183–98.
Wilson, C., and Reader, W. 1958. *Men and Machines*.
Wilson, J. 1864. Reaping machines. *Transactions of the Highland and Agricultural Society of Scotland*, n.s., 19: 123–49.
Wilson Fox, A. 1903. Agricultural wages in England and Wales during the last half century. *Journal of the Royal Statistical Society* 66: 273–348. Also in Minchinton 1968.
Winter, J. M. 1979. Infant mortality, maternal mortality and public health in Britain in the 1930s. *Journal of European Economic History* 8: 439–62.

1982. The decline of mortality, 1870–1950. In Barker and Drake 1982.
1983a. Unemployment, nutrition and infant mortality in Britain, 1920–50. In Winter 1983b.
ed. 1983b. *The Working Class in Modern British History*. Cambridge.
1985. *The Great War and the British People*.
1988. Some paradoxes of the First World War. In Wall and Winter 1988.
Wood, G. E. 1984. Comment on 'real output and the gold standard years.' In Bordo and Schwartz 1984.
1991. Comment on Charles Goodhart. In Capie and Wood 1991.
Wood, G. H. 1909. Real wages and the standard of comfort since 1850. *Journal of the Royal Statistical Society* 72: 91–103.
1910. *The History of Wages in the English Cotton Trade during the Past Hundred Years*. Manchester.
Woods, R. 1982. The structure of mortality in nineteenth century England and Wales. *Journal of Historical Geography* 8: 373–94.
1985. The effects of population redistribution on the level of mortality in nineteenth century England and Wales. *Journal of Economic History* 45: 645–51.
1987. Approaches to the fertility transition in Victorian England. *Population Studies* 41: 283–311.
1989. Population growth and economic change in the eighteenth and nineteenth centuries. In Mathias and Davis 1989.
Woods, R., and Smith, C. W. 1983. The decline of marital fertility in the late nineteenth century: the case of England and Wales. *Population Studies* 37: 207–25.
Woods, R., and Woodward, Y. H. A., eds. 1984. *Urban Disease and Mortality in Nineteenth Century Europe*.
Woods, R., Waterson, P. A., and Woodward, Y. H. A. 1988 and 1989. The causes of the rapid infant mortality decline in England and Wales, 1861–1921. *Population Studies* 42: 343–66 and 43: 113–32.
Worswick, G. D. N. 1984. The sources of recovery in UK in the 1930s. *National Institute Economic Review* 110: 85–93.
Wright, G. 1971. An econometric study of cotton production and trade, 1830–60. *Review of Economics and Statistics* 53: 111–20.
1974. Cotton consumption and the post-bellum recovery of the American South. *Journal of Economic History* 34: 610–35.
Wright, J. F. 1985. Real wage resistance: eighty years of the cost of living. *Oxford Economic Papers* 36 Supplement: 152–67.
Wrightson, J. 1890. The agricultural lessons of 'The Eighties'. *Journal of Royal Agricultural Society*, 3rd. Ser., 1: 275–88.
1906. Comparative economy of different methods of harvesting corn crops. *Journal of the Royal Agricultural Society of England* 67: 98–106.
Wrigley, C. J., ed. 1982. *A History of British Industrial Relations, 1875–1914*. Amherst, Mass.
Wrigley, E. A., and Schofield, R. S. 1981. *The Population History of England, 1541–1871: A Reconstruction*.
Yeager, C. B. 1984. The image of the gold standard. In Bordo and Schwartz 1984.

Youngson, A. J. 1960. *The British Economy 1920–1957*.
1979. *The Scientific Revolution in Victorian Medicine*. New York.
Zarnowitz, V. 1985. Recent work on business cycles in historical perspective: a review of theories and evidence. *Journal of Economic Literature* 23: 523–80.
Zeitlin, J. 1983. The labour strategies of British engineering employers, 1890–1922. In Gospel and Littler 1983.
1985. Industrial structure, employer strategy, and job control in Britain, 1880–1920. In Mommsen and Husung 1985.

List of British Isles cities, towns, villages, parishes, counties, regions and other geographic landmarks cited

Note: in 1974 county boundaries in Britain were redrawn; many were consolidated and renamed. Post-1974 county names and descriptions have been given *only* in those instances where they were cited in the text; otherwise all county references are to the pre-1974 counties and boundaries. Not all counties are included.

MAJOR DIVISIONS AND COUNTRIES

England
The southern portion (excluding Wales) of Great Britain; roughly 50,875 square miles; London is its capital.

Great Britain
England, Wales and Scotland.

Ireland (Eire)
Western island of the British Isles; by a new constitution effective 29 December 1937, Ireland declared itself a 'sovereign, independent, democratic state'; full independence from the British Commonwealth was achieved with the Republic of Ireland Act in 1948; 27,137 square miles; Dublin is the capital.

Northern Ireland
A self-governing state established in 1920 with the Government of Ireland Acts; made up of the former counties of Antrim, Armagh, Down, Londonderry, Tyrone and Ulster; area of 5,238 square miles; a focal point of social, economic and political unrest between Protestants and Catholics; Belfast is the seat of government.

Scotland
The northern part of Great Britain; 29,796 square miles in area; the border with England extends from roughly the Solway Firth to the Cheviot Hills to the river Tweed; composed of the Southern Uplands, the Central Lowlands (frequently referred to in combination as 'the Lowlands'), the Northern and Western Highlands ('the Highlands'), the Hebrides or Western Isles and the Orkney and Shetland Isles; Edinburgh is Scotland's capital.

United Kingdom of Great Britain *and Ireland*
Political union established 1 January 1801; comprised of England and Wales, Scotland and Ireland; superseded by the United Kingdom of Great Britain *and Northern Ireland* on 6 December 1921; the Irish Free State recognised as a free member of the British Commonwealth (until 1937 when Ireland declared its independence).

Wales (Cymru)
Principality in the SW of Great Britain; area of some 8,000 square miles;

commonly divided according to 'North Wales' and 'South Wales'; the Welsh capital is Cardiff.

CITIES, TOWNS AND VILLAGES

Aberdeen
Seaport city and county town of Aberdeenshire, Scotland; 130½ miles N of Edinburgh and 524 miles N of London.

Ayr
Seaport and county town of Ayrshire, Scotland, on river Ayr; 41½ miles SW of Glasgow and 87½ miles WSW of Edinburgh.

Balcarres (House)
In E Fifeshire, Scotland; ¾ miles NW of Colinsburgh.

Banbury
Town in Oxfordshire; 22 miles N of Oxford.

Barnsley
Town in Yorkshire (West Riding); 16 miles N of Sheffield, on river Dearne.

Bedford
County town of Bedfordshire, straddles river Ouse; 49¾ miles NW of London.

Belfast
Principal town of county Ulster in Northern Ireland; 113 miles N of Dublin, across the Irish Sea from Glasgow (135 miles) and from Liverpool (156 miles); site of Queens University.

Billingham
Urban district in SE Durham; 2½ miles NE of Stockton-on-Tees.

Birmingham
City in Warwickshire; 113 miles NW of London; located roughly in the centre of England on the edge of a major coal and iron district; metal manufactures were central to Birmingham's industrial development.

Blackpool
Town in N Lancashire; 16½ miles NW of Preston and 227 miles NW of London by rail.

Blackwell Hall
Seat in S Durham, on river Tees; 1½ miles SW of Darlington.

Bradford
City in Yorkshire (West Riding); 9 miles W of Leeds, 35 miles SW of York and 192 miles from London by rail; England's primary seat for woollens and worsteds manufacture; nicknamed 'Worstedopolis'.

Bristol
Seaport city in Gloucestershire (and Somerset); port 26 miles from Cardiff, Wales, and 71 miles from Swansea, Wales; 117½ miles W of London.

Cambridge
County seat of Cambridgeshire; 57 miles NE of London by rail; most notably the site of Cambridge University and its related colleges.

Cardiff
Seaport and county town of Glamorgan, Wales; 152 miles W of London; voluminous exports of coal and iron from nearby Taff and Rhymney Valleys made through the port; industries also included iron foundries, tinplate manufactures and iron shipbuilding.

Carnarvon
County town of Carnarvonshire, Wales; 246 miles NW of London by rail.

Carron
Village in Stirlingshire, Scotland; near river Carron; ironworks established there in 1760.

Coventry
City of Warwickshire; 19 miles SE of Birmingham and 94 miles NW of London by rail; manufactures included cycles, motors, ribbons, silk, watches, woollens, carpets, cotton, metalwork and iron founding.

Crook
Village in S Durham.

Derby (där′bē)
County town of Derbyshire; 42½ miles NE of Birmingham, 60 miles SE of Manchester and 129 miles NW of London by rail.

Dublin
Metropolis of Eire (Ireland); port 60 miles from Holyhead, Carnarvonshire, Wales, 196 miles from Glasgow.

Dudley (and Ward)
Town in Worcestershire; 8 miles NW of Birmingham; 121½ miles NW of London.

Dundee
Seaport city on the Tay in Angus, Scotland; 59½ miles N of Edinburgh, 84 miles NE of Glasgow, and 452¾ miles NW of London by rail; principal manufactures included jute and linen, shipbuilding, engineering, foundries and brewing.

Dundonald
Village in Ayrshire, Scotland.

Dunkinfield
Municipal borough in Cheshire.

Edinburgh
Capital of Scotland and county town of Midlothian, on the Firth of Forth; 392½ miles N of London; seaport section known as 'Leith'; principal industries included printing, bookbinding, machine-making, rubber and brewing.

Edgbaston
Parliamentary division of Birmingham.

Etruria
Village near Stoke-upon-Trent, N Staffordshire; site of Josiah Wedgwood's earthenware manufactures.

Gainsborough
Town in Lincolnshire; 15 miles NW of Lincoln and 145 miles NW of London; a sub-port of Grimsby.

Gateshead
Town in N Durham on river Tyne, opposite Newcastle; industrial composition mimicked that of Newcastle.

Glasgow
City on the river Clyde in Lanarkshire, Scotland; 47½ miles W of Edinburgh and 401½ miles NW of Euston Station in London by rail; principal industries were textiles, printing, iron manufacture, engineering; regarded as the seat of the Scottish iron trade.

Gleneagles
Place in Perthshire, Scotland; site of grand hotel with golf course and tennis grounds.

Hereford
County town of Herefordshire on river Wye; 144 miles NW of London by rail.

Hull
City at the confluence of the river Hull and the estuary the Humber; 55½ miles SE of Leeds and 173½ miles N from London; one of England's largest ports; also known as 'Kingston-upon-Hull'.

Huntingdon
County town of Huntingdonshire on river Ouse; 59 miles N of London.

Inverness
County town of Inverness-shire, Scotland, at NE end of Caledonian Canal; 192 miles from Edinburgh, 585 miles from London; principal industries included railway repair, shipbuilding, iron founding and woollen cloth.

Keighley (kēth′lē)
Town in Yorkshire (West Riding); 9 miles NW of Bradford; connected to Hull by the Leeds & Liverpool Canal.

Leeds
City on river Aire in Yorkshire (West Riding); 25 miles SW of York, 43 miles NE of Manchester and 186 miles NW of London by rail; site of most major industrial undertakings.

Leicester (les′ter)
Capital city of Leicestershire on river Soar; 99 miles by rail NNW of London; principal centre for a large agricultural market, including wool-producing districts.

Lincoln
County town of Lincolnshire; 120 miles NW of London.

Liverpool
Seaport city in Lancashire on the river Mersey; 31 miles W of Manchester by rail, 201 miles NW of London; chief port for Britain's transatlantic trade.

London
Capital city of England; seat of government for Great Britain; on the Thames; principal financial and commercial centre for Britain; the financial centre is sometimes simply referred to as 'the City'.

Macclesfield
Town in Cheshire; 17½ miles S of Manchester, 166 miles NW of London by rail; adjacent to the Macclesfield Canal.

Manchester
City in Lancashire, separated from Salford by river Irwell; connected to the sea 35½ miles away by the Manchester Ship Canal; 183 miles NW of London.

Marston
Village in Cheshire on river Trent and on Mersey Canal.

Meriden
Village in Warwickshire; 5½ miles NW of Coventry.

Monmouth
County town of Monmouthshire, England; 19 miles S of Hereford.

Newbury
Town in Berkshire on river Kennet; 17 miles SW of Reading, 53 miles WSW of London by rail.

Newcastle-upon-Tyne
City in Northumberland on river Tyne; 268½ miles N of London; being the port

nearest one of the largest coalfields in England, immense quantities of coal were exported from there; played a central role in the coal trade.

Northampton
Capital of Northamptonshire on river Nene; 65¾ miles NW of London; principal seat of boot and shoe manufactures; also host to the Pytchley Hunt in March and November.

Nottingham
Capital of Nottinghamshire; 123½ miles by rail NW of London's St Pancras Station; important industries were lace making and cotton hosiery manufacture.

Oldham
Town in SE Lancashire on river Medlock; 6 miles NE of Manchester.

Oxford
County town of Oxfordshire between rivers Cherwell and Thames; 63 miles from London by rail; principally an educational centre, site of Oxford University.

Prescott
Town in SW Lancashire; 7½ miles E of Liverpool; site of Liverpool Corporation's water supply reservoirs.

Preston
Port and manufacturing town in Lancashire; on the Lancaster Canal near the head of river Ribble's estuary; 28 miles NE of Liverpool and 31 miles NW of Manchester.

Salford
City in Lancashire, W of Manchester; 'it forms practically a part of Manchester'.

Sheffield
City in Yorkshire; 42½ miles SE of Manchester, 158½ miles NW of London; long recognised for its cutlery industry, but had almost every other manufacturing industry, too.

Southampton
Seaport in Hampshire; 79 miles SW of London; one of Britain's major port centres, particularly for passengers.

Southend-on-Sea
Town in Essex on the Thames; 42 miles E of London by rail.

Stirling
County town of Stirlingshire, Scotland on river Forth; 20½ miles NE of Glasgow and 36½ miles NW of Edinburgh by rail.

Turnberry
Place on Ayrshire coast on Turnberry Bay; 56 miles SW of Glasgow by rail.

Warrington
Town in Lancashire; 16 miles WSW of Manchester.

Warwick
County town of Warwickshire on river Avon; 108 miles NW of London.

York
County town of Yorkshire; 188 miles NW of London.

COUNTIES

Ayrshire
Maritime co. in SW of Scotland; mineral deposits included coal, iron, limestone and sandstone – all extensively worked; had manufactures of woollens, cotton, iron and earthenware; also dairying.

Bedfordshire
Inland co. N of London; primarily agricultural, with some manufactures related to agricultural implements; some mineral extraction.

Berkshire (Bark'shir)
Inland co. W of London; agriculture included dairying and crop cultivation; manufactures of agricultural implements and malt making; Reading had a large biscuit enterprise.

Berwickshire
Maritime co. in SE of Scotand; mineral deposits of limestone, coal and copper; coastal location supported an important fishing industry; agriculture limited to a fertile area called 'the Merse'.

Borders
(Post-1974) co. in SE of Scotand; encompasses the former counties of Berwickshire, Roxburghshire, Selkirkshire, Peebles-shire and parts of Midlothian.

Buckinghamshire
Inland co. adjacent NW to London; agriculture centred around grazing in the south and cultivation of wheat, beans, etc., to the north.

Cambridgeshire
Inland co. N of London; large fens and marshlands drained for agriculture.

Cheshire
Maritime co. S of Lancashire; serviced by the Manchester Ship Canal; mineral deposits of salt, coal and ironstone; railway rolling-stock manufacture was an important industry.

Cornwall
Maritime co. at the extreme SW of England; tin and copper mining and manufacture were dominant industries.

Derbyshire
Inland co. in N central England; pasture and crop lands as well as endowments of coal, iron ore, lead, limestone and marble; manufactures included paper making, silk, lace, cotton, brewing and iron founding.

Devon
Maritime co. in SW of England; like Cornwall, tin and copper mines and manufactures, as well as lead, iron and various clays; industries were coarse woollens, linens, lace, paper, and gloves and shoes.

Durham
Maritime co. in N of England; some of England's most important coalfields located here; many various industries, including chemicals, glass, shipbuilding, paper, woollens & worsteds, large ironworks and machine making.

Essex
Maritime co. adjacent NE to London; primarily agricultural with few industries not related to local supply of agricultural implements.

Glamorgan
Maritime co. in S of Wales; commercially the most important Welsh county due to its endowment of coal and iron ore and its convenient seaboard location; home to some of the world's largest ironworks of the time.

Gloucestershire
Co. in W of England; two large coalfields in the west; industries included silk, woollens and cotton, gloves, glass and dairying.

Hampshire
Maritime co. in S of England; also called 'Hants'; rolling countryside supported

sheep and pigs; main industry located at the ports – shipbuilding and shipping services.

Hertfordshire
Inland co. N of London; economy dominated by agriculture: animal husbandry, grains, hay, fruit and vegetable gardens for urban markets; very few manufactures.

Humberside
(Post-1974) co. on the NE English coast; composed the former counties of East Riding, Yorkshire, parts of West Riding, Yorkshire and the Lindsey division of Lincolnshire; 'Humberside North' is that part of the co. N of the Humber, previously East Riding.

Huntingdonshire
Inland co. in E of England; primarily agricutural with market gardens and dairying; manufactures essentially limited to the local supply of implements.

Kent
Maritime co. in SE of England; largely agricultural, producing more hops than the rest of the country; manufactures centred around paper, gunpowder and pottery; late exploitation of a coal measure on the eastern coast.

Lancashire
Maritime co. in the NW of England on the Irish Sea; major industrial area: coal and iron, shipbuilding and immense cotton and textile manufactures.

Limerick
County in Munster province, Ireland; rolling plain considered quite productive; chief manufactures were woollens, paper and milled grains; also town on river Shannon, W Ireland.

Lincolnshire
Maritime co. in E of England; divided into divisions of Holland, Kesteven and Lindsey; primarily agricultural with a few heavy industries of shipbuilding and machine making.

Midlothian
Co. in SE of Scotland on Firth of Forth; formerly Edinburghshire; mineral deposits of coal, shale, ironstone and limestone; principal industries were brewing, paper manufacture and brick and tile making.

Monmouthshire
Maritime co. in W of England, adjacent to border with Wales; some agricultural production (wheat, rye, barley and oats); best known for its large industries centred around iron and coal; occasionally included as part of the 'South Wales' region.

Norfolk
Maritime co. in the E of England; principal industries were fishing and agriculture: livestock – including cart horses and poultry.

Northamptonshire
Inland co.; hilly district with large deposits of iron; dominant industry centred around iron, but also had boot and shoe industries; colloquially 'Northants'.

Northumberland
Most northerly co. in England; coalfields and lead deposits dominated economy; major industrial area with ironworks, shipbuilding and chemicals manufacture.

Nottinghamshire
N central co. in England; several coal mines, but primarily agricultural; hosiery, cycles, woollens and cotton, and iron foundries among the industries.

Oxfordshire
Central inland co.; primarily engaged in agriculture.

Ross and Cromarty
Co. in extreme NW of Scotland; encompassed some mainland areas and islands of the Outer Hebrides and Lewis (except Harris); lowlands cultivated and industry limited to the distillation of whiskey.

Shropshire
Inland co. in W central England; famous for its breed of sheep; cattle and dairying; deposits of coal and ironstone – only heavy industries related to iron.

Staffordshire
Co. in NW central England; two major coalfields; heavy industry drawn to nearby coal; 'the Black Country' well known for all branches of iron and related industries.

Strathclyde
(Post-1974) co. in W Scotland; formerly counties of Argyllshire, Ayrshire, Lanarkshire, Dunbartonshire and parts of Stirlingshire.

Suffolk
Maritime co. in E England; produced agricultural crops of wheat, barley, peas and beans, butter, sheep and cart-horses; manufactures limited to agricultural implements.

Surrey
Inland co. adjacent S to London; some industries: pharmaceuticals, tobacco, calicoes and woollen goods.

Sussex
Maritime co. in SE England; administratively divided into East and West Sussex; coastal lowlands cultivated with grains and hay; primary sheep pastures; manufactures included woollens, paper, gunpowder and brick and tile making.

Sutherland
Maritime co. in extreme N of Scotland; economy dominated by fishing and sheep-grazing.

Western Isles
(Post-1974) co. in far NW Scotland; formerly parts of Ross and Cromarty and Inverness-shire.

Wiltshire
Inland co. W of London; woollens, carpets, cutlery and steel goods, and iron-founding traditional industries; a unique industry was training dogs for truffle-hunting.

Yorkshire
Large co. on NE coast; major deposits of limestone and coal; divided into three Ridings: North, East and West.

North Riding, in N of co.; endowments of limestone, lead, and ironstone; industries related to iron smelting.

East Riding, in SE of co.; primarily agriculture-related industry; included major seaport of Hull.

West Riding, in W and SW of co.; centre of Yorkshire's industry; encompassed the major Yorkshire coalfield in an area 45 miles × 20 miles; industrial centres in West Riding included Barnsley, Bradford, Dewsbury, Halifax, Huddersfield, Leeds and Sheffield.

REGIONS

arable zone

Counties of Yorkshire (East Riding), Lincolnshire, Nottinghamshire, Rutland, Huntingdonshire, Warwickshire, Leicestershire, Northamptonshire, Cambridgeshire, Norfolk, Suffolk, Bedfordshire, Buckinghamshire, Oxfordshire, Berkshire, Hampshire, Hertfordshire, Essex, Middlesex, Surrey, Kent and Sussex.

Black Country

A term used to designate the manufacturing district south of Staffordshire, occupies radius about 10 miles round West Bromwich.

Cyfartha

In northern vicinity of Merthyr Tydfil, Glamorgan, Wales; seat of iron works.

East Anglia

Counties of Huntingdonshire, Cambridgeshire, Norfolk and Suffolk.

east midlands

Counties of Derbyshire, Nottinghamshire, Lincolnshire (Kesteven & Holland divisions), Leicestershire, Rutland and Northamptonshire.

Forest of Dean

WNW in Gloucestershire; forest supplied wood needed for charcoal in early iron making; largely deforested by 1800.

Highlands

General region of Scotland beyond the Grampians; population primarily of Celtic heritage.

Home Counties

Counties of Essex, Kent, London, Middlesex and Surrey; sometimes referred to as 'the Six Home Counties' including Hertfordshire with those above.

Lothians

District on the south side of the Firth of Forth; included the Scottish counties of East Lothian, Midlothian and West Lothian.

midlands

Counties of Derbyshire, Herefordshire, Leicestershire, South Lancashire, Northamptonshire, Nottinghamshire, Rutland, Shropshire, Staffordshire, Warwickshire, Worcestershire; divided into the east midlands and the west midlands.

north-east

Counties of Northumberland, Durham and Yorkshire (North Riding).

North Wales

Counties of Anglesey, Carnarvonshire, Denbighshire, Flintshire, Merioneth and Montgomeryshire.

north-west

Counties of Cumberland, Westmorland and Lancashire (perhaps also including Cheshire).

pastoral zone

Counties of Northumberland, Cumberland, Durham, Yorkshire (North & West Ridings), Westmorland, Lancashire, Cheshire, Derbyshire, Staffordshire, Shropshire, Worcestershire, Herefordshire, Monmouthshire (Wales), Gloucestershire, Wiltshire, Dorsetshire, Somersetshire, Devonshire and Cornwall.

Scottish Lowlands

The Scottish mainland not included in the Highlands; generally applied to the counties south of the Firths of Clyde and Tay; 'eastern': East Lothian,

Midlothian, West Lothian, Peebles-shire, Selkirkshire and Roxburghshire; 'Western': Renfrewshire, Lanarkshire, Ayrshire, Wigtownshire, Kirkcudbrightshire and Dumfries-shire.

south-east

Counties of Bedfordshire, Buckinghamshire, Oxfordshire, Berkshire, Hampshire, Hertfordshire, Essex, (Greater London), Surrey, Kent and Sussex.

South Lancashire

Area in NE England; now Merseyside and Greater Manchester.

South Wales

'Formally' comprised of the counties: Brecknockshire, Cardiganshire, Carmarthenshire, Glamorgan, Pembrokeshire and Radnorshire.

south-west

Counties of Gloucestershire, Wiltshire, Somerset, Dorset, Devon and Cornwall.

West Country

Counties of Cornwall, Devon, Somerset and parts of Wiltshire, Gloucestershire and Dorset.

east midlands

Counties of Shropshire, Staffordshire, Warwickshire, Worcestershire and Herefordshire.

PARISHES

Ash

In Derbyshire, 8 miles SW of Derby.

Banbury

In Oxfordshire, 22 miles N of Oxford.

Blackburn

In Lancashire; 11 miles E of Preston and 210 miles NW of London; one of the principal locales of cotton manufactures.

Bottesford

In N Leicestershire, 7 miles NW of Grantham or in Lindsey, Lincolnshire, 7 miles W of Briggs.

Burslem

In Stoke-on-Trent, N Staffordshire; 20 miles NNW of Stafford by rail; most notably the birthplace of Josiah Wedgwood (1730–95).

Dawlish

In E Devonshire.

Gedling

In Nottinghamshire, 3 miles NE of Nottingham.

Morchard Bishop

In Devonshire, N of Exeter.

Odiham

In NE Hampshire.

Shepshed

In Leicestershire, 4 miles W of Loughborough.

Winlaton

In Durham on river Tyne.

RIVERS, CANALS AND GEOGRAPHIC LANDMARKS

Ayr
River in Ayrshire, Scotland; flows 38 miles W to Firth of Clyde at Ayr.

Bristol Channel
An expansion of the estuary of the river Severn; it is about 85 miles long and from 5 to 43 miles wide; rapid rising of the tide creates a *bore*, or sudden wave.

Boyne
River in Leinster (len'ster), south-eastern province of Ireland; flows 70 miles through countries of Kildare and Meath to the Irish Sea; 'Battle of the Boyne' found James II defeated by William III on 1 July 1690.

Channel Tunnel
Tunnel connecting Folkestone, England, and Calais, France; built beneath the English Channel; frequently beset by financial and political problems since the 1960s; formally termed 'the Eurotunnel', but nicknamed 'the Chunnel'.

Clyde
Scotland's most important river; 91 miles long; even the largest ships could navigate it to Glasgow; many shipbuilding enterprises built along its banks.

Culloden (Moor)
On the border of Nairnshire, a maritime co. of NE Scotland; site of the defeat of Prince Charles Edward and the Highlanders (the Jacobites) by the Duke of Cumberland which signalled the defeat of the Stuarts.

English Channel
Extension of the Atlantic Ocean between S England and N France; connected to the North Sea by the Strait of Dover; fishing grounds for mackerel and oysters; often simply 'the Channel'.

Humber
Estuary of the rivers Ouse and Trent; 38 miles long and 1 to $7\frac{1}{4}$ miles across.

Kentish Weald, *see* Weald

Mersey
North-western river formed by the confluence of rivers Goyt and Tame; empties into the Irish Sea; 70 miles in length; large ships could anchor there.

Thames
Britain's most important river; navigable by a great variety of vessels; vital to London's import/export trade; the Thames from London Bridge to Blackwall was known as the 'Port of London' and the section below London Bridge was known as 'The Pool'.

Wear
River in Durham; 65 miles long; barges could navigate it to Durham.

Weald
A landmark of physical geography covering parts of Kent, Surrey and Sussex counties; previously it was densely forested but was largely stripped of timber to make charcoal for early iron making; later it supported pasturelands, hop cultivation and orchards, particularly in Kent.

LONDON: AREA AND LANDMARKS

East End
Area of London generally associated with poverty and the poorer classes of labour; possibly so-named to contrast with the fashionable West End.

Euston Station

Station built for the London & Birmingham railway; located N central London; recognised for its architecture prior to renovations made by British Rail in the 1960s.

Greater London

1963 redesignation of the counties of London and Middlesex and parts of Surrey, Kent, Essex and Hertfordshire.

Heathrow

Formally London (Heathrow) Airport; opened 31 May 1946 to connect the United States and the United Kingdom by direct air-service; to the W of Greater London.

Spitalfields

Neighbourhood in London's East End; after 1865 French Protestants established silk weaving as an industry there.

Soho

District in W London; centre for Victorian era entertainment, reputable and disreputable alike; also recognised as a neighbourhood of immigrants.

St Pancras Station

London terminal for the midland railway; built in the centre of one of London's slum areas, Agar Town.

Sandown Park

150 acre race course, $\frac{1}{2}$ mile N of Esher Station in Surrey.

Whitehall

Formerly a royal residence; seat of the executive branch of the British government; a street between Trafalgar Square and Parliament Square, and a general designation for the area including the Prime Minister's residence, 10 Downing Street.

Index and glossary

Abel-Smith, B., 135, 283
Abnormal Importations Act, 352
Abramovitz, M., 73
absolute advantage
Greater efficiency than someone else, such as Britain's greater efficiency in both agriculture and manufacturing in the nineteenth century. What is relevant to the question of what Britain should have specialised in doing, however, is comparative advantage (q.v.).
accelerator
The dependence of investment on the amount of the product consumed, as the building of petrol stations depends on the amount of petrol sold. The 'acceleration' refers to the speeding up of flow it causes in an underemployed economy: a rise in investment in one industry causes a rise in income earned in others by the 'multiplier' (q.v.), which then causes still more investment (to service the consumption out of the new income), accelerating the rise in income.
Adams, A. A., 280
Admiralty, 135
Africa, 177
age-specific rate
The frequency of some event in population counting at a specific age. The age-specific death rate, for instance, is the deaths per 1,000 people of age one year; similar rates can be calculated for those ages two years, ten to fifteen years, etc. Marriage, birth and other rates are also used.
age structure, 42–5, 186–7
effect on labour force, 44–5
effects of war on, 46
and fertility, 43
and stock of human capital, 45
welfare implications, 44
The proportion of people at each age. In a rapidly growing population, for example, children will outnumber old people, and the age structure will look, if plotted on a graph, like a triangle with a large base; there will be a high proportion at ages one year, two years, etc.
aggregate supply–aggregate demand model, 325, 327–33, 336, 346, 349
agriculture, 145–72
in business cycles, 261–3
changing role in GDP, 263
declining labour force, 162–3, 171–2
depression, 16, 146–9, 221
factor movements, 165–6
incomes, 146–8
labour costs, 153, 155
output, 145, 164
productivity, 145, 148–9, 171
regional specialisation, 163–5
supply responsiveness, 149–52
technical change, 152–6, 162–3
see also animal husbandry; dairy farming; farm labourers; farms; grain
Air Ministry, 407
air travel, 406–7
alcohol consumption, 279
Aldcroft, D. H., 65, 68, 188, 241, 250, 258, 260, 296, 314, 316
Alford, B. W. E., 63, 74, 77, 78, 88, 299, 404
Allen, R. C., 81, 287
Allen, R. G. D., 375
Amalgamated Engineering Union (AEU), 112
Amalgamated Society of Engineers (ASE), 102, 103, 109, 110–11
Anderson, M., 9, 10, 41, 45, 50, 51
André, D., 149
Andrews, B. P. A., 340
Andrews, P. W. S., 389

Anglo-American War, 198
animal husbandry, 164–5
Argentina, 166, 177–8, 182, 187, 193–4, 203–5, 209, 214, 231
Armstrong, P., 115
Army recruits, 283–4
Ashley, W. J., 65
Ashton, T. S., 222, 241
Ashworth, W., 89
assets, new issues, 190, 191
assets, purchase by trustees, 191–2
Association of Clearing Banks, 241
Atkinson, A. B., 364
Atkinson, T. C., 262
Atlantic economy, 50
Austin, Herbert, 395
Australia, 48, 50, 177, 180–2, 187, 193, 199, 203, 209, 220, 287–8
Austria, 344
autarky
Self-sufficiency, especially of a whole country. Autarky is the opposite of free trade (q.v.).
automobile industry, *see* motor vehicle industry
autonomous spending, autonomous expenditure
Spending that is not affected by the size of income, but by other things, such as optimism about the future, government policy or purchases by foreigners. Part of investment, much of government spending and most of exports are thought to fall in this category. It is the prime mover of income in an underemployed economy: as autonomous expenditure goes, so goes (by the 'multiplier' and 'accelerator') the economy.
average propensity to consume
The ratio of consumption to income. The ratio has in fact little economic significance. The *marginal* propensity (q.v.) determines the strength of consumption spending as a factor in prosperity. Cf. consumption function; multiplier.
Ayr, 163

Bagehot, W., 230–1
Bain, G. S., 92, 93, 95, 97
Baines, D. E., 10, 18, 29–61, 94, 165, 286
bakelite, 399
Baker, W. J., 407
balance of payments
(1) The record of payments by (say) Britain to and from foreigners, including flows of exports and imports, bonds, gifts and so forth.
(2) The net flows of money into the country during a year. It is a line, so to speak, in (1). A positive (or 'in surplus' or 'favourable') balance means that money is on balance flowing into the country. The analogy with a single person's balance is exact: to take the case of a deficit (unfavourable balance), when one's purchases (imports) exceed income (exports), and when borrowing (net borrowing abroad) cannot cover the excess, one must necessarily be running down one's bank balance or stores of cash.
balance of payments equilibrium
Literally, a situation in which the money flowing into or out of a country has no tendency to change from year to year in amount. Usually the term is reserved for the special case of zero net flows: no money flowing in or out.
balance of trade
The value of a nation's exports (both goods and services, textiles and shipping) minus the value of its imports. It is part of the balance of *payments* (q.v.).
Balfour, A. J., 419
Balfour Committee (1928), 336, 399
Balogh, T., 354, 392
banking system, 189–90, 225–9, 239–40
branch, 230, 231
Bank of England, 217, 219, 239, 298, 302–3, 307, 309, 316, 339–40, 342–5, 352–3, 391, 405, 412
lender of last resort, 223, 230–1
Bank Rate
The interest rate the Bank of England charges on loans of short duration to the public (especially other banks). Changing the Bank Rate is one way the Bank can change economic conditions. Cf. discount rate.
bankruptcy, 192
Owing more than one owns; bankruptcy law must adjudicate the claims for whatever assets there are.
Banks, J. A., 41
banks
clearing, 217
commercial, 392–3

failures, 229–30, 416
mergers, 239
role in industry, 229–30, 239
Baring crisis, 227, 231
Barker, T. C., 74, 404
Barnes, H., 280
Barnett, C., 393
Barnsby, G. J., 276
Barro, R. J., 222, 258
Barsky, R. B., 225
base-year prices
The prices used as the point of view in looking at prices or quantities of another year. For example, national income in 1883 'expressed in the prices of 1900 as the base year' will place weights on the various items in the bundle of goods produced in 1883 according to their relative prices in 1900 the base year.
Bassett, P., 90, 116
Batchelor, R. A., 230
Bateman, 156
Batstone, E., 114, 115, 116
Baumol, W., 118, 143
Beaujot, R., 287
Becker, G. S., 42
Bedaux system, 394
Bedfordshire, 163
Beenstock, M., 305, 309, 312, 347, 348, 378, 379, 380
Beeton, Mrs, 127
Belgium, 40, 80, 344
Bellerby, J. R., 149, 171
Benjamin, D., 305, 306, 361–5, 377
Benson, J., 95
Berkshire, 164
Bernanke, B. S., 223, 343, 344, 350
Berry, R. A., 159
Berwick, 163
Beveridge, W. H., 361, 368
Bevin, E., 341
biased technical progress
Improvements in knowledge of how to do things that save on the use of one input especially. The assembly line, for example, saved labour; the hot blast in ironmaking saved coal. Cf. labour saving; technological change.
bicycle industry, 86
bilateral payments
Buying and selling between two countries, strictly. If Britain had to settle her debts with India bilaterally, for example, the value of all exports to India would have to equal the value of all imports, with no possibility of India using (as she did) a surplus with other European countries to finance a deficit with England. You as a carpenter would have to supply the butcher and baker each with carpentry to the exact value of your purchases of meat and bread.
Birmingham, 51, 391
birth control, 39–40
birth rate, 30
see also fertility
Live births per thousand population.
Bloomfield, A. I., 187
Board of Education, 134
Bogart, E. L., 215
bonds, 176, 177
A bond is a promise by a debtor to pay a fixed sum in the future in exchange for the loan of the 'principal' now. If the bond (that is, the loan) can be paid off before the specified date in the future, by giving back the principal with interest, it is said to be 'redeemable at the pleasure of the borrower'. Most bonds are not redeemable.
Booth, A. E., 11, 311, 373
Booth, C., 266
Boreham, A. J., 149
Bowden, S. M., 310
Bowley, A. L., 8, 266, 271–3, 278
Boyer, G. R., 57, 276
Brazil, 177, 193
Bright, J., 166
Bristol, 391
British Broadcasting Corporation (BBC), 406, 420
British disease, 90–2
British empire, 197–216
defence, 210–13
finance of current expenditure, 210
gains
from investment, 204–10
net, 213–15
from trade, 200–4
growth of, 197–8
monetary transfers, 210
subsidy of, 207–8, 209–10, 213
British Iron and Steel Federation, 315
Broadberry, S. N., 295, 299, 308, 310, 312, 316, 328, 338, 340, 350, 353, 363, 382, 385, 408, 409
Broadbridge, S., 182
Brodrick, G. C., 152, 156
Brody, D., 105

Brooklands Agreement (1893), 84, 106, 112, 417
Brown, A. J., 56
Brown, W., 114
Brunner, E., 389
Brunner, K., 221
Buckinghamshire, 160
Buckley, K. A. H., 212
budgetary position, inter-war, 243
budget deficit
Excess of government spending over tax receipts, as during wars. A budget deficit is financed either by borrowing or by printing money. Cf. balanced budget.
Burgess, K., 100, 102, 109
Burnett, J., 279, 281
Burnett-Hurst, A. R., 278
business cycles, 2–3, 221–3
(1870–1913), 247–64
climatic shocks, 260–3
data, 248–50
definitions, 247–8
export model, 222, 254–6
inter-war, 320–3
investment models, 256–8
monetary factors, 258–60
and wages, 103
see also Juglar trade cycle; Kondratieff wave; Kuznets swing
Buxton, N. K., 314
Byron, R. P., 249

Cagan, P., 221
Cain, P. J., 137, 198, 209
Caird, J., 146, 158, 159–60
Cairncross, A. K., 18, 52, 183, 192, 251, 256, 307
Calmfors, L., 384
Cambridgeshire, 164
Cameron, R., 182, 191
Canada, 48, 50, 177–8, 180, 182, 187, 193–4, 199, 201, 203–4, 209, 287–8
Cantillon, R., 63
Capie, F., 217–46, 258–9, 308–9, 318, 337, 343, 347, 348, 378
capital
availability of long-term, 392
human, 45
social overhead, 67, 179, 180, 181–2
supply of, 390–3
(1) Commodities used to make other commodities in the future. Thus, bricks, steel, lathes and the Latin fourth declension are not valued in themselves for direct consumption, but are all used to make things in the future (cars, motor cars, chairs, Latin poetry).
(2) The pile of existing capital, somehow added together into one number. The related but distinct idea is 'investment', i.e. the additions to the stock during a year. The flow of water per minute into a bathtub added up over the number of minutes it has been flowing is the stock of water in the bathtub. Likewise, investment added up is the stock of capital.
(3) In business, the financial resources available for an enterprise; what is put into a project (cf. capital market).
capital accumulation,
Investment, that is, providing more machines or other long-lasting instruments of production.
capital deepening
Providing more machines per labourer. An assembly line producing automobiles is a deepening of capital relative to hand methods. Cf. capital widening; technological change (embodied).
capital formation
Investment (q.v.), i.e. using up resources now to get a return in the future, such as building a railway, educating the people, making ships.
capital gains and losses
Changes in the value of a long-lived asset caused by a rise or fall in its price. If the land tax is raised unexpectedly, for example, land becomes suddenly less desirable and landlords experience a capital loss.
capital intensive
Using much capital (long-lived goods used to produce other goods) relative to labour or land. Relative to a blacksmith's forge, a fully automated continuous processing mill is a capital-intensive way to produce iron nails. Hence, 'capital intensity' as a measure of how much capital is used. Cf. capital deepening; labour intensive.
capital market, 67, 187–8, 190
A market in which IOUs are bought and sold, that is, in which 'capital' in the financial sense is bought and sold. It need not be in a single location, as is the stock exchange. The bond market (located as it were in the minds of all buyers and sellers or bonds) and the

banks, for example, are capital markets, part of the unified capital market of a developed economy.
capital–output ratio, 6
The ratio of the value of machinery, buildings and the like to the value of their output. It is a measure of the importance of capital to an economy and figures in the Harrod–Domar model of economic growth (q.v.).
capital widening
Increasing the number of men equipped with a given amount of capital. An expansion of coastal shipping with no change in the amount of capital per sailor or per ton shipped would be capital widening (as against deepening, q.v.).
Cardiff, 391
Carnarvon, 163
Caron, F., 182
Carré, J.-J., 138, 318
Carrier, N. H., 30, 48
Carr-Saunders, A. M., 404
cartel, 386, 389–90, 404
see also price-fixing agreements
A group of firms organised into a monopoly. Cartels are illegal under English common law.
Casson, M., 63, 304, 378
central bank
The state's bank, such as the Bank of England or (in the USA) the Federal Reserve Bank. A fashionable circumlocution for central bank is 'the monetary authority', i.e. the institution in charge of managing a nation's currency. Cf. monetary policy; money supply.
Central Electricity Board, 405, 406
cereals *see* grain
Ceylon, 177
Chaloner, W. H., 65
Chamberlain, N., 420
Chamberlain–Bradbury Committee, 339
Chambers, J. D., 158
Champernowne, D. G., 249
Chandler, A. D., 65, 71, 101, 179, 190, 293, 395, 397
Channing, F. A., 156
Chapman, A. L., 136, 142, 379
Chapman, S. D., 88
Charles, E., 43
cheap money
In bankers' language, conditions of an ample amount of money-to-lend and the low interest rates (hence cheap) that accompany such conditions. Cf. loanable funds.
Checkland, S., 293
chemical industry, 86–7, 401
Cheshire, 164
children, poverty, 275–6
China, 198, 209
chocolate, 87–8
Church, R. A., 86
Churchill, Winston, 241–2, 339, 340, 341
cigarettes, 87
Clack, G., 115
Clapham, 160
Clark, C., 118, 318
Clark, G., 160–1
Clark, K., 166
classical economic theory, classical economics
Economics from Adam Smith (1723–90) to John Stuart Mill (1806–73). Chiefly British, and most particularly Scottish, with French assistance. It contrasts with the 'neoclassical' (q.v.) economics of the 1870s onward in its emphasis on discovering the laws of motion of capitalist development.
classical vs. Hecksher–Ohlin theories of locational specialisation
Two competing theories of why a country, say Britain in 1860, exports what it does, say cotton textiles. The classical theory, elaborated by English writers from the early 1800s onward, emphasises superior technologies such as the better machines and commercial institutions available in Lancashire than in Bombay; the Hecksher–Ohlin theory, elaborated by Swedish writers from the 1920s onward, emphasises the endowments of resources especially suitable to the export in question, such as the relatively large amount of capital available in Britain.
Clegg, H. A., 95, 103, 105
Cline, W. R., 159
cliometrics
Economics and statistics in the service of history. The word was coined in the late 1950s by Stanley Reiter, a mathematical economist then at Purdue University in the United States, from 'Clio' (the muse of history) and 'metrics' (by analogy with 'econometrics', q.v.). Identical to 'new economic history'.
Clydeside, 59

Coale, A. J., 38, 40
Coal Mines Act (1930), 315, 406
coal mining industry, 85–6, 314, 315, 394, 400, 402
Coase, R., 406
coefficient of variation
A measure of the variability of a set of numbers, the most useful one in descriptive statistics. It is the standard deviation (q.v.) divided by the average. Dividing by the average makes variabilities in differing units comparable with each other, such as the variability from year to year of income compared with that of prices, or the variability of wages from place to place before and after a general rise in their level.
Coker, E. E., 115
cold storage, 169
Cole, A. H., 63, 69
Cole, G. D. H., 88, 102
Cole, W. A., 54, 145
Coleman, D. C., 75, 85
collective bargaining *see* wages
The laws, customs and civilised conventions for handling disputes between employers and unionised employees, especially disputes over the agreed conditions under which the workers shall in future supply labour.
Collins, E. J. T., 153, 154, 163
Collins, M., 189, 230, 239–40, 246, 337, 343, 347
Colonial Stock Act (1900), 192, 206
colonies *see* British Empire
Committee on Trusts (1919), 404
Commonwealth, 308, 405
comparative advantage
Greater relative efficiency than someone else. 'Relative' here means 'relative to the other things one could do'. Thus, Britain had a comparative advantage in manufacturing in the nineteenth century, even when (by the end of the century) other countries could do some manufacturing better absolutely. Contrast 'absolute advantage'.
competition, 19–20, 91
and cotton industry, 106
effect on entrepreneurs, 78–9
and employment relations, 104–6
and engineering industries, 110
and iron and steel industry, 107–8
policy, 403–8
source of instability, 389
and weaving, 106–7
competitive markets
Markets undistorted by monopoly, that is, by concentration of power among either buyers or sellers.
complementary factor
An input that helps another to be useful. Petrol and automobiles are complementary.
conciliation boards, 103
confidence, loss of, 16–17
Conservative governments, 339, 398
Consols
British government *consol*idated stock. Consols were promises to pay lenders to government a low interest rate forever. They were perpetual bonds, for the principal is never paid. Cf. irredeemable bonds.
constant elasticity form
A choice of mathematical equation such that the *elasticity* (q.v.) is constant. The elasticity is constant when it appears as an exponent. For example, $Q = DP^e$ (where e is negative) is a constant elasticity form for a demand curve. The form $Q = D + eP$ is not.
constant returns to scale
A constancy in the cost of a good as its production enlarges. Cf. diminishing returns; economies of scale; scope economies.
consumer demand
The demand for goods by British households as distinct from British firms, the British government or foreigners.
consumer goods, 89, 310
consumer price index
A number measuring prices in general facing consumers. Cf. base-year prices; cost of living index (which last is same as the consumer price index).
consumers' surplus
The excess of what consumers are willing to pay at most for something over what they actually pay. Those consumers who in 1816 actually paid 30 shillings for a yard of cotton cloth would have been willing, if pressed, to pay the same amount in 1830. In fact, however, they only had to pay 9 shillings, earning therefore 21 shillings of consumers' surplus.
consumption
alcohol, 279
data, 269
family, 268

and health, 277–86
inter-war, 330
consumption function
The relation between expenditure on home consumption (as distinct from saving, taxes and imports) and total income. If the consumption function has a steep slope, nearly all new income is spent, and becomes someone else's income. If it is flat, then little is spent. The flatter the slope (called the marginal propensity to consume, q.v.) the smaller therefore will be the 'multiplier' effects (q.v.) of a given stimulus to income.
consumption good
A thing or service, such as a television or a loaf of bread, purchased to satisfy human desire now, as distinct from an investment good (q.v.) purchased to make such consumption goods later, and not for its direct, present satisfaction of desire.
convertibility
In monetary matters, the ability to exchange paper pounds for gold at the official rate. It was suspended during parts of the Napoleonic Wars.
cooperative movement, 88, 394–5
Copp, T., 287
Coppock, D. J., 220
Coppock, J. T., 152
Corley, T. A., 400
corn
free trade, 166–9
see also grain
Corn Laws, 166
The taxes charged on imported wheat and other grains, especially those repealed in large part in 1846.
Cornwall, 49, 164
correlation coefficient
A measure of how closely one number varies with another as price might vary with quantity. A coefficient of +1·0 means perfect direct variation, one of −1·0 perfect inverse variation. When two series have no relation (either direct or inverse) their correlation coefficient is near zero. The notation for a correlation coefficient is R, whence the expression 'R squared' or R^2: the square of R turns out to be the proportion of the variance (q.v.) in one series explained by the other. Strictly speaking, the explanation must be assumed to be a straight line. Cf. regression.
cost-benefit analysis
An assessment using economics of the desirability of some project, such as a railway. The railway may have costs such as smoke pollution beyond the conventional costs such as engines. All costs need to be figured into the analysis. The total benefit is what consumers are willing to pay. It is not merely what they actually pay. Cf. consumers' surplus; social savings.
cost curve, cost function
The expenditure to produce various different amounts of a good. What 'the' expenditure is depends on what definition one has in mind: of 'total' cost (all the expenditures to produce the amount produced), 'average' cost (total cost per unit produced) or 'marginal' cost (the increase of total cost from producing one more unit). The total cost of producing a million yards of cotton gray cloth might be 6 million shillings; this would imply an average cost of 6 shillings a yard. But if it were difficult to expand production the marginal cost of an extra yard might be higher, say 10 shillings a yard.
cost of living indices, 268, 272–4, 382–3
see also prices
A measure of the prices of consumer goods, such as food, housing, health, cars, clothes and so forth.
cost-push inflation
A rise in prices caused by rises in costs, such as oil prices or trade union wages. The existence of such inflation is disputed among economists, as is its opposite, demand-pull inflation.
costs
of early industrialisation, 413
transaction, 388
cotton industry, 82–5, 403
collective bargaining, 102
and competition, 106
productivity, 83
technical backwardness, 84–5
trade, 83, 98, 214
Cottrell, P. L., 27, 174, 177, 188, 189
counterfactual
An event contrary to actual fact, though perhaps possible. 'British income would have been 10 per cent lower in 1865 had the railway never been invented' is a counterfactual: the railway was in actual fact invented, and the counterfactual

makes an assertion about what the world would have been like if it had not. Statements of cause, such as that the railway caused 10 per cent of British national income in 1865, are said to entail counterfactuals. Consequently, analytical economic history of the sort pursued in this book, which wishes to make causal statements, uses counterfactuals.
Courtaulds, 85, 395, 396, 399
covariance
A measure of how closely two things vary together. Over the nineteenth century, for example, British national income and exports have positive, large covariance, which is to say that when exports were high so was income. Like correlation, to which covariance is related mathematically, covariance does not imply the two things are causally connected, or causally connected in one direction.
craft control, 100, 102, 103, 115–16
and effort, 104
legacy of, 113–16
persistence of, 106–12
craft organisation, 91
Crafts, N. F. R., 15, 182, 220, 250, 265, 270, 271, 306, 312–13, 316, 342, 371–2, 384, 408, 410
craft unions
power of, 100, 102
see also trade unions
credit creation, credit multiplier, money multiplier
The lending of banks to business and so forth, especially the loans that banks make beyond the money they have in their vaults to back up the loans. Cf. bank credit; money supply.
cricket, 138
Crisp, O., 191
Cronin, J. E., 98
cross-section
Of facts, given in person-to-person form, or place-to-place; in contrast with time series, which is year-to-year. The general average price of flats in Britain in 1914, 1915, 1916 and so forth is a time series; the price of flats in thirty towns in 1914 considered town-by-town is a cross-section.
crowding-out, 339, 355, 392
The view that investment by the government in dams, roads, housing and so forth would merely push aside private investment, not increase the nation's investment.
Crown Colonies Loan Act (1988), 206
Crowther, M. A., 284
Crystal Palace Exhibition (1851), 153–4
cultural environment, 75–6
Cunliffe Committee, 338
current account
The statement of, say, Britain's foreign trade in goods and services. Contrast the capital account, the trade in loans and the monetary account, the trade in money. Your own current account consists of the goods and services you sell and the goods and services you buy: a plumber exports plumbing services but imports food, housing, haircuts and so forth. Changes in his loans or his bank balance outstanding are other accounts. Cf. balance of payments; balance of trade.
current prices vs. constant prices
'Current price' refers to valuing, say, national product in this year's prices, by simply adding up every good produced in £. 'Constant price' values goods produced at the prices of some base year (q.v.), the better to compare output or income free of the effects of inflation.
cyclical unemployment
People out of work because of a depression. It is identical to demand-deficient unemployment, distinct from frictional unemployment (q.v.). Cf. full employment; unemployment.

dairy farming, 150–2, 164
Dangerfield, G., 17
Daniel, G. H., 61
Daunton, M. J., 100, 104, 106, 135, 142
Davenport-Hines, R., 404
Davey, C., 39
David, P. A., 153–4, 155, 160
Davidoff, L., 12, 13
Davis, L. E., 132, 188, 190, 192, 202, 205–12
Deane, P., 54, 145, 146, 149
death certification, 32
death rate, 30
see also mortality
defence expenditure, 354
British empire, 210–13
pre-Second World War, 311–12
rearmament, 407, 420
shipping lines, 211, 213

deficit financing
The act of financing government expenditure partially through borrowing from the public rather than taxing it.
deflation
(1) A condition of low aggregate demand (q.v.).
(2) A fall in prices, said sometimes to result from (1), but more usually attributed to the money supply (q.v.).
deflator
The index of prices used to express incomes earned in one year in terms of the prices of another year (the base year). The verb, 'deflate', is the use of such a price index. Cf. base-year prices; consumer price index.
Dellheim, C., 75
demand
1930s sources of, 349
see also aggregate supply–aggregate demand model
demand, aggregate
The total demand for all goods and services in the economy. Its actual level will be identical to national income (q.v.). Its planned level depends on the consumption and investment plans of households, governments and firms. Aggregate demand in this second planned sense is what drives the Keynesian model (q.v.) of the determination of the national income.
demand, effective
Equilibrium (q.v.) aggregate demand (q.v.). It is, in other words, the national income, being the amount of spending by households, governments and firms that they were able to effect.
demand curve, derivation, 325–6
The amounts of a good or service that people wish to buy at various different prices per unit of it. At a low price of labour services, for example, businesses and other buyers of labour would like to buy much of it. The extent to which their wish is fulfilled depends on the supply curve (q.v.).
demand-deficient unemployment
People out of work because the society does not wish to buy all of what it produces. Distinguish frictional unemployment, i.e. men out of work temporarily while moving from a job society does not now want to a job it does want. Identical to cyclical unemployment. Cf. unemployment.
demand for labour, 361, 376–80
The number of people businesses wish to hire at some wage. The lower the wage the larger the number demanded.
demand management, 355
The government's attempt to keep the society's spending at the level of full employment (q.v.), neither too high nor too low, by manipulating its own expenditures. Since its expenditures are part of aggregate demand (q.v.), the attempt may theoretically achieve success.
demographic crisis, subsistence crisis
Overpopulation relative to the amount of land available for agriculture, and the misery that results.
Denmark, 146
Department of Scientific and Industrial Research, 398
dependency ratio
The ratio of those who do not work for money (i.e. normally children, old people and some married women) to those who do work for money.
deposits, deposit liabilities, demand deposits
Cheque-drawing privileges; your chequing account.
depreciation, replacement investment
(1) The wearing out of capital.
(2) Expenditure to replace the worn-out capital.
(3) The fund accumulated to allow for the expenditure to replace the worn-out capital.
The three need not be identical. Depreciation is subtracted from 'gross' income to get 'net' income because a fund used to maintain capital is not available for satisfying present wants.
depreciation of a currency
A fall in a currency's value relative to other currencies. Contrast appreciation, a rise in value and devaluation (q.v.), which entails some intent.
Derby, 163
devaluation
A fall in the value of a currency relative to another, with the connotation that the fall was intended and arranged (if not necessarily desired) by a nation's government. Contrast depreciation,

which connotes an unintended fall in value.

deviation from trend, absolute and relative
Of a time series, i.e. a statistic for a series of years, cases in which the statistics are higher or lower than a trend, i.e. higher or lower than what might be expected from a line fitted through the points. A harvest failure in 1816, for example, would be a deviation from the trend of the wheat crop 1800 to 1820. The absolute deviation is the number of bushels below the 1800–20 trend, say, that the crop fell; the relative deviation is the percentage fall. Cf. trend.

Devon, 163
diets, 279

differentials
Usually in reference to wages; differences between wages from one job to another or from one place to another. If the higher wage is compensation for worse conditions or higher skills the differentials have no tendency to disappear, and are called 'compensating' or 'equalising'.

diminishing returns
The fall in the amount of additional output as additional doses of input are applied. The nation's agriculture is subject to diminishing returns as more workers and capital apply themselves to the fixed amount of land. Output does not fall: it merely rises less than it did from previous doses.

Dimsdale, N. H., 234, 295, 304, 309, 339, 340, 348, 357, 378–80
Dingle, A. E., 279
Dintenfass, M., 86

direct investment
An investment in one's own company by contrast with investment in the bonds of other companies ('portfolio investment'). Cunard Lines, Ltd, investing in port facilities for itself in Quebec would be an example of direct investment; Cunard investing in Canadian Pacific Railway bonds would be 'indirect' or portfolio investment.

direct tax
Levied on the people on whom it is believed or intended to fall, such as the income tax. The distinction between direct and indirect taxes, however, 'is practically relegated to the mind of the legislator. What he proposes should be borne by the original payer is called a direct tax, what he intends to be borne by someone else than the original taxpayer is called indirect. Unfortunately, the intention of the legislator is not equivalent to the actual result' (E. R. A. Seligman, *On the Shifting and Incidence of Taxation* (1892), p., 183). Cf. indirect tax.

discounted value, discounted present value, present value
The amount by which one down-values income earned in the future relative to income earned today. If the interest rate were 10 per cent, for example, one would down-value £1 earned next year to 90p relative to £1 earned today; the discounted value would be 10 per cent below the money value.

discount rate, market rate of discount
The percentage reduction of the price of a short-term IOU (e.g. a ninety-day bill) now below its value when it falls due later. For example, a bill worth £100 ninety days from now might sell for £99 today. The rate is usually expressed as the annual percentage interest rate one would earn on buying such a bill for £99 and holding it to maturity (approximately $(12/3) \times (£1/£99) = 4$ per cent; more exactly, allowing for compounding, 3·67 per cent).

diseases
infectious, 32–5, 283
non-infectious, 32
virulence, 32–3

diseconomies of (managerial) scale
Rises in cost as an enterprise becomes too big for the abilities of its managers to manage. Cf. economies of scale.

disintegration
The breaking apart of a unified enterprise, for increased efficiency (contrast integration).

disposable income
National income (q.v.) minus personal taxes plus subsidies and payments of interest on the government debt. It is the income available in someone's bank account or pocket for spending or saving, the government having taken its share of the product earlier.

Distillers, 401

distribution of income
(1) By size: the frequency of rich and poor.
(2) Functional: how income is allotted to labour, to land and to capital.
distribution of wealth
Sometimes elegant variation for distribution of income (q.v.); sometimes, and properly, the frequency among people of wealth, not annual income, of various sizes, that is, of their market worth on some date if sold off.
distributive networks, 23
Divall, C., 393
domestic service, 53–4, 122–5, 126–7
Dominions, 176
Donovan Report (1968), 116
Dowie, J. A., 295, 337, 385, 402
Driffil, J., 384
drug industry, 87
Dublin, 276
Dubois, P., 318
Dumke, R., 149
Dunlop, J. T., 378
Dunning, J. H., 177
durable assets
Long-lived valuable things, such as houses, bonds, jewellery, money skills. The phrase is redundant: 'assets' are by definition long-lived.
durable goods
Long-lived goods, such as houses or machinery giving value or satisfaction over more than one year.
Durham, 35, 36, 100, 138, 411
Dutton, H. I., 102
Dyer, Colonel, 105
Dyhouse, C., 37

earnings
estimations of, 267–8
regional variations, 276
see also wages
East Anglia, 36, 163
econometrics
Mathematical statistics in the service of economics. Not a synonym for 'mathematical economics' (which is mathematics in the service of economics) or 'quantitative economics' (which is any counting in the service of economics) or 'cliometrics' (which is economics in the service of history).
economic adjustment, 22, 305–6, 333–8
Economic Advisory Council, 311
economic depressions
(1920–1), 240
(1929–32), 242, 306–7, 342–7
recovery, 348–50
shallowness of, 343–5
(1930), 323
world, 386
economic fluctuations *see* business cycles
economic growth, 65–6
failure, 66–8
inter-war, 237, 297–8, 302–3, 320–3
measurement of, 2–4
reasons, 4
economic potential
The best that an economy can do in producing output. Cf. efficiency.
economic rent
The excess of one's income over what could be earned in alternative employment. The excess income of an unusually gifted actor over what his ordinary gifts would earn as a civil servant or salesman is economic rent. So, too, is the excess of the income earned by a piece of agricultural land over what its use outside of agriculture would bring. It amounts in this agricultural case to virtually all the 'rent' in the ordinary sense of payments to a landlord. Cf. rent.
economies of scale
The lowerings of cost caused by a rise in output. The 'caused by' is important: mere correlation between lowering cost and rising output is not always an example of economies of scale. The two could happen to correlate by chance; or lowering cost could cause a rise in output (the reverse direction). Cf. constant returns to scale; diminishing returns.
economy, success or failure?, 13–14
Edelstein, M., 130, 173–96, 197–216
Edgerton, D. E. H., 407, 410
educational system, 76–7, 132–4
education and training, 23, 68, 73, 196, 289, 393
Edwardes, M., 90
efficiency, 20–2
economic
The production of the most for given resources of labour, land and capital. If the resources are badly handled ('misallocated') the nation's output is lower than it need be. Cf. specialisation.

iron and steel industry, 80
versus service quality, 135
effort, and craft control, 104
Eichengreen, B., 222, 291–319, 343, 351, 359, 365
elastic
Expansible without much or any rise in its price, as in 'the supply curve of managerial talent is infinitely elastic'.
elasticity
Sensitivity or expansibility. The price elasticity of demand for housing, for instance, is the sensitivity of the quantity of housing people wish to buy to the price of housing. If they change their buying of housing very little when price goes up the demand is said to have a low elasticity, or to be inelastic; if they change it a lot it is said to have a high elasticity, or to be elastic. Supply, too, has an elasticity 'with respect to price' (another way of saying 'price elasticity'). Mathematically speaking, elasticity is the rate of change of, say, quantity demanded (the result) divided by the rate of change of price (the cause).
elasticity of substitution
The sensitivity of the relative use of inputs to changes in their relative prices. The elasticity of substitution between machines and men in shipping, say, would therefore be a measure of how easily machines (say, automatic pilots) could be substituted for men (human pilots).
elastic supply curves or schedules
Schedules of amounts forthcoming at various prices that show the amount to be very expansible at little rise in the price. The supply curve of labour facing the London docks, for example, was very elastic: at a trivial or small rise in the wage offered the employers could get as many additional workers as they wanted. Likewise, a single cotton mill would face an elastic supply schedule of cotton, which is to say that it would get no cotton at all at a price slightly below the going price. From the mill's point of view, then, the price of cotton is fixed.
Elbaum, B., 72, 100, 107, 108, 390
electrical engineering industry, 81, 314, 401, 402, 410
Electricity Commissioners, 405
electricity supply, 188, 406, 409, 420
emigration, 48–50
demographic effects, 45
and living standards, 286–8
post-First World War, 50
urban character of, 49–50
see also migration
employment
distribution, 274–5
effect of wages on, 378
factors determining, 378–80
regional variations, 56–60
rural decline, 53
in service industries, 120, 122–5
employment budget, 311
employment relations
analysis of, 98–100
and foreign competition, 104–6
endogenous
Caused inside the system being analysed. The price of housing is endogenous to the market for housing. Contrast exogenous.
Engel's law
'The poorer a family, the greater the proportion of its total expenditure that must be devoted to the provision of food', as Ernst Engel (not Friedrich Engels) put it in 1857. Cf. income elasticity of demand.
Engineering Employers' Federation (EEF), 105, 111–13
engineering industries, 81–2, 110, 375
lockouts, 102, 109–12, 417
see also electrical engineering industry
entrepreneurs, 388
collaboration, 294–5
effect of competition, 78–9
failure of, 20, 65, 68–78
short-term view, 77
stupidity, 72–3
entrepreneurship
compared to management, 62
in economic theory, 62–4
Managerial skill; or, especially as used by Joseph Schumpeter and other theorists of capitalism in the early twentieth century, *unusual* managerial skill combined with a willingness to take risks and a perspicacity about the future. From the French word meaning simply 'contractor'.
equilibrium
A much-used term in economics, meaning a condition in which no forces of self-interest, arithmetic or whatever

tend to change the situation. If the gap between urban and rural wages is an equilibrium, for instance, there is no natural tendency for it to disappear. A ball at the bottom of a bowl is in equilibrium.

equilibrium growth path for capital
The way capital would pile up in an economy if it grew neither too fast nor too slow (in the opinion of those supplying and demanding it).

equilibrium level of interest rate
The return on borrowing or lending that makes the amount people wish to borrow equal to the amount buyers of labour (owners of cotton mills, buyers of haircuts, students at university) wish to buy.

equilibrium wage
The payment to workers that makes the amount of hours workers as a whole wish to supply equal to the amount buyers of labour (owners of cotton mills, buyers of haircuts, students at university) wish to buy.

equity
(1) Titles of ownership; stock certificates.
(2) The value of ownership in a company; the right of ownership.
(3) A branch of law meant to supplement the common law.

equity interest
The value of a company. Both words are used here in uncommon senses: 'equity' to mean 'the value of ownership' (as in the phrase, 'I have £2,000 of equity in my house left after the mortgage is subtracted from the price of the house'); 'interest' to mean 'legally recognised concern or right'.

Erickson, C., 49
Ermisch, J., 42
Essex, 160, 163, 164, 165

ex ante
The anticipated value; or from the point of view of before the event; or planned. For example, ex ante profits in a venture are always high – for why else would one embark on it? Ex post, alas, they may be low.

excess capacity
The amount that is not produced by producing less than one can. The British economy in 1933 had excess capacity, with millions of workers out of work and thousands of factories idle. Cf. unemployment.

excess demand
(1) In micro-economics, a situation in a market in which the amount people wish to buy is at the existing price larger than the amount (other) people wish to sell.
(2) In macro-economics, a condition in which aggregate demand (q.v., that is, what people wish to spend) is larger than aggregate supply (i.e. what they plan currently to produce).

Exchange Equalisation Account (EEA), 234, 238–9, 326, 391, 420
exchange rates
competitive devaluations, 351
determination of, 340–1
fixed, 218, 236
floating, 234
free float, 326
inter-war, 332
managed float, 236
real and nominal, 234
see also sterling
The value of one country's money in terms of another, such as \$4·86 per pound sterling (the rate during much of the past two centuries). An exchange rate is 'fixed' if the government of one of the countries is willing to buy and sell its currency at the fixed price, in the same way as it might fix the price of wheat.

exogenous
Caused outside the system being analysed. The weather (except smog) is exogenous to the economy: it may cause things in the economy but is not in turn caused by them. The price of housing, in contrast, *is* caused inside the economy. Cf. autonomous spending; contrast endogenous.

expected, expectation, expected value
Statistically speaking, the average of what one anticipates. If one anticipated that the profits on new cotton spindles, say, could be 4, 6 or 8 per cent, each equally likely, then the expected value would be 6 per cent.

expected lifetime income
One's anticipated income over one's remaining life. The concept is useful because decisions by income earners depend presumably on their expected lifetime income, not merely the income

they happen to have this year. A surgeon, for example, would be sensible to buy more than he earns early in his career, in anticipation of high income later. Identical to permanent income.
expenditure tax
Taxes imposed only on the amounts people spend, as distinct from taxes on income, which tax what they save out of the income as well as what they spend. A tax on food would be an expenditure tax, on all income an income tax, on income from bonds a savings tax.
exponential growth
Growth at a constant percentage rate per year, in the manner of compound interest. A straight line upward sloping on an ordinary graph against time has a falling percentage rate of growth, because the constant absolute rise per year is applied to a larger and larger base. An exponential curve would have to be curving up steeper and steeper to maintain the same rate.
exports
cloth, 98
cotton yarn, 98
and exchange rate, 340
growth, 19–20, 301
lack of competitiveness, 374
prices, 300
structure, 98
weak performance, 342
ex post
The realised value or from the point of view of after the event or attained. Cf. ex ante.
externalities, external effects, external economies or diseconomies
Effects you did not directly pay for, such as the pain of smoke in your eye from the local factory or the pleasure of the council's flower garden. The weeds that spread from your neighbour's ill-kept plot in the village fields to your plot is a 'negative' (i.e. bad) externality. The quickening of trade that spreads from the new railway to your business is a positive (i.e. good) externality. An alternative terminology is that external economies are good, external diseconomies bad. Whatever terminology is used, the key idea is the external nature of the event, that is, outside your own control and not directly affected by your activities. Contrast internal economies of scale.

factor, factor of production
One of the inputs into making things, especially the tripartite division into the inputs, land, labour and capital.
factor endowments
The inputs a nation has at its disposal, including labour, machinery, buildings and skills as well as coal, climate and soil. Cf. classical vs. Hecksher–Ohlin.
factor income distribution
The incomes to each of the three classical 'factors' of production, i.e. labour, land and capital. It is also called the functional distribution of income.
factor scarcity hypothesis
The proposition that the relative abundance of, say, labour will determine how much effort is devoted to saving the labour by inventing new processes.
Factory Acts, 289
family size, 45
farmers' incomes, 147–8
farm labourers, 159–63
age structure, 161–2
earnings variation, 159–60
productivity variations, 160–1
farms
landscape, 154
rents, 157
size, 154–5, 163
tenancy-at-will, 158
tenants rights, 157–8
threshold acreage, 153–5
Fearon, P., 250, 258, 260
Federation of British Industry(ies) (FBI), 241, 398, 419
Federation of Master Cotton Spinners' Associations, 106
Feinstein, C. H. xxiv, 2, 3, 15–16, 19, 23, 25–7, 120–1, 123, 126–7, 136, 139, 145–6, 148, 174–5, 210, 212, 220, 222, 248, 253, 255, 263, 267, 270, 272–5, 312, 315–16, 318, 321, 343, 360, 382
Feis, H., 177, 178
Fenton, A., 163
Ferranti, 77
Ferrier, R. W., 87
fertility, 31
and age structure, 43
decline, 38–42
by occupation, 41–2

relationship with infant mortality, 37–8, 40
see also birth rate
Number of children born per woman.
Fertility Census (1911), 41
Fieldhouse, D. K., 197, 198
final goods
Goods used for consumption, investment, government spending or exports, i.e. not used merely to make other goods. Contrast intermediate goods; compare aggregate demand.
financial crises, 230–1
(1914), 233–4
(1931), 243–5
financial intermediaries
Institutions, such as banks and insurance companies, that in effect transfer money from ultimate savers (trade union pensions, buyers of railway bonds and so forth) to ultimate investors (chiefly business and government). The public gets a secure place to put its funds, and a reward in interest.
financial services, 127, 130
see also banking; capital market; insurance; London, City of
Fine, B., 406
firms
accounts, 391
family, 395
free-standing, 178
funding sources, 188
holding company, 397
joint-stock, 70
limited liability, 390
multi-divisional, 396–7
organisational failure, 70–7
restrictive practices, 404
size, 70–1, 315, 391, 401
structure, 396–7, 402–3
theory of, 387–90
vertically integrated, 190
First World War, 217, 419
conscripts, 34–5
demographic effect, 46, 395
economic consequences for UK, 292–5
and the empire, 215–16
finance, 232–4
government intervention, 293–4
innovation, 294
labour movement, 295
wages, 382
fiscal policy, inter-war, 311
Fisher, F. M., 151
Fisher, I., 225, 259
Fitzpatrick, S., 288
fixed capital
Capital that cannot be varied in amount quickly to suit circumstances; the opposite, therefore, of 'working capital', 'variable capital', 'goods in process', 'inventories' or any number of other similar ideas. A railway's lines and sidings are fixed capital; its stock of coal to burn in engines is variable. Cf. fixed cost.
fixed cost, overhead cost
Costs that do not rise as one makes more. The cost of digging the main shaft is a fixed cost for a coal mine, because it is given and unchanging whether the coal raised is much or little or nil. The costs of miners or of pit props, by contrast, do rise as the mine raises more coal. Contrast variable costs.
Fletcher, T. W., 165
Florence, P. S., 74
Floros, N., 363
Floud, R. xix–xxv, 1–28, 34, 77, 82, 269, 283
food
consumption, 32–5
imports, 145, 169–70, 171
industry, 87
Football League, 128
Ford, A. G., 187, 222
Ford, Henry, 254, 258, 397
Ford Motor Company, 113
foreign investment, 19, 25, 27, 67, 173–96, 292
causes of, 173, 180–92
defaults on, 192–3
direct, 177–9
direction of, 176–7
effects of, 173–4
and income distribution, 194–5
institutional and legal factors, 187–92
portfolio, 177–9, 182–3
rates of, 174–6, 180
rates of return on, 181, 182–3, 194
social rate of return, 193–5
and terms of trade, 193–5
Lending to another economy, as Englishmen did to American and Indian railways.
Foreign Office, 135
foreign trade multiplier
The mutual enrichment by expanded trade that takes place when one country

buys from another, setting men to work who spend their income from work on the products of the first country. The successive rounds peter out, leaving income in both countries higher than before trade. The argument, which is an offset to the autarky (q.v.) sometimes favoured by Keynesian economies (q.v.), depends on the existence in both countries of unemployment (q.v.). Cf. marginal propensity to import; multiplier.
Foreman-Peck, J. S., 129, 137, 141, 142, 308, 386–414
Fowler, A., 104
Fowler, L., 104
Fox, W., 161, 165
France, 19, 23, 40, 84–5, 138, 182, 199–200, 204, 211–13, 243, 293, 343, 344, 416
Paris Exhibition (1867), 15–16, 415
franchise, 103, 133, 287
Franco-Prussian War, 197
Fraser, D., 290
Fraser, W. H., 269
Freeman, A., 276
Freeman, R. B., 91
free trade, 21, 166–70, 292
The absence of artificial barriers to exchange among nations such as tariffs and quotas. Britain was officially (and for the most part, practically) a free trade country from the 1840s to the 1930s. No country has literally zero tariffs: Britain's were about 5 per cent of the value of imports in 1880. Contrast autarky.
Fremdling, R., 408
Frenkel, J. A., 183
Freud, Sigmund, 418
frictional unemployment
People out of work on their way from one job to another, that is, in the normal course of trade. Contrast cyclical unemployment; demand-deficient unemployment. Cf. full employment.
Friedlander, D., 35
Friedman, M., 218–19, 221–2, 224–5, 227, 236, 242, 253, 258–60, 345
friendly societies, 282, 283
Frost, R., 392
Fuchs, V. R., 119
full employment
The condition of the economy in which all who wish to work can find it. In such a condition the economy is producing as much as it can of goods and services. In such a condition an increase in the production of lunches can be had only at the cost of decrease in the production of something else. Cf. efficiency; Keynesian; multiplier; unemployment.
full employment surplus
The excess of government spending over tax receipts that would obtain if employment were full, instead of the less than full level it actually is. The purpose is to give a measure of the stimulative strength of fiscal policy (q.v.) independent of the actual level of unemployment. High unemployment will lead to government deficits – apparently stimulative – automatically, by reducing tax revenues, for instance. Yet a given stance of government in the matter of tax rates and spending programmes might in fact be non-stimulative as the economy approaches full employment. To provide a consistent standard of stimulation, then, one uses the full employment surplus.

gains from trade
The advantage the seller and the buyer get from an exchange. Since both enter the exchange voluntarily both can be presumed to benefit, contrary to the non-economist's notion that one person's or one country's gain is another's loss. Cf. consumers' surplus.
Gales, K., 42
Gallagher, J., 198
Gallman, R. E., 138
garden cities
A movement in Britain in the early twentieth century to settle the population in healthy new cities far removed from the great conurbations. Result: Welwyn Garden City.
Garrett, E. M., 42
Garside, W. R., 267, 311, 359
Gartner, L. P., 56
Gayer, A. D., 222
Gazeley, I., 273
Geary, F., 63
GEC, 396, 399
Geddes axe, 339
Gemmell, N., 138, 139
General Strike (1926), 98, 340, 406, 413, 419

Germany, 21, 23, 199, 211–13, 242, 316, 344, 399, 416
competition, 403–4
demography, 40, 56
education, 24, 76–7, 394
entrepreneurship, 64–5, 67, 70, 80, 87
growth, 16–19
investment, 26–7, 204
productivity, 408
trade, 98, 107, 200
Gerschenkron, A., 64
Gibson Paradox, 225
Gilchrist-Thomas steel-making process, 69, 80, 416
Gillespie, J. A., 369
Gittins, D., 42
Gladstone, W. E., 156, 415
Glamorgan, 138
Glasgow, 51, 55, 190, 269
bank failure, 229, 230, 416
Glass, D. V., 39
Gloucestershire, 159
Glyn, A., 115
Glynn, S., 311, 356, 373
Goddard, N., 158
gold
drain, 343
world distribution, 219
Gold and Silver Export Embargo Act (1920), 241
gold devices
The exploitation by the Bank of England of details in the market for gold in order to encourage or discourage the flow of gold into Britain, especially in the late nineteenth century. For instance, though legally bound to pay out English gold coins (sovereigns) for Bank of England notes at a fixed rate, the Bank could pay out foreign coins at whatever rate it could get.
gold exchange standard
The system of valuing paper currencies at fixed amounts of gold or of other currencies whose value is fixed in terms of gold. Thus, the currency of a small country might be backed by reserve holdings of gold or of sterling or dollars.
gold reserves
The holdings of gold by the Bank of England available to maintain the gold value of British paper money. Cf. official reserves.
gold standard, 218–21, 292
abandoned, 243–5, 345, 350–1
benefits of, 241
classical, 217
parity problems, 242, 243, 299
return to, 240–2, 298–300, 338–42
suspension, 419
The system of valuing paper currencies (pounds, dollars, francs) at fixed amounts of gold. Being fixed to gold they are fixed (within limits of transport cost called 'gold points') to each other. The gold standard, then, amounted to a system of fixed exchange rates. Britain was on gold from 1819 to 1914 and from 1925 to 1931. From 1872 to 1931 or 1933 enough other countries were on gold to justify calling it a system.
Gold Standard Act, 340
Goodhart, C. A. E., 231, 233
goodwill
The reputation, trademark, employee morale, good collection of managers or other distinctive features of a firm. As an accounting idea it makes cost equal revenue when revenue is high: if revenue exceeds costs the excess can be called the income of goodwill. As an economic idea it serves a similar function, and is called 'entrepreneurial income'.
Gordon, R. J., 258, 320
Gorton, G., 238
Goschen, G. J., 223, 231
Gourvish, T. R., 290
government
debt, 232, 233, 237, 245
Bonds, or IOUs, issued by government. Cf. budget deficit; Consols.
inaction, 68
intervention, 293–4, 354
see also state
government expenditure, 331, 354–7
growth, 131–3
structure, 132
and war, 134
For purposes of reckoning the national income, the purchases by the government of goods and services valued by consumers. Transfers of income that are not purchases of goods are not part of government spending in this sense: allowances under the Poor Law are not part of spending, nor under some conventions are interest payments on past government borrowings. Under some conventions of measuring national income, indeed, the provision of roads

and police are taken to be depreciation, and are therefore not included in net income.
grain, 150–2, 164
  supply elasticity, 152
Gramlich, E. M., 133
Grant, A. T. K., 392
Greasley, D., 65, 86
Great Depression, 17, 219–21
  (1) The business slump of the 1930s which was in Britain a continuation of a slump in the 1920s.
  (2) In an obsolete and exploded but still widely used sense, the slow growth of 1873–96 – which was not in fact slow real growth but merely a fall in prices.
Great Exhibition (1851), 16, 153–4
Green, A., 195
Gregory, A., 9
Gregory, T. E., 242
Grigg, P. J., 241
gross
  In economic terminology, 'inclusive of something', distinguished from 'net'. Thus gross exports of shipping services from Britain are all British sales of shipping services to foreigners, whereas net exports are all British sales to foreigners minus sales by foreigners to Britain.
gross barter terms of trade
  The ratio of the amount of exports a country gains from trade to the amount of exports it must sacrifice to acquire the imports. The concept was introduced by the American economist Frank Taussig (1859–1940) to allow for tribute payment and immigrants' remittances home as an element in trade. It has proven unsuccessful, and most modern studies focus attention on the net barter terms, simply called *the* terms of trade (q.v.).
gross domestic fixed capital formation
  The expenditure to produce ('form') new machinery, buildings and other slow-to-adjust assets ('fixed capital') located at home ('domestic', as opposed to foreign), and including ('gross') replacements of worn-out capital as well as entirely new capital.
gross domestic product
  The sum of the value of everything produced in Britain, by contrast with things produced by British capital or labour abroad.
gross national income or gross national product
  Gross national income or (what amounts to the same thing) product, or 'GNP', includes as output of the economy the costs of maintenance and replacement of the machinery, buildings, railways, etc., that make up the nation's capital. Net national income or product subtracts out these costs, as not available for consumption or new investment. The difference is usually small. Cf. depreciation.
gross reproduction rate
  A measure of how many children the typical woman will have over her life. It eliminates the effect of varying proportions of women at various ages. Contrast fertility.
growth accounting
  The measuring of the immediate causes of rising national product, as for example: rises in the labour force, in capital per person and in technology.
growth theory
  A branch of economics dealing in an abstract (usually mathematical) form with certain of the causes of the wealth of nations. Despite its encouraging name, it is not empirically based, and is not therefore a theory of any actually achieved economic growth.

Habakkuk, H. J., 66, 75, 153, 181
Haggard, H. R., 151, 162
Hall, A. A., 276
Hall, A. D., 152
Hall, A. R., 180, 209
Handfield Jones, S. J., 220
Hannah, L., 73, 188, 316, 394, 396, 406
Harley, C. K., 68, 99, 223, 259
Harman, Jeremiah, 230
Harnetty, P., 201
Harris, B., 313, 367
Harris, C. C., 151
Harris, J., 289
Harrison, A. E., 86
Harrison, R., 100
Harrod–Domar model
  The extension of Keynesian thinking to the long run, named in honour of the economists who developed it. The model contemplates the possibility that the 'natural' growth of income necessary for full employment (given the growth of

population) may be less or more than the 'warranted' growth necessary to fulfil the plans of savers and investors. If the plans are underfulfilled (i.e. if population growth is too slow to invest the savings that people will make out of income) income will stagnate. Cf. Keynesianism.
Harvey, C. E., 77
Hatry, C., 389, 391
Hatton, T. J., 57, 202, 254, 276, 304, 306, 311, 318, 359–85
Hawke, G. R., 182, 214
Hawtrey, R. G., 222
Hay, J. R., 289
Headrick, D. R., 72
health
and consumption, 277–86
insurance, 289–90
occupational variations, 10
public provision, 32–3
status, 282–3
see also hospitals
Heath, F. G., 161
height, 9, 11, 268–9, 283–4
height studies
The use for history of military, charity and other records that give the height of young people relative to their age. Height is an indicator of nutrition and health. Also known as anthropometric history.
Heim, C. E., 313, 376, 412
Henderson, H. D., 354, 357
Henning, G. R., 400
Hennock, E. P., 11, 88
Herbert, R. F., 63, 64
Hertfordshire, 155
Hicks, J. R., 251, 320
high-powered money, monetary base
The money on which other monies are built, because it depends less on confidence and is therefore used to stand behind other monies. Gold money, for instance, is valuable even when public confidence in cheque money (or 'bank money', q.v.) fails. Therefore, gold stood behind cheque money in the nineteenth century. Today government notes and coin serve the same function. These parts of the 'monetary base' are called 'high-powered' because they are themselves money while also standing behind other money; consequently, a given inflow of gold will allow multiple expansion of all monies. Cf. credit creation; money supply.
Hill, T. P., 119
Hinton, J., 112
Hirst, H., 395
Hitler, A., 420
Hobsbawm, E. J., 96, 100, 105
Hobson, J. A., 181, 185–6
Hodgson, J. A., 339
Hoffman, R. J. S., 65
Holden, K., 353
holidays, seaside, 129
Hopkins, A. G., 197, 198, 209
Hopwood, E., 104
Horsewood, N., 348, 380
hospitals, 34, 134–5
Hounshell, D., 105
household production
The part of national income, sometimes not included in official returns, that is produced outside the market.
housing
boom, 310, 350, 353, 409
conditions, 34
density, 280–1
quality, 281, 289
Howells, P., 356
Howson, S., 309, 339
Huberman, M., 103
Hudson, P., 101
Hughes, T. P., 188
human capital, and age structure, 45
The acquired skill of people, such as their ability to read. It is called 'capital' to draw attention to its similarity to physical capital such as buildings and machines. Like them it is a result of costly investment and yields returns into the future. Cf. capital.
Humphries, J., 353, 409
Hunt, E. H., 55, 57, 103, 160, 276
Huntingdonshire, 164
Huttenback, R. A., 192, 205–12
Hutterites, 38
Hyman, R., 96, 110

ICI (Imperial Chemical Industries), 394, 396, 398, 420
ideological conflict, 412–13
Imlah, J. A. H., 175, 193
immigration
Irish, 55
Jewish, 56
see also migration

imperialism, 197–216
informal, 198, 209
Import Duties Advisory Committee, 308
import penetration, 350
imports
food, 145, 169–70, 171
increasing, 21
inter-war, 302
import substitution, 352
income
agricultural, 146–8
investment, 266–7
labour, 266–7
money–income relationship, 218–19
per capita, 266–7, 270–7
property, 266–7
and savings, 128
see also national income
income effect
The virtual increase in the income of consumers that takes place when a price of something they buy falls. The fall in the price of grain in the late nineteenth century, for example, had two effects on the consumption of grain: by the 'substitution' effect, cheaper grain was substituted for other goods, increasing the amount of grain consumed; by the income effect, less grain was consumed, for richer people (made richer by the price fall) buy proportionately less grain. Cf. Engel's law.
income elasticity of demand
How sensitive the demand for some particular product is to changes in the incomes of demanders. If a 10 per cent rise in income, for example, causes a 5 per cent rise in the quantity of food demanded, then food is said to have an income elasticity of 5/10, or 1/2. Cf. elasticity.
income elasticity of expenditure
How sensitive expenditure (i.e. non-savings) is to a rise of income. If expenditure rose in proportion to income the elasticity would be 1·0; if less than in proportion, less than 1·0. Cf. consumption function; propensity to consume.
incorporation
The formation of a joint-stock company, which is to say a firm of indefinite life, able to act as a legal person, whose liabilities are those of the firm alone, not of the individual holders of shares. Cf. bankruptcy; limited liability; partnerships.
India, 106, 176, 177, 181, 199, 201, 203, 206, 209, 210, 211
Indian Mutiny, 201
indirect tax
Levied 'on' the goods, such as a tax on petrol levied on the station owner, 'in the expectation and intention [as Mill put it] that he shall indemnify himself at the expense of another', i.e. the motorist. Thus are import duties, excises, sales taxes and so forth distinguished from 'direct' taxes, such as the income tax or the land tax. Cf. direct tax.
industrialisation
catching-up process, 66
disadvantages of an early start, 67
industrial policy, 403–8
industrial revolution, second, 65, 71, 397
industrial structure, 92–3, 402–3
holding company, 397
inter-war, 386–414
multi-divisional, 396–7
regional concentration, 100–1
restructuring, 315–17, 405–6
vertical specialisation, 402–3
inequality, 10–13
infant-industry argument
Some industry is claimed to be 'infant', to be nourished and protected from grown-up industries abroad.
infant mortality rates
Deaths per thousand in the first year of life.
inflation, 329
expectations, 225
unanticipated, 259
wartime, 233
A rise in money prices. The rise in one price – say, food – is not inflation, for it may represent merely a growing scarcity of food relative to other goods. Inflation is a growing scarcity of all goods relative to money. Cf. cost-push inflation; current prices vs. constant prices.
inflationary finance
The support of government by the printing of money, as distinct from taxing or borrowing from the public. Cf. balanced budget; budget deficit; government debt.
informal empire
The nations tied to Britain by commerce and foreign policy, especially in Latin

America; 'the empire of free trade', as distinct from the literal empire in Canada, India and so forth.
information, 189, 388, 412
asymmetric
Knowledge that one party to a transaction has that is not shared by another; for example, an employer may know of job opportunities that his workers do not; or a debtor may know of risks that the lender does not. The economics of asymmetric information has recently been much explored.
informational cost
Expense incurred in finding information, as for example the time spent looking up this definition. The cost of discovering the market price is an informational cost, which will be high across high barriers of distance and culture. Cf. adjustment costs.
infrastructure
The capital and the institutions needed for an economy to work well (Latin 'under'): good roads, fair and fast courts of law, honest (or predictably corrupt) government and the like.
Inglis, S., 129
innovation
attitudes towards, 73–4
effect of First World War, 294
entrepreneurs' role, 63–4, 69
see also research and development; technology
input–output analysis
The use of input–output tables (q.v.) to reckon what flows among industries might be in various hypothetical circumstances.
input–output table
An array of the flows of goods around the economy. One column in such an array might be, for example, the steel industry. The steel output is produced by other industries putting in coal, iron ore, railways, machinery, oil, electricity, paper and so forth. One row in such an array might also be steel. The steel output is distributed to the machinery industry (which in turn sells machinery back to steel), to construction, to shipbuilding, to railways and so forth. The table includes only intermediate goods, i.e. goods used to make goods.
insurance, 127–8, 130
see also health insurance
integration, vertical and horizontal, 149
The two ways that large firms are formed: buying up the suppliers of raw materials (vertical) or buying up competitors (horizontal).
interest rates, 223–5
colonial, 205–6
expected, 259
high, 338–9
inter-war, 332
low, 245–6, 309, 327, 352–3
nominal and real, 223–5
parity, 327, 353
and prices, 225
short- and long-term, 223
stable, 224
intermediate goods
Goods used to make goods, as distinct from 'final' goods (q.v.). Steel ingots, railway freight, jet fuel, computer services are all examples. Cf. input–output table; value added.
internal economies of scale
A fall in cost a firm may experience when it expands, as against 'external economies' (coming from outside the firm) or 'internal *dis*economies' (a rise rather than a fall in cost). For example, the spreading of the fixed costs of a large building that occurs when more activity is crammed into it is an internal economy of scale.
International Plate Glass Convention, 404
international trade, 293
cotton, 83, 98, 214
free, 21, 166–70, 292
inter-war, 300–4
international transactions, inter-war, 331
interrelatedness, 67
invention, and innovation
Invention refers to the first implementation of an idea, for example a machine, on an experimental basis; innovation to its introduction into commercial use. There can be a long delay between the two.
inventories, stocks, goods in progress, working capital, variable capital
The physical amounts or money values of materials held for working up. 'Goods in process' is the most illuminating term. The shoemaker's holding of leather, the steel-maker's holding of finished steel, the publisher's holding of paper, ink and finished books are all 'goods in process'.

inventory costs
The expenditure to keep goods in storage awaiting sale, as on a shopkeeper's shelf or in a farmer's barn.
Invergordon Mutiny, 244
investment, 293
crowding-out, 339, 355, 392
industrial, 26–7
inter-war, 314–15, 330, 350
losses home and abroad, 192–3
in management, 71, 92, 111, 113
portfolio, 177–9, 182–3
rates of return on, 183–5
see also foreign investment
Using up resources now to get a return in the future, such as buildings, railways, educating the people and so forth. Investment at home is one of the major parts of national income (q.v., the others being consumption, government spending and investment abroad). It is a more or less productive use of the money value of saving (q.v.) to increase future income. More technically, it is the rate per year at which the existing stock of capital is added to. Cf. capital formation.
investment banking, 189–91
A storehouse of funds that specialises in loaning out its funds to business for long-term projects. In European economic history, the German investment banks of the late nineteenth century are said to have been especially bold and important in German growth, by contrast with the greater caution of British banks.
invisible earnings
In foreign trade, a country's earnings in providing the rest of the world with 'invisible' (i.e. intangible) services, such as shipping, insurance, tourism.
Ireland, 48, 55, 145, 156, 276
Northern, 410
iron and steel industry, 80–1, 107–8
iron law of wages
The proposition, popular in economics *c.*1830, that the wage will never rise above subsistence because workers will give birth to more workers as it does. Cf. demographic crisis; Malthusian trap; natural price of labour.
iron ore, 66
Irving, R. J., 141–2
issues, new
Fresh IOUs, as distinct from ones made in the past and now being traded.
Italy, 48

James, H., 75, 76, 343, 344, 350
Japan, 115, 138, 209, 301
Jeffrey, J. R., 30, 48, 51
Jenkins, D. T., 85
Jenks, L. H., 176
Jevons, W. S., 260, 263
Jewish migrants, 56
Johnman, L., 401
Johnson, P., 128, 187, 268
Joint Industrial Councils, 381
Joint Stock Companies Act (1856), 390–1
joint-stock company
A business that sells certificates of ownership in itself, the 'ownership' being a right to a share (hence 'shares of stock') in profits. Cf. incorporation; limited liability.
Jolly, M., 113
Jones, G., 410
Jones, G. S., 281
Jones, G. T., 83, 106
Jones, H. G., 92, 93, 97–8
Jones, M. A., 49
Jones, M. E. F., 410
Jones index of real cost
An early attempt to measure total factor productivity (q.v.) in selected British industries, developed by G. T. Jones in *Increasing Returns* (Cambridge, 1933). The index measures the fall in cost, holding constant the price of inputs (hence 'real'), that accompanies technological progress. It anticipated by thirty years other so-called 'dual' measures of productivity change (i.e. those using prices instead of quantities).
Juglar, C., 250, 256
Juglar trade cycle, 250–1, 254, 263

Kain, R., 150, 166
Kaldor, N., 117–18, 143, 245
Kalman filter, 261
Katouzian, M. A., 129–30
Kay, J., 389
Kearns, G., 33
Kendall, M., 161
Kendrick, J. W., 149
Kennedy, W. P., 27, 67, 71, 188, 189, 190, 191, 256
Kent, 164
Kesner, R. M., 210

Key Industries Duties, 292
Keynes, J. M., xxiii, 191–2, 225, 239, 241–2, 299, 311, 320, 340, 354–7, 361, 378, 410, 420
Keynesian
Of the school of Keynes (1883–1946) (pronounced 'canes' to rhyme with 'brains'), the famous Cambridge economist and government advisor, whose *General Theory of Employment, Interest and Money* (1936) revolutionised economics. The revolution, presently under heavy counter-attack, advocated the use of government spending and other active policy to offset the cycle of boom and bust. Cf. accelerator; autonomous spending; budget deficit; consumption function; demand, aggregate; demand-deficient unemployment; excess capacity; foreign trade multiplier; full employment; full employment surplus; Harrod–Domar model; multiplier; contrast monetarism, money supply.
Kiddy, 242
Kindleberger, C. P., 67, 73, 74, 146, 151, 188, 244
King, J. E., 102
Kirby, M. W., 406
Kirkaldy, A. W., 232
Kirzner, I. M., 64
Kitson, M., 308, 352
Kleinknecht, A., 254
Klondike, 220
Klovland, J. T., 219
Knight, R., 136, 142, 379
Knodel, J., 37
Kochin, L., 305, 306, 361–5, 377
Kocka, J., 71
Koike, K., 91
Kondratieff, N. D., 250
Kondratieff waves, 250, 253–4
Kravis, I. B., 126, 144
Kredit Anstalt, 244
Kuznets, S., 25, 26, 250, 255
Kuznets cycle, long swing, 11, 250, 251–2, 263
Variations in the rate of growth of some twenty years' duration from peak to peak, discovered by Simon Kuznets. They have been connected to periodic waves in migration, population growth, housebuilding, technological change and frontier settlement. An alternative view is that they do not exist, i.e. that they are statistical artifacts created by random variation in the 'real' (roughly ten-year) business cycle.
Kydland, F. E., 258
Kylsant, Lord, 391

labour, 393–5
aristocracy of, 100
cheap, 67–6, 105
child, 13
conditions, 295
costs, 153, 155, 335, 337–8
demand, 361, 376–80
division of, 12, 93, 402
mobility, 60–1
movement, 295
selection of, 394
shortages, 375
skilled, 99
supply, 100–1, 270, 376–80
white collar, 394
see also farm labourers; trade unions; workers
labour exchanges, 289, 360, 290, 418
labour force
and age structure, 44–5
industrial structure, 22–8
post First World War, 294
quality, 23–4
restructured, 375
women's participation, 93–5
All workers for money income. Housewives, small children, the disabled and others who do not wish to work for money income are therefore not part of the labour force. The unemployed are part of it, since they wish to work for a wage, though they cannot.
Labour governments, 398, 405, 419
labour intensive
Using much labour relative to other inputs, especially capital. A blacksmith's forge is a labour-intensive way to make nails compared with a fully automated nail mill.
labour market, 346
bifurcated, 371
Labour movement
The Labour Party, the trade union movement and the Co-operative movement, working in conjunction.
Labour Party, 133, 295, 412, 417, 418
labour productivity, 4–5, 316, 402
agriculture, 148–9
inter-war, 335
services, 138–9, 141

labour saving
Improvements in knowledge of how to do things that reduce the amount of labour especially. The assembly line is an example, as are machine tools (saving on skilled hand labour). Labour saving is not the same thing as technical progress or productivity change generally, because there is more than labour used to make things – capital, land and materials are used and saved as well. Cf. biased technical progress; productivity.
laissez faire
French phrase meaning 'to leave [alone] to do', that is, the policy of minimal government.
Lancashire, 35, 49, 59, 82–5, 95, 128, 138, 159, 160, 164, 198, 201, 410
Cotton Corporation, 405
Cotton Famine, 37
Lancaster, H. O., 287
Landes, D. S., 23, 65, 69, 73, 77, 188
land intensive
Using much land relative to capital or, especially, labour. Wood was a land-intensive product relative to wheat in the nineteenth century, for example; and agriculture as a whole is obviously land intensive relative to manufacturing.
land–labour ratio
The quotient of the acreage of agricultural land available and the number of workers available to work it.
landowners, 156–9
criticised, 156–7
incomes, 147–8
investment, 158–9
pattern of, 163
Latin America, 176, 185, 204
Law, C. M., 58
Lawrence, B., 134
Lazonick, W., 72, 84, 90–116, 390, 403
leakage of purchasing power
The income saved or spent on imports, that does not directly cause production and employment here at home here and now. It 'leaks' out, which is to say that it is unstimulative, not useless. Cf. Keynesian; multiplier.
learning by doing
The teachings of the best teacher, experience. In other words, it is the improvement in making steel, cotton cloth or whatever that comes with practice. Learning by doing has become a popular way in economics of summarising one source of productivity change, a source that amounts to economies of scale (q.v.).
Lee, C. H., 36, 59–60, 117–44
Leeds, 51
Lees, L. H., 55
leisure activities, growth of, 128
leisure preference
The taste for activities other than working in the market, such as sleeping, painting for pleasure, doing housework. For given preferences a high wage (that is, a high payment for leaving home and going into the market to work) will induce people to take little 'leisure'. Cf. labour force.
Lenin, V. I., 199
Leverhulme, Lord, 394
Levine, A. L., 65, 68, 73, 75
Lewchuk, W., 112, 113, 114, 189, 394, 403
Lewis, W. A., 250, 251, 254, 263, 343
Lewis-Fanning, E., 40
Leybourne, S. J., 220
Liberal government, 289
Liberal Party, 103
Liesner, T., 233
life expectancy, 7, 281, 282–3, 287
The number of years the average person would live if death rates and birth rates were to stay constant. It can be life expectancy 'at birth', 'at age 20' or some other age.
limited liability
The exemption from personal debt of a stock holder in a corporation. The owners of a corporation are not required to hand over their personal assets to clear the debts of the corporation, by contrast with partnerships (such as Lloyds).
Lincoln Bank, 226, 416
Lindert, P., 73, 87, 292
Link, A. N., 63, 64
Lipsey, R. G., 383
liquidity, world-wide scramble for, 231, 244
Little, Assistant Commissioner, 158
Littler, C. R., 394
Liverpool, 51, 55, 130
living standards, 265–90
definition, 265–6
Llewellyn-Smith, H., 366
Lloyd George, D., 354–7, 419
Lloyd-Jones, R., 69
loanable funds
The money available in a society to be invested.

Locke, R., 394
lockouts, engineering industries, 102, 109–12, 417
Logan, W. P. D., 31
London, 276, 410
  capital market, 67, 187–8, 190
  City of, 292, 342
  employment, 53, 59–60
  migrants, 49, 51, 55–6
  poverty, 365–7
London Stock Exchange, 130, 206, 391
Lorenz, E. H., 100
Lorenz curve
  The plot of the per cent (y) of all income of the nation received by the bottom (x) per cent of the income recipients. It is a summary measure of equality or its lack. If 5 per cent of income is received by 5 per cent of the recipients, 50 per cent by 50 per cent, and so forth throughout, then there is perfect equality. On the other hand, if the bottom 90 per cent of the income receivers receive only, say, 1 per cent of the income, there is nearly perfect inequality: 10 per cent receive 99 per cent of all income.
Lothians, 163
Louis, W. R., 198
Lowndes, G. A. D., 44
Lucas, R. E., 221, 258
lumpiness
  The all-or-nothing character of some projects: one either builds a railway line from Manchester to Liverpool all in a lump or one does not; a single rail, or two going half way, is useless. Lumpiness can be an obstacle to the undertaking of a desirable project if an enormous lump must be accumulated before the project is begun. Cf. infrastructure; social overhead capital.
Lund, P. J., 353

Macara, C., 106
McBride, T. M., 127
McClelland, K., 103
McCloskey, D., xix–xxiii, 65–7, 81, 86, 107, 108, 189, 192, 238, 256, 258, 260
McConnell, P., 153, 156, 162
MacDonald, R., 419, 420
McDonald, W., 163
MacInnes, J., 116
MacIntosh, T., 310
McIvor, A., 106
McKendrick, N., 75
McKenna Duties, 292
  High taxes on imports of automobiles, films and other luxuries imposed by the Chancellor of the Exchequer in 1915 as a war measure. When the war was over they were not removed, becoming the substance and symbol of Britain's retreat from free trade.
McKeown, T., 32–5
Mackinnon, M., 265–90
McLean, D., 209
McLean, I. W., 212
McMahon, C. W., 143
Macmillan Committee (1931), 239–40, 244, 311, 342, 392, 420
Macmillan gap, 392
  An assertion by the Committee on Finance and Industry, which reported in 1930–1, that the British capital market channelled funds abroad or into large businesses, leaving little businesses starved of capital.
McQuillan, K., 287
macro-economics
  The part of economics having to do with inflation and unemployment. From another point of view, the macro-economic is what is left over from the micro-economic, i.e. the part having to do with markets, relative prices and scarcity. Although it means 'large', in an economic context 'macro' does not necessarily mean the larger and more important parts of the subject. Unlike micro-economics, there is no settled theory of macro-economics, but many theories with more or less in common: Keynesianism, monetarism and so forth.
Macrosty, H. W., 336
Maddison, A., 120, 131, 296, 297, 318
Maddock, R., 212
Makower, H., 61
Malin, J. C., 85
Malinvaud, E., 318
malnutrition, and unemployment, 313
Malthusian trap
  A situation in which rises of income due to (say) technical progress are offset by rises in population eating the income, leaving the income per head unaltered. It is named in honour of the economist Thomas Malthus (1766–1834), who pointed it out most vividly. Cf. iron law of wages.

management, 388
compared to entrepreneurship, 62
interests of, 395–6
professionalism, 395, 397, 412
management structures, 116
investment in, 92, 111, 113
managerial capitalism, 101
Manchester, 51, 55, 130, 190, 391
Marconi Co., 407

marginal
In most economic usage, 'last'. Thus, the marginal product of labour in wheat is the bushels of wheat produced by adding the last man. Occasionally it will mean, as in common parlance, 'small' or 'inadequate', as when an enterprise is said to earn 'marginal returns'.

marginal cost
The cost of the last unit produced. Cf. cost curve.

marginal efficiency of capital, marginal efficiency of investment, marginal product of capital
Various ideas, technically distinct but all capturing the value of (and therefore the demand for) additional machinery, buildings and so forth in an economy. The marginal efficiency of capital is the demand for capital in the same way that the economy's savings (q.v.) is its supply.

marginal land
The last acre to be brought into production, i.e. the worst land – worst in the combination of fertility and location that makes land valuable.

marginal product of labour (or of capital)
The product of the last labourer to be added (or of the last machine or building); the increase in output to be expected from an additional dose.

marginal propensity to consume
The share of spending on consumption of domestic goods and services (as distinct from savings or imports) out of each additional £ of income. Cf. consumption function; leakage of purchasing power; marginal propensity to import; multiplier.

marginal propensity to import
The share of spending on imports out of each additional £ of income. In the Keynesian model (q.v.) imports, like saving and taxes, do not lead to further income for the nation, and are therefore 'leakages' that drag the economy. Cf. consumption function; leakage of purchasing power; marginal propensity to consume; multiplier. Contrast foreign trade multiplier.

marginal vs. average return
The return on the last bit of investment vs. the return over all previous investments. Since one will choose the high-return investments first, the last investments will have low returns, which is to say that marginal return is less than average.

market equilibrium
Supply equals demand. The participants will not voluntarily change the price or quantity traded once equilibrium is achieved.

marketing, criticised, 71–2

market power
The ability to search for a profitable price, as against taking the price as given (as a small competitor must).

markets
mass, 397
nature of, 66
size, 412
theory of, 387–90
Trades at a (roughly) single price for the same thing. Thus, wheat was traded in a world-wide market during the nineteenth century, housing in a local market. The trades need not be in one place.

market structure
The character of a market in respect of its competitiveness: monopolised, competitive, oligopolistic (Greek 'few sellers') or whatever.

Marks, P. H., 42
Married Women's Property Acts (1870, 1880), 12
Marsh, A. I., 115

Marshallian
Of the school of Alfred Marshall (1842–1924), the Cambridge economist whose *Principles of Economics* (fl. *c.*, 1910) 'led [English economics] out of the valley and on to a sunlit height' (J. A. Schumpeter). Marshall gave English economics, and much of economics whether English or not, its modern form. He is particularly associated with the refinement of supply and demand and the notion of equilibrium it embodies.

Marx, K., 99, 154, 415
Mass, W., 84, 100, 106

mass-production machinery, 113
Mathias, P., 63
Matthews, R. C. O., xxiv, 5–6, 15–16, 19, 23–4, 27, 98, 123, 126, 148, 220, 253–4, 256, 260, 263, 266–7, 304–5, 316, 341, 347, 355–6, 382, 402, 409
May Committee, 345
Maynard, G., 90
Meade, J. E., 249
means testing, 367
mechanical engineering, lockout, 102
Mechi, Alderman, 146
medical intervention, 32–4
Medoff, J. L., 91
Meltzer, A. H., 221, 231
Menderhausen, H., 216
mergers, 71, 190, 315, 316, 388–9
metal-working industries, 114–15
Metcalf, D., 363
Mexico, 193
Michie, R. C., 67, 68, 188, 189, 191
Micklewright, J., 364
micro-economics
  The part of economics having to do with markets, relative prices and scarcity. It does not mean the worm's eye view, or the small (micro) and presumably trivial subjects in economics. A 'micro-economics of unemployment', for example, attempts to explain unemployment in terms of the maximising decisions of individuals rather than in terms of other 'macro-economic' (q.v.) variables such as aggregate demand or the money supply.
Middleton, R., 311, 312, 350, 355
midlands, 165
Midlothian, 155
migration, 23, 46–56
  balance, 30–1
  in business cycle theory, 256
  chain, 47
  costs, 376
  information flow model, 47–8, 49–50
  internal, 23, 50–5, 162, 276
  measurement problems, 51
  push–pull model, 47–8, 49
  regional, 165–6, 376
  return, 48–9
  stage, 49
  see also emigration; immigration
Mills, T. C., 219, 220, 222, 224, 246
Millward, R., 139, 141, 142, 405
Miners' Federation, 96, 406
Mingay, G. E., 158
minimum wage, legal
  A law specifying that no one may be hired for less than a stated sum, as for tailoring, chainmaking and cardboard box making from 1909 on, and for coal mining from 1912 on.
Ministry of Labour, 363, 368, 370–2
Mitchell, B. R., 18, 30–1, 43–4, 92–3, 97–8, 133, 146, 149, 151, 175, 186, 212, 216, 268, 280, 297, 318
Mitchell, W. C., 247
Mitchison, R., 9
mobility
  Movement of resources from one employment to another. If owners of capital have mobility their capital will earn the same return everywhere, for they will move the capital elsewhere if does not. If land is not mobile, as it is not, then land will not earn the same return everywhere.
models, xxi–xxii
Moggridge, D. E., 244, 299, 307, 340–1
monetarism
  The macro-economic theory, associated especially with the American economist Milton Friedman, claiming that the money supply (q.v.) is a prime mover of the level of prices and of income. Cf. high-powered money; monetary policy; quantity theory of money. Contrast Keynesian.
monetary base, inter-war, 237–8, 240
monetary policy
  global nature of, 326–7
  inter-war, 309
  The plans by governments for changing the amounts of money in order to affect unemployment and inflation. Cf. Bank Rate; central bank; fiscal policy; high-powered money; money supply.
monetary transfers, British empire, 210
money
  in business cycle theory, 258–60
  global contraction, 343–4
  and output, 260
  pre-Second World War demand, 219
  real balances, 259–60
  role of, 217–46
  see also interest rates
money–income relationship, 218–19
money market
  All exchanges of which the rate of interest is the price, that is, all borrowing and lending. Sometimes the term is

specialised to mean all such exchanges for short periods (such as three months) among banks, governments and large enterprises.
money–output relationship, 221–3
money supply
  determinants, 227
  expansion, 309, 352–3
  inter-war, 243–4
  and prices, 332
  The sum of all means of payment, such as coin, bank notes, chequing accounts and easily cashable savings accounts. Cf. credit creation; high-powered money; monetary policy. Also called 'stock of money'.
monopoly, 389–90
  of professionals, 404
  One seller. The Post Office in Britain, for example, has a monopoly of letter post.
monopoly power, 404
monopsony
  'One buyer', as monopoly means 'one seller'. The single coal company in a northern village might be a monopsonist in buying labour.
moral hazard, 388, 390–1
morbidity, 33, 282–3
More, C., 99
Morgan, E. V., 232, 293, 339
Morris, M. D., 203
Morris, William, 394, 397
mortality rates, 7–9, 281–2
  by age, 31–2
  falling, 29–32
  reasons for, 32–5
  and income, 35
  infant, 7, 36–8
  and life expectancy, 31
  statistics, 268
  urban penalty, 35
  see also death rate
  Deaths per thousand population, or deaths at a certain age per population of that age.
mortgage
  A loan on the security of houses and land: if the borrower cannot pay the agreed interest, he forfeits the house to the lender.
Morton, J. C., 153
motor vehicle industry, 86, 113–14, 188–9, 394, 401, 403, 410
moving average
  An average over several years, called 'moving' because as years pass the earlier years are dropped from the average and the mid-year of the averages moves. It is a crude way of smoothing out jumps in a series of, say, wheat prices to reveal the underlying trend.
Mowat, C. L., 348
Mowery, D. C., 399
Mukerjee, T., 203, 210
multilateral settlement, multilateral payments
  The usual pattern of buying and selling among all countries. The word 'settlement' arises from the notion that all must in the end settle up, paying for purchases from country Y with receipts from X and Z. Britain's large deficit in trade with the United States around 1910, for example, was made up in the multilateral settlement by a surplus with India, which in turn ran a surplus with the Continent, which in turn ran a surplus with the United States. Multilaterally – i.e. looking at it from literally many sides – the accounts balance.
multinationals, 178–9, 410, 413
multiplier, employment
  The ratio in which new expenditure in an underemployed economy results in a larger rise of income. New exports of steel in 1933, for example, would have earned steelworkers and owners in South Wales more income, which they would spend on, say, bread and housing, thereby giving more income to bread bakers and housebuilders. The multiple effects eventually die out, killed by 'leakages' (q.v.) that do not cause higher British income (e.g. imports or saving). But the flow of income is permanently higher than it was before, at least if the initial rise of expenditure is permanent. The economy must, however, be well below full employment for the effect to work. Cf. accelerator; consumption function; Keynesian.
multiplier, money, 226–7
multiplier-accelerator theory, 256–8
Musson, A. E., 87
Mutch, A., 153, 154

National Confederation of Employers' Organisations, 398

national debt
The loans owed by the state. 'National' is a misnomer, because it is not all loans in the nation but only those owed by the state. The chief source of such indebtedness since the eighteenth century has been the exigencies of war.
National governments, 345, 398, 420
national income, 2–4, 266–7
average, 2–3
distribution, 8, 9, 11, 126, 267
inter-war, 321
per capita, 266–7, 270–7
The sum of the value of everything produced for the nation, taking care not to count the value of, say, coal twice, once when it is mined and again when it is burned to make iron. National income is the sum of every income earned in the nation: workers, capitalists, landlords, bureaucrats. As a first approximation it is equal to national product, for the cost of producing things is someone's income. The taxes on things such as the sales tax on bread, however, make for a difference between what is paid ('at market prices') and what is earned ('at factor costs'). The national income at factor cost, then, is rather lower than national product (which itself may be lowered by removing depreciation; cf. gross national product). The national value added is the sum of all values added. The value added by each firm is the value of the labour and capital it uses, that is, the value of its goods in excess of its purchases from other industries. The sum of all these will be the sum value of labour and capital, i.e. national income.
nationalisation, *see* state ownership
National Shipbuilders, scheme, 411
National Shipbuilders, Security, 406
National Shipbuilders' Society Ltd, 315
natural price of labour
The wage that would result in the long run if the number of labourers always increased (by birth) when they grew to some degree prosperous. Cf. iron law of wages; Malthusian trap.
natural rate of growth
In the Harrod–Domar model (q.v.) the percentage rate at which income would grow if it grew in accord with growing population.
natural rate of unemployment
The percentage of people out of work in normal times, such as people between jobs. It is, therefore, the lowest possible rate of unemployment. Identical to frictional unemployment.
natural resources
The valuable properties of the land, such as coal bearing. 'Resources' unqualified means all inputs to production, not merely natural resources.
Nelson, R. R., 64
neoclassical economics
The modern orthodoxy in economics, as distinct from classical economics (q.v.) before it and modern Marxian, institutionalist or Austrian economics. It emphasises mathematics in method and profit-maximising in substance. In its simplest and most characteristic form it treats as given the technology, taste and resources of an economy, turning its attention to how these interact. The various schools may be distinguished by their respective forefathers; those of neoclassical economics are Adam Smith and his intellectual grandson, Alfred Marshall. Cf. classical economics; Marshallian.
Netherlands, 145, 146
net investment
All investment minus the investment in depreciation; which is to say, the investment that results during a year in a net increase – allowing for replacement as it wears out – of the stock of capital.
net national product, *see* gross national product
What the nation makes excluding that used to repair old machines and buildings.
net output, *see* value added
net overseas assets
The value of what foreigners owe Britain subtracting out what Britain owes them.
Newcastle, stock exchange, 391
Newell, A., 344, 347
Newfoundland, 177
newspaper press, 88
New Survey of London Life and Labour, 365
Newton, M. P., 51
New Zealand, 146, 151, 166, 169, 182, 203, 209
Nicholas, S. J., 71–2, 179, 410

Nickell, S. J., 348, 363, 380
Nolan, P., 116
non-imperialism
  marginal standard, 199–202, 204–8, 211–13, 215–16
  strong standard, 199–200, 202–4, 208–10, 213–14
non-pecuniary benefits
  Good things that happen to you for which you do not pay, such as the pleasure from a neighbour's garden (presuming that you did not pay more to buy your house on account of his garden). Cf. externalities.
Norfolk, 164
normal profits
  The return to the owners of a business just necessary to keep the industry at its best size (namely the size at which supply equals demand). A sudden rise in demand for coal will produce (temporary) super-normal profits to the owners; a sudden fall, subnormal profits.
Norman, Montagu, 342, 391, 412
North, D. C., 132
Northamptonshire, 138, 164
Northumberland, 35, 36, 100, 411
Norway, 48
nuptiality
  The rate of marriage per thousand population at risk.
nutrition, 9, 32–3

O'Brien, A. P., 129, 190
O'Brien, P. K., 213
occupational structure, 92–3
  geographical, 17–18
Oddy, D. J., 34
Odling-Smee, J. C., xxiv, 19, 23, 27, 220, 253, 263, 316
Offer, A., 159, 170, 211, 215, 287
official reserves
  The gold or dollars or Swiss francs or whatever held by the central bank in order to 'back' (i.e. stabilise the value of) the national currency. Cf. gold reserves.
Ó Gráda, C., 11, 145–72
Ojala, E. M., 151
Okhawa, K., 138
Okun relation, 323
Oldham, 130
oligopoly, 137
Olson, M., 151, 389–90, 413
open economy
  A nation affected by economic events abroad, so that prices, interest rates and so forth at home are determined in part abroad. Only very high tariffs or other artificial restrictions on trade can prevent a modern economy from being 'open' in most respects, yet economic models are often 'closed'.
opportunism, 388
opportunity cost
  The value of an alternative given up to pursue another. The value of the alternative is the economist's touchstone in measuring true cost. It may or may not correspond with the measures thrown up by the market place. The 'cost' of some improvement in a farm, for example, might seem at first to be merely the out-of-pocket expenses of the landlord. But if the improvement temporarily disrupts the farm or if the improvements makes impossible some other project (e.g. road widening), then more costs need to be counted to capture the full opportunity cost.
Ormerod, P. A., 305, 363
O'Rourke, K., 276
Orsagh, T. J., 80
Orwin, C. S., 147, 164
Ottawa Conference (1932), 405, 420
output
  composition, 400–2
  growth, 14–16, 296–7
  see also money–output relationship
output, full employment
  The goods made by an economy when all who wish to work do. Cf. full employment.
output gap, 322–4, 327–30
Overend Gurney Crisis (1866), 229
overseas new issues
  New lending to foreigners, especially in the form of IOUs. Thus, new issues are 'portfolio investment' by Englishmen in foreign bonds. Contrast direct investment
Overton, M., 164
overvaluation
  A condition of a currency in which the price at which it is presently selling in terms of other currencies is for some reason too high. The pound sterling, for example, is said to have been overvalued when Britain returned to gold in 1925.

The price of the pound ($4·86) did not fall, because the Treasury would buy up pounds to keep the price up. According to the traditional story, the price level in Britain had to fall to achieve equilibrium at the too high price of pounds.
Oxfordshire, 160, 164

Palmerston, H. J. T., 415
paper, 401
Parker, W. N., xix
partial equilibrium analysis
 Economic thinking that takes one small sector of the economy in isolation, on the argument (sometimes true, sometimes false) that the more remote consequences of a change in question by way of other parts of the economy are unimportant. The other member of the pair is 'general equilibrium analysis'.
participation rate
 The percentage of a group who work in the market instead of at home. It is most commonly applied to women, whose rate has varied markedly from one time or social class to another. Cf. labour force.
partnerships
 Businesses in which the owners share the profits and, by contrast with limited companies, take full responsibility for the debts of the business. Cf. incorporation; limited liability.
Patterson, D. G., 178, 187
pauperism, 269, 284–6
 see also poverty
Payne, P. L., 63, 66, 71, 72, 74, 89
Peacock, A. T., 134
Pearce, I. F., 192, 203
Peden, G. C., 357
Peel, J., 40
Pelling, H., 97, 103, 105
Pember Reeves, M., 268
pensions, old age, 289–90
performance indicators, 1–2
Perkin, H., 63
permanent income
 The income one can count on having, contrasted with 'transitory' income (which includes any unusual unexpected rise or fall in income). The 'permanent income hypothesis' is the notion that the amount people consume (i.e. the amount they do not save) is dependent on their permanent not their transitory income. Identical to expected lifetime income.
Perren, R., 158, 164, 166, 167
Perry, P. J., 147, 150
Petit, P., 119
Phelps Brown, E. H., 220
Phillips, A. D. M., 70
Phillips, A. W., 383
Phillips curve, 323
 An association of high unemployment with low inflation and low unemployment with high inflation named for one of its formulators.
piece-master system, 109–10
Pigou, A. C., 162, 260, 338, 341, 381
Pilgrim Trust, 367, 376
Pilkingtons, 395, 404
Piva, M. J., 288
Platt, D. C. M., 175, 198
police force, 211, 212
Pollard, S., 62–89, 100, 196, 232, 241
Pollins, H., 182
Ponting, K. G., 85
Poor Law Act (1834), 12
Poor Laws, 269, 283, 284, 288, 289–90
 The traditional name until the twentieth century for the regulations of state charity. The 'Old' Poor Law, dating back to Elizabethan times, obtained until 1834, the 'New' thereafter.
Pope, D., 50
population
 age structure, 42–5, 186–7
 growth, 4
  transition model, 29
  see also fertility; mortality
 mobility, 23, 51–3
 see also migration
Porter, J. H., 103, 393
portfolio investment
 abroad, 177–9
 rates of return, 182–3
 Lending in exchange for IOUs such as bonds. Contrast direct investment, in equity, that is to say, shares of ownership. Cf. overseas new issues.
Post Office, 135, 136–7, 142, 144, 406
poverty, 10–11
 causes of, 365–7
 extent of, 278–9
 policy responses, 288–90
 primary, 277–8
 secondary, 278
 see also pauperism
preference securities
 Certificates of partial ownership of a company that are paid off before

'common' stocks if the company goes bankrupt.
Prescott, E. C., 258
Prest, A. R., 280
Preston, 102
Price, R., 92–4, 95, 97
price deflated return
The interest rate earned per year minus the relevant inflation per year. A loan to the government in 1800 that earned 6 per cent by 1801 would really earn only 2 per cent if inflation in the meantime had been 4 per cent because the pounds in which the government repaid £106 for every £100 borrowed would be worth 4 per cent less.
price-fixing agreements, 388–9
see also cartels
price–output trends, 327–30
prices
and interest rates, 225
inter-war fluctuations, 384
and money supply, 332
trends, 268
world-wide fall, 220–1
see also cost of living
primary goods, primary sector
Those coming 'earliest' in the stages of production. It is therefore another word for both 'investment' goods (i.e. goods such as bricks, coal, used to build machinery and buildings) and for agricultural goods (on the idea that agriculture is fundamental). Carrying on, 'secondary' goods are manufactured commodities, such as cloth, glass, processed food and so forth. 'Tertiary' goods are not goods at all, but services, such as barbering and teaching. The sequence from raw materials and agriculture through commodities to human services is in this view a progression from primary to tertiary.
primary producing area
Areas such as America and Australia and Africa that produced in the nineteenth century 'primary' goods (q.v.), i.e. raw materials for Europe's machines.
Prince, H., 150, 166
Princeton Fertility Survey, 38
private return
Rewards from a project that come directly to the investors in the project, by contrast with the more comprehensive returns that include any benefits (subtracting any hurts) that come to people other than those who invested. The profits from a railway line, for example, would be private returns; the rise in the rent of my land when the railway ran by it would have to be added to measure the social rate of return (q.v.). Cf. cost-benefit analysis; social opportunity cost; social saving.
process innovation
The introduction of a new way of making an old thing, as distinct from the introduction of a new thing ('product' innovation).
producers' surplus
The excess of what producers are actually paid over what they would be willing to accept at the least. The idea is analogous, on the other side of the market, to 'consumers' surplus' (q.v.). It is identical to 'rent' (q.v.) and to profit.
product innovation
The introduction of a new thing as distinct from a new way of making an old thing ('process' innovation). The word 'innovation' in both phrases emphasises that it is not invention – i.e. discovery – that is entailed, but bringing into practical use.
production function
The relationship between input and output.
productive potential
The most the society can make under conditions of full employment (q.v.).
productivity
capital, 139
cotton industry, 83
declining growth, 21
gap, 386, 408–10
growth, 5–6, 400, 402
international comparisons, 408–10
inter-war, 321
labour, 4–5, 138–9, 141, 316, 402
regional variations, 410–12
service industries, 138–42
total factor, 4–7, 139–41, 148–9
Output per unit of input, conventionally either of land, labour, capital or some combination of these. The productivity of labour is output per man in some industry or economy. Since it is per man, ignoring other inputs (such as capital or raw materials), it is not usually an

adequate measure of efficiency overall in the use of resources. Cf. total factor productivity.
profit-sharing schemes, 394
propensity to consume
The amount consumed out of the average £ or (a slightly different notion) the additional £ of income. Cf. consumption function; marginal propensity to import; multiplier.
Prothero, R. E. (Lord Ernle), 146
psychic income
Satisfactions not paid for explicitly in money, such as from the neighbour's garden or from the company furniture in one's office. Cf. externalities.
public expenditure *see* defence expenditure; government expenditure
public good
A commodity from the benefits of which no one in the public can be (or in some definitions should be) excluded. National defence is enjoyed by Jones if it is enjoyed by his neighbour Smith, for there is no cheap way by which missiles and tanks protecting Smith can fail to afford Jones some protection.
public utilities
Services such as electricity, telephone, water supply, sewerage, roads, gas, and the like that governments commonly provide directly or regulate closely, on the grounds that the services would otherwise tend to become dangerous monopolies.
Purcell, J., 114

quantity theory of money
The conviction that an increase in general prices is a result of increases in the supply of money. The main alternative theories are those of aggregate demand (q.v.) and of supply. Cf. high-powered money; monetarism; monetary policy.

Railway Act (1921), 405, 419
railways, 131, 141–2, 315
colonial, 204, 207–8
diffusion of, 214
foreign investment in, 179, 181–2
India, 199, 201
rate of return
The interest on a loan generalised to apply to anything that like a loan involves sacrifice now for a reward later. Government bonds, for example, have a rate of return; but so does education or long-distance running. Cf. social rate of return.
raw materials, price of, 378, 380
rayon, 401
Reader, W., 74, 389, 394
real
An economic word meaning 'adjusted for mere inflation or deflation of prices in general'.
real income
Formally, money income expressed in the prices of some year, removing therefore the objection in comparisons of income in say 1800 and 1850 that a pound in 1800 did not buy the same amount as a pound in 1850. Cf. base-year prices; consumer price index; cost of living index.
real national income, real output
The nation's income (or production because what is produced accrues as someone's income) brought back to the £s of some particular year such as 1913. The result allows income to be compared from year to year even if prices have changed between them.
real per capital consumption
The consumption part of the nation's real national income (q.v.) per head, in real terms, i.e. eliminating inflation. The other parts are investment, government spending and exports.
real vs. money wages
Money wages are the pay packet in money; real wages express its purchasing power in the prices of some year. Cf. consumer price index; cost of living index; real.
reaper-and-binder, 156, 162, 416
reaping machine, 152–6, 162
Red Flag Act, 68
rediscounting, discounting
The purchase of IOUs before they are due, giving the original holder money immediately and giving the holder in due course the interest to be earned by holding them. The Bank of England, for example, commonly rediscounted bills (i.e. short-term IOUs) for the banks. The banks had themselves bought the bills (discounted them), and the Bank bought the bills in turn from them (*re*discounted the bills).

redistribution of income
A shift in who gets what as pay or other earnings.
Redlich, F., 64
Redmond, J., 242, 299, 303, 340
re-exports
Goods imported into Britain and then immediately exported abroad without further processing. Under the Navigation Acts Britain was by law endowed with a large re-export trade of products from the colonies bound for foreign countries.
refrigeration, 169
regression analysis, regression equation, curve fitting
Techniques for fitting straight lines through a scatter of points. In finding the straight line that would best summarise the relationship during, 1921–38 between consumption and income, for instance, one is said to 'regress consumption on income', i.e. fit a straight line through points on a graph of annual consumption and income for these years. The simplest and by far the most widely used of the techniques is called 'least squares' or 'ordinary least squares'. The result will be an equation for a straight line, such as: Consumption in £ million at 1938 prices equal £277 million plus 0·44 times income in £ million at 1938 prices. Symbolically, the equation is in general $C = a+bY$. The actual numerical result turns out to say that the line that best fits the scatter of combinations of consumption and income is a constant (£277 million) plus 44 per cent of whatever income happens to be. The 'slope' or 'slope coefficient' or 'regression coefficient' or 'beta' is in this case 0·44. Consumption here is called the 'dependent' variable, income the 'independent' variable, in accord with the notion that consumption is dependent on income. The technique generalises easily to more than one independent variable, in which case it is called 'multiple regression' and amounts to fitting a plane (rather than a line) through points in space (rather than through points on a plane surface). In multiple regression the coefficient 'on' (i.e. multiplying) each independent variable measures the way each by itself influences the dependent variable. The equation fitted in the case mentioned above was in fact Consumption = 277+(0·44) Income+(0·47) Consumption Last Year, which is a multiple regression of this year's consumption on this year's income and last year's consumption. It says that for a given consumption last year each £ of income raised consumption by £0·44; and for a given income each £ of consumption last year raised consumption this year by £0·47. The technique generalises with rather more difficulty to more than one *dependent* variable, in which case it is called 'simultaneous equation estimation'.
Reid, A., 103
relative income hypothesis
The notion that one's consumption (as distinct from savings) depends on one's relative economic position, not absolute wealth. According to the hypothesis the poor will save little (i.e. consume virtually all their income) even though they are in absolute terms as wealthy as, say, the high-saving middle class of a much poorer country. Cf. permanent income.
relative price
As distinct from 'nominal' or 'money' or 'absolute' prices, the price of one good in terms of another good, rather than in terms of money. If farm labour earns 16 shillings a week when wheat sells for 8 shillings a bushel, then the price of a week of labour relative to a bushel of wheat is 2·0 bushels per week. Note the units: they are units of physical amounts, not money. Relative prices are determined by the real effectiveness of the economy, whereas money prices are determined by relative prices and by the dearness of money.
rent, economic rent, pure rent
The return to factors of production in excess of its next best employment. In an industry with no next best employment – for instance, land used in agriculture alone – all the return will be economic rent. A coal seam is another classical example: the seam has no employment other than for coal. Economic rent need not correspond exactly to the amount earned in 'rent' in the ordinary sense of weekly rent for a flat, or even yearly rent for land. For definitions in slightly

different terms: cf. economic rent; producers' surplus.
rentier
The receiver of rent, from French (and pronounced as French). Often with an unfavourable connotation, it means the receiver of income without labour, as the owner of government bonds, for example, or the owner of urban land.
replacement investment, *see* depreciation
The new machinery and buildings installed when the old wear out.
research and development, 398–400
diffusion rate, 399–400
expenditure on, 399
see also innovation; technology
research associations, 398–9
reserve/deposit ratio, 226, 238–9
residual, the
A name for 'total factor productivity' (q.v.) emphasising its character as what rise of output is left over to explain after the rise of inputs has explained what it can.
resource endowment, 66
retailing, 88, 409–10
retail price index, cost of living index
The average of prices in shops, as distinct from prices at the warehouses ('wholesale price index') or in the economy generally ('GNP deflator'). Identical to consumer price index. Cf. base-year prices.
Rew, R. H., 149
Rhee, A., 157
Ricardian theory
Any idea associated with David Ricardo (1772–1823), the English economist who brought the system of Adam Smith to a high degree of logical refinement. The chief of these ideas, and the one usually meant when 'Ricardian' is used without further qualification, is the theory of rent (q.v.), namely, the idea that the demand for something available in limited supply and without alternative employment (such as well-located land) determines its price.
Ricardo, D., 146
Richardson, H. W., 65, 308
Richardson, J. H., 316, 386, 394
Riley, J. C., 282
Rimmer, W. G., 74
risk, 183, 187–8, 412
aversion, 392
lowered by colonial status, 206–7, 208
sharing, 388
risk-adjusted, risk-premium, risk-differentials
In the capital market, the allowance for risk in the annual return on an IOU. The return to common stock in the UK, for example, was well above the return to Indian railway bonds, but the higher return required the greater taking of risk in holding stocks: 'risk-adjusted', in other words, one might conclude that the returns were the same. In the labour market, additional rewards may be necessary to induce people to enter hazardous occupations, such as coal mining.
road building, 408
Robbins, K., 76
Roberts, E., 35, 37, 42
Robertson, P., 100
Robinson, R., 198
Rockoff, H., 220, 230
Rodda, J. C., 262
Rodrik-Bali, G., 219, 227
Rose, L., 37, 74
Rosenberg, N., 105
Rostas, L., 141, 315, 316, 408
Rostow, W. W., 222, 250
Routh, G., 135, 396
Rowan, D. C., 192
Rowe, J. W. F., 49, 94–5, 96
Rowntree, B. S., 11, 161, 265–6, 277–8, 284, 366, 394
Rowthorn, R. E., 251
Royal Agricultural Society, 158
Royal Commission on Education, 134
Royal Commissions on Agriculture, 147, 156–8, 164, 165
Royal Mail Steam Packet Co., 391
Royal Tariff Commission, 147
Rubinstein, W. D., 76, 163, 267
Russia, 204
Russo, J. A., 261

Sachs, J., 309
Salter, W. E. G., 402
Samuel, R., 99
Samuelson, P., 254
Sandberg, L. G., 64, 65, 77, 84–5, 106
Sanderson, M., 77, 399
Sargent, T., 243
Sargent Florence, P., 395
Saul, S. B., 17, 82, 110, 201, 210, 220, 253
Savage, M., 42

Saville, J., 54, 103
savings
  and age structure, 186–7
  and income, 128
  and investment, 24–8
  surplus, 181, 185–7
  Abstention from consumption. Any income a person or a nation does not consume in a year but sets aside to yield future consumption is called 'saving'. Cf. consumption; financial intermediaries; investment; loanable funds.
savings function
  Statement of what causes people to save. The most obvious cause is income: a rich man saves more in total than does a poor man, and perhaps even more as a percentage of his income. Another thing on which savings depend is the interest rate earned on the savings accounts, bonds, stocks, etc., into which savings are put: if interest (after tax and risk) is high, people wish to save more.
savings ratio, savings rate
  The ratio of abstention from consumption to all income; that is, the percentage of all income set aside today to produce income tomorrow.
Say, J. B., 63
Sayer, R. S., 241
Scandinavia, 49
scarcity
  The limited amount of desirable things; the curse of Adam and the central concern of mainstream economics.
Schofield, R. S., xxiv, 40
Schumpeter, J. A., 63–4, 217, 253
Schwartz, A., 218–19, 221–2, 224–7, 230, 236, 242, 253, 258, 259, 260, 345
Scotland, 40, 163, 164, 165, 410
Scottish Football League, 138
Seabourne, T., 231
search theory
  The economics of finding the best deal, the logic of which has only recently been explored seriously. Its main significance is that it offers a rationale for conditions otherwise outside the traditional economic models. A condition of unemployment, for example, may be the best one can do in view of the high costs of search. Cf. asymmetric information
Searle, G. R., 289
Second World War, 385
Select Committee on Revenue Department Estimates, 135
Sells, D., 381
service industries, 23, 89, 117–44, 409–10
  capital/labour ratios, 137
  classification, 118–20
  consumer, 125–9
  consumption expenditure, 126
  efficiency versus quality, 135
  elasticity of demand, 126
  employment data, 120, 122–5
  in growth models, 117–18, 143–4
  market structure, 137–8
  output, 120–2
  producer, 129–31
  productivity, 138–42
  public sector, 131–5
  regional employment, 125
  and regional income, 129
  size of enterprise, 136–7
  wages structure, 135–6
  see also domestic service
shareholders
  control by, 178
  interests of, 395–6
Sheffield, 130, 293, 391
shipbuilding industry, 81, 314, 315, 336, 403
shop stewards, 111–12, 114–15, 116
short-run cost curve
  The expenditure of a company or person to supply something before they have been permitted to adjust their affairs to supply it cheapest. For instance, the short-run cost curve of steel shows what additional steel will cost if no new plants, iron mines or marketing arrangements are permitted. In the long run the cost will be lower, for new plants will be built to service the additional quantity demanded. Cf. cost.
Siegrist, H., 71
Simon, M., 177, 179
Sisson, K., 114
skewed distribution of income
  The profile of how many people earn what yearly incomes, from the poorest to the richest, is known as the income distribution of the society. A graph of such a distribution, i.e. of how many people have each income (£100–£200, £200–£300, etc.), is not normally bell shaped, but squeezed over towards the low end. Such squeezing is known as skewness. Cf. Lorenz curve.

Sloane, P. J., 138
Smith, A., 117, 170
Smith, F. B., 34, 37, 283
Snow, E. C., 282
soap industry, 87
social change, and infant mortality, 36–8
social opportunity costs
The value of alternatives sacrificed by some decision, viewed from the entire society's point of view. A decision to pay one's rent of £100 on a farm, for example, costs the private opportunity cost of the money: the payer cannot then buy that £100-worth of goods. From the social point of view, however, the opportunity cost is zero, because the landlord gains what you lose. There is no real sacrifice entailed in using the land, for (suppose) it has no alternative use outside agriculture. Cf. opportunity cost; rent; Ricardian theory.
social overhead capital
Capital used by the whole society, especially in circumstances in which expenditure on it is large and the ability to charge for its use is small: roads, dams, schools, the diplomatic corps, etc. Identical to infrastructure.
social rate of return, 193–5
The rate of return on a project earned by the entire society, rather than by one group of beneficiaries. The social rate of return to the building of canals, for example, is not merely the return from fares to the owners of the canals (5 per cent on their invested capital, say) but also the return, to shippers and landowners, not captured by the canal owners (an additional 4 per cent, say), for a social rate of return of 9 per cent per year. Cf. externalities; private return.
social savings
The benefit from a project, measured to include all benefits over the entire society. The annual social savings divided by the opportunity costs (q.v.) of the investment would be the social rate of return (q.v.). For purposes of economic history the leading example of calculating social savings is R. W. Fogel's in *Railroads and American Economic Growth* (1964).
Solomou, S. N., 16, 247–64, 308, 352
Solow, B. L., 151
South Africa, 177, 180, 203, 209, 220
specialisation,
The assignment of the relatively best qualified person or other input to the best job. Cf. comparative advantage; efficiency.
specialised factors of production
Inputs that are used in one industry alone. Skilled miners or, still more, the coal seams themselves are highly specialised factors of production. They receive the above-normal or below-normal returns to the industry, being unwilling or unable to move in and out of the industry in response to good and bad times. That is, their earnings are rents. Cf. rent.
specie payments
Giving gold or silver ('specie') in exchange for paper currency. When specie payments are made on demand at a fixed ratio of so much gold or silver per pound or dollar the currency may be said to be 'backed' by specie or to be on a specie standard. Cf. gold reserves; gold standard; official reserves.
speculation, 336
spinning, 83–4
sport, professional, 128–9, 137–8, 143–4
standard deviation
A measure of variability; the square root of the variance (q.v.). Cf. coefficient of variation.
standard of living index
A measure of the incomes of ordinary people reckoned in real terms. Cf. real income; real per capita consumption.
staple products
(1) Basic industries or industries on which the prosperity of the nation is thought to depend, such as coal or cotton
(2) Raw materials. The phrase is used in connection with the 'staples theory' of economic growth which alleges that the enrichment of some countries (notably the 'new' frontier countries, especially Canada and Australia) has depended on exports of raw materials.
state
as customer, 407–8
role in industrial organisation, 387
see also government
state monopoly, 137
state ownership, 404–5, 406, 412–13
STC, 396–7

steel industry, 395
Stephens, H., 153
sterling
  appreciation, 339–41
  depreciation, 307, 351–2
stockbuilding, inventory investment
  Adding to inventories. If shoemakers increase their inventories of unprocessed leather or unsold shoes, then stockbuilding has occurred.
stock exchange
  booms, 391–2
  London, 130, 206, 391
Stone, I., 177
Stone, J. R. N., 249
Stoney, P. J. M., 383
strikes, 98
  see also General Strike
structural change, 17–18
  Changes in the share of different sectors of the economy, such as when industry grows at the expense of agriculture.
Sturmey, R. G., 406
substitution, 144
Suffolk, 164, 165
Summers, L. H., 225
sunspot theory, 260
Supple, B. E., 8, 130–1, 406
supply curve
  derivation, 324–5
  elasticity, 152, 270
  The sensitivity with which the amount supplied responds to changes in price. If some buyer of wheat offered a little more than the going market price, for example, sellers would rush in to supply him. He would face a very high elasticity of supply. On the other hand, if the world as a whole offered a higher price for wheat, very little more would be forthcoming; the world as a whole faces a quite *in*-elastic supply of wheat. Cf. elasticity.
  Keynesian model, 324
  for labour, 100–1, 270, 376–8
  new classical model, 324–5
  price
  The payment that will induce suppliers of milk, labour and bonds to supply milk, labour and bonds.
  see also aggregate supply–aggregate demand model
  The amounts of a commodity forthcoming at various different prices for it. At a low wage, for example, the supply curve of labour will yield a small amount of labour (measured in hours, say), at a high wage a large amount. Cf. demand curve; elasticity.
Surrey, 160
Sutherland, Duke of, 163
Svedberg, P., 177
Switzerland, 84
Symons, J. S. V., 344, 347
Szreter, S., 34

Taff Vale decision, 103
tariffs, 196, 351, 405
  effects on output, 308
  empire, 197, 200–2
  general, 352
  inter-war, 308
  Taxes on goods leaving or (more usually) entering a country.
taxation
  indirect
  Levied 'on' the goods, such as a tax on petrol levied on the station owner, 'in the expectation and intention [as Mill put it] that he shall indemnify himself at the expense of another', i.e. the motorist. Thus are import duties, excises, sale taxes, and so forth distinguished from 'direct' taxes, such as the income tax or the land tax. Cf. direct tax.
  regressive
  Taxes whose burden falls on the poor, as taxes on food are said to be relative to 'progressive' taxes such as those on mink coats and yachts or, more directly, high incomes.
  selective employment, 118
  wartime, 232
Taylor, A. J., 86
Taylor, D., 151, 152
technological change
  An alteration, normally an improvement, in ways of making goods and providing services. The two terms are often used interchangeably, although technical change may be applied to a single small change while technological change implies a wider range of changes. Cf. productivity change.
technology, 17–18
  adaptation, 69–70
  backwardness, 84–5
  progress, 152–6, 162–3, 398–400
  skill-displacing, 105, 110

see also innovation; research and development
Teitelbaum, M. S., 39, 43
telecommunications, 23, 210, 409, 417
Telser, L. G., 389
Temin, P., 66, 151
Terms of Settlement, 111, 112
terms of trade
and aggregate supply curve, 325
deterioration, 20
and foreign investment, 193–5
The price of exports divided by the price of imports. More generally, it is the price of what a country buys relative to what it sells. For example, your wages (the price of your exports) divided by the prices you face in the market (the price of your imports) are your personal terms of trade. Since 'exports' are not a single good with a meaningful price of £3 per cubic yard, say, the value of the terms of trade in one year has no meaning. But a comparison between the terms of trade in say 1880 and 1913 for Britain does have meaning. For example, an 'improvement in the terms of trade' would entail a rise in the price of exports relative to the price of imports; in the case mentioned the ratio rose 16 per cent. In the technical literature of economics this concept is called the net barter terms of trade. Cf. gross barter terms of trade.
Terry, M., 115, 116
tertiary sector
The service portion of the economy. That it is third reflects the view that agriculture and other fruits of the earth are primary, lending this admirable quality to related industries, such as steel. Services in this (untenable) view border on superfluous, and art is mere idle fancy.
textile industry, 314, 336
Thane, P., 290
Thatcher, Margaret, 90, 357
third-generation syndrome, 74
Thirlwall, A. P., 71, 118
Thomas, B., 50, 61, 256, 311–13, 354, 371–1, 375, 407–8
Thomas, M., 320–58, 410
Thomas, R. L., 383
Thomas, T., 355
Thomas, W. A., 250, 251, 391
Thompson, F. M. L., 145, 153, 157
Thomson, D., 265, 288
Thomson, R., 105
threshing machine, 162
Tilly, L. A., 42
time series
Of facts, given in, e.g., year-to-year or month-to-month form; in contrast with cross-section, which is person-to-person or place-to-place. Income of the nation in 1860, 1861, 1862 and so forth is a time series; the incomes of 100 blast furnacemen in 1860 is a cross-section (q.v.).
Titmuss, R. M., 36
Tobacco Trade Advisory Committee, 404
Tolliday, S., 107, 113, 389
total factor productivity (TFP), 21, cf. productivity
The ratio of all outputs to a composite of all inputs. If it rises it signifies a rise in output relative to inputs, greater 'efficiency' in common parlance. It is called 'total' (as distinct from 'partial') productivity because it is *not* merely output per unit of labour alone, or any one input alone. It is the productivity of *all* factions (i.e. inputs) taken together. Other names for it are 'the residual', 'technical progress' or 'productivity charge'.
total vs. variable costs
Total costs are all costs, whereas variable costs are only those costs that vary with output. 'Fixed' costs (such as the site rent of a shop or the mortgage payment on the purchase of machinery) do not vary with output, and are the other element. Cf. cost.
Trace, K., 73, 87, 400
Trade Board Act (1918), 295
Trade Boards, 313, 381, 382
trade unions, 283, 312, 381
attack on, 116
data, 276–7, 360–1
membership, 96–7, 112, 419
New Model, 102, 110
obstruction, 68
see also craft unions; labour; shop stewards
Trade Unions Congress, 418
training, *see* education and training
transactions costs
Expenses of doing business, such as the expense of finding someone to do it with, of negotiating a deal and of making sure the deal is carried out.

transactions demand
The desire to hold money to spend, at once, as distinct from holding it for a rainy day or as an investment.
transitory/windfall income
The part of income that is not one's long-run, expected ('permanent') income. Simple Keynesian theory (q.v.) asserts that the amount spent on consumption depends on this income not permanent income. Simple Friedmanite theory asserts that it depends on permanent income. The one theory assumes people spend what they have; the other assumes they plan, spending only their long-run income, saving the rest. Cf. expected lifetime income.
transport, 23
development of, 129, 131
see also railways; road building
Tranter, N. L., 34
Treadway, R., 38, 40
Treasury, 134–5, 240, 299, 303, 316, 327, 339, 345, 353–5
view
The opinion on how to fight the slump of the 1930s that was associated with the British Treasury. It was anti-Keynesian (q.v.) and cautious.
Treaty of Ghent, 198
Trebilcock, C., 82, 88
trend
Of a statistic for a series of years, the level it might be expected to be at in some year according to a line fitted through many or all the years. The expectation can be formed in various ways, e.g. by a moving average (q.v.) or more elaborately by a regression (q.v.). Cf. deviation from trend.
Turkey, 209
Turner, A. J., 227
Turner, H. A., 114
turning point
The point at which a graph of a time series changes direction. For example, the year 1896 was a turning point of the price level, i.e. the year in which falling prices became rising prices.
t-value, *t*-ratio
Roughly a number in regression analysis (q.v.) that indicates how likely it is that a certain coefficient is zero. The higher the *t*-value the less likely it is. Formally, the *t*-value is the ratio of the coefficient to its standard deviation, i.e. the amount it is likely to vary in two-thirds of the cases. The *t*-value thus measures the number of standard deviations (q.v.) the coefficient is away from zero.

uncertainty, 389
underemployment
Work-spreading to give each person a position but only part of a job. As distinct from simple unemployment, everyone is apparently at work, but not profitably. It is said to characterise poor countries nowadays, and perhaps the traditional parts of Britain once.
unemployment, 11–12
benefit, 305–6, 361, 419
benefit-to-wage ratio, 362–5
casual, 368
a cause of poverty, 365–7
causes of, 304–5, 312, 361–2, 413–14
cyclical, 374
data, 276–7, 359–61
by demographic groups, 364
disciplinary effect, 394
duration, 367–72
effect on income, 267–8
First World War, 215–16
industrial variation, 369
insurance, 290, 360, 362–7
inter-war, 304–6, 321–4, 348, 359–85
and labour costs, 338
long-term, 313, 348, 367, 371–2, 384
and malnutrition, 313
regional variations, 58–9, 364, 372–6
structural, 313, 362, 372–6
temporarily stopped, 368–9
trade union rate, 276–7, 360–1
The amount by which people who seek work are unable to find it. Contrast full employment. Cf. cyclical unemployment; demand-deficient unemployment; frictional unemployment.
Uniform List (1892), 107
Unilever, 401
United States, 101, 177, 202–5, 212, 230, 236, 243, 287, 294, 307, 327
banks, 223
Civil War, 415
competition, 19, 300, 403
entrepreneurship, 64–7, 71, 80, 84, 86
Federal Reserve Board, 343
growth, 16–19
innovation, 21
investment, 18–21, 26–7, 178, 185, 187, 190, 195–6
migration, 48, 50, 56

money supply, 222, 345
multinationals, 410
non-union era, 105
productivity, 138, 141, 386, 408–9, 413
railways, 178, 185, 193–4
Sherman Anti-Trust Act (1890), 388, 417
shop floor management, 113
trade, 98, 107, 110, 181, 199–200
Wall Street Crash, 345
wheat, 169
Urquhart, M. C., 195, 212
Usher, D., 282
utilities
electricity supply, 188, 406, 409, 420
water and gas, 88

vacancies, 61, 369–70
value added
The money amount an industry contributes directly to the making of a good. The 'direct' contribution of the steel industry is the value of the labour, capital and land employed. The raw materials such as coal, iron ore and electricity are purchased from other industries (viz. coal mining, ore mining, electricity generation). These therefore are not value added. Incidentally, the sum of all values added is national income, for it is the sum of all earnings.
Vamplew, W., 128–9, 138, 144
Van de Walle, E., 37, 40
Van Duijn, J. J., 254
variable cost
Costs of a factory, such as leather in a shoe factory, that vary with how much the factory produces. The initial cost of the buildings and machinery, by contrast, is a fixed cost. Cf. fixed cost; total cost.
variance
Variability, but in a particular technical sense. The variance of the incomes of people, for example, is the sum of the squares of the differences between the average income and each person's income. Cf. coefficient of variation; standard deviation.
variation, coefficient of, *see* coefficient of variation
Verdoorn's Law, 117
The generalisation that industries growing quickly are also industries becoming more efficient quickly.
Veverka, J., 131–2
Vichniac, J. E., 107
visible and invisible exports
Visible exports are literally so: goods one can see and touch (and tax). Invisibles are services and therefore not seeable: insurance, shipping, education sold to foreigners, for example. The service of making loans at interest to foreigners is generally put in a third category.
vital registration, 32
Von Tunzelmann, G. N., 316, 402
voting rights, 103, 133, 287

Wachter, K. W., 9
wage drift, 115
wage index, 272
wage lists, 103
wages
adjustment, 305–6
and business cycle, 103
collective bargaining, 102–3, 111, 271, 402
national, 58, 295, 381
workplace, 114
and cost of living index, 382–3
and demand for labour, 376–80
determination, 380–4
effects of benefits on, 362–5, 381–2
estimations of, 267–8
family wage, 95
growth, 270–2
incentive schemes, 394
international comparison, 287
inter-war, 334, 384
piece-rate systems, 109–10, 113–14
regional variations, 56–8
relative, 270
rigidity, 312–13, 345–7, 381
skill differentials, 393
structure, 94–6, 135–6
too high, 362
see also earnings
Wagner's Law, 133–4
Wales, 35, 152, 160, 163, 164, 165, 410
Wall, R., 46
Wallace, N., 243
Walters, A., 90, 222
war
finance, 232–3
and government expenditure, 134
loan, 233
see also First World War; Second World War
Warburton, P., 305, 312, 347, 379, 380
War Loan, 309
War Office, 134

Ward, D., 74
Wardley, P., 88, 137, 138, 139
Waterson, M., 405
Weale, M. R., 16, 249, 250, 253
wealth
The value of one's sellable things. It may be defined narrowly to include only money, houses, bonds, jewels; or broadly to include the value (even if one cannot sell it for a sum now) of future earnings. The nation's wealth does not include bonds and other IOUs of one citizen to another, which cancel out, being one person's debt to another person.
wealth distribution, 126
weaving, 106–7
Webber, A., 219, 222, 224, 226, 228, 233, 235, 238, 258–9, 318
Webster, C., 35
Wehler, H. U., 197
weighted average
The typical value of some measure, adjusted for the relative importance of various items. Thus, the unweighted average of city sizes would count Camberley and London each as cities; the weighted average would count London more times than Camberley, perhaps in proportion to their sizes. Such a procedure would give the size of city in which the typical person lived while the unweighted procedure would give the average population of a list of places called cities.
Weir, R. E., 401
Weiss, T. J., 138
welfare reforms, 289–90
Wengenroth, U., 81
West Africa, 203
Whetham, E. H., 147, 164
White, J. L., 95
Whiteside, N., 359, 369
Whitley Committee (1917), 381
Wicksell, K., 225
Wiener, M. J., 75
Wigham, E., 111
Wigley, T. M. L., 262
Wilkins, M., 177, 178
Wilkinson, E., 406, 411
Wilkinson, F., 100, 102, 107–8
Williamson, J. G., 10, 169, 187
Wilson, C., 65, 74, 87–8, 394
Wilson, J., 153, 155
Wilson, P. A., 404
Wiltshire, 159, 164
Winter, J. M., 35, 36, 43, 46, 313
Winter, S. G., 64
Wiseman, J., 134
women
in domestic service, 124–5
labour force participation, 93–5
rural employment, 53
Wood, G., 217–46
Wood, G. H., 95, 266
Woods, R., 10, 31, 34, 36–7, 41
Woodward, Y. H. A., 34
woollens and worsteds, 85
workers *see* labour
working capital
The capital (q.v.) of a firm in the form of materials to be worked on, cash in hand, inventories of finished products and so forth that can be readily made into cash. Identical to circulating capital.
working hours
reduced, 110, 337–8, 384–5
short-time working, 109
work sharing, 369
Worswick, G. D. N., 143, 305, 308, 309, 310, 363
Wright, G., 202
Wright, J. F., 382
Wrightson, J., 150, 156
Wrigley, E. A. xxiv, 40

Yeager, C. B., 217
York, 278
Yorkshire, 41, 138
North Riding, 160
West Riding, 159, 163, 410
Young, A., 158
Youngson, A. J., 283, 338

Zarnowitz, V., 247
Zecher, J. R., 238, 258
Zeitlin, J., 95, 100, 105, 110–11, 112, 114